Social Security Programs and Retirement around the World

**National Bureau of
Economic Research
Conference Report**

Social Security Programs and Retirement around the World
Disability Insurance Programs and Retirement

Edited by **David A. Wise**

The University of Chicago Press

Chicago and London

DAVID A. WISE is the John F. Stambaugh Professor of Political Economy at the Kennedy School of Government at Harvard University. He is the area director of Health and Retirement Programs and director of the Program on the Economics of Aging at the National Bureau of Economic Research.

The University of Chicago Press, Chicago 60637
The University of Chicago Press, Ltd., London
© 2016 by the National Bureau of Economic Research
All rights reserved. Published 2016.
Printed in the United States of America

24 23 22 21 20 19 18 17 16   1 2 3 4 5
ISBN-13: 978-0-226-26257-4 (cloth)
ISBN-13: 978-0-226-26260-4 (e-book)
DOI: 10.7208/chicago/9780226262604.001.0001

Library of Congress Cataloging-in-Publication Data

Social security programs and retirement around the world : disability
    insurance programs and retirement / edited by David A. Wise.
        pages cm — (National Bureau of Economic Research
    conference report)
    ISBN 978-0-226-26257-4 (cloth : alk. paper) —
    ISBN 978-0-226-26260-4 (e-book) 1. Social security.
    2. Postemployment benefits. 3. Disability retirement. I. Wise,
    David A. II. Series: National Bureau of Economic Research
    conference report.
    HD7091.S6244 2015
    362—dc23
                                                                    2015011454

Relation of the Directors to the
Work and Publications of the
National Bureau of Economic Research

1. The object of the NBER is to ascertain and present to the economics profession, and to the public more generally, important economic facts and their interpretation in a scientific manner without policy recommendations. The Board of Directors is charged with the responsibility of ensuring that the work of the NBER is carried on in strict conformity with this object.

2. The President shall establish an internal review process to ensure that book manuscripts proposed for publication DO NOT contain policy recommendations. This shall apply both to the proceedings of conferences and to manuscripts by a single author or by one or more co-authors but shall not apply to authors of comments at NBER conferences who are not NBER affiliates.

3. No book manuscript reporting research shall be published by the NBER until the President has sent to each member of the Board a notice that a manuscript is recommended for publication and that in the President's opinion it is suitable for publication in accordance with the above principles of the NBER. Such notification will include a table of contents and an abstract or summary of the manuscript's content, a list of contributors if applicable, and a response form for use by Directors who desire a copy of the manuscript for review. Each manuscript shall contain a summary drawing attention to the nature and treatment of the problem studied and the main conclusions reached.

4. No volume shall be published until forty-five days have elapsed from the above notification of intention to publish it. During this period a copy shall be sent to any Director requesting it, and if any Director objects to publication on the grounds that the manuscript contains policy recommendations, the objection will be presented to the author(s) or editor(s). In case of dispute, all members of the Board shall be notified, and the President shall appoint an ad hoc committee of the Board to decide the matter; thirty days additional shall be granted for this purpose.

5. The President shall present annually to the Board a report describing the internal manuscript review process, any objections made by Directors before publication or by anyone after publication, any disputes about such matters, and how they were handled.

6. Publications of the NBER issued for informational purposes concerning the work of the Bureau, or issued to inform the public of the activities at the Bureau, including but not limited to the NBER Digest and Reporter, shall be consistent with the object stated in paragraph 1. They shall contain a specific disclaimer noting that they have not passed through the review procedures required in this resolution. The Executive Committee of the Board is charged with the review of all such publications from time to time.

7. NBER working papers and manuscripts distributed on the Bureau's web site are not deemed to be publications for the purpose of this resolution, but they shall be consistent with the object stated in paragraph 1. Working papers shall contain a specific disclaimer noting that they have not passed through the review procedures required in this resolution. The NBER's web site shall contain a similar disclaimer. The President shall establish an internal review process to ensure that the working papers and the web site do not contain policy recommendations, and shall report annually to the Board on this process and any concerns raised in connection with it.

8. Unless otherwise determined by the Board or exempted by the terms of paragraphs 6 and 7, a copy of this resolution shall be printed in each NBER publication as described in paragraph 2 above.

Erratum:

The names of two coauthors were inadvertently omitted from the introduction. The authors for the introduction are Courtney Coile, Kevin Milligan, and David A. Wise. Courtney Coile is professor of economics at Wellesley College and a research associate of the National Bureau of Economic Research. Kevin Milligan is an associate professor at the Vancouver School of Economics, University of British Columbia, and a research associate of the National Bureau of Economic Research.

Contents

Acknowledgments

Funding for this project was provided by the National Institute on Aging, grant numbers P01-AG005842 and P30-AG012810 to the National Bureau of Economic Research. We thank two anonymous reviewers for detailed and thoughtful comments. The views expressed herein are those of the authors and do not necessarily reflect the views of the National Institute on Aging, the National Institutes of Health, or the National Bureau of Economic Research.

Introduction

David A. Wise

Through the coordination of work by a team of analysts in twelve countries for over fifteen years, the International Social Security (ISS) project has used the vast differences in social security programs across countries as a natural laboratory to study the effects of retirement program provisions on the labor force participation of older persons. A central finding of the project is that in many countries the provisions of social security and related government programs provide strong incentives for workers to leave the labor force at relatively young ages and that reducing the inducement to leave the labor force can lead workers to delay retirement and yield large improvements in the financial position of government budgets. The work to date has also made clear that disability insurance (DI) programs can play a large role in the departure of older persons from the labor force, as many workers pass through DI on their path from employment to retirement.

This is the sixth phase of the ongoing ISS project. This phase is particularly related to the fifth phase (Wise 2012) and the second phase (Gruber and Wise 2004) of the project. This volume continues the focus of the previous volume on DI programs while extending the methodology to study retirement behavior used in the second phase to focus in particular on the effects of the DI programs. The key question this volume seeks to address is: Given health status, to what extent are differences in labor force participa-

David A. Wise is the John F. Stambaugh Professor of Political Economy at the Kennedy School of Government at Harvard University. He is the area director of Health and Retirement Programs and director of the Program on the Economics of Aging at the National Bureau of Economic Research.

For acknowledgments, sources of research support, and disclosure of the author's material financial relationships, if any, please see http://www.nber.org/chapters/c13323.ack.

tion across countries determined by the provisions of disability insurance programs?

The fifth phase presented an analysis of historical trends in our group of countries to set the stage for the more formal analysis of disability insurance programs in the current volume. In that phase, the countries summarized DI program reforms and considered how DI reforms were related to changes in health, in particular as measured by changes in mortality. We also treated DI reforms as natural experiments—not prompted by changes in the health or employment circumstances of older persons—and showed that these "exogenous" reforms often had a very large effect on the labor force participation of older workers.

The second phase, which was based on microeconomic analysis of the relationship between a person's decision to retire and the social security and other program incentives faced by that person, documented the large effects that changing plan provisions would have on the labor force participation of older workers. In that phase the country teams considered the employment implications of increasing retirement program eligibility ages, including the eligibility age for DI, and showed that these changes would have very large effects on employment at older ages. As described in more detail below, the current phase of the project differs from the second in incorporating a more careful modeling of the incentives arising from the DI program and simulating how changes in access to DI might affect labor force participation.

To summarize the findings of the remaining phases: The first phase of the project described the retirement incentives inherent in plan provisions and documented the strong relationship across countries between social security incentives to retire and the proportion of older persons out of the labor force (Gruber and Wise 1999). The third phase (Gruber and Wise 2007) demonstrated the consequent fiscal implications that extending labor force participation would have on net program costs—reducing government social security benefit payments and increasing government tax revenues. The analyses in the first two phases, as well as the analysis in the third phase, are summarized in the introduction to the third phase.

In the fourth phase (Gruber and Wise 2010) we directed attention to the oft-claimed proposition that incentives to induce older persons to retire—inherent in the provisions of social security systems—were prompted by youth unemployment. Many have worried that if the incentives to retire were removed and older persons stayed longer in the labor force, the job opportunities of youth would be reduced. We found no evidence to support this "boxed economy" proposition. In short, we concluded: "the overwhelming weight of the evidence, as well as the evidence from each of the several different methods of estimation, is contrary to the boxed economy proposition. We find no evidence that increasing the employment of older persons will reduce the employment opportunities of youth and no evidence that increasing the employment of older persons will increase the unemployment of youth."

The results of the ongoing project are the product of analyses conducted for each country by analysts in that country. Researchers who have participated in the project are listed below:

Belgium	Alain Jousten, Mathieu Lefebvre, Sergio Perelman, Pierre Pestieau, Raphaël Desmet, Arnaud Dellis, and Jean-Philippe Stijns
Canada	Kevin Milligan, Tammy Schirle, Michael Baker, and Jonathan Gruber
Denmark	Paul Bingley, Nabanita Datta Gupta, Michael Jørgensen, and Peder J. Pedersen
France	Luc Behaghel, Didier Blanchet, Muriel Roger, Thierry Debrand, Melika Ben Salem, Antoine Bozio, Ronan Mahieu, Louis-Paul Pelé, and Emmanuelle Walraet
Germany	Axel Börsch-Supan, Tabea Bucher-Koenen, Hendrik Jürges, Johannes Rausch, Morten Schuth, Lars Thiel, Reinhold Schnabel, Simone Kohnz, and Giovanni Mastrobuoni
Italy	Agar Brugiavini and Franco Peracchi
Japan	Mayu Fujii, Takashi Oshio, Satoshi Shimizutani, Akiko Sato Oishi, and Naohiro Yashiro
Netherlands	Adriaan Kalwij, Arie Kapteyn, and Klaas de Vos
Spain	Pilar García Gómez, Sergi Jiménez-Martín, Judit Vall Castelló, Michele Boldrín, and Franco Peracchi
Sweden	Per Johansson, Lisa Laun, Mårten Palme, and Ingemar Svensson
United Kingdom	James Banks, Carl Emmerson, Gemma Tetlow, Richard Blundell, Antonio Bozio, Paul Johnson, Costas Meghir, and Sarah Smith
United States	Courtney Coile, Kevin Milligan, Jonathan Gruber, and Peter Diamond

An important goal of the project has been to present results that were as comparable as possible across countries. Thus the chapters for each phase were prepared according to a detailed template that we developed in consultation with country participants. In this introduction, we summarize the collective results of the country analyses and borrow freely from the country chapters. In large part, however, the results presented in the introduction could only be conveyed by combined analysis of the data from each of the countries. The country chapters themselves present much more detail for each country and, in addition to the common analyses performed by all countries, often present country-specific analysis relevant to a particular

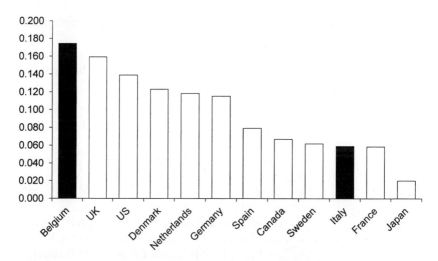

Fig. I.1   Proportion of men age sixty to sixty-four receiving DI benefits in 2009, by country

Note: The data for Belgium and Italy pertain to the number of DI participants divided by the number of active wage earners plus the number of DI participants (rather than the population ages sixty to sixty-four). Data for Germany are for ages fifty-five to fifty-nine. Data for France are for 2007 and for ages fifty-five to fifty-nine and pertain to inactivity due to health reasons. Data for Italy are for 2004. The value for Japan is an estimate.

country. In addition, the country chapters typically present results separately for both men and women.

As we have noted in our past work, the share of the population receiving disability benefits at older ages varies substantially across countries. Figure I.1 shows the share of men ages sixty to sixty-four collecting DI benefits by country in 2009. This value varies by a factor of eight within the participant countries, from 17 percent in Belgium to 16 percent in the United Kingdom, 14 percent in the United States, 6 percent in Italy and France, and 2 percent in Japan. (It is important to note that the data for Belgium and Italy pertain to the number of DI participants divided by the number of active wage earners plus the number of DI participants, rather than the population age sixty to sixty-four. This same caveat applies to figures I.2, I.6, I.7, I.8, and I.9.) It seems unlikely that differences of this magnitude would be driven exclusively, or even primarily, by differences in the health status of the population across countries. In the introduction to the prior phase of the project (Milligan and Wise 2012), we grouped countries according to the share of men collecting disability benefits at age forty-five, which was 2 to 3 percent in one set of countries and 5 to 6 percent in another. By age sixty-four, both groups of countries were exhibiting large differences in the share of men collecting DI (or similar) benefits—among countries with the lower rates of DI usage at age forty-five, for example, participation at age sixty-four ranged from less than 10 percent to over 35 percent. The emergence of these vast differences in the use of DI at older ages among countries with similar rates of disability in middle age strongly suggests that DI usage depends on factors other than health. These statistics also indicate that the DI program serves as a source of retirement income before the social security eligibility age for a sizable share of the population in some countries. It is these observations that lead us to seek a better understanding of how financial incentives from DI programs affect labor supply.

This introduction is organized in several sections. The first section presents background information on DI participation, including changes over time, participation gradients by education and health status, and other relevant statistics. The second section explains the Poterba, Venti, and Wise (PVW) index of health that is used throughout the analysis. The third section explains the estimation procedure that is followed. The last section discusses the simulations based on the estimation results. While the simulations in the second phase of the project emphasized the implications of increasing program eligibility ages, the simulations here emphasize employment (retirement) effects of incentives inherent in the provisions of the country retirement plans, particularly of changing the accessibility of the DI program.

Background

Trends in DI Participation: We begin by documenting changes in DI participation over time. Figure I.2 shows the DI participation rate for men ages sixty to sixty-four by country for selected years from 1970 through 2012 (years of data available for each country vary; data for France and Germany is for ages fifty-five to fifty-nine). Disability insurance participation is not shown for Japan, where DI participation has been extremely low. Similar figures in the individual country chapters show results for men ages fifty to fifty-four and fifty-five to fifty-nine; for women trends in these other groups are often similar to those shown here, though participation levels are lower at younger ages.

Perhaps the most striking feature of these data is the sharp decline in the DI participation rate for older men in many European countries beginning between the late 1980s and the mid-1990s. In five countries—most striking in Sweden, Canada, and the United Kingdom, but also in Italy and Germany—an inverted U-shaped pattern is evident, with DI participation rising until the mid-1990s and falling sharply thereafter. The DI participation rate reached 36 percent in Sweden and 27 percent in the United Kingdom before dropping by 53 and 50 percent respectively over the next fifteen to twenty years. The drop was 50 percent from the peak in Canada, 41 percent in Germany, and 15 percent in Italy. In the Netherlands, Denmark, and Belgium there was also a large decline after the late 1980s, ranging from 32 to 45 percent. In these three countries the time series begins too late to see the rise, but the fall in DI participation is quite evident.

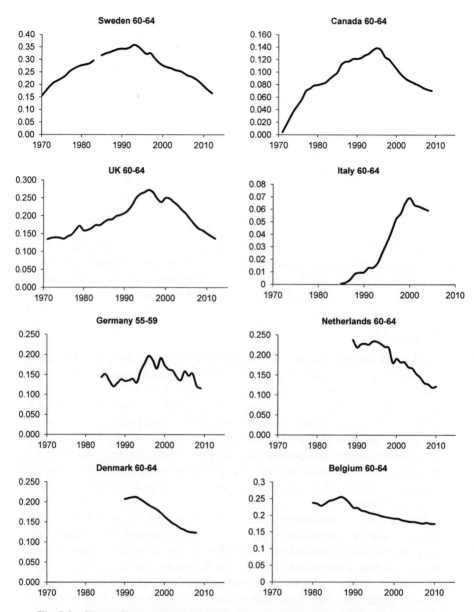

Fig. I.2   Share of men age sixty to sixty-four on DI (fifty-five to fifty-nine in Germany and France), for selected years

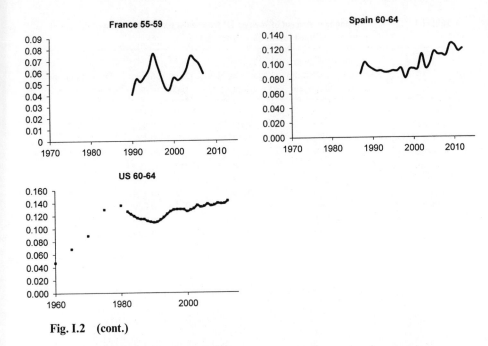

Fig. I.2   (cont.)

In the remaining countries, the pattern is different. In the United States, the DI participation rate for men ages sixty to sixty-four rose from 4.7 to 13.6 percent between 1960 and 1980 and then fell by 3 percentage points during the 1980s from 13.6 to 10.4 percent. Since that time, while DI participation in many European countries has fallen dramatically, the DI participation rate in the United States increased by 30 percent in a trend that shows no signs of stopping. Spain, too, has experienced an increase in the DI participation rate over the past two decades. In France the trend in DI participation between 1990 and 2007 is unclear, although there was a decline in DI participation in the last years of available data.

The changes are summarized in table I.1. The countries are ordered by the decline in the percent on DI with the greatest decline in Sweden and the greatest increase in the United States.

As we discuss subsequently, the dramatic changes in the DI participation rate over time experienced by many countries cannot be explained by changes in health. This feature of the data is documented in substantial detail in the previous phase of the project—the individual country chapters in that volume (Wise 2012) and the introduction to that volume (Milligan and Wise 2012). The rapid changes in the level of DI participation that can be seen in figure I.2 are often associated with reforms in the DI program or in other government programs and are also documented in the prior phase of the project.

In addition to looking at the DI participation rate in isolation, it is instruc-

Table I.1   Change in percent of men on DI from most recent maximum or minimum to year of most recent data (by country)

	Year of most recent minimum (or maximum)	Year of most recent data	DI percent in these years		Percent change between years
Sweden	1993	2012	0.360	0.170	−52.8
Canada	1995	2009	0.139	0.070	−49.6
United Kingdom	1996	2012	0.272	0.137	−49.6
Netherlands	1994	2010	0.219	0.121	−44.7
Denmark	1993	2008	0.212	0.123	−42.0
Germany	1996	2009	0.196	0.115	−41.3
Belgium	1987	2010	0.255	0.174	−31.8
France	2004	2007	0.074	0.059	−20.3
Italy	2000	2004	0.069	0.059	−14.5
Spain	1988	2012	0.102	0.120	17.6
United States	1990	2012	0.109	0.142	30.3

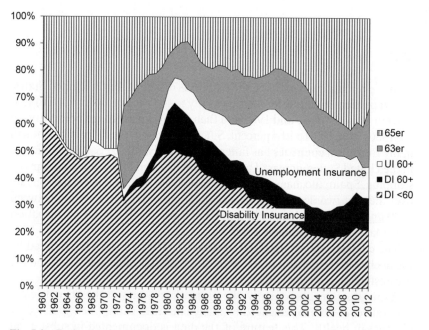

Fig. I.3   Pathways to retirement for men in Germany

tive to consider how the use of different benefit programs as pathways from employment to retirement has changed over time. Figure I.3 provides this information for German men. As the figure makes evident, the proportion of men retiring by way of DI fluctuated widely between 1960 and 2012. For example, the proportion retiring through the two DI programs (for work-

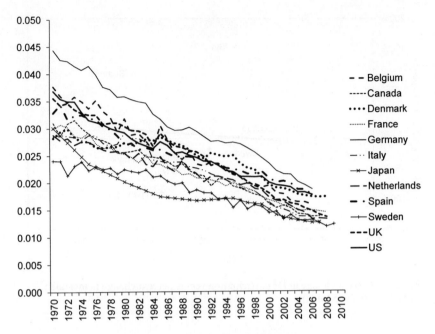

Fig. I.4   Decline in mortality at age sixty-five, by country

ers under and over age sixty, respectively) ranged from a high of 68 percent in 1981 to a low of 28 percent in 2005—a decline of over 58 percent—and then increased by over 14 percent by 2012. This figure also shows that the decline in retirement through DI coincided with an increase in retirement through a special unemployment insurance program for older workers. The decline in the sum of DI plus unemployment insurance (UI) programs between 1981 and 1999 was a more modest 33 percent. This example suggests that government programs may substitute for one another—a decline in participation in one program may be offset by an increase in participation in another program and may not necessarily be associated with an equal increase in labor supply. Therefore it is important to take a holistic view and model the incentives arising from all programs that are potential sources of (early) retirement income, as we aim to do in the analysis that follows.

Trends in DI Participation versus Trends in Health: In the prior phase of the project (Wise 2012), we emphasized the absence of a relationship between DI participation and health, as measured by mortality. Figure I.4, taken from the introduction to this earlier study (Milligan and Wise 2012), shows the decline in mortality at age sixty-five between 1970 and the early twenty-first century for our twelve participating countries. Mortality declined in all of the countries over this period, generally in a similar way. Yet as shown above in figure I.2, DI participation fluctuated widely over the same time period. The juxtaposition of these trends casts doubt on the possibility that

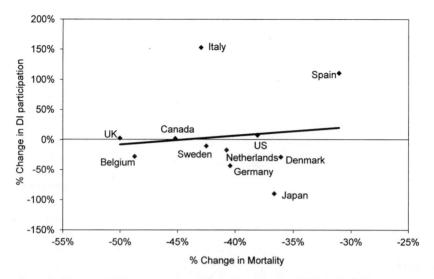

Fig. I.5   Percent change in DI participation versus percent change in mortality, early 1980 to 2005 (men)

changes in DI participation within countries over time are driven by changes in health, at least as measured by mortality. This point is made more directly in figure I.5, also from Milligan and Wise (2012), which plots the change in mortality and the change in DI participation between 1980 and 2005 for the twelve participating countries and finds little evidence of a relationship between them.

Trends in DI Participation versus Trends in Employment: While there is little evidence that changes in health are associated with changes in DI participation, we anticipate that changes in DI participation are associated with changes in employment at older ages. Here we explore the relationship over time by plotting the evolution of DI participation and employment rates at older ages within each country over time. A central goal of this phase of the project is to explore the relationship between DI programs and labor force participation through microeconomic analysis, as discussed below. The time-series data here helps to provide motivation for the formal analysis to follow.

The relationship between DI participation and employment in the participating countries is presented in figure I.6. In this figure the left axis measures employment and the right axis measures DI participation. As discussed above with respect to figure I.2, the DI participation rate for older men follows an inverted U-shaped pattern in a number of countries, rising until the early-to-mid-1990s and then falling, while several additional countries (for whom earlier data was not available) also have a decline in DI participation over the past several decades. The new insight from figure I.6 is that there is

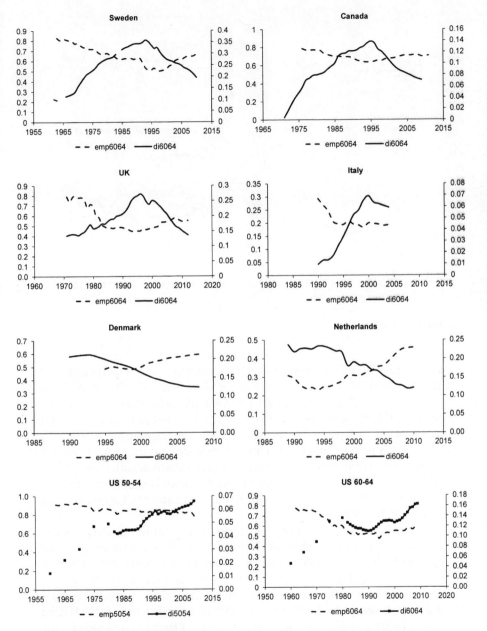

Fig. I.6 Employment and DI rates for men, by country, for the age interval sixty to sixty-four (except where noted)

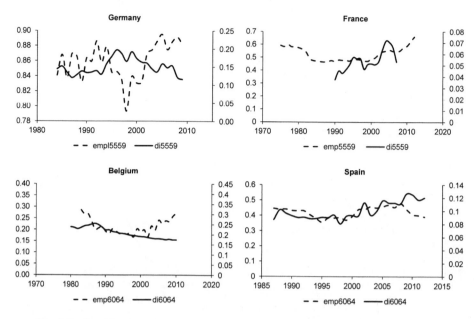

Fig. I.6   (cont.)

an inverse relationship between the DI participation and employment rates in virtually all of these countries. Specifically, in Canada, Denmark, Italy, the Netherlands, Sweden, and the United Kingdom, the relationship is quite clear; as DI participation increases the employment rate falls and as DI participation declines employment increases. The relationship is especially striking in Sweden, Canada, the United Kingdom, and Italy where the peak in DI participation (with a sharp increase and a sharp fall after the peak) is mirrored by a reverse relationship for employment. A similar relationship is also shown for Germany, but with greater fluctuation in the employment and DI trends over time.

In the United States, the story is more complex. For men age sixty to sixty-four, the inverse relationship is evident in the 1970s, but over the past two decades both employment and DI participation have been rising. However, for US men age fifty to fifty-four—the ages at which a large number of men first receive DI benefits—the inverse relationship is clear. A similar relationship (not shown) holds for the fifty-five to fifty-nine age groups in the United States. In three additional countries—Belgium, Germany, and Spain—the data are too noisy or the time series too brief to draw strong conclusions, although the data suggest a negative relationship at the beginning and at the end of the time period for which data are available in Belgium, at the end of the period in Germany, and perhaps at the end of the period in Spain. Nonetheless, the fact that we observe that employment moves in the opposite

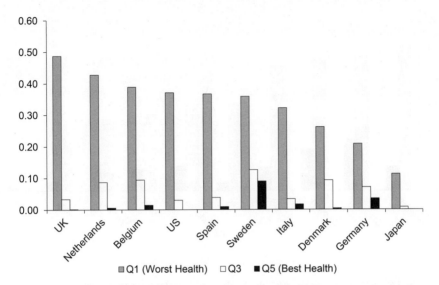

Fig. I.7   Share of men age fifty-five to sixty-four on DI in 2010, by health quintile

Note: The data are from various years, 2008–2011, depending on the availability for each country. Data for Belgium, Denmark, Italy, the Netherlands, and Sweden are for ages fifty to sixty-four. Data for Germany are for ages fifty to fifty-nine.

direction of DI participation in most countries, in periods of both rising and falling DI participation and with the peak in DI participation lining up with the trough in employment in several cases, suggests a noticeable relationship between the two series.

Health and DI Participation: Having explored how DI participation varies across countries over time, and with changes in health and employment over time, we next consider how DI participation varies by health quintile. The description of how the health quintiles are constructed is deferred to the second section of this chapter.

The results are shown in figure I.7 for men age fifty-five to sixty-four. In all countries, there is a substantial DI gradient with respect to health, with those in the lowest health quintile dramatically more likely to be on DI than those in the middle or highest health quintile. This finding is of course consistent with the intended purpose of DI programs to provide income support to individuals with reduced work capacity. The figure also shows, however, that for people with similar levels of health (for example, those in the lowest health quintile in their own country), there are large differences across countries in the probability of being on DI. In the United Kingdom, nearly half of older men in the lowest health quintile are on DI, versus about one-quarter of Danish men and one-tenth of Japanese men in the lowest quintile. Among countries with similar rates of DI in the lowest health quintile—such as the United States, Spain, and Sweden—the share

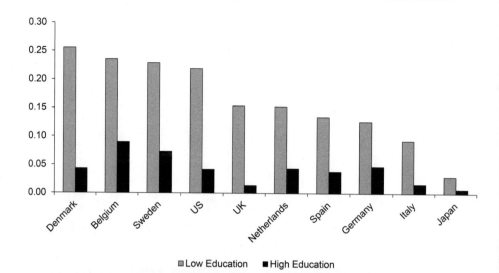

Fig. I.8   Share of men age fifty-five to sixty-four on DI in 2010, by education

Note: Data are from various years, 2008–2011, depending on availability for each country. Data for Belgium, Denmark, Italy, the Netherlands, and Sweden are for ages fifty to sixty-four. Data for Germany are for ages fifty to fifty-nine. Low and high education groups are defined differently across countries.

of men in the middle health quintile who are on DI ranges from 3 percent in the United States to 13 percent in Sweden.

Education and DI Participation: One feature of DI that may not be widely understood is the strong relationship between DI participation and education. Figure I.8 shows the share of men at ages fifty-five to sixty-four who are on DI by level of education across countries; the values for the highest and lowest education groups are shown on the graph, although definition of high and low varies across countries.

In Denmark, Italy, the United States, and the United Kingdom, those individuals in the lowest education group are at least five times as likely to be receiving DI benefits as those in the highest education group. In other countries, the ratio of probabilities is somewhat lower, but still greater than two in every country. Differences in rates of DI participation by education group may reflect the fact that less educated individuals on average are in poorer health than those with more education—a possibility that we explore in more detail below—but likely also reflect economic circumstances such as weaker job prospects or higher replacement DI rates for workers with low lifetime earnings in systems with progressive benefit formulas.

DI Participation by Education and Health: We return to the question of whether differences in DI participation by education are primarily due to health differences by calculating DI participation by health and education for those countries with large enough sample sizes to do so. Figure I.9 shows

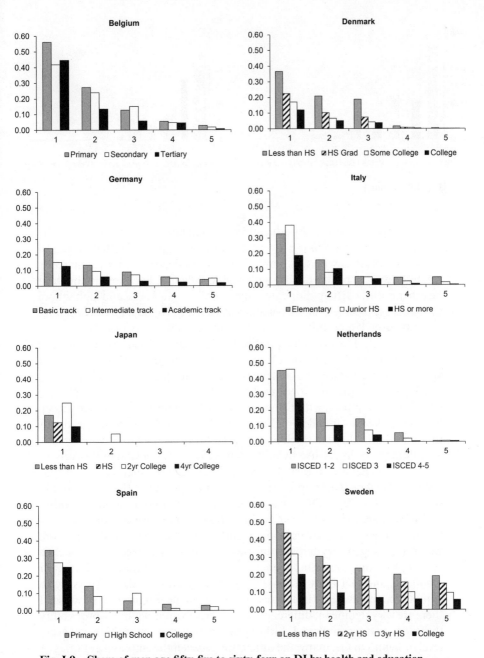

Fig. I.9   Share of men age fifty-five to sixty-four on DI by health and education (by country)

Note: Data for each country are generally pooled across multiple years to increase sample size and precision. Data for Belgium, Denmark, Italy, Netherlands, Spain, and Sweden are for ages fifty to sixty-four. Education groups are defined differently in different countries.

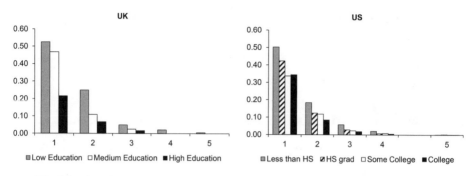

Fig. I.9   (cont.)

the participation percent by education for each health quintile in ten of the participant countries. In the lowest health quintile in the United States, 50 percent of persons with less than a high school degree are DI participants versus only 34 percent of those with a college degree. For those in the third health quintile, participation rates among college graduates and high school dropouts are 6 percent and 2 percent, respectively. In the United Kingdom, there are even larger differences by education in DI use by men in the same health quintile. In the lowest quintile, those in the low education group are over twice as likely to be on DI as those in the high education group (53 versus 22 percent); this is also true in the second quintile (23 versus 4 percent) and third quintile (6 versus 2.5 percent). A similar pattern is evident in the other countries, with Denmark and Sweden having particularly steep gradients, like the United Kingdom, and other countries reflecting gradients more similar to those in the United States. From these figures, we conclude that differences in DI use by education group are not due exclusively to differences in health. Rather, it appears that there are other factors such as differential labor market prospects or earnings potential that may explain the large differences in DI participation by education, conditional on health.

Employment by Health and by Education: Finally, we explore the relationship between employment and health and employment and education, which are likely to vary across countries depending on the provisions of each country's DI program. Employment rates by health quintiles are plotted for Denmark and Germany only—for other countries the data necessary to compute an equivalent time series are not available. Figure I.10 shows that there are very significant differences across health quintiles in the probability that older men are employed. Although employment rates are higher at every level of health in Germany, the difference between the employment rates of those in the lowest and highest health quintiles is roughly the same in both countries, 20 to 25 percentage points.

Figure I.11 presents employment rates at ages fifty-five to sixty-four by level of education, country, and year. This figure shows that there are very

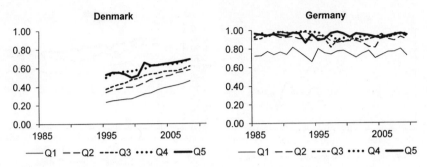

Fig. I.10   Employment by health quintile, for men age fifty-five to sixty-four (by country and year)

Note: Data for Denmark are for ages fifty to sixty-four.

large differences in employment by education. In most countries, the difference in employment between the highest and lowest education groups (where the definition of these groups varies by country) is at least 20 percentage points. Notably, these differences are of a similar magnitude to those seen across health quintiles in figure I.10. Thus education is strongly related to both DI participation and to employment at older ages, consistent with a causal link between employment and application for DI.

Measuring Health

Health is a central component of the analysis. Here we explain briefly the measure that is used and a key property of the measure.

To maintain as much comparability across countries as possible, we use a health index developed by Poterba, Venti, and Wise (PVW) that has previously been used in several contexts (see, e.g., Poterba, Venti, and Wise 2013). The index, as set out by PVW, is the first principal component of twenty-seven health indicators reported in the US Health and Retirement Study (HRS). Much of the analysis reported in this volume makes use of a nexus of comparable studies—the English Longitudinal Study of Aging (ELSA), the Japan Study of Aging and Retirement (JSTAR), and the Survey of Health, Ageing and Retirement in Europe (SHARE), which includes eight of our participant countries: Belgium, Denmark, France, Germany, Italy, the Netherlands, Spain, and the United Kingdom. The similarity of these studies allows us to apply the PVW methodology across countries.

To be more specific, in the current project we use a slightly modified version of the PVW index based on twenty-five indicators that are common to the HRS and to all of the SHARE countries. Japan and the United Kingdom lack data on several of the indicators, so they use the same methodology with the remaining indicators. There are four countries that do not employ the PVW method in constructing health measures for their analysis. One is

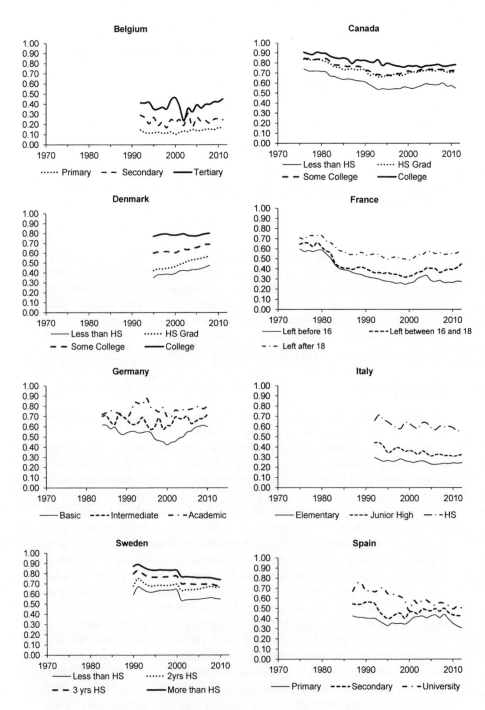

Fig. I.11   Employment by education level, men age fifty-five to sixty-four (by country and year)

Note: Data for Belgium and for Spain are for the age interval sixty to sixty-four.

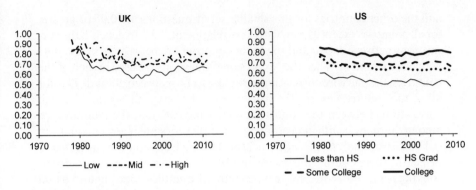

Fig. I.11   (cont.)

Canada, which lacks detailed data on health in any survey that would meet the other requirements of this project and thus uses a simplified health measure (see country chapter for details). The others are Sweden, Denmark, and Germany, who have chosen to use non-SHARE data to obtain a larger sample size for their analyses. For these four countries, therefore, the comparable health measure cannot be used. Nonetheless the comparable health measures for all SHARE countries are included in the discussion below. The health measures in non-health-index-countries are not comparable to the index health measure. Also, in some countries, the precise index used in a country may differ slightly from the index used in this discussion of the properties of the index.

The health measures and the weights (loadings) given to each measure in the index for each country (except Canada) are shown in table I.2A. Comparison of the weights across countries reveals striking consistency among the countries. That is, the ranking of the weights is very similar from one country to the next. This is especially apparent for the United States, the eight SHARE countries, and for the United Kingdom (based on ELSA data).

Table I.2B shows the correlation of the weights for each pair of countries. All but two of the thirty-two pairwise correlations for the United States and the SHARE countries are 0.95 or greater, and many are 0.97 or greater. Correlations between the rankings for the United Kingdom and each of the other countries and the ranking for Japan and each of the other countries are shown on the right-hand side of the table. These correlations are based on the weights for the health indicators that are common to each country. For example, the correlations for Japan are based on the twenty-two indicators that are common to the United States, the SHARE countries, and Japan. The correlations for the United Kingdom are based on the twenty variables that are common to the United Kingdom, the United States, and the SHARE countries. The pairwise correlations between the United Kingdom and the other countries for this smaller set of questions are 0.95 or greater for all countries except Japan, with a correlation of 0.92. In general, the correlations between Japan and the other countries are between 0.88 and 0.93 with one exception. When the "exact same" questions are used in each of the countries, the pairwise correlations are close to 1—between .98 and .99—for all of the countries except the pairwise correlations with Japan. The high correlations between the country loadings indicate that the relationships among the many health indicator responses are very similar across countries.

For ease of analysis the index measures for each country are converted to percentile scores, with 1 the lowest and 100 the highest. For many comparisons the percentile scores are grouped into five quintiles. Many figures based on these quintiles are shown in the background section above.

An important feature of the index is the strong correspondence to survival. For example, based on ELSA data in the United Kingdom, given the health index quintile in 2002 the survival rate in 2011 for persons in the lowest quintile is 59.7 percent, it is 72.6 percent in the second quintile, 81.9 percent in the third, 88.9 percent in the fourth, and 93.9 percent in the highest quintile. Based on HRS data in the United States, given the health index decile in 1992, the survival rate in 2008 ranges from 42.8 percent for those in the bottom decile to 71.4 percent for those in the fifth decile to 89.6 percent for those in the top decile. In the United States, the index in 1992 is also strongly related to future health events such as diabetes, lung cancer, health disease, stroke, hospital stay in 2008, and poor health in 2008 (Poterba, Venti, and Wise 2013).

The following example points to the value of a health measure that can be constructed in a comparable way across countries, and provides some added support to the idea that the resulting health index values are reasonable. In figure I.12, we report the PVW health index by age and country, as measured relative to the US value. At ages fifty to fifty-four, the health of women in the United States is worse than the health of women in most other countries. This finding continues at least through ages sixty to sixty-four, but by the mid-1970s, health in the United States is better than in all countries (with the exception of the United Kingdom). This finding is consistent with the conclusion of many analysts that health in the United States improves after Medicare eligibility at age sixty-five and that expenditure on health care for the oldest old is relatively higher in the United States than in other countries. For men, shown in figure I.13, the general trend is similar but not as dramatic.

Estimation

A central goal of the analysis in this phase of the project is to estimate the relationship between the provisions of each country's retirement programs and the labor supply (or retirement) behavior of older workers in

Table I.2A   The PVW first principal component index for the United States (HRS) and SHARE countries

Question	HRS	Germany	Sweden	Netherlands	Spain	Italy	France	Denmark	Belgium	United Kingdom	Japan
Difficulty walking sev. blocks	0.307	0.276	0.271	0.270	0.264	0.288	0.281	0.265	0.280	0.321	0.311
Difficulty lift/carry	0.293	0.271	0.300	0.297	0.298	0.292	0.284	0.302	0.294	0.312	0.337
Difficulty push/pull	0.288	0.277	0.296	0.299	0.292	0.283	0.289	0.281	0.297	0.309	0.340
Difficulty with an ADL	0.281	0.275	0.279	0.260	0.258	0.273	0.272	0.275	0.279	0.302	0.242
Difficulty climbing stairs	0.276	0.289	0.318	0.297	0.303	0.284	0.296	0.313	0.288	0.290	0.315
Difficulty stoop/kneel/crouch	0.275	0.293	0.292	0.309	0.301	0.288	0.304	0.294	0.289	0.290	0.309
Difficulty getting up from chair	0.266	0.285	0.287	0.275	0.291	0.273	0.265	0.274	0.264	0.282	0.304
Self-reported health fair or poor	0.262	0.285	0.259	0.284	0.265	0.259	0.279	0.299	0.276	0.258	0.211
Difficulty reach/extend arms up	0.224	0.244	0.215	0.202	0.236	0.241	0.227	0.184	0.192	0.223	0.269
Ever experience arthritis	0.197	0.153	0.169	0.176	0.196	0.199	0.185	0.189	0.201	0.216	0.122
Difficulty sitting two hours	0.194	0.218	0.204	0.210	0.213	0.200	0.178	0.211	0.186	0.228	0.277
Difficulty picking up a dime	0.164	0.169	0.173	0.124	0.169	0.193	0.152	0.157	0.137	0.174	0.248
Back problems	0.162	0.180	0.176	0.195	0.196	0.182	0.161	0.186	0.177	n/a	
Ever experience heart problems	0.156	0.129	0.153	0.106	0.122	0.142	0.162	0.123	0.159	0.137	0.094
Hospital stay	0.154	0.152	0.154	0.144	0.108	0.132	0.126	0.135	0.132	n/a	0.109
Home care	0.152	0.143	0.177	0.221	0.160	0.134	0.211	0.193	0.204	0.199	
Doctor visit	0.146	0.208	0.168	0.190	0.184	0.203	0.200	0.183	0.236	n/a	0.082
Ever experience psychological	0.137	0.090	0.064	0.059	0.114	0.080	0.067	0.079	0.087	0.062	0.017
Ever experience stroke	0.132	0.125	0.109	0.105	0.098	0.127	0.124	0.120	0.114	0.108	0.126
Ever experience high blood pressure	0.129	0.121	0.094	0.095	0.108	0.121	0.110	0.084	0.087	0.147	0.075
Ever experience lung disease	0.123	0.085	0.088	0.090	0.097	0.119	0.105	0.132	0.097	0.109	0.040
Ever experience diabetes	0.114	0.114	0.083	0.082	0.094	0.110	0.091	0.067	0.089	0.085	0.071
BMI at beginning of period	0.072	0.077	0.062	0.080	0.079	0.065	0.092	0.059	0.071	n/a	0.026
Nursing home stay	0.070	0.042	0.073	0.085	0.020	−0.002	0.024	0.057	0.024	n/a	
Ever experience cancer	0.060	0.076	0.060	0.061	0.035	0.043	0.038	0.050	0.061	0.044	0.035
N	155,595	5,424	5,615	5,431	4,198	5,416	5,844	4,132	6,739	42,352	

Note: The HRS values are based on data for all HRS cohorts for waves 1992 to 2008. The SHARE values are based on data for 2004 and 2006. The Japan index is based on pooled data from the first and second waves of JSTAR. The United Kingdom values are based on pooled data from 2002, 2004, 2006, and 2008. The precise index used in each country may differ slightly from the indices used here, which are based on the same health measures in each country, with the exception of the United Kingdom and Japan.

Table I.2B   **Correlations or principal component loadings for each pair of countries**

	HRS	Germany	Sweden	Netherlands	Spain	Italy	France	Denmark	Belgium	United Kingdom	Japan
United States	1	0.951	0.961	0.925	0.961	0.962	0.949	0.949	0.939	0.970	0.900
Germany		1	0.968	0.949	0.972	0.974	0.959	0.952	0.953	0.950	0.910
Sweden			1	0.973	0.966	0.955	0.969	0.977	0.961	0.970	0.930
Netherlands				1	0.952	0.919	0.964	0.978	0.964	0.960	0.900
Spain					1	0.978	0.966	0.966	0.961	0.960	0.910
Italy						1	0.965	0.949	0.956	0.970	0.920
France							1	0.968	0.984	0.970	0.880
Denmark								1	0.971	0.960	0.880
Belgium									1	0.970	0.850
United Kingdom										1	0.920
Japan											1

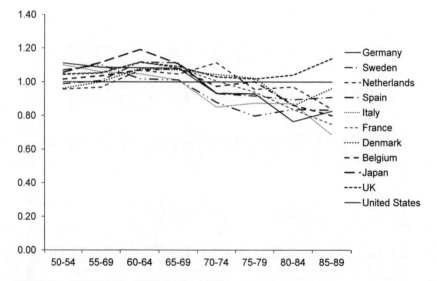

Fig. I.12   The PVW health index by country and age relative to the United States, for women

that country. The analysis in this phase of the project is closely related to the analysis in the second phase.[1] Here, however, we give particular attention to the provisions of DI programs, as well as other pathways to retirement.

More specifically, we want to understand how changing the provisions of a country's DI program (and perhaps other programs) would affect retirement. To explore this, we first need to construct a retirement incentive measure that reflects how the provisions of a country's social security, DI, and other relevant programs provide a greater or lesser return to continued work at a given age for each worker. Next, we assess whether this incentive mea-

1. See, in particular, the discussion on pages 10–15 of Gruber and Wise (2004).

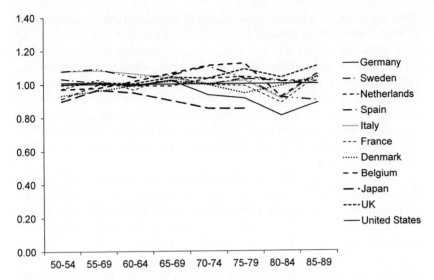

Fig. I.13   The PVW health index by country and age relative to the United States, for men

sure is empirically related to retirement behavior. Finally, we use the results of this estimation to simulate how a change to a country's DI program (and the resulting change in the retirement incentive measure) would be expected to affect retirement.

The key idea that underlies our analysis is the potential gain from postponing retirement from today's age until some future age. This is the incentive to delay retirement. We first explain this incentive measure, assuming that there is only one pathway to retirement. We then explain the issues that arise when there are multiple pathways to retirement (e.g., social security and DI). We then discuss the other covariates included in the country retirement specifications. As the discussion below and in the country chapters makes clear, workers may face very different incentives for continued work depending on the provisions of retirement programs in their country as well as on individual characteristics such as potential earnings, earnings history, family structure, and other attributes.

Retirement Incentive and the Option Value: To begin, assume that there is only one retirement program, social security. When a person retires he (or she) will receive a stream of benefits until death. If the person retires at age t, the present discounted value of benefits, or social security wealth, is given by SSW_t. If the person retires one year later, the present discounted value of future benefits will be SSW_{t+1}. The social security accrual from one year to the next is given by

$$SSW_{t-1} - SSW_t.$$

That is, this measure describes the change in promised future social security benefits from working one additional year. Social security wealth will go up if an extra year of work is translated into a higher flow of benefits in the future, either because of the relationship between social security and lifetime earnings or because of actuarial adjustments that reward later retirement. Social security wealth may go down, though, if the extra benefits that accrue from the extra work are not large enough to compensate for the loss of any retirement benefits in that extra year of work. The net of the future extra benefit entitlement and the loss of benefits in that extra year of work is the one-year accrual.

One shortcoming of the accrual as a measure of retirement incentives is that there could be greater increases in social security wealth from delaying retirement by two years, three years, or more rather than by a single year; beyond some ages benefits may decline—depending on the benefit formula in a given country. The gains associated with work beyond the current year will not be captured by this simple measure. Thus to fully appreciate the incentives inherent in the social security program, we must consider the path of benefits many years into the future. The benchmark approach we use for considering the entire future path of accruals is the "option value" (OV) model.[2] To summarize, this model evaluates the expected present discounted value of incomes for all possible future retirement ages and then measures the "value" of retirement today versus the value of retiring at the optimal date (which may be today, but more likely is in the future). If looking ahead suggests gains from work at some time in the future, there is an incentive for the person to remain in the labor force to take advantage of these gains.

A simplified version of the option value measure at age t can be described by:

$$\text{Simplified OV}_t(r^*) = \left[\begin{pmatrix} \text{discounted} \\ \text{benefits if} \\ \text{retire at } r^* \end{pmatrix} - \begin{pmatrix} \text{discounted} \\ \text{benefits if} \\ \text{retire at } t \end{pmatrix} \right] + \begin{pmatrix} \text{discounted} \\ \text{future wages} \\ \text{through age } r^* \end{pmatrix}.$$

In this formulation, a person considering whether to retire at age t considers the present value of benefits if he retires now (at age t) with the benefits if he retires at some later age. If the person retires at some later age he will gain from future wage earnings and from any gain in future pension benefits. The gain in wage earnings is represented by the last bracket and the gain in pension benefits by the difference between the terms in the first bracket. The age at which the total of the two components is the greatest is denoted by r^*. The option value prescription is that the person will continue to work if this option value is positive. More detail on the option value specification is shown in the appendix on the option value model.

---

2. For a more detailed discussion, see Stock and Wise (1990).

Multiple Pathways to Retirement: The discussion above assumes that there is only one pathway to retirement, but in all countries there are multiple pathways. In the United States there are two pathways—Social Security and disability insurance (DI)—but in other countries there are three or more pathways—the social security "normal" retirement, DI, special unemployment insurance programs, or a special early retirement program. To estimate the OV incentive on retirement with multiple programs, we follow an instrumental variables-like approach. For each program, we first estimate the OV measure for that program, essentially assuming that the worker will retire through that program and the only decision is at what age to retire. Next, we estimate the probability that the person assigns to each program as a possible pathway to retirement. Finally, we calculate the "inclusive OV," which is the weighted average of the OVs for each of the possible programs. The probabilities to be assigned to each program are determined by the relationship between individual attributes and the likelihood that a particular program was chosen by similar workers in the past. For example, in the United States, the probability weight for the DI plan is determined by the probability that a person in each of four education levels was on DI anytime at ages sixty and sixty-four in the relevant year (estimated using HRS data for the years 1992 to 2010). The exact method used for each country is described in the country chapters. This approach is an "instrumental variable" estimate of the expected OV faced by a given person.

Figure I.14 shows the OVs by age for each country. The OV calculations are based on the detail in the appendix. For illustration, consider the programs in the United States and in Belgium. The United States has only two programs, DI and Social Security (SS). Belgium has four programs—Social Security, DI, unemployment insurance (UI), and early retirement (CER). Notice that in the United States, the OV of delaying retirement is much larger under the SS program than under the DI program. That is, the gain from delaying retirement is much greater under the SS program. Thus persons who consider the DI program as a route to retirement have a much greater incentive to retire at a young age than persons who consider SS as the only pathway to retirement. The inclusive OV is the weighted average of the SS and DI OVs. In the United States, the average DI weight is small so the inclusive OV is close to the SS OV. The OVs in Belgium are quite different. First note that the program OVs in general are much lower in Belgium than in the United States. Second, note that the inclusive OV is much lower in Belgium than in the United States. At age fifty, for example, the inclusive OV in the United States is about 33,200 but is only about 12,500 in Belgium. Thus it would appear that the average gain to delaying retirement is much less in Belgium than in the United States.

It is important to understand that the estimated effect of the inclusive OV on retirement—thought of as an instrumental variable estimate of the OV effect on retirement—is taken as the effect of the OV on retirement

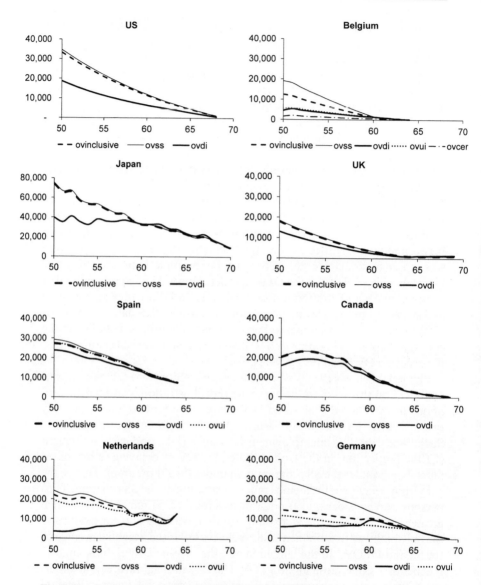

Fig. I.14   Option values and inclusive OV by age, by country

and used in all estimates of the effects of program provisions and changes in program provisions on retirement. For example, this estimate is used to predict (simulate) the effect on retirement of having access only to the DI versus access only to the social security program.

Estimation and Additional Covariates: Although the inclusive OV incentive measure is the key variable in the estimation, other individual attributes

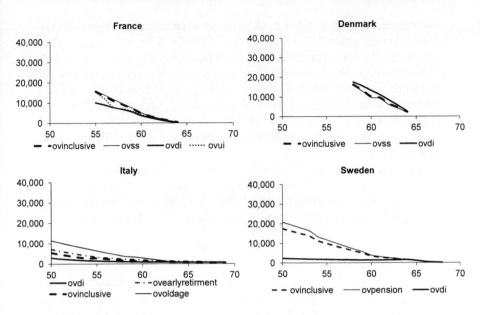

Fig. I.14   (cont.)

are also included. First recall that the OV depends on estimated individual earnings as described above. In addition, the specification for each country includes health—typically controlling for health quintile based on the PVW index described above. One might expect health to be particularly important when contemplating retirement under the DI pathway. The specification also includes education level, gender, whether the person is married, whether the spouse works, total non-social security assets, and occupation indicator variables. There is some variation depending on data availability in each country.

Finally, each specification controls for age. Two versions are included. One includes indicator variables for each age, and the other includes age as a single continuous variable. The inclusion of age is particularly important when evaluating the effect of the OV on retirement. Quoting from the introduction to phase 2 of the project:

> A crucial issue in the analyses in this volume is identification—that is, determination of the separate effect of each variable on retirement, as distinct from each of the other variables. Determining the effect of plan incentives on retirement is a key goal, but other individual attributes also influence the decision to retire. For example, persons are more likely to prefer retirement to work as they age. A linear age variable will potentially capture this effect, but only if preferences for leisure evolve linearly with age. (Gruber and Wise 2004, 12)

We return to this issue when discussing simulations below.

Parameter Estimates: For each country, estimates are reported for several alternative specifications. For example, in some specifications separate indicator variables are included for each age; in others, a single linear age effect is included. In some specifications health quintile indicators are included, and in other specifications a single variable for health percentile is included. For some countries the sample sizes are large enough to obtain separate estimates by health quintile and by education level; in others, including most of the SHARE countries (if the SHARE data are used), the sample sizes are not large enough to estimate separate parameters by health quintile or by education.

The most important coefficient is the estimated effect of the inclusive OV on the probability of retirement. The country estimates of this retirement incentive effect are sensitive to the differential variance in the OVs across countries. To account for this, the estimated effect of a one standard deviation change in the OV is reported in square brackets as well as the effect of a unit (10,000 "utility" units) change in the OV. In addition, in some specifications the percent gain in the OV from delaying retirement is estimated instead of the OV itself—the percent gain from delaying retirement at age a is measured by the OV of delaying retirement at age a divided by the utility associated with retirement at age a. Like the standard deviation of the OVs, this measure may be more comparable across countries than OV units and thus help to make the results more comparable across countries.

Estimates for each of the countries are reported in table I.3. Estimates are reported for two specifications. The first is the fourth specification in the first table of estimates presented in each of the country chapters. The second is the effect of the percent gain in the OV from delaying retirement. Several features of the estimates stand out. First, the estimated option value incentive measure is highly statistically significant in each of the countries, with the exception of Spain and Germany (using SHARE data). In these countries the sample sizes are apparently too small to obtain statistically significant results. The German estimates based on the much larger Socio-Economic Panel Survey (SOEP) data file are highly significant. Second, there is considerable variation across countries in the estimated effects. Even excluding the statistically insignificant estimates for two countries and the smallest estimates for the United Kingdom and Sweden, the estimated effects for the remaining countries vary by a factor of seven. In two countries the estimated effect of a unit (10,000) increase in the OV is to reduce the retirement rate by about 11 percent or more. In five countries the effect on retirement is between 3 and 5 percent. In the United Kingdom and Sweden the estimated effect is less than 1 percent. The estimated effect of a standard deviation change in the incentive measure also varies across countries, but less than the unit increase estimate. In eight countries these estimates are between 4 and 9 percent. In the remaining three countries with statistically significant estimates the values are between 1 and 3 percent. Third, in most countries there is very little difference in the estimated effect of the incentive

Table I.3 The effect of the retirement program incentive effect, inclusive OV, on retirement, by specification

Specification	Netherlands	Belgium	France	Germany	Denmark	United States	Japan
(1): Specification (4), with age dummies							
Estimate	-0.119	-0.106	-0.046	-0.0423	-0.0433	-0.0331	-0.0217
Standard error	(-0.049)	(-0.033)	(-0.006)	(-0.0031)	(0.0005)	(.0011)	(0.006)
Effect of OV std. change	[-0.091]	[-0.079]	[-0.042]	[-0.0525]	[-0.0438]*	[-0.056]	[-0.045]
(2): Percent gain: Specification (4), with age dummies							
Estimate	-0.060	-0.313	-0.038	-0.0186	-0.0806	-0.0593	-0.0384
Standard error	(-0.072)	(-0.082)	(-0.012)	(-0.0016)	(0.0015)	(.0124)	(0.0122)

Specification	Canada	United Kingdom	Italy	Sweden	Spain	Germany (SHARE)
(1): Specification (4), with age dummies						
Estimate	-0.0166	-0.006	-0.049	-0.0015	-0.005	-0.020
Standard error	(0.0021)	(-0.001)	(0.020)	(0.000)	(-0.017)	(-0.015)
Effect of OV std. change	[-0.041]	[-0.028]	[-0.023]	[-0.0126]	[-0.004]	[—]
(2): Percent gain: Specification (4), with age dummies						
Estimate	-0.0451	-0.148	-0.0315	—	-0.036	—
Standard error	(0.0108)	(0.022)	(-0.0005)	—	(-0.046)	—

Table I.4   **Estimated incentive measure effects by health quintile for selected countries**

	United States	United Kingdom	Germany (SOEP)	Denmark	Sweden
OV: Worst health quintile	−0.0594	−0.008	0.0902	−0.0639	−0.0022
Standard error	(0.0038)	(0.002)	(0.0105)	(0.0015)	(0.0001)
Effect of OV std. change	[−0.073]	[−0.062]	[−0.0707]	[0.065]	[−0.0145]
OV: Second quintile	−0.0353	−0.006	−0.0453	−0.0490	−0.0018
Standard error	(.0026)	(−0.002)	0.0067	(0.0014)	(0.0000)
Effect of OV std. change	[−0.052]	[−0.040]	[−0.0576]	[0.0285]	[−0.0142]
OV: Third quintile	−0.0336	−0.003	−0.0285	−0.0342	−0.0013
Standard error	(0.0023)	−0.002	−0.0043	(0.0011)	(0.0000)
Effect of OV std. change	[−0.056]	[−0.030]	[−0.0628]	[0.0256]	[−0.0118]
OV: Fourth quintile	−0.0234	−0.005	−0.0195	−0.0282	−0.001
Standard error	(.0018)	(−0.002)	(−0.005)	(0.0009)	(0.0000)
Effect of OV std. change	[−0.044]	[−0.050]	[−0.0628]	[0.0186]	[−0.0098]
OV: Best health quintile	−0.0197	−0.007	−0.0219	−0.0372	−0.0009
Standard error	(.0017)	(−0.002)	(−0.005)	(0.0010)	(0.0000)
Effect of OV std. change	[−0.037]	[−0.081]	[−0.0320]	[0.0283]	[−0.0097]

Notes: Germany (SOEP), Denmark, and Sweden do not use the PVW health index so that health comparability across all of the countries is not assured, although in each country the available measures can be used to rank persons by health.

measure in the specification with age indicators compared to the otherwise identical specification but with a single linear age measure—these estimates can be seen in the country chapters. Finally, the estimated effects of other covariates vary substantially from one country to the other and many of the estimated effects are not statistically different from zero. The many estimates based on several additional specifications are shown in the country chapters.

Although it is clear that persons in poor health are more likely to retire early through the DI pathway, whether the effect of the incentive measure on retirement should vary in one direction or another with health is not clear a priori. Some evidence, however, is provided in the country data. Table I.4 shows the estimated incentive measure effect by health quintile for several countries with sample sizes large enough to distinguish estimates by health. In four of the five countries the estimated effect of the incentive measure declines with health. In the United States the effect declines continuously from −0.0594 for those in the worst health to −0.0197 for those in the best health, in Germany from −0.0902 to −0.0219, in Denmark from −0.639 to −0.0373, and in Sweden from −0.0022 to −0.0009. In each of these countries the result is also shown clearly by comparing the effect of a standard deviation change in the OV for those in the best versus those in the worst health, shown by the estimates in the square brackets. The United Kingdom is an exception, showing essentially no relationship between the incentive measure and health. Recall that the health measures used in Germany, Denmark, and Sweden are based on the few selected health measures in the data files used in those countries and are not comparable to the PVW index measure used the United States and the United Kingdom. Nonetheless, the health measures used in the other three countries can be used to rank persons by health quintile. Note that the relationship between the incentive measure and health should not necessarily be expected to be the same in all countries. For example health is the central criteria for eligibility for DI in the United States, while the relationship may be less strict in other countries that may give more weight to labor market conditions, for example, to determine DI eligibility. The descriptive data above show a strong correspondence between health quintile and DI participation in each country, although the strength of the relationship varies from country to country, as shown in figure I.9.

Simulations

Each of the country chapters includes a series of simulations. Some simulations show the fit of the estimated specifications. For all countries these simulations show that the models predict well the proportion of persons that has retired by age. Other simulations are descriptive—for example, showing employment by education or health by age. The most important simulations are used to predict the effect of the retirement program incentive effects on retirement. It is helpful to recall first the simulations that were done in the second phase of the project.

The most important simulations in the second phase were used to predict the effect of increasing retirement program eligibility ages. We describe here two simulations—S1 and S3—that were reported in the introduction to the second phase (Gruber and Wise 2004). Both simulations show the effect of increasing the eligibility ages, but the estimation specification and the simulation methods differ. Simulation S1 is based on estimation that controlled for a linear measure of age in the specification and only the OV incentive measure (and the associated variables that determine the OV incentive) is used in the simulation.[3] Simulation S3 uses age indicator variables in the estimation and, in addition, uses adjusted age indicators to simulate retirement under the program changes.[4] The percent reduction in the proportion of men

3. The estimation in this earlier volume was also based on OV, though as noted above, the current analysis features a more careful modeling of DI and other pathways to retirement (thus, the OV measure used in phase 2 is not exactly the same as the OV inclusive measure used in the new simulations described below).

4. The estimated age indicator effects, as well as the program incentive effects, are used to predict the effect of the program changes. For example, for the three-year eligibility delay, the age indicator for a given age is taken to be the estimated age indicator three years prior to the given age. The age sixty indicator, for example, is taken to be the estimated age fifty-seven indicator. The result is that under the *three-year eligibility delay*, the projected retirement rate at age sixty is *approximately* the same as the current program age fifty-seven retirement rate. The spike at the early retirement age under the current program, for example, shows up three years later under the reform. This approach assumes that *all* of the estimated age effects can be attributed to the eligibility age program provisions. (The ages include the age at which persons are eligible for one or more programs, as well as the "normal" retirement age.)

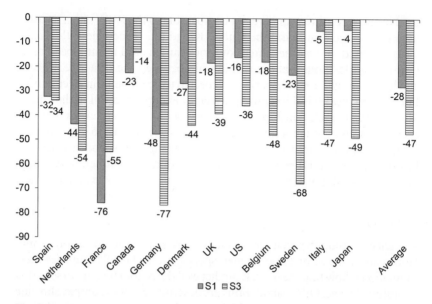

Fig. I.15   Three-year delay OV-S1 and OV-S3

out of the labor force (OLF) is shown in figure I.15. This figure reproduces the data in figure 16 of Gruber and Wise (2004, 29), and the details of the construction of the figure are discussed there.

For the S1 simulation, the incentive measure for a country (the OV) is recalculated based on the OV that incorporates the implications of the delayed eligibility age. The shaded bars show the effect of only the change in the incentive implications of the three-year delay. The average reduction in the proportion of men out of the labor force (OLF) is large—28 percent. Underlying the average, however, are large differences across countries. For four countries the reduction was greater than 32 percent, for two countries the reduction was less than 4 percent, and was between 16 and 28 percent for the remaining countries. The simulated reduction in the proportion of men OLF is much larger if age indicators are used in estimation and the age effects for each age are moved up three years to correspond with the three-year increase in all program eligibility ages.

It is not surprising that the effects of increases in the eligibility ages are large. For example, this simulation implies that the early retirement age in the United States increased from sixty-two to sixty-five and under S3 this reduced the OLF proportion by 36 percent. In most countries (although not in the United States because DI was not included in the analysis) increasing the eligibility age for retirement would also change the eligibility age for DI by three years as well.

Now in this phase, with emphasis on DI, increasing the eligibility age for

DI seems implausible in many if not most countries. Here we do not change the eligibility age, but instead ask how employment is affected differentially by the provisions of the DI pathway compared to the provisions of the regular social security pathway, and we consider the effect of changes in the provisions of DI programs, especially changes in eligibility stringency. The simulations are all based on the country estimates in table I.3, specification (4). For each simulation the first stage is to calculate OVs corresponding to the programs or program changes that are being compared. Then the estimated effect of the OV incentive effect from table I.3, specification (4) (together with the estimates for other variables in the specification) are used to simulate retirement at each age under each program or program change for each person in the sample. Then the implications for years of employment between ages fifty and sixty-nine are calculated.

Each country has reported the results of three simulations. The first simulation is intended to evaluate the effect of the differential incentive effects inherent in the provisions of each pathway on retirement—if all persons faced only one of the pathway options. For the United States there are only two pathways—Social Security or DI. For other countries there are three or more pathways. Each country has used the table I.3, specification (4) coefficients to predict each individual's probability of retirement for each pathway—using the DI OVs and then using the SS OVs for the United States. These estimates can also be found in the individual country chapters. For the Netherlands, for example, there are three pathways—disability, unemployment, and retirement. The retirement probabilities (hazard rates) by age and the cumulative proportion of persons still working (survival rates) by age are shown in figure I.16. Separate lines are shown for each pathway in each country. The distance between the lines for the different pathways varies across countries, depending on the differences in the strength of the retirement incentives across the pathways.

For illustration, consider the retirement rates and the survival rates for the Netherlands compared to the United States. The retirement rates are much greater in the Netherlands than in the United States—at age sixty the retirement rates are 0.1 or lower for each pathway; in the Netherlands the retirement rates are close to three times as great, all greater than 0.27. Corresponding to the higher retirement rates at each age, the survival rate at each age is much higher in the United States than in the Netherlands. For example, at age sixty in the United States employment is much higher than in the Netherlands—between 0.47 and 0.59 in the United States and between 0.21 and 0.38 in the Netherlands, depending on the pathway to retirement. The survival rates are only comparable across countries if the process begins at age fifty and are only shown for these countries. The hazard rates are provided for all countries for which the data are available.

For each program the countries have calculated the mean predicted retirement by age and have used these data to calculate the expected years of work

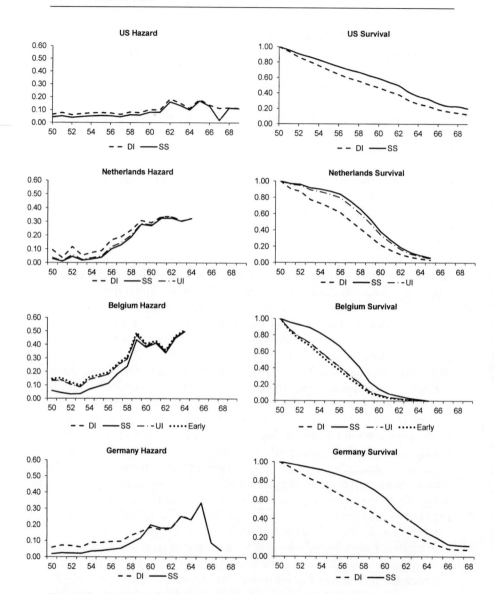

Fig. I.16   Retirement hazard rates and cumulative survival rates by age and by country

between ages fifty and fifty-nine. For the United States, for example, the average years of work over the fifty to sixty-nine age interval is simulated to be 10.18 years if everyone faced the DI OVs and 11.93 years if everyone faced the SS OVs. That is, on average, people work 17.3 percent more years when faced with the incentives inherent in the SS option rather than the incentives inherent in the DI option. In the Netherlands the simulated years of work

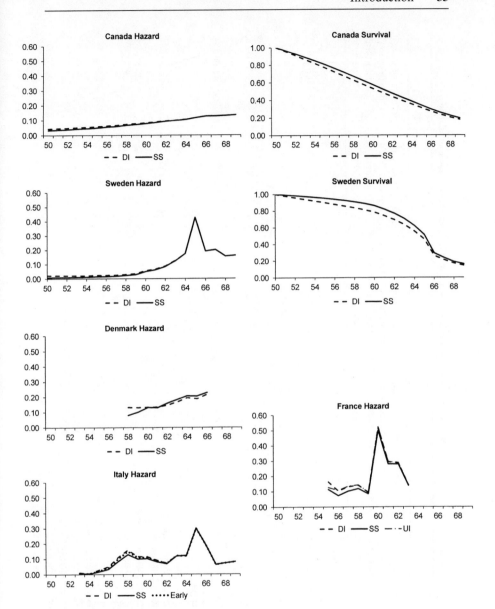

Fig. I.16   (cont.)

in the fifty to sixty-five age interval is 7.40 under the DI pathway, 9.02 under the unemployment pathway, and 7.47 under the retirement pathway. These simulated years worked between ages fifty and sixty-nine for other countries are shown by pathway in table I.5.

It is important to understand that these differences indicate the marginal effect of the DI incentive compared to the regular retirement incentive, hold-

Table I.5 Simulations: Effect of incentive measures alone on years of work between ages specified for each country (three simulations)

Country	Retirement programs compared	Simulations			
		Yrs. of work if *all* persons faced the same retirement pathway option	Yrs. of work if *all DI participants* had faced the same retirement pathway	Yrs. of work if two-thirds to DI and one-third to SS pathway	Yrs. of work if one-third to DI and two-thirds to SS pathway
United States 50–69	(1) DI = base	10.18	8.33	8.75	9.17
	(2) SS	11.93	9.64		
	Percent change vs. base	17.3	15.7	5.1	10.1
Canada	(1) DI yrs. of work	11.31	10.22	10.41	10.61
	(2) SS yrs. of work	11.91	10.83		
	Percent change (2)/(1)	5.3		1.9	3.8
United Kingdom 50–69	(1) DI	10.7	9.13	9.39	9.51
	(2) SS	11.3	9.79		
	Percent change (2)/(1)	5.6	7.2	2.8	4.2
Germany 50–67	(1) DI = base	9.49	8.94	10.19	11.06
	(2) UB	10.32	9.96		
	(3) OA	13.98	13.62		
	Percent change (3)/(1)	47.2			
	Percent change (2)/(1)	8.7			
	Percent change (3)/(2)	35.5			
	Percent change vs. base				
Netherlands 50–65	(1) DI = base	7.40	7.02	13.0	23.8
	(2) UE	9.02			
	(3) Retire	9.47	8.94	7.56	8.52
	Percent change (3)/(1)	28.0			
	Percent change (2)/(1)	21.9			
	Percent change (3)/(2)	5.0			
DI N = 23	Percent change vs. base			7.69	21.37

Belgium				
50–64				
(1) CER	5.36	4.53		
(2) DI = Base	5.65	4.66	4.68	5.48
(3) UI	5.71	4.65		
(4) OAP	7.54	5.51		
Percent change (4)/(1)	40.67			
Percent change (4)/(2)	33.45			
Percent change (4)/(3)	32.05			
Percent change vs. base			0.43	17.60
France				
55–64				
(1) UE	4.09	4.293		
(2) DI = base	4.96	4.188	4.384	4.554
(3) Normal retirement	5.50	4.766		
Percent change (3)/(1)	34.4			
Percent change (2)/(1)	21.3			
Percent change (3)/(2)	10.8			
Percent change vs. base			4.68	8.74
Denmark				
57–69				
(1) DI = base	4.50	3.6	3.67	3.73
(2) SS	4.80	3.8		
Percent change vs. base	6.7	5.6	1.9	3.6
Italy				
(1) DI = base	12.00	6.9	7.04	7.09
(2) Old age	12.67	7.25		
(3) Early retirement	12.31	7.26		
Percent change (3)/(1)	5.6			
Percent change (2)/(1)	2.6			
Percent change (3)/(2)	2.9			
Percent change vs. base			2.0%	2.8%
Sweden				
50–69				
(1) DI = base	13.17	11.35	5.06	10.06
(2) Old age	13.93	11.89	11.55	11.73
Percent change vs. base	5.8	4.8	1.8	3.3

Notes: For Germany the SOEF does not report DI application, thus estimates for persons in the worst health quintile are used in the right three columns of the table. For Japan there are too few DI applicants to simulate reliable estimates. For Spain none of the incentive estimates is significant, thus the simulations are not reported.

ing constant all other individual attributes included in the specification. In particular, it holds constant the estimated age dummies. For countries with multiple pathways the process would be repeated for each of the pathways. To be specific, we estimate the incentive effect of a retirement program—the effect of OVinclusive—with an equation like this:

$$R = k + a\,\text{OVinclusive} + b\,\text{Age} + c\,\text{Health} + d\,\text{Education} +$$

We estimate $\hat{a}, \hat{b}, \hat{c}, \hat{d}$ and so forth. The estimate $\hat{a}$ (the estimates reported in table I.3) is an IV estimate of the effect of the OV on retirement. For simulation we take $\hat{a}$ as *the* estimate of the effect of OV on retirement and use it for all of the simulations. With a one-year increase in age the effect on retirement is given by $dR/d\text{Age} = \hat{a}(d\text{OV}/d\text{Age}) + \hat{b}\,\text{Age}$, where the first term is negative ($\hat{a}$ is negative) and the second term positive—that is, the first term reduces the incentive to delay retirement and the second term increases the preference for retirement with advancing age. The likelihood of retiring advances with age because a reduction in the OV of continuing work is reinforced by the concomitant increase in age. If age is excluded from the specification, then to fit the retirement data the coefficient on OV will have to increase, and if the OVinclusive is eliminated from the specification the coefficient on age will have to increase to fit the retirement data. This is the identification issue mentioned above. In order to identify the correct effect of the incentive measure we must have an age specification that captures the true increase in preference to retire with age. One feature of the estimates that increases our confidence in the incentive estimates is that they are virtually the same whether the single linear age or indicators for each age are used to estimate the effect of age on the preference to retire.

Instead of making calculations for all persons in the sample, the second and third simulations consider only persons who were observed to have chosen the DI option. The second simulation asks how much years of work would have changed for this group had the group faced the OVs of the regular retirement option instead of the OVs of the DI program. For the United States, among all those who applied for DI, years worked under the SS option is 15.7 percent greater than under the DI option (9.64 years versus 8.33 years; these values are lower than those for the full sample likely because DI applicants are less healthy than the population at large). For all those who received DI, work under the SS option would have been 16.2 percent greater under the SS option then under the DI option (9.87 years versus 8.49 years).

Recall again that in phase 2 of the project we simulated the effect of delaying all program eligibility ages by three years, including the eligibility ages for DI and unemployment programs. In one of these simulations we used estimates with age dummies and in another we used estimates based on continuous age. These simulations suggested very large reductions in retirement, especially the simulations using age dummies in the estimation.

The simulations proposed here do not consider raising the DI eligibility age, but rather direct attention to the incentive effects—the OVs—of the program provisions, and stringency provisions, conditional on the estimated age "preference" effects. It should not be surprising that the employment effect of changing the OV incentive effects is typically much smaller than changing the program eligibility ages. Increasing the eligibility age for DI for three years, for example, means that no one can claim DI benefits for these three years and thus cannot be on the DI program. This would cause great hardship to those who are truly disabled and undermine the insurance role of DI. That is why we do not consider changing the age of eligibility for the DI programs as we did in phase 2.

The aim of the third simulation is to get an idea of the effect on retirement of greater stringency in DI acceptance. As in the second simulation, we focus on DI recipients (or applicants, if available). From that simulation, we have an estimate of expected working life if everyone follows the DI path and if everyone follows the SS path. We now make similar calculations to show the effect of making it harder for this group of people who are interested in using DI to access the program—in effect changing the eligibility stringency. To do this, we first randomly assign two-thirds of the group to the DI path and one-third to the SS path, calculate everyone's expected probability of retirement, sum by age, and use that to generate an expected work life from ages fifty to sixty-nine, as described above. We then repeat the process but randomly assign one-third to the DI path and two-thirds to the SS path. (If there are more than two paths the simulations are done for different combinations of programs, making different assumptions about which program persons use, if not to DI.) In the United States, the expected work life is 8.328 years if everyone takes the DI path (from the second simulation described above), 8.749 years with two-thirds on the DI path, 9.166 years with one-third on the DI path, and 9.635 years with all on the SS path (again from the second simulation). Not surprisingly, shutting down the DI path for one-third of this sample has about one-third the effect of shutting it down for the full sample of DI applicants/recipients. Again, the idea of this simulation is to simulate the work effect of making DI harder to access for a share of the population.

The results of the simulations for most of the countries are reported in table I.5. The retirement programs that are compared for each country are shown in the first column of the table. The countries in the table are ordered by the average number of years worked—between the ages shown—for persons who retire under the "standard" retirement program—ranging from 11.93 years in the United States and 11.3 years in the United Kingdom to 4.8 years in Denmark.

The second column shows the years of work if all persons faced the same pathway option, using all the pathways available in a given country. For the

United States, the years of work after age fifty would be 10.18 if everyone faced the DI incentives and 11.93 if everyone faced the social security incentives, a difference of 17.3 percent. The results differ across countries—for example, the change in years of work for Canada is only 6.7 percent, which is one-third the magnitude of the change in the United States. This in part reflects the size of the DI plan in Canada relative to the United States.

The next column repeats the exercise, but uses the sample of disabled individuals only. The base number of years worked for this sample is smaller in all countries, and the percent impact of varying the incentives of this sample is smaller than for the entire sample in column (2).

The last two columns show the results of the simulation that randomly assigns the incentives, to simulate the effect of making it more difficult for some DI applicants to access the program. The patterns in the results are expected from the calculations—when two-thirds of the sample is assigned to the DI incentives, the results look closer to the column (2) results than when only one-third of the sample is assigned DI incentives. Overall, the simulations suggest that DI programs have a noticeable impact on retirement across countries.

Conclusions

This volume is the sixth phase of the ongoing project on retirement programs around the world. The focus is on the importance of disability programs (DI) and, in particular, the retirement incentive effects of DI programs compared to other retirement programs. This is the second of two phases on DI programs. The first DI phase (the fifth phase of the continuing project) presented analysis of historical trends in our group of countries intended to set the stage for the more formal analysis in the current volume. In the first DI phase, the countries summarized DI program reforms and considered how DI reforms were related to changes in health, in particular, measured by change in mortality. We also considered DI reforms as natural experiments that showed that exogenous reforms can have a very large effect on the labor force participation of older workers. The current phase is also closely related to the second phase of the project, also based on microeconomic analysis of the relationship between a person's decision to retire and the program incentives faced by that person. In particular, in the second phase the countries considered the employment implications of increasing retirement program eligibility ages, including the eligibility ages for DI programs. The analysis showed that increasing eligibility ages would have very large effects on employment at older ages.

In contrast, the current phase focuses on the retirement incentive effects of program provisions without considering changes in program eligibility ages. We give attention to the provisions of DI programs as well as the provisions of other pathways to retirement. The goal is to understand how changing the provisions of country DI programs in particular would change retirement. Each country estimated the relationship between program provisions and retirement incentives in their country using an extension of the option value model used in the second phase of the program.

Several noticeable findings are based on background summary data. First, the proportion of men ages sixty to sixty-four collecting disability benefits ranges widely across countries, ranging from 17 percent in Belgium to 16 percent in the United Kingdom, 14 percent in the United States, 6 percent in Italy and France, and 2 percent in Japan—including Belgium and Italy that use a DI proportion different from the other countries. Second, the data show that in all countries, with the exception of the United States, there was large variation over time in DI participation rates with substantial decline in participation beginning in the early to mid-1990s in many countries. For example, in Canada participation in the sixty to sixty-four age group declined 49.6 percent between 1995 and 2009. In the United Kingdom, DI participation declined 49.6 percent between 1996 and 2012. In the United States, on the other hand, DI participation between 1990 and 2012 increased by over 30 percent. Third, variation in DI participation over time was unrelated to trends in health, which improved consistently over time based on declines in mortality. Fourth, and perhaps most striking, DI participation in all countries is very strongly related to education level, even controlling for health. Fifth, descriptive data show a noticeable inverse relationship between DI participation and employment over time.

The measurement of health is a central component of the analysis. To maintain as much comparability across countries as possible we use the health index developed by Poterba, Venti, and Wise (PVW). The index as set out by PVW is the first principal component of twenty-seven health indicators reported in the United States Health and Retirement Study (HRS). The index can be duplicated (approximately) through the nexus of comparable studies—the English Longitudinal Study of Aging (ELSA), the Survey of Health, Ageing and Retirement in Europe (SHARE), and the Japan Study of Aging and Retirement (JSTAR). These surveys include each of the twelve participating countries except Canada. For reasons of sample size, however, alternative data sources have been used in Sweden, Denmark, and Germany and these data do not provide sufficient health data to construct the PVW index.

Estimation is based on the regression counterpart to the Stock-Wise option value analysis in which retirement is based on the gain (the option value) of delaying retirement. A unique feature of the estimation in this phase is the "inclusive option value" that allows estimation based on the provisions of all pathways to retirement in each country. Two features of the estimates stand out. First, the estimated option value incentive measure is highly statistically significant in each of the countries with the exception of two countries—Spain and Germany (SHARE)—where the SHARE country data files were not large enough to support precise estimation. Second, the estimated effect of the OV incentive measure is substantial in most countries. For example, a one standard deviation increase in the option value (used as a standard measure across countries) reduces the estimated retirement rate by between 4 and 6 percent in six countries, by between 8 and 9 percent in two countries, and between 1 and 3 percent in three countries.

The most important results are in the form of simulations. First, simulations show that the model estimates fit the data very well—which is to be expected in specifications in which age indicators are estimated. Second, simulations of retirement rates by age and survival in the labor force show very large variation across countries. Third, perhaps the most important simulations show the importance on retirement of differences in the provisions of each pathway to retirement in each country. These differences are estimated first by simulating the number of years worked between ages fifty and sixty-nine if all persons faced only one of the pathways to retirement. For example, in the United States, years worked would be 10.18 if all persons faced the DI pathway provisions. If all persons faced the Social Security pathway, the average would be 11.93 years, an increase of 17.3 percent. In Belgium there are four pathways with estimated hours of work between ages fifty and sixty-nine of 5.36, 5.65, 5.71, and 7.54 for the CER, DI, UI, and old-age pension (OAP) pathways, respectively. Hours of work on the OAP pathway exceed hours on the CER, DI, and UI pathways by 40.67 percent, 33.45 percent, and 32.05 percent, respectively.

Fourth, simulations show the effect on retirement of increasing the stringency of admission to the DI program. This simulation is especially relevant given the large reduction in DI participation in many countries since the late 1980s and the mid-1990s. For example, if one-third of the persons now on DI in the United States were instead eligible only for the Social Security program, the hours of work of current DI participants would be increased by 5.1 percent; if two-thirds were eligible for the Social Security program only hours of work of current DI recipients would be increased by 10.1 percent. A comparable increase in the stringency of access to the DI program in the Netherlands would increase the years of work of current DI recipients by 7.69 percent and 21.37 percent, respectively.

With large increases in life expectancy in all participating countries there is considerable interest in prolonging working lives. Indeed, there has been a large increase in the employment of men in most of the participating countries since the late 1980s and the mid-1990s—the same period over which DI participation has been declining in most countries. Future increases in working lives will depend on the capacity to work, which may depend on individual attributes such as education. The capacity to work will be the topic of the next phase of the International Social Security project.

Appendix

Appendix on the OV Incentive Measure

Under the option value formulation, the value at age t of retirement at age r is given by

$$V_t(r) = \sum_{s=t}^{r-1} \beta^{s-t} E_t(Y_s^\gamma) + \sum_{s=r}^{S} \beta^{s-t} E_t(kB_s(r))^\gamma,$$

using the Stock-Wise specification. Here Y is future wage income and B is social security benefit income, which depends on the retirement age r. For simplicity, the probabilities of being alive to collect the income or the benefits have been suppressed. In this formulation, a person considering whether to retire at age t considers the present value of benefits if he retires now (at age t) with the benefits if he retires at some later age. If the person retires at some later age he will gain from future wage earnings and from any gain in future pension benefits.

If r^* is the retirement year that gives the maximum expected gain, the option value is given by

$$OV_t(r^*) = \sum_{s=t}^{r-1} \beta^{s-t} E_t(Y_s^\gamma) + \left[\sum_{s=r^*}^{S} \beta^{s-t} E_t(kB_s(r^*))^\gamma - \sum_{s=t}^{S} \beta^{s-t} E_t(kB_s(t))^\gamma \right]$$

$$= \begin{pmatrix} \text{discounted utility} \\ \text{of future wage} \end{pmatrix}$$

$$+ \left[\begin{pmatrix} \text{discounted utility} \\ \text{of benefits if} \\ \text{retire atr*} \end{pmatrix} - \begin{pmatrix} \text{discounted utility} \\ \text{of benefits if} \\ \text{retiree att} \end{pmatrix} \right].$$

Considering this equation, we can see that there are two ways to calculate the option value used in the analyses in this volume: one way is to use prior estimated values for the utility parameters γ, β, and k. Instead, we assume these values: $\gamma = 0.75$, $\beta = 0.03$, and $k = 1.5$, which are somewhat different from estimates obtained by Stock and Wise (1990), especially the assumed value of β, which is much smaller than their estimate.

References

Gruber, Jonathan, and David A. Wise. 1999. *Social Security Programs and Retirement around the World.* Chicago: University of Chicago Press.

———. 2004. *Social Security Programs and Retirement around the World: Micro-Estimation*. Chicago: University of Chicago Press.

———. 2007. *Social Security Programs and Retirement around the World: Fiscal Implications*. Chicago: University of Chicago Press.

———. 2010. *Social Security Programs and Retirement around the World: The Relationship to Youth Employment*. Chicago: University of Chicago Press.

Milligan, Kevin, and David A. Wise. 2012. "Introduction and Summary." In *Social Security Programs and Retirement around the World: Historical Trends in Health, Employment, and Disability Insurance and Reforms*, edited by David A. Wise. Chicago: University of Chicago Press.

Poterba, James, Steven Venti, and David A. Wise. 2013. "Health, Education, and the Postretirement Evolution of Household Assets." *Journal of Human Capital* 7 (4): 297–339. PMCID: PMC4043284.

Stock, James, and David Wise. 1990. "Pensions, the Option Value of Work, and Retirement." *Econometrica* 58:1151–80.

Wise, David A. 2012. *Social Security Programs and Retirement around the World: Historical Trends in Health, Employment, and Disability Insurance and Reforms*. Chicago: University of Chicago Press.

1

Disability Insurance Incentives and the Retirement Decision
Evidence from the United States

Courtney Coile

1.1 Introduction

The rolls of the US Disability Insurance (DI) program have risen dramatically since the program's inception in 1956. Over the past two decades, the share of the population age twenty-five to sixty-four receiving DI benefits more than doubled, from 2.3 percent in 1989 to 5.1 percent in 2012 (Figure 1.1). The growth of the program is likely to continue, stabilizing at 7 percent of the nonelderly population, according to one projection (Autor and Duggan 2006a). The rising number of DI beneficiaries has jeopardized the program's ability to pay benefits, with annual benefit expenditures reaching $140 billion in 2012 and the DI trust fund projected to be depleted by 2016. As the trustees of the program recently warned, "lawmakers need to act soon to avoid reduced payments to DI beneficiaries three years from now" (OASDI Trustees 2013).

Concerns about the DI program have been amplified by the observation that the program's growth does not appear to be driven by worsening population health. Over the period that DI participation doubled, the fraction of people reporting themselves to be in poor health or suffering from a work-limiting health problem was unchanged, if not declining (Milligan 2012; Duggan and Imberman 2008). These trends have led to renewed interest

Courtney Coile is professor of economics at Wellesley College and a research associate of the National Bureau of Economic Research.

This chapter was prepared for the NBER International Social Security project. I thank the organizers and other country teams for their suggestions. I also thank Peter Diamond, Jonathan Gruber, and Kevin Milligan, authors of US analyses in earlier volumes of the *Social Security and Retirement around the World* series that helped to inform the current chapter. For acknowledgments, sources of research support, and disclosure of the author's material financial relationships, if any, please see http://www.nber.org/chapters/c13351.ack.

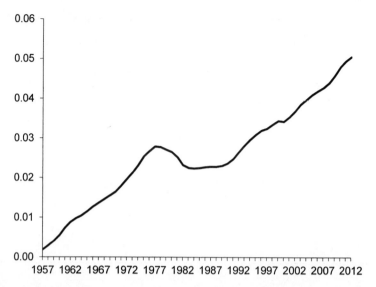

Fig. 1.1   DI beneficiaries as a share of population, age twenty-five to sixty-four (1957–2012)

Source: Authors' calculations based on table 5.D3 from the Social Security Annual Statistical Supplement and population data from the US Census Bureau (www.census.gov).

in understanding the causes of the rise in the DI rolls, as well as its consequences. The effect of DI on labor supply has been a subject of interest since Bound (1989, 1991) and Parsons (1991) reached different conclusions from comparisons of the earnings of accepted and rejected DI applicants. More recent work by Maestas, Mullen, and Strand (2013), French and Song (2012), and Chen and van der Klaauw (2008) has made use of plausibly exogenous variation in DI receipt coming from random assignment of DI applicants to medical examiners or similar sources.

This study takes a different approach to exploring the effect of the DI program on labor supply, specifically labor force withdrawal or retirement. The methodology employed here builds on Coile and Gruber (2004, 2007), who construct several measures of the financial incentives for additional work arising from the structure of the Social Security (SS) program. One measure is the "option value" (OV), which captures the *gain* in utility resulting from retiring at the optimal future date, over and above the utility available by retiring today. Those studies find that having a larger financial incentive for continued work is associated with a reduced probability of retirement. However, these studies ignore the DI program, treating Social Security (and private pensions) as the only possible pathway to retirement.

In the current study, I construct an "inclusive" option value measure that incorporates the financial incentives arising from both SS and DI, and estimate models that relate this new measure to the retirement transitions of workers age fifty to sixty-nine, using data from the Health and Retirement Study (HRS). To explore the effect of incentives on retirement conditional on health, I control for health using an index developed in Poterba, Venti, and Wise (2013). I explore whether the effect of incentives on retirement varies by health and education, both of which are strongly related to the probability of DI receipt. Finally, to put the magnitude of the findings into context and gauge the relevance of DI to retirement decisions, I use the regression estimates to simulate the effect of reducing access to DI.

I have several key findings. First, the probability of DI receipt is strongly linked to education, even conditional on health. Second, the inclusive OV measure has a negative and significant effect on the probability of retirement; the effect is robust to choice of specification and varies by education and health. Finally, the simulations suggest that reducing access to DI would have large effects on the labor force participation of DI applicants.

The remainder of the chapter is structured as follows. In the next section, I provide background on the US DI program and the past literature on DI and labor supply. Next, I describe the empirical strategy, notably how the inclusive OV measure is constructed, as well as the data used. I present descriptive statistics on the probability of DI receipt, and then present the main regression results. I conclude with a simulation of the effect of reducing access to DI and a discussion of the implications of the findings.

1.2   Background

1.2.1   Institutional Features of Social Security and Disability Insurance

Disability insurance in the United States is part of the Social Security program. Eligibility for DI and the calculation of DI benefits is similar to that for SS, with a few key differences.

Workers become eligible for Social Security retired worker benefits after ten years (forty quarters) of covered employment, which now encompasses most sectors of the economy. Benefits are determined by first calculating the Average Indexed Monthly Earnings (AIME), an average of the individual's highest thirty-five years of earnings, indexed by a national wage index. Next, a progressive linear formula is applied to the AIME to get the primary insurance amount (PIA), where ninety cents of the first dollar of earnings is converted to benefits but only fifteen cents of the last dollar. Finally, the PIA is multiplied by an adjustment factor for claiming before or after the normal retirement age ([NRA]; currently sixty-six, but rising slowly to sixty-seven for those born in 1960 or later) to obtain the monthly benefit amount. Benefits are first available at age sixty-two but may be claimed as late as age seventy, and the adjustment factor for early or delayed claiming is considered to be roughly actuarially fair.[1] Before the NRA, workers face an earnings test if their earnings exceed a threshold amount, $15,480, in 2014. Benefits are available for spouses and survivors of retired workers, though a spouse who is also qualified for retired worker benefits receives only the larger of the benefits to which she (or he) is entitled. For the median earner, the Social Security replacement rate is 47 percent of average lifetime earnings (Biggs and Springstead 2008).

While receipt of retired worker benefits upon claiming is automatic for an insured worker, the DI application process is more complex. First, in order to be disability insured, a worker must meet both "recent work" and "duration of work" tests, working in at least five of the last ten quarters (less if disabled by age thirty) and for up to forty quarters over the worker's lifetime (depending on age at disability). An insured worker applying for DI must be determined to have a disability, defined as the "inability to engage in substantial gainful activity (SGA) by reason of any medically determinable physical or mental impairment(s) which can be expected to result in death or which has lasted or can be expected to last for a continuous period of not less than twelve months."[2] The review of a DI application can be a lengthy, multistep process—the initial decision is made by an examiner at a state disability determination (DDS) office, but denied applicants have up to four levels of appeal available to them. One recent study found that although only one-third of applicants were allowed in the initial determination, nearly two-thirds were ultimately awarded benefits (Maestas, Mullen, and Strand 2013). Successful DI applicants begin receiving benefits five months after disability onset, and are eligible for Medicare after two years. Beneficiaries who earn more than the SGA threshold, $1,070 per month in 2014, lose DI eligibility.

The disability screening process has been subject to changes over time. In the late 1970s, DDS offices tightened medical eligibility criteria in response to growing DI enrollments, resulting in a sharp increase in initial denial rates (Gruber and Kubik 1997). A 1980 law increased the number of "continuing disability reviews" (CDRs), leading to the termination of benefits for 380,000 individuals over the next three years (Rupp and Scott 1998). These actions generated a public backlash that led Congress to enact new legislation in 1984. While the new law did not change the statutory definition of disability, it shifted the focus of screening from medical to functional criteria, instructing examiners "to place significant weight on applicants' reported pain and discomfort, to relax its strict screening of mental illness and to consider multiple nonsevere ailments (impairments) as constituting

1. Shoven and Slavov (2013) estimate that returns to delayed claiming have increased over time, particularly since 2000, while Munnell and Sass (2012) argue that the actuarial fairness of the Social Security adjustment factor has changed little over time. Coile et al. (2002) show there is a financial and utility gain from claiming delay for many individuals.

2. Social Security Act, Title II, Section 216 (http://www.ssa.gov/OP_Home/ssact/title02/0216 .htm#act-216-i), accessed May 11, 2015.

a disability during the initial determination decision, even if none of these impairments was by itself disabling" (Autor and Duggan 2006b, 8). The 1984 law also put more weight on medical evidence provided by applicants' own health care provider and less on that from the Social Security Administration's medical examination.

Several differences between SS retired workers and DI benefits are relevant for the discussion of financial incentives below. First and foremost, DI benefits are available (to a successful applicant) from the age of disability onset, while retired worker benefits are available only starting at age sixty-two. Second, DI benefits are not subject to reduction for early claiming; thus, a worker claiming retired worker benefits at age sixty-two would receive 75 percent of their PIA (based on current rules), while a worker who was awarded DI benefits at age sixty-two (or any other age) would receive 100 percent of their PIA.[3] Finally, there are some small technical differences in the calculation of the two benefits, such as a lower number of years of earnings and different indexing year (both due to the shorter career) used in the calculation of the AIME and PIA for DI benefits.

1.2.2   Relevant Past Literature

This chapter, like nearly any study of the US DI program, is motivated at least in part by the growth over time in DI enrollments, and thus the literature exploring the reasons for this trend is of interest. Changes in the stringency of medical screening are clearly one important factor. As figure 1.1 illustrates, fluctuations in DI enrollment over time match up with the dates of screening changes, with the DI participation rate falling by 20 percent between 1977 and 1984 (from 2.8 percent of the nonelderly population to 2.2 percent) following the initial tightening of eligibility criteria and increase in CDRs and rising again sharply following the 1984 law. The composition of the DI population has also shifted dramatically in the past two decades, with the number of beneficiaries with musculoskeletal and mental disorders growing by over 300 percent while the number with cancer and heart disease grew by only 30 percent; the explosive growth in the former group is consistent with the 1984 law's relaxed screening of mental illness and greater emphasis on pain and workplace function (Autor and Duggan 2006a).

Economic and demographic factors have also been put forward as possible explanations for the time-series trend. Autor and Duggan (2003) point out that the value of DI relative to potential labor market earnings has risen since the late 1970s because of the interaction between the DI benefit formula and rising income inequality, whereby DI benefits become relatively

3. The rise in the NRA makes it more attractive for early retirees to apply for DI when they retire, since the actuarial reduction for claiming retired worker benefits at age sixty-two is rising over time from 20 percent (for those born before 1938) to 30 percent (for those born starting in 1960). Li and Maestas (2008) find that the increase in the NRA has led to an increase in DI applications, particularly among those in poor health.

more generous if an individual's earnings growth lags behind the average growth of earnings in the economy. Over the past two decades the increase in DI enrollment has been largest for those without a high school degree, consistent with their weakening position in the economy (Katz and Autor 1999). Another potential explanation is rising women's labor force participation, which has made more women eligible for DI. As illustrated below, women's DI participation rates rose more rapidly over this period than did men's, lending some credence to this theory; however, Autor and Duggan (2006a) estimate that increased attachment to the labor force explains only one-sixth of the increase in women's DI participation over time, suggesting that other factors may matter more. Finally, as mentioned above, changes in health do not appear to be a major driver of the growth in DI enrollment, since mortality rates have fallen over time while other health measures have generally been either flat or improving.

A second strand of the literature that is highly relevant for the present analysis concerns the effect of the DI program on labor supply. The long-term decline in the labor force participation of older men that began after the end of World War II (before stabilizing and ultimately reversing starting in the early 1990s) coincided with the rapid growth of the DI program in its first two decades of existence, prompting analysts to explore the effect of DI on men's labor force participation as far back as Parsons (1980). Estimating the effect of the DI program on labor supply is difficult because the counterfactual—how much DI recipients would have worked in the absence of the DI program—is unobservable. Comparing the labor force participation of DI recipients with that of the population at large is fraught because DI recipients are in worse health and may differ in other unobservable ways, introducing bias in the estimation.

Bound (1989) offers a novel solution, using the postdecision earnings of rejected DI applicants as an upper bound estimate of the work capacity of successful applicants, the former group presumably being in better health than the latter. Finding that rejected DI applicants had labor force participation rates of less than 50 percent, Bound concludes that the work capacity of successful applicants is low. Subsequent papers (Parsons 1991; Bound 1991) have raised and debated potential problems with this approach. Rejected applicants may need to remain out of the labor force for years to avoid jeopardizing their appeals and may also suffer depreciation of human capital due to the interruption in their work career (which would not occur in the absence of a DI program). Lahiri and Wixon (2008) found that rejected DI applicants also tend to have intermittent work histories, further calling into question their use as a comparison group.

More recent contributions to this literature have surmounted the usual endogeneity problem by identifying plausibly exogenous sources of variation in DI receipt. Maestas, Mullen, and Strand (2013) exploit variation in the allowance rates of DI examiners at the initial stage in the DI determination process. They find that among the roughly one-quarter of applicants on the margin of program entry, employment would have been nearly 30 percentage points higher in the absence of DI benefits. These effects are heterogeneous, ranging from no effect for the most impaired to a 50 percentage point effect for the least impaired. French and Song (2012) employ a similar methodology, using variation that arises from random assignment of DI cases to administrative law judges, a later stage in the DI determination process. Chen and van der Klaauw (2008) employ a regression discontinuity approach based on discrete changes in eligibility standards at various ages (e.g., age fifty-five) that are codified in the Medical-Vocational Guidelines and used for applicants when a disability determination cannot be made on medical grounds alone. The latter two papers obtain estimates roughly similar to those of Maestas, Mullen, and Strand (2013). Gruber (2000) differs slightly from the other papers in this group in that he focuses on the generosity of DI benefits. Making use of a differential increase in benefits in Quebec versus the rest of Canada in the 1980s to estimate a differences-in-differences model, he finds an elasticity of labor force nonparticipation with respect to DI benefits in the range of 0.3.

The approach employed in this chapter takes a different tack, building on the analysis in Coile and Gruber (2001, 2004, 2007). As explained in more detail below, this approach involves calculating the financial incentive to continued work through the SS and DI programs (option value) and estimating its effect on retirement decisions. Rather than comparing labor supply outcomes of DI recipients and nonrecipients, as most of the above-referenced papers do, the approach taken here compares the labor supply outcomes of those with more and less to gain from continued work. As explained at greater length in the Coile and Gruber papers, there is substantial heterogeneity in the option value measure.[4] While some of this heterogeneity arises from differences in characteristics such as age, marital status, and earnings (which may influence retirement decisions but can be included as control variables), much of it also arises from factors such as nonlinearities in the Social Security benefit formula and how they interact with the particulars of an individual's earnings history. As we argue in those earlier papers, this is a fruitful source of variation for estimating the effect of Social Security on retirement. The innovation in this chapter, relative to those earlier studies, is to incorporate DI incentives in to the option value measure through the construction of the "inclusive option value" measure.

4. This is also true of the purely financial-based incentive measures that play a bigger role in these earlier studies, namely the "accrual," or increase in lifetime present discounted value (PDV) of Social Security benefits arising from an additional year of work, and "peak value," or change in PDV associated with working from the present age to the age at which PDV is maximized.

1.3   Empirical Approach

1.3.1   Data

The data for the analysis comes from the Health and Retirement Study (HRS). The HRS began in 1992 as a survey of individuals then age fifty-one to sixty-one (born in 1931–1941) and their spouses, with reinterviews of these individuals every two years. Over time, new cohorts have been added to the survey to maintain a national panel of individuals over age fifty and their spouses.[5] To date, 11 waves of data (1992–2012) have been collected; as the 2012 data has only recently been made available, this chapter uses the 1992–2010 data. The chapter uses the RAND HRS data file, a cleaned data set that links information over time and across family members and defines variables consistently over time.

A key feature of the HRS is that it includes Social Security earnings histories for most respondents.[6] This allows for the calculation of SS and DI benefit entitlements, which depend on the entire history of earnings. The HRS also contains richly detailed health information that is used in constructing the health index, as detailed below.

The size of the HRS—over 30,000 individuals have appeared in one or more survey wave over the years—as well as the fact that it is a panel allows for the construction of a large sample of person-year observations. Specifically, the estimation sample includes observations for all men and women in any year from 1992 to 2009 in which they met three criteria: (a) they were age fifty to sixty-nine during the year; (b) they were in the labor force at the beginning of the year; and (c) they were observed in the subsequent survey wave, in order to be able to determine whether or not they retired that year. Thus an individual who was, for example, age fifty when first observed in the HRS in 1998 and retired in 2008 at age sixty would contribute eleven person-year observations to the sample, so long as he remained in the survey until 2010 (to determine whether he retired in 2008). The final sample includes 70,675 observations from 10,570 individuals.

The labor supply outcome of interest in the chapter is retirement. Retirement is defined based on the labor force status reported at each wave, an individual being classified as retired when he or she has transitioned from working or unemployed at the previous wave to out of the labor force in the current wave, with the year of retirement assigned based on the date the individual reports at the current wave. Retirement is treated as an absorbing

---

5. The Asset and Health Dynamics among the Oldest Old (AHEAD) cohort (born before 1924) was added to the survey in 1998, when the previously separate AHEAD survey was merged with the HRS. The War Babies (1942–1947) and Children of the Depression (1924–1930) cohorts were also added in 1998. The Early Baby Boomer cohort (1948–1953) joined the survey in 2004 and the Mid-Baby Boomer cohort (1954–1959) in 2010.

6. These data are restricted and available by application only.

state, so that once an individual reports himself as out of the labor force after age fifty, any subsequent employment spells are not used in the analysis.

1.3.2   Pathways to Retirement

While in some other developed countries early retirement or unemployment insurance benefits offer a viable means of income support from the time a worker leaves his or her job until he or she becomes eligible for social security benefits, in the United States there are only two relevant pathways from employment to retirement: the traditional Social Security ([SS]; meaning retired worker) path and the disability insurance (DI) path.[7]

As noted above, SS benefits are available starting at age sixty-two. In the construction of the incentive measures, described in more detail below, SS benefits are treated as being claimed at the later of age sixty-two or when the individual retires. Although claiming is a separate decision from retirement and an individual could theoretically claim benefits either before retirement (once he or she has reached age sixty-two) or after, this assumption seems reasonable given that the SS earnings test, which is still in place for workers until they reach the NRA, depresses preretirement benefit claiming (Gruber and Orszag 2003) and that it is relatively rare for individuals to delay SS benefit receipt after retirement (Coile et al. 2002).

The DI benefits are treated as being claimed at the time of labor force withdrawal, since there is no advantage to (or even mechanism for) delayed claiming.[8] While this may be a reasonable assumption, it is clearly not realistic to assume that everyone can be a successful DI applicant. There is a medical screening process, and though it may be imperfect (as evidenced by the large number of denied applicants who are successful upon appeal, for example), some individuals—those in worse health, also potentially those who are older or in certain occupations due to the use of vocational guidelines in some cases—would be expected to have a higher probability of

7. Unemployment insurance (UI) benefits are typically available for only six months and only to insured workers who are laid off, limiting their value as a source of early retirement income. Coile and Levine (2007) suggests that UI benefits are not empirically important for the retirement decision, finding that workers who reach age sixty-two in a period of high unemployment are more likely to retire, but that the generosity of UI benefits has no effect on retirement transitions. They conclude that SS may be more relevant than UI in protecting older workers from the impact of a late-career employment shock. In addition, in theory, private pensions should be incorporated in the analysis as well, not as a distinct path to retirement but as an income source available to those individuals in the sample who are eligible for defined benefit (DB) pensions, whether they retire along the SS or DI path. Coile and Gruber (2007) calculate incentive measures using SS income only and using both SS and pension income and obtain very similar regression estimates from the two sets of measures, providing some justification for their omission here.

8. Successful applicants are eligible for benefits after a five-month waiting period from the onset of disability, as discussed earlier, but this detail is ignored in the analysis. The DI applicants often spend more than five months waiting for their final disability determination, but benefits are paid retroactively.

a success. A discussion of how the uncertainty in access to DI benefits is incorporated into the empirical analysis is deferred to the following section.

1.3.3   Option Value Calculations

To review, the goal of the analysis is to develop a retirement incentive measure that will reflect the financial incentives for continued work arising from both the SS and DI programs and to estimate its effect on retirement. To explain the chapter's approach, in this section I first describe the standard SS-only option value measure used in prior analyses (Coile and Gruber 2004, 2007). I then explain how this will be expanded to an "inclusive OV" measure that incorporates DI benefits, including how the uncertainty about an individual's ability to access DI is addressed. Finally, I explain other details relevant to the calculation of the inclusive OV measure.

The option value (OV) approach was pioneered by Stock and Wise (1990) in order to model retirement incentives for workers with defined benefit (DB) pensions. Because DB pensions can have nonmonotonic accrual patterns, for example, very large returns to work in the year that pension vesting occurs or that the individual reaches the pension plan's normal retirement age, the one-year change in the present discounted value (PDV) of pension wealth resulting from an additional year of work (the "accrual") fails to capture the fact that by working this year, the employee is effectively purchasing an option to work in a future year with a larger accrual. Although nonmonotonicities in the accrual of SS benefits do not tend to be as large or frequent as those found for DB pensions, Coile and Gruber (2001) nonetheless show that they exist for SS as well.

Option value is a forward-looking measure of the utility *gain* arising from working to the optimal future retirement date, in excess of the utility available by retiring today. Traditionally, OV has included only SS (and sometimes pension) benefits, but since the present analysis analyzes DI incentives as well, I use the notation OVSS to indicate the traditional measure that only includes SS. The OVSS calculation begins as follows:

$$OVSS(R)_{ii} =$$

(1) $$\left[\sum_{t=0}^{R} \frac{1}{(1+\delta)^t} \text{probalive}_{it}(\text{wage}_{it})^\gamma + \sum_{t=R}^{T} \frac{1}{(1+\delta)^t} \text{probalive}_{it}(k * \text{SSben}(R)_i)^\gamma \right]$$

$$- OVSS(R_0),$$

where R refers to a future retirement date, R_0 refers to today, and T is the final period in which the individual could be alive. Also, $OVSS(R)$ is essentially the sum of earnings until time R and of SS benefits (which are a function of R) from time R to time T, discounted for time preference and survival probability, where δ reflects the discount rate, γ reflects the curvature of the utility function, and k reflects the greater utility individuals receive from retirement income due to the utility of leisure. Unlike Stock and Wise (1990), who obtain values for the utility parameters by a structural estimation of their model, we assume that these three parameters take on the values of 0.03, 0.75, and 1.5, respectively.[9]

Equation (1) reflects the utility gain associated with retiring at some future date R, so the individual must repeat this calculation for all possible values of R and estimate:

$$(2) \quad \text{OVSS}_i = \max_R \{\text{OVSS}(R_1)_i, \text{OVSS}(R_2)_i, \ldots, \text{OVSS}(R_{\max})_i\},$$

where OVSS is the gain in utility arising from delaying retirement and receipt of SS benefits from the present time until the optimal date, the date at which utility is maximized. In our analysis, age sixty-nine is treated as the last possible retirement age considered by the worker.

Having made this calculation for OVSS, it is straightforward to calculate OVDI in the same manner, temporarily ignoring the possibility that the DI path may be difficult to access for many individuals. In essence the OVDI calculation tells us, if one is going to retire via the DI program, what the optimal date (age) at which to do so is and how large the utility gain is from waiting until that optimal date.

Having calculated OVSS and OVDI brings us to two related questions. First, how can we construct a single incentive measure that incorporates both?[10] Second, what is the appropriate way to account for the fact that not everyone who might want to will be able to choose to retire down the DI path? It turns out that both questions have the same answer, which is to construct an inclusive OV measure that is a weighted average of the two individual measures, as follows:

$$(3) \quad \begin{aligned} \text{OVInclusive}_i &= (\text{DIprobability}_i * \text{OVDI}_i) \\ &\quad + ((1 - \text{DIprobability}_i) * \text{OVSS}_i), \end{aligned}$$

where OVInclusive is the key regressor in our retirement regressions. The obvious question that arises in its calculation is what value to use for DIprobability. In theory, this measure should reflect the probability that the DI path is a realistic option for a given individual. Our approach is to calculate the probability that people age fifty-five to sixty-four are receiving DI by year, sex, and education cell, and use these cell probabilities. This approach has the practical advantage that it requires relatively little data, making it feasible to apply in contexts where rich data such as the HRS is

9. An informal grid search over a range of possible values for the three parameters suggests that the likelihood function is relatively flat with respect to parameter choice.

10. One very relevant reason for preferring a single measure in the current context is that the results presented here will be combined with those from the other countries participating in the NBER International Social Security project, and the number of pathways may differ across countries. One of the important benefits of having analysts in a large number of countries undertake the same analysis (as nearly as possible) is the insights that can be derived when results are combined.

not available. While it would be possible, using the HRS, to go beyond this approach to estimate a predicted probability that any given individual would go on DI, incorporating health information that is surely relevant to DI application and receipt, an advantage of using cell averages is that it avoids the use of these potentially endogenous covariates. Additionally, since some regression specifications interact our incentive measure with health, it is awkward to also have health embedded in the construction of the incentive measure. In essence, one can think of this as similar to an instrumental variables approach, where we limit ourselves to the variation that is more plausibly exogenous to retirement to obtain a cleaner, if less precise, estimate of DIprobability. The actual values used for DIprobability are reported below.

Finally, I briefly discuss a few salient technical details relevant to the calculation of OVInclusive; more information about these calculations can be found in the appendix to Coile and Gruber (2001). The worker's potential future earnings must be projected to age sixty-nine in order to calculate OVSS and OVDI, as earnings enter directly in the OV measures. Following Coile and Gruber (2004), I grow real earnings by 1 percent per year from the last observed value. I estimate PIAs for all possible future retirement dates using a program that incorporates the Social Security benefits rules and has been cross-checked against the Social Security Administration's ANYPIA model. The appropriate actuarial adjustment factor is applied in the calculation of SSBen(R). For married workers, OVSS and OVDI incorporate dependent spouse and survivor benefits, allowing for the probability that at any given age, either or both spouses may be surviving. The inclusion of spousal benefits is complicated by the fact that a spouse who is qualified for retired worker benefits is entitled to the greater of this or her dependent benefit, which will depend on her retirement date. A full modeling of joint retirement decisions is beyond the scope of this chapter, so I assume that any working wives (or husbands) retire at age sixty-two for the purpose of incorporating dependent benefits on the spouse's record, a seemingly reasonable assumption, given that the median retirement age is sixty-two for married women who were working at age fifty.

1.3.4   Health Quintiles

An important goal of the larger project of which this chapter forms a part is to ask: Given health status, to what extent are differences in labor force participation within and across countries determined by the provisions of DI programs? To be able to answer this, it is necessary to control for health in the analysis, preferably in a way that incorporates as much information as possible and can be replicated across countries.

The approach adopted here, which builds on Poterba, Venti, and Wise (2013) and is described at length elsewhere in this volume, is to construct a health index based on twenty-seven questions, including self-reported health diagnoses, functional limitations, medical care usage, and other health indicators. To do so, one first obtains the first principal component of these indicators, which is the "weighted average of indicators where weights are chosen to maximize the proportion of the variance of the individual health indicators that can be explained by this weighted average." The estimated coefficients from the analysis are then used to predict a percentile score for each respondent, referred to as the health index. An individual's health index value typically will vary by HRS survey wave, as updated health information points are incorporated. As Poterba, Venti, and Wise (2013) demonstrate, the health index is strongly related to mortality and to future health events such as stroke and diabetes onset, though not to new cancer diagnosis. In the analysis below, respondents are divided into health quintiles based on their health index scores.

1.4   Results

1.4.1   Descriptive Analysis: DI Participation Rates

Before turning to the regression results, I present some figures on DI participation. Figures 1.2A and 1.2B show participation rates for men and women ages fifty to sixty-four since 1982, using data on DI beneficiaries from the Social Security Administration and population data from the US Census Bureau. Trends over time for older workers mirror those seen in figure 1.1 for the population at large. By 2012, one in seven men ages sixty to sixty-four (14.2 percent) is on DI, as is one in ten men at ages fifty-five to fifty-nine (10.6 percent), and one in fourteen at ages fifty to fifty-four (7.1 percent). The DI participation rates for older women have risen even more dramatically than for older men in the last three decades, doubling for the age sixty to sixty-four group, from 5.6 percent in 1982 to 11.4 percent in 2012, and tripling for women age fifty to fifty-four, from 2.0 percent in 1982 to 6.4 percent in 2012.

Figures 1.3A through 1.3D show rates of DI receipt by education and health for men and women ages fifty-five to sixty-four. These and subsequent figures use data from the HRS;[11] representative years from 1992 through 2008 are shown on the graph, though calculations are made for all years. The first thing to note is that the values shown on figures 1.3A and 1.3B are the DIprobability values used in the construction of OVInclusive, as they are year-sex-education cell average participation rates.

Figure 1.3A shows a substantial DI participation gradient by education, with the lowest education group, high school dropouts, being five to six times more likely to be on DI than the highest education group, college

---

11. The data in these figures reflect all HRS respondents in the relevant age group, and are not limited to workers.

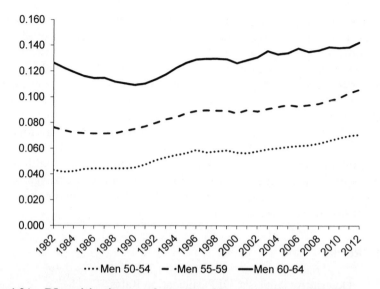

····Men 50-54 — ·Men 55-59 ——Men 60-64

Fig. 1.2A   DI participation rates for men age fifty to sixty-four, 1982–2012

Source: Authors' calculations based on table 5.D3 from the Social Security Annual Statistical Supplement and population data from the US Census Bureau (www.census.gov).

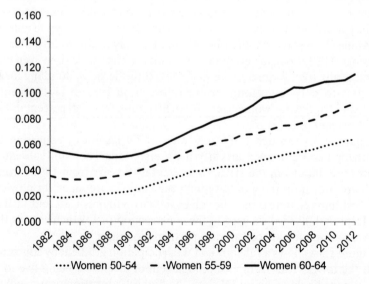

····Women 50-54 — ·Women 55-59 ——Women 60-64

Fig. 1.2B   DI participation rates for women age fifty to sixty-four, 1982–2012

Source: Authors' calculations based on table 5.D3 from the Social Security Annual Statistical Supplement and population data from the US Census Bureau (www.census.gov).

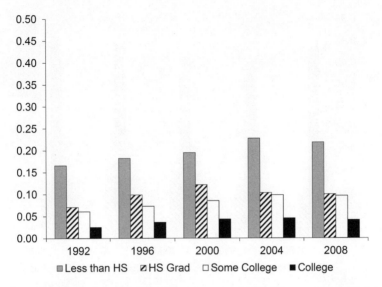

Fig. 1.3A **Probability men age fifty-five to sixty-four in HRS have received DI, by education and year**

Source: Authors' calculations from the HRS.

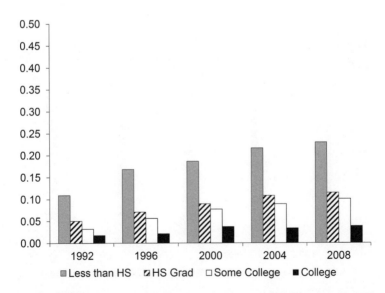

Fig. 1.3B **Probability women age fifty-five to sixty-four in HRS have received DI, by education and year**

Source: Authors' calculation from the HRS.

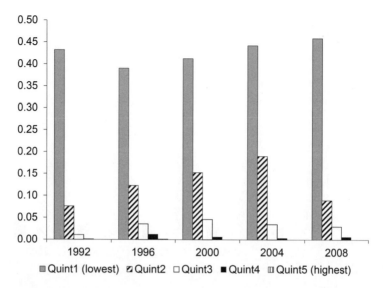

Fig. 1.3C Probability men age fifty-five to sixty-four in HRS have received DI, by health quintile and year

Source: Authors' calculation from the HRS.

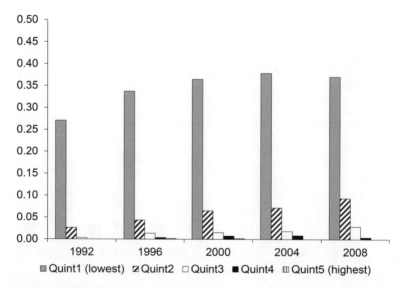

Fig. 1.3D Probability women age fifty-five to sixty-four in HRS have received DI, by health quintile and year

Source: Authors' calculation from the HRS.

graduates; in 2008, the rates were 22 percent for the former group and 4 percent for the latter. The rise in DI rates over time that was evident in earlier figures is present here as well for all education groups; the DI participation rate for high school graduates, for example, rises by 41 percent from 1992 to 2008, from 7.1 percent to 10.0 percent. Figure 1.3B shows that the DI participation gradient by education is, if anything, steeper for women; the rise in DI over time is also more pronounced, consistent with earlier figures.

Figures 1.3C and 1.3D repeat the exercise, stratifying by health quintile (as defined above) rather than by education group. The DI participation gradient with respect to health is much steeper than that for education. This is not terribly surprising, in that there is a medical screening process for DI, so those in worse health (measured using data from the current survey wave) should be more likely to be on DI. Among men ages fifty-five to sixty-four in 2008, 46 percent of those in the lowest health quintile were on DI versus 9 percent for the second quintile, 3 percent for the third, and essentially no one in the top two quintiles. The strong relationship between DI receipt and the health index would seem to provide some reassurance that both the health index we construct is a useful summary statistic for health status and that the DI medical screening process is at least somewhat successful in identifying the least healthy. The graph for women is very similar, though the probability of being on DI for those in the lowest health quintile is somewhat lower, only 37 percent in 2008.

One question raised by these figures is whether the correlation between education and DI receipt seen in figures 1.3A and 1.3B primarily reflects the effect of health, since low socioeconomic status is known to be correlated with poor health (Smith 1999), or whether there is a relationship between education and DI receipt even conditional on health. This question is answered in figures 1.3E and 1.3F, which show the probability of DI receipt by education and health, averaged across all years. The education gradient is substantially smaller, but remains nontrivial, with male high school dropouts in the lowest health quintile being 46 percent more likely to be on DI than college graduates in the same health quintile (50 percent vs. 34 percent), while female high school dropouts are 66 percent more likely to be on DI (38 percent vs. 23 percent). The education gradient is equally strong, if not stronger, in higher health quintiles, though the absolute rates of DI participation are quite small in the top two quintiles. Thus, we can conclude that education has a robust relationship with DI receipt. This is consistent with rising income inequality being one of the explanations for the rise in the DI rolls, as mentioned above. It is also consistent with finding that DI applications and awards tend to rise with the unemployment rate (Autor and Duggan 2003), since less educated workers experience higher rates of unemployment.

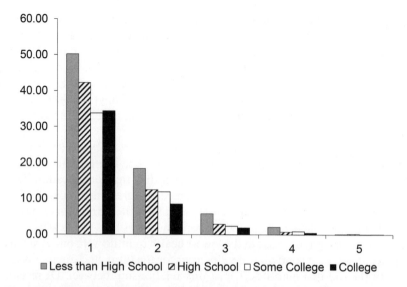

Fig. 1.3E   DI participation by health quintile and education, men fifty-five to sixty-four, 1992–2009

Source: Authors' calculations from the HRS.

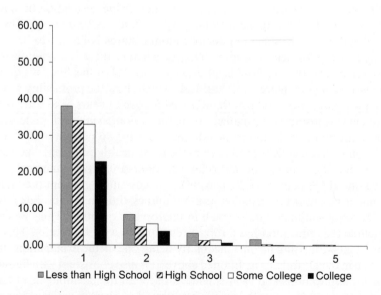

Fig. 1.3F   DI participation by health quintile and education, women fifty-five to sixty-four, 1992–2009

Source: Authors' calculations from the HRS.

1.4.2   Descriptive Analysis: Incentive Measures

Before examining the regression results, it is useful to take a closer look at the incentive measures that are the key regressors in those models. Figures 1.4A and 1.4B show the mean values of the OV measures by age for men and women. These figures are constructed by taking a sample of workers at age fifty and computing their incentive measures at all future ages through age sixty-nine; there is no concern of sample selection (e.g., higher income workers being less likely to retire) as the sample ages, as mean OV is calculated using data for all workers, regardless of their ultimate retirement decision.

Starting with figure 1.4A, the first thing to note is that the mean for all of the OV measures (OVSS, OVDI, and OVInclusive) is positive, indicating that on average there is some utility gain associated with remaining in the labor force until the optimal future retirement date, whether the individual is contemplating retirement along the SS or DI path. For all measures, the mean value is declining with age, reflecting the fact that the closer one gets to the optimal retirement date, the smaller the utility gain associated with waiting until that date to retire.[12] As far as the magnitudes, the OV measures are in utility units rather than in currency units, so the values do not have an easy interpretation, though higher values reflect a larger gain from retirement delay. The values of OVDI are lower than those for OVSS, for reasons I explain below, but have the same pattern of declining with age. The values for OVInclusive are much closer to those of OVSS than OVDI; this is expected, given that OVInclusive is a weighted average of the two and the average DIprobability in the sample is approximately 10 percent, putting more emphasis on OVSS in the calculation. The values for women, shown in figure 1.4D, are lower than for men, as women's lower average earnings mean that they have less to gain from retirement delays (recall that the OV measures incorporate the value of earnings through retirement as well as the value of SS or DI benefits after retirement). However, the decline with age and relative magnitudes of the different measures display the same patterns observed for men.

Some additional insight into these measures, and particularly into the relationship between OVSS and OVDI, can be gleaned from figures 1.4C and 1.4D. These report a simpler measure, the PDV of lifetime SS or DI benefits associated with each possible retirement date. The PDV measures reflect the financial (not utility) gain from additional work if one retires along either the SS or DI path, and include only changes in the value of benefits and not the additional wages that may result from additional work.

As figure 1.4C indicates, PDVSS rises moderately with additional work through age sixty-two, the age of SS eligibility, as additional years of earn-

---

12. By construction, OV cannot be negative, but it will be zero once the individual has passed his or her optimal retirement date.

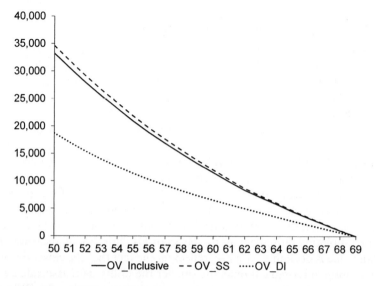

Fig. 1.4A   Mean OV by age for men

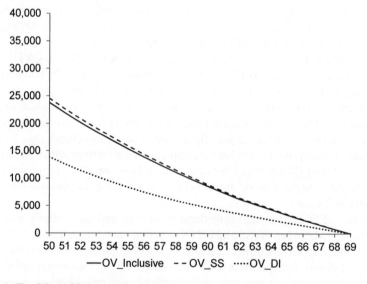

Fig. 1.4B   Mean OV by age for women

ings may replace zeroes or low-earnings years in the SS benefit calculation. After age sixty-two, the PDVSS grows more slowly, as an additional year of work is accompanied by a delay in the SS benefit claim that results in the loss of one year of SS benefits (lowering the PDV) but also in a higher actuarial adjustment and permanently higher SS benefits once receipt commences

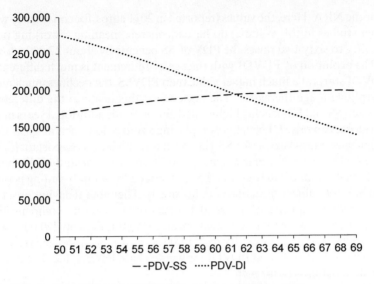

Fig. 1.4C   Mean PDV-SS and PDV-DI by age, men (2011 euros)

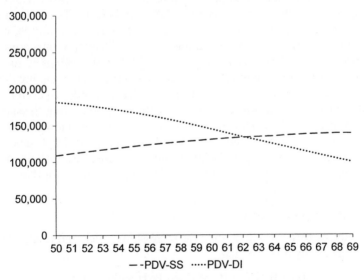

Fig. 1.4D   Mean PDV-SS and PDV-DI by age, women (2011 euros)

(raising the PDV); at the mean, the net of these two effects is positive, but modestly so.[13] With a 3 percent discount rate, the series essentially peaks at or

13. These results will be sensitive to the choice of the discount rate, since the cost of remaining in the labor force for an additional year is borne now and the benefit is received in the future.

near the NRA. Here, the values (reported in 2011 euros, for consistency with other studies in this volume) do have a concrete meaning—working from age fifty to sixty-two raises the PDV of SS benefits by about 27,000 euros.

The evolution of PDVDI with the age of retirement is much different—PDVDI starts at a much higher value than PDVSS, but declines much more sharply with age thereafter. The reasons for this relate to the differences between SS and DI benefits highlighted above. While additional years in the workforce can raise DI benefits by replacing a zero or low-earnings year with a higher-earnings year, as for SS, this effect is relatively less important for DI because DI uses a shorter averaging period.[14] More importantly, DI benefits are available immediately upon DI award (after a five-month waiting period) and are not subject to actuarial adjustment. Therefore delaying onset of DI benefit receipt means a loss of benefits today, with no compensating increase in future benefits. For men, mean PDVDI falls from 270,000 euros if retirement occurs at age fifty to 151,000 euros if it occurs at age sixty-six. As expected, PDVSS and PDVDI for women have lower values but display the same patterns as for men.

Returning to figures 1.4A and 1.4B, OVDI can be positive (and declining with age) even when PDVDI peaks at a retirement age of fifty because the OV measures include earnings as well as SS or DI benefits. The replacement rates from SS and DI are fairly low, both in absolute terms and by international standards, and so even though the OV calculation puts a greater value on a dollar of retirement income than a dollar of earnings because of the utility of leisure, it may still be optimal to delay retirement along the DI path even if DI benefits are immediately available in order to accumulate additional years of earnings. Nonetheless, the key point is that the sharply different profiles of PDVSS and PDVDI explain the much lower values of OVDI relative to OVSS in figures 1.4A and 1.4B—there is simply much less to be gained by remaining in the labor force for those retiring along the DI path, relative to the gains available from delaying retirement for those retiring along the SS path.

1.4.3   Regression Results

Finally, we turn our attention to the regression models and results. These models generally take the form:

$$(4) \qquad R_{it} = \beta_0 + \beta_1 OV_{it} + \beta_2 AGE_{it} + \beta_3 Health_{it} + \beta_4 X_{it} + \varepsilon_{it},$$

where retirement (R_{it}) is a dummy variable equal to 1 if the individual retires during the year (reports being out of the labor force at the following survey

---

14. To elaborate on this, a fifty-year-old considering retiring now through the SS path would likely have zeroes in the calculation of his PIA for SS benefits, as he is unlikely to have thirty-five years of covered earnings by this point. By contrast, for a fifty-year-old considering retiring now through the DI path, the PIA would be calculated based on only the highest twenty-three years of earnings, so it is less likely that this calculation would include zeroes.

year and specifies this year as the year of retirement); OV_{it} is the inclusive option value described above. We also use a "percent change" version of this variable by dividing the option value by the level of utility available by retiring today. The variable AGE represents either a set of age dummies or a linear variable for the individual's age. The variable Health represents either a set of quintile dummies or the continuous health index. Finally, we include as a set of other controls (X_{it}) the individual's marital status, citizenship status, education, occupation, industry, and the spouse's employment status.

The main regression results are presented in table 1.1A. The first key finding is that OVInclusive has a negative and statistically significant effect on earnings. An increase of 10,000 units (which is somewhat smaller than the mean value of OV, which is 14,526) would reduce the probability of retirement by 3.3 percentage points, or about 40 percent relative to the baseline retirement rate of 7.9 percent. The estimates also suggest that a one standard deviation change in the OV (a 14,770-unit change) would lower the probability by 5.6 percentage points. This result is quite consistent across specifications—using age dummies versus linear age or health quintiles versus the continuous health index has little effect on the results.

The other coefficients on table 1.1A are much as expected. Health is an important determinant of retirement. In the models using health quintiles, relative to the poorest health group (omitted), those in higher health quintiles are 2.8 to 3.9 percentage points less likely to retire in any given year. The pattern of the four health quintile dummies suggests that the healthiest group has the lowest probability of retirement, though the difference between the lowest quintile and all others is more important than the differences between any of the other quintiles. The linear health index similarly suggests that better health (which is indicated with a larger index value) makes one less likely to retire, though the implied retirement gradient with respect to health is flatter using this continuous measure than that found using the quintiles. The probability of retirement rises with age, and the age dummies (not shown) exhibit the expected spikes at ages sixty-two and sixty-five.

In table 1.1B, the standard OVInclusive measure is replaced with the percent change version of this measure. The results suggest that a 100 percent increase in OVInclusive would reduce the probability of retirement by 5.9 percentage points. A 100 percent increase in OVInclusive, evaluated at the mean, would represent something like a 14,000-unit increase. Thus, it seems about right that this effect (5.9 percentage points) is roughly similar to the one standard deviation change effect (5.6 percentage points), since that simulates a similar change in OVInclusive.

The next set of tables explore whether the effects seen in tables 1.1A and 1.1B vary by health. In theory, it is not clear whether the impact of a given change in OVInclusive should have a bigger or smaller effect for someone in poor health. On the one hand, poor health may make individuals less likely

Table 1.1A Effect of inclusive OV on retirement

	Specification							
	(1)	(2)	(3)	(4)	(5)	(6)	(7)	(8)
OV_inclusive	-0.0333	-0.0325	-0.0338	-0.0331	-0.0332	-0.0325	-0.0338	-0.0331
	(.0011)	(.0011)	(.0011)	(.0011)	(.0011)	(.0011)	(.0011)	(.0011)
	[-.056]	[-.055]	[-.057]	[-.056]	[-.056]	[-.055]	[-.057]	[-.056]
Health quint 2 (second lowest)	-0.0282	-0.0281	-0.0260	-0.0259				
	(.0022)	(.0021)	(.0022)	(.0021)				
Health quint 3	-0.0302	-0.0302	-0.0283	-0.0283				
	(0.0022)	(0.0022)	(0.0022)	(0.0022)				
Health quint 4	-0.0353	-0.0349	-0.0326	-0.0323				
	(.0022)	(.0021)	(.0022)	(.0022)				
Health quint 5 (highest)	-0.0388	-0.0385	-0.0362	-0.0360				
	(.0022)	(.0021)	(.0022)	(.0022)				
Health index					-0.0007	-0.0007	-0.0006	-0.0006
					(.00004)	(.00004)	(.00004)	(.00004)
Age	0.0017		0.0019		0.0015		0.0016	
	(.0002)		(.0002)		(.0002)		(.0002)	
Age dummies		Included		Included		Included		Included
Female			-0.0031	-0.0031			-0.0037	-0.0037
			(.0022)	(.0022)			(.0022)	(.0022)

	(1)	(2)	(3)	(4)	(5)	(6)
Married	0.0044	0.0040			0.0040	0.0037
	(.0025)	(.0025)			(.0025)	(.0025)
Spouse works	-0.0151	-0.0146			-0.0149	-0.0144
	(.0022)	(.0021)			(.0022)	(.0021)
Total assets	0.0002	0.0000			0.0002	0.0000
(in millions of euros)	(.0013)	(.0013)			(.0013)	(.0013)
Occup. dummies	Included	Included			Included	Included
Educ.: <High school	0.0170	0.0157			0.0170	0.0159
	(.0040)	(.0039)			(.0040)	(.0039)
Educ.: High school	0.0100	0.0091			0.0100	0.0092
	(.0031)	(.0031)			(.0031)	(.0031)
Educ.: Some college	0.0023	0.0016			0.0021	0.0015
	(.0032)	(.0031)			(.0032)	(.0031)
No. of observations	67,228	67,228	67,228	67,228	67,228	67,228
Mean ret. rate	0.079	0.079	0.079	0.079	0.079	0.079
Mean of OV	14,526	14,526	14,526	14,526	14,526	14,526
Std. dev. of OV	14,770	14,770	14,770	14,770	14,770	14,770

Notes: Coefficients are marginal effects of a 10,000-unit change in OV from probit models. Standard errors are shown in parentheses. The effect of a one standard deviation change in OV is shown in brackets (this is estimated as the effect of increasing inclusive OV from the current value −0.5 std. dev. to the current value +0.5 std. dev.).

Table 1.1B   Effect of percent gain in inclusive OV on retirement

	Specification			
	(1)	(2)	(3)	(4)
Percent gain in OV	−0.0578	−0.0555	−0.0615	−0.0593
	(.0118)	(.0114)	(.0129)	(.0124)
Linear age	X		X	
Age dummies		X		X
Health quintiles	X	X	X	X
Other Xs			X	X
No. of observations	63,564	63,564	63,564	63,564
Mean ret. rate	0.079	0.079	0.079	0.079
Mean of % gain in OV	0.687	0.687	0.687	0.687
Std. dev. of % gain in OV	1.135	1.135	1.135	1.135

Note: Models are the same as models 1–4 in table 1.1. Coefficients are marginal effects. Standard errors are shown in parentheses.

to respond to economic incentives, as health becomes the most important factor in the retirement decision. On the other hand, the incentives may be more important for individuals in poorer health because they are more actively considering retirement, while those in good health may just plan to continue working until they reach some critical age, such as sixty-two. The results presented in tables 1.2A, 1.2B, and 1.2C support the second hypothesis, as the responsiveness to the incentives is higher for those in poor health. For example, in table 1.2A (specification [1]), the impact of a 10,000-unit increase in the option value would be to lower retirement probability by 6.2 percentage points for those in the lowest health quintile, but only by 2.0 percentage points for those in the top quintile. This pattern of results is similar across specifications and for both the option value and percentage gain in option value formulations.

In tables 1.3A and 1.3B, the effect of OVInclusive is allowed to vary by education group. Workers with lower education will have lower lifetime earnings, and thus can expect to receive a higher replacement rate (though lower benefits in absolute terms) from DI and SS relative to that experienced by higher-income workers, due to the progressive nature of the benefit calculation. This, along with the increased likelihood that less educated workers are in poor health (which has already been found to increase the responsiveness to incentives) may make less educated workers more responsive to financial incentives.

Tables 1.3A and 1.3B confirm this hypothesis. More highly educated individuals are less responsive than lower-educated individuals to the same incentive. For example, in table 1.3A (specification [1]), the impact of a 10,000-unit increase in the option value would be to lower retirement probability by 6.3 percentage points for high school dropouts, but only by 2.0

Table 1.2A   **Effect of inclusive OV on retirement by health quintile**

	No. of obs.	Mean ret. rate	Mean of OV	Std. dev. of OV	Specification			
					(1)	(2)	(3)	(4)
OV: Lowest quintile (worst health)	13,701	0.132	10,632	11,818	−0.0617	−0.0608	−0.0604	−0.0594
					(.0038)	(.0038)	(.0038)	(.0038)
					[−0.076]	[−0.075]	[−0.074]	[−0.073]
OV: 2nd quintile	13,525	0.081	12,702	13,232	−0.0347	−0.0338	−0.0363	−0.0353
					(.0027)	(.0027)	(.0027)	(.0026)
					[−0.050]	[−0.049]	[−0.053]	[−0.052]
OV: 3rd quintile	13,398	0.074	14,205	14,149	−0.0339	−0.0328	−0.0346	−0.0336
					(0.0024)	(0.0023)	(0.0023)	(0.0023)
					[−0.055]	[−0.054]	[−0.057]	[−0.056]
OV: 4th quintile	13,476	0.062	16,103	15,579	−0.0239	−0.0232	−0.0240	−0.0234
					(.0019)	(.0019)	(.0019)	(.0018)
					[−0.043]	[−0.042]	[−0.044]	[−0.044]
OV: Highest quintile (best health)	13,128	0.054	17,192	15,847	−0.0197	−0.0192	−0.0202	−0.0197
					(.0017)	(.0017)	(.0017)	(.0017)
					[−0.036]	[−0.035]	[−0.037]	[−0.037]
Linear age					X	X		
Age dummies							X	X
Other Xs						X	X	X

Notes: Models are the same as models 1–4 in table 1.1, but are estimated separately by health quintile; each coefficient on the table is from a different regression. Coefficients are marginal effects of a 10,000-unit change in OV from probit models. Standard errors are shown in parentheses. The effect of a one standard deviation change in OV is shown in brackets (this is estimated as the effect of increasing inclusive OV from the current value −0.5 std. dev. to the current value +0.5 std. dev.).

Table 1.2B Effect of percent gain in inclusive OV on retirement by health quintile

	No. of obs.	Mean ret. rate	Mean of % OV	Std. dev. of % OV	Specification			
					(1)	(2)	(3)	(4)
OV: Lowest quintile (worst health)	12,802	0.132	0.561	0.850	-0.0641 (.0319)	-0.0620 (.0308)	-0.0674 (.0345)	-0.0653 (.0334)
OV: 2nd quintile	12,739	0.081	0.607	1.050	-0.0598 (.0185)	-0.0566 (.0172)	-0.0631 (.0201)	-0.0599 (.0187)
OV: 3rd quintile	12,713	0.074	0.639	0.684	-0.0772 (0.0060)	-0.0738 (0.0058)	-0.0806 (0.0059)	-0.0774 (0.0057)
OV: 4th quintile	12,829	0.062	0.698	0.773	-0.0531 (.0052)	-0.0510 (.0051)	-0.0564 (.0050)	-0.0544 (.0049)
OV: Highest quintile (best health)	12,481	0.054	0.793	1.866	-0.0390 (.0047)	-0.0374 (.0045)	-0.0407 (.0046)	-0.0393 (.0044)
Linear age					X			
Age dummies						X	X	X
Other Xs						X		X

Notes: Models are the same as models 1–4 in table 1.1, but are estimated separately by health quintile; each coefficient on the table is from a different regression. Coefficients are marginal effects. Standard errors are shown in parentheses.

Table 1.2C   **Effect of inclusive OV on retirement with health index interaction**

	Specification			
	(1)	(2)	(3)	(4)
OV	−0.0392	−0.0387	−0.0396	−0.0391
	(.0034)	(.0034)	(.0033)	(.0033)
	[−0.065]	[−0.065]	[−0.067]	[−0.066]
OV*health index	0.00009	0.00010	0.00009	0.00009
	(.00005)	(.00005)	(.00005)	(.00005)
Health index	−0.0008	−0.0008	−0.0007	−0.0007
	(.00006)	(.00006)	(.00006)	(.00005)
Linear age	X		X	
Age dummies		X		X
Other Xs			X	X
No. of observations	67,228	67,228	67,228	67,228
Mean ret. rate	0.079	0.079	0.079	0.079
Mean of OV	14,526	14,526	14,526	14,526
Std. dev. of OV	14,770	14,770	14,770	14,770

Notes: Models are the same as models 5–8 in table 1.1, with the addition of an OV*health index interaction. Coefficients are marginal effects of a 10,000-unit change in OV from probit models. Standard errors are shown in parentheses. The effect of a one standard deviation change in OV is shown in brackets (this is estimated as the effect of increasing inclusive OV from the current value −0.5 std. dev. to the current value +0.5 std. dev.).

percentage points for college graduates. The results are generally robust across specifications, though in table 1.3B, where the incentive measure is defined in terms of a percentage change, the coefficients for high school dropouts are small and statistically insignificant.

Overall, our regression results confirm the findings of Coile and Gruber (2004, 2007) that the financial incentives for continued work arising from the structure of the Social Security system—now construed broadly to include both SS retired worker benefits and DI benefits—have a significant effect on retirement decisions. The effect is in the expected direction, in that workers with a larger financial incentive to delay retirement are more likely to do so, and its magnitude suggests that a large change in financial incentives will have a large impact on the probability of retirement. In addition, I find that the impact of financial incentives on retirement is strongest for those in poor health and those with less education, potentially reflecting a greater salience of financial incentives for groups that may tend to begin to consider retirement at relatively younger ages.

1.5   Simulations and Discussion

One of the benefits of constructing an inclusive measure that incorporates the financial incentives from both SS and DI is that it can be used to simulate

Table 1.3A Effect of inclusive OV on retirement by education group

					Specification			
	No. of obs.	Mean ret. rate	Mean of OV	Std. dev. of OV	(1)	(2)	(3)	(4)
OV: < High school	10,756	0.109	8,697	9,139	−0.0633	−0.0603	−0.0647	−0.0614
					(.0054)	(.0053)	(.0053)	(.0051)
					[−0.062]	[−0.059]	[−0.064]	[−0.061]
OV: High school	24,006	0.086	12,444	12,077	−0.0413	−0.0405	−0.0430	−0.0421
					(.0023)	(.0023)	(.0023)	(.0023)
					[−0.055]	[−0.054]	[−0.058]	[−0.057]
OV: Some college	15,541	0.070	16,033	14,893	−0.0293	−0.0285	−0.0305	−0.0297
					(0.0019)	(0.0019)	(0.0019)	(0.0019)
					[−0.050]	[−0.049]	[−0.053]	[−0.052]
OV: College	16,925	0.060	19,715	18,560	−0.0201	−0.0198	−0.0204	−0.0202
					(.0013)	(.0013)	(.0013)	(.0013)
					[−0.043]	[−0.043]	[−0.044]	[−0.044]
Linear age					X		X	
Age dummies						X		X
Health quintiles						X	X	X
Other Xs					X	X	X	X

Notes: Models are the same as models 1–4 in table 1.1, but are estimated separately by education group; each coefficient on the table is from a different regression. Coefficients are marginal effects of a 10,000-unit change in OV from probit models. Standard errors are shown in parentheses. The effect of a one standard deviation change in OV is shown in brackets (this is estimated as the effect of increasing inclusive OV from the current value −0.5 std. dev. to the current value +0.5 std. dev.).

Table 1.3B   **Effect of percent gain in inclusive OV on retirement by education group**

	No. of obs.	Mean ret. rate	Mean of % OV	Std. dev. of % OV	Specification			
					(1)	(2)	(3)	(4)
OV: < High school	9,864	0.109	0.550	2.171	−0.0229	−0.0213	−0.0242	−0.0224
					(.0165)	(.0154)	(.0174)	(.0162)
OV: High school	22,875	0.086	0.602	0.668	−0.0785	−0.0756	−0.0858	−0.0829
					(.0085)	(.0082)	(.0087)	(.0084)
OV: Some college	14,989	0.070	0.767	0.955	−0.0581	−0.0564	−0.0628	−0.0611
					(.0046)	(.0044)	(.0046)	(.0044)
OV: College	15,836	0.060	0.819	0.840	−0.0487	−0.0475	−0.0515	−0.0504
					(.0037)	(.0037)	(.0037)	(.0037)
Linear age					X		X	
Age dummies						X		X
Other Xs							X	X

Notes: Models are the same as models 1–4 in table 1.1, but are estimated separately by education group; each coefficient on the table is from a different regression. Coefficients are marginal effects. Standard errors are shown in parentheses.

the effect of changes to the DI program. Such simulations are also another way to gauge whether the magnitude of the estimated effects seems sensible. Note that the simulations discussed below are not intended to reflect likely real-world changes to the DI program, but rather to give some sense of the program's importance for labor supply decisions.

I undertake several simulations, all of which essentially amount to reducing the likelihood that workers are able to access the DI path. The results of the simulations are shown in figures 1.5A and 1.5B. The first set of bars on figure 1.5A show the predicted work life expectancy if individuals may only consider retiring along the SS path versus along the DI path. To elaborate on how this calculation is made, I first use the regression estimates from table 1.1A specification (4), to predict each individual's probability of retirement using OVDI (or equivalently, setting DIprobability to 1 and recomputing OVInclusive) and using OVSS (setting DIprobability to 0). I then sum the predicted probability of retirement by age for the whole sample under each scenario and retain the mean value, using this to generate a survival function and using the survival function to estimate the average expected remaining work life.

This calculation yields the prediction that on average, individuals age fifty would work for an additional 11.9 years if SS were the only pathway to retirement versus 10.2 years if DI were the only path. Relative to the expected work life (after age forty-nine) when DI is the only path, workers work 17.3 percent longer when they must retire through SS—this figure is reported on figure 1.5B.

The second set of bars repeats this calculation using only those individuals who ever apply for DI. In general, they are in worse health, so their projected remaining work life is smaller than that for the full sample, whether contemplating retiring via SS or DI. But the increase in work life when access to the DI path is turned from off to on is fairly similar to that for the whole sample, 15.7 percent. The remaining two calculations are similar but reflect the fact that it is unlikely that the DI program would be eliminated entirely in the real world. Rather, it is more likely that the medical screening might be tightened, as it was in the late 1970s. Thus I estimate the effect if access to DI were lost for two-thirds of DI applicants (third set of columns) or for one-third of DI applicants (last set of columns). Naturally, the projected effects of these program changes are smaller than that of eliminating DI entirely—they are projected to increase the labor supply of the DI applicant pool by 10.1 percent and 5.0 percent, respectively. Since DI applicants make up only a fraction of the total population, the effect on aggregate labor supply (not estimated here) would be smaller.

In conclusion, this study revisits the question of how retirement incentives arising from the structure of Social Security affect retirement decisions, expanding on earlier work that focused on Social Security retired worker

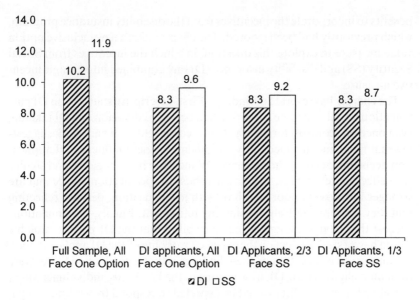

Fig. 1.5A Expected years of work life on SS versus DI path

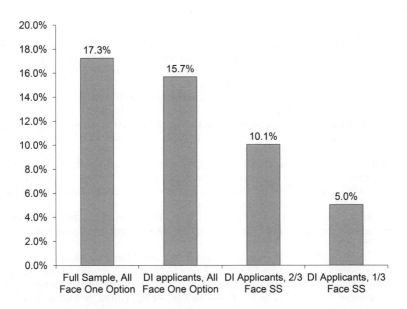

Fig. 1.5B Change in expected work life

benefits to incorporate the incentives from the disability insurance program, which previously had been ignored. The chapter uses a new inclusive option value measure to explore this question, in which the incentives from Social Security (SS) and disability insurance (DI) are combined into a single incentive measure.

The chapter has several key findings. First, descriptive statistics on DI participation reveal that there is a strong link between education and DI take-up, even once one controls for health. This is consistent with past work suggesting that rising income inequality and unemployment influence DI application decisions. Second, the inclusive OV measure has a negative and significant effect on retirement. Effects are robust to specification choice and are stronger for those in poor health or with low education, perhaps reflecting that they are more actively considering retirement. Finally, the simulations suggest that a large change in the probability that the DI path is available would have a sizable effect on the expected work life of the DI applicant pool. An important implication of these findings is that if the United States were to tighten eligibility for DI, as was done in the late 1970s, individuals still in the labor force at age fifty would be expected to respond by working longer, though there would almost certainly be heterogeneity in workers' ability to respond in this way and losses in lifetime income as a result.

References

Autor, David H., and Mark G. Duggan. 2003. "The Rise in the Disability Rolls and the Decline in Unemployment." *Quarterly Journal of Economics* 118 (1): 157–206.
———. 2006a. "The Growth in the Social Security Disability Rolls: A Fiscal Crisis Unfolding." *Journal of Economic Perspectives* 20 (3): 71–96.
———. 2006b. "The Growth in the Social Security Disability Rolls: A Fiscal Crisis Unfolding." NBER Working Paper no. 12436, Cambridge, MA.
Biggs, Andrew G., and Glenn R. Springstead. 2008. "Alternative Measures of Replacement Rates for Social Security Benefits and Retirement Income." *Social Security Bulletin* 68 (2): 1–19.
Bound, John. 1989. "The Health and Earnings of Rejected Disability Insurance Applicants." *American Economic Review* 79 (3): 482–503.
———. 1991. "The Health and Earnings of Rejected Disability Insurance Applicants: Reply." *American Economic Review* 81 (5): 1427–34.
Chen, Susan, and Wilbert van der Klaauw. 2008. "The Effect of Disability Insurance on Labor Supply of Older Individuals in the 1990s." *Journal of Econometrics* 142 (2): 757–84.
Coile, Courtney, Peter Diamond, Jonathan Gruber, and Alain Jousten. 2002. "Delays in Claiming Social Security Benefits." *Journal of Public Economics* 84 (3): 357–86.
Coile, Courtney C., and Jonathan Gruber. 2001. "Social Security Incentives for Retirement." In *Themes in the Economics of Aging*, edited by David A. Wise, 311–54. Chicago: University of Chicago Press.
———. 2004. "The Effect of Social Security on Retirement in the United States."

In *Social Security Programs and Retirement around the World: Micro-Estimation*, edited by Jonathan Gruber and David A. Wise, 691–730. Chicago: University of Chicago Press.

———. 2007. "Future Social Security Entitlements and the Retirement Decision." *Review of Economics and Statistics* 89 (2): 234–46.

Coile, Courtney, and Phillip B. Levine. 2007. "Labor Market Shocks and Retirement: Do Government Programs Matter?" *Journal of Public Economics* 91 (10): 1902–19.

Duggan, Mark, and Scott Imberman. 2008. "Why Are the Disability Rolls Skyrocketing? The Contribution of Population Characteristics, Economic Conditions, and Program Generosity." In *Health at Older Ages: The Causes and Consequences of Declining Disability among the Elderly*, edited by David Cutler and David Wise, 337–79. Chicago: University of Chicago Press.

French, Eric, and Jae Song. 2012. "The Effect of Disability Insurance Receipt on Labor Supply: A Dynamic Analysis." Working Paper no. 2012–12, Federal Reserve Bank of Chicago.

Gruber, Jonathan. 2000. "Disability Insurance Benefits and Labor Supply." *Journal of Political Economy* 108 (6): 1162–83.

Gruber, Jonathan, and Jeffrey D. Kubik. 1997. "Disability Insurance Rejection Rates and the Labor Supply of Older Workers." *Journal of Public Economics* 64 (1): 1–23.

Gruber, Jonathan, and Peter Orszag. 2003. "Does the Social Security Earnings Test Affect Labor Supply and Benefit Receipt?" *National Tax Journal* 56 (4): 755–73.

Katz, Lawrence F., and David H. Autor. 1999. "Changes in the Wage Structure and Earnings Inequality." In *Handbook of Labor Economics,* vol. 3, part A, edited by Orley C. Ashenfelter and David Card, 1463–1555. Amsterdam: Elsevier.

Lahiri, K., J. Song, and B. Wixon. 2008. "A Model of Social Security Disability Insurance Using Matched SIPP/Administrative Data." *Journal of Econometrics* 145 (1–2): 4–20.

Li, Xiaoyan, and Nicole Maestas. 2008. "Does the Rise in the Full Retirement Age Encourage Disability Benefits Applications? Evidence from the Health and Retirement Study." MRRC Working Paper no.198, Michigan Retirement Research Center.

Maestas, Nicole, Kathleen Mullen, and Alexander Strand. 2013. "Does Disability Insurance Receipt Discourage Work? Using Examiner Assignment to Estimate Causal Effects of SSDI Receipt." *American Economic Review* 103 (5): 1797–829.

Milligan, Kevin. 2012. "The Long-Run Growth of Disability Insurance in the United States." In *Social Security Programs and Retirement around the World: Historical Trends in Mortality and Health, Employment, and Disability Insurance Participation and Reforms*, edited by David A. Wise, 359–89. Chicago: University of Chicago Press.

Munnell, Alicia H., and Steven A. Sass. 2012. "Can the Actuarial Reduction for Social Security Early Retirement Still Be Right?" Issues in Brief no. ib2012-6, Center for Retirement Research at Boston College.

OASDI Trustees. 2013. *The 2013 Annual Report of the Board of Trustees of the Federal Old-Age and Survivors Insurance and Federal Disability Insurance Trust Fund.* http://www.ssa.gov/oact/tr/2013/tr2013.pdf.

Parsons, Donald O. 1980. "The Decline in Male Labor Force Participation." *Journal of Political Economy* 88 (1): 117–34.

———. 1991. "The Health and Earnings of Rejected Disability Insurance Applicants: Comment." *American Economic Review* 81 (5): 1419–26.

Poterba, James, Steven Venti, and David A. Wise. 2013. "Health, Education, and the Post-Retirement Evolution of Household Assets." *Journal of Human Capital* 7 (4): 297–339.

Rupp, Kalman, and Charles Scott. 1988. "Determinants of Duration on the Disability Rolls and Program Trends." In *Growth in Disability Benefits: Explanations and Policy Implications*, edited by Kalman Rupp and David Stapleton. Kalamazoo, MI: Upjohn Institute for Employment Research.

Shoven, John B., and Sita Nataraj Slavov. 2013. "Recent Changes in the Gains from Delaying Social Security." NBER Working Paper no. 19370, Cambridge, MA.

Smith, James P. 1999. "Healthy Bodies and Thick Wallets: The Dual Relation between Health and Economic Status." *Journal of Economic Perspectives* 13 (2): 145–66.

Stock, James H., and David A. Wise. 1990. "Pensions, the Option Value of Work, and Retirement." *Econometrica* 58 (5): 1151–80.

2

Effect of Pensions and Disability Benefits on Retirement in the United Kingdom

James Banks, Carl Emmerson, and Gemma Tetlow

2.1 Introduction

Employment rates of older workers in the United Kingdom fell sharply during the 1980s, but have been increasing steadily since the mid-1990s. As figure 2.1 shows, the employment rate of men between the ages of fifty-five and fifty-nine fell from over 90 percent in the late 1960s to just 67 percent by 1995 before increasing again to 77 percent just prior to the most recent recession. Employment rates of older men are now similar in the United Kingdom to the levels seen in Canada, for example, but are somewhat higher than those seen in France and lower than those in Denmark and Sweden. Among older women, employment rates fell sharply during the recession of the early 1980s but have increased steadily since then and are now at the highest levels that have ever been seen in modern times. Sixty-six percent

James Banks is professor of economics at the University of Manchester and Deputy Research Director of the Institute for Fiscal Studies. Carl Emmerson is Deputy Director of the Institute for Fiscal Studies. Gemma Tetlow is program director of work on pensions, saving, and public finances at the Institute for Fiscal Studies.

This chapter forms part of the International Social Security project at the NBER. The authors are grateful to Richard Blundell and to the other participants of that project for useful comments and advice. We are also grateful to the Joseph Rowntree Foundation and the ESRC-funded Centre for the Microeconomic Analysis of Public Policy at IFS (grant number RES-544-28-5001) for funding this project. Data from the Family Expenditure Survey (FES), the Labour Force Survey (LFS), and the English Longitudinal Study of Ageing (ELSA) were made available by the UK Data Archive. The ELSA was developed by a team of researchers based at the National Centre for Social Research, University College London, and the Institute for Fiscal Studies. The data were collected by the National Centre for Social Research. The funding is provided by the National Institute of Aging in the United States, and a consortium of UK government departments coordinated by the Office for National Statistics. Responsibility for interpretation of the data, as well as for any errors, is the authors' alone. For acknowledgments, sources of research support, and disclosure of the authors' material financial relationships, if any, please see http://www.nber.org/chapters/c13334.ack.

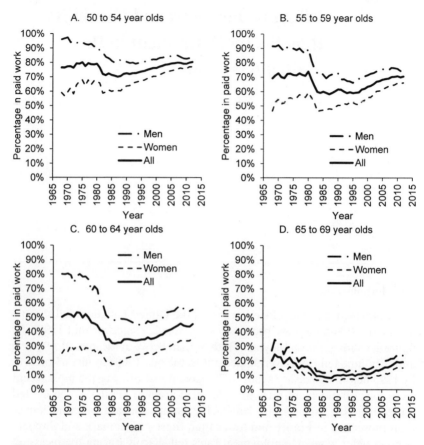

Fig. 2.1   Employment rates of older men and women, 1968–2012

Source: Family Expenditure Survey (1968–1982) and Labour Force Survey (1983–2012).

Note: Tables 2A.1–2A.3 in the appendix provide the figures underlying these graphs and also provide figures for the overall employment rate of fifty to sixty-nine-year-olds over time.

of women age fifty-five to fifty-nine and 35 percent of those age sixty to sixty-four are now in employment. This is still lower than the employment rates of older women in Denmark and Sweden, but higher than those seen in France and the Netherlands.

Employment rates differ substantially between those in better and worse health. As figure 2.2 shows, over 80 percent of men age fifty to fifty-nine who are in the best three health quintiles are in employment, compared to only around 25 percent of those in the worst health. A slightly less steep health gradient is seen for women ages fifty to sixty-nine in figure 2.3. For both men and women, the health gradient diminishes with age. For example, while there is roughly a 20 percentage point drop in employment rates between the fifty-five to fifty-nine age group and the sixty to sixty-four age group

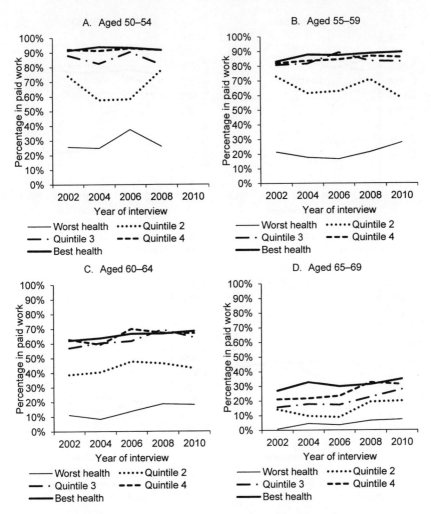

Fig. 2.2 Employment rates of men by health, 2002–2003 to 2010–2011
Source: English Longitudinal Study of Ageing, waves 1–5. Weighted using cross-sectional weights.
Notes: In 2002, 2006, and 2008, the ELSA sample is representative of those age fifty and older. However, in 2004 and 2010, it is only representative of those age fifty-two and older. The sample size of fifty to fifty-four-year-old men in 2010 is too small to allow us to report employment rates separately by health quintile for this group.

for men in the top three health quintiles, among men in the worst health quintile employment rates fall between the same ages by only around 10 percentage points. (The definition of health used here is explained in detail in section 2.3.2.)

In this chapter, we examine how far these differences in employment rates across health groups (and, within a health group, between the United King-

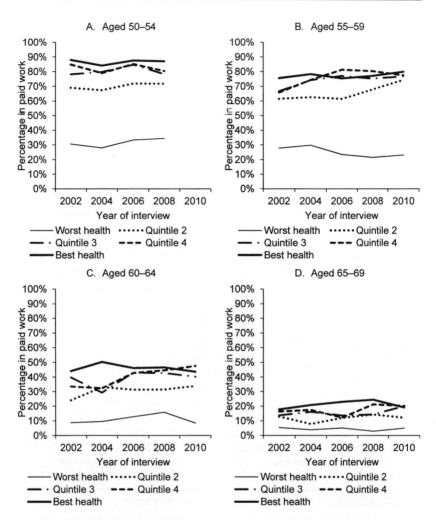

Fig. 2.3   Employment rates of women by health, 2002–2003 to 2010–2011

Source: English Longitudinal Study of Ageing, waves 1–5. Weighted using cross-sectional weights.

Notes: In 2002, 2006, and 2008, the ELSA sample is representative of those age fifty and older. However, in 2004 and 2010, it is only representative of those age fifty-two and older. The sample size of fifty to fifty-four-year-old women in 2010 is too small to allow us to report employment rates separately by health quintile for this group.

dom and other countries) can be explained by the availability of publicly funded disability insurance (DI) and financial incentives provided by other retirement income schemes in the United Kingdom. Unlike in many other countries, publicly funded DI in the United Kingdom provides a flat-rate payment to qualifying individuals rather than a payment that depends on the level of previous earnings. The financial disincentives to work provided by the system, therefore, differ substantially across individuals with different potential labor market earnings.

We estimate a reduced-form model of retirement behavior in the United Kingdom, including measures of the option value of remaining in paid work emanating from state and private pensions and the publicly funded DI system. The model is estimated using data from the first five waves of the English Longitudinal Study of Ageing (ELSA) covering the period from 2002–2003 to 2010–2011. We define "retirement" as any movement out of paid work. We find that the financial incentives from retirement income schemes—as described by an option value measure—are significantly related to individuals' retirement decisions. The estimated impact of these financial incentives is found to be robust to the different specifications that we consider: a one standard deviation increase in the option value of remaining in work leads to a 2.7–3.1 percentage point reduction in the probability of retiring over the next year (depending on the specification used); this compares to a mean retirement rate of 17.9 percent among our sample as a whole. We also find no statistically significant evidence that responsiveness to these financial incentives varies either by an individual's health or education.

Given the nature of the United Kingdom's disability insurance program, most of this financial incentive is driven by state and private pensions rather than by the availability of the DI benefits. Simulations in which we change the stringency of the DI system suggest that a complete relaxation of DI eligibility criteria would reduce the average number of years worked between the ages of fifty and sixty-nine by 0.6 years (or a 7 percent reduction) for both men and women. Meanwhile, abolishing the DI system altogether would increase the average number of years worked by just 0.1 years (or less than 1 percent). However, the effects would be somewhat larger for those who are most likely to claim DI. For example, among the subsample of individuals who are observed to retire using the DI pathway, we estimate that a complete relaxation of the stringency criteria would reduce the number of years worked by 8.5 percent.

Section 2.2 describes key features of the UK pension and social insurance systems that affect incentives to remain in work at older ages. Section 2.3 describes our empirical methodology, including outlining how we incorporate real-life retirement incentives into our reduced-form model and describing the data used. Section 2.4 presents the results of our retirement regressions, showing how responsive individuals' labor force participation is to the financial incentives they face and how this differs across those with different levels of health and education. Based on the results presented in section 2.4, section 2.5 provides some illustrative simulations of employment rates under alternative assumptions about the stringency of the DI regime and focusing on different subgroups of the population; in particular, we simulate retirement rates assuming that everyone/no one is able to qualify for DI and we show the effect of these assumptions both for the sample as a whole and for the subsample who are observed to claim DI at some point. Section 2.6 concludes.

Throughout this chapter, all monetary values are expressed in euros in 2012 prices, using the sterling/euro exchange rate prevailing at the time of writing and adjusting cash amounts measured at different points in time using the Consumer Price Index (CPI).

2.2   Institutional Background

In the United Kingdom, individuals potentially have access to four sources of income after retirement. First, they may be eligible to receive a state pension. Second, they may also get income from a private pension—either one provided by a previous employer or a scheme that they set up on their own. Third, if individuals are judged to have sufficiently poor health, they may qualify for disability-related benefits. Finally, people who are out of work may also qualify for income-tested benefits. Each of these different income sources potentially provides incentives for individuals to remain in or leave work as they get older. This section provides a brief description of each of these elements in turn, in particular focusing on where there is variation across individuals and over time in the incentives to move out of paid work, which can be used to analyze the impact of these incentives on actual retirement behavior.

2.2.1   State Pension System

The UK state pension consists of two parts.[1] The first-tier pension (known as the basic state pension [BSP]) is based on the number of years (but not on the level) of contributions made. A full BSP in 2012–2013 was worth £107.45 a week (17 percent of average full-time weekly earnings, or around €130). This amount is currently indexed each year by the greatest of inflation, earnings growth, or 2.5 percent, and is payable from the state pension age onward.[2]

People receive the full amount of the BSP if they have at least thirty years during their working lives (that is, from age sixteen up to state pension age) in which they have made a "contribution."[3] Contributions include (among other things) being employed or self-employed, caring for children or disabled adults, and receiving unemployment or disability benefits. These

1. A full description of the UK state pension system can be found in Bozio, Crawford, and Tetlow (2010).
2. Individuals can choose to defer receipt of their state pension; they receive a 10.4 percent uplift to their pension income for each year that they defer receipt.
3. Men (women) who reached the state pension age before 2010—some of whom are included in our sample—needed forty-four (thirty-nine) years of contributions to qualify for the full award.

contribution conditions are sufficiently broadly defined that most men and women now reaching the state pension age can qualify for the full award.

The second-tier pension, now known as the state second pension (S2P), is related to earnings across the whole of working life (from 1978 onward); enhancements are also awarded for periods since April 2002 spent out of work due to some formal caring responsibilities. The second-tier pension scheme replaces 20 percent of earnings within a certain band. The maximum total weekly benefit that could have been received from the second-tier pension by someone reaching the state pension age in 2012–2013 was about £160 (€190). However, historically, the majority of employees have opted out of this second-tier pension and instead built up a private pension (of approximately equal value) in return for paying a lower rate of payroll tax (National Insurance Contributions [NICs]). Therefore, the majority of pensioners receive far less than £160 a week in second-tier pension income from the state.

In the United Kingdom a state pension can be received once an individual has reached the state pension age, but not before. Importantly, there is no earnings test for receipt of the state pension; that is, the amount received is not reduced if the individual also has earned income.[4] Between 1948 and April 2010, the state pension age was sixty-five for men and sixty for women. Since April 2010 the state pension age for women has been rising[5] and the intention is that by 2018 it will be equalized at age sixty-five for both men and women. Thereafter the state pension age for both men and women is set to rise further, reaching age sixty-six in 2020 and age sixty-eight by the middle of this century.

Effect of State Pensions on Incentives to Work or Retire

The UK state pension system does not, for the majority of individuals, have a large impact on the marginal financial incentive to remain in, or to leave, paid work. There is some incentive for individuals to continue "contributing" to the system until they reach the state pension age, as additional contributions will increase the amount of state pension income that they will receive. However, once an individual has accrued thirty years of BSP entitlement, the marginal accrual of additional pension declines. Furthermore, individuals can potentially accrue extra state pension entitlement not only through paid work but also through nonwork activities. The fact that the same amount of state pension can be received from the state pension age regardless of whether the individual has actually left the labor market

4. The earnings test was abolished in 1989.
5. Cribb, Emmerson, and Tetlow (2013) find that the rise in the female state pension age from sixty to sixty-one between April 2010 and April 2012 led to a significant increase in labor supply among both the women directly affected by the reform and among men married to those directly affected by the reform.

means that there is no financial incentive from the state pension system to leave the labor market at this point. While the state pension age is the single-most common age for men and women to withdraw from the labor market, most leave at some other age.

The UK state pension system does not, therefore, provide sharp financial incentives for specific individuals to retire at a particular point in time. How-ever, previous legislation (passed in 1975, 1986, 1995, and 2000) has changed the generosity of the state pension significantly, with the changes varying by individuals' date of birth, sex, caring responsibilities, and earnings. The first and last of these four reforms significantly increased the average generosity of the state pension system, while the intermediate two significantly reduced it. These changes have generated differences in the lifetime wealth of individuals born at different points in time and therefore potentially induced differences in retirement ages across cohorts.[6] The state pension system has been increasingly generous to low earners and some groups not in paid work in more recent years, but the generosity of the system to higher earners peaked among those reaching state pension age in 2000. Our data cover cohorts born between 1933 and 1958, who will reach state pension age between 1993 and 2024 and have all faced slightly different state pension legislation.

2.2.2   Private Pension System

More important in terms of its impact on financial incentives to work at older ages is the private pension system. Because of the relatively low level of state pension provision in the United Kingdom, private pension saving has always played an important role. In 2011–2012, 60 percent of employees between ages fifty-five and fifty-nine had some form of private pension cov-erage, with 53 percent of employees having an employer-sponsored scheme (either defined benefit or defined contribution) and 12 percent having an individually arranged (defined contribution) personal pension; 5 percent of employees age fifty-five to fifty-nine have both types of scheme.[7]

For some of these individuals, part of this private pension provision will be a direct substitute for state pension provision since, as mentioned above, many individuals choose to opt out of the second-tier state pension and instead save in a private pension. This has been possible for members of defined benefit schemes since 1978 and was also possible for defined con-tribution scheme members between 1987 and 2012. Figure 2.4 shows the numbers of fifty to fifty-nine-year-old employees contracted out into differ-ent types of private sector pension arrangements each year since 1997. The figure shows the gradual decline in defined benefit pension scheme member-

6. See Disney and Emmerson (2005) for details of the reforms and the change in income at the state pension age (SPA) for individuals from different cohorts and different earnings and employment histories.

7. Source: Chapter 6 of Department for Work and Pensions, *Family Resources Survey 2011/12*, July 2013 (https://www.gov.uk/government/statistics/family-resources-survey-201112).

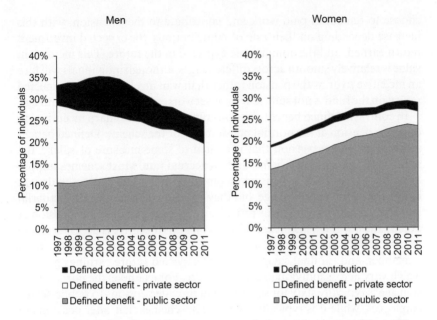

Men   Women

Fig. 2.4   Contracting out in private sector second-tier pensions among fifty to fifty-nine-year-old employees, by sex and year

Sources: Department for Work and Pensions tabulation tool (http://tabulation-tool.dwp.gov.uk/NIRS/live/tabtool.html). Human Mortality Database.

Note: Figures relate to main coverage during the financial year.

ship among private sector employees and the increasing numbers covered by public sector defined benefit schemes, which was due to the growth in public sector employment over this period.

Many employees have additional private pension saving, either in defined benefit or defined contribution pensions, above the minimum required second-tier pension coverage.[8]

Effect of Private Pensions on Incentives to Work or Retire

Different types of private pension arrangements can and do lead to significant differences in the financial incentives that those in paid work face to start drawing their pension at particular ages. Those in defined contribution pensions can typically expect to see the value of their pension rise if they

8. Until December 2012, in the United Kingdom people were required to annuitize at least 75 percent of all pension funds by the age of seventy-five. This requirement covers not only occupational pensions, but also individually arranged personal pensions. Therefore, in this chapter we treat all defined contribution pensions as providing a retirement income stream rather than treating them as a standard financial asset. This is different from the approach used in the analysis of the United States, where individual retirement accounts (IRAs) are treated as financial assets.

choose to remain in paid work and contribute to their pension, with this increase depending on their rate of contributions, the expected investment return earned, and the annuity rate expected in the future. This increase in value is relatively smooth across different ages, although individuals will face an incentive to draw the pension rather than wait any longer if the expected return on the fund is not sufficient to offset worsening annuity rates with age.

In contrast, defined benefit pensions typically provide sharp incentives to draw the pension at the normal pension age for the scheme. Defined benefit schemes provide a pension that is related to some measure of salary, the number of years in the scheme, and an accrual rate. Most schemes impose an actuarial reduction to pension income if an individual chooses to draw it before the normal pension age, but they typically do not offer any actuarial increase for late drawing. This provides an incentive to draw the pension at exactly the normal pension age. How strong this incentive is depends on the precise parameters of the pension scheme, how long an individual has been a member, and (in final salary schemes) expected future earnings growth, which vary across individuals and over time. For example, the normal pension age is typically sixty for schemes that provide pensions to public-sector employees, while it is typically sixty-five in schemes that offer pensions to private-sector workers (and for many who joined public sector schemes after around 2005).

Until April 2006, employees were not legally allowed to draw a pension from an employer while continuing to work for that same employer. Therefore, up to this point, these incentives to draw a pension at a particular time translated quite directly into incentives to leave work (or at least leave one's current employer) at that point as well. However, since April 2006 it has been possible for an individual to continue working for an employer while also drawing a pension from them. Therefore, from that point onward the incentive to draw a private pension at a particular age continued to exist but it became (in theory, at least) disconnected from the decision about whether or not to remain in paid work. In the empirical analysis below we include time dummies in our regressions to allow for behavior to differ over time, potentially as a result of this and other policy reforms.

2.2.3   Disability Benefits

Other features of the benefit system also affect the financial incentives that different individuals face to be in paid work at particular ages. Potentially the most important of these is the system of out-of-work support for those deemed to be in poor health. This subsection provides a brief summary of the key features of the UK disability benefit system and some trends over time in the numbers claiming these benefits and the generosity of the system. Further details of reforms to the disability benefits in the United Kingdom over the period since 1948 can be found in Banks et al. (2012), with a brief summary (taken from that publication) provided in box 2.1.

Box 2.1   Reforms to the UK disability insurance system, 1948 to present day

1948	Introduction of sickness benefit. Flat-rate benefit, no distinction by duration of claims.
1966	Introduction of earnings-related sickness benefit.
1971	Introduction of invalidity benefit (IVB). Higher rate for duration above six months.
1972 reform	Introduction of invalidity allowances. Supplements for becoming disabled at younger age.
1980	Abolition of earnings-related sickness benefit.
1983/1986	Introduction of statutory sick pay.
1995 reform	Incapacity benefit (IB) replaces IVB. New claimants receive less generous IB, which is taxable (unlike IVB). "Own occupation" test replaced by "any occupation" test. Regional medical test instead of personal doctor. No longer paid to people over state pension age.
2001 reform	Increased contribution requirement to qualify for IB. Introduction of means testing with regard to pension income.
Pathways-to-work expansion 2003–2008	Piloting of a package of reforms consisting in increased conditionality, increased support, and increased financial incentives to return to work.
2008 reform	Employment support allowance (ESA) replaces IB for new claimants.
2010 reform	ESA is applied to all existing IB claimants.

Source: Banks et al. (2012).

A notable feature of the disability benefit system in the United Kingdom is the weak link between the benefits that an individual can receive and the contributions they have paid in the past. Or, in other words, the relatively small amount of disability insurance that the state provides to many employees. Although eligibility for certain types of disability benefits is dependent on past social insurance contributions, the amount received is a flat rate, regardless of the level of previous earnings. As a result, there is very little disability insurance provided by the state for those on average or high earnings, since the flat rate of benefit is much lower than the amount they could have expected to earn. In addition, those on low incomes may qualify for means-tested support if they do not meet the contribution conditions. The amount of insurance provided was reduced further in April 2012 by a reform that limited the amount of time that some claimants could receive non-means-tested disability benefits to one year. However, the data we use in this chapter only cover the period up to 2011.

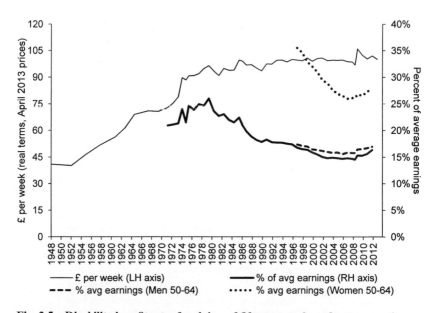

Fig. 2.5   Disability benefit rates for claims of fifty-two weeks or longer, over time

Source: Department for Work and Pensions, Annual Abstract of Statistics 2012, July 2013, Department for Work and Pensions, London (https://www.gov.uk/government/publications /abstract-of-statistics-2012). Labour Force Survey, 1997–2012.

Note: Rates shown are for sickness benefit (July 1948 to October 1972), invalidity benefit ([IVB]; October 1973 to April 1994), incapacity benefit ([IB]; April 1995 to April 2008), and employment and support allowance ([ESA]; October 2008 to April 2013). Rate shown is applicable from week fifty-two of claim, without any dependent additions, and for ESA (i.e., post-October 2008) includes the work-related activity addition. Average earnings for men and women age fifty to sixty-four are calculated excluding the top and bottom 1 percent of earners.

The low level of disability benefits, relative to earnings, for most workers is shown in figure 2.5. This shows the level of the principal disability benefit[9] over time, both after inflation (as measured by the Retail Price Index [RPI]) and relative to average earnings. Until 1974, the level of these benefits was uprated on an ad hoc basis. From 1974 to 1980 the increase was formally linked to the greater of price inflation and earnings growth. This led to the value of these benefits peaking relative to earnings in the late 1970s at 25 percent of average earnings. This was still a relatively low level of disability insurance for those on average and above average earnings by international standards; for example, the systems in place in the Netherlands, Spain, and the United States all provide a higher level of earnings replacement to higher earners than is available in the United Kingdom. Since the late 1970s, the

9. Figure 2.5 shows the long-term rate of disability benefit, which is the rate that has been payable to individuals who have been receiving disability benefits for at least fifty-two weeks. For much of this period, lower rates of benefit were payable for shorter claim durations.

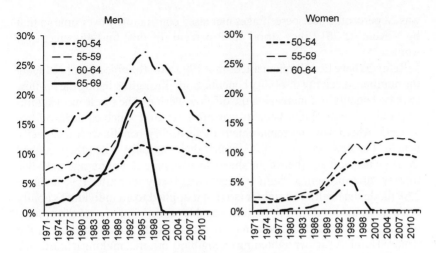

Fig. 2.6   Proportion receiving disability benefits over time, by sex

Sources: Authors' calculations using data on numbers of disability benefit claims from Anyadike-Danes and McVicar (2008), Department for Work and Pensions tabulation tool (http://tabulation-tool.dwp.gov.uk/NIRS/live/tabtool.html), and data on population by age group from the Office for National Statistics.

Note: Figures show the percentage claiming IVB, IB, or ESA.

level of these benefits has been formally linked to inflation (as measured by the RPI up until April 2010, and by the Consumer Price Index [which tends to increase less quickly than the RPI] from April 2011 onward). This has meant that, in real terms, the benefit has remained at about £100 (€120) per week but, as average earnings have in the United Kingdom tended (until recently) to increase more quickly than prices, the value of disability benefits has fallen to around 15 percent of average earnings.

The last forty years have also seen dramatic changes in the numbers of individuals receiving disability benefits. This is shown, by both sex and age group, in figure 2.6. The proportion of older men receiving disability benefits increased substantially between 1970 and the mid-1990s, with strong growth among those age sixty to sixty-nine throughout this period and among those age fifty to fifty-nine over the period from 1985 to 1995. The proportion of women age fifty to sixty-four receiving disability benefits also increased substantially between 1985 and 1995. These trends are largely unrelated to trends in health and disability, but have instead been driven both by economic factors and changes in the stringency of the system; Banks et al. (2012) provide more analysis of the drivers of these trends.

Another striking trend, not shown in figure 2.6, is the nature of health problems among disability benefit claimants. In May 1995, 19 percent of working-age men who were receiving disability benefits were receiving them because of mental or behavioral conditions; the equivalent figure for women was 28 percent. These percentages increased continuously over time so that by November 2012 they stood at 43 percent for men and 45 percent for women.[10]

Reforms have been implemented since 1995 with the objective of reducing the numbers receiving disability benefits, both through reducing the on-flow to these benefits and increasing the off-flow. Perhaps the single most significant reform to disability benefits was probably that which came into force in 1995, which saw the replacement of invalidity benefit with incapacity benefit. For new claimants this stopped their eligibility when they reached the state pension age (hence the sharp drop in male claimants age sixty-five to sixty-nine and female claimants age sixty to sixty-four after 1995 in figure 2.6), made the health test tighter (so that it applied to an individual's ability to do any paid work as opposed to suitable work), and moved the administration of this test from personal doctors to medical staff working at the regional level. A further tightening of eligibility criteria, making it harder for individuals to move directly from unemployment benefit to disability benefit, was implemented in 2001. The replacement of incapacity benefit with employment support allowance from October 2008 saw a further attempted tightening in the eligibility criteria; this involved a change in the medical test and greater requirements and support for some of those receiving Employment Support Allowance (ESA) to seek to manage their health condition and to prepare for a return to the labor market. As figure 2.6 shows, from 1995 onward the proportion of older working-age men receiving disability benefits has declined sharply, with particularly large falls at older ages, while the proportion of older working-age women receiving these benefits has stopped increasing.

The combination of changes in the generosity of disability benefits (shown in figure 2.5) and the change in the numbers in receipt of these benefits (shown in figure 2.6) have led to large changes in public spending on these benefits. This is shown in figure 2.7. In 1948–1949, less than 0.4 percent of national income was spent on disability benefits; this rose to 1.0 percent of national income at the start of the 1990s before peaking at 1.6 percent of national income in the mid-1990s. Since then, spending on disability benefits has fallen as a share of national income (and fallen relative to economy-wide inflation); it is now projected that by 2017–2018, the UK government will spend 0.6 percent of national income on these benefits, which would be the lowest level of spending as a share of national income on disability benefits since the mid-1960s.[11]

---

10. Figures cited refer to the primary health condition, as recorded under the International Classification of Diseases summary code, for each disability benefit recipient. Source: Authors' calculations using the Department for Work and Pensions tabulation tool (http://tabulation-tool.dwp.gov.uk/100pc/tabtool.html).

11. Figures relate to spending on sickness benefit, invalidity benefit, severe disablement allowance, income support on grounds of disability, incapacity benefit, and employment and support

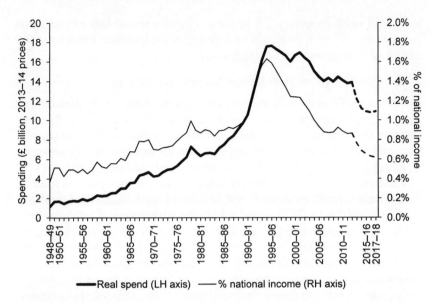

Fig. 2.7   Total spending on disability benefits in the United Kingdom, 1948–1949 to 2017–2018

Source: Department for Work and Pensions, Benefit Expenditure and Caseload Tables, March 2013 (https://www.gov.uk/government/publications/benefit-expenditure-and-caseload-tables -2013).

Note: Figure shows spending on sickness benefit, invalidity benefit, severe disablement allowance, income support on grounds of disability, incapacity benefit, and employment and support allowance.

Effect of Disability Benefits on Incentives to Work or Retire

Disability benefits will provide a disincentive to remain in paid work for those whose health is sufficiently poor that they are likely to qualify for these benefits. However, the level of disability benefits provided by the state in the United Kingdom is so low that the financial return to moving out of paid work onto disability benefits will be fairly minimal for all but the lowest earners. Therefore, for moderate and higher earners, the availability of disability benefits may not serve as a strong disincentive to remaining in paid work in the United Kingdom, even if the (medical) test of eligibility was very weak. However, for very low earners, the flat-rate benefits could provide a reasonably high level of earnings replacement and thus the financial disincentives to working for this group could be considerable and would depend on how likely they think it is that they would qualify for these benefits if they were to

allowance. Source: Department for Work and Pensions, Benefit Expenditure and Caseload Tables, March 2013 (https://www.gov.uk/government/publications/benefit-expenditure-and -caseload-tables-2013).

leave paid work. In section 2.5 we present simulations of how employment rates among different groups would change if the qualification criteria for disability benefits were relaxed/tightened.

2.2.4   Unemployment Benefits and Means-Tested Support

The final policies directly affecting financial incentives around retirement age are those coming from the rest of the tax and benefit system. Most of these do not vary, or exhibit relatively little variation, by age. The key one that does vary by age and could be significant for some groups is the system of means-tested support for those on low incomes and not in paid work.

Those not in poor health who are below the female state pension age and are actively seeking paid work can be eligible for Jobseeker's Allowance (JSA), which in 2013–2014 is paid at £71.00 (€80) per week. Those who have made sufficient contributions are able to receive this for up to six months, while a means-tested payment of the same amount is available beyond this point (and is available immediately for those who have not made sufficient contributions). For those who are above the female state pension age (or with a partner over the female state pension age), the means-tested payment (known as Pension Credit) is more generous: the weekly amount is much higher (£142.70 per week, or around €170) and there is no requirement for recipients to be actively seeking paid work. As figure 2.8 shows, only a small proportion of older men and women receive JSA, but a greater number of individuals over the female state pension age are in receipt of the means-tested Pension Credit.

Effect of Means-Tested Out-of-Work Benefits on Incentives to Work

Out-of-work benefits will reduce the financial incentive to work. The relatively low level of JSA available before the state pension age, which is limited to six months' duration, in addition to the job search requirements will mean that this financial disincentive to work will be small for many workers; this is reflected in the relatively low numbers of men and women receiving these benefits. For those above the female state pension age—or with a partner above the female state pension age—the more generous Pension Credit will provide a stronger financial disincentive to be in paid work and one that is potentially important, at least for lower-wage workers.

2.2.5   Other Institutional Factors Affecting Employment Rates of Older People

Until October 1, 2006, it was possible for employers in the United Kingdom to make a worker redundant (or refuse to hire them) purely on the grounds of their age, although the government had made cautious efforts to discourage such practices.[12] New legislation in 2006 prevented employ-

---

12. See Wunsch and Raman (2010) for a more detailed discussion.

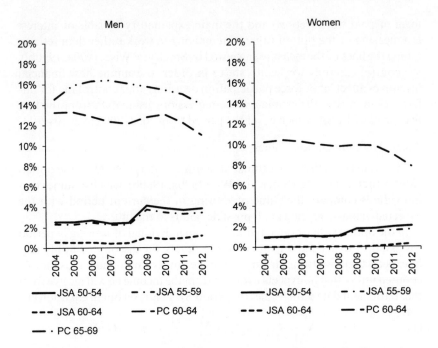

Fig. 2.8   Proportion receiving Jobseeker's Allowance and Pension Credit over time, by sex

Sources: Authors' calculations using claims data from Department for Work and Pensions tabulation tool (http://tabulation-tool.dwp.gov.uk/NIRS/live/tabtool.html) and data on population by age group from the Office for National Statistics.

Note: Figure shows the percentage claiming Jobseeker's Allowance (JSA) and Pension Credit (PC).

ers doing this to workers under age sixty-five.[13] This new legislation was, however, quickly challenged by older workers in the European Court of Justice. Although the ECJ (and subsequently the UK High Court) ruled the legislation was lawful, the UK government reviewed the policy and eventually abolished the ability to impose compulsory retirement ages altogether. Since April 2011, employers have no longer been able to make employees redundant on the grounds of age alone.[14]

2.3   Empirical Approach

The next section presents the results of regressions in which the dependent variable is an indicator of whether or not an individual ceases doing any

13. Employment Equality (Age) Regulations 2006, http://www.legislation.gov.uk/uksi/2006/1031/contents/made.

14. There are a small number of exceptions to this where employers can prove that a compulsory retirement age is objectively justified by the demands of the job.

form of paid work (retires) and the main explanatory variable of interest is a measure of the option value of remaining in work rather than retiring (along the lines of the measure suggested by Stock and Wise [1990a, 1990b]). We control carefully for health status in order to examine how financial incentives affect labor force participation decisions after controlling for differences in health. We estimate these regressions using data from the first five waves of ELSA, which cover the period from 2002–2003 to 2010–2011.

2.3.1   Defining Option Values

The model of retirement estimated in this chapter is based on the option value retirement model (Stock and Wise 1990a, 1990b), which assumes that individuals compare the value of retiring in the current period with the expected value of retiring at all possible points in the future.

In the option value model, the value to an individual of retiring in period r is assumed to depend on, among other things, the discounted utility that he expects to derive from earnings up to the point of retirement plus the discounted utility that he expects to derive from the income he will receive from that retirement date until he dies (in period S). This is set out in equation (1).

$$(1) \qquad V_t(r) = \sum_{s=t}^{r-1} \frac{1}{(1+\delta)^{s-t}} \pi_{st} Y_s^\gamma + \sum_{s=r}^{S} \frac{1}{(1+\delta)^{s-t}} \pi_{st}(kB_s(r))^\gamma.$$

We assume that, due to the disutility of work, utility from one unit of income while working (Y_s) is lower than utility from one unit of income in retirement (B_s): specifically, we assume that k takes the value 1.5. We also assume that the coefficient of relative risk aversion (γ) is 0.75, which picks up the diminishing marginal utility of additional income (either in retirement or during working life). We assume that δ is equal to 0.03 and that there is a probability (π_{st}) that an individual who is alive in period t survives to period s, which depends on an individual's age and sex.

The option value at time t is the difference between the maximum utility ($V_t(r^*)$) that can be obtained from retirement in the future (in period r^*) and the utility that can be derived from retirement in the current period ($V_t(t)$), shown in equation (2).

$$(2) \qquad OV_t(r^*) = V_t(r^*) - V_t(t).$$

The value of retiring at a particular point in time will depend on what set of benefits an individual expects to be able to receive after he retires. In this chapter, we are specifically interested in distinguishing between the stream of benefits that would be received if an individual qualified for disability benefits and the stream of benefits that would be received otherwise. We calculate the option value for each of these "pathways" separately and then construct a combined measure of the option value, which is equal to the weighted sum of the option values of the individual pathways. The weights used depend on the likelihood of an individual choosing (and being allowed to choose) a particular pathway. This weighted option value measure, summarized in equation (3), is the variable that we then include in our regression models. Subsection 2.3.3 describes in more detail the pathways that we consider and the weights we use.

(3) $$\overline{OV_t(r^*)} = \omega OV_t^1(r^*) + (1 - \omega)OV_t^2(r^*).$$

2.3.2   Data

We use data from ELSA, which provides detailed information on a range of individual circumstances that are essential for our estimation strategy. In particular, the survey contains detailed information on individuals' participation in paid work, their private pension scheme membership, their current health status, and information on family structure and partner's income and wealth (which affect entitlement to means-tested benefits).

Our base sample is all those who were between ages fifty and sixty-nine and doing some paid work in any of the first four waves of ELSA, which were collected between 2002–2003 and 2008–2009. The outcome of interest is whether these individuals moved out of paid work over the next two years, that is between wave t and wave t +1; in other words, we examine exits from paid work that happened between 2002–2003 and 2010–2011. Our pooled sample comprises 10,290 person-year observations on 4,909 unique individuals.

The ELSA provides detailed information on accrued rights to private pensions, including the accrued value of and current contributions to defined contribution pensions and existing tenure in and detailed rules of defined benefit schemes. This information allows us to calculate the financial incentives to leave paid work that are provided by these schemes, which (as described in section 2.2) are a very important component of the financial incentives facing (both healthy and unhealthy) older workers in the United Kingdom, given the relatively ungenerous state pension and publicly funded disability insurance systems, particularly to moderate and higher earners.

The ELSA also measures a wide range of indicators of individuals' health, covering both subjective and objective measures. Based on a range of measures of health, we estimate a health index for each wave of the survey using a principal components analysis, similar to that suggested by Poterba, Venti, and Wise (2011, 2013; henceforth [PVW]). The continuous index that we use is the first principal component of twenty-three health indicators from ELSA data. The indicators chosen are those that most closely approximate the measures used by PVW. However, we are unable to include measures of back problems, hospital and nursing home stays, and doctor visits, which are not asked about in a comparable way in ELSA. Table 2.1 sets out the results of estimating this index for each of the first five waves of ELSA. The index estimated varies across individuals and over time for the same individuals, since it is based on measured health at each wave.

Table 2.1   First principal component index for the United Kingdom

	2002–2003	2004–2005	2006–2007	2008–2009	2010–2011
Has difficulty:					
Walking quarter of a mile	0.284	0.295	0.299	0.304	0.297
Lifting or carrying	0.278	0.279	0.284	0.284	0.284
Pushing or pulling	0.274	0.277	0.275	0.276	0.279
Climbing several flights of stairs	0.266	0.276	0.273	0.276	0.275
Stooping/kneeling/crouching	0.263	0.272	0.273	0.269	0.273
Getting up from a chair	0.255	0.264	0.265	0.265	0.266
Reaching/extending arms	0.203	0.197	0.204	0.200	0.204
Sitting for two hours	0.211	0.212	0.216	0.208	0.215
Picking up a 5p piece	0.149	0.150	0.159	0.152	0.155
with any ADL	0.272	0.275	0.273	0.272	0.277
Receives help at home	0.156	0.169	0.180	0.185	0.175
Self-rated health: Fair, bad, very bad	0.253	—	0.236	—	—
Self-rated health: Fair, poor	0.255	0.241	—	0.246	0.244
Ever been diagnosed with:					
Arthritis	0.200	0.213	0.212	0.205	0.210
Psychological conditions	0.049	0.060	0.065	0.061	0.059
Stroke	0.080	0.093	0.091	0.094	0.090
Hypertension	0.083	0.171	0.162	0.148	0.136
Lung disease	0.092	0.093	0.096	0.102	0.096
Cancer	0.033	0.038	0.042	0.044	0.039
Heart problems	0.114	0.116	0.123	0.125	0.120
Diabetes	0.071	0.079	0.084	0.086	0.080
BMI	0.070	0.091	0.110	0.119	0.099
BMI^2	0.079	0.097	0.106	0.117	0.101
BMI missing	0.054	0.043	−0.031	−0.028	0.004
Any pain	0.253	0.255	0.239	0.235	0.249
Moderate/severe pain	0.259	0.263	0.246	0.248	0.258

Notes: The wording of the question about self-rated health differs across the waves of ELSA. In all waves except wave 3 respondents were asked to rate their health on a five-point scale from "excellent" to "poor"; this is the same wording that is used in the Health and Retirement Survey (HRS). In wave 3, respondents were asked to rate their health on a five-point scale from "very good" to "very bad"; this version of the question was also included in wave 1. In the principal components analysis, we define as in "bad health" those who reported "fair" or "poor" on the HRS scale, or "fair," "bad," or "very bad" on the scale used in wave 3.

The health measures included in the index are deliberately chosen—from among a large range of other possible measures—because they are closely associated with labor force participation. The strong relationship between this measure of health and employment rates for both men and women is shown in figures 2.2 and 2.3, respectively. However, the mix of indicators used is such that women are on average assessed to have "worse" health than men at each age using this measure—as shown in figure 2.9, which shows the average percentile of the distribution of this health index for men and

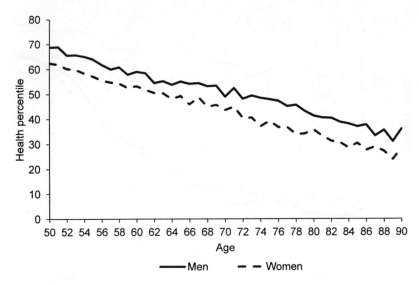

Fig. 2.9   Average health percentile, by age and sex
Source: English Longitudinal Study of Ageing, waves 1–5, unweighted.

women of different ages. Figure 2.9 also demonstrates that health declines on average with age.

Employment rates by health are documented in figures 2.10A and 2.10B. This takes all individuals age fifty and over and presents the proportion in work by health quintile. Even at the age of fifty, more than half of men and women who are in the worst health quintile are not in paid work; this compares to only around 10 percent of those in the best health. As a result, the analysis presented in this chapter cannot explain the factors underlying labor force exits for many of those in the worst health who have already withdrawn from paid work at younger ages (or have never entered the labor market in the first place). The sample we use (of those who are in work at age fifty or above) will be biased toward a relatively healthy group of individuals within the cohorts we study.

Our regression analysis also includes a number of other covariates derived from the ELSA data. In particular, we divide individuals into three groups based on the age that they left full-time education: left school at or before the age of fifteen, post-fifteen but no college, and some college.[15] We also include indicators of whether an individual is in a couple and whether the partner was working at baseline, whether the individual was self-employed at baseline, and we include a measure of the family's net nonpension wealth. Net nonpension wealth includes the value of financial, housing, and other physical assets, less the value of any outstanding secured and unsecured debts.

15. For the cohorts considered here, schooling was compulsory up to the age of fifteen.

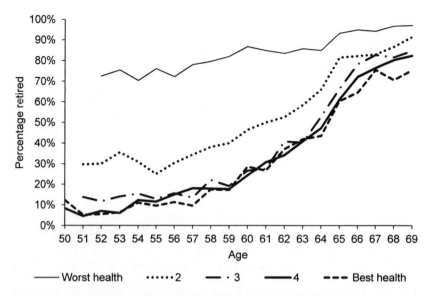

Fig. 2.10A   Prevalence of retirement among older men, by health

Source: The ELSA waves 1–5, unweighted.

Note: Employment rates for some age/health groups are not shown due to small sample sizes (<30 observations).

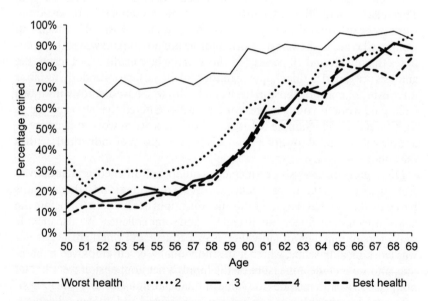

Fig. 2.10B   Prevalence of retirement among older women, by health

Source: The ELSA waves 1–5, unweighted.

Note: Employment rates for some age/health groups are not shown due to small sample sizes (<30 observations).

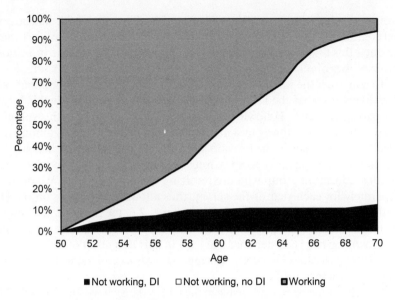

Fig. 2.11   Prevalence of pathways to retirement among those in work at age fifty
Source: The ELSA waves 1–5, pooled (unweighted).
Note: Prevalence of pathways is calculated by aggregating two-year transition probabilities
calculated from the sample at each age who were initially working.

2.3.3   Pathways to Retirement

To calculate the option value of remaining in work, we need to examine
the stream of income that individuals receive from the age that they appear
in the survey until they die. This income stream will depend on the age at
which they retire and the pathway that they retire through.

In this chapter we consider two pathways to retirement. The first pathway
we refer to as the "DI pathway" and entails individuals claiming disability
benefits as soon as they retire; the other (non-DI) pathway assumes that
individuals will not be eligible for disability-related benefits when they retire.
Along both pathways, individuals are assumed to claim any private pension
to which they are entitled at the point they retire and any state pension to
which they are entitled at the state pension age.[16] We also assume that families claim any means- and asset-tested benefits that they are entitled to in
each year. Along the DI pathway we also assume that individuals qualify for
and claim disability-related benefits. Although there is a contributory condition for receipt of working-age DI benefits, this is minimal and virtually all
those who are working in our baseline sample would satisfy it.

Figure 2.11 shows how use of the two pathways evolves with age, starting

---

16. If an individual retires before the age at which they can first claim their private pension
(before the state pension age), they are assumed to have to wait and claim their private (state)
pension at the earliest possible age.

from a population who are all in work at age fifty. Since the ELSA data do not yet contain a long enough panel to follow any one cohort from age fifty to age seventy, this figure is constructed by patching together two-year transition probabilities observed among different cohorts within the ELSA sample.

To construct the weighted option value measure, we need an estimate of how likely it is that the DI pathway will be open to an individual if he or she chooses to retire. Following the approach used throughout this volume, we weight the DI pathway by a measure of the prevalence of DI among the stock of individuals in the relevant age range. Specifically, we calculate the fraction of men age fifty to sixty-four (and women age fifty to fifty-nine) in each education group who are receiving disability benefits. We do this separately for each year of the survey, thus allowing the weight on the DI pathway to vary over time. As shown in figure 2.6, the proportion of older men receiving DI has been declining since 1995 (while the increase among older women has been stemmed), at least in part as a result of reforms over the last two decades aimed at reducing the on-flow and increasing the off-flow from these benefits.

The same time trends are visible in the ELSA data, shown in figures 2.12A and 2.12B. The decline in DI receipt among men is particularly pronounced among those with the lowest levels of education, although DI receipt remains much more prevalent among this group than among those with higher levels of education. For example, in 2002, 17.6 percent of low-educated men age fifty to sixty-four who were not in paid work were receiving disability benefits; this compares to 7.2 percent among the middle education group and just 2.5 percent among the most highly educated. Among women, overall rates of DI receipt have been quite stable between 2002 and 2010. However, this overall pattern hides an upward trend among the lowest education group, among whom the rate of DI receipt rose from 8.6 percent in 2002 to 12.9 percent in 2010.

The prevalence rates shown in figures 2.12A and 2.12B are the weights we use in constructing our weighted option value measure.

2.3.4   Constructing Option Values

As described in subsection 2.3.1, the (utility) value to an individual of retiring at a particular point in time is a function of the earned income that he will receive until he retires and the retirement income he receives thereafter. We estimate the value of retiring at each age from fifty to sixty-nine, using the formula outlined in equation (1). The option value is then calculated as the difference between the value of retiring at the age that maximizes this value function and the value of retiring immediately. A number of assumptions are required to estimate earned income in the future and the future stream of retirement income that would be received from state and private pensions and disability benefits, conditional on the year of retirement. This subsection outlines the main assumptions we have made.

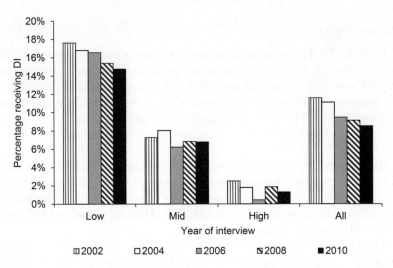

Fig. 2.12A Prevalence of DI receipt among men age fifty to sixty-four, by education level

Source: English Longitudinal Study of Ageing, waves 1–5. Weighted using cross-sectional weights.

Notes: In 2002, 2006, and 2008, the ELSA sample is representative of those age fifty and older. However, in 2004 and 2010, it is only representative of those age fifty-two and older.

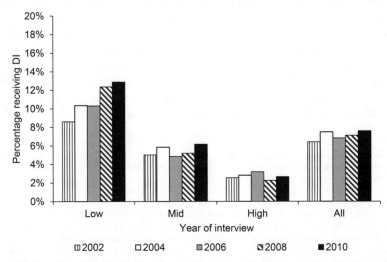

Fig. 2.12B Prevalence of DI receipt among women age fifty to fifty-nine, by education level

Source: English Longitudinal Study of Ageing, waves 1–5. Weighted using cross-sectional weights.

Notes: In 2002, 2006, and 2008, the ELSA sample is representative of those age fifty and older. However, in 2004 and 2010, it is only representative of those age fifty-two and older.

Future Earnings

In the ELSA data we observe current earnings for our baseline sample. In constructing the option value measures, we assume that those who remain in paid work will receive the same real-terms income in every future year; the exception to this is that we assume individuals receive 2.5 percent a year real-earnings growth between the ages of fifty and fifty-four.

State Pension Income

As described in section 3.2, state pension entitlements depend on an individual's contributions to the system over the whole of their working life. The measures of state (and private) pension rights that we use in this chapter are described in more detail in Crawford (2012). Here we provide a brief summary of the main assumptions.

The ELSA data do not contain a full record of respondents' labor market behavior.[17] Therefore, we have had to make some assumptions about past behavior and earnings in order to impute state pension rights. We assume that all sample members have continuously been in paid work since leaving full-time education. Previous earnings are calculated by assuming that individuals have always earned the same multiple of group-specific median earnings as they are earning when they are observed in ELSA. Median earnings profiles were estimated using repeated cross-sectional data from the Family Expenditure Survey, allowing for differences by sex, cohort, and education level.[18] Given these employment and earnings histories, we calculate state pension entitlements by applying the rules of the system, which vary by date of birth, and for men and women born on the same date.

Table 2.2 shows that the men in our regression sample have on average €121,500 of accrued state pension rights, compared to €110,800 for women. Table 2.3 shows that on average these men could accrue at most a further €8,000 of state pension wealth by continuing to work, while the women in

17. A life history interview, including questions on labor market behavior, was fielded in wave 3. However, only wave 3 respondents were eligible for this and not all responded. It does not, therefore, provide us with comprehensive information on all individuals in our baseline sample. Therefore, we have not made use of these data here.

18. Our assumption that all individuals have been continuously employed since leaving full-time education is likely to overstate accrued state pension rights on average. On the other hand, our assumption about the level of past annual earnings may lead us to underestimate accrued state pension rights. This is because, if individuals have cut their hours of work or taken on a less demanding, lower-paid job in the run-up to retirement, we have assumed that the pay in this job (observed in ELSA) is indicative of their earlier earnings. Bozio et al. (2010) compared figures for state pension wealth estimated using the method we use here to those estimated from administrative data and found that the median error, for those interviewed in the first wave of ELSA, was an overestimation of 7.1 percent. The median error was larger for women (12.5 percent) than for men (3.4 percent). Given that maximum entitlement to the basic state pension is capped after thirty years of contributions, this overstatement of accrued rights will also tend to result in an underestimation of potential future accrual (and thus option values).

Table 2.2 **State and private pension wealth (thousands of €, 2012 prices)**

	Men	Women	All
State pension wealth			
Mean	121.5	110.8	116.4
25th percentile	81.6	73.6	78.8
Median	111.3	111.6	111.4
75th percentile	154.6	145.2	149.8
Private pension wealth			
Mean	233.6	107.5	173.1
25th percentile	32.7	0.0	10.3
Median	136.3	35.5	76.8
75th percentile	325.8	142.7	238.7
Total pension wealth			
Mean	355.1	218.2	289.4
25th percentile	158.4	106.3	126.3
Median	265.1	162.0	206.5
75th percentile	448.9	271.6	364.0
Sample size	5,353	4,937	10,290

Source: ELSA, waves 1–4, pooled.

Table 2.3 **Maximum accrual of state and private pension wealth (thousands of €, 2012 prices)**

	Men	Women	All
State pension accrual			
Mean	8.0	4.3	6.2
25th percentile	0.0	0.0	0.0
Median	6.3	0.0	2.4
75th percentile	11.5	6.7	9.9
Private pension accrual			
Mean	16.4	11.4	14.0
25th percentile	0.0	0.0	0.0
Median	1.1	0.0	0.0
75th percentile	19.6	15.1	17.1
Total pension accrual			
Mean	24.1	15.7	20.0
25th percentile	4.1	0.0	0.1
Median	13.5	7.7	10.8
75th percentile	28.9	22.1	25.4
Sample size	5,353	4,937	10,290

Source: ELSA, waves 1–4, pooled.

Notes: This table shows the change in the (gross) present discounted value of state/private/total pension rights that individuals could expect to get if they continued to work after the year of interview.

our sample could accrue on average a maximum of €4,300. However, there is considerable heterogeneity in this. For example, more than half of women in our sample cannot accrue any further state pension entitlement by working for longer—in large part this is because these women have a state pension age of sixty and so cannot accrue any further pension rights after that point.

Private Pension Income

In order to calculate the current value and potential future accrual of private pensions in the ELSA sample, less information is required on past earnings and employment than was required to calculate state pension rights. The vast majority of defined benefit pension schemes in the United Kingdom (at least during the period covered by the data we use here) were final salary schemes. Therefore, current salary combined with information on scheme tenure and rules (which are asked directly in the survey) are sufficient to estimate defined benefit pension wealth. In order to calculate the potential value of future accrual, we also need to use the aforementioned assumption about future earnings growth. In the UK defined benefit pensions typically provide a survivor benefit to the surviving spouse equal to 50 percent of the original beneficiary's pension. Our treatment of this is discussed on page 110.

The current value of defined contribution pension funds is also asked directly in the ELSA survey. Future accrual of defined contribution pension rights will depend on the level of future contributions (from both the employee and the employer), the investment return on the fund, and any changes in annuity prices.

Table 2.2 shows that on average men in our regression sample have €233,600 of private pension wealth—or nearly twice as high as their accrued state pension wealth. Women, on the other hand, have a similar level of average private pension wealth (€107,500) as state pension wealth (€110,800). Potential future accrual of private pension wealth is higher on average than potential accrual of state pension wealth, as shown in table 2.3.

Disability Benefit Income

Along the DI pathway, individuals are also assumed to be able to receive disability-related benefits. During the time period covered by our data (2002 to 2011), these benefits included Incapacity Benefit and (from 2008) Employment Support Allowance for working-age individuals; these are worth around £100 (or €120) a week in current prices. These benefits can be claimed up to, but not beyond, the state pension age. From the state pension age onward, those in poor health may qualify for disability additions to the main means-tested benefits. We allow for this in the calculation of our option value measures.

Unemployment Benefits, Means-Tested Support

As described in section 2.2, non-means-tested unemployment insurance payments are only available prior to the state pension age for a maximum of six months in the United Kingdom. We do not factor these into our option value measures, as they do not provide any significant financial incentives to individuals to leave paid work permanently. Much more important—to low earners, at least—is the availability of (non-time-limited) means-tested benefits, which we factor into the value of both retirement pathways.

Entitlement to means-tested benefits depends on total family income (and assets). Therefore, in order to calculate how much means-tested benefit income an individual might receive if they were not working, we need to make some assumptions about their partner's earnings and other income as well. To calculate family means-tested benefit income, if the individual's partner is in work at baseline, we assume that he/she remains in work until their state pension age. If the partner is not working at baseline, we assume they remain out of work.[19]

For each future year along each pathway to retirement we calculate the means-tested benefit income that the family would be entitled to by applying the rules of the benefit system to the income (from state and private pensions and disability benefits) that the family would have in a particular year under each possible assumption about the timing of retirement. There is also an asset test for receipt of means-tested benefits in the United Kingdom—that is, assets above a certain threshold are assumed to generate an income, which results in the withdrawal of some or all of the benefit. Therefore, we also assess the family's net financial wealth holdings against this asset test; we assume that families' wealth remains constant in real terms in the future. The two main means-tested benefits that we model are Income Support (for working-age individuals) and Pension Credit (for those over the female state pension age), as described in section 2.2. Both of these benefits contain an additional payment for disabled individuals, which we allow for in our calculations of the value of the DI pathway.

Net Income

We calculate sample members' net income from all of the above sources by calculating their liability to income tax and employee social insurance contributions (the latter only applies to earnings received while below the state pension age). This allows us to take into account the fact that additional accrual of pension rights would be valued less by someone who faced

---

19. This assumption reduces the computational complexity of the problem. However, it should be noted that the partner retiring at the state pension age may not be the utility (or income) maximizing choice for the couple.

a high marginal tax rate in retirement than by someone who faced a lower marginal rate.

Survival Probabilities

The value of future income depends on the probability that an individual (or their partner, in the case of survivor benefits in defined benefit schemes) survives long enough to receive the income. We use official period life tables to calculate these survival probabilities.[20] For single individuals, we weight income in future years by the probability that the individual survives to that age (p_{st} in equation [1]). For couples, the income that is received will depend on whether one or both of the partners survives. We, therefore, augment equation (1) to allow for two states of the world: respondent and spouse alive and respondent only alive. The weight (π_{st}) applied to income in each state is shown in equation (4). We assume that individuals place no weight on income received by their spouse after they die—that is, we exclude survivor benefits from our analysis.

$$
(4) \qquad \pi_{st} = \begin{cases} \pi_{st}^R \pi_{st}^P & \text{both alive} \\ \pi_{st}^R (1 - \pi_{st}^P & \text{respondent only alive} \end{cases},
$$

where π_{st}^R denotes the probability that the respondent survives from period t to period s and π_{st}^P denotes the probability that their spouse survives.

Describing Option Values

The incentives to remain in, or leave, paid work induced by different retirement income schemes depend on the precise rules of the scheme. The option value of retirement will also depend on the earnings that an individual could receive if they carried on working.

As described in section 2.2, defined benefit pensions typically incentivise members to remain in the scheme until the normal pension age but to leave thereafter, as such schemes usually apply an actuarial reduction to benefits drawn before the normal pension age but do not offer an uplift for late drawing. In contrast, defined contribution pensions tend to provide smoother and for most of those in our sample—given the assumptions we have made about investment returns, contributions, and annuity rates—upward-sloping accrual profiles. To illustrate this, figures 2.13A and 2.13B show how the average present discounted value of future state and private pension income varies with retirement age for men and women (respectively) who were age fifty-one in the first wave of ELSA.

Figures 2.14A and 2.14B show, for men and women respectively, how the average option value of remaining in work is estimated to evolve with

---

20. Source: Office for National Statistics, Interim Life Tables, England 2007–2009. http://www.ons.gov.uk/ons/rel/lifetables/interim-life-tables/2009–2011/rft-england.xls.

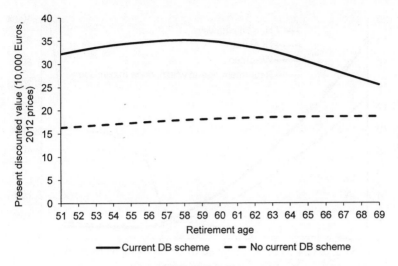

Fig. 2.13A   Evolution of present discounted value of pension income with age, men age fifty-one

Source: The ELSA wave 1, weighted.

Note: Sample is men age fifty-one in ELSA wave 1. Sample sizes: 68 with DB schemes and 87 without.

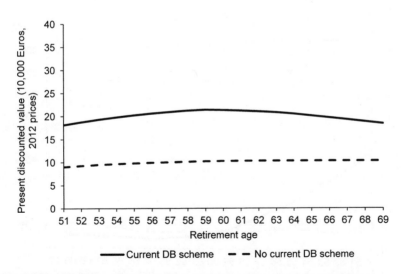

Fig. 2.13B   Evolution of present discounted value of pension income with age, women age fifty-one

Source: The ELSA wave 1, weighted.

Note: Sample is women age fifty-one in ELSA wave 1. Sample sizes: 68 with DB schemes and 114 without.

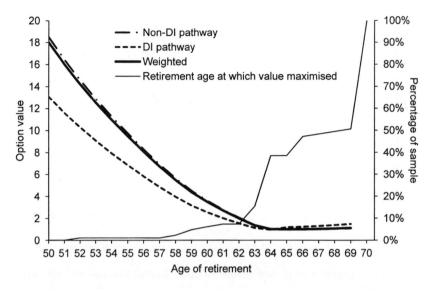

Fig. 2.14A   Evolution of option values with age, men initially at age fifty in 2002–2003

Source: The ELSA wave 1, weighted.

Note: Sample is men age fifty in ELSA wave 1. Sample size = 77.

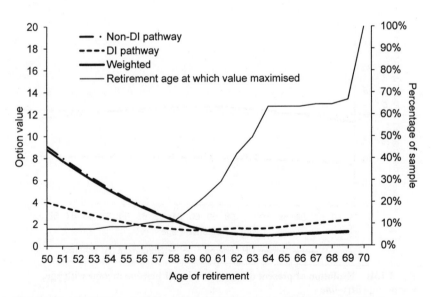

Fig. 2.14B   Evolution of option values with age, women initially at age fifty in 2002–2003

Source: The ELSA wave 1, weighted.

Note: Sample is women age fifty in ELSA wave 1. Sample size = 87.

age—starting from a sample of individuals who were age fifty in the first wave of the survey. The option value is—by definition—always nonnegative. However, it can fall to zero before the age of seventy if retirement income is sufficiently high (and/or the disutility of work is sufficiently large) that an individual values retirement at least as highly as continued work, despite missing out on additional years of earnings. To illustrate this, figures 2.12A and 2.12B also show the cumulative distribution function of the age at which the value of retiring peaks for this cohort of men and women.

For 49 percent of our sample of men and 33 percent of women, the option value of continuing to work remains positive until the age of sixty-nine. (As described above, we have—by construction—prevented individuals from considering retirement beyond this age.) For a further 23 percent of men the value of retirement peaks for retirement at the state pension age (i.e., working until age sixty-four). The spike in the value of retirement at the state pension age for women is less pronounced in figure 2.12B; this is because this cohort of women are affected by the gradual increase in the female state pension age and so the sample described here have state pension ages that range from sixty-one years to sixty-one years and eleven months. Working until (but not beyond) the age of sixty, sixty-one, or sixty-two maximizes the option value for 25 percent of women in this sample.

Table 2.4 shows the distribution of option values among our regression

Table 2.4	Distribution of option values		
	Men	Women	All
Option value: Non-DI pathway			
Mean	9.4	6.0	7.8
25th percentile	2.1	0.7	1.3
Median	7.3	4.1	5.5
75th percentile	13.6	8.9	11.4
Standard deviation	10.5	7.5	9.4
Option value: DI pathway			
Mean	6.4	3.7	5.1
25th percentile	0.4	0.0	0.1
Median	4.0	1.5	2.5
75th percentile	9.2	5.0	7.2
Standard deviation	9.3	6.5	8.2
Inclusive option value			
Mean	9.1	5.9	7.5
25th percentile	1.9	0.7	1.2
Median	6.9	3.9	5.3
75th percentile	13.1	8.6	11.0
Standard deviation	10.4	7.4	9.3
Sample size	5,353	4,937	10,290

Source: ELSA, waves 1–4, pooled.

Note: Option values are calculated based on monetary figures measured in thousands of euros in 2012 prices.

sample for both the pathways we consider and also shows the distribution of the inclusive option value measure. Option values are higher on average for men than women, but there is considerable variation in option values among both men and women: the mean inclusive option value is 9.1 for men and 5.9 for women, with a standard deviation of 10.4 and 7.4, respectively. Table 2A.6 in the appendix provides descriptive statistics on the other covariates included in our regressions for the regression sample.

2.4   Results

This section presents the results from estimating reduced-form models of retirement. These examine the impact of the calculated option value (which are in 1,000s of utils, based on monetary figures measured in euros in 2012 prices) on the likelihood of moving out of paid work between consecutive waves of ELSA—that is, over a two-year period.[21] The estimates are produced using a probit model and we report in the tables the mean marginal effect of the option value and the other controls of interest, taken across all the individuals in the sample. As set out above, the data used are from the first five waves of ELSA, and our standard errors (reported in parentheses in the tables in this section) allow for clustering at the individual level.

Table 2.5 reports our main estimates of the impact of option value on the likelihood of an individual moving out of paid work over the subsequent two years for eight different specifications. The first column includes, alongside the estimated option value, controls for the estimated health quintile (which are defined across all individuals in paid work unlike those in section 2.3, which were defined across all individuals) and linear age. A one-unit increase in option value is found to reduce the likelihood of an individual leaving paid work over the next two years by 0.7 percentage points (ppts) and this effect is statistically different from zero at the 1 percent level. Those in the worst quintile of health are found to be 6.9 ppts more likely to leave the labor market than those in the middle quintile of the estimated health distribution. The second column contains a more flexible set of controls for age (with age dummies interacted by sex being included in the model instead of controlling just for age linearly), but this is found to have very little effect on the other coefficients of interest.

Columns (3) and (4) are equivalent to columns (1) and (2), except these also include a richer set of controls for other characteristics. Those who are married and whose spouse is not working are found to be more likely to retire than single individuals, while those who are married with a spouse who is working are found to be the least likely to retire. Financial (nonpension)

---

21. The results from alternative specifications, which includes the percentage increase in utility from delaying retirement rather than the absolute increase in value, on the right-hand side can be found in appendix tables 2A.7 to 2A.9.

Table 2.5   Effect of inclusive option value on retirement

Variables	(1)	(2)	(3)	(4)	(5)	(6)	(7)	(8)
Option value	-0.007***	-0.006***	-0.007***	-0.006***	-0.006***	-0.006***	-0.007***	-0.006***
	[0.001]	[0.001]	[0.001]	[0.001]	[0.001]	[0.001]	[0.001]	[0.001]
	[0.061]	[0.054]	[0.062]	[0.056]	[0.060]	[0.053]	[0.061]	[0.055]
	{0.031}	{0.027}	{0.031}	{0.028}	{0.030}	{0.027}	{0.031}	{0.028}
Worst health	0.069***	0.072***	0.070***	0.072***				
	[0.011]	[0.011]	[0.011]	[0.011]				
Health quintile 2	0.015	0.015	0.017	0.017				
	[0.011]	[0.011]	[0.011]	[0.011]				
Health quintile 4	-0.014	-0.012	-0.015	-0.013				
	[0.012]	[0.012]	[0.012]	[0.012]				
Best health	-0.003	-0.002	-0.005	-0.004				
	[0.012]	[0.012]	[0.012]	[0.012]				
Health index					-0.020***	-0.020***	-0.020***	-0.020***
					[0.002]	[0.002]	[0.002]	[0.002]
Age	0.016***	Dummies	0.016***	Dummies	0.016***	Dummies	0.016***	Dummies
	[0.001]		[0.001]		[0.001]		[0.001]	
Female	0.018**		0.015*	0.004			0.014*	
	[0.008]		[0.008]	[0.055]			[0.008]	

(continued)

Table 2.5 (continued)

Variables	(1)	(2)	(3)	(4)	(5)	(6)	(7)	(8)
Married			0.027***	0.028***			0.028***	0.028***
			[0.009]	[0.009]			[0.009]	[0.009]
Spouse working			-0.043***	-0.042***			-0.042***	-0.041***
			[0.008]	[0.008]			[0.008]	[0.008]
Net wealth			0.002	0.003			0.002	0.002
			[0.004]	[0.004]			[0.004]	[0.004]
Low education			-0.020**	-0.021**			-0.023**	-0.024**
			[0.010]	[0.010]			[0.010]	[0.010]
Mid-education			-0.015	-0.015			-0.015	-0.016
			[0.010]	[0.010]			[0.010]	[0.010]
Self-employed			-0.039***	-0.037***			-0.039***	-0.037***
			[0.010]	[0.010]			[0.010]	[0.010]
Sample size	10,290	10,290	10,290	10,290	10,290	10,290	10,290	10,290

Notes: Coefficients are marginal effects from probit models. Standard errors are shown in parentheses and are clustered at the individual level. Age dummies are interacted with sex. Dummies also included for interview wave. Figures in square brackets show the effect on retirement of a one standard deviation change in option value; figures in curly brackets show the one-year retirement probability counterparts to these figures. The mean two-year retirement rate for the regression sample is 17.9 percent; the mean option value is 7.545 and the standard deviation of the option value is 9.269.

***Significant at the 1 percent level.

**Significant at the 5 percent level.

*Significant at the 10 percent level.

wealth is not found to have a statistically significant effect on retirement, while those with lower levels of education qualifications are found to be less likely to retire than those with higher levels of qualifications. Finally, self-employed people are found to be nearly 4 ppts less likely to retire than employees. The estimated impact of option value, and of different health quintiles, on retirement rates are not affected by the inclusion of these additional controls.

Columns (5), (6), (7), and (8) are analogous to the first four columns, except instead of controlling for the estimated health quintile, they instead control directly for the estimated health index (linearly). Those with higher values of the health index—that is, those with better health—are found to be less likely to retire. The estimated marginal effect of option value on retirement—and indeed the estimated impact of the other controls included in columns (7) and (8)—are unaffected by controlling for the estimated health index in this different way.

Each of the specifications presented in table 2.5 suggest that, on average, a one-unit increase in the option value leads to a reduction in the likelihood of an individual retiring over the next two years by 0.6–0.7 ppts. In order to quantify this better, the table presents (in square brackets) the impact on retirement of a one standard error change in the estimated option value.[22] Depending on the specification, this suggests that such a one standard error change in the option value is associated with retirement probabilities over the next two years being reduced by between 5.3 ppts and 6.2 ppts (i.e., column [6] and column [3]). This is a large impact—the mean retirement probability across the sample is 17.9 percent. Converting these to the chances of retiring over the next year, this is suggesting that a one standard deviation change in the option value would reduce retirement probabilities by between 2.7 ppts and 3.1 ppts, relative to a 9.4 percent average retirement probability.

Table 2.6 presents the impact of option value on retirement estimated separately for each health quintile. Columns (1) to (4) are equivalent to the first four columns of table 2.5. Option value is found to have a statistically significant impact on retirement among all five health quintiles, but there is no evidence that the size of this impact varies across any of the quintiles: that is, we have not found evidence that, for example, those in better health respond more strongly to the financial incentives to retire than those in the worst health. Again there is no evidence that the estimated impact of the option value varies across the four models.

The same pattern is found using the four models reported in table 2.7. Instead of estimating the impact of option value on retirement separately by health quintile, the results reported in table 2.7 instead pool all of the data but include an interaction between the estimated option value with

---

22. This is calculated by taking the mean difference between the simulated retirement probability across our sample under the scenario where every individual's option value is reduced by half the standard error of the option value (0.5 * 9.269) and the scenario where every individual's option value is increased by half the standard error.

Table 2.6 Effect of inclusive option value on retirement, by health quintile

Variables	(1)	(2)	(3)	(4)	Sample size	Mean ret. rate	Mean OV	S.d. of OV
OV: Worst health	-0.009***	-0.009***	-0.008***	-0.008***	2,120	0.260	5.829	7.474
	(0.002)	(0.003)	(0.002)	(0.002)				
	[0.064]	[0.066]	[0.060]	[0.062]				
	{0.033}	{0.034}	{0.030}	{0.031}				
OV: 2nd quintile	-0.006***	-0.005***	-0.007***	-0.006***	2,054	0.185	6.653	7.050
	(0.002)	(0.002)	(0.002)	(0.002)				
	[0.045]	[0.038]	[0.047]	[0.040]				
	{0.023}	{0.019}	{0.024}	{0.020}				
OV: 3rd quintile	-0.005**	-0.003	-0.006***	-0.003*	2,067	0.167	7.152	8.479
	(0.002)	(0.002)	(0.002)	(0.002)				
	[0.040]	[0.023]	[0.047]	[0.030]				
	{0.020}	{0.012}	{0.024}	{0.015}				
OV: 4th quintile	-0.005***	-0.005***	-0.005***	-0.005***	2,031	0.139	8.853	10.398
	(0.002)	(0.002)	(0.002)	(0.002)				
	[0.056]	[0.052]	[0.054]	[0.050]				
	{0.028}	{0.026}	{0.027}	{0.025}				
OV: Best health	-0.007***	-0.006***	-0.007***	-0.007***	2,018	0.141	9.341	11.725
	(0.002)	(0.002)	(0.002)	(0.002)				
	[0.082]	[0.074]	[0.087]	[0.081]				
	{0.042}	{0.038}	{0.044}	{0.041}				
Linear age	✓							
Age dummies		✓	✓	✓				
Health quintiles	✓	✓	✓	✓				
Other covariates			✓	✓				

Notes: Coefficients are marginal effects from twenty separate probit models. Standard errors are shown in parentheses and are clustered at the individual level. Other covariates in each specification are as described in table 2.5. Figures in square brackets show the effect on retirement of a one standard deviation change in option value; figures in curly brackets show the one-year retirement probability counterparts to these figures.

***Significant at the 1 percent level.
**Significant at the 5 percent level.
*Significant at the 10 percent level.

Table 2.7   Effect of inclusive option value on retirement, interacting option value with health quintile

Variables	(1)	(2)	(3)	(4)
Option value	−0.006***	−0.005***	−0.006***	−0.005***
	(0.001)	(0.001)	(0.001)	(0.001)
OV*health index	−0.000	−0.000	−0.000	−0.000
	(0.000)	(0.000)	(0.000)	(0.000)
Health index	−0.018***	−0.018***	−0.018***	−0.018***
	(0.003)	(0.003)	(0.003)	(0.003)
Linear age	✓		✓	
Age dummies		✓		✓
Health quintiles	✓	✓	✓	✓
Other covariates			✓	✓
Sample size	10,290	10,290	10,290	10,290
Mean ret. rate	0.179	0.179	0.179	0.179
Mean OV	7.545	7.545	7.545	7.545
S.d. of OV	9.269	9.269	9.269	9.269

Notes: Coefficients are marginal effects from probit models. Standard errors are shown in parentheses and are clustered at the individual level. Age dummies are interacted with sex. Dummies also included for interview wave.
***Significant at the 1 percent level.
**Significant at the 5 percent level.
*Significant at the 10 percent level.

the estimated health quintile. A one-unit increase in option value is found to reduce the chances of an individual retiring over the next two years by 0.5–0.6 ppts (very slightly below the 0.6–0.7 ppts reported in table 2.5), with no evidence found that this effect varies by estimated health. The estimated marginal effects are once again found to be stable across the four specifications reported in table 2.7.

We also estimate separate models by level of education. The results are reported in table 2.8 and show that higher option values are associated with lower retirement rates in each of the three education groups. We also find that the retirement decisions of those with middle levels of education—that is, those who completed some postcompulsory education, but did not go on to do a degree—appear, if anything, to be more responsive to the option value that they face than either those with lower or those with higher levels of education. (In some cases the impact on retirement probabilities of a one standard deviation change in the option value is found to be larger for those with high education, but this arises because the distribution of option values is more dispersed among this group than among the other education groups.) Once again we find that the estimated impact of the option value is not sensitive to which of the four models is used.

The predicted retirement hazards using the results from column (4) of table 2.8 are shown in figure 2.15A for men and in figure 2.15B for women.

Table 2.8 Effect of inclusive option value on retirement, by education level

Variables	(1)	(2)	(3)	(4)	Sample size	Mean ret. rate	Mean OV	S.d. of OV
OV: Low education	-0.006***	-0.005***	-0.006***	-0.005***	4,045	0.197	5.801	7.256
	(0.002)	(0.002)	(0.002)	(0.002)				
	[0.047]	[0.038]	[0.045]	[0.036]				
	{0.024}	{0.019}	{0.023}	{0.018}				
OV: Mid-education	-0.008***	-0.008***	-0.008***	-0.008***	4,005	0.172	7.587	8.165
	(0.002)	(0.001)	(0.001)	(0.001)				
	[0.067]	[0.065]	[0.069]	[0.067]				
	{0.034}	{0.033}	{0.035}	{0.034}				
OV: High education	-0.006***	-0.005***	-0.005***	-0.005***	2,240	0.161	10.618	12.836
	(0.001)	(0.001)	(0.001)	(0.001)				
	[0.071]	[0.064]	[0.071]	[0.064]				
	{0.036}	{0.033}	{0.036}	{0.033}				
Linear age	✓		✓					
Age dummies		✓		✓				
Health quintiles	✓	✓	✓	✓				
Other covariates			✓	✓				

Notes: Coefficients are marginal effects from twelve separate probit models. Standard errors are shown in parentheses and are clustered at the individual level. Other covariates in each specification are as described in table 2.5. Figures in square brackets show the effect on retirement of a one standard deviation change in option value on the two-year retirement probability; figures in curly brackets show the one-year retirement probability counterparts to these figures.

***Significant at the 1 percent level.
**Significant at the 5 percent level.
*Significant at the 10 percent level.

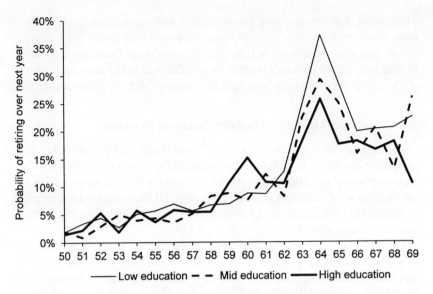

Fig. 2.15A   Predicted retirement hazards, by education level (men)
Note: These retirement hazards are calculated using the regression coefficients reported in specification (4) in table 2.8.

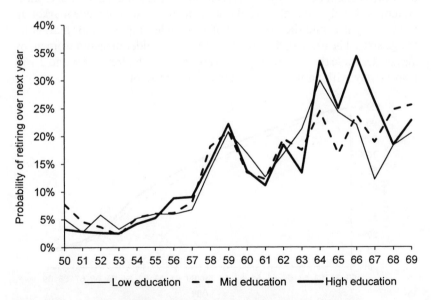

Fig. 2.15B   Predicted retirement hazards, by education level (women)
Note: These retirement hazards are calculated using the regression coefficients reported in specification (4) in table 2.8.

This shows that retirement in the two years from ages fifty-nine to sixty is more common for highly educated men than men with lower levels of education and that the reverse is true over the two years from age sixty-four. In contrast, among women there is little difference in the retirement probabilities over the two years from ages fifty-nine to sixty by education group.

2.5   Simulating Alternative Disability Insurance Programs

In order to provide a clearer sense of how the probability of being able to receive disability benefits affects individuals' retirement behavior, this section examines predicted retirement rates under alternative scenarios for the likelihood of receiving disability benefits. All the simulations presented in this section are based on the estimates from the fourth (i.e., the richest) specification in table 2.5.

Under the current system our model suggests that those in work at age fifty will, on average, work for a further 10.9 years before retiring. On average, men in work at age fifty are predicted to work longer before retiring (12.0 years) than women (10.0 years). The first two situations we compare are, in one dimension, the extreme possibilities: first a system in which everyone would be able to retire onto the DI pathway—that is, regardless of health, everyone not in paid work is able to receive disability benefits—and second a system under which no one is able to retire onto the DI pathway. Since disability benefits can only be received up to the state pension age, these systems will only affect the likelihood of men leaving the labor market up to age sixty-five, and the likelihood of women leaving the labor market up to age sixty. The estimated employment levels of older men and women, by age, under these two different systems are shown in figures 2.16A and 2.16B respectively, with pooled results shown in figure 2.16C.

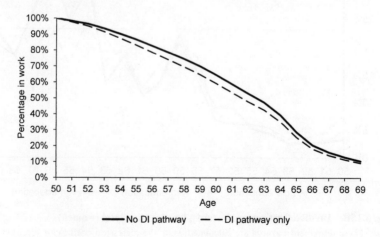

Fig. 2.16A   Employment survival curve for men, assuming there is only one pathway
Note: These survival curves are calculated using the coefficients from specification (4) in table 2.5.

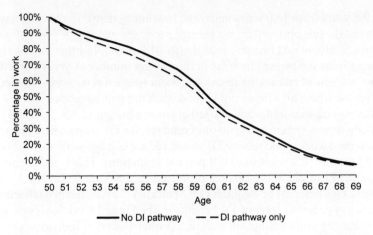

Fig. 2.16B   Employment survival curve for women, assuming there is only one pathway

Note: These survival curves are calculated using the coefficients from specification (4) in table 2.5.

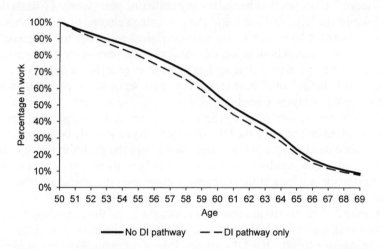

Fig. 2.16C   Employment survival curve (men and women), assuming there is only one pathway

Note: These survival curves are calculated using the coefficients from specification (4) in table 2.5.

For men, moving to the system where no one can retire onto the DI pathway makes no apparent difference to the average number of years worked (it stays at 12.0 years). But under the alternative extreme where everyone is able to retire onto the DI pathway, it falls to 11.4 years. In other words, moving from a system where everyone is able to move onto DI to one where no one is able to is estimated to increase the average number of years that men will work by 5.5 percent.

If all women in work at age fifty were able to retire onto the DI pathway, then the average predicted number of years of work from age fifty would fall (to 9.5 years from 10.0 years under the baseline system). If no women were able to take this option then the average predicted number of years of work from age fifty would increase slightly (to 10.1 years). In other words, there is an estimated 6 percent increase in the average number of years worked by older women when moving from the system where no one is able to receive DI to one where all women not in paid work are able to receive DI.

Combining men and women together (shown in figure 2.16C), we find that moving from a system where no one could receive DI to one where everyone not in paid work could receive DI would reduce average years worked from 11.0 years to 10.4 years (or a 5.9 percent reduction). This is much smaller than, for example, the estimates produced in this volume for the United States (17.3 percent) or Belgium (12.2 percent). This difference reflects the much less generous level of DI benefits in the United Kingdom compared to either the United States or Belgium (rather than that individuals in the United Kingdom are less responsive to financial incentives than individuals in these other countries).

Figure 2.17 shows the change in the number of years worked (the darker series and the left-hand axis) and the percentage change in the number of years worked (the lighter series and the right-hand axis) for all possible likelihoods of individuals being able to take the DI pathway into retirement. For example, this shows that an 8 percent chance of being able to receive disability benefits would leave the average number of years worked between ages fifty and sixty-nine unchanged.

Finally we explore whether there are groups of individuals for whom varying the availability of the DI pathway has a particularly large impact on their labor market behavior. Specifically we vary the likelihood with which individuals would be able to receive disability benefits were they to move out of paid work, but look at the outcomes only among those who are observed to receive disability benefits at some point in our sample.

Figure 2.18 shows the number of years worked, and the percentage change in the number of years worked, for all possible likelihoods of individuals being able to take the DI pathway into retirement. For this group of individuals—that is, those who are observed to receive disability benefits at some point in our data—a 20 percent likelihood of being able to take the DI pathway would leave the average number of years worked between ages fifty and sixty-nine unchanged.

2.6   Conclusions

This chapter has documented differences in employment rates of men and women between ages fifty and sixty-nine by health and explored how these employment rates are affected by financial incentives to leave the labor market. The measure of financial incentives builds on the existing literature by incorporating potential income from disability benefits alongside that from

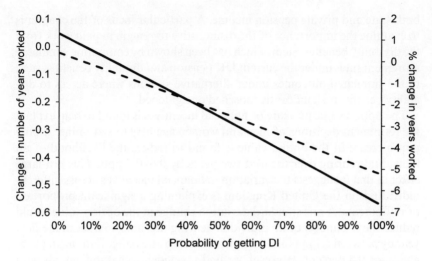

Fig. 2.17   Relationship between probability of getting DI and number of years worked between age fifty and sixty-nine, all individuals

Notes: These survival curves are calculated using the coefficients from specification (4) in table 2.5. Percentage change in years worked is calculated relative to the predicted employment rates using the actual DI probability.

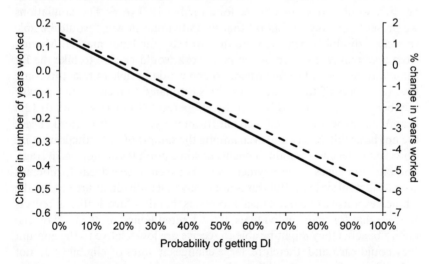

Fig. 2.18   Relationship between probability of getting DI and number of years worked between age fifty and sixty-nine, DI recipients only

Notes: These survival curves are calculated using the coefficients from specification (4) in table 2.5. Percentage change in years worked is calculated relative to the predicted employment rates using the actual DI probability.

both state and private pension income. A particular focus of the chapter is to examine the importance of the disincentive to remain in paid work from the disability benefit system, which has been shown by comparing simulated retirement rates under the current UK pension and disability benefit system to the simulated outcomes under alternative systems where access to disability benefits is significantly loosened or tightened.

The option value measure of financial incentives is found to help explain the retirement decisions of men and women age fifty to sixty-nine. A one-unit increase in the option value is found to reduce the likelihood of an individual retiring over the next two years by 0.6–0.7 ppts. This is a large effect in that it suggests the variation in financial incentives across different individuals in the United Kingdom is explaining a significant proportion of retirements. A one standard deviation change in the option value would reduce the likelihood of an individual leaving the labor market in the next year by between 2.7 ppts and 3.1ppts, relative to an average retirement probability of 9.4 percent. However, we find no evidence that individuals with different levels of health respond to our measure of financial incentives differently; so, for example, we do not find evidence that those in poor health are less responsive to the financial incentives that they face than those with better health.

Under the current system our model suggests that men in work at age fifty would work, on average, for a further 12.0 years while women in work at age fifty would work, on average, for a further 10.0 years. The simulations we present vary the likelihood that an individual in work would be able to receive disability benefits were they to leave the labor market. Moving from a system where everyone in paid work would be able to take the DI route into retirement to one where no one would be able to take this route (i.e., regardless of their actual health) is estimated to increase the average numbers of years worked by men by 5.5 percent (from 11.4 years to 12.0 years) and by women by 6.0 percent (from 9.5 years to 10.1 years). These are not large differences and even among the sample of individuals who are observed to receive disability benefits at some point we do not, on average, find big differences in employment rates between these extremely different counterfactual systems. But this is not to say that individuals are not, on the whole, responsive to the financial incentives that they face. Rather it reflects the fact that for many individuals in the United Kingdom the level of disability benefits they might be able to receive are low relative to the amount they could earn and, therefore, large changes in rates of eligibility do not induce large effects on overall employment.

Appendix

Additional Tables and Figures

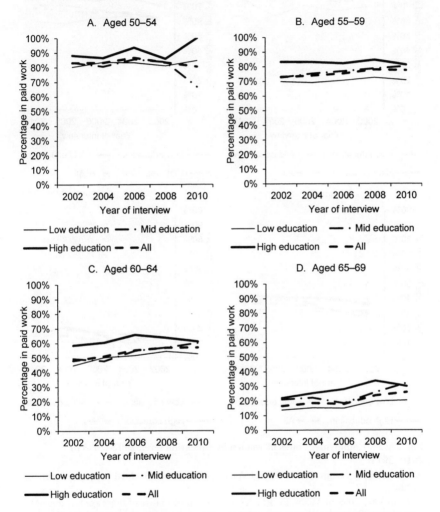

Fig. 2A.1   Employment rates of men by education level, 2002–2003 to 2010–2011
Source: English Longitudinal Study of Ageing, waves 1–5. Weighted using cross-sectional weights.
Note: In 2002, 2006, and 2008, the ELSA sample is representative of those age fifty and older. However, in 2004 and 2010, it is only representative of those age fifty-two and older.

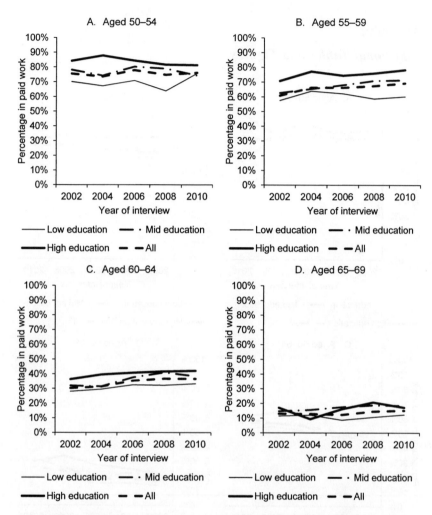

Fig. 2A.2 Employment rates of women by education level, 2002–2003 to 2010–2011

Source: English Longitudinal Study of Ageing, waves 1–5. Weighted using cross-sectional weights.

Note: In 2002, 2006, and 2008, the ELSA sample is representative of those age fifty and older. However, in 2004 and 2010, it is only representative of those age fifty-two and older.

Table 2A.1   **Employment rates of older men over time, by age**

	50–54	55–59	60–64	65–69	All 50–69
1968	96.1	91.4	80.0	27.1	77.0
1969	96.8	91.3	79.9	34.8	77.5
1970	97.4	92.3	80.4	32.6	77.4
1971	93.9	89.9	79.3	32.2	75.7
1972	95.1	87.9	74.0	24.5	73.4
1973	93.8	91.2	78.8	29.0	75.2
1974	93.0	89.9	80.0	29.7	74.4
1975	93.8	89.9	78.1	25.2	73.5
1976	92.8	88.8	78.3	23.7	72.6
1977	92.3	90.0	76.2	19.4	70.7
1978	92.9	87.9	68.0	21.9	70.0
1979	91.2	86.1	71.5	22.5	68.8
1980	91.4	89.8	69.3	20.6	68.6
1981	88.0	81.6	59.8	18.6	63.3
1982	86.9	76.0	58.5	16.9	61.8
1983	83.9	72.8	51.4	12.9	58.1
1984	82.9	73.7	49.3	12.7	58.2
1985	81.2	71.7	47.8	11.8	57.0
1986	79.7	69.3	48.0	11.8	55.0
1987	80.9	71.2	47.8	11.3	53.9
1988	81.9	72.0	48.9	13.0	53.9
1989	81.8	73.4	48.8	13.5	54.6
1990	80.4	72.6	48.4	13.8	55.2
1991	79.6	68.6	47.3	13.7	54.9
1992	79.9	68.7	46.2	13.7	52.7
1993	79.1	67.5	44.9	12.4	53.1
1994	79.7	67.2	44.8	13.4	53.8
1995	80.2	66.2	45.1	14.1	54.5
1996	80.5	68.1	45.2	12.7	56.0
1997	81.2	69.0	47.3	14.1	57.1
1998	81.7	70.6	46.4	14.4	57.7
1999	82.2	70.7	47.2	15.0	57.6
2000	82.1	71.5	47.7	14.1	58.3
2001	83.1	72.5	48.7	14.6	59.0
2002	83.4	73.0	49.5	15.6	60.5
2003	83.8	74.2	53.2	17.5	60.3
2004	83.8	74.7	53.7	17.3	61.5
2005	84.7	75.7	54.1	18.8	61.6
2006	84.6	75.4	54.7	20.0	61.5
2007	85.0	74.9	56.9	20.5	61.9
2008	83.9	76.6	58.1	21.6	60.8
2009	82.9	76.4	55.9	21.7	60.9
2010	82.6	76.0	54.5	23.9	59.8
2011	83.0	74.4	54.4	22.9	60.5
2012	83.9	75.6	55.4	23.9	58.1

Source: Family Expenditure Survey (1968–1982) and Labour Force Survey (1983–2012).

Table 2A.2 **Employment rates of older women over time, by age**

	50–54	55–59	60–64	65–69	All 50–69
1968	59.1	46.5	25.0	14.2	37.3
1969	56.8	52.8	28.0	15.6	38.7
1970	59.3	54.5	26.1	13.9	39.4
1971	62.3	51.5	30.4	14.1	40.2
1972	58.2	52.1	27.6	12.8	39.1
1973	64.3	55.3	29.9	13.4	41.1
1974	66.9	55.8	29.7	15.8	42.9
1975	67.9	54.7	25.9	13.7	41.3
1976	63.9	55.6	28.7	13.4	41.1
1977	67.8	57.9	28.3	10.9	41.8
1978	64.6	57.0	26.8	12.5	41.0
1979	67.2	56.2	27.2	10.0	40.9
1980	66.9	59.5	24.1	12.1	41.0
1981	65.6	56.1	26.1	10.8	39.6
1982	58.7	52.6	23.0	7.5	36.5
1983	59.4	46.4	19.4	6.5	33.3
1984	60.8	46.9	19.8	6.6	34.1
1985	60.0	47.2	17.4	6.2	32.7
1986	60.6	47.4	17.7	5.7	32.7
1987	60.5	48.1	18.1	5.2	32.8
1988	60.4	47.8	18.5	5.3	32.4
1989	62.7	49.2	21.1	6.8	34.5
1990	63.6	50.5	21.7	7.2	35.5
1991	63.9	50.6	22.4	6.6	35.7
1992	65.6	51.7	23.0	7.5	37.8
1993	66.3	51.2	23.7	7.5	38.7
1994	66.8	52.6	24.2	7.3	39.8
1995	67.4	52.4	24.8	7.5	39.7
1996	67.8	51.4	24.5	6.9	40.8
1997	68.9	50.9	25.4	7.8	42.0
1998	69.6	53.1	24.1	7.8	42.9
1999	70.4	54.2	24.3	8.5	43.5
2000	70.4	56.2	25.6	8.2	44.2
2001	71.4	56.3	27.3	7.9	45.1
2002	72.3	58.1	27.6	8.8	45.8
2003	73.3	60.4	28.1	9.8	46.1
2004	73.8	60.6	29.5	9.6	47.1
2005	74.3	61.7	30.6	10.3	48.1
2006	74.8	62.7	32.4	11.4	47.8
2007	75.4	63.8	32.6	11.0	48.2
2008	76.2	64.2	33.9	12.0	48.4
2009	75.8	64.9	33.5	14.3	48.8
2010	75.8	66.0	33.6	15.3	48.9
2011	77.1	66.0	33.7	15.3	49.5
2012	77.1	66.2	35.9	15.2	44.2

Source: Family Expenditure Survey (1968–1982) and Labour Force Survey (1983–2012).

Table 2A.3 **Employment rates over time (men and women), by age**

	50–54	55–59	60–64	65–69	All 50–69
1968	76.5	69.3	50.3	20.1	56.1
1969	76.4	71.3	51.6	24.4	57.0
1970	77.3	72.7	52.5	22.7	57.5
1971	77.3	70.1	51.9	22.5	56.7
1972	76.3	69.4	50.2	18.2	55.6
1973	79.3	72.3	53.3	20.5	57.5
1974	79.2	72.4	53.0	22.2	57.7
1975	80.1	71.5	49.8	19.0	56.3
1976	77.4	71.4	52.1	18.0	55.8
1977	79.5	72.7	49.8	14.9	55.2
1978	78.7	71.6	46.3	16.7	54.8
1979	78.6	71.1	45.6	15.9	54.0
1980	79.0	74.0	44.4	16.1	54.0
1981	76.3	68.8	41.1	14.4	50.8
1982	72.0	64.2	40.0	11.8	48.5
1983	71.2	59.9	34.5	9.4	45.2
1984	72.3	59.3	34.7	9.4	45.6
1985	71.3	60.1	32.2	9.1	44.2
1986	70.8	59.3	31.7	8.4	43.3
1987	70.1	58.3	32.3	8.2	42.9
1988	70.6	59.3	32.3	8.0	42.7
1989	72.1	60.4	34.7	9.7	44.1
1990	72.5	61.7	34.8	10.1	44.9
1991	72.0	61.5	34.6	9.9	44.9
1992	72.6	60.2	34.1	10.4	45.0
1993	72.6	59.2	33.9	9.8	45.7
1994	73.2	59.7	34.1	10.2	46.6
1995	73.7	59.2	34.6	10.7	46.9
1996	74.1	59.5	34.6	9.7	48.2
1997	74.9	59.7	36.0	10.8	49.4
1998	75.5	61.7	34.9	10.9	50.0
1999	76.2	62.2	35.4	11.6	50.3
2000	76.1	63.6	36.2	11.0	51.0
2001	77.1	64.1	37.6	11.1	51.8
2002	77.7	65.3	38.2	12.1	52.9
2003	78.5	67.1	40.1	13.5	53.0
2004	78.7	67.5	40.9	13.4	54.0
2005	79.3	68.5	41.8	14.4	54.6
2006	79.5	68.9	43.1	15.5	54.4
2007	79.9	69.2	44.2	15.5	54.8
2008	79.8	70.2	45.7	16.6	54.3
2009	79.2	70.4	44.3	17.9	54.7
2010	79.1	70.8	43.7	19.4	54.1
2011	79.9	70.1	43.6	19.0	54.8
2012	80.4	70.7	45.3	19.3	51.0

Source: Family Expenditure Survey (1968–1982) and Labour Force Survey (1983–2012).

Table 2A.4   **Percentage of men age fifty to sixty-four receiving disability insurance, by education and health quintile**

Education	Health quintile					
	Worst	2	3	4	Best	All
Low	58.88	22.84	6.02	1.68	1.16	16.55
Mid	48.49	14.98	4.15	0.90	0.57	6.85
High	18.18	3.55	2.27	0.61	0.21	1.56
All	53.74	17.67	4.59	1.12	0.65	9.85

Source: English Longitudinal Study of Ageing, waves 1–5, pooled (unweighted).

Table 2A.5   **Percentage of women age fifty to fifty-nine receiving disability insurance, by education and health quintile**

Education	Health quintile					
	Worst	2	3	4	Best	All
Low	41.84	6.44	2.26	1.46	0.74	10.94
Mid	29.29	6.81	1.64	0.68	0.32	5.42
High	25.86	8.13	2.06	1.54	0.00	2.70
All	36.46	6.80	1.96	1.15	0.36	7.15

Source: English Longitudinal Study of Ageing, waves 1–5, pooled (unweighted).

Table 2A.6   **Descriptive statistics on regression sample**

Percent (except where otherwise stated)	Men	Women	All
Age (years)	57.6	57.1	57.4
	(4.5)	(4.3)	(4.4)
Married	73.1	61.5	67.5
	(44.4)	(48.7)	(46.8)
Spouse working	62.9	56.3	59.7
	(48.3)	(49.6)	(49.0)
Low education	40.4	38.1	39.3
	(49.1)	(48.6)	(48.8)
Mid-education	35.6	42.6	38.9
	(47.9)	(49.4)	(48.8)
High education	24.0	19.3	21.8
	(42.7)	(39.5)	(41.3)
Self-employed	23.5	13.1	18.6
	(42.4)	(33.8)	(38.9)
Net wealth (thousands)	225.4	177.5	202.4
	(1131.4)	(707.9)	(952.3)
Sample size	5,353	4,937	10,290

Note: Standard deviations are shown in parentheses.

Table 2A.7   **Effect of percentage gain in value from delaying retirement**

Variables	(1)	(2)	(3)	(4)
Percent gain in OV	–0.171***	–0.157***	–0.162***	–0.148***
	[0.023]	[0.022]	[0.023]	[0.022]
Linear age	✓		✓	
Age dummies		✓		✓
Health quintiles	✓	✓	✓	✓
Other covariates			✓	✓
Sample size	10,290	10,290	10,290	10,290
Mean ret. rate	0.179	0.179	0.179	0.179
Mean % gain	0.281	0.281	0.281	0.281
S.d. of % gain	0.338	0.338	0.338	0.338

Notes: Coefficients are marginal effects from probit models. Standard errors are shown in parentheses and are clustered at the individual level. Other covariates are as described in table 2.5.

***Significant at the 1 percent level.

**Significant at the 5 percent level.

*Significant at the 10 percent level.

Table 2A.8   Effect of percentage gain in value from delaying retirement, by health quintile

Variables	(1)	(2)	(3)	(4)	Sample size	Mean ret. rate	Mean % gain	S.d. of % gain
Percent gain: Worst health	-0.175***	-0.178***	-0.163***	-0.166***	2,120	0.260	0.243	0.341
	(0.054)	(0.053)	(0.053)	(0.053)				
Percent gain: 2nd quintile	-0.123**	-0.098*	-0.120**	-0.094*	2,054	0.185	0.260	0.291
	(0.050)	(0.050)	(0.050)	(0.050)				
Percent gain: 3rd quintile	-0.197***	-0.159***	-0.179***	-0.141***	2,064	0.167	0.263	0.318
	(0.053)	(0.050)	(0.053)	(0.051)				
Percent gain: 4th quintile	-0.154***	-0.146***	-0.130***	-0.121***	2,031	0.139	0.318	0.361
	(0.048)	(0.045)	(0.048)	(0.046)				
Percent gain: Best health	-0.208***	-0.183***	-0.207***	-0.184***	2,018	0.141	0.325	0.365
	(0.052)	(0.050)	(0.052)	(0.050)				
Linear age	✓		✓					
Age dummies		✓		✓				
Health quintiles	✓	✓	✓	✓				
Other covariates			✓	✓				

Notes: Coefficients are marginal effects from twenty separate probit models. Standard errors are shown in parentheses. Other covariates in each specification are as described in table 2.5. Standard errors are clustered at the individual level.

***Significant at the 1 percent level.

**Significant at the 5 percent level.

*Significant at the 10 percent level.

Table 2A.9   Effect of percentage gain in value from delaying retirement, by education level

Variables	(1)	(2)	(3)	(4)	Sample size	Mean ret. rate	Mean % gain	S.d. of % gain
Percent gain: Low education	-0.195***	-0.173***	-0.179***	-0.159***	4,045	0.197	0.249	0.297
	(0.041)	(0.039)	(0.041)	(0.039)				
Percent gain: Mid-education	-0.177***	-0.167***	-0.169***	-0.161***	4,005	0.172	0.294	0.354
	(0.037)	(0.036)	(0.037)	(0.036)				
Percent gain: High education	-0.145***	-0.130***	-0.127***	-0.115***	2,240	0.161	0.317	0.372
	(0.042)	(0.041)	(0.041)	(0.040)				
Linear age	✓		✓					
Age dummies		✓		✓				
Health quintiles	✓	✓	✓	✓				
Other covariates			✓	✓				

Notes: Coefficients are marginal effects from twelve separate probit models. Standard errors are shown in parentheses and are clustered at the individual level. Other covariates in each specification are as described in table 2.5.

***Significant at the 1 percent level.

**Significant at the 5 percent level.

*Significant at the 10 percent level.

References

Anyadike-Danes, M., and D. McVicar. 2008. "Has The Boom in Incapacity Benefit Claimant Numbers Passed its Peak?" *Fiscal Studies* 29 (4): 415–34.
Banks, J., R. Blundell, A. Bozio, and C. Emmerson. 2012. "Disability, Health and Retirement in the United Kingdom." In *Social Security Programs and Retirement around the World: Historical Trends in Mortality and Health, Employment, and Disability Insurance Participation and Reforms*, edited by D. Wise, 41–77. Chicago: University of Chicago Press.
Bozio, A., R. Crawford, C. Emmerson, and G. Tetlow. 2010. "Retirement Outcomes and Lifetime Earnings: Descriptive Evidence from Linked ELSA-NI Data." DWP Working Paper no. 81, Department for Work and Pensions. https://www.gov.uk /government/uploads/system/uploads/attachment_data/file/214382/WP81.pdf.
Bozio, A., R. Crawford, and G. Tetlow. 2010. "The History of State Pensions in the UK: 1948 to 2010." IFS Briefing Note no. BN105, Institute for Fiscal Studies. http://www.ifs.org.uk/.
Crawford, R. 2012. "ELSA Pension Wealth Derived Variables (Waves 2 to 5): Methodology." UK Data Archive Study no. 5050, English Longitudinal Study of Ageing. http://www.esds.ac.uk/doc/5050/mrdoc/pdf/5050_ELSA_PW_methodology .pdf.
Cribb, J., C. Emmerson, and G. Tetlow. 2013. "Incentives, Shocks or Signals: Labour Supply Effects of Increasing the Female State Pension Age in the UK." Working Paper no. W13/03, Institute for Fiscal Studies, London.
Disney, R., and C. Emmerson. 2005. "Public Pension Reform in the United Kingdom: What Effect on the Financial Well-Being of Current and Future Pensioners?" *Fiscal Studies* 26 (1): 55–81.
Poterba, J. M., S. F. Venti, and D. A. Wise. 2011. "Family Status Transitions, Latent Health, and the Post-Retirement Evolution of Assets." In *Explorations in the Economics of Aging*, edited by D. A. Wise, 23–69. Chicago: University of Chicago Press.
———. 2013. "Health, Education, and the Post-Retirement Evolution of Household Assets." NBER Working Paper no. 18695, Cambridge, MA.
Stock, J., and D. Wise. 1990a. "The Pension Inducement to Retire: An Option Value Analysis." In *Issues in the Economics of Aging*, edited by D. Wise, 205–24. Chicago: University of Chicago Press.
———. 1990b. "Pensions, the Option Value of Work and Retirement." *Econometrica* 58 (5): 1151–80.
Wunsch, C., and J. V. Raman. 2010. "Mandatory Retirement in the United Kingdom, Canada and the United States of America." TAEN Discussion Paper, The Age and Employment Network, London. http://www.taen.org.uk/uploads/resources /Combined_dissertation_final_formatted.pdf.

3

Option Value of Disability Insurance in Canada

Kevin Milligan and Tammy Schirle

3.1   Introduction

As Canadians approach retirement, there are two principal paths to be taken. First, a person may choose to work until entering retirement, at which time they will rely on public pension income and other private savings. For most Canadians, public pension income becomes available as early as age sixty and the normal retirement age is sixty-five. Second, depending on eligibility, a person may work, take up disability benefits available through the public pension system, and then make the transition to regular public pension benefits when they reach age sixty-five.

We are interested in understanding the importance of the financial incentives for work and retirement that are embedded in Canada's public retirement and disability benefit systems. We are also interested in accounting for the relative importance of financial incentives as it depends on individuals' health and socioeconomic status. To this end we extend the research presented in Baker, Gruber, and Milligan (2004), which focused on the financial incentives for retirement in the structure of the Canada and Quebec Pension Plans' (C/QPP) regular retirement benefits. In this study, we have introduced the possibility of receiving Canada and Quebec Pension Plan Disability

Kevin Milligan is an associate professor at the Vancouver School of Economics, University of British Columbia, and a research associate of the National Bureau of Economic Research. Tammy Schirle is associate professor of economics and director of the Laurier Centre for Economic Research & Policy Analysis (LCERPA) at Wilfrid Laurier University.

This chapter was prepared for the NBER International Social Security project. We thank the organizers and other country teams for their suggestions. We especially thank Michael Baker for his work on previous stages of this project on which this current chapter is built. For acknowledgments, sources of research support, and disclosure of the authors' material financial relationships, if any, please see http://www.nber.org/chapters/c13325.ack.

Benefits as a potential path into retirement. In doing so, we also look more closely at the impact of self-assessed health status on the responsiveness of the retirement decision.

Unlike several other Organisation for Economic Co-operation and Development (OECD) countries, the Canadian system for disability benefits is quite limited. To qualify for C/QPP disability, a person must have a "severe and prolonged" medical condition. In determining eligibility, a person's age, employment opportunities, or socioeconomic status is not taken into account. Furthermore, disability benefits are not permanent—an eligible person must convert their disability benefits to a retirement benefit at age sixty-five. While the person's C/QPP retirement pension benefits will account for time taken away from the labor force with a disability, it is not typically the case that taking the disability path will substantially alter future retirement benefit amounts (after age sixty-five). Rather, the financial incentives along the two paths to retirement are quite similar.

In this context, we find that the financial incentives embedded in the C/QPP system have a significant and even substantial effect on the likelihood of entering retirement. The incentives are not driven by the provisions specific to the C/QPP disability benefits. Rather, the financial incentive effects largely reflect incentives contained in the C/QPP retirement benefit calculations. Furthermore, we find that the impact is driven by those with lower self-assessed health.

The chapter proceeds as follows. First, we provide background information on the Canadian retirement income and disability system, including both the institutions and some descriptive graphs to investigate the important trends in the data. Next we lay out our empirical approach, including descriptions of our data and estimation strategy. We then explain our results and go through some simulations to explore the implications of our estimates. Finally, we conclude by placing our results in the context of other evidence and the policy environment.

3.2   Background

We provide in this section the relevant background on the institutions of the Canadian retirement and disability policy environment.[1] We also provide graphical illustration of some important trends to help place our work in context.

In Canada, seniors can receive public pension income from two programs—the Old Age Security (OAS) program and the Canada and Quebec Pension Plans (C/QPP). The OAS provides a modest pension to all individuals over age sixty-five that meet residency requirements. The OAS

---

1. For more details on Canada's public pensions, see Baker, Gruber, and Milligan (2004) and Milligan and Schirle (2006, 2013).

pension is supplemented with the Guaranteed Income Supplement (GIS), which is an income-tested benefit for those receiving the OAS pension. The OAS program also provides a supplement (known as the Allowance) to spouses of OAS pensioners and widows age sixty to sixty-four. About one-third of Canadian seniors receive either GIS or Allowance benefits. The OAS program had not changed significantly for three decades. However, gradual increases in the ages of eligibility by two years will begin in April 2023. Also, in July 2013 the option to defer the OAS pension was introduced, with an actuarial adjustment applied for each month (up to sixty months) that the OAS pension is deferred.

The Canada and Quebec Pension Plans offer three types of benefits—retirement, survivor, and disability. The C/QPP is funded with a payroll tax applied to earnings above a "Year's Basic Exemption" and below a "Year's Maximum Pensionable Earnings" (YMPE). The C/QPP retirement pension offers a defined benefit pension, with a monthly benefit based on an individual's earnings history from age eighteen (or 1966) up to the time benefits are claimed (from age sixty to age seventy). Some allowances are made for low-earnings years, years with a disability, and years spent caring for young children. The normal retirement age is sixty-five, and an actuarial adjustment is applied for early or late benefit take-up. The C/QPP benefit is designed to replace up to 25 percent of lifetime average earnings (below the YMPE). In 2013, the maximum benefit for an individual claiming benefits at age sixty-five was CAD $1,021.50.

Core components of the C/QPP have not changed significantly since the 1980s. In 1998–1999, the formula that defined the maximum C/QPP benefit changed slightly, effectively lowering the maximum monthly benefit.[2] Recently, a few important changes were made to the C/QPP retirement benefit. First, a schedule of gradual increases in the actuarial adjustments began in 2011 and will be fully phased in by 2017 (see Laurin, Milligan, and Schirle 2012). Second, beginning in 2012 individuals can continue contributing to the C/QPP after taking up the retirement benefit, as contributions toward a separate postretirement benefit. Third, a work interruption (at least one month of no earnings) is no longer required to initiate C/QPP benefits after 2011.

The C/QPP also provides a survivor benefit to the surviving spouse of C/QPP contributors. The benefit amount has two components—a flat-rate portion, and an earnings-related portion that depends on the deceased spouse's earnings history from age eighteen until the time C/QPP benefits are claimed. Both components of the benefit depend on the claimant's age. The maximum benefit depends on whether the recipient is also receiving a C/QPP

2. Until 1997 the benefit formula had used an average of the past three years' YMPE to update lifetime earnings to current levels. In 1998 the past four years' YMPE was used, and from 1999 on the past five years' YMPE was used.

retirement or disability pension, with a maximum combined retirement and survivor pension equal to CAD $1,021.50 (the maximum retirement pension).

The C/QPP also administers a disability benefit available to C/QPP contributors under age sixty-five. The disability benefit also has two components—a flat-rate portion and an earnings-related portion based on the individual's earnings history from age eighteen and the year in which a disability occurs. Before 1997, a person was eligible if they contributed for at least two of the three years or five of the ten years preceding the onset of the disability. After 1997, the minimum contribution requirement is four of the previous six years. The maximum monthly disability benefit is higher than the maximum retirement benefit, set at CAD $1,212.90 in 2013. The maximum combined survivor and disability benefit is equal to the maximum disability benefit. At age sixty-five, the C/QPP benefits are converted to a retirement benefit. In the retirement benefit calculation, years in which the individual received C/QPP disability benefits are not counted as part of the earnings history.

The administration of disability benefits was significantly altered in September 1995, with more stringent eligibility requirements put in place. After the reforms, an individual must have a medical condition that is "severe and prolonged" to qualify for benefits. A medical report from a physician is required. A major change in 1995 was that socioeconomic factors were no longer considered in adjudicating applications and no special consideration would be given to applicants age fifty-five and over.[3] (For more detail on the historic development of the DI part of the C/QPP, see Baker and Milligan [2012].)

It is apparent that these changes significantly affected disability benefit eligibility. In figure 3.1, we can see that disability benefit receipt by individuals age fifty to sixty-four rose steadily until 1995, when 14 percent of men and 8 percent of women age sixty to sixty-four received CPP disability benefits. For men, disability benefit receipt declines sharply after the reforms, so that in 2009 only 7 percent of men age sixty to sixty-four are receiving benefits. For women disability receipt also declines after the reforms, however, the effect of the reforms on the rate of receipt is offset by the general upward trend in women's employment rates (figure 3.2). With greater attachment to the labor force, more women meet the minimum contribution requirements for disability benefits than before.

There were important changes in the employment rates of both men and women over time. In figure 3.2, we see that for women there is a general increase in the employment rate among those age fifty to sixty-four since

3. See http://www.oag-bvg.gc.ca/internet/English/parl_oag_199609_17_e_5048.html, paragraph 17.66.

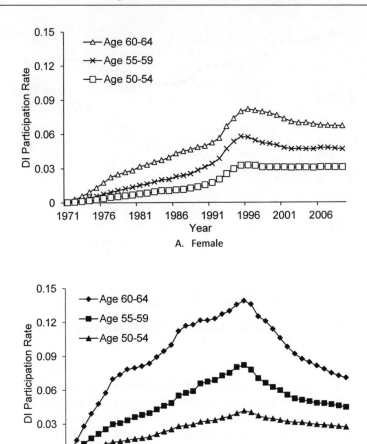

Fig. 3.1   CPP disability benefit receipt by sex and age, 1971–2009
Source: CPP Statistical Bulletin for DI counts; CANSIM database population counts.

the 1970s, with larger increases after the mid-1990s. Men's employment rates, on the other hand, fell steadily until the early 1990s after which their employment rates rose steadily. By 2009, the gender gap in employment rates among seniors had narrowed substantially—with 62 percent of women and 70 percent of men age fifty to sixty-four employed.

The recent increases in older individuals' employment rates in Canada have many explanations. One important factor is education. In figure 3.3, we see that more educated men and women are more likely employed. Although the likelihood of being employed among university-educated men does not

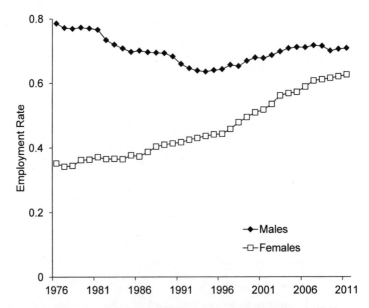

Fig. 3.2   Employment rates of individuals age fifty to sixty-four, 1976–2011
Source: Labour Force Survey public use microdata files.

show a clear upward trend after the mid-1990s, the portion of men and women that are university educated has increased substantially.[4] The likelihood of employment among university-educated women increased steadily since the 1970s, but only increased since the mid-1990s for less educated groups of women. These broader trends for women are generally ascribed to cohort effects—the women entering the older age groups since the mid-1990s are the same women driving large increases in younger women's participation after the 1960s (see Schirle 2008).

Interesting to consider is the inverse relationship that appears between the employment rates of older men, particularly those with a high school education, and the rates of disability benefit receipt among men. Unfortunately the Canadian administrative data on disability insurance (DI) use does not allow us to examine the education levels of individuals receiving CPP disability benefits, so we are not able to report tabulations describing potential relationships between education, health, and disability benefit receipt. We expect, however, that more stringent eligibility requirements (that no longer account for socioeconomic circumstances in determining disability status)

---

4. From tabulations based on Statistics Canada Cansim Table 282–0004 (Labour Force Survey), in 1995 13 percent of men and 7 percent of women age fifty-five to sixty-four had a university degree. In 2009, 23 percent of men and 19 percent of women age fifty-five to sixty-four had a university degree.

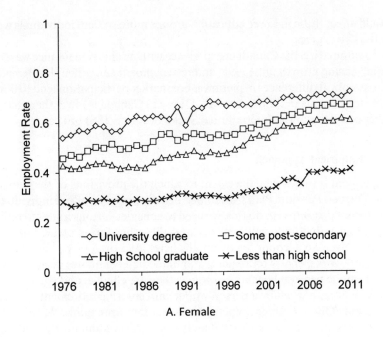

A. Female

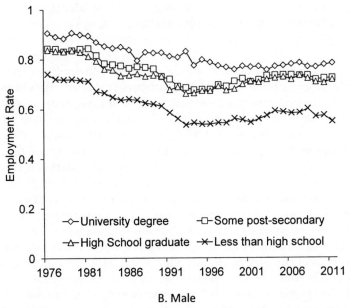

B. Male

Fig. 3.3 Employment rates of men and women age fifty to sixty-four, by education (1976–2011)

Source: Labour Force Survey public use microdata files.

would affect those in lower-education groups more so than individuals with university degrees.

To summarize, the Canadian experience with disability insurance was one of increasing growth until 1995, and retrenchment since then. For females, across-cohort differences in lifetime labor market participation tend to dominate movements in DI use. Overall, DI use in Canada is lower than that of other countries in the International Social Security (ISS) project.

3.3 Empirical Approach

Our goal is to describe the extent to which the provisions of the Canada and Quebec Pension Plan's disability benefit program affect individuals' retirement decisions. To do this, we need to consider various routes to retirement that individuals will consider and the other forms of income they may receive. We account for two paths here: (a) a disability path whereby a person works, enters retirement, and immediately initiates disability and other public pension benefits as soon as they are eligible; and (b) a regular retirement path whereby a person works until entering retirement and then initiates C/QPP retirement benefits as soon as they are eligible. We then consider the retirement incentives that individuals will account for, derived from each program's provisions, by calculating the option value (OV) associated with delayed retirement on each path to retirement.

3.3.1 Data

Unfortunately, Canada lacks the data necessary to accurately calculate individuals' incentives to retire and/or participate in the disability insurance program. The best data source we have available for this study is the Survey of Labour and Income Dynamics (SLID), which is a panel data set conducted as an annual survey. The SLID panel surveys started in 1993. Individuals belonging to the households sampled in the first year of the panel are interviewed each year for six years. A new panel is started every three years, so that two panels are underway each year after 1995. Approximately 50,000 individuals are interviewed each year, covering the entire population. Around one-third of this sample is in the fifty to sixty-nine age range. The SLID survey provides us with fairly deep information on the labor market activities and earnings of an individual, as well as a few health questions.

The focus of our analysis is the period 1996–2009. Separate samples of males and females age fifty to sixty-nine are drawn from each year. The sample is selected conditional on positive employment earnings, so that incentives for retirement conditional on being employed are examined. Work is defined as having positive earnings in two consecutive years. If an individual has positive earnings in one year and zero earnings in the next, the year of positive earnings is defined as the retirement year. Given this structure, we are only able to use retirements that take place in the first five years of each panel and the last year a retirement observation is formed is 2008.

3.3.2   Pathways to Retirement

In Canada, there are only two pathways to retirement to consider. First, we consider individuals who work, retire, and begin collecting CPP/QPP retirement benefits at their first age of eligibility after retirement. We refer to this as the retirement path. Second, we consider individuals who work, are disabled and collect CPP/QPP disability benefits, and then begin collecting CPP/QPP retirement benefits at age sixty-five. We refer to this as the disability path. In both cases, an individual who was eligible for an employer-provided pension will begin collecting that pension as soon as they retire.

Other pathways are feasible for Canadians, but would not likely be taken. For example, individuals could work, use employment insurance (EI) benefits, and then retire, collecting CPP/QPP retirement benefits at their first opportunity. The EI system, however, has fairly strict job search requirements for those not temporarily laid off and will not pay benefits to those who quit their jobs or were justifiably fired. Those fired are paid benefits only in special cases (including those for whom short-term disability was the reason for quitting). It must be the case, however, that individuals intend to return to work and benefits are paid for a limited time. Sickness benefits are only available for fifteen weeks. Regular EI benefits are available for fourteen to forty-five weeks, depending on the individual's work history and local unemployment rates.

Also, individuals may access provincial social assistance programs if they do not meet the age/marital status requirements of GIS and Allowance programs. Most provinces, however, require social assistance recipients without young children to engage in a job search. Moreover, the programs do not provide generous benefits.

3.3.3   Weighting the Pathways

The pathway probabilities applied in option value calculation (described in more detail below) are based on the Canada Pension Plan Statistical Bulletin and census population counts. We have information to calculate the number of individuals receiving disability benefits per population by five-year age group and sex. This age- and sex-specific disability rate in each year is used in weighting the two pathways. The resulting weights for the disability path are presented in figure 3.4. Note that take-up of C/QPP disability benefits is not an option after age sixty-five, so that the weight placed on the disability path for the sixty-five to sixty-nine age group is set to zero. The weight placed on the retirement path is then (1 − disability rate).

3.3.4   Health Quintiles

The information in SLID is not detailed enough for the creation of a meaningful health index. Instead, we rely on individuals' reported self-assessed health. For all years 1996 and later, individuals are asked to describe their current state of health as excellent, very good, good, fair, or poor. Note

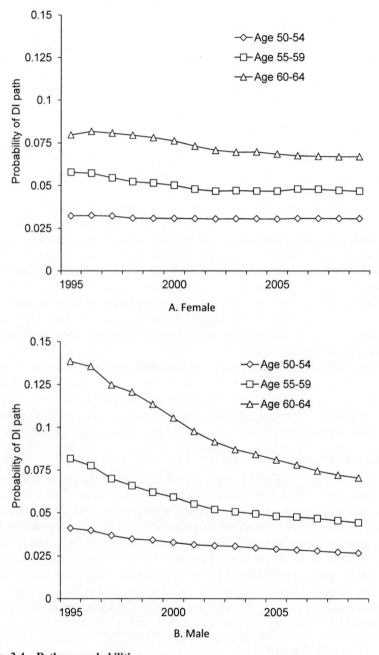

Fig. 3.4   Pathway probabilities
Source: CPP Statistical Bulletin for DI counts; CANSIM database population counts.

that individuals are asked to report on their health in the month of January following the income year.

There are a few questions in SLID that capture an individual's self-reported disability status, however, the nature of the question varies over time. Prior to 1999, the questions were designed to capture whether a person was permanently unable to work. Starting in 1999, questions were designed to more generally reflect activity limitations. As such, we do not attempt to make use of this health information here.

Figure 3.5 graphs the labor market exit rate by self-assessed health category, separately for females and for males. This variable is of particular importance since it will define our dependent variable for the regression analysis, which comes later. While there are five categories available in the SLID (poor, fair, good, very good, excellent), we combined poor and fair for the purposes of this graph because of low sample sizes in some age cells. The result is four lines, representing poor-fair, good, very good, and excellent self-assessed health. For both females and males, the poor-fair category stands noticeably apart from the other three lines. Exit rates are higher for those with weaker health. In contrast, those with good, very good, or excellent health are clustered quite close together.

3.3.5   Option Value Calculations

For each pathway (P = retirement or disability) and each potential retirement age (R), we calculate the present discounted value at age t of the flow of indirect utility derived from all income sources as

$$(1) \quad PDV_t(R,P) = \sum_{s=t}^{R-1} \frac{1}{(1+\delta)^{s-t}} \pi_{s|t}(Y_s)^\gamma + \sum_{s=R}^{T} \frac{1}{(1+\delta)^{s-t}} \pi_{s|t}(kB_s(R))^\gamma ,$$

where p is the probability of surviving to age s, Y_s represents labor income, B_s represents nonlabor income, and all income sources are in real terms. The discount rate (d) is set at 0.03, the risk aversion parameter (g) is 0.75, and the parameter $k = 1.5$ accounts for the disutility of labor. We assume the last age a person is alive is 102. The earliest retirement age considered is age fifty and the last retirement age is sixty-nine. Note that for married couples, the probability of joint survival is used and the income received by surviving spouses (e.g., survivor benefits) is accounted for.[5]

The value of delaying retirement until age $R > t$ rather than retiring immediately at age t is

$$(2) \quad \begin{aligned} OV_t(R,P) = &\sum_{s=t}^{R-1} \frac{1}{(1+\delta)^{s-t}} \pi_{s|t}(Y_s)^\gamma + \sum_{s=R}^{T} \frac{1}{(1+\delta)^{s-t}} \pi_{s|t}(kB_s(R))^\gamma \\ &- \sum_{s=t}^{T} \frac{1}{(1+\delta)^{s-t}} \pi_{s|t}(kB_s(t))^\gamma. \end{aligned}$$

5. Survival probabilities are based on the 2000–2002 life tables from Statistics Canada.

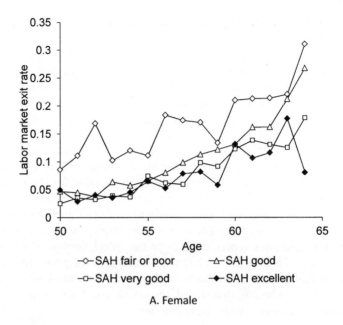

A. Female

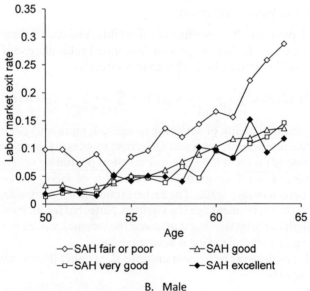

B. Male

Fig. 3.5 Exit rates by self-assessed health status
Source: Authors' calculations using the SLID.

The option value of each pathway then represents the utility that can be gained by delaying retirement. Let $R^* > t$ represent the retirement age that would maximize the utility that can be gained by delaying retirement. Then the maximum option value for a given pathway P is simply

(3) $$OV_t(P) = OV_t(R^*, P) - OV_t(t, P).$$

An *inclusive* option value is then derived as a weighted average of the pathways' maximum option values, using the weights described in the previous section. That is,

(4) $\quad OV_t(\text{inclusive}) = \omega_d OV_t(\text{Disability}) - (1 - \omega_d)OV_t(\text{Retirement}).$

We estimate the option value for all individuals in our SLID sample (ages fifty to sixty-nine, 1996–2009) separately for women and men. We have 78,350 person-year observations.

Although SLID provides us with fairly deep information on the labor market activities and earnings of an individual, it does not provide the information required to accurately calculate the indirect utility flows (equation [1]) for each individual. Annual income is reported, and is often drawn directly from individuals' tax records (though individuals have the option of self-reporting income).[6] We do not have access to individuals' full earnings histories. The SLID income data also lacks detail. For instance, SLID does not differentiate between CPP/QPP retirement, disability, or survivor benefits. There is also no distinction between (employer-provided) registered pension plan (RPP) benefits and registered retirement income fund (RRIF) payments. The RRIF payments could reflect payments from a defined contribution RPP or withdrawals from individual Registered Retirement Savings Plans (RRSPs) that must eventually be converted to RRIFs.

Given our data limitations, we impute income derived from many sources—including past earnings, investment income, and employer-sponsored pension income—based on the information we have available and calculate the benefits that individuals may receive based on policy rules existing at the time that expectations are formed. Details of these calculations are as follows.

Earnings—Histories and Forecasts

Earnings forecasts are required for the option value calculation, as individuals delaying retirement will receive earnings and those earnings will in part determine later retirement benefit entitlements. To forecast earnings, we assume the observed wages (at time t) will increase with inflation. That

---

6. The distribution of income among those opting to share income tax information is clearly different from those who self-report, but the implications of this for research are not entirely clear. See Brochu, Morin, and Billette (2014).

is, we assume zero real wage growth. Inflation projections are taken from the Canadian Pension Plan (CPP) Actuarial Reports.

Earnings histories are required for the calculation of C/QPP benefit entitlements. To construct the earnings history, we take the observed earnings from SLID and backcast earnings based on age and sex specific median-earnings growth rates. Our growth estimates are based on the age- and sex-specific median earnings observed from the Survey of Consumer Finances ([SCF]; 1973–1997) and SLID (1998–2009). The SCF was only conducted every second year until 1981, so we interpolate the missing year values by taking an average of previous and subsequent year's median earnings. For years prior to 1973, we backcast median earnings based on the growth in the industrial composite of average weekly wages.[7]

Benefit Entitlement and Tax Payable

We estimate the after-tax expected value of C/QPP retirement, disability, and survivor benefits, OAS pensions, and GIS/Allowance entitlement for each individual and their spouse based on the policy rules in place in the year considered (t).

The C/QPP benefit entitlements are based on the earnings histories described above. While we account for C/QPP provisions that allow low-earnings years to be dropped from the earnings history when determining average earnings, we have not accounted for time spent caring for young children since we have little information on this in SLID. After initiating benefits, C/QPP benefits rise with inflation and are held constant in real terms. Interactions between the three C/QPP programs are accounted for. For the disability path calculations, we require C/QPP disability benefit recipients to convert their disability benefit to the C/QPP retirement benefit at age sixty-five, accounting for years of disability in the earnings history. For survivor benefits, the cap on total C/QPP benefits is applied.

For the calculation of C/QPP survivor benefits that an individual would receive upon the death of their spouse, simplifying assumptions were required to make the calculations tractable. The difficulty lies in the fact that for each year into the future the spouse survives, another year is added to their earnings history for the survivor benefit calculation. To keep this simple, we assume an individual forms the expectation for potential survivor benefits in the future based on the survivor benefits they would receive if their spouse died the next year.

In the calculation of C/QPP disability benefits, we do not account for benefits available to dependent children under age eighteen and children that are students age eighteen to twenty-four.

---

7. Based on 11-516-XIE Series E49-59 ("Average Weekly Wages and Salaries, Industrial Composite, by Province, 1939 to 1975"), accessed at http://www.statcan.gc.ca/pub/11-516-x /sectione/E49_59-eng.csv, May 3, 2012.

Individuals are assumed to meet OAS and GIS residency requirements. To be entitled to full OAS benefits, a person must have resided in Canada for forty years, otherwise the OAS benefit is prorated and special provisions apply (offering additional benefits) in the calculation of GIS. The OAS clawbacks on individual income (at a rate of 15 percent for income over CAD $70,954 in 2013) and GIS/Allowance clawbacks on a couple's income (50 percent for GIS benefits and 75 percent for Allowance benefits) accounts for all forecasts of income discussed in this section, including spouse's income. We have not assigned Allowance benefits to widows and widowers ages sixty to sixty-four; rather, they are treated the same as other single individuals. We account for GIS and Allowance earnings exemptions.

To obtain an after-tax income, we calculate the amount a person can expect to pay in federal and provincial income taxes each year, using the Canadian Tax and Credit Simulator (CTaCS) calculator (Milligan 2012) and the policy rules in place in the year considered (t). To make the calculations more tractable we have calculated the tax payable on individual income until at least age seventy.[8] When calculating future taxes, we assume federal and Quebec income tax brackets, and amounts for major tax credits, increase with inflation. We then set further projections of tax payable to increase with inflation. This aligns with the assumption that individuals are retired by age seventy and all income sources are increasing only with inflation thereafter. This imposes the assumption that all tax parameters set in dollar amounts will also increase with inflation.

Spouses

We also create a full earnings history and projections for a spouse, which is used to determine their C/QPP and other benefit entitlements. As we are not modeling a joint retirement decision, we impose the behavioral assumption that a spouse will retire at age sixty, or immediately if the spouse is already over age sixty. This assumption is made to keep the benefit calculations tractable. We also assume the spouse cannot take the disability path and only takes the retirement path. Otherwise, forecasted spousal income is calculated using almost the same methods as for the individual.

Other Income Sources

We also require projections of individual (and their spouse's) future nonlabor income. We project future nonlabor income based on conditional means estimated from the 2001 census. First, we impute other income (representing investment and other money income) based on 2001 mean other income conditional on sex (male/female) and age (fifty to fifty-four, fifty-five

8. More precisely, we have calculated taxes up to year 2019, at which point all individuals in our sample have reached at least age seventy. When calculating spouse's tax payable, we will have some error for younger spouses in the most recent years of our data.

to fifty-nine, sixty to sixty-four, sixty-five to sixty-nine, and seventy and older). We assigned the same amount whether in or out of the labor force in order to focus attention on the public pension benefits. Without this assumption, the imputed income would be pivotal to the determination of option value since the other income would "turn on" only once someone retires. Once a spouse has died, we assume the surviving spouse will begin receiving 75 percent of the deceased spouse's other income.

We also impute an employer-provided pension to those in SLID who appear to contribute to an employer-provided plan, based on the 2001 census mean retirement pension income conditional on age and sex. Note the census pension income variable does not differentiate between RPP, RRSP, and RRIF income. The age- and sex-specific means are then applied to all individuals who indicated in SLID that they either contribute to an RPP or they had a pension plan with their job once they turn age sixty. Once a spouse has died, we assume the surviving spouse will begin receiving 75 percent of the deceased spouse's pension.

The resulting mean option value, by age, for Canadian women and men is presented in figure 3.6. Note the mean is based on a cross section of people in our SLID sample at each age. While there is clearly a substantial gap in option values at each age between the retirement and disability paths, the low probability of entering the disability path implies a negligible gap between the retirement path option values and the inclusive option value (which averages across the paths using the probabilities as weights). For women, we see that the utility to be gained from working until an optimal retirement age tends to decline with age. For men, the option value increases slightly from ages fifty to fifty-five and declines thereafter.

To get a more complete picture of the shape of the incentives, we present in figure 3.6 the total discounted present value of lifetime benefits by age of retirement. This is different from option value because it does not account for future earnings at all, and it is measured in dollars rather than in utility terms. Also, we are showing here the lifetime total value of benefits rather than the difference between current and future benefits, as is done for option value. The results here indicate that the present value of benefits for both women and men peak at around age fifty-seven, and that the benefits from retiring through DI are on an average lifetime basis much higher at most ages than through the standard retirement path. The DI and non-DI paths converge at age sixty-five because DI benefits are transformed to regular CPP/QPP benefits at that age, so there is no longer any difference.

A contrast between figure 3.6 and figure 3.7 is that for option value in figure 3.6 very few reach the point of optimal retirement (when option value is at zero) until late in their sixties, while in figure 3.7 many see declines in their discounted present value of pension wealth decline from their late fifties. The difference comes from the utility basis of option value. Even though the discounted pension wealth may be falling, the value of future earnings

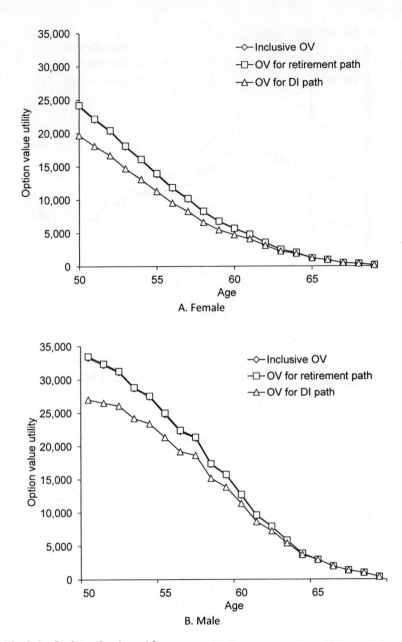

Fig. 3.6 Option value (mean) by age
Source: Authors' calculations using the SLID.

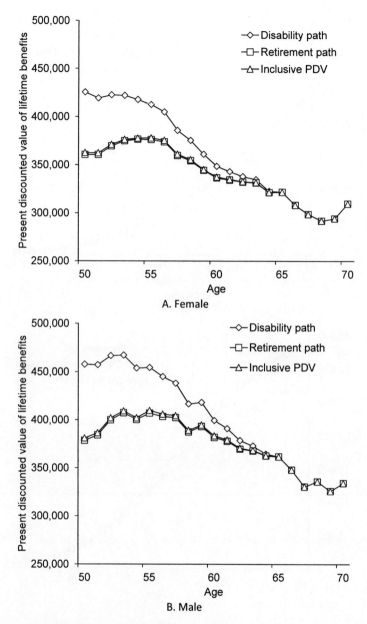

Fig. 3.7   Present discounted value by age
Source: Authors' calculations using the SLID.

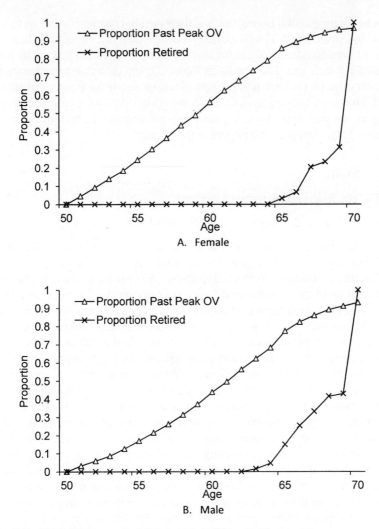

Fig. 3.8   Share having reached the maximum OV and retirement, by age
Source: Authors' calculations using the SLID.

(which is taken into account through the utility calculations of option value) makes it optimal to continue work. How these different factors are weighed depends on the preference parameters (discount rate, preference for leisure, risk aversion) that are chosen for the optional value calculations. We use the parameters that are common to all countries in the project in order to have our calculations on the same basis. We experimented with alternative sets of parameters, finding our regression coefficients were not particularly sensitive to other reasonably similar sets of parameters.

Figure 3.8 shows the proportion having retired at each age and compares that to the proportion having reached their optimal retirement date as calculated by option value. The proportion retired comes from applying observed hazard rates to a fictional cohort starting at age fifty to see how many have retired by each age. The results in figure 3.8 indicate that retirements by option value do not match the observed retirement distribution particularly well. However, in order to maintain comparability to other countries in the project, we maintain this calculation of option value based on the set of parameters common to all papers in the project.

3.4   Results

The equations estimated take the form

$$(5) \qquad R_{it} = \beta_0 + \beta_1 OV_{it} + \beta_2 AGE_{it} + \beta_3 RPP_{it} + \beta_4 X_{it} + \upsilon_{it},$$

where entry to retirement (R_{it}) is set equal to 1 if we see the individual retire (a year of no earnings following a year of positive earnings); OV_{it} is the inclusive option value described above. We also use a "percent change" formulation of this variable by dividing the option value by the present level of utility. Here AGE represents either a set of age dummies or a linear variable for the individual's age, and also includes the age difference between spouses; RPP represents variables that indicate whether the person and their spouse appear eligible for employer-sponsored pension benefits. Finally, we include as a set of controls (X_{it}) the individual's marital status, immigrant status, education, occupation, industry, and the spouse's employment status.

The main results are presented in tables 3.1A and 3.1B for the female and male samples, respectively, using the inclusive option value incentive measure. The inclusive option value has a statistically significant, negative effect on the probability of entering retirement. An increase of 10,000 units in the option value decreases the probability of retirement by 2–3 percentage points for women and 1 to 1.5 percentage points for men. The results are fairly robust to the choice of specification. The effect of the option value does not depend on the specification of age. The effect of the option value falls by about one-third when the broader set of controls is included in the estimating equation in columns (3) and (4).

Other coefficients have the expected effects. Those with better health are substantially less likely to leave the labor force. For example, in column (1) of table 3.1A, the coefficient on having excellent self-assessed health is –0.071, which suggests a 7.1 percentage point decrease in the probability of exiting compared to those with poor health (the excluded category). The effect of better health is slightly larger for women than for men. The other notable significant results are for the presence of a firm pension plan for oneself and for the spouse. Those with their own pension are less likely to exit. This simple dummy variable combines any dynamic incentive with any wealth effect of a pension, so this negative coefficient likely reflects strong incentives

Table 3.1A   Effect of inclusive OV on retirement, female sample

	(1)	(2)	(3)	(4)
Number of obs.	35,409	35,409	35,409	35,409
Retirement rate	0.094	0.094	0.094	0.094
Mean of OV	13,303	13,303	13,303	13,303
Inclusive OV	−0.0316***	−0.0321***	−0.0245***	−0.0250***
	[0.0027]	[0.0027]	[0.0028]	[0.0028]
Impact of one SD change	−0.0568	−0.0574	−0.046	−0.0469
Health fair	−0.0391***	−0.0386***	−0.0306***	−0.0300***
	[0.0063]	[0.0063]	[0.0051]	[0.0051]
Health good	−0.0661***	−0.0656***	−0.0489***	−0.0484***
	[0.0069]	[0.0069]	[0.0064]	[0.0063]
Health very good	−0.0849***	−0.0843***	−0.0627***	−0.0619***
	[0.0078]	[0.0077]	[0.0077]	[0.0075]
Health excellent	−0.0710***	−0.0709***	−0.0511***	−0.0506***
	[0.0058]	[0.0058]	[0.0054]	[0.0053]
Age	0.0059***		0.0031***	
	[0.0005]		[0.0005]	
Age dummies		Included		Included
Married/common law			0.0167***	0.0169***
			[0.0046]	[0.0046]
Immigrant			0.0041	0.0041
			[0.0048]	[0.0047]
Spouse age difference			0.0025***	0.0025***
			[0.0005]	[0.0006]
Finished high school			0.0111*	0.0100*
			[0.0058]	[0.0057]
Some postsecondary			0.0045	0.0041
			[0.0046]	[0.0046]
University degree			0.0147*	0.0146*
			[0.0077]	[0.0076]
Has firm pension plan			−0.0167***	−0.0160***
			[0.0038]	[0.0038]
Spouse has firm pension			0.0175***	0.0171***
			[0.0057]	[0.0057]
Spouse employed			−0.0054	−0.005
			[0.0046]	[0.0046]
Occupation dummies			Included	Included
Industry dummies			Included	Included

Notes: Coefficients are the marginal effects of a 10,000-unit change in OV from probit models. Standard errors clustered on individuals are in brackets. For inclusive OV, beneath the standard errors we report the impact of a one standard deviation change in inclusive OV in retirement, calculated by the difference in predicted probability perturbing inclusive OV by plus and minus one-half of a standard deviation.

***Significant at the 1 percent level.
**Significant at the 5 percent level.
*Significant at the 10 percent level.

Table 3.1B   **Effect of inclusive OV on retirement, male sample**

	(1)	(2)	(3)	(4)
Number of obs.	42,941	42,941	42,941	42,941
Retirement rate	0.077	0.077	0.077	0.077
Mean of OV	16,469	16,469	16,469	16,469
Inclusive OV	−0.0166***	−0.0163***	−0.0129***	−0.0128***
	[0.0022]	[0.0022]	[0.0024]	[0.0024]
Impact of one SD change	−0.0465	−0.0454	−0.0376	−0.0374
Health fair	−0.0305***	−0.0313***	−0.0247***	−0.0253***
	[0.0049]	[0.0048]	[0.0041]	[0.0040]
Health good	−0.0495***	−0.0503***	−0.0398***	−0.0406***
	[0.0054]	[0.0055]	[0.0050]	[0.0049]
Health very good	−0.0631***	−0.0641***	−0.0500***	−0.0510***
	[0.0063]	[0.0063]	[0.0062]	[0.0062]
Health excellent	−0.0527***	−0.0533***	−0.0411***	−0.0417***
	[0.0050]	[0.0050]	[0.0045]	[0.0044]
Age	0.0053***		0.0028***	
	[0.0005]		[0.0006]	
Age dummies		Included		Included
Married/common law			0.0028	0.0024
			[0.0039]	[0.0039]
Immigrant			−0.0004	−0.0002
			[0.0036]	[0.0036]
Spouse age difference			0.0013***	0.0013***
			[0.0004]	[0.0004]
Finished high school			−0.0043	−0.0042
			[0.0041]	[0.0041]
Some postsecondary			0.0039	0.0042
			[0.0034]	[0.0034]
University degree			0.0069	0.0073
			[0.0055]	[0.0055]
Has firm pension plan			−0.0163***	−0.0162***
			[0.0034]	[0.0034]
Spouse has firm pension			0.0153***	0.0155***
			[0.0047]	[0.0047]
Spouse employed			−0.004	−0.0031
			[0.0037]	[0.0036]
Occupation dummies			Included	Included
Industry dummies			Included	Included

Note: Coefficients are the marginal effects of a 10,000-unit change in OV from probit models. Standard errors clustered on individuals are in brackets. For inclusive OV, beneath the standard errors we report the impact of a one standard deviation change in inclusive OV in retirement, calculated by the difference in predicted probability perturbing inclusive OV by plus and minus one-half of a standard deviation.

***Significant at the 1 percent level.

**Significant at the 5 percent level.

*Significant at the 10 percent level.

Table 3.1C   **Effect of percent change in OV on retirement, female sample**

	(1)	(2)	(3)	(4)
Number of obs.	34,674	34,674	34,674	34,674
Mean retirement rate	0.094	0.094	0.094	0.094
Mean % gain in OV	0.328	0.328	0.328	0.328
Percent gain in OV	–0.1229***	–0.1255***	–0.0887***	–0.0906***
	[0.0121]	[0.0122]	[0.0115]	[0.0116]
Linear age	X		X	
Age dummies		X		X
SAH controls	X	X	X	X
Other Xs			X	X

Note: Coefficients are the marginal effects of a 100 percent change in the ratio of OV to peak value. Standard errors clustered on individuals are in brackets. The four models presented are the same as in table 3.1A.
***Significant at the 1 percent level.
**Significant at the 5 percent level.
*Significant at the 10 percent level.

Table 3.1D   **Effect of percent change in OV on retirement, male sample**

	(1)	(2)	(3)	(4)
Number of obs.	42,127	42,127	42,127	42,127
Mean retirement	0.077	0.077	0.077	0.077
Mean % gain in OV	0.514	0.514	0.514	0.514
Percent gain in OV	–0.0398***	–0.0387***	–0.0299***	–0.0298***
	[0.0095]	[0.0093]	[0.0095]	[0.0094]
Linear age	X		X	
Age dummies		X		X
SAH controls	X	X	X	X
Other Xs			X	X

Note: Coefficients are the marginal effects of a 100 percent change in the ratio of OV to peak value. Standard errors clustered on individuals are in brackets. The four models presented are the same as in table 3.1B.
***Significant at the 1 percent level.
**Significant at the 5 percent level.
*Significant at the 10 percent level.

to stay in the labor force to continue accruing future firm pension income. For the spouse's pension, there is only a wealth effect as one's own continued work would not increase the future pension income from the spouse's pension. So, the positive coefficient here suggests that the wealth effect goes in the expected direction—higher wealth through the presence of a spousal pension means earlier retirement, all else equal.

Tables 3.1C and 3.1D present the results for the percent-change version of option value. The specifications here are the same as in tables 3.1A and 3.1B. To be concise, we present only the coefficient on the percent gain in OV. Because these percent change measures are scale independent, they should be more comparable to the other countries in the project. The reported coefficients for males and females are of the expected negative sign. The first column in table 3.1C reports a coefficient of −0.12, which suggests that an increase in the percent option value of 10 percent would lead to a 1.2 percentage point drop in the likelihood of retirement. The relative magnitudes of the estimates across tables 3.1C and 3.1D are similar to the relative magnitudes seen in tables 3.1A and 3.1B.

The next set of tables breaks down the sample into subsamples defined by self-assessed health status. Tables 3.2A, 3.2B, 3.2C, and 3.2D look at females and males using the option value and percent gain in option value formulations. One way to think about the impact of health on the response to incentives is to consider that poor health may make the decisions of individuals less elastic with respect to economic incentives, as health imperatives become more important than economic calculations. On the other hand, the incentives may be much more salient for individuals in poorer health because they are actively confronting a choice of when to retire, while those in good health just continue to work. The results presented in tables 3.2A through table 3.2D support the second of these hypotheses, as the responsiveness to the incentives is much higher for those in poor health than those in strong health. For example, in table 3.2B, specification (1), the impact of a 10,000-unit increase in the option value would be to lower retirement probability by 6.38 percentage points for those in poor health, but only 1.28 percentage points for those in excellent health. This pattern of results holds across specifications, sexes, and for both the option value and percentage gain in option value formulations.

To look further into this phenomenon, we pool the sample together again across all health categories and try interacting the option value incentive measure with the level of self-assessed health. These results are presented in tables 3.3A, 3.3B, 3.3C, and 3.3D using the same progression of specifications, sexes, and option value versus percent gain in option value results. Here, the results show little difference across health groups. For example, in table 3.3A, the coefficient on the interaction of OV and "Health Fair" has a coefficient of −0.0174, which is not statistically significant. This means that those with fair health do not have a statistically significantly larger response to a unit change in OV than do those in the excluded health category (poor health). The base effects of OV at −0.0252 and of health (−0.0320 for fair health) are still strongly statistically significant and not much changed from the corresponding estimates in the first column of table 3.1A.

At first glance, the results from tables 3.2A–D do not appear to be in accord with tables 3.3A–D. Tables 3.2A–D show evidence that samples selected on being in low health have much stronger responses to OV than

Table 3.2A   Effect of inclusive OV on retirement by health status, female sample

	Observations	Mean retirement rate	Mean of OV	Std. dev. OV	Specification			
					(1)	(2)	(3)	(4)
Health poor	828	0.244	8,955	14,527	-0.0726***	-0.0715***	-0.0553***	-0.0530***
					[0.0237]	[0.0230]	[0.0221]	[0.0189]
Health fair	2,985	0.152	9,952	13,314	-0.0689***	-0.0724***	-0.0602***	-0.0581***
					[0.0139]	[0.0136]	[0.0110]	[0.0103]
Health good	10,287	0.101	12,245	14,482	-0.0503***	-0.0503***	-0.0334***	-0.0335***
					[0.0047]	[0.0046]	[0.0046]	[0.0046]
Health very good	13,665	0.077	13,951	15,879	-0.0185***	-0.0185***	-0.0157***	-0.0159***
					[0.0038]	[0.0039]	[0.0038]	[0.0039]
Health excellent	7,644	0.074	15,429	17,066	-0.0215***	-0.0222***	-0.0208***	-0.0211***
					[0.0036]	[0.0035]	[0.0035]	[0.0034]
Age control					Linear	Dummies	Linear	Dummies
Extended controls							Yes	Yes

Note: Coefficients are the marginal effects of a 10,000-unit change in OV from probit models. Standard errors clustered on individuals are in brackets. Extended controls are those included in columns (3) and (4) of table 3.1A.

***Significant at the 1 percent level.

**Significant at the 5 percent level.

*Significant at the 10 percent level.

Table 3.2B Effect of inclusive OV on retirement by health status, male sample

	Observations	Mean retirement rate	Mean of OV	Std. dev. OV	Specification			
					(1)	(2)	(3)	(4)
Health poor	11,31	0.203	13,470	17,063	−0.0638***	−0.0598***	−0.0449**	−0.0431**
					[0.0179]	[0.0172]	[0.0204]	[0.0194]
Health fair	4,046	0.126	14,686	17,078	−0.0426***	−0.0396***	−0.0288***	−0.0252***
					[0.0082]	[0.0079]	[0.0068]	[0.0061]
Health good	12,596	0.080	19,071	22,666	−0.0163***	−0.0161***	−0.0093***	−0.0098***
					[0.0032]	[0.0031]	[0.0029]	[0.0029]
Health very good	16,068	0.063	21,831	23,098	−0.0119***	−0.0115***	−0.0131***	−0.0127***
					[0.0032]	[0.0032]	[0.0020]	[0.0019]
Health excellent	9,100	0.061	24,649	27,054	−0.0128***	−0.0123***	−0.0084**	−0.0081**
					[0.0039]	[0.0037]	[0.0039]	[0.0037]
Age control					Linear	Dummies	Linear	Dummies
Extended controls							Yes	Yes

Note: Coefficients are the marginal effects of a 10,000-unit change in OV from probit models. Standard errors clustered on individuals are in brackets. Extended controls are those included in columns (3) and (4) of table 3.1B.

***Significant at the 1 percent level.
**Significant at the 5 percent level.
*Significant at the 10 percent level.

Table 3.2C   Effect of inclusive OV on retirement by health status, female sample

					Specification			
	Observations	Mean retirement rate	Mean of % OV	Std. dev. % OV	(1)	(2)	(3)	(4)
Health poor	805	0.256	0.256	0.502	-0.1779** [0.0901]	-0.1785** [0.0898]	-0.1814** [0.0762]	-0.1466** [0.0661]
Health fair	2,914	0.153	0.260	0.380	-0.2636*** [0.0524]	-0.2820*** [0.0520]	-0.2267*** [0.0408]	-0.2194*** [0.0387]
Health good	10,052	0.101	0.309	0.399	-0.2103*** [0.0203]	-0.2105*** [0.0201]	-0.1284*** [0.0184]	-0.1287*** [0.0183]
Health very good	13,391	0.078	0.335	0.398	-0.2103*** [0.0203]	-0.2105*** [0.0201]	-0.1284*** [0.0184]	-0.1287*** [0.0183]
Health excellent	7,512	0.074	0.375	0.440	-0.0786*** [0.0157]	-0.0824*** [0.0155]	-0.0753*** [0.0149]	-0.0760*** [0.0144]
Age control					Linear	Dummies	Linear	Dummies
Extended controls							Yes	Yes

Note: Coefficients are the marginal effects of a 10,000-unit change in OV from probit models. Standard errors clustered on individuals are in brackets. Extended controls are those included in columns (3) and (4) of table 3.1A.

***Significant at the 1 percent level.
**Significant at the 5 percent level.
*Significant at the 10 percent level.

Table 3.2D Effect of inclusive OV on retirement by health status, male sample

	Observations	Mean retirement rate	Mean of % OV	Std. dev. % OV	Specification			
					(1)	(2)	(3)	(4)
Health poor	1,116	0.204	0.382	0.502	-0.1853***	-0.1724***	-0.1426**	-0.1395**
					[0.0564]	[0.0536]	[0.0718]	[0.0682]
Health fair	3,949	0.127	0.388	0.488	-0.1082***	-0.1013***	-0.0592**	-0.0518**
					[0.0332]	[0.0305]	[0.0213]	[0.0213]
Health good	12,317	0.081	0.470	0.582	-0.0375***	-0.0376***	-0.0199**	-0.0214**
					[0.0130]	[0.0126]	[0.0093]	[0.0092]
Health very good	15,790	0.062	0.527	0.603	-0.0266***	-0.0252***	-0.0328***	-0.0311***
					[0.0097]	[0.0097]	[0.0074]	[0.0071]
Health excellent	8,955	0.061	0.611	0.778	-0.0290*	-0.0272*	-0.0175	-0.0167
					[0.0159]	[0.0151]	[0.0120]	[0.0115]
Age control					Linear	Dummies	Linear	Dummies
Extended controls					Yes	Yes	Yes	Yes

Note: Coefficients are the marginal effects of a 10,000-unit change in OV from probit models. Standard errors clustered on individuals are in brackets. Extended controls are those included in columns (3) and (4) of table 3.1B.

***Significant at the 1 percent level.
**Significant at the 5 percent level.
*Significant at the 10 percent level.

Table 3.3A   **Effect of inclusive option value on retirement with health interactions, female sample**

	Specification			
	(1)	(2)	(3)	(4)
OV	−0.0252***	−0.0264***	−0.0217**	−0.0224***
	[0.0093]	[0.0091]	[0.0087]	[0.0084]
OV*health fair	−0.0174	−0.0166	−0.0150	−0.0148
	[0.0129]	[0.0127]	[0.0119]	[0.0117]
OV*health good	−0.0234**	−0.0226**	−0.0155	−0.0154*
	[0.0105]	[0.0103]	[0.0095]	[0.0092]
OV*health very good	0.0004	0.001	0.0014	0.0016
	[0.0101]	[0.0100]	[0.0092]	[0.0089]
OV*health excellent	0.0015	0.0020	0.0037	0.0037
	[0.0103]	[0.0102]	[0.0092]	[0.0089]
Health fair	−0.0320***	−0.0318***	−0.0239***	−0.0233***
	[0.0090]	[0.0091]	[0.0081]	[0.0079]
Health good	−0.0548***	−0.0546***	−0.0398***	−0.0393***
	[0.0092]	[0.0091]	[0.0088]	[0.0085]
Health very good	−0.0851***	−0.0850***	−0.0634***	−0.0629***
	[0.0101]	[0.0101]	[0.0102]	[0.0099]
Health excellent	−0.0720***	−0.0720***	−0.0529***	−0.0525***
	[0.0073]	[0.0073]	[0.0068]	[0.0066]
Age control	Linear	Dummies	Linear	Dummies
Extended controls			Yes	Yes
Number of observations	35,409	35,409	35,409	35,409
Mean retirement rate	0.094	0.094	0.094	0.094
Mean of OV	13,303	13,303	13,303	13,303
Std. deviation of OV	15,616	15,616	15,616	15,616

Note: Models are the same as those in table 3.1A, with the addition of interaction terms for the inclusive option value and health status. Coefficients are the marginal effects of a 10,000-unit change in OV from probit models. Standard errors clustered on individuals are in brackets.
***Significant at the 1 percent level.
**Significant at the 5 percent level.
*Significant at the 10 percent level.

do individuals in better health. Tables 3.3A–D, on the other hand, show little difference in responsiveness across health groups. To reconcile these results, it must be understood that the samples in tables 3.2A–D are selected on health, but the other characteristics of the individuals in the different health categories are not random. That is, people in low health typically have lower education and have lower lifetime earnings, among other factors. The results in tables 3.3A–D suggest that it is not health itself that was driving the differing responses to OV in tables 3.2A–D. Instead, it was some other difference that is correlated with health. In tables 3.3A–D, when these factors are controlled, we see only the extra responsiveness by health to OV. To

Table 3.3B   **Effect of inclusive option value on retirement with health interactions, male sample**

	Specification			
	(1)	(2)	(3)	(4)
OV	−0.0164***	−0.0164***	−0.0174**	−0.0176**
	[0.0057]	[0.0057]	[0.0071]	[0.0070]
OV*health fair	−0.0082	−0.0076	−0.0046	−0.0039
	[0.0075]	[0.0074]	[0.0085]	[0.0084]
OV*health good	0.0007	0.0011	0.0078	0.0080
	[0.0063]	[0.0062]	[0.0073]	[0.0072]
OV*health very good	0.0005	0.0008	0.0029	0.0031
	[0.0066]	[0.0065]	[0.0072]	[0.0071]
OV*health excellent	−0.0002	0.0000	0.0058	0.0059
	[0.0074]	[0.0073]	[0.0080]	[0.0079]
Health fair	−0.0258***	−0.0271***	−0.0221***	−0.0232***
	[0.0071]	[0.0070]	[0.0070]	[0.0067]
Health good	−0.0502***	−0.0513***	−0.0464***	−0.0474***
	[0.0072]	[0.0072]	[0.0075]	[0.0074]
Health very good	−0.0637***	−0.0649***	−0.0523***	−0.0536***
	[0.0089]	[0.0089]	[0.0096]	[0.0096]
Health excellent	−0.0527***	−0.0534***	−0.0451***	−0.0457***
	[0.0076]	[0.0075]	[0.0075]	[0.0074]
Age control	Linear	Dummies	Linear	Dummies
Extended controls			Yes	Yes
Number of observations	42,941	42,941	42,941	42,941
Mean retirement rate	0.077	0.077	0.077	0.077
Mean of OV	20,827	20,827	20,827	20,827
Std. deviation of OV	23,551	23,551	23,551	23,551

Note: Models are the same as those in table 3.1A, with the addition of interaction terms for the inclusive option value and health status. Coefficients are the marginal effects of a 10,000-unit change in OV from probit models. Standard errors clustered on individuals are in brackets.
***Significant at the 1 percent level.
**Significant at the 5 percent level.
*Significant at the 10 percent level.

investigate this further, we turn next to an assessment of the effects of OV across education groups.

The last set of tables compare the OV results across education groups. Those with lower education are more likely to self-assess their health as not so strong, and they also tend to have lower lifetime earnings. More physical labor might lead to an earlier need to contemplate retirement than those with office jobs typical among those with higher education. Lower lifetime earnings may make lower educated individuals more responsive to the financial incentives in public pensions, as public pensions will make up a larger share of their retirement incomes.

Table 3.3C   **Effect of percent change option value on retirement with health interactions, female sample**

	Specification			
	(1)	(2)	(3)	(4)
Percent change OV	−0.0146	−0.0179	−0.0169	−0.0178
	[0.0162]	[0.0168]	[0.0157]	[0.0156]
Percent OV*health fair	−0.0404***	−0.0398***	−0.0319***	−0.0320***
	[0.0101]	[0.0101]	[0.0094]	[0.0094]
Percent OV*health good	−0.0467***	−0.0464***	−0.0323***	−0.0326***
	[0.0064]	[0.0064]	[0.0057]	[0.0057]
Percent OV*health very good	−0.0225***	−0.0223***	−0.0157***	−0.0160***
	[0.0051]	[0.0052]	[0.0046]	[0.0045]
Percent OV*health excellent	−0.0209***	−0.0209***	−0.0134***	−0.0137***
	[0.0060]	[0.0060]	[0.0050]	[0.0049]
Health fair	−0.0195**	−0.0194**	−0.0132	−0.0121
	[0.0095]	[0.0094]	[0.0094]	[0.0094]
Health good	−0.0414***	−0.0411***	−0.0286***	−0.0276***
	[0.0085]	[0.0085]	[0.0084]	[0.0082]
Health very good	−0.0713***	−0.0711***	−0.0504***	−0.0494***
	[0.0089]	[0.0088]	[0.0089]	[0.0086]
Health excellent	−0.0626***	−0.0626***	−0.0443***	−0.0436***
	[0.0069]	[0.0068]	[0.0065]	[0.0064]
Age control	Linear	Dummies	Linear	Dummies
Extended controls			Yes	Yes
Number of observations	34,674	34,674	34,674	34,674
Mean retirement rate	0.094	0.094	0.094	0.094
Mean of OV	0.328	0.328	0.328	0.328
Std. deviation of OV	0.411	0.411	0.411	0.411

Note: Models are the same as those in table 3.1A, with the addition of interaction terms for the percent option value and health status. Coefficients are the marginal effects of a 100 percent change in percent OV from probit models. Standard errors clustered on individuals are in brackets.
***Significant at the 1 percent level.
**Significant at the 5 percent level.
*Significant at the 10 percent level.

Tables 3.4A, 3.4B, 3.4C, and 3.4D show these results for subsamples by education group. The first two tables show women and men using the option value, while the third and fourth tables show the results using the percent gain in option value. The four specifications shown across each table are the same four as shown in tables 3.1A–D. Each row of these tables shows results from separate regressions on subsamples defined by education groups.

The results across all specifications and samples show a decreasing responsiveness of individuals to the option value pension incentive when education increases. More highly educated individuals are less responsive

Table 3.3D   Effect of percent change option value on retirement with health interactions, male sample

	Specification			
	(1)	(2)	(3)	(4)
Percent change OV	0.0312***	0.0298***	0.0214**	0.0205**
	[0.0080]	[0.0079]	[0.0088]	[0.0088]
Percent OV*health fair	−0.0333***	−0.0323***	−0.0272***	−0.0265***
	[0.0054]	[0.0054]	[0.0055]	[0.0054]
Percent OV*health good	−0.0237***	−0.0230***	−0.0147***	−0.0144***
	[0.0033]	[0.0032]	[0.0031]	[0.0031]
Percent OV*health very good	−0.0235***	−0.0228***	−0.0196***	−0.0192***
	[0.0039]	[0.0039]	[0.0030]	[0.0029]
Percent OV*health excellent	−0.0247***	−0.0241***	−0.0167***	−0.0165***
	[0.0034]	[0.0034]	[0.0028]	[0.0028]
Health fair	−0.0015	−0.0037	0.002	0.0001
	[0.0092]	[0.0089]	[0.0105]	[0.0101]
Health good	−0.0273***	−0.0288***	−0.0245***	−0.0256***
	[0.0070]	[0.0069]	[0.0070]	[0.0069]
Health very good	−0.0395***	−0.0411***	−0.0259***	−0.0272***
	[0.0082]	[0.0081]	[0.0079]	[0.0079]
Health excellent	−0.0329***	−0.0340***	−0.0259***	−0.0267***
	[0.0069]	[0.0069]	[0.0066]	[0.0065]
Age control	Linear	Dummies	Linear	Dummies
Extended controls			Yes	Yes
Number of observations	42,127	42,127	42,127	42,127
	0.077	0.077	0.077	0.077
Mean retirement rate	0.514	0.514	0.514	0.514
	0.635	0.635	0.635	0.635
Mean of OV	42,127	42,127	42,127	42,127
	0.077	0.077	0.077	0.077
Std. deviation of OV	0.514	0.514	0.514	0.514

Note: Models are the same as those in table 3.1B, with the addition of interaction terms for the percent option value and health status. Coefficients are the marginal effects of a 100 percent change in percent OV from probit models. Standard errors clustered on individuals are in brackets.

***Significant at the 1 percent level.
**Significant at the 5 percent level.
*Significant at the 10 percent level.

than lower-educated individuals to the same incentive. The result is strongly robust across specifications.

Overall, our regression results have confirmed earlier findings showing that Canada's retirement system has an influence on retirement decisions. Additionally, we find that the impact of the retirement income system on retirement decisions is strongest for those in weakest health, and those with lower levels of education. In both cases, this may reflect a stronger salience

Table 3.4A   Effect of inclusive option value on retirement by education group, female sample

					Specification			
	Observations	Mean retirement rate	Mean of OV	Std. dev. OV	(1)	(2)	(3)	(4)
High school dropout	7,400	0.122	7,272	9,711	-0.0567***	-0.0577***	-0.0497***	-0.0496***
					[0.0103]	[0.0098]	[0.0098]	[0.0093]
Completed high school	6,296	0.100	12,001	14,310	-0.0359***	-0.0376***	-0.0288***	-0.0285***
					[0.0056]	[0.0053]	[0.0060]	[0.0056]
Some postsecondary	15,249	0.085	13,876	14,684	-0.0315***	-0.0315***	-0.0246***	-0.0246***
					[0.0034]	[0.0033]	[0.0032]	[0.0031]
University degree	5,185	0.077	21,203	21,253	-0.0178***	-0.0175***	-0.0118***	-0.0113***
					[0.0043]	[0.0041]	[0.0038]	[0.0035]
Age control					Linear	Dummies	Linear	Dummies
Extended controls							Yes	Yes

Note: Coefficients are the marginal effects of a 10,000-unit change in OV from probit models. Standard errors clustered on individuals are in brackets. Extended controls are those included in columns (3) and (4) of table 3.1A.

***Significant at the 1 percent level.

**Significant at the 5 percent level.

*Significant at the 10 percent level.

Table 3.4B   **Effect of inclusive option value on retirement by education group, male sample**

					Specification			
	Observations	Mean retirement rate	Mean of OV	Std. dev. OV	(1)	(2)	(3)	(4)
High school dropout	11,274	0.103	12,509	13,103	-0.0433***	-0.0421***	-0.0314***	-0.0312***
					[0.0046]	[0.0046]	[0.0043]	[0.0042]
Completed high school	6,067	0.068	19,733	21,236	-0.0192***	-0.0186***	-0.0100***	-0.0095***
					[0.0040]	[0.0038]	[0.0030]	[0.0026]
Some postsecondary	16,371	0.070	20,615	18,806	-0.0158***	-0.0154***	-0.0113***	-0.0111***
					[0.0039]	[0.0038]	[0.0042]	[0.0041]
University degree	7,384	0.065	32,132	35,709	-0.0103***	-0.0097***	-0.0094***	-0.0085***
					[0.0026]	[0.0023]	[0.0015]	[0.0013]
Age control					Linear	Dummies	Linear	Dummies
Extended controls							Yes	Yes

Note: Coefficients are the marginal effects of a 10,000-unit change in OV from probit models. Standard errors clustered on individuals are in brackets. Extended controls are those included in columns (3) and (4) of table 3.1B.

***Significant at the 1 percent level.

**Significant at the 5 percent level.

*Significant at the 10 percent level.

Table 3.4C   Effect of percent change in option value on retirement by education group, female sample

	Observations	Mean retirement rate	Mean of OV	Std. dev. OV	Specification			
					(1)	(2)	(3)	(4)
High school dropout	7,213	0.122	0.196	0.267	-0.1725***	-0.1806***	-0.1405***	-0.1403***
					[0.0405]	[0.0397]	[0.0368]	[0.0357]
Completed high school	6,163	0.099	0.296	0.410	-0.1403***	-0.1482***	-0.1061***	-0.1058***
					[0.0248]	[0.0239]	[0.0249]	[0.0230]
Some postsecondary	14,986	0.085	0.341	0.388	-0.1248***	-0.1242***	-0.0900***	-0.0897***
					[0.0152]	[0.0151]	[0.0127]	[0.0125]
University degree	5,099	0.078	0.498	0.545	-0.0723***	-0.0709***	-0.0445***	-0.0425***
					[0.0207]	[0.0200]	[0.0170]	[0.0159]
Age control					Linear	Dummies	Linear	Dummies
Extended controls							Yes	Yes

Note: Coefficients are the marginal effects of a 100 percent change in percent OV from probit models. Standard errors clustered on individuals are in brackets. Extended controls are those included in columns (3) and (4) of table 3.1A.

***Significant at the 1 percent level.

**Significant at the 5 percent level.

*Significant at the 10 percent level.

Table 3.4D   **Effect of percent change in option value on retirement by education group, male sample**

					Specification		
	Observations	Mean retirement rate	Mean of OV	Std. dev. OV	(1)	(2)	(3)	(4)
High school dropout	11,046	0.104	0.319	0.373	-0.1238*** [0.0202]	-0.1212*** [0.0197]	-0.0846*** [0.0167]	-0.0857*** [0.0160]
Completed high school	5,951	0.068	0.495	0.592	-0.0383** [0.0158]	-0.0359** [0.0151]	-0.0207** [0.0097]	-0.0192** [0.0089]
Some postsecondary	16,097	0.070	0.499	0.517	-0.0291** [0.0145]	-0.0282** [0.0141]	-0.0226* [0.0135]	-0.0226* [0.0134]
University degree	7,271	0.065	0.781	0.941	-0.0289*** [0.0089]	-0.0272*** [0.0080]	-0.0259*** [0.0055]	-0.0234*** [0.0049]
Age control					Linear	Dummies	Linear	Dummies
Extended controls							Yes	Yes

Note: Coefficients are the marginal effects of a 100 percent change in percent OV from probit models. Standard errors clustered on individuals are in brackets. Extended controls are those included in columns (3) and (4) of table 3.1B.

***Significant at the 1 percent level.
**Significant at the 5 percent level.
*Significant at the 10 percent level.

of public retirement benefits and greater physical need to contemplate retirement.

3.5   Understanding the Results and Implications

We now turn to some simulations to assess the magnitudes of our results and the implications in particular for disability insurance. In our simulations, we use estimates from tables 3.1A (for women) and 3.1B (for men), specification (4). We take the estimated coefficient on OV from this specification and use it for the simulations. Each simulation involves imposing some different counterfactual pension or disability insurance regime and recalculating the option value. Then, taking the new option value, we use the estimated coefficients from tables 3.1A and 3.1B, specification (4) to predict retirement probabilities for each individual in the data set.

The counterfactual scenarios we examine here should not be considered as direct policy options. Instead, we think of these simulations as a way to gauge the magnitude of our results and to compare results across countries in the project.

We consider four different simulations. We first imagine an individual for whom disability insurance is not an option, so the only incentives that matter are on the non-DI path. Second, we take an individual who represents the complementary case—only considering the DI option value. We do this simulation for two different samples. The first sample contains all individuals. The second sample is selected based on self-assessed disability status reported in the SLID. For these individuals, we expect the DI incentives may be more salient. So, the two samples and the two simulated incentives make for four total sets of simulations.

We present first the hazard rates for the two sets of incentives and the two samples. The predicted probability for each individual is calculated using either the DI path only or the non-DI path only, and the resulting probabilities are aggregated across all individuals or across only those who self-report as disabled. Figure 3.9 shows the resulting hazards, which is formed by taking the individual predicted retirement probabilities averaged by age for each simulation.

The lower two lines in each of the panels of figure 3.9 show the results for the full sample. The "All DI" line shows the results when all emphasis is put on the DI path; the "All non-DI" shows the results when all emphasis is put on the non-DI path. For women at age fifty, the difference in the predicted probabilities between the two paths is about 1 percentage point—4.5 percent versus 3.5 percent. For men, the gap is smaller at 0.65 of a percentage point. The difference between the incentives closes at age sixty-five because DI benefits transform to CPP retirement benefits at that age. So, the difference between the lifetime value of benefits for a sixty-four-year-old retiring through DI or non-DI is quite small, reflecting only one year of different

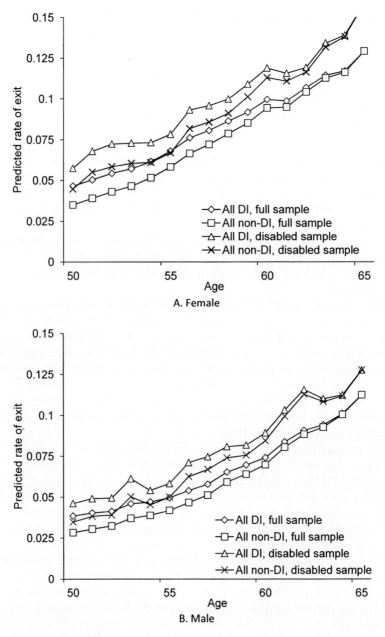

Fig. 3.9   Hazard rates
Source: Authors' calculations using the SLID.

benefits received before age sixty-five. Figure 3.9 also shows higher simulated exit rates at each age for the disabled sample. The difference between the all DI and the all non-DI path is very similar to the full sample.

Figure 3.10 takes these hazard rates and constructs a survival curve. Starting with a full 1.0 share of people working at age fifty, the curve shows how many survive after accounting for the exits suggested by the hazard rates from figure 3.9. The same four simulations are shown for women and for men. The difference in survival rates comparing across the all DI and the all non-DI lines looks fairly small in all cases. However, it is possible to aggregate across ages by adding the survival rates at each age together. The resulting number provides a projection of the number of years of work that can be expected after age fifty under each simulation.

The aggregated predictions for years of work are presented in figure 3.11. For this figure, we show not only the all DI and all non-DI simulations, but also two intermediate simulations. Here, we randomly assign the DI incentives to two-thirds of the observations and the non-DI incentives to the rest. Then, we repeat with only one-third getting the DI incentives. As above, we show results for the full sample and the disabled sample.

The results show a modest difference ranging from the all DI to the all non-DI simulation. The predicted years of work under all DI for women is 10.5 years, but under all non-DI it is 11.2 years, for a gain of 0.7 years. As a percentage of the 10.5 years, this represents a potential increase in labor supply over these ages of 8 percent if people shifted from a focus on DI to a focus on the non-DI incentives. For men, the equivalent change is from 11.9 years to 12.5, for a percentage increase of 5 percent in years worked over this age range. For both men and women, the number of years worked in the disabled sample is smaller, but the difference across simulations is similar.

These results suggest a modest impact of DI in Canada. This may reflect the relatively small scale of the program in Canada compared to other countries, and also relatively high stringency of the system after 1995.

3.6   Conclusion

This chapter has studied the retirement decisions of Canadians and the influence of the retirement income and disability insurance systems on those decisions. We confirm and extend the results of previous research that has shown retirement decisions to be dependent upon the incentives embedded in the public programs available to Canadians. In particular, we are able here to incorporate the DI aspect of the Canadian system into the analysis along with the retirement income elements. In addition, we show how the results vary by health status and education, finding that lower health and lower education Canadians are more sensitive to the retirement incentives.

We also present simulation results, comparing what would happen if individuals paid more attention to the DI or the non-DI incentives they may

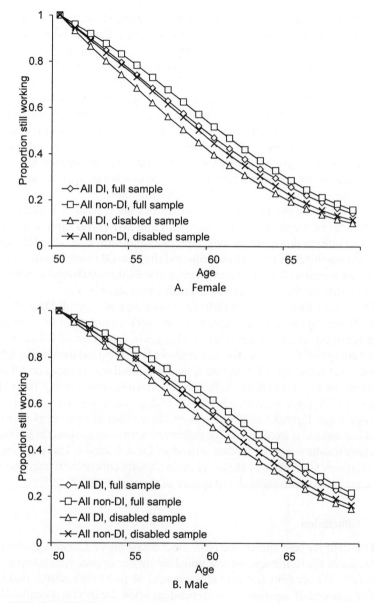

Fig. 3.10 Survival rates
Source: Authors' calculations using the SLID.

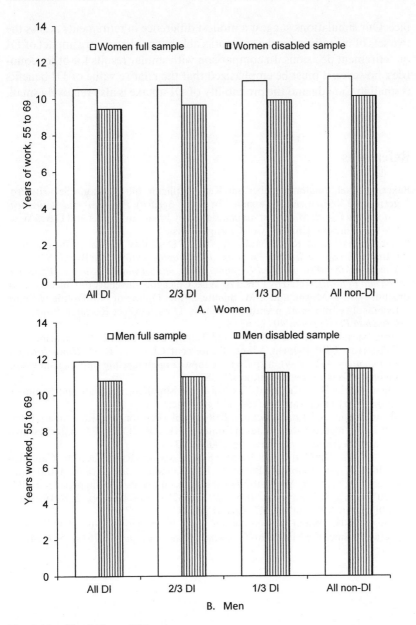

Fig. 3.11   Simulation results
Source: Authors' calculations using the SLID.

face. Our simulations suggest a modest difference in retirements across the two sets of incentives, implying a noticeable but not large extra impact of DI on retirement decisions. In comparison with similar results for other countries, however, it must be emphasized that the relative value of DI benefits is small in Canada and the probability of DI uptake is also relatively small.

References

Baker, Michael, Jonathan Gruber, and Kevin Milligan. 2004. "Income Security Programs and Retirement in Canada." In *Social Security Programs and Retirement Around the World: Micro-Estimation*, edited by Jonathan Gruber and David Wise, 99–152. Chicago: University of Chicago Press.
Baker, Michael, and Kevin Milligan. 2012. "Disability Insurance Programs in Canada." In *Social Security Programs and Retirement around the World: Historical Trends in Mortality and Health, Employment, and Disability Insurance Participation and Reforms*, edited by David A. Wise. Chicago: University of Chicago Press.
Brochu, P., L.-P. Morin, and J.-M. Billette. 2014. "Opting or Not Opting to Share Income Tax Information with the Census: Does it Affect Research Findings?" *Canadian Public Policy* 40 (1): 67–83.
Laurin, Alexandre, Kevin Milligan, and Tammy Schirle. 2012. "Comparing Nest Eggs: How CPP Reform Affects Retirement Choices." *C. D. Howe Institute Commentary* 352 (May). http://www.cdhowe.org/comparing-nest-eggs-how-cpp-reform-affects-retirement-choices/17887.
Milligan, Kevin. 2012. Canadian Tax and Credit Simulator. Software and documentation. http://faculty.arts.ubc.ca/kmilligan/ctacs/.
Milligan, Kevin, and Tammy Schirle. 2006. "Public Pensions and Retirement: International Evidence in the Canadian Context." HRSDC-IC-SSHRC Skills Research Initiative Working Paper Series no. 2006-A-13.
———. 2013. "The Retirement Income System and the Risks Faced by Canadian Seniors." CLSRN Working Paper no. 120, Canadian Labour Market and Skills Researcher Network. April. http://www.clsrn.econ.ubc.ca/workingpapers/CLSRN%20Working%20Paper%20no.%20120%20-%20CLSRN%20Retirement%20Program%20Synthesis%20Report.pdf.
Schirle, T. 2008. "Why Have the Labour Force Participation Rates of Older Men Increased Since the Mid-1990s?" *Journal of Labor Economics* 26 (4): 549–94.

Health Status, Disability, and Retirement Incentives in Belgium

Alain Jousten, Mathieu Lefebvre, and Sergio Perelman

4.1 Introduction

In previous volumes of this NBER series on *Social Security Programs and Retirement around the World*, Pestieau and Stijns (1999), Dellis et al. (2004), Desmet et al. (2007), Jousten et al. (2010), and Jousten, Lefebvre, and Perelman (2012) documented how the Belgian social protection landscape offers a variety of pathways to retirement before reaching the normal retirement age (NRA) that is currently fixed at age sixty-five. For contractual wage earners, who represent the majority of the Belgian workforce, these early exit routes include an early exit option in the old-age pension scheme (OAP), conventional early retirement (CER), unemployment insurance (UI), and disability insurance (DI).

In this chapter, we focus our attention on the potential link between health status, disability insurance, and retirement for contractual wage earners ages fifty to sixty-four. Jousten, Lefebvre, and Perelman (2012) already explored the link between aggregate indicators of health and disability, on the one hand, and retirement on the other. The present study extends the analysis by taking a cross-sectional approach at the individual worker level.

Alain Jousten is professor of economics at the University of Liege, HEC Management School and Tax Institute, and a research fellow of the Institute for the Study of Labor (IZA) and of NETSPAR. Mathieu Lefebvre is assistant professor of economics at the University of Strasbourg. Sergio Perelman is honorary professor of economics, University of Liege, HEC Management School, and CREPP.

The authors acknowledge financial support from the SBO-project FLEMOSI (funded by IWT Flanders) and the Belspo project EMPOV (TA/00/45). We thank Lut Vanden Meersch (RIZIV-INAMI) for giving us access to the data on DI participation and Ekaterina Tarantchenko for useful discussions and assistance. All remaining errors are our own. For acknowledgments, sources of research support, and disclosure of the authors' material financial relationships, if any, please see http://www.nber.org/chapters/c13324.ack.

For this purpose we use the Belgian sample of SHARE, the Survey of Health, Ageing and Retirement in Europe, which has been collected since 2004.[1] The survey is a cross-national panel database of microdata on health, socioeconomic status, and social and family networks of European individuals age fifty and older conducted since 2004–2005. It covers a broad range of variables of special interest for this study such as information on employment, health, and the household context. We use detailed self-reported information on health to compute a continuous health index and retrospective data to compute retirement incentives. We also construct an option value (OV) indicator as in Stock and Wise (1990) to compare the relative values of continued work versus retirement. We then use both of these indicators as independent variables in a microestimation of retirement decisions by means of a probit model.

While Dellis et al. (2004) relied on administrative records on Belgian workers, our estimation is based on SHARE survey data. One distinct advantage of SHARE is the availability of a rich set of health indicators (both subjective and objective); a distinct disadvantage is a significantly smaller availability of information on careers as compared to the pension register data.

This chapter is organized into several sections. The following section presents some stylized facts on disability participation among people age fifty to sixty-four. Our empirical approach is described in section 4.3, including a detailed description of the construction of a synthetic health index and the option value indicator. A rich set of probit models are estimated and results are reported in section 4.4. Section 4.5 provides microsimulations of some stylized reform scenarios. Section 4.6 concludes.

4.2   The Role of Disability Insurance

The role of DI has been changing quite substantially over time—as can be documented using administrative data. Jousten, Lefebvre, and Perelman (2012) provided a detailed discussion of the role of DI in the retirement landscape. Figures 4.1 and 4.2 summarize the trend in DI participation as

1. This paper uses data from SHARE wave 4, release 1.1.1, as of March 28, 2013, or SHARE waves 1 and 2, release 2.5.0, as of May 24, 2011, or SHARELIFE release 1, as of November 24, 2010. The SHARE data collection has been primarily funded by the European Commission through the 5th Framework Programme (project QLK6-CT-2001–00360 in the thematic programme Quality of Life), through the 6th Framework Programme (projects SHARE-I3, RII-CT-2006–062193, COMPARE, CIT5-CT-2005–028857, and SHARELIFE, CIT4-CT-2006-028812) and through the 7th Framework Programme (SHARE-PREP, N° 211909, SHARE-LEAP, N° 227822 and SHARE M4, N° 261982). Additional funding from the US National Institute on Aging (U01 AG09740-13S2, P01 AG005842, P01 AG08291, P30 AG12815, R21 AG025169, Y1-AG-4553-01, IAG BSR06-11 and OGHA 04-064) and the German Ministry of Education and Research as well as from various national sources is gratefully acknowledged (see www.share-project.org for a full list of funding institutions).

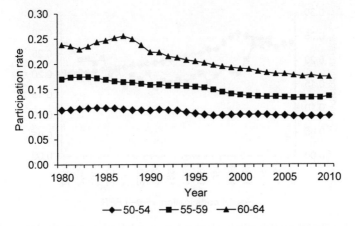

Fig. 4.1   **The DI participation rate, men age fifty to sixty-four (1980–2010)**
Source: INAMI-RIZIV administrative records.
Note: The DI participation rates are obtained as percentage of beneficiaries as a share of the
eligible wage-earner population in the age cohort.

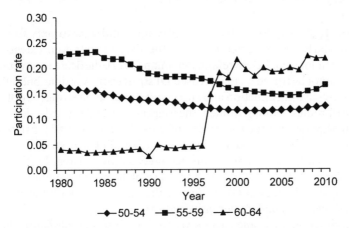

Fig. 4.2   **The DI participation rate, women age fifty to sixty-four (1980–2010)**
Source: INAMI-RIZIV.
Note: The DI participation rates are obtained as percentage of beneficiaries as a share of the
eligible wage-earner population in the age cohort.

observed in administrative data for the population of wage earners (age fifty
and older), by age group and sex.[2]

For men, DI participation rates decreased over time for the three age cat-

---

2. The DI participation rate for a given age group is calculated using administrative records.
The numerator is composed of the number of DI recipients who were awarded a DI benefit
based on a work spell as a contractual wage earner. The denominator includes all active wage
earners, as well as all social security beneficiaries (excluding pensioners) who are receiving
benefits based on a work spell as a contractual wage earner.

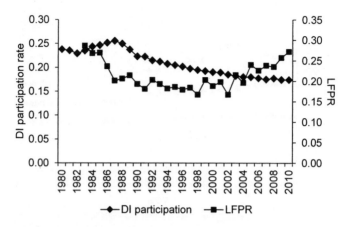

Fig. 4.3   The DI participation and labor force participation, men age sixty to sixty-four (1980–2010)

Sources: INAMI-RIZIV and Eurostat.

Note: The DI participation rates are obtained as percentage of beneficiaries as a share of the eligible wage-earner population in the age cohort.

egories fifty to fifty-four, fifty-five to fifty-nine, and sixty to sixty-four, with a particularly strong decrease among the sixty to sixty-four category. As reported in Jousten, Lefebvre, and Perelman (2012), the decreasing evolution of DI cannot be traced to an increased DI stringency over time, but rather to the progressive introduction and successive decreases in stringency of other early exit routes. Among women, the longer-run trend toward a decrease in DI participation for the age groups fifty to fifty-four and fifty-five to fifty-nine has more recently been reversed, with a likely link with stricter eligibility criteria in early retirement options as indicated by Jousten, Lefebvre, and Perelman (2012). Therefore, as in the case of men, the evolution is less in relation with changes in DI stringency than in relation with the evolution of eligibility rules under alternative pathways.

The situation for women ages sixty to sixty-four is an outlier to this picture, and predominantly driven by changes in the normal retirement age (NRA). Before 1997, the NRA was sixty years for women, de facto leading to very few active women beyond this age. From 1997 to 2009, women's normal age of retirement was progressively increased by one year of age every three calendar years so as to reach an NRA of sixty-five for women in 2009—the same as has been applicable for men for the last decades.[3] This explains the fast increase in DI rates among women in this age category.

Figures 4.3 and 4.4 present the labor force participation rate and the DI

---

3. The alignment of the normal age of retirement for women to that of men was decided in response to two judgments of the European Court of Justice from 1993 ruling that differential criteria by sex constitute discrimination.

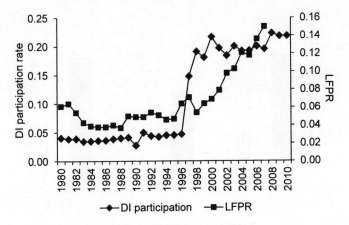

Fig. 4.4   The DI participation and labor force participation, women age sixty to sixty-four (1980–2010)

Sources: INAMI-RIZIV and Eurostat.

Note: The DI participation rates are obtained as percentage of eligible wage-earner population in the same age cohort.

participation rate for the older age group of sixty to sixty-four. While the DI participation for women follows the labor force participation for the reason explained above, it is not the case for men, where trends are opposite in the later part of the observation period. This apparent lack of synchronization between the variables can be traced to several causes, two of which are particularly marked. First, multiple early retirement pathways exist and interact, hence leading to a weakening of the link between each one of them and the aggregate labor market outcomes. Second, since the late 1990s a reversal of the longstanding trend toward lower effective retirement could be observed all across a wide variety of countries (see the previous volumes of this series), and this to a large degree irrespective of the incentive structure prevailing in any specific country.

Disability insurance has a very diverse impact on the various subgroups of the population—particularly when comparing along the education and health dimensions. As Belgium does not have any systematically collected administrative data on those topics, we turn to SHARE to derive some stylized facts. Figures 4.5 and 4.6 illustrate the evolution over the period ranging from the first wave of SHARE (2004–2005) to the last one available to date (2010–2011).[4] They summarize the DI probabilities for male and female wage earners, respectively, within the fifty to sixty-four age group stratified by education level. Overall, there is a strong negative gradient between edu-

---

4. Three waves of SHARE are useable for this analysis: waves 1 (2004–2005), 2 (2006–2007), and 4 (2010–2011). Wave 3 conducted in 2008–2009 (known as SHARELIFE) does not include questions on individuals' current situation, but mainly retrospective questions.

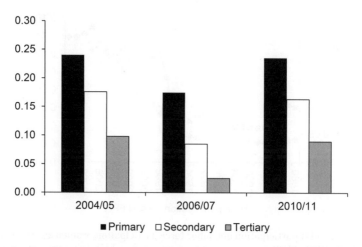

Fig. 4.5   The DI probability by education, male wage earners age fifty to sixty-four
Source: Authors' calculation based on SHARE data (waves 1, 2, and 4).
Note: The DI probability is obtained as the number of individuals receiving DI benefits in the wage-earner population (active or unemployed).

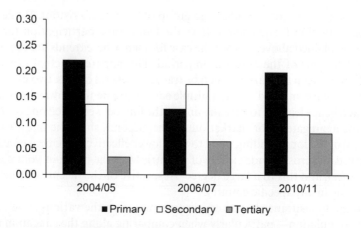

Fig. 4.6   The DI probability by education, female wage earners age fifty to sixty-four
Source: Authors' calculation based on SHARE data (waves 1, 2, and 4).
Note: The DI probability is obtained as the number of individuals receiving DI benefits in the wage-earner population (active or unemployed).

cation level and DI probability for wage earners. The sole exception is the case of women in 2006–2007 (SHARE wave 2), where the DI probability is higher for the intermediate category than for the less educated, likely due to a small-sample problem.

Figures 4.7 and 4.8 illustrate the evolution of DI probabilities among men and women, respectively, by health quintiles. Without entering in the details

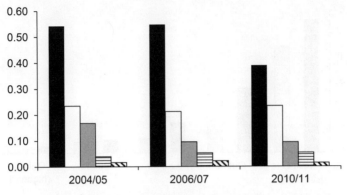

Fig. 4.7   The DI probability by health quintiles, male wage earners age fifty to sixty-four

Source: Authors' calculation based on SHARE data (waves 1, 2, and 4).

Note: The DI probability is obtained as the number of individuals receiving DI benefits in the total population.

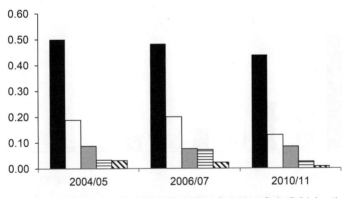

Fig. 4.8   The DI probability by health quintiles, female wage earners age fifty to sixty-four

Source: Authors' calculation based on SHARE data (waves 1, 2, and 4).

Note: The DI probability is obtained as the number of individuals receiving DI benefits in the total population.

of health quintiles computations, which will be presented in detail in section 4.4.3, we observe in these figures that DI probabilities are positively related to health in SHARE, but above all that for people in the lower health quintile the DI probability reaches values as high as 50 percent in some survey waves.

Figures 4.9 and 4.10 combine the two factors of health and education and display the DI probability when crossing these two variables. We observe, in

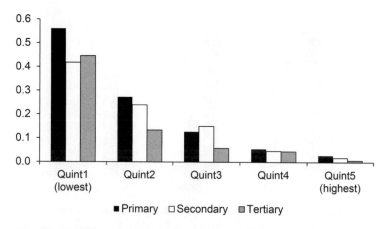

Fig. 4.9   The DI probability by health quintiles and education, male wage earners age fifty to sixty-four

Source: Authors' calculation based on SHARE data (waves 1, 2, and 4).

Note: The DI probability is obtained as the number of individuals receiving DI benefits in the total population.

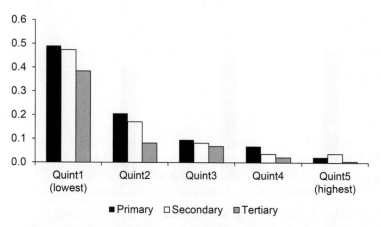

Fig. 4.10   The DI probability by health quintiles and education, female wage earners age fifty to sixty-four

Source: Authors' calculation based on SHARE data (waves 1, 2, and 4).

Note: The DI probability is obtained as the number of individuals receiving DI benefits in the total population.

addition to the effect of health on DI probability, a more mixed pattern of education within each health quintile.

Finally, table 4.1 shows the employment rate of individuals age fifty to sixty-four as computed based on the combined SHARE waves 1, 2, and 4. Employment increases along the health gradient, both for men and women, and is positively correlated with education.

Table 4.1   Employment rate at age fifty-five to sixty-four by health and education

	Primary	Secondary	Tertiary		
By education level					
Men	0.419	0.555	0.657		
Women	0.312	0.424	0.594		
	Quint 1 (lowest)	Quint 2	Quint 3	Quint 4	Quint 5 (highest)
By health quintile					
Men	0.248	0.434	0.580	0.640	0.675
Women	0.147	0.346	0.418	0.526	0.512

Source: Authors' calculation based on SHARE data (waves 1, 2, and 4).

4.3   Empirical Approach

As mentioned before, our main goal is to understand the influence of health status and the provisions of social protection schemes on retirement decisions. For this purpose we estimate a discrete-time retirement model in which exit from the labor market ($R_i = 1$) is explained by social protection incentives, health, and other covariates.

For individual i:

$$(1) \qquad \Pr[R_i = 1] = \Pr[X_i'\beta + \delta OV_i + \gamma H_i],$$

where X_i' is a vector of independent variables, OV_i is a social security incentive, an option value measure, and H_i is a measure of health status.

In our econometric analysis, we use the first two waves of data from SHARE collected in 2004–2005 and 2006–2007 for Belgium. The third wave of data, known as SHARELIFE (collected in 2008–2009), asked all previous respondents (waves 1 and 2) and their partners to provide information not on their current situation, but on their entire life histories. This provides retrospective information on childhood, health, living, and professional career. We combine the first two waves with the retrospective data from SHARELIFE to obtain a full career history for each individual.[5] For individuals surveyed in any wave we can observe when they exited the labor market and through which pathways. This means that while there are usually two years between each wave, we can observe year-to-year transitions. The advantage is that instead of seeing an individual just once between two waves, we follow him along the years between two waves and we know his actual status in each year. We restrict the sample to the individuals who are between ages fifty and sixty-four. In each wave (1 or 2) we select those

---

5. The SHARE wave 4 data was also available but not usable for this purpose given that wave 3, SHARELIFE, did not report detailed information on health and on other key variables for this study.

individuals who were employed as wage earners and exclude retired, unemployed, sick, and disabled. We also exclude individuals for whom retrospective information is not available in SHARELIFE. Finally, we drop all the records for the years that are subsequent to the year when the individual exited the labor force. Our analytical sample consists of 1,210 observations.

Two crucial steps in our analysis relate to the derivation of a synthetic health measure and the calculation of a summary indicator of retirement incentives. For the former, we rely on a continuous health index computed using a principal component analysis based on nearly twenty-five self-reported health indicators. For the latter, we rely on an "inclusive" version of the concept of option value, de facto a weighted average of the option values for each pathway to retirement. We detail the approach below.

4.3.1   Measurement of Health Status

Identifying the effects of health on retirement is complicated because people's health is not directly observable. The use of surveys wherein people report subjective self-assessments of their physical capacity can often be misleading. Indeed, it is a subjective assessment and there is no reason to expect that such assessments are entirely comparable across individuals. Also, answers may not be independent of the outcomes we wish to study. For example, individuals who are inactive often have an incentive to report worse than actual health. In such situations, subjective health indicators measure leisure preferences rather than true health status.

It is thus preferable to use objective indicators of health. The issue is to find objective measures that are correlated with work capacity and that truly reflect the individual's ability to work. The SHARE data contain a variety of objective and subjective measures of health. Using objective measures of physical ability in addition to self-reported health status, we propose to derive a latent health index similar to Poterba, Venti, and Wise (2010). To construct the index we use responses to twenty-four questions and obtain the first principal component of these underlying indicators of health. The first principal component is the weighted average of the health indicators, where the weights are chosen to maximize the proportion of the variance of the indicators that can be explained by the first principal component.[6]

All data from waves 1, 2, and 4 of SHARE are used to calculate the principal components, with ages ranging from 50 to 101. These are then in a second step applied to all observations of waves 1 and 2 that are the basis for our econometric analysis—de facto attributing a health index for each individual in each one of the two waves under study. Thus an individual may experience changes of the health status across the survey waves. The health score obtained from the first principal component is converted into

---

6. The list of health questions used in the principal component analysis is available in appendix table 4A.1, as well as the correlation coefficients corresponding to the first component.

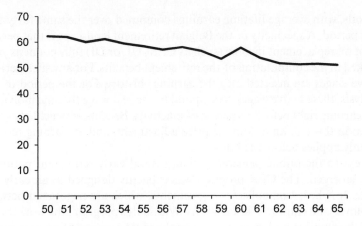

Fig. 4.11   Average health percentile by age
Source: Authors' calculation based on a two-step procedure. First, the underlying principal components are calculated based on twenty-four health questions drawn from SHARE waves 1, 2, and 4 for the age range 50–101. Second, these estimates are then applied to individuals of waves 1 and 2 in the age range fifty to sixty-five.

percentile scores for each observation with 1 the worst health and 100 the best. Later on in the analysis we group persons by health status quintiles using this score. Figure 4.11 displays the average health percentile in Belgium by age for individuals age fifty to sixty-five. We observe in this figure that, as expected, the health indicator decreases with age, with a blip at age sixty. Further, it is perfectly plausible for the average health percentile to remain above the 50 percent markup until the statutory retirement age—with progressively lower levels observed above that age.

4.3.2   Pathways to Retirement

Wage earners face several typical pathways to retirement. A first pathway consists of an immediate transfer from work into the old-age pension system (OAP). The OAP currently allows claiming early retirement as of age sixty, when some career requirements are met. The normal retirement age, at which anybody can claim OAP benefits independently of career requirements, is currently set at age sixty-five for both men and women. Notice that during the first two waves of SHARE data collection from 2004 to 2005 the normal retirement age for women was still under the transitory regime, reaching sixty-three for the first wave and sixty-four for the second.

Benefits correspond to 75 percent of average lifetime earnings for one-earner couples and to 60 percent for singles—with two-earner couples having the right to a top-up to the said 75 percent if the secondary earner's pension is smaller than this household supplement. Claiming early does not imply any actuarial adjustment of benefits as compared to claiming at NRA.

A full career corresponds to forty-five years of earnings or assimilated periods, with average lifetime earnings computed over the same forty-five-year period. A specificity of the Belgian retirement landscape is that periods spent on replacement income (such as CER, UI, or DI) fully count as years worked in the computation of the retirement benefits. For any such periods, fictive wages are inserted into the earnings history. For the period of our analysis, these fictive wages correspond to the real wage that the individual was earning right before his period of inactivity. Benefits are shielded against inflation through an automatic price adjustment, and an earning test frequently applies before the NRA.

Next to the public pension system, several early retirement pathways have emerged. The CER program was explicitly designed as an early exit route. It is based on collective agreements, which are negotiated between employee and employer associations. Within this program, the workers exit the labor market and receive an unemployment compensation paid by the UI system and a bonus paid by the employer, which equals half of the difference between the individual's last net wage and the special unemployment benefit applicable to CER beneficiaries. Both benefits and reference wage have caps and floors. The CER program implies that workers cannot draw public pension benefits before the NRA, at which age he is automatically rolled over into the OAP system. The generally applicable eligibility rule sets out that they have to satisfy a minimum age of fifty-eight and a career of at least twenty-five years, but exceptions exist that allow some workers to exit through CER as early as age fifty with as little as a career of ten years.

Regular UI benefits represent a second effective exit route into retirement. In Belgium there is no generally applicable time limit for UI benefit receipt, except for the automatic rollover provision of the unemployed into retirement upon reaching the NRA. The level of these benefits depends on the family status and the duration of the unemployment spell. In theory, they are equal to 60 percent of the previous net wage if the individual is single or has family dependents. If the spouse or partner has income, benefits are equal to 55 percent of last net wage. In practice, they have caps and floors that vary according to the duration of the unemployment spell, de facto somewhat weakening the mechanical nature of the mentioned replacement rates.

Within the group of unemployed, special rules are applicable to some categories of older workers, a system known as old-age unemployment (OAU) as documented in Jousten, Lefebvre, and Perelman (2012). While the system has played an important role in the Belgian retirement landscape, we do not explicitly take it into account in our analysis for two reasons. First, in SHARE data, OAU is observationally indistinguishable from UI. Second, successive policy changes over the course of the last decade have effectively dismantled the system as a stand-alone program and brought it back into the realm of the regular UI. In fact, the two key benefits of the system as compared to regular UI have been decoupled and significantly tightened:

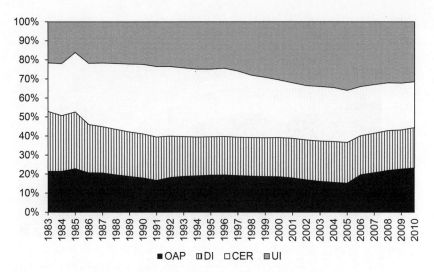

Fig. 4.12   Pathways to retirement—male wage earners, age fifty to sixty-four (%)
Sources: INAMI, ONEM, ONP, and Belgostat.
Note: The denominator is the number of individuals in the same age group who were covered under the wage-earner regime and are currently inactive. The numerator is the split of these people across the various social security programs in the age group fifty to sixty-four.

a waiver from the general job search requirement and the conditions for benefiting from a seniority supplement.

Last but not least, though a priori exclusively targeted at those withdrawing from the labor market for reasons of bad health, DI may also serve as an early exit route. The eligibility is based on loss of earnings capacity. In order to be eligible, the worker has to suffer from a loss of earnings capacity of 66 percent over a period of twelve months. The benefit level is a function of the household status and is equal to 65 percent of reference wage if the worker has dependents. It is reduced to 53 percent if the insured lives alone and to 45 percent if the individual cohabits. As for unemployment, benefits are payable up to the NRA with automatic rollover into OAP occurring at that age.

Figures 4.12 and 4.13 provide empirical evidence on the importance of the various programs across time for men and women, separately. The percentages are computed as the proportion of all social protection beneficiaries, within the fifty- to sixty-four-years-old category, in a particular program at each year. We see the role of the various pathways in absorbing the change in one or another—with UI effectively playing the role of program of last resort.

For men we observe over the last years an increase in the proportion of pensioners (OAP). For women, figure 4.13, we observe on the contrary a dramatic decrease in the proportion of pensioners, due to the progressive

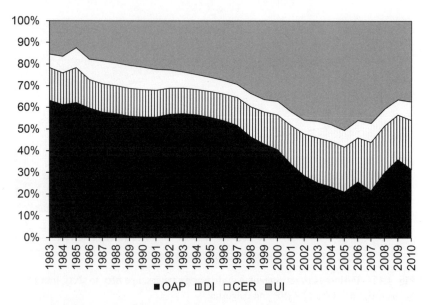

Fig. 4.13   Pathways to retirement—female wage earners, age fifty to sixty-four (%)
Sources: INAMI, ONEM, ONP, and Belgostat.

Note: The denominator is the number of individuals in the same age group who were covered under the wage-earner regime and are currently inactive. The numerator is the split of these people across the various social security programs in the age group fifty to sixty-four.

postponement of the NRA from sixty to sixty-five compensated mainly by unemployment (UI) and, in a lower proportion, by disability (DI). Over the transition period, from 1997 to 2009, the number of women age fifty- to sixty-four years old and beneficiaries of these programs increase more than 50 percent.

4.3.3   Weighting the Pathways to Retirement

As described above, there are four potential pathways to retirement for wage earners in Belgium. Our empirical strategy relies on the computation of a financial indicator that summarizes the incentives associated with the four pathways. The idea is to calculate for each of these pathways to retirement an incentive measure that is aggregated into one final inclusive measure using path-specific weights.

Since we cannot observe each individual's exact eligibility for the various exit routes, we are not able to determine the probability that a given pathway is a realistic option for the individual. Instead we impute to each pathway a weight that is, on average, a realistic prospect for the population age fifty and older. The weights are based on administrative data. We use the share of the population for the age group fifty to sixty-four that is either on disability (DI), unemployment (UI), or early retirement (CER). Old-age

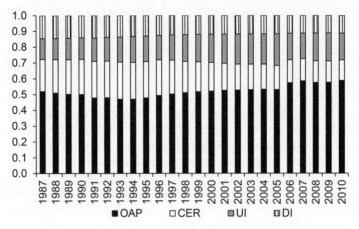

Fig. 4.14   Pathway weights by year—male wage earners, age fifty to sixty-four
Sources: INAMI, ONEM, and Belgostat.

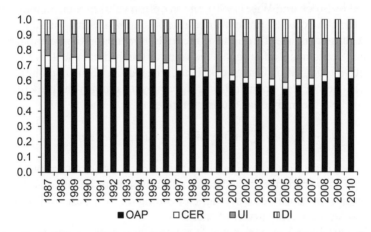

Fig. 4.15   Pathway weights by year—female wage earners, age fifty to sixty-four
Sources: INAMI, ONEM, and Belgostat.

pension (OAP) takes the residual such that the sum of the weights is equal to one. The fifty to sixty-four age window corresponds to the main ages at risk of retirement in Belgium. Figures 4.14 and 4.15 present these weights for the last twenty years. Interestingly, we observe for men a decrease of the weight of disability but an increase for women due to the postponement of women's normal age of retirement.

4.3.4   Option Value Calculations

Thanks to the data from SHARELIFE we are able to reconstruct the individual's career history and thus, ultimately, to calculate the entitlements to benefits. The SHARELIFE survey asks the respondents to provide start and end dates of each paid job they had, the characteristics of the job, as well as the first monthly wage. For those who are still employed at the time of the interview, the last monthly wage is also asked. All these amounts are after taxes.

This information is used to construct a panel with one wage observation per year for each individual, from the first job until the interview year. For simplicity we convert all amounts to 2008 euro dollars. The wage path is obtained using linear interpolation of wages for the years where we lack wage information. During unemployment, sickness, and disability as well as early retirement periods, fictive wages equal to the last observed wage are assigned, as required by calculation rules of public pension. As a result, we can project each individual's entitlements under the four exit routes based on each individual's own earnings history.

As indicated before, our financial incentive measure (OV) is a forward-looking measure based on the concept of option value of retirement, as defined by Stock and Wise (1990). In the option value model, an individual evaluates the expected present discounted value of income for all possible future retirement ages through a route to retirement and then compares the value of retirement today versus the value at the optimal age. It is based on a utility-maximization framework. Under the reduced form formulation, the value at age a of retirement h, $V_a(h)$, is given by (to simplify the presentation, we hide here the individual's subscript index i):

$$(2) \qquad V_a(h) = \sum_{s=a}^{h-1} \theta(s)\rho^{s-a}W_s^\gamma + \sum_{s=h}^{\infty} \theta(s)\rho^{s-a}[kB_h(s)]^\gamma$$

where $\theta(s)$ is the survival probability at age s, ρ is the rate of time preference, and $B_h(s)$ is the benefit expected at age s if the worker retires at age h; W_s is the earnings from continued working. Depending on the household situation, $\theta(s)$ also accounts for survivor benefits.[7]

The variable γ is a parameter of relative risk aversion and is set equal to 0.75. Finally, the parameter k expresses the relative weight of utility of retirement income and is set equal to 1.5.

Letting h^* be the year in the future at which the individual maximizes her/his expected value of retiring, the option value (OV) is then defined as the difference in utility terms between retiring at the best point in the future (h^*) or now (a):

$$(3) \qquad OV_a(h^*) = V_a(h^*) - V_a(a)$$

We rely on an inclusive version of the option value that is a weighted average of the option value associated to each potential route (pathway)

---

7. We use a discount rate of 3 percent, which is very often used in the literature. Mortality tables by sex for the Belgian population are used to compute $\theta(s)$. The source is the Human Mortality Database (www.mortality.org).

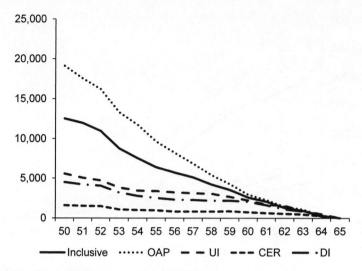

Fig. 4.16   Mean OV by age—male wage earners
Source: Authors' calculations based on SHARE data.
Note: The lines correspond to a cohort of fifty-year-olds that we follow as it ages.

to retirement. In order to compute the OV for each pathway to retirement, we need to make a projection of individual-level wages. In our analysis, we assume a real growth of wages of 0 going forward. Using this information and the whole career information compiled from SHARELIFE, we compute expected benefit flows for every pathway to retirement (DI, UI, CER, and OAP) for each possible age of retirement up to the NRA. Finally, we integrate expected benefits and expected wages in equations (2) and (3) to derive the option value for each retirement pathway.

Figures 4.16 and 4.17 show the mean OV for each pathway for men and women. The pattern is downward sloping for each OV as well as for both men and women. That is, that the utility to be gained from working one more year tends to decline with age and gets closer to zero at the NRA. The positive nature of the OV over the whole age range is mainly due to the utility term associated with wage income and the benefit formulae applicable under the various Belgian social security programs. Figures 4.16 and 4.17 show that the incentive to stay in the labor force when having an option to exit through CER, UI, and DI is rather weak at ages below sixty, as the OV indicator is flat over the entire age range. It is only when focusing on the OAP route that retirement before sixty is a highly uninteresting option—as for the latter case, the individual would be getting zero income until the age of sixty (the early retirement age of the OAP system).

The inclusive OV indicator summarizes these path-specific OV's into a single measure using the previously derived weights. For each individual and for each possible age of retirement, inclusive OV is calculated. The mean of the inclusive OV by age is plotted in figures 4.16 and 4.17 by means of a

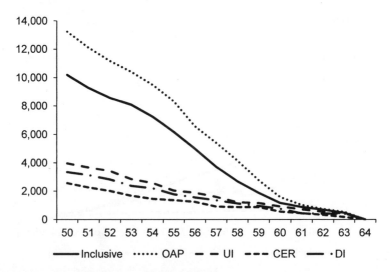

Fig. 4.17   Mean OV by age—female wage earners
Source: Authors' calculations based on SHARE data.
Note: The lines correspond to a cohort of fifty-year-olds that we follow as it ages.

continuous curve, for men and women, respectively. Unsurprisingly, given the weight structure, the OV associated with OAP exerts a predominant effect on the inclusive OV indicator, hence leading to an overall incentive to delay retirement.

4.4   Results

In this section we present a series of results obtained from binary probit estimations. The dependent variable is the binary retirement indicator: it is equal to one if the individual exits the labor force within the year, and zero otherwise. In each specification, we include the inclusive OV as a summary measure of financial incentive, to which we add a series of control variables that vary depending on the specification. Marginal effects are presented.

In specifications (1) and (2) in table 4.2, we only include the inclusive OV as well as a health indicator in the specification. For heath, we use dummies for each health quintile (based on the previously defined health index). Specification (1) uses linear age, while specification (2) is set up with age dummies. In specifications (3) and (4), we include a richer set of sociodemographic variables such as gender, the level of education, as well as dummies for marital status and active spouses. Furthermore, to capture wealth effects, we include the total household financial assets.

Specification (5) conceptually deviates from the previous ones in that it does not contain any linear or age dummy effect. The rationale for this alternative is related to an identification problem in all of these regressions:

Table 4.2 Effect of inclusive OV on probability of retirement

	1	2	3	4	5	6	7	8	9	10
OV inclusive (10,000s)	-0.133***	-0.128***	-0.110***	-0.106***	-0.205***	-0.134***	-0.130***	-0.111***	-0.107***	-0.209***
	(-4.11)	(-3.95)	(-3.35)	(-3.22)	(-7.13)	(-4.11)	(-3.97)	(-3.36)	(-3.25)	(-7.23)
	[-0.101]	[-0.094]	[-0.084]	[-0.079]	[-0.153]	[-0.102]	[-0.095]	[-0.087]	[-0.079]	[-0.156]
Health quint 2 (second lowest)	-0.036	-0.030	-0.035	-0.028	-0.037	—	—	—	—	—
	(-1.33)	(-1.08)	(-1.35)	(-1.04)	(-1.39)					
Health quint 3	-0.049*	-0.046*	-0.043*	-0.039*	-0.047*	—	—	—	—	—
	(-1.86)	(-1.72)	(-1.66)	(-1.62)	(-1.78)					
Health quint 4	-0.040	-0.035	-0.037	-0.031	-0.032	—	—	—	—	—
	(-1.46)	(-1.23)	(-1.40)	(-1.13)	(-1.16)					
Health quint 5 (highest)	-0.051**	-0.045*	-0.053**	-0.047*	-0.062**	—	—	—	—	—
	(-1.97)	(-1.65)	(-2.16)	(-1.86)	(-2.54)					
Health index	—	—	—	—	—	-0.004	-0.003	-0.004	-0.003	-0.003
						(-0.74)	(-0.54)	(-0.76)	(-0.60)	(-0.53)
Age	0.020***	—	0.020***	—	—	0.020***	—	0.020***	—	—
	(5.13)		(5.02)			(5.23)		(5.16)		
Age dummies	—	Included	—	Included	—	—	Included	—	Included	—
Male	—	—	0.009	0.013	0.028	—	—	0.010	0.013	0.029
			(0.40)	(0.60)	(1.32)			(0.44)	(0.62)	(1.35)
Married	—	—	0.053**	0.059***	0.057**	—	—	0.052**	0.057***	0.056**
			(2.41)	(2.74)	(2.56)			(2.31)	(2.63)	(2.49)

(continued)

Table 4.2 (continued)

	1	2	3	4	5	6	7	8	9	10
Spouse works	—	—	-0.058***	-0.060***	-0.077***	—	—	-0.056***	-0.058***	-0.075***
			(-2.67)	(-2.78)	(-3.55)			(-2.60)	(-2.71)	(-3.47)
Total assets	—	—	0.001**	0.001**	0.001**	—	—	0.001**	0.001**	0.001**
			(2.44)	(2.38)	(2.31)			(2.39)	(2.35)	(2.23)
Secondary education	—	—	-0.058**	-0.048*	-0.049*	—	—	-0.061**	-0.051*	-0.051*
			(-2.15)	(-1.78)	(-1.79)			(-2.23)	(-1.86)	(-1.88)
Tertiary education	—	—	-0.106***	-0.104***	-0.087***	—	—	-0.108***	-0.106***	-0.089***
			(-4.48)	(-4.43)	(-3.47)			(-4.60)	(-4.57)	(-3.56)
N	1,210	1,210	1,210	1,210	1,210	1,210	1,210	1,210	1,210	1,210
Mean ret. rate	0.112	0.112	0.112	0.112	0.112	0.112	0.112	0.112	0.112	0.112
Mean of OV	5,978	5,978	5,978	5,978	5,978	5,978	5,978	5,978	5,978	5,978
Std. dev. of OV	4,285	4,285	4,285	4,285	4,285	4,285	4,285	4,285	4,285	4,285

Notes: Coefficients are marginal effects from probit models. The T-statistics are shown in parentheses. The effect of one standard deviation change in OV is shown in brackets (this is estimated as the effect of increasing inclusive OV from the current value -0.5 standard deviations to the current value $+0.5$ standard deviations).

***Significant at the 1 percent level.

**Significant at the 5 percent level.

*Significant at the 10 percent level.

Which is the pure effect of age on retirement, independent of the effect of pension schemes rules? The data we use does not allow us to address this identification issue, many more waves of SHARE would be necessary. Hence, in specifications (1) to (4), the age dummies or the linear age trend capture a mix of both.

In specification (5) we take an extreme alternative by estimating the effect of OV under the assumption that any age-of-eligibility effect is fully taken into account by the inclusive OV variable. Implicitly, this also implies that we give the inclusive OV incentive variable a maximum role, though it does not by itself address the identification problem—it just takes a slightly different view. The approach turns out to be particularly useful when trying to gauge the effect of reform simulations (see the next section).

Finally, specifications (6) to (10) are similar to the five first specifications except that it includes a different indicator for the health status of individuals. In this second batch of specifications, health is introduced as the linear health index obtained from the principal component analysis rather than the relative position in the population by quintile.

The incentive measure turns out to be strongly significant in all specifications. The effect is negative, as expected, which means that a larger value of continued work leads to lower probability of retirement. In brackets, we also report the effect of a one standard deviation change in the OV as the coefficient on the OV can be sensitive to the mean and the variance of the OV. The results are similar to those for the coefficient on OV. In line with expectations, specifications (5) and (10) show a much bigger effect of the inclusive OV as it now captures the full scope of incentives that are otherwise partially captured by the age term.

Regarding health, results are somewhat unexpected. Individuals in the fifth quintile are significantly less likely to retire (at thresholds of 5 or 10 percent, according to the specification) than individuals in the first quintile. Only for some specifications and for a 10 percent significance level, individuals of the third quintile also display similar features. When looking at specifications with the health index, no significant pattern can be distinguished as a function of the health index. This even holds true when interacting the incentive measure with the health index as in table 4.3.

Our findings with regard to the influence of health status have clear policy relevance: they show that the link between health and retirement in Belgium is either weak or not significant. This stands in sharp contrast to the analysis of section 4.2, indicating the importance of performing econometric analysis instead of relying on mere correlations.

While the gender dummy is insignificant, other variables have strong impacts: age plays a significant role. Education also has a strong explanatory power, with higher education leading to significantly lower retirement probabilities. Being married has a positive impact on the likelihood of retirement, while having an active spouse reduces the retirement probability. Household

Table 4.3   Effect of inclusive OV with health index interaction

	1	2	3	4
OV	−0.135***	−0.131***	−0.113***	−0.109***
	(−4.17)	(−4.02)	(−3.44)	(−3.32)
	[−0.058]	[−0.054]	[−0.048]	[−0.046]
Health*OV	−0.017	−0.016	−0.018	−0.017
	(−1.05)	(−0.99)	(−1.17)	(−1.14)
Health index	0.003	0.004	0.003	0.004
	(0.33)	(0.41)	(0.36)	(0.45)
Linear age	X		X	
Age dummies		X		X
Other Xs			X	X
N	1,210	1,210	1,210	1,210
Mean ret. rate	0.112	0.112	0.112	0.112
Mean of OV	5,978	5,978	5,978	5,978
Std. dev. of OV	4,285	4,285	4,285	4,285

Notes: Models are the same as models 5–8 in table 4.2, with the addition of an OV*health index interaction. Coefficients are marginal effects from probit models. The *T*-statistics are shown in parentheses. The effect of one standard deviation change in OV is shown in brackets (this is estimated as the effect of increasing inclusive OV from the current value −0.5 standard deviations to the current value +0.5 standard deviations).

***Significant at the 1 percent level.
**Significant at the 5 percent level.
*Significant at the 10 percent level.

financial wealth also leads to a higher probability of retirement—in line with intuition.

Table 4.4 is analogous to specifications (1) to (4) of table 4.2 but instead of the inclusive OV, we use the percent gain in the utility from delaying retirement till the optimal retirement date. The underlying idea is simple: a similar level of OV can represent very different realities for different individuals, as they may have very different starting positions in terms of initial incomes and well-being. Hence, we define this percent gain in the utility of delayed retirement as the ratio of OV to the level of utility the individual would obtain if he were to immediately retire.[8]

The estimated coefficients on the incentive variable again turn out highly significant and robust to the specification choice. The observed effect of the financial incentive variable is much stronger than in table 4.2, indicating that the relation to initial levels of well-being matter in the Belgian retirement landscape.[9]

8. In terms of the terminology of the previous section, this corresponds to dividing expression (3) by expression (2), the latter evaluated upon immediate retirement.
9. We have tested alternative specifications including the two terms of this ratio as separate variables and have not found any stable relation. Results can be obtained from the authors upon request.

Table 4.4   **Effect of percentage gain in inclusive OV on probability of retirement**

	1	2	3	4
OV change	−0.389***	−0.388***	−0.320***	−0.313***
	(−4.63)	(−4.59)	(−3.91)	(−3.82)
Linear age	X		X	
Age dummies		X		X
Health quintiles	X	X	X	X
Other Xs			X	X
N	1,210	1,210	1,210	1,210
Mean ret. rate	0.112	0.112	0.112	0.112
Mean of % OV	0.252	0.252	0.252	0.252
Std. dev. of % OV	0.169	0.169	0.169	0.169

Notes: Models are the same as models 1–4 in table 4.2. Coefficients are marginal effects from probit models. The *T*-statistics are shown in parentheses.
***Significant at the 1 percent level.
**Significant at the 5 percent level.
*Significant at the 10 percent level.

4.5   Implication of the Results

4.5.1   Fit of the Model

Figures 4.18 and 4.19 compare by age, for men and women separately, the predicted retirement probabilities to the actual probabilities. The predicted probabilities are obtained from the full specification with health quintiles and age dummies (specification [4] in table 4.2). It will be our baseline for the simulations hereafter. The predictions follow closely the change in the actual probabilities, both for men and women. Although not reported here, the predictions made on the basis of estimations with a linear age are not so good. This indicates that the age dummies are important to capture some of the nonlinearities that the incentives or the health cannot capture, such as the key role played by eligibility ages.

Figures 4.20 and 4.21 display the simulated labor market survival process for men and women, separately. These figures are derived using the cross-sectional actual and predicted retirement probabilities of the preceding figures to simulate the survival for a hypothetical cohort of fifty-year-olds to whom we apply these cross-sectional retirement probabilities as they age. Implicitly, this assumes that the currently observed age patterns of retirement remain valid for the hypothetical cohort going forward to the future.[10]

Figure 4.22 relates the effective retirement behavior to what could be expected from our OV measures. It plots the cumulative retirement probabilities and the cumulative percentage of individuals who, according to our

10. This calculation ignores the effect of mortality.

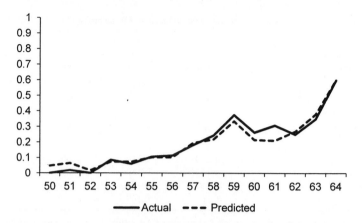

Fig. 4.18   Actual versus predicted retirement probabilities, male wage earners
Source: Authors' calculation based on SHARE data.

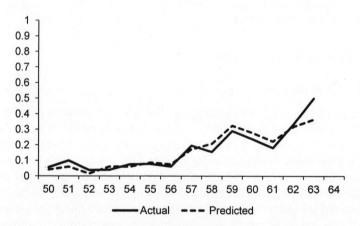

Fig. 4.19   Actual versus predicted retirement probabilities, female wage earners
Source: Authors' calculation based on SHARE data.
Note: The SHARE sample does not include any female wage earners working beyond the age of sixty-three.

incentive measures, have reached the maximum utility. It shows that a large majority of wage earners in Belgium retire before they have reached the utility maximizing age of retirement as predicted by the model.

4.5.2   Simulations

Using our estimations results of section 4.4, we investigate the effect of a change in the Belgian retirement architecture on retirement behavior. We use specification (4) of table 4.2 as our reference.

The first type of simulation (simulation [1]) considers that all persons in

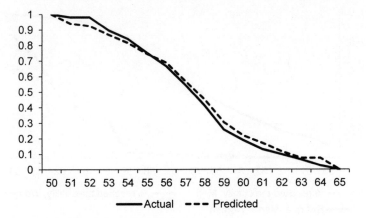

Fig. 4.20   Simulated labor market survival probabilities, male wage earners
Source: Authors' calculation based on SHARE data.
Note: The curves represent simulated labor market survival probabilities for a cohort of fifty-year-olds, to whom we apply the cross-sectional retirement probabilities of figure 4.18.

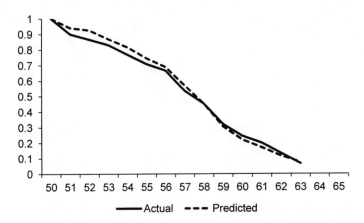

Fig. 4.21   Simulated actual versus predicted labor market survival probabilities, women
Source: Authors' calculation based on SHARE data.
Note: The curves represent simulated labor market survival probabilities for a cohort of fifty-year-olds, to whom we apply the cross-sectional retirement probabilities of figure 4.19. No account is taken of actual mortality.

the sample face only one of the four exit routes rather than a weighted combination of all. Expressed differently, we simulate the impact on retirement behavior of restricting access—and thus OVs—to one of the programs: OAP, CER, UI, or DI. We apply the estimated coefficients of the inclusive OV to these path-specific OVs. Implicitly, we thus view our estimates from the previous section as being instrumented estimates of the true relations—

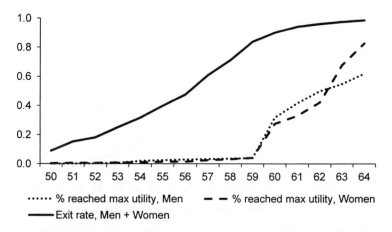

Fig. 4.22   Share of wage earners having reached maximum utility and cumulative retirement probability by age
Source: Authors' calculation based on SHARE data.

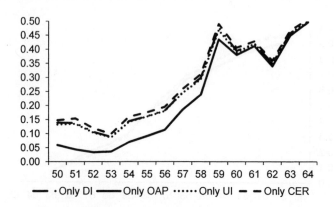

Fig. 4.23   Retirement probabilities by pathway
Source: Authors' calculation based on SHARE data.

with the population-wide averages serving as instruments for true individual eligibility. Figure 4.23 summarizes the results in terms of retirement hazards by age under the alternative scenarios. In line with figures 4.16 and 4.17, the strongest differences appear between the OAP and the other pathways with OAP leading to substantially lower hazard rates. Restricting access to CER, UI, or DI would lead to only marginally different retirement patterns. Figure 4.24 provides another look at the same underlying information. As for figures 4.20 and 4.21, it again represents the simulated labor market survival for a hypothetical cohort of fifty-year-olds facing the same retirement hazards in the future as the cross-sectional data reveals at present. Table 4.5 provides a simple summary statistic based on the same information as figure

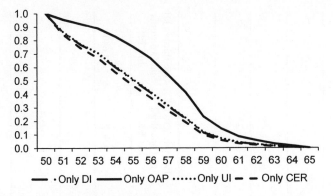

Fig. 4.24   Survival probabilities by pathway

Source: Authors' calculation based on SHARE data.

Note: The curves represent simulated labor market survival probabilities for a cohort of fifty-year-olds, to whom we apple the cross-sectional retirement probabilities of figure 4.23. No account is taken of actual mortality.

4.24: the expected remaining years of work after age fifty. It shows that the average expected remaining working life differs by more than two years, or expressed in relative terms by approximately 40 percent between the most generous pathway (CER) and the least generous pathway (OAP), with UI and DI falling in between.

A second type of simulation (simulation [2]) focuses exclusively on reforms that affect the people who are observed to be exiting through the DI pathway. The idea is simple: if we restrict the availability of DI, it will most directly affect those currently on the beneficiary rolls. Hence, the second type of simulation explores how this specific subgroup would react to changes in the program generosity that it faces. A priori, one could expect this population to be less responsive to financial incentives if the system actually (partially or completely) achieves its goal of covering people with a loss of earnings ability. The results are again summarized in table 4.5. Overall, DI recipients are significantly less responsive to changes in their incentives than the overall population. This would point to significant differences in their characteristics as compared to the population at large. Also, these simulations show that the differences between DI, CER, and UI are sufficiently marginal so as not to have any noticeable effect in terms of average retirement age.

In a third set of simulations (simulation [3]), we still focus on those who retired through DI, but this time with a less categorical policy implementation. In order to mimic the effect of a tightening of the eligibility criteria, we randomly assign a fraction of them (one-third or two-thirds) to the DI path and the remainder is excluded from DI. To reflect the communicating vessels idea, we successively explore the assignment of these people who are refused DI to the various programs. Allocating them to CER or UI means

Table 4.5   Effects of incentive measures alone on years of work between fifty and sixty-four

Simulation 1:

	DI (years of work)	OAP (years of work)	UI (years of work)	CER (years of work)
If all persons faced the same retirement pathway option	5.651	7.544	5.708	5.358

Simulation 2:

	DI (years of work)	OAP (years of work)	UI (years of work)	CER (years of work)
If all DI recipients faced the same retirement pathway option	Two-thirds to DI and one-third to OAP	One-third to DI and two-thirds to OAP	Two-thirds to DI and one-third to UI	One-third to DI and two-thirds to UI
	4.655	5.508	4.652	4.529

Simulation 3:

	Two-thirds to DI and one-third to OAP	One-third to DI and two-thirds to OAP	Two-thirds to DI and one-third to UI	One-third to DI and two-thirds to UI	Two-thirds to DI and one-third to CER	One-third to DI and two-thirds to CER
If all DI recipients faced a mixed of pathway	4.684	5.476	4.659	4.531	4.663	4.640

Simulation 4:

	DI (years of work)	OAP (years of work)	UI (years of work)	CER (years of work)
If all persons faced the same retirement pathway option (no control for age)	4.168	8.033	4.268	3.682

that access to these programs is not tightly monitored, hence leading to a shift between social security programs. Allocating them to OAP can be seen as a residual approach, whereby these individuals would be kept at bay from the UI and DI programs, de facto depriving them of current income until the early retirement age under OAP rules.

Simulations (2) and (3) illustrate that differences between CER, UI, and DI are sufficiently small so as to lead to absolutely marginal effects when shifting people between these programs. There is an immediate policy relevance of this finding: when limiting access to DI without strictly enforcing access conditions for UI and CER, we should broadly expect a mere shift from one program to another—without any positive labor market response. It is only by enforcing the access conditions to these programs that the reform of the DI system can have an effect.

Finally, we explore a fourth set of simulations (simulation [4]) applying the policy change of simulation (1) on the basis of the estimates of specification (5) of table 4.2. Essentially, the idea is to see to which degree the inclusion or exclusion of age in the regression will influence the effect of reforms to the incentive structure. Given the significantly stronger estimates for the inclusive OV variable under specification (5) of table 4.2 (as compared to specification [4]), we unsurprisingly find a significantly stronger impact of the reform scenario in terms of the average remaining working life. Our results show that not controlling for age gives much lower work expectancy for the generous exit paths (CER, UI, and DI) and higher work expectancy for the OAP route—leading to an increase of more than 100 percent of remaining work years between the most generous and the least generous route. Simulation (5) thus provides a way of gauging the maximum effect that one can expect to obtain from a reform of eligibility of these programs. It shows that the reference simulations can be seen as conservative estimates of the likely real-world effects.

4.6   Conclusion

The present chapter set out to explore the link between health status, disability programs, and retirement in Belgium. We documented that disability trends in Belgium are largely disconnected from the employment and labor market participation of older workers ages fifty and older. In Belgium, it turns out that it is rather the CER and UI programs than DI that shape labor market behavior over time and across individuals.

While simple cross-tabulations of health and retirement probability tend to indicate a strong correlation, econometric analysis shows that such a relation does not uphold in a more complete estimation when controlling for a rich set of other variables. This finding is of quite some policy relevance, as it means that health is not a key driver of retirement in Belgium.

The regression analysis also shows that financial incentives as captured by the (inclusive) option value of retirement play a substantial role in explaining retirement behavior. Simulations based on these estimates document that by tightening the eligibility conditions for early retirement programs (CER, UI, and mostly DI), one can substantially increase the number of years an individual would stay active on the labor market. Our simulations also show that any tightening of such eligibility criteria in a given early retirement program would need to be associated with strict monitoring of access to the other early exit routes, as else the total effect would be marginal at best.

Appendix

Table 4A.1   The first principal component index for Belgium

Question	1st component
Difficulty walking 100 m	0.286
Difficulty lifting/carrying weights over 5 kg	0.296
Difficulty pushing/pulling large objects	0.306
Difficulty climbing stairs	0.281
Difficulty stooping/kneeling/crouching	0.283
Difficulty getting up from chair	0.261
Difficulty reaching/extending arms above shoulder	0.199
Difficulty sitting two hours	0.193
Difficulty picking up a small coin from a table	0.139
Body mass index	0.010
Limited activities	0.327
Self-reported health fair or poor	0.284
Number of nights stayed in hospital (last 12 months)	0.125
Number of weeks receiving professional nursing care (last 12 months)	0.180
Number of weeks stayed in a nursing home	0.038
Visit to a medical doctor (last 12 months)	0.237
Ever treated for depression	0.084
Doctor told you had stroke	0.110
Doctor told you had arthritis	0.197
Doctor told you had high blood pressure	0.078
Doctor told you had chronic lung disease	0.108
Doctor told you had diabetes	0.092
Doctor told you had cancer	0.067
Bothered by pain in back, knees, hips, or other joints	0.176

References

BNB-Belgostat. 2013. Online Database on Economic Indicators for Belgium. http://www.nbb.be/belgostat.

Dellis, A., R. Desmet, A. Jousten, and S. Perelman. 2004. "Micro-Modeling of Retirement in Belgium." In *Social Security Programs and Retirement around the World: Micro-Estimation*, edited by J. Gruber and D. Wise, 41–98. Chicago: University of Chicago Press.

Desmet, R., A. Jousten, S. Perelman, and P. Pestieau. 2007. "Microsimulation of Social Security Reforms in Belgium." In *Social Security Programs and Retirement around the World: Fiscal Implications for Reform*, edited by J. Gruber and D. Wise, 43–82. Chicago: University of Chicago Press.

Eurostat. European Labour Force Surveys 1983–2011. Luxembourg: Eurostat. http://ec.europa.eu/eurostat/en/web/microdata/european-union-labour-force-survey.

INAMI-RIZIV. 2013. "Statistiques des indemnités." Brussels: INAMI-RIZIV.

Jousten, A., M. Lefebvre, and S. Perelman. 2012. "Disability in Belgium: There is More Than Meets the Eye." In *Social Security Programs and Retirement around the World: Historical Trends in Mortality and Health, Employment, and Disability Insurance Participation and Reforms*, edited by D. Wise, 251–76. Chicago: University of Chicago Press.

Jousten, A., M. Lefebvre, S. Perelman, and P. Pestieau. 2010. "The Effects of Early Retirement on Youth Unemployment: The Case of Belgium." In *Social Security Programs and Retirement around the World: The Relationship to Youth Employment*, edited by J. Gruber and D. Wise, 47–76. Chicago: University of Chicago Press.

ONP-RVP. 2013. "Statistiques annuelles des bénéficiaires de prestations." Brussels: ONP-RVP.

Pestieau, P., and J. P. Stijns. 1999. "Social Security and Retirement in Belgium." In *Social Security and Retirement around the World*, edited by J. Gruber and D. Wise, 37–71. Chicago: University of Chicago Press.

Poterba, J., S. Venti, and D. Wise. 2010. "The Asset Cost of Poor Health." NBER Working Paper no. 16389, Cambridge, MA.

Stock, J., and D. Wise. 1990. "Pensions, the Option Value of Work, and Retirement." *Econometrica* 58 (5): 1151–80.

Health, Disability Insurance, and Labor Force Exit of Older Workers in the Netherlands

Adriaan Kalwij, Klaas de Vos, and Arie Kapteyn

5.1 Introduction

During the last two decades, social security programs and pension schemes in many developed countries have been redesigned to create stronger incentives for continued work at older ages (Gruber and Wise 2004; Wise 2012). In the Netherlands, the country investigated in this chapter, such reforms are likely to have contributed to the increase in the labor force participation (LFP) of the age fifty-five to sixty-four population from less than 30 percent in the mid-1990s to 45 percent in 2007 (Euwals, de Mooij, and van Vuuren 2009; Kapteyn and de Vos 1999; Van Oorschot 2007). In a previous chapter for the International Social Security project (de Vos, Kapteyn, and Kalwij 2012), we found that disability insurance (DI) receipt appears unrelated to the general health of the population and that over the last two decades rela-

Adriaan Kalwij is an associate professor at the Utrecht University School of Economics. Klaas de Vos is a senior researcher in the quantitative analysis department at CentERdata, Tilburg University. Arie Kapteyn is professor of economics and founding director of the Dornsife Center for Economic and Social Research, University of Southern California, and a research associate of the National Bureau of Economic Research.

This paper uses data from SHARE; release 2.5.0 of waves 1 and 2 and release 1 of wave 4. The SHARE data collection has been primarily funded by the European Commission through the 5th Framework Program (project QLK6-CT-2001-00360 in the thematic program Quality of Life), through the 6th Framework Program (projects SHARE-I3, RII-CT-2006-062193, COMPARE, CIT5-CT-2005-028857, and SHARELIFE, CIT4-CT-2006-028812), and through the 7th Framework Program (SHARE-PREP, N° 211909, SHARE-LEAP, N° 227822 and SHARE M4, N° 261982). Additional funding is also gratefully acknowledged from the US National Institute on Aging (P01AG022481-06, U01 AG09740-13S2, P01 AG005842, P01 AG08291, P30 AG12815, R21 AG025169, Y1-AG-4553-01, IAG BSR06-11 and OGHA 04-064) and the German Ministry of Education and Research, as well as from various national sources (see www.share-project.org for a full list of funding institutions). For acknowledgments, sources of research support, and disclosure of the authors' material financial relationships, if any, please see http://www.nber.org/chapters/c13331.ack.

tively fewer older workers have exited the labor market through DI. Furthermore, we concluded that this reduction could in part be attributed to stricter DI eligibility rules. In this chapter, we take a closer look at this conclusion and use Dutch individual-level data to examine whether, conditional on health status, the exit probability from the labor force can be explained by the provisions of the DI program. In particular, and this has not been done in previous papers, we disentangle the effects of DI eligibility from DI generosity on the exit probability from the labor force. Disentangling these two effects is of major importance for policymakers; if their aim is to reduce the number of DI recipients, the former refers to stricter medical screening of individuals who apply for DI, while the latter refers to reducing DI benefits for those who qualify for DI.

Our main findings are (a) the probability of exiting the labor force appears to be affected by health shocks and not much by baseline health, (b) disability benefits (or generosity) have no discernible impact on the exit from employment, and (c) restricting access to the disability insurance scheme does affect labor force exit.

The chapter proceeds as follows. Section 5.2 describes the main trends in employment and DI participation and summarizes the main reforms in the DI program during the past four decades. Furthermore, it introduces the Dutch branch of the Survey of Health, Ageing and Retirement in Europe (SHARE)—to be called SHARE-NL from now on—and presents DI participation rates by year, gender, level of education, and health quintile. Section 5.3 describes the pathways to retirement and outlines the empirical framework for analyzing the impact of health, the inclusive option value of continued work, and socioeconomic variables on the probability of exiting the labor force. Section 5.4 presents the estimation results and section 5.5 discusses these results and their implications. Section 5.6 concludes.

5.2   Background

5.2.1   Overall Trends in DI Participation and Program Reforms

In our earlier paper (de Vos, Kapteyn, and Kalwij 2012) we discussed in detail the historical trends in DI participation and the successive attempts to reform the legislation with the aim of reversing the trend of continuously increasing numbers of DI beneficiaries. A series of reforms in the DI legislation started in the early 1980s, aimed both at decreasing DI generosity by lowering the replacement rate and at limiting the access to the program by imposing stricter criteria for entry and stricter reevaluation rules. However, only the most recent overhaul of the DI legislation culminating in the introduction of a new DI program replacing the old program in 2006 appears to have succeeded in reversing the upward trend in the DI participation rates

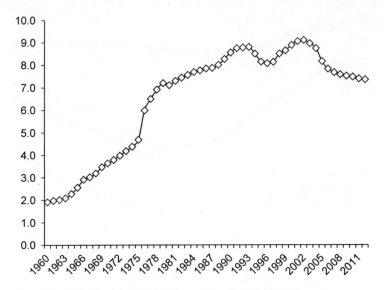

Fig. 5.1   DI recipients as percent of population ages fifteen to sixty-five
Source: Statistics Netherlands (CBS; statline:cbs:nl).

(figure 5.1). In fact by 2009, as shown by Burkhauser and Daly (2011), the number of DI beneficiaries per worker in the Netherlands, which for a long time was among the highest in the developing world, decreased below the comparable figure for the United States.

The main differences between the system in place until the early 1990s and the current system can be summarized as follows. Earlier, entry into DI happened virtually automatically after one year of illness, during which one received up to 100 percent of the last wage as a sickness benefit. When partially disabled, access to DI was equally easy. Once on DI, one was likely to stay on until the retirement age of sixty-five. Currently, entry into DI happens only after strict screening after two years of illness. During this illness period one receives 70 percent of the last wage, paid for by the employer, and there is an elaborate reintegration program to stimulate the return to work. Access to DI (at a replacement rate of 75 percent, which is slightly higher than the previous 70 percent) until the pension age is only granted to persons who are deemed fully and permanently disabled. For the partially and temporary disabled different rules apply, with incentives that maximize the probability of reentry into the labor force.

The trend emerging from figure 5.1 may be related to figure 5.2 showing the employment rates of males and females in two age groups from 1970 onward. It is particularly striking that employment of both women and men age fifty-five to sixty-five has increased substantially since the mid-nineties.

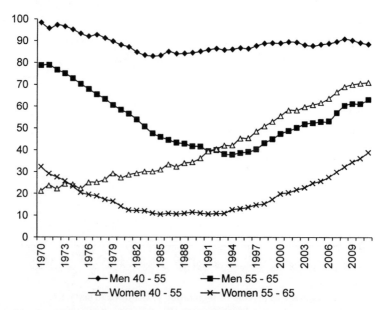

Fig. 5.2   Employment by age and gender (1970–2011)
Source: Statistics Netherlands (CBS; statline:cbs:nl).

The increasing trend for women age forty to fifty-five is likely to largely reflect a cohort effect, as female labor force participation has grown dramatically since the 1970s.

During the last decade, the increase in the employment rates of the older age groups is accompanied by a decrease in the DI participation.[1] The trend is strongest among men, as shown in figures 5.3 and 5.4. Among women, showing large increases in LFP, the decrease in DI recipiency is less noticeable (figures 5.5 and 5.6).

5.2.2   Disability Insurance (DI) Participation by Level of Education and Gender

Our individual-level data are drawn from the first, second, and fourth waves of the Survey of Health, Ageing and Retirement in Europe (SHARE), a harmonized, multidisciplinary and representative cross-national panel survey covering the population age fifty and older in twenty European countries. We use the Dutch branch of SHARE (SHARE-NL). The Dutch waves were conducted in 2004, 2007, and 2011. The SHARE survey includes information on socioeconomic status (e.g., employment, income, and education), health (e.g., self-reported subjective health and doctor diagnosed conditions,

1. More detailed employment rates by age and gender are added in figures 5A.1 and 5A.2 in the appendix.

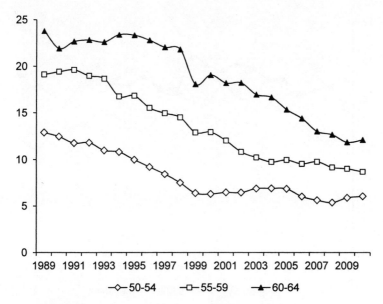

Fig. 5.3   DI recipients as percent of total population by age (men)
Source: Statistics Netherlands, Income Panel Survey (IPO).

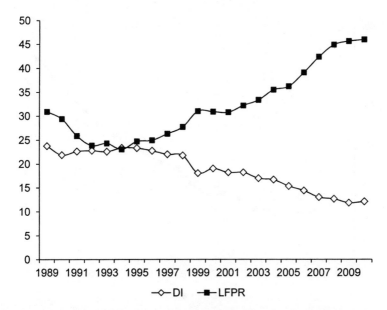

Fig. 5.4   Disability and labor force participation among men ages sixty to sixty-four
Source: Statistics Netherlands, Income Panel Survey (IPO).

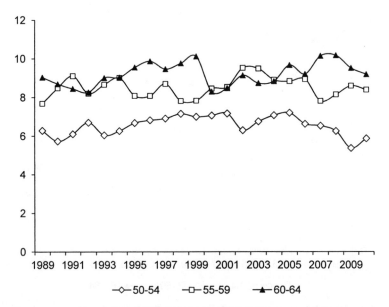

Fig. 5.5   DI recipients as percent of total population by age (women)
Source: Statistics Netherlands, Income Panel Survey (IPO).

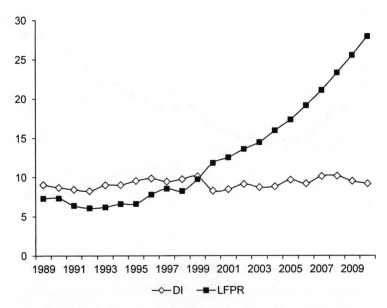

Fig. 5.6   Disability and labor force participation among women ages sixty to sixty-four
Source: Statistics Netherlands, Income Panel Survey (IPO).

Table 5.1   **Number of observations, level of education, and labor market status by age and gender**

	Men				Women			
	2004	2007	2011	All years	2004	2007	2011	All years
Age category No. obs.								
50–54	249	199	132	580	300	274	215	789
55–59	279	238	184	701	337	296	250	883
60–64	241	214	263	718	241	241	316	798
50–64	769	651	579	1,999	878	811	781	2,470
Level of education (%)								
ISCED 1–2	42	37	37	37	58	51	41	49
ISCED 3	29	29	29	30	21	24	30	25
ISCED 4–5	29	34	34	33	21	25	29	25
All	100	100	100	100	100	100	100	100
Labor force status (%)								
Retired	19	25	19	21	47	42	34	41
Employed	64	63	67	65	40	46	53	47
Unemployed	4	2	4	4	3	2	3	2
Disabled	13	10	10	11	10	10	10	10
All	100	100	100	100	100	100	100	100

Notes: No. obs. = number of observations. The percentages are based on weighted frequencies.

physical and cognitive functioning, and behavioral risks), and psychological conditions (e.g., mental health, well-being, and life satisfaction).

For our analysis we select individuals age fifty to sixty-four and, after removing observations with missing information on key variables (about 25 percent), our final sample consists of 1,263 men (1,999 year observations) and 1,509 women (2,470 year observations). Although SHARE-NL aims to be a representative sample for the age fifty and older Dutch population, table 5.1 shows that it includes, for instance, relatively few individuals age fifty to fifty-four. A comparison with official statistics (Statistics Netherlands; statline.cbs.nl) reveals that this group is indeed relatively underrepresented in our sample and in particular in 2011. For instance, the share of men age fifty to fifty-four (as a percentage of men age fifty to sixty-four) in 2011 is about 35 percent in the population and only 23 percent in our sample (details are in table 5A.1 of the appendix). This underrepresentation is mainly due to a relatively low response among individuals who turned fifty in between survey years and who, having reached the SHARE-eligibility age, have been invited to participate in the survey for the first time. This lack of representativeness appears to be mainly age related. To obtain population estimates we have constructed weights based on the population age-gender distribution provided by Statistics Netherlands (appendix table 5A.1). All descriptive tables are based on weighted frequencies.

The level of education is defined according to the 1997 International Stan-

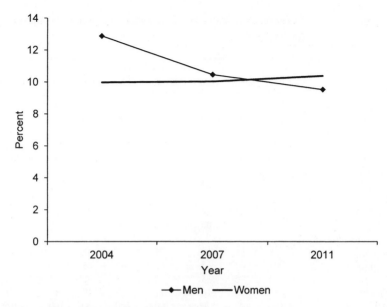

Fig. 5.7   DI participation by year and gender

dard Classification of Education ([ISCED]; MEA 2011). The ISCED 1–2 will be referred to as a low level of education, ISCED 3 as medium level of education, and ISCED 4–5 as a high level of education. Labor force status is self-assessed by the respondents and we distinguish the states "retired" (including nonparticipation), "employed" (including self-employed), "unemployed," and "long-term sick or disabled." We refer to this latter state as DI (disability insurance) participation.

We have constructed a health index based on self-assessed health limitations that will be explained in more detail in the next section. Important here is that based on this health index we determine if an individual is in poor health (lowest health quintile), in excellent health (highest health quintile), or in between.

Table 5.1 shows some stylized facts about the Netherlands, such as higher levels of education for men than for women, although women in the younger cohorts are closing this gap. The table shows relatively minor differences between the respective waves in labor force participation of men. The steep decrease in the percentage of retired women reflects a cohort effect and is paralleled by increasing labor force participation. For men, we observe a slight decrease in DI participation over the years (see also figure 5.7) which, arguably, may be due to the DI reforms in recent years. For women, no appreciable change in DI-participation is observed, which may in part be due to the strong increase in female employment. This may have resulted in an increase in DI participation in absolute numbers that has offset the rela-

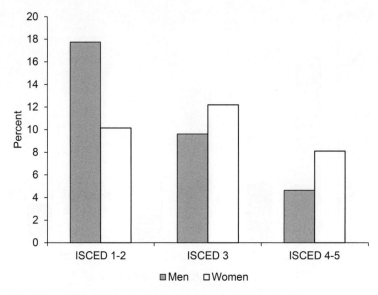

Fig. 5.8   DI participation by level of education and gender (all waves)

tive reduction (among labor force participants) in DI-recipiency due to DI reforms. Figure 5.8 shows a strong educational gradient in DI-participation for men, but less so for women. Figures 5.9 and 5.10 basically show the same patterns by year.

Tables 5.2 and 5.3 show employment rates for, respectively, men and women by year, age, education, and health quintile. Table 5.2, for men, shows an increasing employment rate with level of education and with health quintile for virtually all age categories and years. In line with figure 5.2, the employment rates of men age sixty to sixty-four have increased over time and for all levels of education. Moreover, the table shows that there has been a strong increase in the employment rate among the lowest health quintile for men, which may be due to stricter screening for DI eligibility. Indeed, the gradient in employment by health quintile (as summarized by the ratio of employment rates of the highest and lowest health quintiles) has fallen quite substantially between 2004 and 2011 for all age groups. For women (table 5.3) very similar patterns are observed, albeit at lower levels of employment.

5.2.3   Disability Insurance (DI) Participation by Health Status

As mentioned above, we have constructed a health index of which details will be explained in the next section. Table 5.4 and figures 5.11 and 5.12 show that DI participation is highest among individuals in bad health. This holds for both men and women (43 percent and 32 percent, respectively). Conversely, for those in excellent health, DI participation is only 1 percent. Within a health category, except for the highest, DI participation is higher

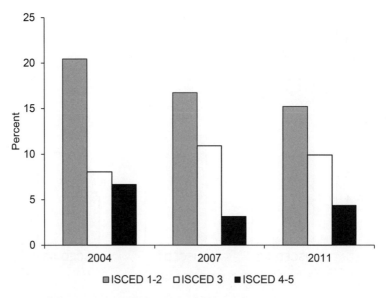

Fig. 5.9 Male DI participation by level of education and year

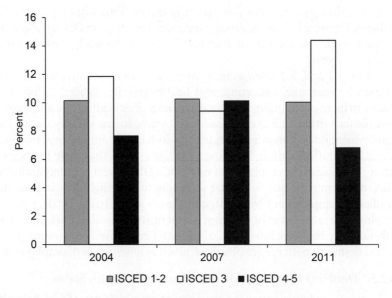

Fig. 5.10 Female DI participation by level of education and year

Table 5.2   Male employment rate by year, age, education, and health quintile

	2004	2007	2011		2004	2007	2011
				Age 50–54			
ISCED 1–2	0.76	0.76	0.84	Health quint 1 (lowest)	0.48	0.46	0.75
ISCED 3	0.86	0.87	0.88	Health quint 2	0.86	0.85	0.88
ISCED 4–5	0.92	0.96	0.92	Health quint 3	0.79	0.91	0.96
				Health quint 4	0.95	0.98	0.85
				Health quint 5 (highest)	0.95	0.94	0.92
				Age 55–59			
ISCED 1–2	0.63	0.63	0.72	Health quint 1 (lowest)	0.32	0.47	0.45
ISCED 3	0.81	0.75	0.72	Health quint 2	0.71	0.53	0.75
ISCED 4–5	0.86	0.78	0.89	Health quint 3	0.78	0.72	0.85
				Health quint 4	0.87	0.82	0.86
				Health quint 5 (highest)	0.85	0.87	0.91
				Age 60–64			
ISCED 1–2	0.18	0.18	0.27	Health quint 1 (lowest)	0.12	0.14	0.21
ISCED 3	0.28	0.30	0.39	Health quint 2	0.22	0.25	0.39
ISCED 4–5	0.35	0.29	0.45	Health quint 3	0.24	0.20	0.46
				Health quint 4	0.30	0.33	0.36
				Health quint 5 (highest)	0.31	0.29	0.40

Table 5.3   Female employment rate by year, age, education, and health quintile

	2004	2007	2011		2004	2007	2011
				Age 50–54			
ISCED 1–2	0.43	0.58	0.64	Health quint 1 (lowest)	0.26	0.41	0.47
ISCED 3	0.56	0.74	0.71	Health quint 2	0.60	0.66	0.67
ISCED 4–5	0.80	0.83	0.83	Health quint 3	0.57	0.68	0.85
				Health quint 4	0.65	0.83	0.76
				Health quint 5 (highest)	0.67	0.83	0.93
				Age 55–59			
ISCED 1–2	0.31	0.32	0.47	Health quint 1 (lowest)	0.20	0.15	0.34
ISCED 3	0.49	0.46	0.63	Health quint 2	0.45	0.32	0.63
ISCED 4–5	0.69	0.65	0.77	Health quint 3	0.57	0.53	0.83
				Health quint 4	0.50	0.63	0.74
				Health quint 5 (highest)	0.58	0.60	0.61
				Age 60–64			
ISCED 1–2	0.10	0.13	0.16	Health quint 1 (lowest)	0.06	0.08	0.16
ISCED 3	0.14	0.26	0.28	Health quint 2	0.22	0.26	0.23
ISCED 4–5	0.28	0.19	0.21	Health quint 3	0.09	0.11	0.17
				Health quint 4	0.09	0.25	0.26
				Health quint 5 (highest)	0.23	0.17	0.19

Table 5.4   **DI participation by level of education and health quintile**

| Cells: (%) | Health quintile | | | | | |
	(lowest) 1	2	3	4	(highest) 5	All
Men						
ISCED 1–2	45	18	14	6	1	18
ISCED 3	46	10	7	2	1	10
ISCED 4–5	28	10	4	0	1	5
All levels	43	14	9	3	1	11
Women						
ISCED 1–2	29	7	3	3	1	10
ISCED 3	41	4	3	2	1	12
ISCED 4–5	27	11	5	2	1	8
All levels	32	7	3	2	1	10

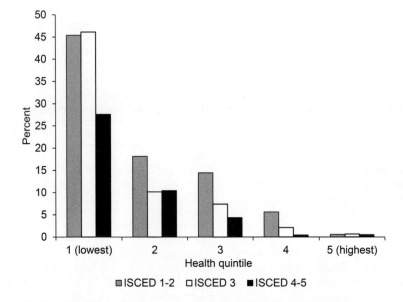

Fig. 5.11   Male DI participation by level of education and health quintile

among low-educated than high-educated men. For women, this gradient is less apparent and this may in part be explained by differences in female employment rates across education groups and types of occupations.

5.3   Empirical Approach

As discussed in the introduction, we are interested in whether, conditional on health status, there are differences in labor force exit rates that can be

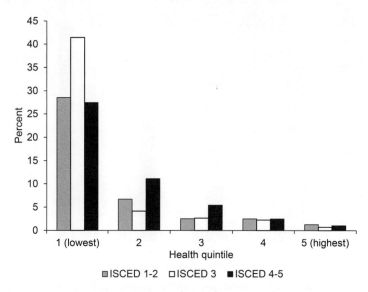

Fig. 5.12   Female DI participation by level of education and health quintile

explained by the provisions of the disability insurance (DI) program. More-over, we wish to disentangle the effects of DI eligibility from DI generosity on exit from the labor force. For this purpose we estimate a transition model in which the probability of exiting the labor force depends, among other fac-tors, on their health and the option value of continued work. An exit from the labor force can be into retirement, into unemployment, or into DI. We do not observe whether a worker is eligible for each of these exit states but use information that enables us to calculate the probability that a worker is eligible for a certain exit route. If a worker is eligible for a specific exit route, the option value of continued work will affect a worker's choice to actu-ally take this exit route or another exit route, and withdraw from the labor force. In short, the three main ingredients of the empirical model are (a) the eligibility probabilities of the exit routes, (b) the health status of the worker, and (c) the option values of the different exit routes. These ingredients are, in the same order, discussed in the following subsections. Before doing so, we first discuss the pathways to retirement.

5.3.1   Pathways to Retirement

The Netherlands has a statutory retirement age of sixty-five, at which most labor contracts are terminated and unemployment, disability, and assistance benefits are terminated as well.[2] After age sixty-five all individuals receive

2. Starting in 2013, the statutory retirement is to be increased gradually. The legislation underlying this increase was introduced rather suddenly in 2012. It is not taken into account in the calculation of the option values in section 5.3.4.

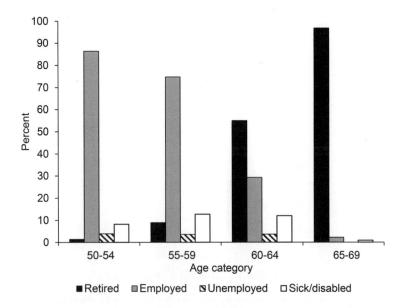

■ Retired   ■ Employed   ◨ Unemployed   □ Sick/disabled

Fig. 5.13   Male labor force status by age category

a public pension benefit (independent of past earnings) and, in most cases, an occupational pension that depends on earnings history. Individuals can be (self-) employed after age sixty-four, next to receiving a pension income. Labor force participation after age sixty-five is still very low, as illustrated by figures 5.13 and 5.14, which show labor force status by age and gender. After age sixty-five, about 97 percent of individuals are retired.

The dominant feature of the figures is that for both men and women there is a steep decline in the employment rate and a concomitant increase in the retirement rate with age. The DI participation increases from about 8 percent among men age fifty to fifty-four to 12 percent among men age sixty to sixty-four. Women show similar increases, but at somewhat later ages. As also discussed in the previous section, figures 5.15 and 5.16 show that there has been a decrease in DI participation for men over the survey years and that for women the dominant feature is an increase in employment and, consequently, a decrease in the share of women in retirement (which includes nonparticipation).

To gain a better understanding of the observed patterns in figures 5.13–5.16, we turn our attention to pathways to retirement. We select a subsample consisting of workers and examine their labor force status in the next wave. Thus we restrict the sample to employed individuals (including self-employed) in 2004 and 2007 and report on their labor force status in, respectively, 2007 and 2011. This subsample contains 468 observations for

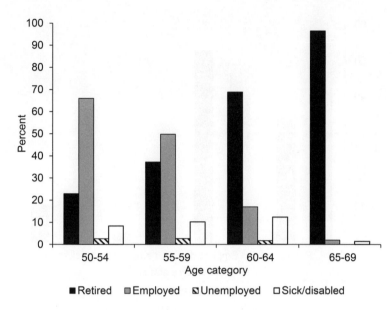

Fig. 5.14   Female labor force status by age category

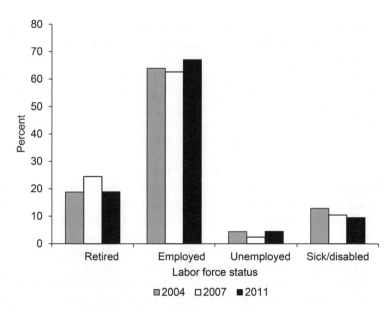

Fig. 5.15   Male labor force status over time (ages fifty to sixty-four)

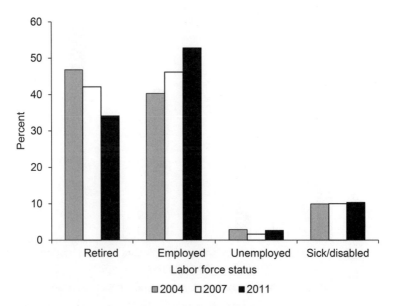

Fig. 5.16   Female labor force status over time (ages fifty to sixty-four)

men and 398 for women. The number of observations falls sharply with age: we observe eighty-seven workers (men and women combined) who are fifty years old and only nine workers who are sixty-four years old. Figures 5.17 and 5.18 show different pathways out of employment. One observes that the retirement route gains in prominence with age. Between two waves, about 2 percent of working men experience a transition into unemployment. For women, this is 4 percent. About 2 percent of working men and 3 percent of working women are on DI benefits in the next wave.

5.3.2   The Likelihood of Different Pathways

The eligibility probabilities of the exit routes are determined using a stock estimator based on labor force states disaggregated by year, gender, and level of education. As will be explained in section 5.3.4, these probabilities are needed to construct the inclusive option value of remaining in employment (see introduction, this volume). Table 5.5 reports these estimated probabilities that add up to 1 across the three different exit routes. For instance, a woman with a medium level of education (ISCED 3) in 2007 is assumed to have a probability of 0.895 to be eligible for the retirement route, a probability of 0.011 to be eligible for the unemployment route, and a probability of 0.094 to be eligible for disability insurance. Loosely interpreted, in this case she believes that, if she would want to exit the labor force, it is least likely she will be eligible for unemployment benefits (1.1 percent), slightly more

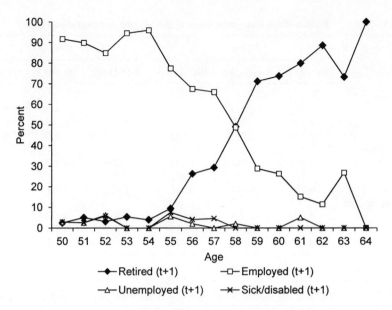

Fig. 5.17 Pathways out of the labor force for men (the percentages of male workers at a given age who are retired, employed, unemployed, or sick/disabled in the next wave)

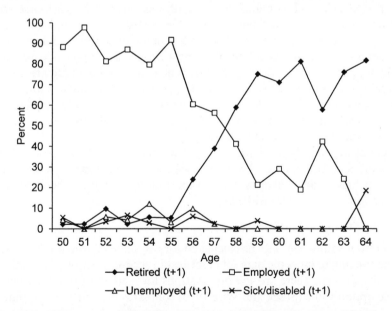

Fig. 5.18 Pathways out of the labor force for women (the percentages of female workers at a given age who are retired, employed, unemployed, or sick/disabled in the next wave)

Table 5.5   Estimated exit route probabilities by gender, year, and level of education

	Men			Women		
	ISCED 1–2	ISCED 3	ISCED 4–5	ISCED 1–2	ISCED 3	ISCED 4–5
Retirement						
2004	0.738	0.873	0.911	0.873	0.848	0.890
2007	0.792	0.865	0.964	0.877	0.895	0.884
2011	0.797	0.857	0.915	0.877	0.830	0.898
Unemployment						
2004	0.058	0.046	0.022	0.026	0.034	0.034
2007	0.041	0.026	0.004	0.021	0.011	0.014
2011	0.050	0.044	0.041	0.022	0.026	0.034
Disability benefits						
2004	0.204	0.080	0.067	0.101	0.118	0.077
2007	0.167	0.109	0.032	0.103	0.094	0.101
2011	0.152	0.099	0.044	0.100	0.144	0.068

likely she is eligible for disability insurance benefits (9.4 percent), and most likely she is eligible for retirement (89.5 percent).

5.3.3   Health Index and Health Quintiles

The SHARE-NL contains many health measures such as self-assessed limitations of activities of daily living, self-reported health status, and objectively measured grip strength. Health has many dimensions and we construct a measure of general health using a principal components analysis. The weights corresponding to the first principal component are presented in table 5.6. Based on these weights we construct a health index and next transform it into percentiles, where 0 is worst health and 100 is best health. Figures 5.19 and 5.20 show some stylized facts that may provide face validity for the thus constructed general health measure. First, overall, health declines with age. Second, the health of women is, on average, worse than that of men. And third, the health of low-educated individuals is worse than that of highly educated individuals of the same age, although there appears to be some convergence with age.

5.3.4   Option Value Calculations

Option values can only be calculated for respondents who are working. The starting point is the data set described in section 5.3.1 of a subsample of 824 workers; there are 450 observations for men and 374 for women.[3] The option value (Stock and Wise 1990) compares the value of continued

3. We have trimmed the data set by excluding forty-two observations corresponding to the top and bottom 2.5 percent of the option value distribution, to avoid our results being affected by extreme values.

Table 5.6   **The first principal component from a principal component analysis of health-related variables**

Explanatory variables	1st component
Difficulties walking several blocks	0.2764
Difficulties to lift or carry something	0.3030
Difficulties to push or pull something	0.2917
Difficulties with an ADL (activity of daily living)	0.2986
Difficulties climbing stairs	0.3105
Difficulties to stoop, kneel, or crouch	0.3093
Difficulties getting up from chair	0.2852
Self-reported health(1 = fair/poor)	0.2862
Difficulties to reach/extend arms up	0.2120
Ever experienced arthritis	0.1693
Difficulties sitting two hours	0.2085
Difficulties picking up a coin	0.1470
Back problems	0.1871
Ever experienced heart problems	0.1341
Hospital stay	0.1336
Home care	0.1276
Doctor visit	0.1063
Ever experienced psychological problems	0.0627
Ever experienced stroke	0.1161
Ever experienced high blood pressure	0.0853
Ever experienced lung disease	0.0959
Ever experienced diabetes	0.0911
BMI	0.0949
Nursing home stay	0.1077
Ever experienced cancer	0.0483

working to the value of exiting the labor market. The value function at time 0 (the current age) of exiting the labor market at a particular future age, R, via route i is:

$$(1) \quad V_i(R) = \sum_{t=0}^{R} \frac{1}{(1+d)^t} \pi_t (wage_t)^\gamma + \sum_{t=R+1}^{T} \frac{1}{(1+d)^t} \pi_t (k \times ben_{it}(R))^\gamma,$$

where d is the discount rate, π_t is the probability of surviving until age t,[4] $wage_t$ is the wage when working in year t and $ben_{it}(R)$ is the benefit received in year t when retiring at age R via route i. We choose the common parameter values $d = 0.03$, $\gamma = 0.75$ and $k = 1.5$. Furthermore, we restrict retirement ages to between fifty and sixty-nine, assume future real earnings to be constant, and ignore spouse and survival benefits. Because detailed information on pension accumulation and entitlements is not available, the calculations are based on stylized parameters approximating the average of the entitle-

4. Note that age is defined here in years from the present; for instance, if someone is currently fifty-five, then $t = 3$ refers to age fifty-eight.

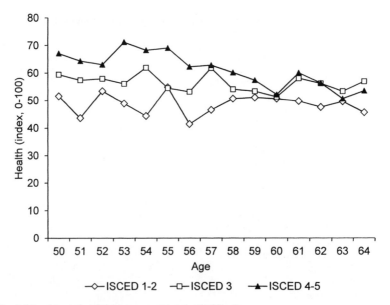

Fig. 5.19   Men's health by age and level of education

ments in the most common pension funds. Benefits by retirement exit route are calculated assuming that occupational pensions are based on final earnings, with an actuarially fair accrual for late take-up.[5] Moreover, we assume that persons born before 1950 may benefit from a more generous (early) retirement plan than later cohorts.

The option values (OVs) at any given age are defined as the value of continued work (until the age when the maximum value is reached, that is, the value of R that maximizes [1]) minus the value of exiting the labor market now into a particular state and staying in that state until age sixty-five and being retired afterward. The higher the OV value, the higher is the payoff of remaining employed and not exiting the labor force. The OVs for the exit states (early) retirement, unemployment, and disability insurance are shown in figure 5.21. The OV inclusive is an average of the OVs corresponding to each of the exit routes, weighted with the exit route probabilities obtained from the stock estimator as shown in table 5.5. Thus, the OVs of each exit state are weighted with the eligibility probability for that state.

This figure shows, first, that it is always beneficial to continue working (all OVs are positive). All exits (before the maximum age of seventy) result in loss

5. Although nowadays most pension funds use average lifetime earnings as the basis for pension benefits calculations, most SHARE-NL respondents have built up their pension in a final earnings system.

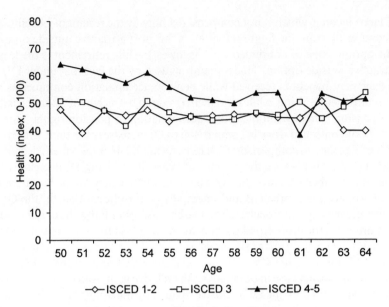

Fig. 5.20   Women's health by age and level of education

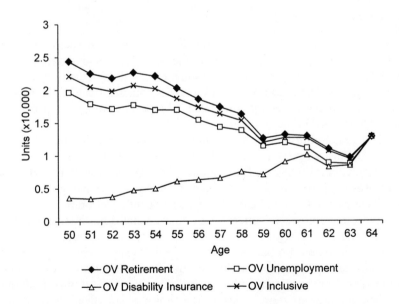

Fig. 5.21   Average option values for continuing employment for each exit route by age

of labor income, which is not compensated fully by the receipt of benefits. A second result from the figure is that DI is the most attractive outside option (the option value of continued work is lowest), while retirement is the least attractive outside option. This is mainly caused by the fact that under DI, a replacement benefit is received while pension accumulation continues as if one continued working, while retirement results in the receipt of an actuarially fair pension benefit without further accumulation of pension rights. Third, the OV of continued work in comparison to DI increases over time, while the OVs of working in comparison with retirement and unemployment decrease with age. This is because the number of years of receiving DI decreases, as does the number of years during which no further pension accumulation occurs under the retirement and unemployment options. Fourth, the OVs converge when age approaches sixty-five because, essentially, the closer one is to retirement, the more equal the benefits received via the various exit routes will be. When exiting at age sixty-five or later, all exit routes are the same.

In addition to using OV inclusive (i.e., the absolute gain from delaying retirement), we also use in our analysis the relative gain from delaying retirement as measured by the OV inclusive divided by the utility of exiting at the current age (variable relative gain in OV).

5.4   Results

The impact of health, the inclusive option value, and socioeconomic variables on the probability of exiting the labor force is analyzed using a probit model. The empirical specification includes all ingredients discussed in section 5.3. The data used in this analysis consist of the 824 men and women (see previous section) and table 5.7 reports summary statistics for all variables used in the analysis.

The regression results of eight different specifications in table 5.8 show that the inclusive option value (OV inclusive) has a negative and statistically significant effect on the exit from employment. An increase of 10,000 units decreases the probability of retirement by about 12 percentage points in specification (8). Current health has no significant effect on the exit probability from employment. Interestingly, marital status has a large and significant effect. Compared to a single person, a married individual has about a 14 percent higher probability of exiting employment. This may suggest that joint leisure time plays an important role in the retirement decision, for instance, for traveling together or spending time with (grand) children.

These findings are quite robust to the choice of specification-age dummies versus linear age, including health quintiles versus a continuous health index, including or excluding other covariates.

Looking at the effect of OV inclusive by health quintile (table 5.9), the effect of OV inclusive is only consistently significant across specifications for those in good health. The fourth specification also shows a significant effect

Table 5.7   **Summary statistics**

Variable (N = 824)	Mean	Standard deviation
Not employed next wave	0.307	0.462
Observed in wave 1 (2004)	0.563	0.496
Observed in wave 2 (2007)	0.437	0.496
Inclusive option value (OV)/10,000	1.801	0.868
Relative gain in OV	0.868	0.436
Health index (0–1)	0.590	0.254
Age (in years)	55.074	3.415
Gender (1 = male, 2 = female)	1.454	0.498
Married (1 = married or cohabitating, 0 otherwise)	0.864	0.343
LN(household income)	10.757	0.657
LN(earnings)	10.227	0.674
Low level of education (ISCED 1–2)	0.328	0.470
Medium level of education (ISCED 3)	0.284	0.451
High level of education (ISCED 4–5)	0.388	0.488

for individuals with worst health, but obviously this effect is not robust with respect to the different specifications. That OV is most important for those in good health is intuitive, as it implies that financial incentives have the largest effect for those in better health. Although financial incentives are likely to also matter for individuals in less than good health, these individuals may have less opportunity to continue work if their health limits the kind or amount of work they can do.

Instead of OV inclusive (i.e., the absolute gain from delaying retirement), table 5.10 presents specifications that include the relative gain from delaying retirement as measured by the OV inclusive divided by the utility of exiting at the current age. The table shows that without controlling for covariates the coefficients are again highly significant, but they are not robust to controlling for covariates.

To further examine the explanation that OV matters more when health is better, we include an interaction effect between OV and health using specifications (5)–(8), that is, with the continuous health index. The main results of this exercise are in table 5.11 and do not show significant interaction effects. Comparing this to the results in table 5.9, therefore, suggests that the interaction between OV and health is mainly concentrated at the group with the very best health.

When examining the effect of OV inclusive on the exit probability by levels of education, the largest effect is found for highly educated individuals (table 5.12). However, this finding may not be robust as it only holds for specifications (1)–(3) and not for specification (4), which includes age dummies and all covariates.

Finally, the results in tables 5.13 and 5.14 are based on the relative gain measure and yield the same conclusions as when using the OV inclusive

Table 5.8   Estimation results for eight specifications

Specification Variables	(1) m.e.	(1) s.e.	(2) m.e.	(2) s.e.	(3) m.e.	(3) s.e.	(4) m.e.	(4) s.e.	(5) m.e.	(5) s.e.	(6) m.e.	(6) s.e.	(7) m.e.	(7) s.e.	(8) m.e.	(8) s.e.
OV																
Inclusive/10,000	-0.089	0.023	-0.082	0.023	-0.147	0.047	-0.119	0.049	-0.089	0.023	-0.081	0.023	-0.148	0.047	-0.119	0.049
A std. dev. change in OV	-0.068		-0.063		-0.113		-0.091		-0.068		-0.062		-0.114		-0.091	
Health quint 2 (2nd lowest)	0.046	0.073	0.066	0.076	0.053	0.074	0.072	0.078								
Health quint 3	0.008	0.067	0.046	0.072	0.015	0.068	0.052	0.073								
Health quint 4	0.026	0.067	0.042	0.069	0.023	0.067	0.035	0.069								
Health quint 5 (highest)	0.045	0.069	0.081	0.072	0.053	0.069	0.088	0.073								
Health index (range 0–1)									0.021	0.067	0.045	0.068	0.021	0.068	0.043	0.069
Age	0.067	0.006			0.060	0.008			0.067	0.006			0.021	0.068		
Age dummies			Included				Included				Included				Included	
Female					0.041	0.040	0.039	0.040					0.042	0.040	0.041	0.040
Married					0.134	0.042	0.145	0.041					0.132	0.042	0.141	0.042
LN(household income)					-0.047	0.029	-0.054	0.029					-0.046	0.029	-0.051	0.029
LN(earnings)					0.110	0.055	0.086	0.056					0.112	0.055	0.088	0.056
ISCED level 3					-0.079	0.041	-0.084	0.041					-0.077	0.041	-0.083	0.041
ISCED level 4 or 5					-0.014	0.045	-0.013	0.046					-0.015	0.045	-0.018	0.046
n	824		824		824		824		824		824		824		824	
Joint significance health quintiles (p-values)	0.916		0.808		0.873		0.707									

Note: Marginal effects (m.e.) from probit models for the probability of leaving employment.

Table 5.9   **Estimation results for four specifications; option value interacted with health**

Specification	n	Mean exit rate	Mean OV	Std. dev. OV	m. e. (1)	(2)	(3)	(4)
OV: 1st quintile (worst health)	73	0.274	1.475	0.760	−0.148 (0.084) [−0.112]	−0.174 (0.104) [−0.132]	−0.333 (0.193) [−0.253]	−0.545 (0.264) [−0.414]
OV: 2nd quintile	138	0.370	1.521	0.793	−0.122 (0.068) [−0.097]	−0.151 (0.087) [−0.120]	−0.095 (0.145) [−0.076]	−0.018 (0.222) [−0.014]
OV: 3rd quintile	183	0.279	1.829	0.802	−0.027 (0.045) [−0.021]	0.002 (0.050) [0.002]	−0.072 (0.098) [−0.058]	−0.091 (0.109) [−0.073]
OV: 4th quintile	223	0.309	1.881	0.833	−0.020 (0.047) [−0.017]	0.009 (0.058) [0.008]	−0.068 (0.090) [−0.056]	−0.039 (0.111) [−0.033]
OV: 5th quintile (best health)	207	0.300	1.993	0.969	−0.150 (0.039) [−0.146]	−0.149 (0.040) [−0.145]	−0.237 (0.088) [−0.230]	−0.216 (0.089) [−0.209]

Note: Standard errors are in parentheses and the marginal effects for a one standard deviation change in the inclusive option value (OV) are in brackets. The models estimated include as explanatory variables age, gender, marital status, education, income, and earnings (as in table 5.8).

Table 5.10   **Estimation results for four specifications, OV specified as a relative gain (OV inclusive divided by the utility of exiting now)**

Specification Variables	m. e. (1)	(2)	(3)	(4)
Relative gain in OV	−0.148 (0.055)	−0.140 (0.055)	−0.071 (0.071)	−0.060 (0.072)
Linear age	X		X	
Age dummies		X		X
Health quintiles	X	X	X	X
Other covariates			X	X
No. of observations	824	824	824	824
Mean exit rate	0.307	0.307	0.307	0.307
Mean gain in OV	0.868	0.868	0.868	0.868
Std. dev. gain in OV	0.436	0.436	0.436	0.436

Note: Standard errors are in parentheses.

Table 5.11   **Estimation results; OV specified as a relative gain interacted with health**

Specification	n	Mean exit rate	Mean gain	Std. dev. gain	(1)	(2)	(3)	(4)
Relative gain in OV: 1st quintile (worst health)	73	0.274	0.728	0.370	−0.419 (0.220)	−0.640 (0.289)	−0.439 (0.284)	−0.957 (0.435)
Relative gain in OV: 2nd quintile	138	0.370	0.747	0.425	−0.314 (0.149)	−0.439 (0.196)	−0.220 (0.187)	−0.292 (0.274)
Relative gain in OV: 3rd quintile	183	0.279	0.857	0.380	0.210 (0.132)	0.223 (0.147)	0.282 (0.163)	0.234 (0.180)
Relative gain in OV: 4th quintile	223	0.309	0.920	0.448	0.031 (0.109)	0.104 (0.129)	0.051 (0.132)	0.124 (0.156)
Relative gain in OV: 5th quintile (best health)	207	0.300	0.951	0.472	−0.317 (0.093)	−0.298 (0.095)	−0.226 (0.139)	−0.174 (0.140)

The header "m. e." spans columns (1)–(4).

Note: Standard errors are in parentheses. The models estimated include as explanatory variables age, gender, marital status, education, income, and earnings (as in table 5.8).

Table 5.12   **Estimation results; OV inclusive interacted with continuous health index**

Specification	(5)	(6)	(7)	(8)
OV inclusive	−0.088 (0.023) [−0.077]	−0.080 (0.023) [−0.070]	−0.147 (0.047) [−0.128]	−0.118 (0.049) [−0.102]
OV inclusive*health index	−0.024 (0.086)	−0.028 (0.086)	−0.016 (0.088)	−0.017 (0.087)
Health index	0.015 (0.071)	0.038 (0.071)	0.017 (0.072)	0.039 (0.072)
Linear age	X		X	
Age dummies		X		X
Other covariates			X	X
Number of observations	824	824	824	824
Mean exit rate	0.307	0.307	0.307	0.307
Mean OV inclusive	1.801	1.801	1.801	1.801
Std. dev. OV inclusive	0.868	0.868	0.868	0.868

The header "m. e." spans columns (5)–(8).

Note: Standard errors are in parentheses and the marginal effects for a one standard deviation change in the inclusive option value (OV) are in brackets.

Table 5.13   **Estimation results; OV interacted with education**

Specification	n	Mean exit rate	Mean OV	Std. dev. OV	m. e. (1)	(2)	(3)	(4)
OV inclusive: ISCED 1–2	253	0.352	1.338	0.633	−0.075 (0.055) [−0.047]	−0.073 (0.056) [−0.046]	−0.129 (0.124) [−0.081]	−0.135 (0.128) [−0.085]
OV inclusive: ISCED 3	227	0.248	1.813	0.795	−0.045 (0.040) [−0.036]	−0.045 (0.049) [−0.036]	−0.165 (0.093) [−0.131]	−0.122 (0.112) [−0.097]
OV inclusive: ISCED 4–5	299	0.313	2.184	0.903	−0.114 (0.036) [−0.103]	−0.132 (0.047) [−0.119]	−0.145 (0.063) [−0.131]	−0.101 (0.080) [−0.091]

Note: Standard errors are in parentheses and the marginal effects for a one standard deviation change in the inclusive option value (OV) are in brackets. The models estimated include as explanatory variables age, gender, marital status, education, income, and earnings (as in table 5.8).

Table 5.14   **Estimation results; relative gain interacted with education**

Specification	n	Mean exit rate	Mean gain	Std. dev. gain	m. e. (1)	(2)	(3)	(4)
Relative gain in OV: ISCED 1–2	270	0.352	0.705	0.336	−0.216 (0.121)	−0.230 (0.124)	−0.280 (0.189)	−0.329 (0.195)
Relative gain in OV: ISCED 3	234	0.248	0.919	0.422	0.012 (0.097)	0.005 (0.115)	0.031 (0.142)	0.021 (0.163)
Relative gain in OV: ISCED 4–5	320	0.313	0.967	0.482	−0.147 (0.089)	−0.127 (0.109)	−0.067 (0.097)	−0.025 (0.118)

Note: Standard errors are in parentheses. The models estimated include as explanatory variables age, gender, marital status, education, income, and earnings (as in table 5.8).

measure: when using specification (4) they show the strongest impact of the relative gain of continued working among individuals in the lowest health quintile and among low-educated individuals.

5.5   Understanding the Results and their Implications

5.5.1   The Model Fit

To asses model fit we use specification (4), which is most flexible as it includes age dummies and allows for a nonlinear relation between health and the exit probability. We have converted the exit rates to yearly exit rates. Figures 5.22 and 5.23 show that the observed and predicted exit rates from employment within one year by age and gender are fairly close, which is not surprising as age dummies are included in the model.

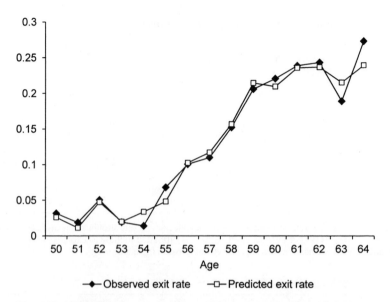

Fig. 5.22   Model fit for men by age (exit rates from employment within one year)

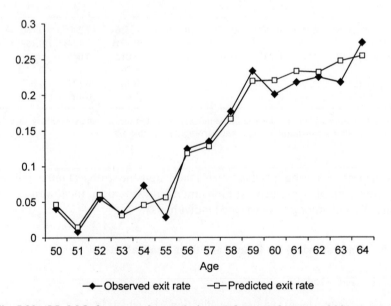

Fig. 5.23   Model fit for women by age (exit rates from employment within one year)

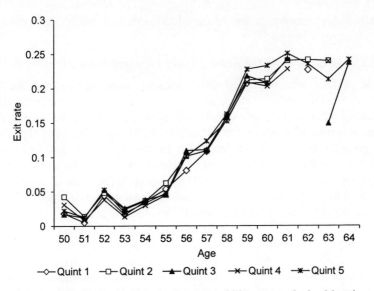

Fig. 5.24   Predicted exit rate from employment within one year by health quintile (men)

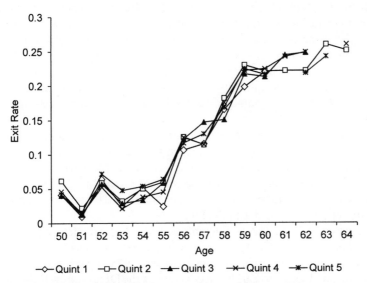

Fig. 5.25   Predicted exit rate from employment within one year by health quintile (women)

5.5.2   Implications of the Results: Graphical Description of Results

The predicted (yearly) exit rates, based on specification (4) (table 5.8), by health quintile in figures 5.24 and 5.25 show that the exit rates vary little by health quintile, as one would expect in light of the estimation results. Differences by level of education reveal that exit rates from employment are relatively high among the low-educated individuals, in particular at younger ages (figures 5.26 and 5.27).

5.5.3   Implications of the Results: Counterfactual Simulations

We perform counterfactual simulations to assess the impact of health, education, DI eligibility rules, and DI generosity on the exit probability (keeping other explanatory variables unchanged). For this we use the estimation results of specification (4), table 5.8. Figure 5.28 shows that there are no noteworthy effects of health on the exit probability and figure 5.29 shows that having a medium level of education reduces the exit rate from employment. In figures 5.30 and 5.31 we simulate the effect of a change in the disability benefits. These figures show that even large changes in the disability benefits have virtually no impact on labor force exit.

Figures 5.32 and 5.33 show, respectively, the exit probability from and the survival probability in employment under the assumption that all individuals are entitled to the benefits of only one particular exit route. This means that we assume in the OV-DI scenario that all individuals are eligible for DI benefits (and not for any other benefits), in the OV-retirement scenario that all individuals are only entitled to (early) retirement benefits, and in the OV-unemployment benefits scenario that all individuals are entitled to only unemployment benefits (and not to DI or retirement benefits).[6] As these figures show, the OV-DI scenario yields the largest exit probability and the lowest survival probability, which means that if all individuals would be entitled to DI, that is, that there is no medical screening, more people would exit employment before age sixty-five. Conversely, if no individual would be entitled to DI benefits, more people would remain employed until the age of sixty-five.

We can quantify this effect by calculating the expected number of years of work until age sixty-five. The expected number of years of work in the OV-DI scenario is equal to 7.40, in the OV-retirement scenario it is equal to 9.47, and in the OV-unemployment scenario it is equal to 9.02 years. This implies 1.62 additional years of work if everyone faced the retirement option compared to if everyone faced the DI option.

Next we consider this latter difference only for those who left employment for DI. There are only twenty-three such individuals in our sample. For these individuals the difference is only slightly higher: 1.92 years (expected number of years of work equal to 7.02 when only having the DI option and 8.94 years when only having the retirement option). Finally, we examine the effect of restricting access to DI in a more gradual way. Again we consider only those

---

6. Some individuals, for example the self-employed, may not have contributed to an occupational pension scheme and, therefore, have no early retirement benefits and their income after retirement is assumed to consist of the state pension only (starting at age sixty-five). Likewise, persons who did contribute to an occupational pension scheme but choose to retire before the relevant early retirement age are assumed to receive no pension until age sixty-five.

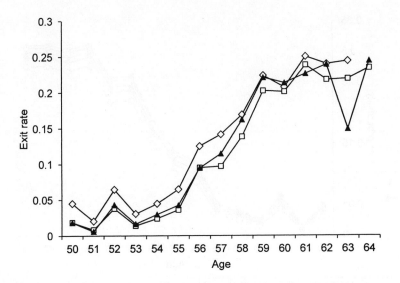

Fig. 5.26 Predicted exit rate from employment within one year by level of education (men)

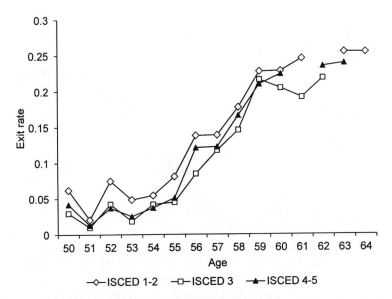

—◇—ISCED 1-2   —□—ISCED 3   —▲—ISCED 4-5

Fig. 5.27 Predicted exit rate from employment within one year by level of education (women)

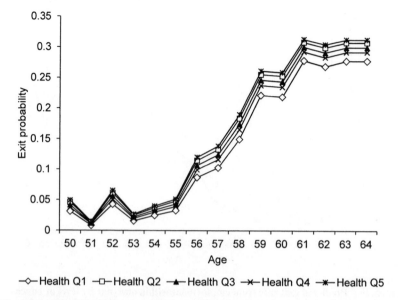

Fig. 5.28   Simulated effect of health on the exit probability from employment within one year

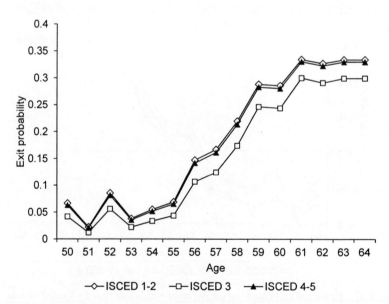

Fig. 5.29   Simulated effect of education on the exit probability from employment within one year

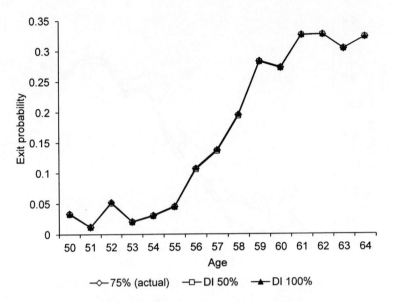

Fig. 5.30 Simulated effect of DI benefits on the exit probability from employment within one year

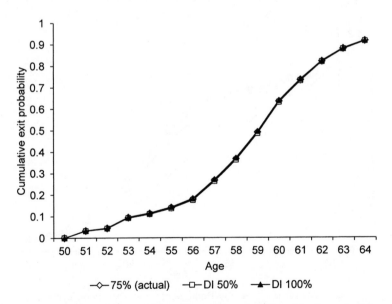

Fig. 5.31 Simulated effect of DI benefits on the probability of having exited from employment

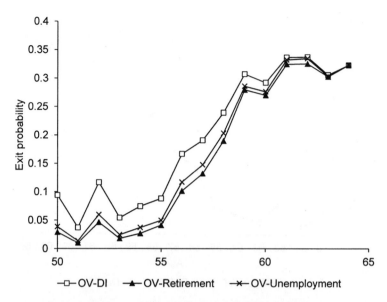

Fig. 5.32 The simulated exit probability from employment within one year when assuming all individuals are entitled to either DI (disability insurance), retirement, or unemployment benefits

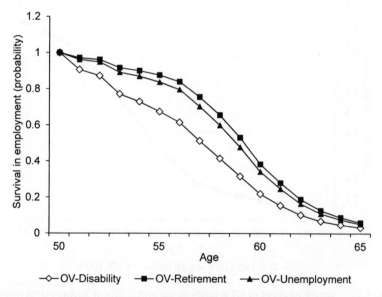

Fig. 5.33 The simulated survival probability in employment when assuming all individuals are entitled to either disability, retirement, or unemployment benefits

Table 5.15   **Estimation results including health shock**

Specification	m. e.			
	(5)	(6)	(7)	(8)
OV inclusive	−0.086	−0.078	−0.148	−0.118
	(0.023)	(0.023)	(0.047)	(0.049)
Health index	−0.049	−0.020	−0.049	−0.021
	(0.076)	(0.078)	(0.077)	(0.079)
(Adverse) health shock	0.136	0.122	0.134	0.120
	(0.070)	(0.071)	(0.071)	(0.072)
Linear age	X		X	
Age dummies		X		X
Other covariates			X	X
Number of observations	824	824	824	824
Mean exit rate	0.307	0.307	0.307	0.307
Mean OV inclusive	1.801	1.801	1.801	1.801
Std. dev. OV inclusive	0.868	0.868	0.868	0.868
Mean health index (0–1)	0.590	0.590	0.590	0.590
Std. dev. health index	0.254	0.254	0.254	0.254
Mean health shock (−1,1)	0.029	0.029	0.029	0.029
Std. dev. health shock	0.268	0.268	0.268	0.268

Note: Standard errors are in parentheses.

who left for DI and examine what would have happened if only two-thirds, one-third, or nobody was eligible for DI but instead had only the (early) retirement option. In the actual situation all are eligible for DI. Similar to the above, based on the exit probabilities we can calculate the expected years of work for these four scenarios. The expected number of years of work is equal to 7.02, 7.56, 8.52, and 8.94 years when randomly assigning, respectively, 100 percent to be DI eligible, 66.7 percent being DI eligible (and the remaining 33.3 percent eligible for retirement), 33.3 percent being DI eligible, and 0 percent being DI eligible. In line with the previous results, this shows that restricting access to DI increases the expected years of work.

5.5.4   Health Shocks

The finding that exit routes are unaffected by current health may appear puzzling, as health is likely to play a role in the labor force exit decision as has been found, for instance, by Schuring et al. (2013) for the Netherlands. To examine this further we define a health shock as the difference between the health index in the current wave and the health index in the next wave. If the health shock is positive it means a deterioration of health (an adverse health shock). Table 5.15 shows the results in which we added an adverse health shock variable to the models (5)–(8). The results show that an adverse health shock results in a higher probability of exiting the labor force.[7]

One might, of course, suspect that health shocks are endogenous, in the sense that retirement would negatively affect health rather than the other way around. The literature on the relation between health and retirement is ambiguous, with several papers finding that retirement has no adverse health effects (e.g., Kalwij, Knoef, and Alessie 2013; Neuman 2008) or even a positive effect on health (e.g., Charles 2004; Hemingway et al. 2003; Coe and Zamarro 2011; Bloemen, Hochguertel, and Zweerink 2013). Other papers, however, conclude that retirement may have a negative impact (e.g., Kuhn, Wuellrich, and Zweimueller 2010; Behncke 2012; Dave, Rashad, and Spasojevic 2008). If it is the case that retirement is good for health, then the effects of health on retirement in table 5.15 could actually be an underestimation of the effect of health shocks. However, given the inconclusive state of the literature, the estimates in table 5.15 have to be interpreted with care.

5.6   Conclusion

In this chapter we examined to what extent the exit probability from the labor force can be explained by the provisions of the DI program. In particular we disentangled the effects of DI eligibility from DI generosity on this exit probability. For this we mainly used data from the Dutch branch of the Survey of Health, Ageing and Retirement in Europe, which was conducted in 2004, 2007, and 2011.

Concerning the relation between health and labor force exit, we find that the effect of a health shock on the probability of exiting the labor force is marginally significant (at the 10 percent level).

We find no discernible impact of disability benefits on the exit from employment, but restricting access to the disability insurance scheme does affect labor force exit and increases, on average, the years people remain in employment until the age of sixty-five. These findings suggest that if policymakers aim to reduce the number of DI recipients they may choose stricter medical screening of individuals who apply for DI rather than reducing DI benefits for those who qualify for DI.

---

7. All estimates are significant at the 5 percent level according to a one-sided t-test.

Appendix
Additional Table and Figures

Table 5A.1   **The age distribution by gender and year in SHARE (the Netherlands) and in the Dutch population**

	Men			Women		
	2004 (%)	2007 (%)	2011 (%)	2004 (%)	2007 (%)	2011 (%)
SHARE-NL						
50–54	32	31	23	34	34	28
55–59	36	37	32	39	37	32
60–64	31	33	45	27	29	40
50–64	100	100	100	100	100	100
Population						
50–54	37	36	35	37	36	35
55–59	36	35	32	36	35	32
60–64	26	29	33	27	29	33
50–64	100	100	100	100	100	100

Source: For population, Statistics Netherlands (CBS; statline.cbs.nl).

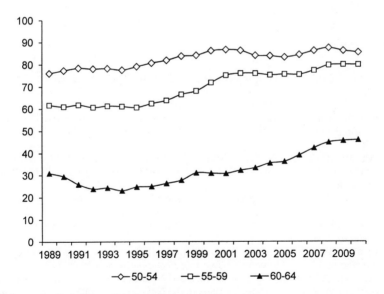

Fig. 5A.1   Employment rates of older men by age group
Source: Statistics Netherlands, Income Panel Survey (IPO).

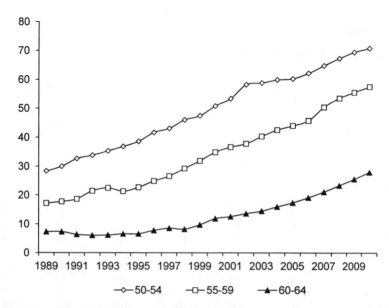

Fig. 5A.2   Employment rates of older women by age group
Source: Statistics Netherlands, Income Panel Survey (IPO).

References

Behncke, S. 2012. "Does Retirement Trigger Ill Health?" *Health Economics* 21:282–300.
Bloemen, H., S. Hochguertel, and J. Zweerink. 2013. "The Causal Effect of Retirement on Mortality: Evidence from Targeted Incentives to Retire Early." IZA Discussion Paper no. 7570, Institute for the Study of Labor. http://ftp.iza.org/dp7570.pdf.
Burkhauser, R. V., and M. Daly. 2011. *The Declining Work and Welfare of People with Disabilities.* Washington, DC: American Enterprise Institute for Public Policy Research.
Charles, K. K. 2004. "Is Retirement Depressing? Labor Force Inactivity and Psychological Well-Being in Later Life." *Research in Labor Economics* 23:269–99.
Coe, N., and G. Zamarro. 2011. "Retirement Effects on Health in Europe." *Journal of Health Economics* 30 (1): 77–86.
Dave, D., I. Rashad, and J. Spasojevic. 2008. "The Effects of Retirement on Physical and Mental Health Outcomes." *Southern Economic Journal* 75:497–523.
De Vos, K., A. Kapteyn, and A. Kalwij. 2012. "Disability Insurance and Labor Market Exit Routes of Older Workers in the Netherlands." In *Social Security and Retirement around the World: Historical Trends in Mortality and Health, Employment, and Disability Insurance Participation and Reforms*, edited by David A. Wise, 419–47. Chicago: University of Chicago Press.
Euwals, R., R. de Mooij, and D. van Vuuren. 2009. "Rethinking Retirement: From

Participation Toward Allocation." CPB Special Publication no. 80, CPB Netherlands Bureau for Economic Policy Analysis.

Gruber, J., and D. A. Wise, eds. 2004. *Social Security Programs and Retirement around the World: Micro-Estimation.* Chicago: University of Chicago Press.

Hemingway, H., M. Marmot, P. Martikainen, G. Mein, and S. Stansfeld. 2003. "Is Retirement Good or Bad or Mental and Physical Health Functioning? Whitehall II Longitudinal Study of Civil Servants." *Journal of Epidemiology and Community Health* 57:46–49.

Kalwij, A., M. Knoef, and R. Alessie. 2013. "Pathways to Retirement and Mortality Risk in the Netherlands." *European Journal of Population* 29 (2): 221–38.

Kapteyn, A., and K. de Vos. 1999. "Social Security and Retirement in the Netherlands." In *Social Security and Retirement around the World*, edited by Jonathan Gruber and David A. Wise, 269–304. Chicago: The University of Chicago Press.

Kuhn, A., J. P. Wuellrich, and J. Zweimueller. 2010. "Fatal Attraction? Access to Early Retirement and Mortality." IZA Discussion Paper no.5160, Institute for the Study of Labor. http://ftp.iza.org/dp5160.pdf.

Mannheim Research Institute for the Economics of Aging (MEA). 2011. Release Guide 2.5.0 Waves 1 & 2 (www. share-project.org).

Neuman, K. 2008. "Quit Your Job and Get Healthier? The Effect of Retirement on Health." *Journal of Labor Research* 29:177–201.

Schuring, M., S. J. Robroek, F. W. Otten, C. H. Arts, and A. Burdorf. 2013. "The Effect of Ill Health and Socioeconomic Status on Labor Force Exit and Re-Employment: A Prospective Study with Ten Years Follow-Up in the Netherlands." *Scandinavian Journal of Work, Environment & Health* 39 (2): 134–43.

Stock, James H., and David A. Wise. 1990. "Pensions, the Option Value of Work, and Retirement." *Econometrica* 58 (5): 1151–80.

Van Oorschot, W. 2007. "Narrowing Pathways to Early Retirement in the Netherlands." *Journal of Poverty and Justice* 15:247–55.

Wise, D. A., ed. 2012. *Social Security and Retirement around the World: Historical Trends in Mortality and Health, Employment, and Disability Insurance Participation and Reforms.* Chicago: University of Chicago Press.

6

Retirement, Early Retirement, and Disability
Explaining Labor Force Participation after Fifty-Five in France

Luc Behaghel, Didier Blanchet, and Muriel Roger

6.1 Introduction

The link between health status and retirement has long been neglected in the French pension debate. The French system offers early retirement possibilities to people suffering from handicap or invalidity, but they never had the importance they have taken in some other countries. The reason is twofold: (a) an age at normal retirement that used to be low compared to international standards, and (b) the preeminence of two other pathways, unemployment insurance and public early retirement schemes, for exits at still lower ages. A large fraction of people wishing to retire early because of poor health conditions could do so without explicitly invoking this factor. It is at the most in ex post self-assessments of retirement motives that health considerations seemed to play a significant role (see Barnay and Jeger 2006), but with the well-known difficulty of correcting such assessments from justification biases.

This situation has started evolving over the last decade. Four reforms have been conducted that have or will strongly reduce possibilities to leave as early as age sixty, and specifically the 2010 reform that has shifted the minimum age to sixty-two, with only limited derogations for earlier exits. Simulta-

Luc Behaghel is a researcher at the French National Institute for Agricultural Research (INRA) and the Paris School of Economics. Didier Blanchet belongs to the French National Statistical Institute (INSEE). Muriel Roger is a researcher at the Banque de France, the French National Institute for Agricultural Research (INRA), and the Paris School of Economics.

This chapter presents the views of the authors and should not be interpreted as reflecting the views of the Banque de France or INSEE. For acknowledgments, sources of research support, and disclosure of the author's or authors' material financial relationships, if any, please see http://www.nber.org/chapters/c13327.ack.

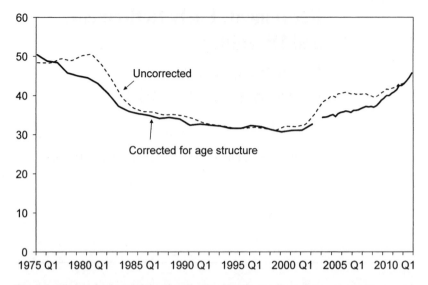

Fig. 6.1   Labor force participation for the fifty-five to sixty-four age group

Source: Labor Force Survey and Minni (2012).

Note: The thin line reports the gross labor force participation rate. The thick line reports a LFP rate corrected for changes in age structure within the fifty-five to sixty-four age bracket. For instance, starting in 2001–2002, the gross rate is pushed above its basic trend by the arrival of the first baby boom cohorts at age fifty-five. The corrected rate neutralizes this temporary phenomenon. The break in 2002–2003 corresponds to the shift from the annual to the continuous time Labor Force Survey.

neously, access to public early retirement schemes has been dramatically reduced: except for some very specific categories of workers, these schemes are currently under extinction. Some tightening of rules also took place within the unemployment route; until recently, recipients of unemployment allowances over a certain age were exempted from seeking employment, making their condition very close to the one of pre- or fully retired workers. This exemption was abolished in 2012.

All these changes have started producing significant results in terms of employment or labor force participation rates in the fifty-five to sixty-four age group (see figure 6.1). In this context, interest for the health/retirement connection has now emerged as a much more central issue. This issue can be considered from two opposite points of view.

- From the budgetary point of view of those who seek to maximize the impact of past reforms on actual retirement ages, one potential pre-occupation is the risk of seeing the invalidity route to retirement progressively expand as an alternative to those other routes that are-progressively shut down or made much less attractive. This substitution effect is well known: reducing opportunities offered by one route or a subset of existing routes generally leads to a redirection of flows toward other pathways, limiting the ex post efficiency of the initial policy.

- From the opposite social point of view of individual well-being, one can conversely argue that bad health is a legitimate motive for benefiting from an early exit and that it should be more systematically taken into account in the design of retirement policies.

The second issue is closely related to two other ones: (a) the question of knowing how retirement schemes should take into account the hardness of past or current working conditions that very often constitute prominent determinants of health status, and (b) the question of knowing how these same pension rules should take into account differences in life expectancy that are generally tied to bad health conditions. France is a country that benefits from a relatively high average life expectancy, but where mortality differentials are quite large across social groups. Global policies that aim at uniform increases in retirement ages ignoring these penibility/health/mortality differentials raise obvious problems of fairness and this has probably contributed to part of the resistance encountered by some reforms. The 1993 and 2003 reforms have partially avoided this problem because they chose to postpone retirement ages by changing conditions on past contribution records, hence essentially affecting skilled and healthier workers having started working and contributing at older ages. Such is also the strategy followed by the new 2013 reform. The 2010 reform, on the other hand, by raising uniformly the minimum retirement age, affected more than proportionately less skilled workers (Blanchet and Le Minez 2012) that were, up to now, the main beneficiaries of the French low minimum age at retirement, and who could consider this as a fair compensation for their generally much shorter life horizons.

The two apparently opposite budgetary and social points of view concerning the health/retirement issue are not contradictory. An optimal design of retirement schemes requires adequate pathways for individuals that deserve specific treatments, be it for bad health or any other relevant motive, accompanied with some checking that such pathways are not used by individuals for whom they have not been targeted.

To help thinking about such optimal schemes, some positive knowledge of how health and retirement decisions currently interfere is an obvious intermediate step. It is to this question that the present chapter contributes, looking at how various exit routes have been used in the past by French senior workers according to their observed health status. The chapter will be organized in five sections. Section 6.2 will come back to the general description of the disability and sickness leave route to retirement in France and how its share in global transitions to retirement has changed over time. Section 6.3 presents the empirical method used to estimate the exit rate from the labor market of older workers according to their health status. Results are given in section 6.4 and section 6.5 is devoted to some simulations of how older workers' retirement behavior would change, for a given health status, when the relative generosity of the different retirement routes changes.

6.2 Background

The development of the French pension system took place in several steps throughout the twentieth century. The first large-scale system was developed in 1920, (*retraites ouvrières et paysannes*) then replaced in 1941 during World War II by the AVTS (*Allocation aux Vieux Travailleurs Salariés*) under the Vichy government. It provided early retirement for workers above age sixty excluded from the labor force either for health or economic reasons. But the real birth of the pension system we are still living in today occurred just after World War II, when a large welfare state started being developed with a specific part devoted to old age. The initial value for the normal retirement age had been set at sixty-five, considered as the typical average threshold at which individuals started being unable to maintain their standards of living through labor force participation, be it for health or other reasons, and thus had to become eligible for old-age benefits.

However, specific health conditions were also taken into account by the designers of the welfare system and still provide the basic structure of what will be called here the "invalidity" pathway to retirement. Before age sixty, people suffering from health troubles implying work limitations are eligible for disability insurance benefits (*pension d'invalidité*). Then, reaching sixty, these people already benefiting from invalidity insurance directly shift to old-age disability benefits (*retraite pour ex-invalides*). Individuals declared unable to work at age sixty, but who did not previously benefit from invalidity benefits, are also eligible for old-age disability benefits (*retraite pour inaptitude*). For quite a long time, however, this second category remained highly selective: it required a disability rate of 100 percent, was limited to people having worked for at least thirty years, and provided a benefit being, at the maximum, equal to 40 percent of the average of past wages.[1] This was higher than the rate of replacement for people claiming early retirement at age sixty without this invalidity motive, but remained little attractive.

For several years, the global generosity of the whole pension system remained limited. Until the end of the 1960s, poverty remained widespread among older age groups. A reaction took place during the 1970s, and several changes progressively increased the coverage and level of pension benefits. This period was also a relatively dynamic period for the development of the *pension d'inaptitude*, in a context marked by strong union pressure in favor of lowering the normal retirement age to sixty for the entire population. During the 1970s that demand remained unsatisfied, but the Boulin reform

---

1. The disability rate measures the intensity of limitations encountered by the disabled person.

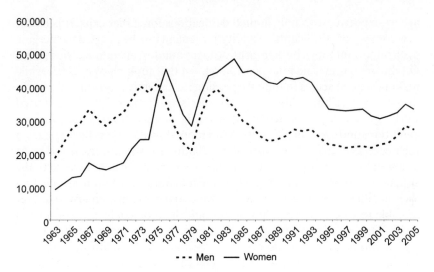

Fig. 6.2   *Pensions d'inaptitude*: **Total flows**
Source: CNAV in Omnès (2006).

in 1971 opened several possibilities for earlier exits for various categories of the population, including a move toward less selective and more generous rules for the *pension d'inaptitude*: the threshold for the rate of invalidity was lowered to 50 percent, the condition of having worked thirty years or more was suppressed, and benefits were increased to 50 percent of the average wage, that is, in line with a normal full-rate pension.

This mechanically led to an increased importance of this route, but, as shown in figure 6.2, the incidence of this change was more pronounced for women because men, at the same period, had also started benefiting from the development of another early retirement route financially more attractive, that is, unemployment and early retirement initially developed to cope with severe reductions of activity that had taken place in some traditional industries such as the steel industry, but that progressively expanded as a major instrument offered to employers and employees for facilitating all forms of early exits from the labor force. This unemployment and early retirement route initially concerned workers in the sixty to sixty-four age group.

After 1983 access to a full pension at age sixty became possible for the large majority of the population, the only condition being to have contributed to the pension system for at least 37.5 years. In this context, claiming for a *pension d'inaptitude* became useless for a large share of people. Those who still had a reason to rely on this route were people reaching the age of sixty in bad health and with incomplete careers.

This situation has started to evolve again over the last decade. Four reforms have been conducted that have strongly reduced the possibilities to leave as early as age sixty, specifically the 2010 reform that has shifted the minimum age to sixty-two, with only limited derogations for earlier exits. It is in this new context that the health/invalidity/retirement link has started reemerging as an important topic, both from an academic and an operational viewpoint. On the operational side the pension reform that took place in 2003, while making general access to full-rate pensions at age sixty more difficult, introduced new possibilities for exits before age sixty for workers having started working very early, expected to suffer, on the average, from harder working conditions and lower health status than more skilled workers having started their careers at much later ages. This 2003 reform was also expected to be followed by negotiations between social partners specifically devoted to the situation of workers suffering from difficult working conditions affecting their health status. Although these negotiations remained unable to deliver tangible results, this shows how important the problem is now considered to be. The issue implicitly or explicitly reemerged with the 2010 reform. Opponents to the reform pointed at consequences of a uniform increase in the minimum retirement age for all workers including those with bad health, low life expectancies, or who have experienced bad working conditions. A partial answer to this concern has been to finally maintain the threshold of age sixty for people with a level of impairment of at least 50 percent.

6.3   Empirical Strategy

Stylized facts concerning the relative importance of the French disability and sickness leave route are already well known. Behaghel et al. (2012) have shown that, until now, alternative routes have exempted French workers from massively relying on disability motives for early exits over the past decades, but put forward that a decrease in the generosity of other routes may induce people in bad health to claim disability benefits. Results of these authors are mostly on substitution effects between the several retirement pathways available to old age workers. In the sequel, the objective is to go some steps further, by looking in more detail at how retirement behavior is affected by the availability of the various routes out of the labor force and how this availability interacts with actual health status. We shall consider incentives provided by disability insurance (DI) programs, but also by old-age specific unemployment or early retirement benefits, in addition to those provided by normal pension rules.

Some difficulties arise when one wants to estimate the causal links between retirement and health at old age. Labor force attachment, health, and relative gains associated with the different pathways may be driven by common unobservable factors like abilities, preferences, or family events. For instance, the disability and sickness leave route is advantageous for those with short careers. Following the choices made in previous waves of the International Social Security (ISS) program, we rely on an option value (OV) indicator (Stock and Wise 1990) of the incentives to leave the labor market to disentangle the effect of health versus incentives in the retirement behavior. The option value indicator measures the value to continue working compared to the value provided by other options in a dynamic framework. The OV indicator is labeled "inclusive" in the sense that it tries to provide a synthetic weighted summary of the option values associated with each possible path to retirement.

The inclusive OV summarizes the main characteristics of the French retirement system and alternative routes into a single indicator. Among the many difficulties of such an exercise, one stems from the intrinsic complexity of the French system and of the various routes offered to workers considering leaving the labor force. To keep things tractable, we restrict ourselves to "normal retirement" for wage earners or civil servants. Concerning access to old age unemployment support and preretirement, a one-by-one inclusion of all the possibilities that have existed over the period is beyond the scope of this chapter and would probably be of little interest, given the very aggregate nature of the index we are trying to build. Our approach is instead to proxy all these routes by the dominant one for each period, giving to this route a global weight equal to the total flow of early retirees or unemployed for each period.

The incentive indicator for the disability and sickness leave pathway has been simulated following assumptions that will be described later. Once this is made, we shall be able to compute an inclusive option value as:

$$OV_t^{inc}(t) = \alpha_{DI}OV_t^{DI}(t) + \alpha_{UER}OV_t^{UER}(t) + (1 - \alpha_{DI} - \alpha_{UER})OV_t^{normal}(t),$$

where OV_t^{inc} is the inclusive option value, OV_t^{DI} is the option value for the disability and sickness leave pathway, OV_t^{UER} is the option value for the unemployment and early retirement pathway, OV_t^{normal} is the option value for normal retirement and where α_{DI} and α_{UER} are the relative weights of the DI and unemployment and early retirement pathways.

Because the main objective of the chapter is to disentangle the impact of incentives and health status on labor force participation, we introduce simultaneously the OV and individual health indicators in regressions explaining employment status. The generic equation that is estimated is therefore:

$$Pr(\text{retire} = 1) = \Phi(\beta OV^{inc} + \gamma I^{health} + \delta X),$$

with retire equal to 1 for individuals not in employment, OV^{inc} the inclusive option value, I^{health} the individual health indicator, and X some individual characteristics. Regressions are also performed separately by health quintiles. The sample includes individuals still employed in the previous year. The estimations are conducted with probit specifications and standard errors clustered at the individual level.

The labor force participation and health indicators are taken from the French data of the Survey of Health, Ageing and Retirement in Europe. The SHARE survey is a multidisciplinary and cross-national panel database of microdata on health, socioeconomic status, and social and family networks of more than 85,000 individuals age fifty or older from nineteen European countries. The sample size for France is around 3,000 households interviewed every two years since 2004. Data collected include information on individual labor market status and numerous health variables: self-reported health, health conditions, physical and cognitive functioning, health behavior, and use of health care facilities. Data on labor force participation are issued from SHARELIFE, the third wave of data collection for SHARE. This wave provides some complementary information on people's life histories. The health indicator is based on waves 1 and 2 of the survey.

Before moving to the results, we detail the components of the regression model in the following subsections. The first subsection is devoted to the presentation of the pathways, the second to the weighting of these different pathways, the third to the computation of the option values, the fourth to the presentation of the health indicator, and the last to the presentation of the main characteristics of the employment data.

6.3.1   Pathways to Retirement and Participation in the Labor Force

We summarize the pathways to retirement in three categories: the normal retirement pathways (main route), the disability and sickness leave pathways (routes of interest), and the unemployment and early retirement pathway (others). Because the unemployment and early retirement pathway is not the focus of the chapter, we decided to aggregate these two retirement routes that actually display some common characteristics.

The main characteristics of the disability and sickness leave route have been already presented in section 6.2. We only recall here the main features of the system. Before age sixty, the *pension d'invalidité* is for individuals with a disability rate over two-thirds. Workers can also be on long-term sickness leaves. After age sixty, people may be eligible to the *pension d'inaptitude* for a disability rate over one-half if they did not get a *pension d'invalidité* before age sixty. These people are treated as full-rate pensioners even if they do not fulfill conditions for the full rate.

For the normal retirement route, we consider the first pillar to be basic pension and the second pillar to be complementary pensions for private-sector employees, and the one-pillar pension for civil servants. The basic pension is linked to age at retirement and to N, the number of years of contribution to the pension scheme. Until 2009, major changes have concerned the condition on N for getting the full rate before age sixty-five (now forty-one years instead of 37.5 in 1992), the replacement rate at this full rate, and the penalties and bonuses for retiring before or after this full rate. In 2009 the mandatory age was shifted to seventy and, in 2010, the minimum retirement age was shifted to sixty-two. Accordingly, the age for getting the full rate without the requested value of N was also increased by two

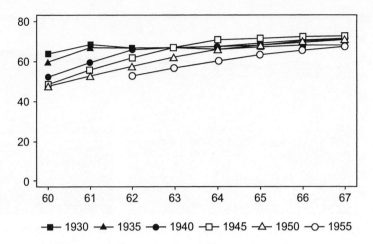

Fig. 6.3   Changes over cohorts for the normal retirement pathway

Source: Authors' computation based on the PENSIPP microsimulation model.

Note: The graph presents the relationship between replacement rates and age at retirement for one illustrative case of worker in six successive cohorts. These illustrative workers are supposed to have worked as wage earners in the private sector and paid at the current social security ceiling only since the age of twenty-four. This age has been chosen to illustrate how the initial rules penalized workers with careers too short to get a full-rate pension at age sixty. The last cohort is affected by the change in the minimum age at retirement, raised from age sixty to sixty-two by the 2010 reform.

years, shifting from sixty-five to sixty-seven. The 2013 reform has again affected the condition on N rather than the age bracket for access to retirement. Figure 6.3 provides a very synthetic view of the recent changes in the main parameters of the pension scheme illustrating how past reforms have changed the relationship between retirement age and the replacement rate for an individual that, under pre-1993 conditions, was already unable to get the full rate at age sixty.

The unemployment and early retirement pathway provides a given percentage of the reference wage at an age that, in the past, has varied between fifty-six and fifty-seven. Here, we have retained a stylized profile for this eligibility age and a fixed replacement rate of 60 percent. We consider a fixed replacement rate, which is the characteristic of most of these programs. The major differences concern eligibility ages, not fully homogenous across subroutes and not constant over the past decades. People in early retirement or on unemployment go on validating years of contribution when over fifty-five years of age until they are entitled to the full-rate pension.

Figure 6.4, from Behaghel et al. (2012), shows the pathways to retirement of men and women from 1983 to 2003. We see a decrease in the share of people still in employment just before their sixtieth birthday and an increase in the shares of people in early retirement or benefiting from unemployment

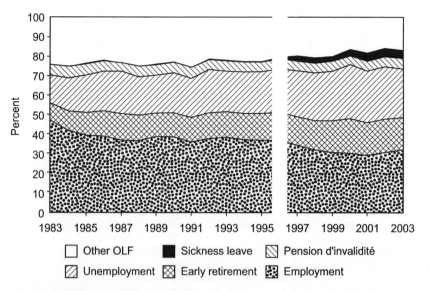

Fig. 6.4   Pathways to retirement, men and women
Source: Behaghel et al. (2012).
Note: Pathways are proxied by the situation at age fifty-nine (source: Enquête Emploi) corrected with administrative data on unemployment (source: Unédic), early retirement (source: Dares), and complemented with administrative data on sickness leave (source: CNAM) and inflows from *pension d'invalidité* to *pensions d'inaptitude* (source: CNAV). Break in the series: Data on sickness leave are missing before 1997; before that date, workers in sickness leave are recorded as employed.

insurance benefits. All over the period, the number of people going through disability insurance or sickness leave is not negligible, but remains small, amounting to between 5 percent and 8 percent of the population.

6.3.2   Weighting the Pathways to Retirement

The retrospective presentation of the pathways underlines the changes over the last decades. People from different cohorts experience different opportunities at the end of their working lives. Pathways in figure 6.4 are proxied by the situation at age fifty-nine in the French Labor Force Survey corrected with administrative data on unemployment and early retirement and complemented with administrative data on sickness leave and inflows from pension *d'invalidité* to pension *d'inaptitude*. We have the information at the population level. To disaggregate the pathways by gender or education, we use another French survey mixing information on disability and labor market histories to compute the relative weights of the retirement pathways, by cohorts, over the last decades.

The data are taken from the French survey *Santé et Itinéraire Profession-*

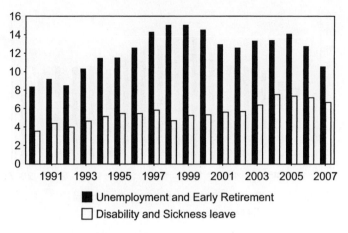

Fig. 6.5   Pathway probabilities by year

nel (Health and Labor Market history). The survey provides current and retrospective information on health and labor market status for 14,000 individuals aged twenty to seventy-four in 2006. All successive spells in labor market histories and all major health events in individuals' lives are reported.[2] Moreover, the survey provides general socioeconomic information on the characteristics of households and information pertaining to periods before entry in the labor market. We select a subsample of spells corresponding to the states experienced by the individuals of the sample from ages fifty-five to sixty. The states are classified in four categories: employment, disability or sickness leave, early retirement or unemployment (with unemployment benefits), and retired or out of the labor force.

We make several assumptions to compute the relative weights. We consider that the DI path is relevant for everybody and not only for those who seem to have ex ante some obvious (observed) reasons to consider the choice of applying for DI. The amount of information required to be able to know if the DI path is a realistic prospect for an individual may be very high and the assumptions we should have to make very strong. We thus impute to each individual, considering a few individuals' characteristics, the mean value of the cell, that is, the probability to experiment each pathway for all individuals having the same characteristics. The probabilities are calculated using the share of the population for the combined age groups fifty-five to sixty on each state at a given point in time.

Figure 6.5 provides the stock estimator of the pathway probabilities by

2. Due to the complexity of some labor market trajectories, unemployment and inactivity under one year are not sampled.

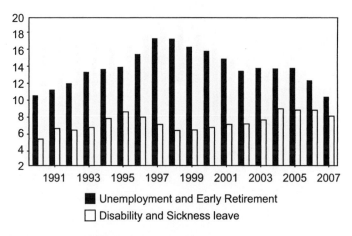

Fig. 6.6   Pathway probabilities by year (men)

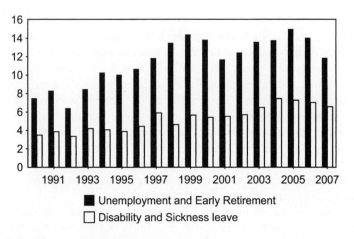

Fig. 6.7   Pathway probabilities by year (women)

year between 1990 and 2007. The share of the disability and sickness leave route increases from less than 4 to nearly 8 percent over the period. However, the level remains quite low. Also, the share of the unemployment and early retirement route nearly doubles during the period, but on a higher level. It goes from 8 to nearly 16 percent, being the highest around 1998 when the disability and sickness leave route exhibits a slight decrease after eight years of monotonous increase.

The decline in the disability and sickness leave route around 1998 is mostly due to men (figure 6.6). It occurs at the same time as an increase in the probability to leave the labor force through the unemployment and early retirement route. Trends for women (figure 6.7) are less clear. This is the case for

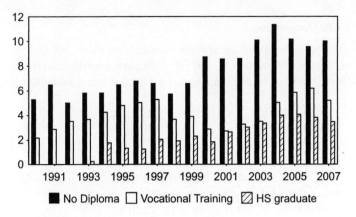

Fig. 6.8   Probability of DI path by education group

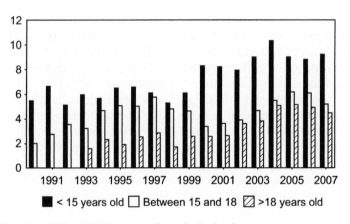

Fig. 6.9   Probability of DI by age at the end of school

most indicators on the labor market over the period, with two phenomena occurring at the same time: changes in the relative situation of older workers on the labor market on the one hand, and the increase in women's labor force participation over the past decades on the other hand.

Retirement routes are also distinct by education level. Figures 6.8 and 6.9 draw the pathway probabilities by education and age at leaving school. The probability to experiment DI is higher for the less educated. At the beginning of the period, the more educated (or those having left school later) did not use the disability or sickness leave route. Their propensity to claim disability pensions increased over the period. Around 2000, the use of DI for the most graduated workers nearly equals the one of individuals with vocational training. The difference by education is more relevant than by gender.

6.3.3   OV Computation

We will hereafter detail the specific assumptions made, for each pathway, to compute the OV indicators. The OV indicators are based on the net present values (NPV) of retiring at age r, computed at age t, and given by:

$$V_t(r) = \sum_{s=t}^{r-1} \pi_{s/t}\beta^{s-t}Y_s^{\gamma} + \sum_{s=r}^{\omega} \pi_{s/t}\beta^{s-t}(kB_s(r))^{\gamma}.$$

With parameters $\beta = 0.97$ (discount factor), $\gamma = 0.75$ and $\kappa = 1.5$ (preference for leisure), and with $\pi_{s/t}$ the probability of being still alive at age s conditional upon being alive at t, Y labor income and $B_s(r)$ the pension benefit that depends upon retirement age r.

The option value of not retiring at t is given by:

$$G_t = V_t(r^*) - V_t(t),$$

where r^* is the age that maximizes $V_t(r)$.

The normal retirement route consists of the normal basic pension (*régime général*) plus complementary pensions (ARRCO-AGIRC) for wage earners in the private sector, or the one-pillar pension applying to civil servants. For these pension schemes, the minimum eligibility age is sixty (the current shift to sixty-two is without any incidence for the population under review). For the calculation of the incentive, an individual retiring before the age of sixty is supposed to live without resources until the minimum age and then retire immediately even if he does not reach the additional condition required for the pension to be a full-rate pension. Hence, his NPV will include a zero component until age sixty, followed by a positive component from sixty to death, at a level that will depend upon whether this individual did or did not reach the full rate at sixty.

For the invalidity route that covers the two subcases of *pension d'invalidité* and *pension d'inaptitude*, an individual exiting through this route at any age before sixty is entitled to 50 percent of a reference wage truncated to the social security ceiling, without any condition concerning the length of his past career. The exact formula for this reference wage is the mean wage over the ten best years of this person's career, after truncation. Here, for simplicity, we retain the truncated value of this person's last wage. Then, when reaching the minimum retirement age of sixty, this person is reoriented toward the *inaptitude* subroute, that is, a computation of a full-rate normal pension (including complementary pensions) even if this person does not totalize the number of years of contribution required for the full rate under normal provisions.

The last route, the unemployment and early retirement route (hereafter UER), offers leaving at an age that, depending upon year of exit, has been alternatively equal to fifty-six or fifty-seven, with a level of benefit applying to one's last wage truncated to 200 percent of the social security ceiling, with two different rates applied to the share of this last wage below and over the social security ceiling. People exiting through this route then go on accumulating years of participation to normal social security and start getting their pensions as soon as they reach conditions for this pension to be a full rate one. This route only applies to wage earners in the private sector. Since it is not possible to voluntary quit the labor force at, for example, age fifty-five and wait until the eligibility age for this UER route, exits through the UER route are treated as equivalent to exits through the normal route, that is, full inactivity until the minimum retirement age.

Table 6.1 shows computations associated with the normal route for an individual considering different ages to leave the labor force when his current age is fifty-five.

This person is a private-sector worker born in 1930, having started working at age seventeen. If he had chosen to leave the labor force at fifty-five (in 1985), he would have had to wait until sixty to get a pension of only 10,948 equivalent euros per year. The "55" column shows the resulting sequence of discounted utility flows by year: zero utility until age fifty-nine included, then a utility at age sixty of $(\kappa*10,498)^\gamma/\gamma$ that, with $\kappa = 1.5$ and $\gamma = 0.75$ is equal to 1,874, hence, after correction for survival and discounting, a contribution to intertemporal well-being of 1,510. The sum of all these contributions from age fifty-five to the maximum life span was 20,955. The same person still at age fifty-five, but contemplating leaving at sixty could expect at this age a much larger pension of 15,170, the gap being due to the five additional years of contributions to both the general regime and complementary schemes. In such a case, the discounted sum of utility flows includes nonzero values corresponding to net labor income between fifty-five and fifty-nine, followed by the flows resulting from the new benefit level, hence a much larger NPV of 37,828.

Considering retirement at still older ages did not lead to large additions to this person's pension benefits, given the rules that applied to this cohort. For this person, having started work in 1947 at age seventeen and continuing to work until age fifty-nine warranted a full-rate pension at sixty. Beyond this age, further increments due to postponing had only small consequences for the level of benefits: they were almost exclusively the result of the accumulation of additional points in complementary schemes. Nevertheless, in this example, retiring later always resulted in a higher NPV, despite the choice of a relatively high preference for leisure. The value κ equal to 1.5 means that, in the short run, the individual is better off once retired instead of working as soon as his replacement rate is higher than 66 percent, and such is the case here after age sixty. But the resulting short-run loss in well-being in case of postponement remains more than compensated by the fact of getting a slightly higher pension all over the retirement period. As a result, viewed

Table 6.1   Computation of incentives, an illustration

			Age of potential retirement										
			55	56	57	58	59	60	61	62	63	64	65
Permanent pension once fully retired			10,498	12,206	13,703	14,199	14,683	15,170	15,685	15,980	16,453	16,730	17,138
Net wage if working			19,079	19,497	19,748	20,147	20,191	20,786	21,068	21,191	21,293	21,230	21,256
Age	Life probs.	Disc. life probs.											
55	1	1	0	2,164	2,164	2,164	2,164	2,164	2,164	2,164	2,164	2,164	2,164
56	0.988	0.959	0	0	2,111	2,111	2,111	2,111	2,111	2,111	2,111	2,111	2,111
57	0.976	0.92	0	0	0	2,043	2,043	2,043	2,043	2,043	2,043	2,043	2,043
58	0.963	0.881	0	0	0	0	1,987	1,987	1,987	1,987	1,987	1,987	1,987
59	0.949	0.843	0	0	0	0	0	1,903	1,903	1,903	1,903	1,903	1,903
60	0.934	0.806	1,510	1,691	1,844	1,894	1,942	1,990	1,860	1,860	1,860	1,860	1,860
61	0.919	0.769	1,442	1,615	1,761	1,809	1,855	1,901	1,949	1,794	1,794	1,794	1,794
62	0.902	0.734	1,375	1,540	1,679	1,725	1,769	1,812	1,858	1,885	1,718	1,718	1,718
63	0.885	0.699	1,310	1,467	1,600	1,643	1,685	1,726	1,770	1,795	1,835	1,643	1,643
64	0.867	0.665	1,246	1,395	1,522	1,563	1,602	1,642	1,684	1,707	1,745	1,767	1,559
65	0.848	0.631	1,183	1,325	1,445	1,484	1,522	1,560	1,599	1,622	1,658	1,678	1,709
...													
95	0.02	0.006	11	13	14	14	15	15	15	16	16	16	17
96	0.013	0.004	7	8	9	9	9	10	10	10	10	10	11
97	0.008	0.002	5	5	6	6	6	6	6	6	6	6	7
98	0.005	0.001	3	3	3	3	4	4	4	4	4	4	4
99	0.004	0.001	2	2	2	2	2	2	2	3	3	3	3
100	0.002	0.001	1	1	1	2	2	2	2	2	2	2	2
Sum of flows			20,955	25,629	29,866	32,601	35,257	37,828	38,347	38,534	38,872	38,951	39,106
Option value			18,151										

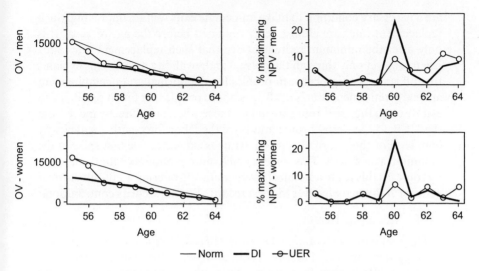

Fig. 6.10   Mean OVs and percent maximizing NPVs of retiring at each age

from age fifty-five, the age maximizing the NPV was sixty-five, and the
option value of going on working at fifty-five was NPV(55,65) – NPV(55,55)
= 39106 – 20955 = 18151, reported in the bottom cell of the table.

How are these incentive measures distributed among the whole population under review and for the three different routes considered in this study?
The left-side panels of figure 6.10 show mean OVs associated to these three
routes for men and women from our sample, respectively. By construction,
OVs at age fifty-five are the same with the normal and the UER route, and
then a break is observed for these OVs at fifty-six and fifty-seven for the
UER route, while OVs for the normal route decline much more gradually.

The disability and sickness leave route, after age fifty-six or fifty-seven,
has characteristics that are very similar to the UER route, replacement rates
being roughly similar. Therefore, the main difference is the fact that this route
does not entail any age condition, hence a much lower option value of going
on working for people having access to this route as soon as age fifty-five.

Graphs in the right-side panels give the percentages of people for which
OVs turn negative at each age, that is, those reaching an age where leaving
the labor force provides a discounted utility flow higher than the one potentially derived from retiring at any later age. Despite the relative generosities
of benefits offered through the invalidity and UER routes, these proportions remain low or even zero until the minimum retirement age. The reason
is again that, for the specification of γ and κ, staying in the labor force is
always preferable to exiting as long as the replacement ratio falls short of
the inverse of the κ parameter that measures preference for leisure. Here, κ
is equal to 1.5, meaning that net replacement rates higher than 66 percent

are a necessary condition to make immediate exits welfare improving. Such replacement rates are almost never obtained before the age of sixty. It is only after the minimum retirement age that such replacement rates start occurring, yet only through the normal and invalidity routes. This explains the full superposition between profiles for the normal and unemployment and early retirement routes at all ages: those people that find it profitable to exit through the UER route are in fact those who could directly move from the UER to the normal route and leave the labor force with a sufficiently high level of their normal pension, with, as expected, one first spike at the minimum age of sixty. This spike is much more pronounced for the invalidity route, as this route amounts to systematically offering a full-rate normal pension at this age whatever the past record of social security contributions.

6.3.4   Measuring Health

The health index is computed using the SHARE data following the methodology developed by Poterba, Venti, and Wise (2010) on the American Health and Retirement Survey data. The authors assume that latent health is revealed by responses to the long list of questions asked in the survey relative to health status and changes in health status. The health index is then defined as the first principal component of these selected health measures. It is a weighted average of the health indicators with weights chosen to maximize the proportion of the variance of the individual health index that can be explained by this first principal component. This methodology has been replicated with twenty-five questions from the SHARE questionnaire. (Details on the selected questions and on the weights are provided in the appendix and in the introduction of this volume.)

The percentiles of health, by age and sex, are given in figures 6.11A and 6.11B.[3] Percentile 1 corresponds to the worst health and percentile 100 to the best. Unsurprisingly, the health index is decreasing with age and is higher for women than for men.

6.3.5   Employment Data

Data on labor market states are issued from SHARELIFE, the third wave of data collection for SHARE. This wave provides some complementary information on people's work histories. The data collection for SHARELIFE took place between the fall of 2008 and summer of 2009. Over a sample of 2,483 individuals for France, we consider 1,121 individuals employed at age fifty-four for whom we have information on past careers and on health indicators. Following them from age fifty-four until retirement provides information on 6,274 annual spells. For each observation we have additional information on gender, age at leaving school, occupation (executive or nonexecutive), degree, marital status, and assets of the household.

Regressions are made on the whole sample, but also on a subsample cor-

---

3. The figures are drawn using the lowess smoother of Stata.

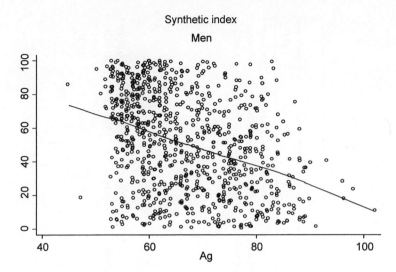

Fig. 6.11A   Percentiles of health index by age, men

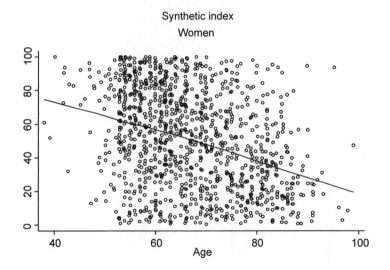

Fig. 6.11B   Percentiles of health index by age, women

responding to health quintiles or education levels. The size of the subsample, the number of observations, and the mean retirement rates will be detailed in tables of results with the coefficients of the regressions.

6.4   Results

Table 6.2A displays the results of probit models of the transition to non-employment between ages fifty-five and sixty-four. Transition to nonem-

Table 6.2A   Effect of inclusive OV on retirement

	Retire							
	(1)	(2)	(3)	(4)	(5)	(6)	(7)	(8)
OV_inclusive	-0.047***	-0.046***	-0.047***	-0.046***	-0.047***	-0.046***	-0.048***	-0.046***
	(0.006)	(0.006)	(0.006)	(0.006)	(0.006)	(0.006)	(0.006)	(0.006)
	[-0.044]	[-0.042]	[-0.044]	[-0.042]	[-0.044]	[-0.042]	[-0.044]	[-0.042]
Health quintile 2 (second lowest)	-0.041***	-0.041***	-0.041***	-0.042***				
	(0.010)	(0.010)	(0.010)	(0.010)				
Health quintile 3	-0.031***	-0.031***	-0.034***	-0.034***				
	(0.011)	(0.010)	(0.010)	(0.010)				
Health quintile 4	-0.029***	-0.030***	-0.028***	-0.029***				
	(0.011)	(0.011)	(0.011)	(0.011)				
Health quintile 5	-0.059***	-0.057***	-0.060***	-0.058***				
	(0.010)	(0.010)	(0.010)	(0.010)				
Health index					-0.010***	-0.010***	-0.010***	-0.010***
					(0.002)	(0.002)	(0.002)	(0.002)
Men			0.018**	0.017**			0.018**	0.017**
			(0.009)	(0.008)			(0.009)	(0.008)

	Linear	Dummies	Linear	Dummies	Linear	Dummies	Linear	Dummies
Married					0.035***	0.034***	0.034***	0.034***
					(0.009)	(0.008)	(0.009)	(0.008)
Educ.: vocational					0.016	0.017	0.015	0.016
(ref.: no diploma)					(0.011)	(0.011)	(0.011)	(0.011)
Educ.: HS graduate and above					-0.007	-0.006	-0.006	-0.005
					(0.010)	(0.010)	(0.010)	(0.010)
Total assets					0.049	0.043	0.044	0.039
(in million euros)					(0.043)	(0.042)	(0.044)	(0.043)
Age	Linear	Dummies	Linear	Dummies	Linear	Dummies	Linear	Dummies
No. of observations	6,274	6,274	6,274	6,274	6,274	6,274	6,274	6,274
No. of subjects	1,121	1,121	1,121	1,121	1,121	1,121	1,121	1,121
Mean retirement rate	0.124	0.124	0.124	0.124	0.124	0.124	0.124	0.124
Mean of OV	15,055	15,055	15,055	15,055	15,055	15,055	15,055	15,055
Std. dev. of OV	10,255	10,255	10,255	10,255	10,255	10,255	10,255	10,255

Note: Coefficients are marginal effects of a 10,000-euro change in OV. The effect of a one standard deviation change in OV is shown in brackets. Robust standard errors in parentheses.

***Significant at the 1 percent level.

**Significant at the 5 percent level.

*Significant at the 10 percent level.

ployment is considered hereafter equivalent to retirement: the transition into employment from any other state of the labor market is rare in this age group, so we consider that leaving the labor market after fifty-five in France is an absorbing state. We include various sets of controls in models (1) to (8). The first four models are estimated using dummy variables for health quintiles. The last four replicate the same specifications, but include the health index under a linear assumption instead of health quintiles. The values of the inclusive OV in the regressions are in units of 10,000 euros.

Results on the inclusive OV are unchanged when we change the specification of the health indicator. The coefficient of the inclusive OV has the expected negative sign and is highly significant, that is, individuals with higher incentives to delay retirement will effectively do it. The results remain remarkably robust to the various sets of controls. Coefficients for the inclusive OV are between –0.046 and –0.048. The effect on the probability of retirement of a one standard deviation change in the OV is given within brackets in table 6.2A, under the estimated coefficient. Since this standard deviation is roughly equal to 10,000 euros, our unit for measuring OVs, these simulated effects have the same order of magnitude as estimated coefficients. They range between –0.042 and –0.044. Considering the mean level of probabilities to retire, that is, 0.124, this implies a decrease of nearly 30 percent for these probabilities: this impact is quite large, but it corresponds to a change in incentives that is itself quite large, amounting to two-thirds of the mean inclusive option value.

Estimates for control variables imply that people in better health tend to retire at older ages. All coefficients on health quintiles are negative and significant in specifications (1) to (4), that is, individuals in a health quintile higher than the first (worst health quintile) tend to remain longer in the labor market. However, there is no clear trend and a linear assumption on the health effect might be rejected. Coefficients of health quintiles 2 to 5 tend to exhibit an inverted U-shaped pattern.

Probabilities to retire are also higher for men and married people. The higher probabilities for men may result from higher pension entitlement due to longer careers not fully captured by incentive variables. Concerning married people, higher propensities to retire can be due to joint retirement decisions of spouses, especially for women (Sédillot and Walraet 2002). On the other hand, coefficients for wealth and education are not significant at the 5 percent level when these variables are introduced in the regressions. A higher education level decreases the probability to retire, as could be expected, but the results are hardly significant, probably because financial motivations to postpone for more skilled people are, here, appropriately captured by the OV indicator.

Figures 6.12A, 6.12B, 6.13A, and 6.13B display predicted versus actual retirement behavior by age. Predicted hazards and survivals are simulated by age using the estimated coefficients of specification (8) where age effects

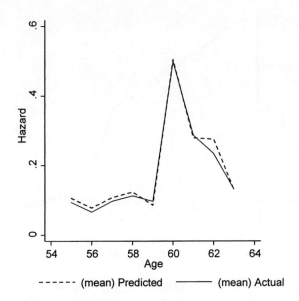

Fig. 6.12A   Model fit hazard, men

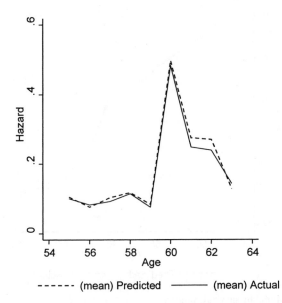

Fig. 6.12B   Model fit hazard, women

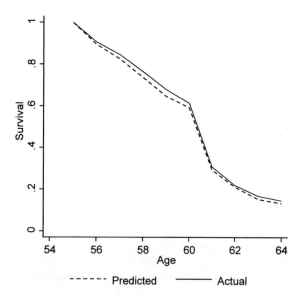

Fig. 6.13A   Model fit survival, men

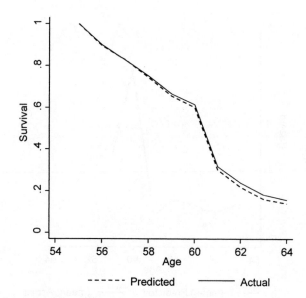

Fig. 6.13B   Model fit survival, women

Table 6.2B   **Effect of percent gains in inclusive OV on retirement**

	Retire			
	(1)	(2)	(3)	(4)
Percent gain in OV	–0.039***	–0.037***	–0.040***	–0.038***
	(0.013)	(0.012)	(0.012)	(0.012)
Age	Linear	Dummies	Linear	Dummies
Health quintiles	X	X	X	X
Other Xs			X	X
No. of observations	6,274	6,274	6,274	6,274
No. of subjects	1,121	1,121	1,121	1,121
Mean retirement rate	0.124	0.124	0.124	0.124
Mean of % gain in OV	0.624	0.624	0.624	0.624
Std. dev. of % gain in OV	0.683	0.683	0.683	0.683

Note: Robust standard errors in parentheses.
***Significant at the 1 percent level.
**Significant at the 5 percent level.
*Significant at the 10 percent level.

are captured by dummies rather than with a linear specification. Age effects are introduced to capture progressive changes in preferences for retirement when people get older, but also some possible attraction effects for some specific retirement ages: using dummies is better suited for capturing this second category of age effects. As a general rule, using dummies rather than a linear trend by age does not affect the estimated impact of the OV indicator, but leads, effectively, to a much better fit reflected on these figures 6.12A, 6.12B, 6.13A, and 6.13B. However, there remains a slight underestimation of survival rates and an overestimation of hazard rates around age sixty-two. Results are the same by gender.

Table 6.2B replicates the specifications (1) to (4) (health quintiles) of table 6.2A for a different OV indicator. This alternative indicator is computed by averaging, over the three potential routes, the percentage gains from delaying retirement measured by the corresponding OVs at this age *a* divided by net present values of retiring, through this route, at this age *a*. Averages are computed using the same relative weights as the ones used for the initial inclusive OV. This new set of estimations confirms that the estimated impact of financial indicators is almost the same whatever the set of control variables introduced in the model.

Tables 6.3A and 6.3B display estimates for the same models as in tables 6.2A and 6.2B, but separately for the five health quintiles. The mean retirement rate is decreasing with the level of health from 0.159 for the worst health quintile to 0.096 for the best health quintile. This means that individuals in better health retire at older ages. The effect of financial incentives provided by the pension system is higher in the middle of the health distribu-

Table 6.3A **Effect of inclusive OV on retirement by health quintile**

	No. of obs.	Mean ret. rate	Mean of OV	Std. dev. OV	Specification			
					(1)	(2)	(3)	(4)
OV: Lowest quintile (worst health)	1,260	0.159	14,233	9,513	−0.040** (0.017) [−0.036]	−0.041** (0.016) [−0.033]	−0.040** (0.018) [−0.035]	−0.041** (0.017) [−0.034]
OV: 2nd quintile	1,253	0.122	13,872	9,370	−0.074*** (0.014) [−0.061]	−0.071*** (0.013) [−0.060]	−0.071*** (0.014) [−0.060]	−0.068*** (0.013) [−0.058]
OV: 3rd quintile	1,257	0.134	14,711	10,072	−0.049*** (0.014) [−0.046]	−0.043*** (0.014) [−0.042]	−0.049*** (0.015) [−0.046]	−0.042*** (0.015) [−0.041]
OV: 4th quintile	1,245	0.128	15,910	10,642	−0.047*** (0.012) [−0.046]	−0.049*** (0.012) [−0.045]	−0.053*** (0.012) [−0.053]	−0.054*** (0.012) [−0.051]
OV: Highest quintile (best health)	1,208	0.096	16,803	11,125	−0.019* (0.010) [−0.021]	−0.017* (0.010) [−0.020]	−0.017 (0.011) [−0.019]	−0.015 (0.010) [−0.018]
Linear age					X		X	
Age dummies						X		X
Other Xs							X	X

***Significant at the 1 percent level.
**Significant at the 5 percent level.
*Significant at the 10 percent level.

Table 6.3B **Effect of percent gain in inclusive OV on retirement by health quintile**

	No. of obs.	Mean ret. rate	Mean of gain	Std. dev. gain	Specification			
					(1)	(2)	(3)	(4)
OV: Lowest quintile (worst health)	1,260	0.159	0.721	0.904	−0.012 (0.019)	−0.014 (0.018)	−0.012 (0.019)	−0.014 (0.018)
OV: 2nd quintile	1,253	0.122	0.611	0.584	−0.083*** (0.026)	−0.084*** (0.025)	−0.079*** (0.026)	−0.080*** (0.025)
OV: 3rd quintile	1,257	0.134	0.569	0.537	−0.056* (0.029)	−0.046* (0.027)	−0.059** (0.030)	−0.049* (0.027)
OV: 4th quintile	1,245	0.128	0.628	0.812	−0.034 (0.031)	−0.041 (0.030)	−0.040 (0.032)	−0.046 (0.030)
OV: Highest quintile (best health)	1,208	0.096	0.623	0.605	−0.023 (0.019)	−0.017 (0.018)	−0.023 (0.019)	−0.016 (0.018)
Linear age					X		X	
Age dummies						X		X
Other Xs							X	X

***Significant at the 1 percent level.
**Significant at the 5 percent level.
*Significant at the 10 percent level.

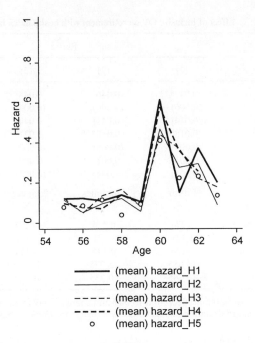

Fig. 6.14   Predicted hazard by health quintiles

tion (table 6.3A). Changes in the probability of retirement associated with a change of one standard deviation for incentives is –0.06 in the second quintile, between –0.04 and –0.05 in the third and fourth quintiles, and around only –0.02 in the fifth quintile. It is as if choices for individuals in very good health were less dependent on financial incentives, both because good health may be associated with better working conditions that reduce propensity to retire or, quite the opposite, because very good health offers opportunities for alternative projects or activities during the retirement period. The low coefficient for the lowest quintile is less counterintuitive as people in bad health may be constrained to retire whatever the financial conditions. The regressions with the gain variable confirm the results of the OV incentive indicator, but generally less significant. Coefficients are significant only for the second and third health quintiles, that is, in the middle of the health distribution. Predicted hazards by health quintile are given in figure 6.14.

Table 6.3C presents the results of models directly including the interaction between health status and the incentive variable, with a linear specification for the health variable. This specification is more constrained than the previous one and less informative: the negative interaction between health and inclusive OV is not statistically significant, but coefficients of the OV inclusive variable remain the same as in specifications (5) to (8) of table 6.2A.

Last, in tables 6.4A and 6.4B, we present estimations including interac-

Table 6.3C   Effect of inclusive OV on retirement with health index interaction

| | Retire | | | |
	(1)	(2)	(3)	(4)
OV_inclusive	−0.047***	−0.046***	−0.048***	−0.046***
	(0.006)	(0.006)	(0.006)	(0.006)
	[−0.044]	[−0.041]	[−0.044]	[−0.042]
Health index	−0.018***	−0.018***	−0.021***	−0.020***
	(0.007)	(0.006)	(0.007)	(0.007)
OV*health index	−0.001	−0.001	0.000	0.000
	(0.005)	(0.004)	(0.005)	(0.005)
Age	Linear	Dummies	Linear	Dummies
Other Xs			X	X
No. of observations	6,274	6,274	6,274	6,274
No. of subjects	1,121	1,121	1,121	1,121
Mean retirement rate	0.124	0.124	0.124	0.124
Mean of OV	15,055	15,055	15,055	15,055
Std. dev. of OV	10,255	10,255	10,255	10,255

Note: Coefficients are marginal effects of a 10,000-unit change in OV from probit models. The effect of a one standard deviation change in OV is shown in brackets. Robust standard errors in parentheses.
***Significant at the 1 percent level.
**Significant at the 5 percent level.
*Significant at the 10 percent level.

tions between education levels and the incentive variables, either the inclusive OV (table 6.4A) or the gain indicator (table 6.4B). Unsurprisingly, the more educated people are, the lower is the mean retirement rate and the higher is the mean of the OV incentive indicators. The effect of changes in the probability of retirement associated with a one standard deviation of the inclusive OV is nearly twice as large for high school graduates or above (nearly −0.06 for a mean retirement rate of 0.109) compared to high school dropouts (around −0.03 for a mean retirement rate of 0.138). Results are not very sensitive to the specification of the model. The general pattern is the same with the gain indicator, but with results that are generally less significant.

6.5 Simulations

Results of the previous section have shown that health and incentives provided by the pension system simultaneously impact on individual retirement behavior. We will now simulate changes in the retirement behavior, for a given level of health, for alternative scenarios concerning pension or disability and sickness leave entitlements.

Because the share of disability and sickness leave among the retirement pathways is quite low in France (figures 6.4 to 6.8), the part of this specific

Table 6.4A   **Effect of inclusive OV on retirement by education group**

	No. of obs.	Mean ret. rate	Mean of OV	Std. dev. OV	Specification			
					(1)	(2)	(3)	(4)
OV: < High school	2,150	0.138	12,352	8,782	−0.033*** (0.012) [−0.028]	−0.030** (0.012) [−0.024]	−0.035*** (0.012) [−0.029]	−0.031*** (0.012) [−0.025]
OV: Vocational	1,265	0.132	15,804	9,301	−0.041** (0.017) [−0.036]	−0.045*** (0.017) [−0.038]	−0.040** (0.019) [−0.035]	−0.044** (0.019) [−0.037]
OV: High school graduate and above	1,932	0.109	18,010	11,964	−0.059*** (0.007) [−0.060]	−0.055*** (0.007) [−0.058]	−0.058*** (0.007) [−0.061]	−0.054*** (0.007) [−0.059]
Linear age					X		X	
Age dummies						X		X
Other Xs							X	X

***Significant at the 1 percent level.
**Significant at the 5 percent level.
*Significant at the 10 percent level.

Table 6.4B   **Effect of percent gain in inclusive OV on retirement by education group**

	No. of obs.	Mean ret. rate	Mean of OV	Std. dev. OV	Specification			
					(1)	(2)	(3)	(4)
OV: < High school	2,150	0.138	0.575	0.638	−0.010 (0.019)	−0.007 (0.019)	−0.011 (0.020)	−0.008 (0.019)
OV: Vocational	1,265	0.132	0.610	0.513	−0.052* (0.030)	−0.057* (0.030)	−0.048 (0.031)	−0.053* (0.031)
OV: High school graduate and above	1,932	0.109	0.621	0.584	−0.104*** (0.018)	−0.095*** (0.017)	−0.100*** (0.018)	−0.092*** (0.017)
Linear age					X		X	
Age dummies						X		X
Other Xs							X	X

***Significant at the 1 percent level.
**Significant at the 5 percent level.
*Significant at the 10 percent level.

path in the inclusive OV is quite slight. Thus, we have to simulate large changes in the availability of this subroute to observe some impact on the inclusive OV and on retirement behavior.

We first simulate retirement behaviors as if only one exit route were available, normal retirement, unemployment and early retirement, or DI. Then, we add two "mixed" scenarios. These two scenarios use unchanged probabilities to exit through the unemployment and early retirement pathway,

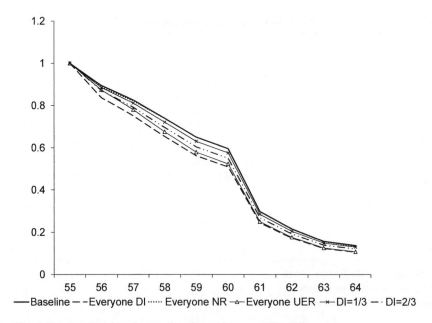

Fig. 6.15   Survival functions under alternative scenarios, full sample

but probabilities differ concerning exits through the DI pathway for the remaining people, one-third and two-thirds, respectively.

These scenarios are applied first to the whole population and then to the subsample of individuals more directly concerned by DI, that is, those for which the incentive to retire is higher through the DI route than through the normal route, hereafter the "DI" subsample. These are the people whose OVs are lower under DI than under normal retirement at the time of effective retirement.

Simulated results are provided in figures 6.15 (whole sample) and 6.16 (DI subsample), using survival functions. They are summarized in table 6.5 using average years spent at work under the various scenarios, compared both to actual numbers and to the simulated baseline scenario. More precisely, the indicators provide the mean cumulative number of years of work from age fifty-five to retirement, for each scenario. Column (1) provides results for the whole population and column (2) for the DI subsample.

Graphs of survival functions show that all alternative scenarios are bracketed within the two polar cases where only the normal route is accessible or where the DI route is available to 100 percent of the population.

When the whole sample is considered, average years of work computed under the baseline scenario are close to the actual figure, 5.509 and 5.652, respectively.

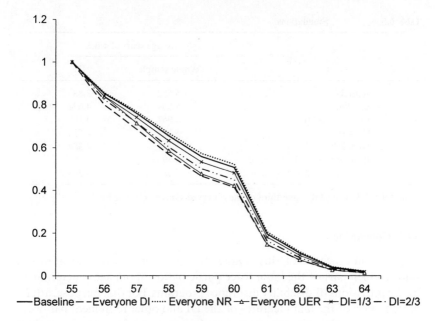

Fig. 6.16   Survival functions under alternative scenarios, DI sample

The average years of work over ages fifty-five to sixty-four if everyone retires through the normal retirement route is simulated equal to 5.495, which is almost the same as the baseline value. This result is explained by the predominant weight of the normal retirement route in the incentives OV indicator. It is lower than the observed average years of work in our sample, 5.652. The simulated average years of work drops to 4.957 if everyone retires through the DI route. Years of work are nearly 14 percent greater under the regular retirement incentives than under the DI incentives. Disability insurance is the route that implies the lowest number of years of work after age fifty-five. Even in the simulation where everyone would have access to unemployment and early retirement at the end of their careers, the mean number of years of work between fifty-five and sixty-four would be higher (equal to 5.089).

Moving to the DI subsample, average years of work are always lower. The difference in actual averages is quite high: 5.652 for the whole sample and 3.886 for the DI subsample. The estimated model predicts a higher number of years worked after age fifty-five, equal to 4.692. Simulations made on this subsample exhibit the same patterns of results as the ones made on the whole sample: the highest number or years of work for incentives of the direct retirement route (4.766), the lowest number of years of work for DI (4.188), and each situation between these brackets.

Table 6.5   Simulations

| | Average years of work | |
	Whole sample	DI
Actual	5.652	3.886
Baseline	5.509	4.692
Everyone in DI	4.957	4.188
DI = 1/3	5.387	4.554
DI = 2/3	5.231	4.384
Everyone normal retirement	5.495	4.766
Everyone in unemployment	5.089	4.293

Note: DI = 1/3 means DI = one-third of the observed sum of (DI + SS).

6.6   Conclusion

The main objective of this chapter was to estimate, for a given health status, which part of the labor force participation at old age is determined by the provisions of disability insurance programs. For that purpose, after a presentation of the main features of the DI and other retirement pathways for older workers in France we estimated the impact of the pension and DI schemes on exits from the labor market, controlling for health status and using a synthetic option value indicator. The OV and health indicators are introduced simultaneously in a probit equation, modeling the probability to make a transition from employment to nonemployment after age fifty-five. The model is estimated on the French data of the European SHARE survey. We conclude, unsurprisingly, that a decrease in the generosity of the pension and DI schemes (i.e., a higher value of the OV) induces people to stay on the labor market and that people in better health tend to retire at older ages.

In the OV approach, DI incentives enter as a component of a larger inclusive OV indicator. In order to isolate the impact of DI, we relied on simulations. First, we present extreme situations simulating what individuals' retirement behavior would have been if each of the three exit routes had applied to all individuals, then some mixed scenarios with various relative importance of the DI pathway. We show that average years of work between ages fifty-five and sixty-four are nearly 14 percent greater when regular retirement incentives are applied to the whole population than when DI rules are systematically applied. We then conduct the same analysis on a subsample of individuals considered as having higher probabilities to be eligible to DI, that is, a DI subsample. The average years of work are always lower for this subsample. The difference in the actual averages is quite high: 5.652 for the whole sample and 3.886 for this selected DI subsample. Simulations made on this subsample exhibit the same patterns as for the whole sample: the highest number or years of work for incentives of the direct retirement route, the lowest number of years of work for DI, and each situation between these brackets.

Of course, such simulations remain theoretical and somewhat disconnected from recent changes in retirement policies in France. As shown in figure 6.1, the French LFP rates for the fifty-five to sixty-four age group have started reincreasing significantly since the middle of the first decade of the twenty-first century, essentially due to successive reforms in the normal retirement route, accompanied by stricter rules for the unemployment and early retirement pathway. Less impact on retirement age could be awaited from reforming a disability and sickness leave pathway that, until now, has remained relatively well focused on those people whose health status really deserve specific dispositions: a tightening of these rules would have been socially problematic with low financial returns at the global level.

The main contribution of the chapter has been to illustrate how financial incentives and health status indeed interact to determine retirement behavior, using original SHARE data complemented with other statistical information. Improving our knowledge of both monetary and nonmonetary determinants of retirement behavior is of major importance for the ex post and ex ante evaluation of both past and future reforms.

Appendix

Table 6A.1   **Coefficients of the health index**

Difficulty walking several blocks	0.281	Ever experienced heart problems	0.162
Difficulty lift/carry	0.284	Hospital stay	0.126
Difficulty push/pull	0.289	Home care	0.211
Difficulty with an ADL	0.272	Doctor visit	0.200
Difficulty climbing stairs	0.296	Ever experienced psychological problems	0.067
Difficulty stoop/kneel/crouch	0.304	Ever experienced stroke	0.124
Difficulty getting up from chair	0.265	Ever experienced high blood pressure	0.110
Self-reported health fair or poor	0.279	Ever experienced lung disease	0.105
Difficulty reach/extend arms up	0.227	Ever experienced diabetes	0.091
Ever experienced arthritis	0.185	BMI at beginning of period	0.092
Difficulty sitting two hours	0.178	Nursing home stay	0.024
Difficulty pick up a dime	0.152	Ever experienced cancer	0.038
Back problems	0.161		

Note: Values are based on data from 2004 to 2006, 5,844 observations.

References

Barnay, T., and F. Jeger. 2006. "Quels dispositifs de cessation d'activité pour les personnes en mauvaise santé?" *Questions d'Economie de la Santé* n° 108. http://www.irdes.fr/Publications/Qes/Qes108.pdf.

Behaghel, L, D. Blanchet, T. Debrand, and M. Roger. 2012. "Disability and Social Security Reforms: The French Case." In *Social Security Programs and Retirement around the World: Historical Trends in Mortality and Health, Employment, and Disability Insurance Participation and Reforms*, edited by D. Wise. Chicago: University of Chicago Press.

Blanchet, D., and S. Le Minez. 2012. "Joint Macro/Micro Evaluations of Accrued-to-Date Pension Liabilities: An Application to French Reforms." DESE Working Paper no. g2012–14. Institut National de la Statistique et des Études Économiques. http://www.insee.fr/en/publications-et-services/docs_doc_travail/G2012-14.pdf.

Minni, C. 2012. "Emploi et chômage des 55–64 ans en 2011." *Dares-Analyses*, n° 049. http://travail-emploi.gouv.fr/IMG/pdf/2013-083.pdf.

Poterba, J. M., S. F. Venti, and D. A. Wise. 2010. "The Asset Cost of Poor Health." NBER Working Paper no. 16389, Cambridge, MA.

Sédillot, B., and E. Walraet. 2002. "La cessation d'activité au sein des couples: y-a-t-il interdependence des choix?" *Economie et Statistique* 357 (1): 79–102.

Stock, J. H., and D. A. Wise. 1990. "The Pension Inducement to Retire: An Option Value Analysis." In *Issues in the Economics of Aging*, edited by David A. Wise, 205–30. Chicago: University of Chicago Press.

7

Health, Financial Incentives, and Early Retirement
Microsimulation Evidence for Germany

Hendrik Jürges, Lars Thiel, Tabea Bucher-Koenen,
Johannes Rausch, Morten Schuth,
and Axel Börsch-Supan

7.1 Introduction

The aim of this chapter is to study the interrelated roles of financial incentives and health in the decision to retire early within the context of the German pension system. It continues and expands earlier research on early retirement in Germany (Börsch-Supan and Schnabel 1999; Börsch-Supan et al. 2004; Börsch-Supan, Kohnz, and Schnabel 2007) by taking health into account in a more systematic way. Too little is yet understood about the role that health plays compared to financial incentives. In Germany, at least, there is hardly any time-series correlation between old-age labor force participation and objective measures of population health such as mortality rates (Börsch-Supan and Jürges 2012). Moreover, in a cross-national perspective there is hardly any relationship between disability benefit (DI) receipt and average population health (Börsch-Supan 2005). On the other hand, health does seem to contribute quite a bit to explain within-country variation in early retirement at any point in time. In particular, mental health problems (which are only weakly related to mortality) are increasingly found to trigger retirement at very early ages such as forty-five or fifty (Börsch-Supan and Jürges 2012).

Hendrik Jürges is professor of health economics and management at the Schumpeter School of Business and Economics, University of Wuppertal. Lars Thiel is a researcher at the Schumpeter School of Business and Economics, University of Wuppertal. Tabea Bucher-Koenen is a senior researcher at the Munich Center for the Economics of Aging. Johannes Rausch is a researcher at the Munich Center for the Economics of Aging. Morten Schuth is a researcher at the Munich Center for the Economics of Aging. Axel Börsch-Supan is director of the Munich Center for the Economics of Aging and professor of economics at the Technical University of Munich.

For acknowledgments, sources of research support, and disclosure of the authors' material financial relationships, if any, please see http://www.nber.org/chapters/c13328.ack.

In the present chapter, we aim at a more systematic treatment of health in retirement decisions by incorporating health in a microsimulation model of retirement. While bad health appears to be an important driver of the decision to leave the labor force within countries and in a given year, it is, of course, not the only one. Generous early retirement benefits—initially conceived to support older workers who are too ill to work or who have trouble finding work for a variety of reasons—may also create disincentives to remain in the labor force until the regular retirement age for healthier workers and workers who have no trouble finding work. Thus, one important contribution of the present study is to estimate the effect of financial incentives on retirement behavior in a very similar way as has been done before, but to differentiate explicitly between individuals of different health states.

The question addressed is: Do financial incentives to retire affect healthy individuals in the same way as they affect less healthy individuals? This is an empirical question. Theoretical predictions are ambiguous. On the one hand, one can argue that individuals' labor supply is less elastic when they are sick. At the extreme, individuals may not be able to do any type or amount of work. Then financial incentives will not matter for the labor supply decisions and pension reforms that reduce the generosity of early retirement provisions, for example, will only hurt those individuals financially but not affect behavior. In contrast, healthy individuals who are able to work and have a choice could be lured into retiring early if provisions are too generous.

On the other hand, it is also possible that many healthy working individuals below the regular retirement age are actually not looking into early retirement possibilities because they are doing well and like their work. These individuals might even be ignorant about the various ways to leave work and the related financial incentives. Early retirement incentives or changes in these incentives might then have less effect than among sick individuals who have health problems that make employment more burdensome (but who are still able to work). The latter group of individuals might look into early retirement possibilities and labor supply decisions could eventually be driven by program generosity. Obviously, the answer to this research question has policy implications because pension reforms that reduce the generosity of early retirement benefits will affect the different types of individuals under both scenarios.

This is particularly interesting in the context of the German pay-as-you-go pension system that has undergone a number of changes since its inception in 1957 (described in more detail in the next section). Until the early 1980s, the system has been made more and more generous, thus creating more and more incentives to retire early. Among men, average retirement age reached its historical minimum in 1984 at only 58.2 years. Low labor market participation among older workers, together with low fertility rates, rising life expectancy, and sluggish labor markets have led to falling numbers of contributors and rising numbers of beneficiaries and cast serious doubts on the financial sustainability of the system. Since 1992, in a continuous effort to save the system, both conservative and social-democratic-led governments have passed a number of major and minor reforms that have reduced the generosity of the system.

Our microsimulations, based on individual survey data spanning more than twenty-five years from 1984 to 2010, take into account all of these reforms that provide the institutional variation that is necessary to identify the effect of system generosity on retirement decisions. Obviously, pension reforms have many different aspects: mandatory retirement ages, credit periods for disability, replacement rates, actuarial adjustment factors, stringency of the disability award process in case of disability benefits, and so on. We try to capture as many of these aspects as possible in a single measure, the option value (OV) of postponing retirement by one year (Stock and Wise 1990), that is, the change in expected discounted lifetime utility when one decides not to retire at a given age. We estimate the effect of this option value on retirement in regressions explaining annual retirement of German men and women age fifty to sixty-nine, overall, by health status and by education.[1]

We base these regressions on two sets of individual microdata: the German Socio-Economic Panel (SOEP) 1984–2010 and the Survey of Health, Ageing and Retirement in Europe (SHARE) 2004–2012.

The SOEP data have the great advantage of capturing a time period during which major reforms of the German pension systems in 1992, 2001, 2004, and 2007 were conducted (see section 7.2.1). This institutional variation greatly helps in obtaining significant results and for the detailed study of interaction and stratification effects. The main advantage of the SHARE data is a much richer health measurement and the comparability to SHARE-based estimations from other European countries. It is also illuminating to compare results within Germany between the two samples. The major disadvantage of the SHARE data is their still rather short length of just four panel waves. This limits the number of retirement transitions, which are crucial for the econometric identification. We therefore provide the SHARE-based estimates mainly for reasons of comparability with other chapters in this volume and as a robustness check with a more refined health measure. Interaction effects, detailed stratification results, and simulations of policy reforms are exclusively based on the SOEP sample.

With the estimated effect of the option value on retirement at hand, we simulate changes in the generosity of the pension system to understand how these changes would affect average retirement age. Since our specific interest

1. In an earlier draft of this paper we started all analyses at the age of forty-five, as this seemed more appropriate for the analysis of disability benefit uptake in Germany. However, this would have compromised comparability of our results with other country analyses in this volume. Thus, we decided to use fifty as a starting age. However, we note that a large proportion of DI recipients enter (at least partial) retirement before that age.

in this chapter is on the interrelated roles of health and financial incentives, the focus of our simulations is on disability pensions. In Germany, these pensions provide fairly generous benefits for those who are not eligible for an old-age pension (mostly individuals under the age of sixty) and who are unable to work for health reasons. We describe these benefits in more detail below. Each year about 20 percent of all new pension recipients receive disability pensions and the average age of first-time DI recipients is fifty among men and fifty-one among women.

In an earlier microsimulation study for Germany, Börsch-Supan et al. (2004) have modeled the effect of changes in the mandatory retirement age or changes in adjustment factors by first computing how these changes affect the option value to postpone retirement and then predict retirement behavior using these new option values. The focus of the current study is to model changes in the stringency of the disability pension award process. Since there is no simple quantitative measure of this important policy variable, we have chosen a somewhat different approach. We have computed option values separately for three different pathways to retirement: disability, prolonged unemployment, and regular retirement. We then combine these option values into one "inclusive" option value using the actual proportion of pensioners who have taken either path as a relative weight. Weights are based on year-sex-education cells and should reflect the perceived likelihood of being able to retire through a specific path (and thus of the actual stringency of the award process for disability pensions, for example).

In our simulations, we vary these weights and compute counterfactual option values under various scenarios. One extreme variant is to set the weight of the disability pension option value to zero. Thus, we increase the stringency of the award process to infinity and effectively block the disability benefit pathway. As we show below, the predicted average retirement age will then increase by only 0.6 years among men and by 0.2 years among women. In contrast, reducing the stringency of the award process, for instance, by assuming that everyone who applies would get disability benefits, reduces the estimated retirement age by 1.5 years among men and by 2.5 years among women.

The chapter is organized as follows: in the next section, we give a brief introduction into the history and the most salient features of the German public pension system. Section 7.3 describes our two micro data sets and documents trends in disability and early retirement in the last twenty-five years. In section 7.4, we describe our approach to estimating the effect of health and financial incentives on retirement behavior. In particular, we discuss the computation of the continuous health index and the inclusive option value of postponing retirement. In section 7.5 we show our retirement regression results, again with a focus on health and option values. Section 7.6 contains a more detailed discussion and interpretation of our empirical results, especially with respect to the goodness of fit of the model and the measured incentive effect of the option value. This section also shows the results of our simulations of the effect of pension reforms on retirement behavior. The final section concludes.

7.2   The German Pension System

We begin this section by a short description of the German statutory public pension system (*Deutsche Rentenversicherung*) and its major reforms in the last fifty years. We focus on the most salient aspects, in particular those related to disability insurance and other early retirement options. More detailed descriptions can be found, for example, in Börsch-Supan and Wilke (2007) and Börsch-Supan (2011). The German pension system covers 85 percent of the German workforce, most of them working in the private sector. Six percent of the workforce (25 percent of the public sector employees) is made up of civil servants such as police, teachers, administrators, or university professors. Civil servants have their own separate and more generous pension system, which we do not describe here. Nine percent of the workforce are self-employed and are mostly self-insured.

7.2.1   History of the German Pension System

The current pay-as-you-go pension system was introduced in 1957. The basics are simple. There are two types of pensions: old-age pensions and disability pensions. Eligibility for an old-age pension begins when one reaches the mandatory retirement age (which was sixty-five for both men and women until recently), conditional on a minimum number of contribution years but independent of the ability to work. Eligibility for a disability pension begins when one becomes partly or fully unable to work, independent of age, but again conditional on a small minimum number of contribution years.

These simple basics are complicated by a number of variants of old-age pensions with usually lower retirement ages but stricter criteria in terms of contribution years (see table 7.1). Already introduced in 1957 were old-age pensions for women and old-age pensions for the unemployed, and both could be drawn at age sixty if contribution requirements were met. Thus, until the first major reform of the pension system in 1972, there were only three pathways into retirement: regular old-age pensions, old-age pensions after long-term unemployment, and work disability. About half of all workers retired early due to disability. Since unemployment was at a historic low in the 1960s and early 1970s, retirement via unemployment accounted for only 2 percent of all entries into retirement. About 10 percent of women retired early on old-age pensions for women. In 1972, before the major reform took effect, the average retirement age for those retiring on old-age pensions was 65.1 among men and 62.7 among women. The average retirement age on disability was about 57.8 among men and 59.8 among women (see figure 7A.1 in the appendix).

Table 7.1   Variants of pension benefits

	Earliest age	Years of contribution	Other	Introduced
	No limit	5 (3 in last 5 years)	Work capacity less than 3 hours per day (less than 6 for partial DI)	1957
Regular old-age	65	5	None	1957
For unemployed	60	15 (8 in last 10 years)	At least 52 weeks unemployed	1957
For women	60	15 (10 after age 40)		1957
For long-term insured	63	35	Actuarial adjustment since 19xx	1972
For disabled workers	60	35	No actuarial adjustment	1972

The 1972 reform introduced two further variants of "early" old-age pensions and thus marked a significant increase in generosity. First, workers with at least thirty-five contribution years became eligible for old-age pensions already at age sixty-three *without actuarial adjustment*. Second, old-age pensions for disabled workers were introduced, also conditional on thirty-five contribution years, with an earliest entry age of sixty-two that was later reduced to age sixty. Both options became an instant success among men, with roughly 30 percent of all workers having taken either path to retirement. Average retirement ages on old-age pensions gradually decreased to 62.5 among men and 61.9 among women in 1980. The new retirement options partly substituted for the disability pathway, and the average age among those retiring on disability benefits dropped to 54.4 among men and 57.7 among women.

The next set of reforms was enacted in 1984. First, there was an increase in generosity—aimed primarily at women—by reducing the eligibility requirement for regular old-age pensions (at age sixty-five) from fifteen to five contribution years. At the same time, restrictions on the eligibility for disability pension were strengthened. This included the introduction of a minimum of three contribution years in the last five years and stricter medical examinations. Also, this part of the reform primarily affected women who often did not meet the stricter requirements. Hence within two years, from 1984 to 1986, the number of women retiring through the disability path decreased by 62 percent while the number of women retiring at age sixty-five essentially doubled.

In face of a looming demographic crisis, serious attempts to cut back on the generosity of the German pension system started in 1992. First, pension benefits were anchored to net rather than to gross wages. This change broke the vicious cycle of increasing pension benefits in response to increasing contribution rates. Second, actuarial adjustments of benefits to retirement age were introduced, albeit only gradually from 1998 onward. As intended, their introduction reduced incentives to retire early, and retirement age and labor force participation of older individuals has indeed increased since then.

Further adjustments to make the German pension system sustainable were decided in 2004 and 2007. In 2004, the pension benefit indexation formula was modified to account for demographic developments (Commission for Sustainability in Financing the Social Security Systems 2003). In 2007, a gradual increase in the normal retirement age from sixty-five to sixty-seven years to be phased in between 2012 and 2029 was decided. Retirement ages for other variants of old-age pensions were increased as well. For instance, the age limit for old-age pensions for the disabled will be shifted to sixty-five years, and old-age pensions for women were effectively phased out.

7.2.2   The Benefit Formula

Pension benefits B are computed as the product of four factors:

$$(1) \qquad\qquad B = E \times Z \times R \times A,$$

where E for *Entgeltpunkte* (earnings points) represents *relative* lifetime earnings. One year of social security contributions of the average wage earner yields exactly one earnings point. Thus, a worker who has entered the labor force at age twenty, worked continuously while receiving average pay, and retires at age sixty-three has a total of 43 earnings points. To compensate the loss in earnings due to nonemployment before becoming eligible for old-age pension, workers who retire on DI get awarded additional earnings points for each year they retire before becoming eligible for old-age pensions for the disabled (credit periods). In order to compensate DI recipients for the introduction of actuarial adjustments, credits for nonemployment years have become more generous. Until 2004, full credit was awarded for each missing year until age fifty-five, and one-third credit for each year between ages fifty-five and sixty. Since 2004, full credits are awarded until age sixty.

Z for *Zugangsfaktor* represents the actuarial adjustment for retirement age. Before the introduction of actuarial adjustments, Z was equal to one for every pension type. Even today, adjustments are not actuarially fair. Adjustment factors were set discretionarily at 3.6 percent for each year of earlier retirement (but 6 percent for each working year after age sixty-five) and thus some 1.5 percentage points lower than current life tables and a 3 percent discount rate would imply (Börsch-Supan and Schnabel 1999). Table 7.2 describes the situation in 2010, the end of the observation period in most of our empirical analyses. It shows an overview of retirement ages and adjustment factors by benefit type and retirement age. Note that disability pensions and old-age pensions for the disabled are the most generous in terms of actuarial adjustment. In contrast to all other pension types, where the 3.6 percent reduction is made for each year workers retire before

Table 7.2   **Benefit types, retirement ages, and adjustment factors (2010)**

Benefit type	< 56	57	58	59	60	61	62	63	64	65	66	67	68	69
					Old-age pensions (OA)									
Regular										1.000	1.060	1.120	1.180	1.240
					Early old-age pensions options (OA)									
For long-term employed								0.928	0.964	1.000	1.060	1.120	1.180	1.240
For previously unempl.					0.820	0.856	0.892	0.928	0.964	1.000	1.060	1.120	1.180	1.240
For the disabled					0.892	0.928	0.964	1.000	1.000	1.000	1.060	1.120	1.180	1.240
For women					0.820	0.856	0.892	0.928	0.964	1.000	1.060	1.120	1.180	1.240
					Disability pension (DI)									
Disability pension	...	0.892	0.892	0.892	0.892	0.928	0.964	1.000	1.000	1.000	1.060	1.120	1.180	1.240

age sixty-five, the pivotal age for disability pensions and old-age pensions for the disabled is sixty-three. Moreover, for retirement ages younger than sixty there is no further adjustment to disability benefits.

R for *Rentenartfaktor* represents the type of benefit (worker, widow, orphan). It is 1 for workers' pensions, 0.6 for widow pensions, and 0.2 for orphans. Widow and orphan pensions are partly means tested. The details are again fairly complex and we refrain from describing them here because widow pensions are not taken into account in our empirical analyses.

A for *Aktueller Rentenwert* represents the current average pension value. This is the amount in euros a retiree receives for each earnings point. As described above, *A* was anchored to gross wages until 1992 and to net wages thereafter. Since 2004, the development of *A* also depends on the development of the system dependency ratio, that is, the ratio of pensioners to workers.

7.2.3   Unemployment Benefits at Older Ages

When analyzing the role of financial benefits and health in retirement decisions, we will also take into account unemployment benefits at older ages. Retiring via unemployment has come to be an important pathway to retirement. This pathway may be attractive to some because unemployment benefits at older ages are generally more generous than those for younger unemployed. In short, there are two types of unemployment benefits in Germany, UB1 and UB2. The UB1 benefits amount to 60 percent (households without children) to 67 percent (households with children) of last net earnings for a period between twelve and thirty-two months, depending on age (details are shown in table 7A.1 in the appendix). When UB1 expires, and workers are still unemployed, they receive UB2 for an unlimited period, that is, essentially until becoming eligible for pensions. Until 2004, UB2 amounted to 53 percent (without children) or 60 percent (with children) of last net earnings. In the major reform of the German welfare system in 2004, UB2 has been turned into a lump-sum welfare payment of currently €382 per month. To this lump-sum payment, benefits for housing and heating are added based on actual costs.

7.3   Data and Descriptives

In this section, we introduce our two main data sources, SOEP and SHARE, describe our health measures, and provide an overview of the trends in German DI participation.

7.3.1   The SOEP Data

Our main data source for detailed estimation and microsimulation is the German Socio-Economic Panel survey (SOEP), an ongoing household panel survey of the German population similar in scope to the Panel Study of Income Dynamics (PSID) (see Wagner, Frick, and Schupp [2007] for a detailed description). The SOEP started in 1984 in West Germany and covered some 6,000 households. Since then, the sample size has been increased several times (notably after reunification) and now consists of roughly 19,000 individuals in 11,000 households. Individual interviews are conducted with all household members age seventeen and older. The survey covers a wide range of subjects, but the focus was and still is on labor market experience and earnings. This includes retrospective employment histories starting at age fifteen, so that it is also possible to reconstruct retirement pathways ex post for years in which a panel member has not yet been interviewed. It also allows us to identify if individuals retire directly from employment or if they first go through a spell of unemployment.

The large number of years, the large sample size, and the availability of detailed employment biographies has motivated us to use the SOEP for our analysis. However, the downside of using the SOEP is the measurement of health. In the first decade of SOEP, there were hardly any questions on health. Through the years the SOEP has broadened in scope, and now also includes fairly detailed health measurements. Yet in order to make use of the full length of the panel, we decided not to restrict our analytic samples to years with detailed health information.

We constructed our sample using as a starting point all West German respondents ages fifty to sixty-nine in 1984 to 2009. Individuals become part of the analytic sample in the year in which they turn fifty and stay in the sample until they retire, die, or are lost to follow-up in any other way. Moreover, the sample is restricted to public and private sector employees. Civil servants or the self-employed are not included.

7.3.2   The SHARE Data

The Survey of Health, Ageing and Retirement in Europe (SHARE) is a pan-European data set designed to analyze the process of population ageing using cross-national comparisons within Europe and between Europe, America, and Asia. While SHARE currently includes twenty European countries, covering the area from Sweden to Greece and Portugal to Estonia, this chapter only uses the German data. The SHARE survey covers the interplay between economic, health, and social factors in shaping living conditions of older people. Also, SHARE provides very detailed health measures, ranging from self-rated health over large sets of limitations in daily living and doctor-reported conditions to biomarkers and performance measures.

In wave 3, the SHARE panel data has been enriched with detailed accounts of the respondents' life histories (SHARELIFE). By integrating this retrospective view, the living conditions in the preceding decades become accessible, thus granting various insights going back as far as into childhood, especially employment histories with several anchors in which earnings are measured.

We construct a panel of respondents based on the SHARE/SHARELIFE data for East and West Germany. The information from the three panel waves (2004, 2006, and 2010–2012) is combined with information on working status and income from the life histories in SHARELIFE. Since SHARE focuses on respondents older than fifty, the majority of individuals included in our sample are older than fifty years of age. We keep a small number of respondents' spouses older than forty-five years. The exact way of calculating the job information from SHARELIFE is explained in section 7.4.3.

We construct a panel of 813 individuals observed from 2004 to 2012. Of those individuals we are only keeping individuals either working in the complete observation period or transitioning from work to retirement while we observe them. We are left with 383 individuals. On average, individuals are observed for six periods (minimum four years, maximum eight years).

7.3.3   Measuring Health

We measure health by using the health index proposed by Poterba, Venti, and Wise (2010), which is constructed by performing a principal component analysis using data from waves 1, 2, and 4 of SHARE for Germany. The obtained continuous health index is computed separately for each wave and is the first principal component of twenty-four health indicators (see table 7.3). The functional limitations in walking, carrying, and pulling have the highest factor loadings.

The raw scores of the index are then used to group individuals into health quintiles in each wave. Individuals assigned to the lowest quintile have the worst health and those assigned to the highest quintile have the best health. As we are interested in the transition to retirement for a given year in the observation period, we replace the health index for years in which no SHARE survey took place with the value of the health index from the last wave relative to a given year (e.g., we took the values for the health index computed in 2004 for the health index in 2005, and so on).

In SOEP, we build our health index on three health variables that are available since the first wave of SOEP. First, there is "health satisfaction," measured on a 0 to 10 scale. This is clearly a subjective measure that appears to be similar to self-rated health and has been used as a measure of subjective health before (e.g., Riphahn 1999; Romeu Gordo 2006). Second, we have information on health care utilization—the number of doctor visits in the last three months and, third, the number of nights spent as an inpatient in a hospital in the last calendar year. We combine the information in these health variables by a similar principal components analysis as for the SHARE data. Included in this computation are all SOEP respondents ages fifty to sixty-nine from 1984 to 2010. Raw health values for each person are then converted to percentiles. In the retirement regressions below, health is added in quintiles (where low values mean bad health and high values mean good health).

Table 7.3   **First principal component index of health based on SHARE Germany**

Health measure	Wave 1	Wave 2	Wave 4
Difficulty walking sev. blocks	0.292	0.269	0.288
Difficulty lift/carry	0.235	0.294	0.303
Difficulty push/pull	0.260	0.287	0.311
Difficulty wih an ADL	0.283	0.275	0.284
Difficulty climbing stairs	0.265	0.269	0.267
Difficulty stoop/kneel/crouch	0.294	0.290	0.269
Difficulty getting up from chair	0.284	0.288	0.273
Self-reported health fair or poor	0.294	0.274	0.269
Difficulty reach/extend arms up	0.255	0.247	0.260
Ever experience arthritis	0.156	0.141	0.184
Difficulty sitting two hours	0.218	0.231	0.171
Difficulty picking up a coin	0.138	0.187	0.173
Back problems	0.190	0.172	0.151
Ever experience heart problems	0.157	0.167	0.156
Hospital stay	0.157	0.161	0.153
Doctor visit	0.226	0.197	0.210
Ever experience psychological problems	0.110	0.087	0.112
Ever experience stroke	0.131	0.132	0.124
Ever experience high blood pressure	0.137	0.115	0.095
Ever experience lung disease	0.104	0.072	0.065
Ever experience diabetes	0.104	0.122	0.121
BMI at beginning of obs. period	0.092	0.080	0.116
Nursing home stay	0.115	0.083	0.072
Ever experience cancer	0.069	0.073	0.092
N	2,953	2,480	1,489

Source: Based on SHARE waves 1, 2, and 4 for Germany.

Figure 7.1, panel (a) shows the average health index percentile separately for men and women ages fifty to sixty-nine. Men are on average healthier than women (at all ages), and health generally deteriorates with age. It is instructive to read this figure horizontally. For instance, we find that women reach the 50th percentile of health at the age of about fifty-two. Men reach this percentile at fifty-five years. In that sense, one can speak of a health gap between women and men that is equivalent to being seven years older. Panel (b) shows the average health percentile by education group jointly for men and women. This graph reflects the familiar education gradient in health (e.g., Jürges 2009; Kemptner, Jürges, and Reinhold 2011). Nevertheless, the steepness of the gradient is surprising. For instance, we find that according to our index, fifty-two-year-old basic track graduates are on average as healthy as sixty-eight-year-old academic track graduates, that is, the health gap is sixteen years. Moreover, the graph also suggests that the education-related health gap is actually increasing in age.

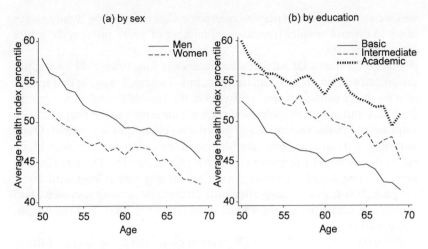

Fig. 7.1   **Average health percentile by age and sex**

7.3.4   Trends in DI Participation 1984–2009

We now describe the development of disability pension receipt and early retirement in general from 1984 to 2009. In contrast to earlier work, we use survey data from SOEP for this description. We decided not to report trends in DI participation, that is, the *stock* of DI recipients from official statistics for several reasons: First, the official statistics are not available by age or education or any other covariates, most importantly health. Second, a break in the official time series in 1992 (due to a reallocation of pensioners across pension types) gives rise to huge spurious "reform effects" that do not reflect actual pathways.

However, using the SOEP has also its disadvantages. First, it does not show the actual pension type a retiree receives. Rather, we identify respondents who retired on disability benefits by the combination of age (younger than sixty) and their self-reported labor force status (retired). At ages sixty and older, we are only able to say whether respondents draw any pension, but not if this is health related. Second, since the SOEP started in 1984, we have only limited information on years before 1984. Labor force participation before the start of the panel can be approximated by labor market biographies, which are available beginning at age fifteen for all respondents. However, we found the results to be quite implausible when compared to official statistics. This may be due to recall bias or sample selection issues. To avoid such problems, we decided to begin our description in 1984 and we use data from the employment biography pertaining to the last calendar year only. Third, when looking at population subgroups, the number of observations in some cells can become small and the aggregate statistics that we discuss in this section may become somewhat noisy. Thus, it only makes sense to discuss broader trends over a number of years, not specific values for specific years.

Figure 7.2 shows DI participation rates over time since 1984 by sex, age groups, education groups, and health status. The average age at first receipt of a disability pension is about fifty, hence we decided to look at age groups forty-five and older.[2] Participation rates are measured as the proportion of respondents in the respective age group who claim they are retired. Quite naturally, participation rates are highest in the oldest age group and lowest in the youngest age group (see panel [a]). Generally, DI participation appears to be slightly increasing over time among men at least until about the year 2000 and decreasing afterward. In contrast, among women we find decreasing participation rates until about the year 2000, and then again some increase.

Panel (b) of figure 7.2 shows DI participation rates by education. Education is measured by an individual's school-leaving certificate according to the three different secondary school tracks in Germany: basic, intermediate, and academic track. This is the most straightforward way to distinguish education groups in the context of the German education system. After being taught together in primary school for four years, students are assigned to one of three secondary school tracks that are usually taught at separate schools. The selection process depends on a mix of formal exams, grades in primary school, recommendations by the class teacher, and parental choice. Of the three tracks, *Hauptschule* is the basic track leading to a basic school-leaving certificate after nine or ten years of schooling (depending on the federal state). *Realschule* is a more demanding intermediate track that leads to a school-leaving certificate after grade 10. Having finished school, both students from the basic track and the middle track usually start an apprenticeship or a school-based vocational training. *Gymnasium* is the academic track leading to a general university-entrance diploma (*Abitur*) after grade 12 or 13. Earlier studies show that secondary track choice has strong implications for the entire life course (Dustmann 2004; Jürges and Schneider 2011). Our findings are consistent with the earlier studies. We observe a clear education gradient in DI participation, particularly among men. However, the gradient is less clear among women. Only in the last ten years do we observe a systematic gap between those with academic track education and those with intermediate or basic track education. One reason why we observe a clearer gradient among men might be that men with basic education often work in physically demanding jobs. The general pattern of DI participation over

2. Note that not only are we unable to identify DI participants older than fifty-nine in our data, doing so will also make less sense than in the US context because many individuals older than fifty-nine are eligible for regular pensions. However, for comparison with other countries, we show early retirement rates for the fifty-five to sixty-four age group in figure 7A.2 in the appendix.

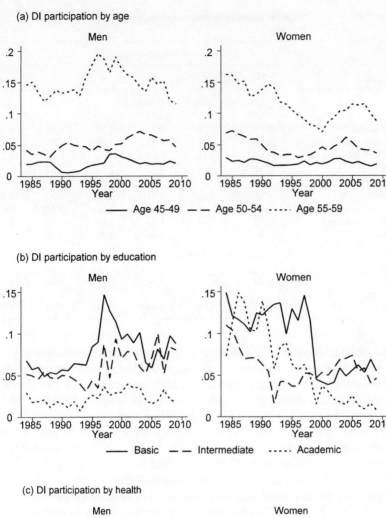

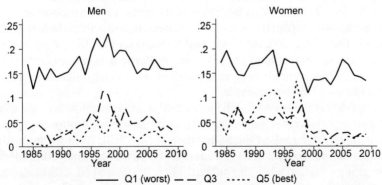

Fig. 7.2 DI participation over time by sex, age groups, education, and health

Source: Authors' own computations using SOEP data.

Table 7.4   DI participation by health, education, and sex (ages forty-five to
                  fifty-nine)

	Health quintile (%)					
Education	1	2	3	4	5	All
Panel (a). SOEP 1984–2009						
Men						
Basic track	20.04	10.80	6.73	3.33	2.56	9.51
Intermediate track	12.08	6.87	4.57	3.60	2.95	5.83
Academic track	11.02	4.00	1.85	1.44	0.81	3.25
All	17.20	8.47	4.98	2.79	2.08	7.19
Women						
Basic track	16.50	7.28	5.21	3.86	5.32	8.44
Intermediate track	14.68	5.46	3.43	2.15	3.25	5.61
Academic track	11.73	3.66	1.51	1.65	0.38	3.74
All	15.49	6.27	4.04	2.93	3.65	6.92
Panel (b). SHARE 2004–2012						
Men						
All	21.43	11.36	5.68	2.41	0.89	6.54
Women						
All	19.61	1.69	2.94	3.53	0.80	4.38

time among basic track graduates actually matches the temporal pattern of musculoskeletal diseases as a primary diagnosis for disability benefit uptake. As shown in Börsch-Supan and Jürges (2012), musculoskeletal conditions were the most common primary diagnosis between about 1990 and 2000, but their relevance has greatly diminished since then.

Panel (c) of figure 7.2 shows DI participation rates by health level, where health is measured by a continuous index and subsequently divided into quintiles from bad to good health (described briefly in section 7.3.3). We omit the second and fourth quintile for improved clarity of the graph. While we generally find a graded relationship between health and DI participation, with the least healthy individuals having the highest DI participation rates, the relationship appears to be highly nonlinear. Individuals in the first health quintile (i.e., those with the worst health levels) have by far the highest DI participation rates, around 15 to 20 percent. Participation rates in the third quintile are also somewhat elevated, but there is not much difference between the middle and the best quintile.

Considering the strong link between health and education, we also show DI participation rates jointly by health and education groups (see panel [a] of table 7.4, based on the SOEP data 1984–2010). Even within health groups, we find an education gradient in DI participation, and within education groups, we find a health gradient. Thus, health and education interact strongly when explaining DI participation rates in Germany. The same holds for retirement rates among the fifty-five to sixty-four-year-olds (see table 7A.2 in the appendix).

The SHARE data exhibit a similar pattern of DI participation as in SOEP (see panel [b] of table 7.4: participation rates are much higher for the lowest health quintile and strongly decrease thereafter). However, SHARE has a lower overall participation rate for both men and women, and the difference between the first and the higher health quintiles is more pronounced. This may be due to the more precise definition of DI possible with SHARE where the type of pension is part of the question battery on benefit recipiency. Moreover, the data covers a much later sample, 2004–2012, when DI rules were less generous than between 1984 and 1995.

To put the development of DI participation in context, we now describe the development of employment at large at older ages. This analysis is based on the SOEP data in order to depict the long-term trends. Figure 7.3 shows employment rates among older individuals over time by age group, sex, education, and health. Employment among men ages forty-five to fifty-four is fairly stable over time. The small ups and downs reflect general developments on the German labor market, for instance high unemployment rates in the mid-1990s, which are also mirrored in the trough in employment in the fifty-five to fifty-nine age group. As shown in table 7A.1, unemployment benefits in this age group were particularly generous during that period. The most significant trends in employment can be found among men ages sixty to sixty-four. After a long decline to about 45 percent in the early twenty-first century, they have increased steeply. This is a consequence of general improvements on the labor market, but also of the labor market and pension reforms of the early twenty-first century. Among women, labor force participation has been continuously rising in all age groups. This finding mainly reflects rising female labor force participation among younger cohorts.

Employment at older ages exhibits a clear gradient by education. The gap in employment rates between individuals who graduated from the academic track and individuals who graduated from the basic track rises clearly with age. In 2009, the difference in employment rates was about 4 percentage points in the forty-five to forty-nine age group, but 25 percentage points in the sixty to sixty-four age group. However, the gap appears to have narrowed in the last decade, mainly because of steeply rising labor force participation rates among the less educated in the sixty to sixty-four age group.

As expected, labor force participation by health is also clearly graded. Individuals in the healthiest quintile have the highest labor force participation rates and those in the least healthy quintile have the lowest participation rates. As with education, we find that the gap widens as individuals get older. In 2009, for instance, the percentage difference in employment rates between the healthiest and the sickest 20 percent in the forty-five to forty-nine age group was only 6 percentage points. In the sixty to sixty-four age group, the

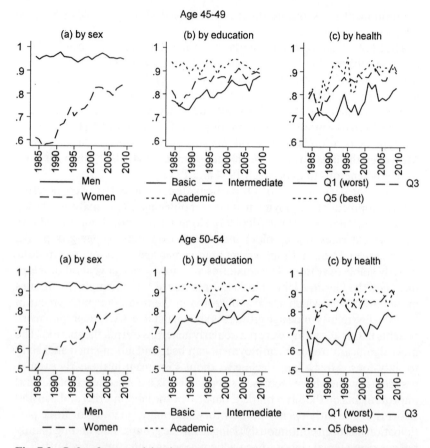

Fig. 7.3   **Labor force participation rates at ages forty-five to sixty-nine by sex, education, and health quintiles**
Source: Authors' own computations using SOEP data.

same difference was 21 percentage points. Note, however, that since the year 2000, employment rates are also increasing among the sickest respondents in the oldest age group.

7.4   Empirical Approach

In this section we explain our empirical approach to estimating the effects of health and financial retirement incentives on exiting the labor force and the data used for our estimations. The general regression specification is:

$$(2) \qquad h_{it} \equiv p(l_{it+1} = 0 | l_{it} = 1) = f(H_{it}, OV_{it}, X_{it}, \varepsilon_{it}).$$

We estimate the probability of leaving employment (i.e., retiring immediately or becoming first unemployed and then retiring) in year $t + 1$ con-

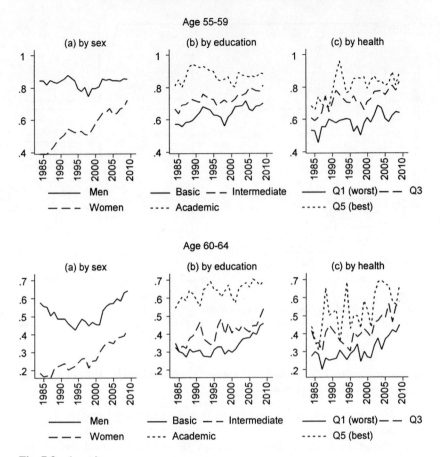

Fig. 7.3   (cont.)

ditional on working in year t as a function of individual health H in year t, of the option value of continuing to work OV in year t, and a set of individual specific covariates: age, sex, education, occupation (SOEP only), asset income (SOEP only), household wealth, and spouse's employment status. We generally specify $f(\ )$ as a probit model and report marginal effects. In the following, we describe the empirical specification of our main explanatory variable, the option value of postponing retirement, as well as the dependent variable, exit from the labor force.

7.4.1   Pathways to Retirement

The financial incentives that are relevant in the decision to retire are summarized in the inclusive option value to postpone retirement, as described in the next subsection. The first step is to compute for each working individual

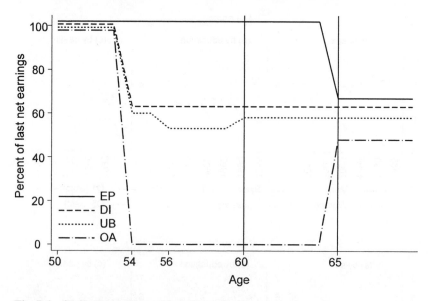

Fig. 7.4   Stylized earnings and benefits paths

Note: EP = continuous employment, DI = disability pension, UB = unemployment benefits, and OA = old-age pension.

the future stream of expected earnings and pension benefits that arises from each of the following pathways:

1. Continue working for another year and receive labor market income, then decide again.

2. Retire on disability benefits, receive those benefits until the regular retirement age, and then switch to a regular old-age pension. Retiring on DI includes receiving old-age pensions for the disabled.

3. Leave work and register as unemployed, receive unemployment benefits or other welfare payments until one becomes eligible for an old-age pension, especially old-age pension for the unemployed. We assume that nobody who registers as unemployed will get back into work.

4. Leave work and receive neither earnings nor welfare payments until eligible for an old-age pension. Then draw a regular pension based on one's earnings points obtained during employment.

Thus, we consider three main pathways to retirement: disability pensions, unemployment, and old-age pensions. To illustrate the value of each path in terms of pension and/or welfare benefits, figure 7.4 shows in stylized form the potential benefit streams for a male worker considering retirement at age fifty-four as a percentage of the last net earnings. To simplify the exposition, we assume a constant average pension value. If the worker retires on DI at age fifty-four, he will receive about 63 percent of his last net earnings for the rest of his life. If the worker becomes unemployed, he will remain so until age sixty and then switch to old-age pensions for the unemployed. During the first year of unemployment he will receive UB1, then UB2, which is lower than UB1. If the worker simply retires without drawing unemployment benefits or disability benefits, he will receive nothing until he becomes eligible for old-age pensions, for instance, at age sixty-five when he has less than thirty-five contribution years.

7.4.2   Option Value Calculations

To measure the effect of pension system generosity on early retirement and disability uptake, we compute the inclusive option value of remaining one year longer in employment. "Inclusive" means that all alternative pathways to retirement are included in a single OV measure by appropriate weighting. The inclusive option value is computed in several steps.

Estimating Individual Earnings and Benefit Streams

First, we take all respondents who are between fifty and sixty-nine years old in any year between 1984 and 2009 in SOEP and between 2004 and 2012 in SHARE, respectively. For each of these respondents we compute, for each year and for each potential retirement age, the (expected) earnings and benefit streams from each possible pathway to retirement: disability pension, unemployment, and regular old-age pension. We only consider earnings and benefit streams of the individual decision maker and do not include survivor pensions (in contrast to the United States, there are no spouse benefits).

Individual earnings streams can be divided in three periods: presurvey participation, during survey participation, and postsurvey participation. Whereas we are able to observe earnings during participation directly for a certain number of years (contemporaneous earnings), we need to infer individual presurvey and postsurvey earnings by appropriate backcasts and forecasts, respectively. The key ingredients in individual earnings backcasts and forecasts are for the SOEP data:

1. Historical average gross earning for backcasts and predicted average gross earnings for forecasts. Both historical averages and forecasts (until 2025) are derived from official statistics of the German statutory pension insurance scheme (Deutsche Rentenversicherung Bund 2012). After 2025, we project average earnings with a 1 percent real growth rate.

2. Historical average tax and contribution rates for backcasts and predicted tax and contribution rates for forecasts. These are taken from statistics published by the Federal Ministry of Finance (2013) and the German statutory pension insurance scheme (Deutsche Rentenversicherung Bund 2012), respectively.

3. Individual earnings relative to average earnings. We estimate relative earnings for each individual in our data by running a fixed-effects regression

of contemporaneous (gross) log earnings, separately for men and women, on a third-order polynomial in age. The individual-specific intercept (fixed effect) from this regression measures the deviation of an individual's earnings from average earnings.

4. Individual labor market biographies dating back to age fifteen. These are taken from the SOEP employment calendars and biographies.

Based on contemporaneous information on earnings, backcasts, and forecasts, we compute earnings of each individual $(\hat{Y}_{it})$ as

$$(3) \qquad \hat{Y}_{it} = \begin{cases} E_{it} \cdot \alpha_i \cdot (g\,\bar{Y}_t - \bar{T}_t - \bar{C}_t) & \text{if} \qquad t < t^{\min(i)} \\ Y_{it} & \text{if} \quad t^{\min(i)} \le t \le t^{\max(i)} \ , \\ \tilde{E}_{it} \cdot \alpha_i \cdot (g\,\tilde{Y}_t - \tilde{T}_t - \tilde{C}_t) & \text{if} \qquad t > t^{\max(i)} \end{cases}$$

where E_{it} indicates whether individual i was employed (= 1), unemployed (= 0.6) or out of the labor force (= 0) in year t, and $\tilde{E}_{it}$ represents future employment status; α_i is the individual specific effect obtained from the fixed effects earnings regressions; g is a gender adjustment factor equal to 0.9 for women and 1.1 for men reflecting gender differentials in average earnings due to discrimination or productivity differences. Further, $\bar{Y}_t$ are historical average gross earnings in year t, $\bar{T}_t$ is the historical average tax rate in year t, and $\bar{C}_t$ is the historical average contribution rate to social security, health, and unemployment insurance. Likewise, $\tilde{Y}_t$ are predicted average gross earnings in year t, $\tilde{T}_t$ is the predicted average tax rate in year t, and $\tilde{C}_t$ is the predicted average contribution rate to social security, health, and unemployment insurance. We use the predicted social security contribution rates published by the German statutory pension system, but as predicted tax rates we simply use the 2010 values; $t^{\min(i)}$ and $t^{\max(i)}$ are the first and last year an individual is observed in the SOEP. Earnings forecasts are made until 2035 (when the youngest cohort in our data reaches age seventy).

In SHARELIFE the respondents are asked to recall any job spell, which lasted six months or longer, using the so-called *Life History Calendar* (see Schröder 2011). In addition, the first wage at the beginning of each job, characteristics specific to each spell (e.g., occupation, industry, part-time work, etc.), the current wage if the respondent is still working (at the time of the interview), and the last wage at the end of the main job (if the respondent is a retiree in 2008–2009) are obtained during the course of the interview.

We use the methodology applied by Weiss (2012) to obtain the complete earnings history for each respondent for the German subsample of SHARELIFE:

1. In a first step, we take the imputed current wage from wave 1 and wave 2 to replace missing values for the current wage in SHARELIFE (for employment spells that started before wave 1 or wave 2). The remaining missing values for first wage, current wage, and last wage of the main job were

imputed using predictive mean matching (first introduced by Little [1988]). Thus, we end up with complete data on the first job of each job spell, the current job, and the last wage of the main job, which are necessary to project the annual wage during each employment spell.[3]

2. In a second step, we regress the logarithm of the current wage (last wage of the main job, respectively) on potential labor market experience and its quadratic form, years of schooling and characteristics that are specific to the respective employment spell, that is, dummy variables for type of industry and for white-collar jobs. All explanatory variables are interacted with potential labor market experience and its quadratic form.[4]

3. The obtained estimated regression coefficients and the first wage of each job spell are then used to predict the wage at the end of each employment spell. Having the wage at the beginning and at the end of an employment spell and the length of each spell at hand we are able to calculate the annual growth of wages during an employment spell.

4. As a last step, we use the growth rate to compute the wage for each year during an employment spell.

Weiss (2012) checked the validity of the wage prediction procedure using data from the SOEP. The provided evidence shows that this method for predicting wage works rather well.

Net wages are translated into gross wages by using historical tax and social security contribution rates. Earnings points are calculated by comparing gross wages to historic average wages.

Finally, we use the same method for SOEP and SHARE to make benefit forecasts for each individual at each planning age from fifty to sixty-nine until 2060, when the youngest cohort reaches age 100. We use the above earnings histories to compute disability pensions, unemployment benefits (UB1 and UB2), and old-age pensions at each retirement based on the relevant legislation.

The Option Value of Postponing Retirement

To compute the option value of continuing work in utils, we first convert income from work Y into utility using the instantaneous utility function $u(Y) = Y^\gamma$ with parameter $\gamma = 0.75$. Then we convert retirement income and/ or unemployment benefits B into utility using the instantaneous utility function $v(B) = (kB)^\gamma$ with parameter values $\gamma = 0.75$ and $k = 1.5$, where k reflects the relative value of leisure. These utility parameters are the same as in all other country chapters of this volume to ensure comparability. The choice

---

3. Observations were dropped for individuals whose wages at the end of the main job are coded in a foreign currency or are not codeable. Amounts given in German marks (DM) and East German marks are converted into euros.
4. Potential labor market experience is defined as the age in year t minus years of education and age at school entry.

of 1.5 is based on earlier US estimates (Gruber and Wise 2004) and appears to be very low for European countries. See, for example, Börsch-Supan et al. (2004), who use a grid search algorithm and obtain maximum likelihood estimates between 2.5 and 3.5 for Germany. This difference is exacerbated by a lower choice of γ than in Börsch-Supan et al. (2004).

Next we compute the expected future lifetime utility at some planning age a from retiring at any future age R as

$$(4) \qquad \mathrm{EU}_i(B)_a^R = \sum_{t=a}^{R-1} \frac{1}{(1+r)^{t-a}} s_{it} u(Y_{it}) + \sum_{t=R}^{T} \frac{1}{(1+r)^{t-a}} s_{it} v(B_{it}),$$

where s_{it} is the conditional probability of being alive in year t (obtained from life tables of the Federal Statistics Bureau) and r is a discount rate arbitrarily set to 3 percent. Here, Y_{it} and B_{it} are earnings and benefits, respectively, in year t at age $a + t$.

The first part of equation (4) reflects expected and discounted utility during one's working life and the second part reflects expected and discounted utility during one's retirement years. In our computations, the maximum attainable age T is arbitrarily set to 100. In $t = 0$ (at some planning age), the gain in expected lifetime utility from continuing working until age R (compared to receiving benefit B from the next period onward) is equal to

$$(5) \qquad \mathrm{OV}_i(B)_a^R = \mathrm{EU}_i(B)_a^R - \mathrm{EU}_i(B)_a^{a+1}.$$

Thus, the option value of not retiring on benefit B at some planning age a is equal to the maximum gain (across all R) from delaying retirement:

$$(6) \qquad \mathrm{OV}_i(B)_a = \max_R [\mathrm{OV}_i(B)_a^R].$$

Clearly, the larger the OV at any given planning age, the stronger the incentive to postpone retirement.

7.4.3   Weighting the Pathways—The Inclusive Option Value

The option value described in the preceding subsection is computed for a specific type of benefit, that is, for some specific pathway to retirement. However, since individuals in Germany have several options of retiring early, we want to estimate a weighted average of all option values to capture the overall incentive effect to retire. The weights should reflect the probability that either of these paths is a realistic pathway to retirement. Using the employment biographies in the German SOEP data, we estimate these weights—by year, sex, and education level—as the shares of the already retired population age fifty to sixty-nine who have retired through either of the following pathways:

1. Entering retirement on disability benefits (DI path). These are men and women who have changed directly from employment to retirement before the age of sixty and men who have changed from employment to retirement

at age sixty to sixty-three. Formally, the latter group retires on old-age pensions for the disabled, but we classify these as retired through DI.

2. Entering retirement via unemployment (UB path). These are women who were unemployed before retiring at age sixty or older and men who were unemployed before retiring at age sixty-two and older.

3. Retiring on old-age pensions (OA path). These are women who change directly from employment to retirement at age sixty and older and men who change from employment to retirement at age sixty-three and older.

We compute the inclusive option value of not retiring at age a as the weighted average of the three relevant option values:

$$
(7) \quad \mathrm{OV}_i(a) = \pi(\mathrm{DI}) \times \mathrm{OV}_i(\mathrm{DI})_a + \pi(\mathrm{UB}) \times \mathrm{OV}_i(\mathrm{UB})_a + \pi(\mathrm{OA}) \\ \times \mathrm{OV}_i(\mathrm{OA})_a.
$$

Here, $\pi(\mathrm{DI})$, $\pi(\mathrm{UB})$, and $\pi(\mathrm{OA})$ are the weights of the three pathways and OV(DI), OV(UE), and OV(OA) are the respective option values.

For the SHARE data, we use the same approach with two deviations:

- We also include the basic pension intended to provide a minimum standard of living (*Grundsicherung*), which was introduced into the pension system in 2003. After calculating the expected earnings-related pension, we check if this pension is above the minimum level. If not, pension benefits are topped up to this level.
- For all pathways we check if the respective pathway via DI or unemployment gives higher utility than the regular old-age pension. The assumption for this procedure is that this pathway can always be chosen. Only if DI or unemployment would deliver higher utility is the weighting applied.

Based on the SOEP data, figure 7.5, panel (a) shows the option values (in 10,000 utils) of not retiring from each of the three pathways at each planning age between fifty and sixty-nine, separately, for men and women. Several points are worth being highlighted. First, average option values are always larger than zero, that is, given our parameterization of the utility function (standard across all country chapters in this volume) and continuing to work always increases expected lifetime utility, even at ages sixty-five and older. Thus, it seems surprising that anyone actually retires. This pattern is identical when looking at OVs calculated from the SHARE data (not shown here).

The relative attractiveness of each pathway is reflected in the value of the OV conditional on age: the smaller the OV, the more attractive a pathway. For men up to age sixty, retiring on DI is the most attractive option on average, followed by unemployment and old-age pension. Considering the stylized benefit streams shown in figure 7.3, this is not surprising. The increase in the DI option value at age sixty seems puzzling at first sight. The reason for

(a) Average option values by retirement path

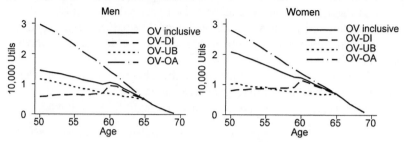

(b) Average present discounted value of income stream by retirement path

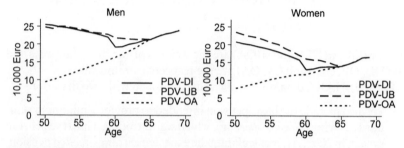

Fig. 7.5   Average option values of postponing retirement and discounted income streams at planning ages from fifty to sixty-nine

Notes: Panel (a): Average option values of postponing retirement via disability (DI), unemployment (UB), or old-age pension (OA) path at planning ages from fifty to sixty-nine. Panel (b): Average present discounted values of earnings/benefit streams when retiring via disability (DI), unemployment (UB), or old-age pension (OA) path at planning ages from fifty to sixty-nine. Panels (c) and (d): Average inclusive option value by education and health quintile.

this jump is that from age sixty onward individuals actually do not receive DI proper, but old-age pensions for the disabled (OA-DI). In contrast to those planning to retire on DI (at ages younger than sixty), individuals planning to retire at any future age on OA-DI will not be credited further earnings points for the years they were unable to work.

A summary of the present discounted value of the earnings and benefit stream from either pathway is shown in panel (b) of figure 7.5. These figures clearly illustrate the generosity of both DI and UE. The present discounted value of the earnings/benefit stream even falls with age because of the increase in pension benefits. The present discounted value of the old-age pension options rises continuously until the arbitrarily chosen end of the decision period.

Figure 7.5 also shows the inclusive option value by age and education (panel [c]) and by age and health (panel [d]). There are substantial differences in option values across education groups, particularly among men. Basic track graduates have lower inclusive option values (thus higher incen-

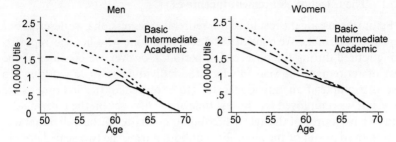

(c) Average inclusive option values by education

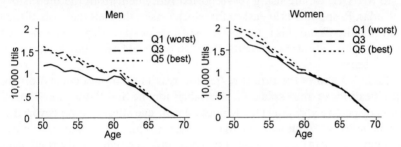

(d) Average inclusive option values by health quintile

Fig. 7.5   (cont.)

tives to retire) than intermediate or academic track graduates at every age. Of course, this difference is due mainly to disparities in earnings streams across education groups. The variation across health quintiles is not as large, but it is clearly present. Individuals in the lowest health quintile (worst health status) have lower option values or higher early retirement incentives. This reflects differences in earnings across health groups, that is, an income gradient in health. Our analysis does not say anything about whether low earnings are due to bad health or bad health due to low earnings, as this is beyond the scope of this chapter.

7.5   Results

Our analytical SOEP sample consists of a panel of 4,109 working individuals with a total of 21,000 observations. The SHARE sample is much smaller with 813 individuals' contribution to 2,118 observations in four waves. As mentioned before, each individual becomes part of the analytical sample at age fifty and remains in the sample until he or she self-reports as retired, becomes sixty-nine years old, dies, or is lost to follow-up for other reasons.[5]

5. In SHARE, a small number of spouses of respondents are between ages forty-five and fifty.

7.5.1   The Effect of Retirement Incentives

Before discussing the results of our retirement regressions, we describe our dependent variable. We consider as a retiree anyone who has self-reported being retired during the observation period. However, we consider as the year of retirement the year in which the individual stopped working. To give an example: if an individual claims to be retired for the first time at age sixty, but was employed for the last time at age fifty-seven, the individual is said to have retired at the age of fifty-eight, no matter if the individual was unemployed or out of the labor force or both during the two years between ending employment and becoming a retiree.

In SHARE we are using self-reported retirement from the life history calendar. Respondents are asked for which reason they left their job. If they said "I retired" and this is the last job spell we observe, they are considered retired. This definition is identical to the other SHARE-based studies in this volume.

Table 7.5 shows the probit regression results (marginal effects) of five specifications of the explanatory variables for the SOEP and the SHARE data, respectively. Model (1) includes a linear age effect and no covariates, (2) includes age dummies and no covariates, (3) includes a linear age effect and covariates, (4) includes age dummies and covariates, and (5) includes sex-specific age dummies and covariates. Model (4) is the common specification in this volume, of which we discuss the quantitative results. In general, results are clearer when using age dummies, but the qualitative findings are robust across the different specifications.

The OV coefficient reflects the percentage point effect of increasing the inclusive option value by 10,000 utils. Note that these are marginal effects evaluated at the means of the explanatory variables. The effect is highly significant in all specifications based on the SOEP data. This also holds for the estimates based on the SHARE data when age is specified as a set of dummy variables (columns [2] and [4]). A 10,000-util increase in the option value reduces the probability of retirement by approximately 4.2 percentage points in the SOEP data and by 2 percentage points in the SHARE data. Put in relative terms, this means that a 73 percent increase in the option value relative to the overall mean of 13,770 reduces retirement hazards by about 80 percent compared to the overall average of 5.3 percent in the SOEP data. The SHARE-based estimate is substantially smaller: a similar 76 percent increase in the option value relative to the overall mean of 13,065 reduces retirement hazards by only about 36 percent compared to the overall average of 5.5 percent.

The smaller effects in SHARE compared to SOEP may have various reasons. The SHARE data include the topping-up of low pensions via social assistance (*Grundsicherung im Alter*), which makes the option value flat for individuals with low pensions. Moreover, the samples are different: SHARE

Table 7.5 **Probit regressions explaining the decision to retire (marginal effects), option value enters in absolute value**

	Specification				
	(1)	(2)	(3)	(4)	(5)
Panel (a). SOEP					
Option value (10,000 utils)	−0.0317	−0.0349	−0.0379	−0.0423	−0.0421
	(0.0029)	(0.0027)	(0.0034)	(0.0031)	(0.0033)
	[−0.0323]	[−0.0407]	[−0.0404]	[−0.0521]	[−0.0525]
Health quintile 2	−0.0140	−0.0127	−0.0136	−0.0122	−0.0118
	(0.0025)	(0.0022)	(0.0024)	(0.0021)	(0.0020)
Health quintile 3	−0.0179	−0.0153	−0.0173	−0.0150	−0.0148
	(0.0025)	(0.0022)	(0.0024)	(0.0021)	(0.0021)
Health quintile 4	−0.0181	−0.0158	−0.0170	−0.0150	−0.0147
	(0.0025)	(0.0022)	(0.0024)	(0.0021)	(0.0021)
Health quintile 5	−0.0162	−0.0140	−0.0153	−0.0133	−0.0131
	(0.0026)	(0.0023)	(0.0025)	(0.0022)	(0.0021)
Linear age	X		X		
Age dummies		X		X	X
Age dummies × sex					X
Covariates			X	X	X
No. obs.	21,027	20,915	21,027	20,915	20,915
Mean retirement rate	0.052	0.053	0.052	0.053	0.053
Mean OV	13,704	13,771	13,704	13,771	13,771
Std. dev. OV	7,549	7,513	7,549	7,513	7,513
Panel (b). SHARE					
OV (10,000 utils)	−0.010	−0.022	−0.007	−0.020	−0.018
	(0.005)	(0.006)	(0.005)	(0.007)	(0.007)
Health quintile 2	−0.022	−0.031	−0.022	−0.032	−0.034
	(0.011)	(0.015)	(0.011)	(0.015)	(0.015)
Health quintile 3	−0.017	−0.022	−0.017	−0.021	−0.026
	(0.011)	(0.015)	(0.011)	(0.016)	(0.016)
Health quintile 4	−0.020	−0.026	−0.019	−0.026	−0.028
	(0.011)	(0.016)	(0.012)	(0.016)	(0.016)
Health quintile 5	−0.020	−0.026	−0.021	−0.028	−0.030
	(0.011)	(0.015)	(0.011)	(0.015)	(0.015)
Age linear	X		X		
Age dummies		X		X	X
Age dummies × sex					X
Controls			X	X	X
N	2,118	2,118	2,118	2,118	2,118
Mean retirement rate	0.083	0.083	0.083	0.083	0.083
Mean OV	13,065.62	13,065.62	13,065.62	13,065.62	13,065.62
Std. dev. OV	8,612.53	8,612.53	8,612.53	8,612.53	8,612.53

Table 7.6   **Probit regressions explaining the decision to retire (marginal effects), option value enters in relative terms**

	Specification				
	(1)	(2)	(3)	(4)	(5)
OV utility gain	−0.0132	−0.0137	−0.0130	−0.0139	−0.0131
	(0.0073)	(0.0074)	(0.0074)	(0.0077)	(0.0073)
Health quintile 2	−0.0166	−0.0164	−0.0162	−0.0161	−0.0157
	(0.0027)	(0.0025)	(0.0027)	(0.0025)	(0.0025)
Health quintile 3	−0.0220	−0.0210	−0.0209	−0.0203	−0.0201
	(0.0026)	(0.0025)	(0.0026)	(0.0025)	(0.0024)
Health quintile 4	−0.0221	−0.0214	−0.0208	−0.0205	−0.0201
	(0.0027)	(0.0025)	(0.0026)	(0.0025)	(0.0024)
Health quintile 5	−0.0204	−0.0197	−0.0191	−0.0187	−0.0187
	(0.0027)	(0.0026)	(0.0027)	(0.0025)	(0.0025)
Linear age	X		X		
Age dummies		X		X	X
Age dummies × sex					X
Covariates			X	X	X
No. obs.	21,027	20,915	21,027	20,915	20,915
Mean ret. rate	0.0522	0.0525	0.0522	0.0525	0.0525
Mean OV gain	0.6020	0.6050	0.6020	0.6050	0.6050
Std. dev. OV gain	0.5404	0.5403	0.5404	0.5403	0.5403

includes respondents from East Germany and has a substantially later sample. Finally, the precision of measurement is different; SHARE has a more encompassing health measure, while SOEP has more precise earnings histories (see below).

The numbers in square brackets in panel (a) show the average effect of a one standard deviation change in the inclusive option value—computed as the average predicted retirement probability when the option value is 0.5 standard deviations larger than its actual value minus the average predicted retirement probability when the option value is 0.5 standard deviations smaller than its actual value, averaged across all observations. The estimates indicate that a one standard deviation increase in OV reduces retirement rates by about 5.9 percentage points or nearly 100 percent of the average. The difference between the effect sizes found for the two alternative specifications can be partly explained by a strongly nonlinear (concave) relationship between OV and retirement hazards. The larger the option value at baseline, the smaller the effect of one util.

Yet another estimated specification of the relation between the inclusive option value and the probability to retire can be found in table 7.6, shown for the SOEP data only. Here we show the effect of the utility gain if labor force participation is continued until the optimal age relative to the utility when retiring at the planning age. In other words, this is the *percentage gain in future lifetime utility* from choosing the optimal retirement age instead of retiring now. This measure has a few advantages over the absolute number of utils. For instance, absolute option values very much reflect the individual's income level. A 10,000-utils option value of postponing retirement may thus mean a lot more (have a stronger incentive effect) to a low-income than to a high-income worker. Related to this, the relative utility gain might be more useful in international comparisons when income levels differ across countries.

The reported coefficients reflect the effect size of a *100 percent* lifetime utility gain from postponing retirement. Again, results show a decline in retirement rates when the lifetime utility gain from postponing retirement rises. Our estimates show that doubling this gain is linked with a 1.3 percentage point or 20 percent decrease in retirement hazard rates. Note, however, that standard errors are much larger (relative to the point estimates) than before, so that the coefficients are significant at the 10 percent level only.

7.5.2   The Effect of Health

We now turn to the effect of health on retirement rates. Table 7.5 shows the coefficients of health quintile dummies with those in the worst health quintile being the reference group. Respondents in higher quintiles are in better health. Our results clearly show that health has a significant relationship with retirement rates. Healthier individuals have lower retirement rates. The results also show that the relationship is highly nonlinear. Respondents in the baseline quintile have about 1.2 to 1.5 percentage points higher retirement hazard rates than those in the second to fifth quintiles (among which there is no big difference) in the SOEP sample. The SHARE sample exhibits a substantially larger effect of health on retirement, indicating that respondents in the baseline quintile have about 2.1 to 3.2 percentage points higher retirement hazard rates than those in the second to fifth quintiles. It is noteworthy that the nonlinear shape of the health effects is very similar for both the SOEP and the SHARE sample. Compared to the overall average retirement rate of 5.3 (8.3) percent, this suggests having a severe health shock and moving from the fifth to the first health quintile would increase retirement probabilities by more than 20 percent (35 percent) in SOEP (SHARE, respectively). "Mild" health shocks, for example moving from the fourth to the second health quintile, do not seem to have any effect on retirement rates. The larger marginal effects in the SHARE data compared to the SOEP, together with the substantially smaller effects of the option value, may reflect the more encompassing health measure in the SHARE data. The SOEP-based estimates of the financial incentives may therefore be an upper bound. Since the earnings histories in the SOEP are probably more precisely estimated than those based on the SHARELIFE data, the SHARE-based estimates of the financial incentives may rather be a lower bound.

7.5.3. The Effect of Financial Incentives by Health Status

Having established independent effects of health and financial incentives on retirement rates, it is natural to ask whether the two interact. Specifically, the question is whether healthier individuals are more or less responsive to financial incentives. Casual reasoning suggests that the labor supply of sick individuals should be less elastic than the labor supply of healthy individuals simply because sick individuals' choices are constrained by bad health. On the other hand, one might argue that individuals who are in bad health and consider early retirement might be more responsive to financial incentives than healthy individuals who have no plans to retire early. Both effects are not mutually exclusive and may even cancel each other out.

Table 7.7, based on the SOEP data, shows the effect of the inclusive option value on retirement rates separately for each health quintile. This is estimated from separate retirement regressions for each of the health quintiles. We have estimated the effect of a 10,000-util increase, of one *within-quintile*

Table 7.7	Marginal effects of inclusive option value on the decision to retire (obtained from probit models) by health quintile					
		Specification				
		(1)	(2)	(3)	(4)	(5)
HQ1	Option value	−0.0690	−0.0761	−0.0792	−0.0902	−0.0894
		(0.0088)	(0.0086)	(0.0110)	(0.0105)	(0.0107)
	Std. dev. effect	[−0.0498]	[−0.0582]	[−0.0587]	[−0.0707]	[−0.0722]
	Option value gain	−0.0207	−0.0221	−0.0146	−0.0164	−0.0147
		(0.0163)	(0.0163)	(0.0151)	(0.0152)	(0.0142)
HQ2	Option value	−0.0351	−0.0364	−0.0439	−0.0453	−0.0469
		(0.0076)	(0.0068)	(0.0079)	(0.0067)	(0.0074)
	Std. dev. effect	[−0.0331]	[−0.0413]	[−0.0458]	[−0.0576]	[−0.0579]
	Option value gain	−0.0043	−0.0046	−0.0049	−0.0055	−0.0062
		(0.0099)	(0.0093)	(0.0091)	(0.0088)	(0.0085)
HQ3	Option value	−0.0296	−0.0272	−0.0314	−0.0285	−0.0123
		(0.0040)	(0.0039)	(0.0045)	(0.0043)	(0.0029)
	Std. dev. effect	[−0.0369]	[−0.0508]	[−0.0444]	[−0.0628]	[−0.0722]
	Option value gain	−0.0232	−0.0230	−0.0206	−0.0214	−0.0111
		(0.0132)	(0.0119)	(0.0133)	(0.0122)	(0.0056)
HQ4	Option value	−0.0155	−0.0173	−0.0173	−0.0195	−0.0235
		(0.0050)	(0.0044)	(0.0058)	(0.0050)	(0.0066)
	Std. dev. effect	[−0.0369]	[−0.0508]	[−0.0444]	[−0.0628]	[−0.0722]
	Option value gain	−0.0199	−0.0196	−0.0203	−0.0203	−0.0234
		(0.0091)	(0.0083)	(0.0097)	(0.0088)	(0.0104)
HQ5	Option value	−0.0151	−0.0158	−0.0219	−0.0219	−0.0123
		(0.0053)	(0.0049)	(0.0057)	(0.0050)	(0.0031)
	Std. dev. effect	[−0.0189]	[−0.0268]	[−0.0218]	[−0.0320]	[−0.0341]
	Option value gain	−0.0193	−0.0179	−0.0272	−0.0248	−0.0139
		(0.0088)	(0.0080)	(0.0097)	(0.0086)	(0.0051)

standard deviation increase and of a 100 percent increase in future lifetime utility.

The qualitative results are robust across all specifications, but not across different measures of the early retirement incentives. Let us begin by looking at the marginal effect of a 10,000-util increase in the option value to postpone retirement, that is, when the incentives are specified in absolute terms. Here, we find the biggest effect of the inclusive option value in the first health quintile. The estimated effects decrease up to the fourth quintile and then increase again (slightly). These findings appear to be consistent with the notion that sick individuals for whom early retirement is a more salient option are also more influenced by the financial incentives. At this point one should also keep in mind that average option values are positive everywhere and that those in good health have particularly high option values. Thus, making early retirement more or less attractive will probably not make a large difference to them. In contrast, those in worse health have lower option values anyway, so that changes in option values matter more. The opposite mechanism—sick individuals being so constrained in their labor supply decisions that financial incentives hardly matter—seems less prevalent.

The estimated effects of a one within-quintile standard deviation change in the OV are qualitatively similar to those discussed in the preceding paragraph. However, the decline in the OV effect across quintiles is weaker. This may be partly due to the fact that the OV standard deviation is larger among the healthy (and richer) than among the unhealthy. In contrast to the findings above, where the sickest quintile stood out, it seems that it is now the healthiest quintile that is much less responsive to early retirement incentives than the rest. Finally, when looking at another relative incentive measure, the percent gain in lifetime utility, we find no clear pattern. If anything, the incentive effect seems to be slightly increasing with health status.

It is, of course, unfortunate that different specifications yield somewhat different conclusions. The choice of specifications is rather ad hoc, and we have no theory that would tell us which specification to prefer. We believe a fair summary of the results shown in table 7.6 is that there is hardly any evidence that the labor supply of the sickest quintile is the *least elastic* at the extensive margin. Rather, depending on specification of the incentive variable, their reaction to financial incentives is at least as strong as the reaction of the healthier quintiles—if not stronger.

7.5.4   The Effect of Financial Incentives by Education Level

Our final set of results, again based on SOEP data, relates to differences in retirement behavior by education groups. As noted above, a good way to distinguish education levels in Germany is by type of school-leaving certificate or type of secondary school track attended: basic track, intermediate, and academic track. We have already seen that employment rates are lower for the less educated. Correspondingly, retirement rates are generally larger

Table 7.8   Marginal effects of inclusive option value on the decision to retire
                   (obtained from probit models) by education

		Specification				
		(1)	(2)	(3)	(4)	(5)
Basic	Option value	−0.0344	−0.0392	−0.0471	−0.0511	−0.0504
		(0.0062)	(0.0063)	(0.0068)	(0.0067)	(0.0072)
	Std. dev. effect	−0.0240	−0.0291	−0.0340	−0.0391	−0.0394
	Option value gain	−0.0063	−0.0068	−0.0069	−0.0069	−0.0064
		(0.0067)	(0.0070)	(0.0071)	(0.0073)	(0.0065)
Intermediate	Option value	−0.0415	−0.0409	−0.0467	−0.0457	−0.0423
		(0.0050)	(0.0047)	(0.0051)	(0.0049)	(0.0050)
	Std. dev. effect	−0.0477	−0.0518	−0.0592	−0.0627	−0.0615
	Option value gain	−0.0205	−0.0212	−0.0238	−0.0254	−0.0228
		(0.0125)	(0.0122)	(0.0135)	(0.0134)	(0.0125)
Academic	Option value	−0.0270	−0.0230	−0.0296	−0.0238	−0.0171
		(0.0044)	(0.0033)	(0.0046)	(0.0034)	(0.0027)
	Std. dev. effect	−0.0406	−0.0620	−0.0463	−0.0686	−0.0734
	Option value gain	−0.0505	−0.0387	−0.0512	−0.0398	−0.0298
		(0.0220)	(0.0172)	(0.0209)	(0.0159)	(0.0116)

among the less educated. Of workers who completed the basic track, about 5.5 percent retire annually, whereas of workers who completed the academic track, only 4.7 percent retire annually. As we have seen above, differences in average inclusive option values across education groups are substantial (see figure 7.5, panel [d]), reflecting well-known differences in lifetime income by education group.

In terms of the strength of the option value effect on retirement rates, we find sizable differences across education groups and across specifications (see table 7.8). When estimating the percentage point effect of a 10,000-util increase using our standard specification (4), the size of the coefficient drops from 5.1 percentage points among basic track graduates to 2.4 percentage points among academic track graduates. However, when we standardize the effect size, for instance, by looking at the effect of one *within-education group* standard deviation increase in future lifetime utility, we tend to find the opposite result: academic and intermediate track graduates actually become more responsive than basic track graduates. This can be partly explained by the fact that the standard deviation in the utility gain is nearly twice as large in the highest than in the lowest education group. Also, when we look at the effect of a 100 percent lifetime utility gain, it is stronger among the better educated than among the less educated.

7.6   Understanding the Results and Their Implications

After having established that the health and financial incentive effects are qualitatively similar in the two data sets, we now exploit the longer time horizon and the richer policy variation in the SOEP data to better understand the implications of our results for pension policy.

7.6.1 The Model Fit

Our first step in understanding the above results is to show how well our estimated models fit the actual retirement behavior. Figure 7.6 compares, separately for men and women, the actual and predicted retirement hazard rates and the actual and predicted labor force survival rates (starting at age fifty). Note that the y axis for hazard rates is on a logarithmic scale. Both actual and predicted log retirement rates are practically the same. This was to be expected since our preferred regression specification contains age dummies interacted with sex that should be able to pick up much of the variation in retirement across the age distribution. Hazard rates increase almost linearly until age sixty-five. In other words, retirement hazards increase exponentially with age. The spikes at younger ages are due to sampling variation, but the spikes at older ages (sixty, sixty-three, or sixty-five) can be explained by the provisions of the pension system. At age sixty many women could retire on old-age pensions for women and men could retire on either old-age pensions for the unemployed or for the disabled. Age sixty-five is the regular retirement age.

Figure 7.6, panels (e) to (h), show predicted retirement hazard rates for men and women by health quintile and by education. Again, this is shown on a log scale. The figures show that the main difference in retirement rates is between the first (least healthy) health index quintile and the other health quintiles. This holds across the entire age range but seems to be particularly pronounced below the age of sixty, that is, where the most salient early retirement option is DI. Differences in predicted retirement hazards by age also clearly show an education gradient. Academic track graduates have the lowest retirement hazards across most of the age distribution. The difference is very pronounced among men. In contrast, there is hardly any difference among women older than fifty-six.

7.6.2 Relationship between OVs and Retirement

We have seen above that the average inclusive option values are always positive. Thus, on average, there are at every age financial incentives to continue working. Another way to study the relationship between option values and retirement behavior is to find—for each individual—the age at which the incentive to retire reaches a maximum (hence the inclusive option value reaches a minimum) and to compute the cumulative proportion of respondents who have reached that age. Then we compare this proportion with the cumulative proportion of individuals who have retired. If reaching the minimum of one's option value to postpone retirement affected actual retirement behavior strongly, we should see something like a one-to-one relationship between the two series. Figure 7.7 shows that the two series are positively related but at the end of the observation period (at age sixty-nine) only 20

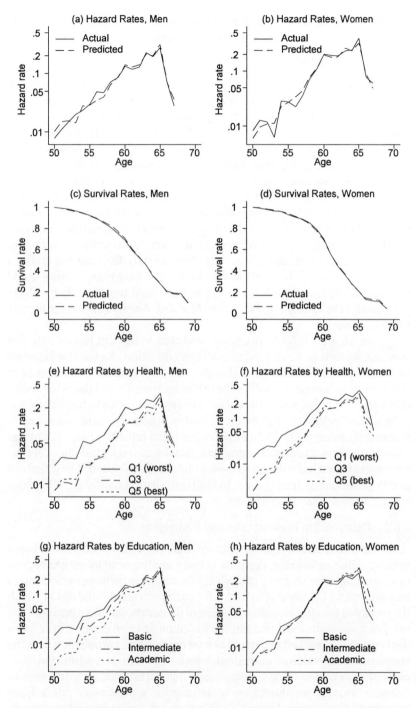

Fig. 7.6 **Model fit. Actual versus predicted average retirement rates and survival rates by sex, education, and health**

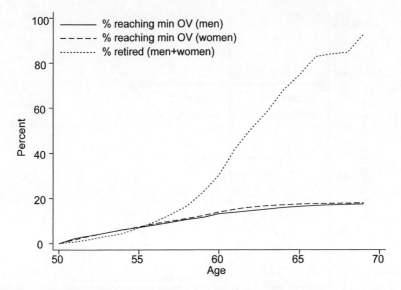

Fig. 7.7   Percent of individuals who have reached the minimum option value (maximum retirement incentive) and actual retirement rate (by age)

percent of individuals have reached their OV minimum, whereas more than 90 percent have retired. Thus, the predictive value of the OV for aggregate retirement rates seems limited.

7.6.3   Simulation of Pension Reform

In this section we show the result of a number of simulated changes to the pension system and compare them to the status quo. We will simulate four different scenarios by varying the option value to postpone retirement for each individual. First, we assume that everyone is able to retire on DI if they want to (maximum lenience), by giving a weight of one to the DI path and zero weight to the alternatives (100 percent DI probability). Second, we simulate the other extreme by taking away the possibility to retire on DI completely and giving zero weight to the DI path in the inclusive option value (0 percent DI probability, maximum stringency). Since in contrast to, for example, the United States, we have more than two retirement paths, and it is not a priori clear how to distribute the DI probability that prevails in the status quo to the other two paths. One possibility is to change the probabilities of the unemployment and the old-age pension path so that they remain proportional to the status quo. A behavioral interpretation of this possibility is that workers who are denied the DI path will partly choose the UB path and partly chose the OA path. We believe this is unrealistic. Rather, we think that workers will try to get on the "next best" retirement path, which is UB. Thus, in the 0 percent DI probability scenario, we keep the original OA weight constant but increase the UB weight.

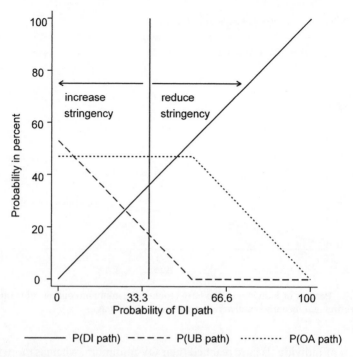

Fig. 7.8   Simulation of pathway probabilities

Further, we model two intermediate scenarios by assuming a one-third and a two-thirds probability of receiving DI upon application. Again, this begs the question of how to choose the relative weights of the other two paths. We illustrate our modeling decision in figure 7.8. The x axis shows the assumed variation in DI probabilities and the y axis the implied DI, OA, and UB pathway probabilities. The vertical line shows the overall status quo probabilities. Starting from the status quo and increasing the stringency of the award process means going left, decreasing stringency means going right. When we increase the stringency, we assume that all workers who are denied DI consider taking the UB path instead. When we reduce the stringency, we assume that first workers who would otherwise have taken the "next best" UB path will consider DI. Only if there are no workers left from the UB path do workers who have taken the OA path consider taking the DI path.

Retirement hazards and labor force survival rates are predicted using our baseline estimation equation (specification [4] in table 7.4). The results of our simulations can be seen in figure 7.9. Retirement hazard rates are largest under a 100 percent DI probability regime and smallest under a 0 percent DI probability regime. The other regimes are in between.

To summarize the data shown in figure 7.9, we summed up the survival rates from age fifty to age sixty-nine to get at the expected number of work-

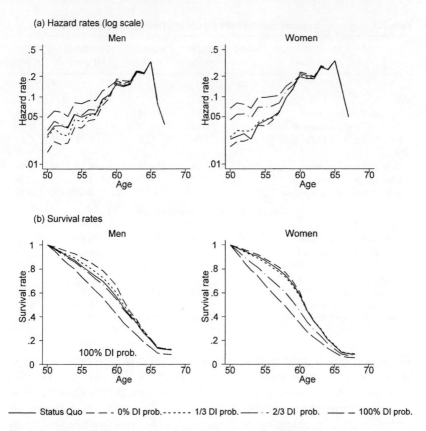

Fig. 7.9   Simulated log hazard and survival rates under different scenarios (all individuals)

ing years at age fifty associated with each scenario. This is shown in table 7.9, part (a). The average number of working years over the fifty to sixty-nine age interval in our sample is 11.5 years among men and 11 years among women, which implies an average retirement age of 61.5 and 61 years, respectively. Note that this is very close to the average in administrative data as shown in figure 7A.1 in the appendix. Closing the DI path altogether will increase the number of working years by about 0.6 years among men but only 0.2 years among women. Opening up the DI path for everyone, for instance by reducing the stringency of the award process, so that everyone who would apply would be accepted, would decrease the average number of working years by 1.6 years among men and 2.4 years among women. Compared to the overall length of retirement of about seventeen years (Deutsche Rentenversicherung Bund 2012), these changes appear to be moderate.

Next, we restrict the sample to the group of people who should have the most reason to apply for disability benefits, namely workers in bad health.

Table 7.9   **Expected years of work (at age fifty) under various scenarios**

	Status quo	0% DI prob.	One-third DI prob.	Two-thirds DI prob.	100% DI prob.
Part (a). Full sample					
Men					
Expected years of work	11.49	12.13	11.68	11.29	9.94
Abs. diff. w.r.t. status quo		0.64	0.19	−0.20	−1.55
Rel. change w.r.t. status quo		1.06	1.02	0.98	0.87
Women					
Expected years of work	11.41	11.58	11.33	10.15	9.05
Abs. diff. w.r.t. status quo		0.17	−0.09	−1.26	−2.36
Rel. change w.r.t. status quo		1.01	0.99	0.89	0.79
Part (b). Ever in first health quintile					
Men					
Expected years of work	11.01	11.81	11.32	10.80	9.46
Abs. diff. w.r.t. status quo		0.80	0.31	−0.21	−1.55
Rel. change w.r.t. status quo		1.07	1.03	0.98	0.86
Women					
Expected years of work	10.99	11.15	10.88	9.61	8.46
Abs. diff. w.r.t. status quo		0.16	−0.11	−1.38	−2.53
Rel. change w.r.t. status quo		1.01	0.99	0.87	0.77

We do not show hazard rates but report only the average number of working years in association with our scenarios (table 7.9, part [b]). For this analysis, we include only individuals who were in the first health quintile at least once during the entire observation period. As it turns out, however, the estimated effect of changing the stringency of the disability benefits is only slightly smaller than the effect estimated for the full sample. This somewhat unexpected finding may be due to the fact that the common specification used for our simulations does not allow for differences in the size of incentive effects by health status.

7.7 Conclusion

In the light of continuing demographic change and ailing labor markets, pension reform remains high on the political agenda in many countries. Owing to a number of recent reforms, the German pension system appears to be on a more financially sustainable path today than it used to be ten or fifteen years ago. However, these reforms have reduced the generosity of the pension system and thus rescinded what many Germans used to view as considerable welfare state achievements. Reducing generosity has two effects on the social security budget (Börsch-Supan, Kohnz, and Schnabel 2007): a direct (mechanical) effect, by changing contributions and benefits for a given work history, and an indirect effect through behavioral responses to the reform, that is, more contributions and less benefits due to longer working lives. These two effects can also be found on the level of the individual worker, and their relative strength depends on the elasticity of labor supply, which in turn may depend to a considerable extent on individual health.

The aim of this chapter was to expand and complement earlier micro-simulation studies on the German pension system by a more systematic treatment of health and disability. More than 20 percent of the workforce eligible for public pensions enters retirement first on disability pensions, at an average age of only slightly more than fifty years. While disability uptake rates have been fairly constant in the last three decades, important changes can be found with respect to the type of health problems that trigger early retirement. Retirement on disability pensions due to cardiovascular health problems has declined from nearly 40 percent to less than 10 percent and has been largely replaced by retirement due to mental health problems, which now are the primary diagnosis for disability in more than 40 percent of all early retirees (Börsch-Supan and Jürges 2012).

We address two new questions in this chapter: First, to what extent do financial incentives to retire—measured by the option value to postpone retirement by one year—affect the retirement decisions of sick or disabled individuals? Put differently, does bad health reduce an individual's labor supply elasticity at the extensive margin? The answer to this question has important policy implications. If the sick and disabled are not responsive to financial incentives because their labor supply has become inelastic, policies that aim at reducing the generosity of disability benefits and providing less incentives to retire early are only partially successful. They may primarily hurt those for whom disability pensions are an important part of the welfare system. In contrast, if disability pension recipients respond to reductions in generosity by postponing retirement, these reductions are less harmful than in the first case. Unfortunately, our empirical results with respect to that question are somewhat ambiguous, but the least common denominator is that among the least healthy financial incentives *do not matter less* than among healthier segments of the workforce.

Given this result our next question is, how do changes to the stringency of the disability award process affect labor supply and average retirement age? Simulating the effect of those changes in stringency, such as stricter medical requirements, can be quite challenging. Therefore, we took a very simple approach and varied the likelihood of receiving disability pensions from 0 to 100 percent, that is, from a totally restrictive to a totally lenient reward process, and compared the average retirement age or the average length of the remaining working life to the status quo. We found that increasing the stringency of the award process so that the DI path is closed altogether will increase the expected retirement age by only 0.6 years among men and 0.2 years among women, based on SOEP data. In contrast, reducing the stringency to the extent that every applicant would be accepted would decrease the average number of working years quite substantially, namely, by 1.6

years among men and 2.4 years among women. These simulated changes seem moderate, in particular considering the fact that the SHARE-based elasticities were even smaller. However, what needs to be taken into account is that our simulations make an important assumption: individuals who are denied the DI path consider taking the next best path to early retirement (which is unemployment). Thus, making the disability benefit award process more stringent without closing this other fairly generous early retirement route would not greatly increase labor force participation in old age.

There are several methodological caveats requesting further research. First, the SHARE data exhibit a substantially smaller marginal effect of the option value, and at the same time larger effects of the health variables, compared to the estimates based on the SOEP data. This may reflect the more encompassing health measure in the SHARE data. On the other hand, earnings histories are probably better captured by the SOEP data than by SHARELIFE. The SOEP-based estimates of the financial incentives may therefore be an upper bound, while the SHARE-based estimates may rather represent a lower bound.

Second, the utility parameters embedded in the option value have not been estimated but are fixed at values based on earlier US estimates. While this ensures comparability to all other country chapters in this volume, the choice of the parameter describing the value of leisure appears to be very low for European countries. In future work, these parameters should be estimated by maximum likelihood methods.

Third, and finally, the chosen functional form of the estimation equation is a combination of a probit model (and its underlying random utility logic) with an option value that has its own utility function embedded; in particular, a very specific functional form of the trade-off between labor and leisure. While this pragmatic approach has worked well in many circumstances, it is not an internally consistent model of labor supply that has failed in other circumstances (see Börsch-Supan 2012). Further research is necessary to shed light on the environments in which our approach is a reliable approximation of an internally consistent model.

Appendix

Table 7A.1   **Eligibility for UB1: Maximum number of months by age and year**

Age	until 1984	1985	1986–1987	1988–1997	1998–1/2006	2/2006–2007	since 2008
				Years			
<45					12		
45					18		
46		12	16	22			12
47							
48					22	12	
49							
50			20	26			
51	12						
52							15
53							
54		18			26		
55							
56			24	32			18
57						18	
58					32		24
>58							

Table 7A.2   **Retirement rates by health, education, and sex (age fifty-five to sixty-four)**

Education	1	2	3	4	5	All
		Health quintile (%)				
Men						
Basic track	46.93	41.38	33.40	27.95	25.75	37.64
Intermediate track	35.90	30.37	28.79	22.50	21.97	28.30
Academic track	30.98	20.78	18.04	16.46	13.87	19.92
All	42.85	35.61	28.75	23.64	21.62	32.09
Women						
Basic track	36.68	29.42	24.63	23.77	23.05	29.37
Intermediate track	37.95	27.23	24.05	19.97	21.72	27.21
Academic track	33.10	22.56	17.51	15.38	12.47	20.91
All	36.57	28.18	23.52	21.59	20.94	27.86

Source: Calculation combines data from 1984–2009 SOEP.

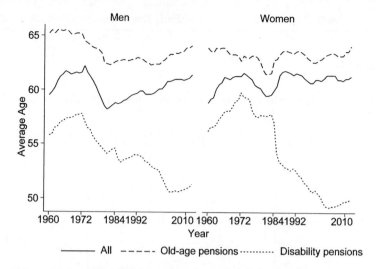

Fig. 7A.1   Average retirement ages, West Germany (1960–2012)

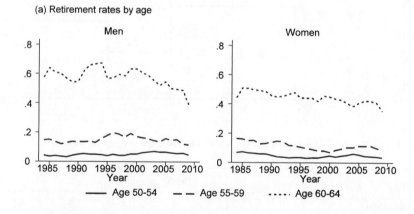

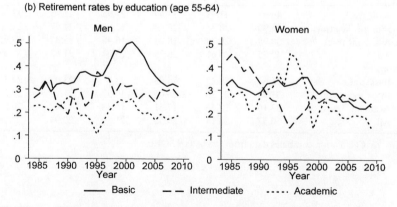

Fig. 7A.2   Retirement rates over time by sex, age groups, education, and health
Source: Authors' own computations using SOEP data.

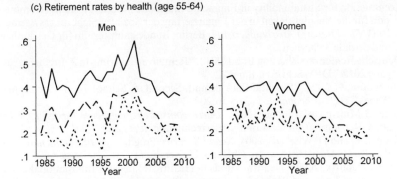

Fig. 7A.2   (cont.)

References

Börsch-Supan, A. 2005. "Work Disability and Health." In *Health, Ageing, and Retirement in Europe—First Results from the Survey of Health, Ageing and Retirement in Europe*, edited by A. Börsch-Supan et al., 253–58. Mannheim, Germany: Mannheim Research Institute for the Economics of Aging.
———. 2011. „Gesamtwirtschaftliche Wirkungen der Rentenreformen." In *Handbuch der gesetzlichen Rentenversicherung SGB VI*, edited by E. Eichenhofer, H. Rische, and W. Schmähl, 251–305. Munich: Luchterhand Verlag Gmbh.
———. 2012. "Note on the Stock-Wise Utility Function Used in their Option-Value Analysis." Discussion Paper, Munich Center for the Economics of Aging.
Börsch-Supan, A., and H. Jürges. 2012. "Disability, Pension Reform, and Early Retirement in Germany." In *Social Security Programs and Retirement around the World: Historical Trends in Mortality and Health, Employment, and Disability Insurance Participation and Reforms*, edited by D. Wise. Chicago: University of Chicago Press.
Börsch-Supan, A., S. Kohnz, and R. Schnabel. 2007. "The Budget Impact of Reduced Early Retirement Incentives on the German Public Pension System." In *Social Security Programs and Retirement around the World: Fiscal Implications of Reform*, edited by J. Gruber and D. Wise, 201–52. Chicago: University of Chicago Press.
Börsch-Supan, A., and R. Schnabel. 1999. "Social Security and Retirement in Germany." In *Social Security and Retirement around the World*, edited by J. Gruber and D. Wise. Chicago: University of Chicago Press.
Börsch-Supan, A., R. Schnabel, S. Kohnz, and G. Mastrobuoni. 2004. "Micro-Modeling of Retirement Decisions in Germany." In *Social Security Programs and Retirement around the World: Micro-Estimation*, edited by J. Gruber and D. Wise. Chicago: University of Chicago Press.
Börsch-Supan, A., and C. B. Wilke. 2007. "The German Public Pension System: How It Will Become an NDC System Look-Alike." In *Pension Reform—Issues and Prospects for Non-Financial Defined Contribution (NDC) Schemes*, edited by Robert Holzmann and Edward Palmer, 573–610. Washington, DC: The World Bank.

Commission for Sustainability in Financing the Social Security Systems (Kommission für die Nachhaltigkeit in der Finanzierung der Sozialen Sicherungssysteme). 2003. *Final Report (Abschlußbericht)*. Berlin: Bundesministerium für Gesundheit und Soziale Sicherheit.

Deutsche Rentenversicherung Bund. 2012. "Rentenversicherung in Zeitreihen. Ausgabe 2012." DRV-Schriften Band 22.

Dustmann, C. 2004. "Parental Background, Secondary School Track Choice, and Wages." *Oxford Economic Papers* 56:209–30.

Federal Ministry of Finance. 2013. *Durchschnittsbelastung nach Tarifen 1958 bis 2014*. Retrieved from www.bmf-steuerrechner.de/uebersicht_ekst/.

Gruber, J., and D. Wise, eds. 2004. *Social Security Programs and Retirement around the World: Micro-Estimation*. Chicago: University of Chicago Press.

Jürges, Hendrik. 2009. "Healthy Minds in Healthy Bodies. An International Comparison of Education-Related Inequality in Physical Health among Older Adults." *Scottish Journal of Political Economy* 56 (3): 296–320.

Jürges, Hendrik, and Kerstin Schneider. 2011. "Why Young Boys Stumble: Early Tracking, Age and Gender Bias in the German School System." *German Economic Review* 12 (4): 371–94.

Kemptner, Daniel, Hendrik Jürges, and Steffen Reinhold. 2011. "Changes in Compulsory Schooling and the Causal Effect of Education on Health: Evidence from Germany." *Journal of Health Economics* 30:340–54.

Little, R. J. A. 1988. "Missing-Data Adjustments in Large Surveys." *Journal of Business and Economic Statistics* 6:287–96.

Poterba, J., S. Venti, and D. Wise. 2010. "The Asset Cost of Poor Health." NBER Working Paper no. 16389, Cambridge, MA.

Riphahn, Regina T. 1999. "Income and Employment Effects of Health Shocks. A Test Case for the German Welfare State." *Journal of Population Economics* 12 (3): 363–89.

Romeu Gordo, L. 2006. "Effects of Short- and Long-term Unemployment on Health Satisfaction: Evidence from German Data." *Applied Economics* 38 (20): 2335–50.

Schröder, M. 2011. "Retrospective Data Collection in the Survey of Health, Ageing and Retirement in Europe." SHARELIFE Methodology. Mannheim, Germany: Mannheim Research Institute for the Economics of Aging.

Stock, J. H., and D. A. Wise. 1990. "The Pension Inducement to Retire: An Option Value Analysis." In *Issues in the Economics of Aging*, edited by D. A. Wise, 205–30. Chicago: University of Chicago Press.

Wagner, Gert G., Joachim R. Frick, and Jürgen Schupp. 2007. "The German Socio-Economic Panel Study (SOEP)—Scope, Evolution, and Enhancements." *Schmollers Jahrbuch* 127 (1): 139–69.

Weiss, C. T. 2012. "Two Measures of Lifetime Resources for Europe using SHARELIFE." SHARE Working Paper Series no. 06–2012.

8

Health, Disability Insurance, and Retirement in Denmark

Paul Bingley, Nabanita Datta Gupta, Michael Jørgensen, and Peder J. Pedersen

8.1 Introduction

Labor force participation of older persons varies greatly both between countries and within countries over time. Individual health status, labor market conditions, and social security program provisions all play a role in this. Disability insurance (DI) programs are at the interface between social security provisions, labor market conditions, and health and may play an important role for many persons as they move from employment to retirement from the labor market. In principle, it may be the case that changes in DI participation rates reflect changing health and changing labor market conditions. However, trends in DI participation appear to be unrelated to changes in mortality and health. Differences in health between countries would need to be much larger than those revealed in comparable survey data in order to account for differences in DI participation (Milligan and Wise 2012). In many countries, DI effectively provides early retirement benefits before eligibility for other social security programs begin. This begs the main question: Given health status, to what extent are the differences in labor force participation for seniors across countries determined by the provisions of

Paul Bingley is a research professor at the Danish National Centre for Social Research. Nabanita Datta Gupta is professor of economics at Aarhus University. Michael Jørgensen is a senior pension analyst at ATP in Denmark. Peder J. Pedersen is professor of economics at Aarhus University.

This chapter is part of the International Social Security project at the NBER. The authors are grateful to the other participants of that project for useful comments and advice. We are also grateful to the Danish Strategic Research Council (dsf-09-070295) for financial support. The views expressed herein are those of the authors and do not necessarily reflect the views of the National Bureau of Economic Research. For acknowledgments, sources of research support, and disclosure of the authors' material financial relationships, if any, please see http://www.nber.org/chapters/c13326.ack.

DI programs? Answering this question is a challenge because measuring health is notoriously difficult and DI programs interact with social security provisions in different ways across countries.

Social security programs in general have been shown to provide strong incentives for older workers to exit from the labor market at certain ages (Gruber and Wise 2004). In the 2004 volume, incentives were characterized by an option value (OV) model that allows the expected future consequences of current work decisions to be accounted for (Stock and Wise 1990). This was implicitly an inclusive option value, in the sense that different pathways to retirement were included in a single summary measure of expected future consequences. Several countries with extensive DI programs, such as Sweden (Palme and Svensson 2004) and Denmark (Bingley, Datta Gupta, and Pedersen 2004), included a DI retirement pathway probabilistically as part of the inclusive option value. In the current volume, because DI programs are of primary interest, for the sake of greater comparability, DI pathways contribute to inclusive option values in a similar way across all countries.

In order to control for health one needs to follow individuals over time either with repeated survey questions about self-assessed health or administrative data about health care usage. Different countries have different health data sources. Even the European countries participating in SHARE, which follow a survey protocol to maximize comparability across countries might have different modes of response between populations, which makes comparison response-by-response difficult. Most other countries in the volume use self-assessed health from surveys, whereas Sweden and Denmark use administrative records of health care usage for the sake of much greater sample sizes. Each of the studies calculates a single health index on the basis of the first principal component of their own sets of health measures. Most of the analyses are conducted on the basis of quintiles of these indices.

Identification of incentive effects requires variation in pension program provision between individuals, and ideally within individuals over time by way of pension program changes or reform. We choose an observation period 1996–2008. That is from the first year that we can observe health care usage spanning the population based on administrative records, through the announcement of a major pension program reform in 1998, and beyond full enactment of the new law in 2006.

From our descriptive analyses we can see clear gradients in DI participation rates by health quintile and by level of completed schooling. Those in worse health and with less schooling are more likely to receive DI at some point from age fifty. The gradient of DI participation across health quintiles is almost twice as steep as across levels of schooling. We find that pension program incentives in general are important determinants of retirement age. Individuals in poor health are significantly *more* responsive to economic incentives than those in better health, and those with low schooling are significantly *more* responsive to economic incentives than those with long schooling. Hence low schooling and poor health are associated with greater DI participation, and those with low schooling and poor health are also most responsive to economic incentives.

The remainder of the chapter is organized as follows. Section 8.2 shows background trends in labor force and DI participation over time by schooling and health. Section 8.3 presents the empirical approach, describing pathways to retirement, how they are weighted, describing the health index and the option value calculations. Section 8.4 presents results from estimating option value models of retirement controlling for health in various ways. Section 8.5 shows goodness-of-fit measures and conducts counterfactual simulations to illustrate some implications of the results. Section 8.6 summarizes and concludes.

8.2   Background

Previous studies have shown how trends in labor force participation for seniors have only a weak relationship with changes in mortality and other measures of health over time and across countries (Milligan and Wise 2012). Neither did there appear to be any relationship between the development of DI programs and changes in mortality and measures of health. These findings were on the basis of a broad view of disaggregated data covering a dozen countries and spanning several decades. In the current chapter we want to analyze how individual retirement behavior in Denmark is related to DI provisions, when controlling for individual variations in health and other characteristics. As background for this microanalysis, in this section we describe trends over time in DI participation, labor force participation and employment by age, and correlate these with individual characteristics: gender, health status, and educational attainment.

In the population eighteen to sixty-four years old, the share receiving DI has been fairly constant at around 7 percent since 1990 (Organisation for Economic Co-operation and Development [OECD] 2008). This is quite low and stable relative to the situation in neighboring Nordic countries (OECD 2009). However, the relatively low DI participation rate in Denmark needs to be viewed in the context of competing transfer programs. Between 1992 and 1996, an early pension benefit (*overgangsydelse*) was available for the long-term unemployed age fifty to fifty-nine. This program removed many from the labor market who might otherwise have applied for DI. In 1998, an existing wage subsidy program for the disabled was expanded and relaunched (*flexjob*). The disabled with some remaining work capacity were thus encouraged to stay in the labor market rather than exit on DI.

Another relevant aspect in the development of DI in Denmark over recent years is the rather stable overall participation rate, with a growing proportion of new young claimants entering the program with psychiatric diagnoses (OECD 2013). A final aspect of DI in Denmark is that only very few reenter the labor market having once received DI (Høgelund and Holm 2006). This is surprising in light of Jonassen, Larsen, and Høgelund (2009), who find that of those with functional disabilities in 1995, 50 percent had improved functional ability in 2008. This was especially the case for the young and those starting out with a psychiatric functional disability.

Time series of DI participation rates are shown in figure 8.1A for age groups fifty to fifty-four, fifty-five to fifty-nine, and sixty to sixty-four for men, and women are shown in figure 8.1B. Women have higher mean DI participation rates than men, and older groups have higher DI participation rates than younger groups. The youngest group has stable DI participation throughout the period for both genders, at 8 percent for men and 12 percent for women. Disability insurance participation has declined markedly for those age sixty to sixty-four, falling from 21 to 13 percent for men and a dramatic 36 to 17 percent for women. In the post-2008 years, not shown in figures 8.1A and 8.1B, DI shares are stable for the fifty and older group until 2013.

The DI participation rates of figures 8.1A and 8.1B are now set alongside employment rates in figures 8.2A, 8.2B, 8.2C, 8.2D, 8.2E, and 8.2F, which show time series for age groups fifty to fifty-four, fifty-five to fifty-nine, and sixty to sixty-four, separately for men and women. A high degree of symmetry is evident, especially in the older group, whereby falls in DI participation are about two-thirds of the size of employment increases. Indeed, since 1999 employment is more common than DI participation for women age sixty to sixty-four. Overall, the share in retirement in this age group is higher than the share in employment, however, as the share of women in a SS program for early retirement is 40 percent of the age group by the end of the period we analyze.

Associations with health status and schooling levels are shown in the next three figures. Figures 8.3A and 8.3B show DI participation rates for age group fifty-five to sixty-four by schooling for selected years, separately for men and women. There is a clear gradient in schooling in that those with lower education have higher rates of DI participation. Graduating high school approximately halves the DI rate, falling from 24 to 13 percent for men and from 35 to 17 percent for women in 1996. Subsequent educational attainment is associated with an approximately 3 percent reduction in DI rates for those with some college and another 3 percent reduction for graduating college. There is no discernible change in the educational gradient over time.

In the following illustrations and for most of the econometric analysis, health status is characterized by quintiles of a health index. Calculation of the index is described in section 8.3.3. Figure 8.4A shows DI participation rates for age group fifty-five to sixty-four by health quintile for selected years for men, and women are shown in figure 8.4B. There is a clear gradient in health in that those with worse health have higher rates of DI participation.

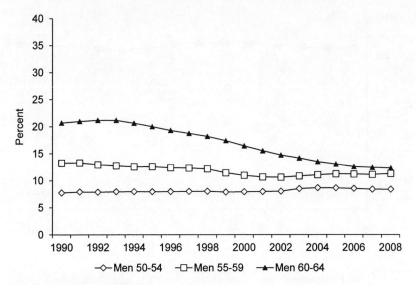

Fig. 8.1A   DI participation by age group, men

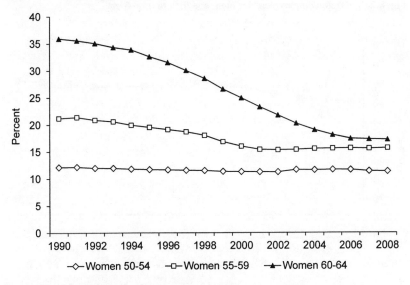

Fig. 8.1B   DI participation by age group, women

Our quintile grouping resolves into three different DI rates, the worst quintile followed by quintiles 2 and 3 together with a lower DI rate, followed by better health quintiles with almost no DI recipients. The fall in DI rate from best health quintile to 2 and 3 is more marked than for schooling, falling from 48 to 25 percent for men and from 61 to 37 percent for women in 1996. There is no discernible change in the health gradient over time.

Fig. 8.2A   DI and employment for men, age fifty to fifty-four

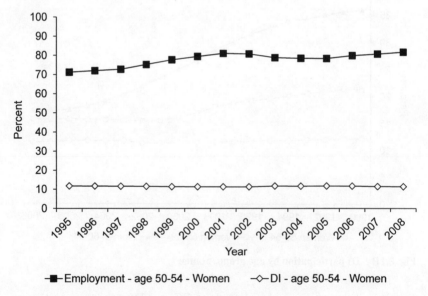

Fig. 8.2B   DI and employment for women, age fifty to fifty-four

Fig. 8.2C   DI and employment for men, age fifty-five to fifty-nine

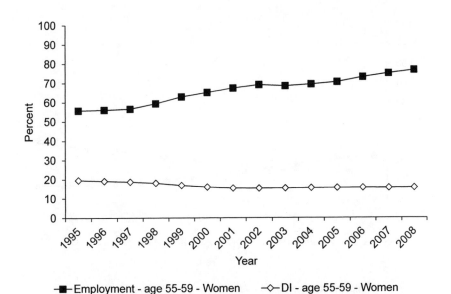

Fig. 8.2D   DI and employment for women, age fifty-five to fifty-nine

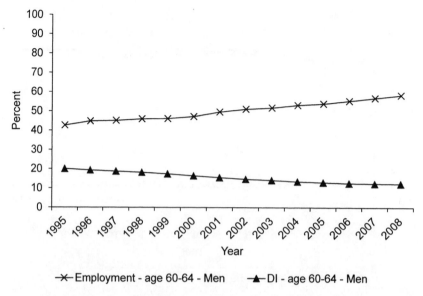

—✕—Employment - age 60-64 - Men   —▲—DI - age 60-64 - Men

Fig. 8.2E   DI and employment for men, age sixty to sixty-four

—✕—Employment - age 60-64 - Women   —▲—DI - age 60-64 - Women

Fig. 8.2F   DI and employment for women, age sixty to sixty-four

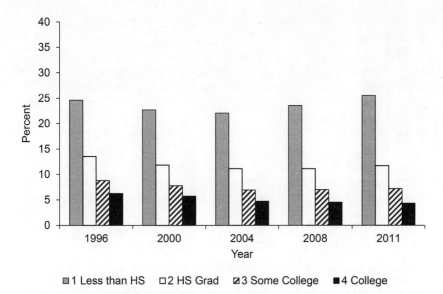

Fig. 8.3A   Men age fifty-five to sixty-four who have received DI by education and year

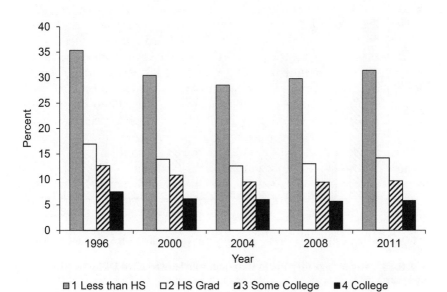

Fig. 8.3B   Women age fifty-five to sixty-four who have received DI by education and year

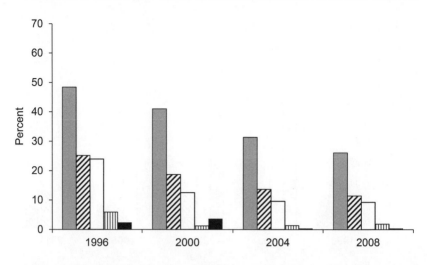

Fig. 8.4A   Men age fifty-five to sixty-four who have received DI by health and year

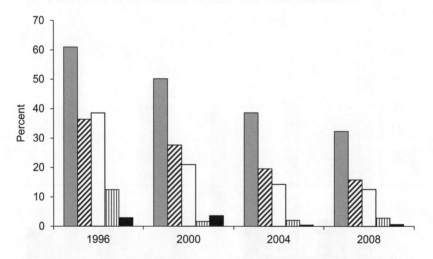

Fig. 8.4B   Women age fifty-five to sixty-four who have received DI by health and year

The joint distribution of DI participation rates by schooling and health quintile together is shown in table 8.1 for age group fifty-five to sixty-four (men in the upper pane and women in the lower pane). Subpopulations with worst health and lowest schooling have highest DI participation rates, at 46 percent for men and 55 percent for women. At the opposite corner of the

Table 8.1   **Percent DI receipt age fifty-five to sixty-four by heath quintile and education**

	health quintile					
	1 (low)	2	3	4	5	All
Men						
1 Less than HS	45.58	25.63	22.84	4.03	2.14	20.63
2 HS grad	30.16	12.97	9.25	1.81	0.94	10.70
3 Some college	22.75	8.56	6.08	1.81	1.10	7.01
4 College	17.22	6.98	4.11	1.23	0.73	4.71
All	34.11	16.06	12.72	2.41	1.30	12.83
Women						
1 Less than HS	55.11	35.59	33.46	7.32	2.50	28.91
2 HS grad	32.92	15.63	11.96	2.44	0.86	12.66
3 Some college	25.78	11.43	8.30	1.83	0.69	9.51
4 College	16.98	7.28	5.05	1.33	0.49	5.66
All	42.12	23.55	20.72	4.25	1.48	19.02

table, men and women in the best health and with a college degree both have a DI rate of less than 1 percent. Within each health quintile there is still a marked schooling gradient in DI participation rates. Similarly, within each educational level there is still a marked health gradient. Health is the most important marginal distribution, with 17 percent of men and women receiving DI of those in worst health with a college degree, whereas only 2 percent of men and women in best health and less than high school participate in DI.

Information from table 8.1 is further split by selected years in figure 8.5A, which presents DI participation rates for the age group fifty-five to sixty-four jointly by schooling and health for men, and women are shown in figure 8.5B. The joint gradient in DI participation rates by health and schooling is maintained proportionally throughout, with worst health and lowest schooling men and women in 1996 at 57 percent, falling to 37 percent by 2008. The fall of one-third for this group over twelve years is similar in magnitude to the DI participation rate difference for those in worse health between some high school and some college.

In the final two sets of background figures, employment rates are associated with schooling and health. Figure 8.6A shows employment rates for age group sixty to sixty-four by schooling over time for men, and women are shown in figure 8.6B. Men have higher employment rates than women. Indeed, men with some college have similar employment rates to women with a college degree, and men with a high school degree have similar employment rates to women with some college. There are similar upward trends in employment rates for the three education groups without a college degree. In 2008, for example, the range of mean employment rates across levels of schooling is narrower for men, ranging from 48 to 80 percent, than for women, ranging from 26 to 70 percent.

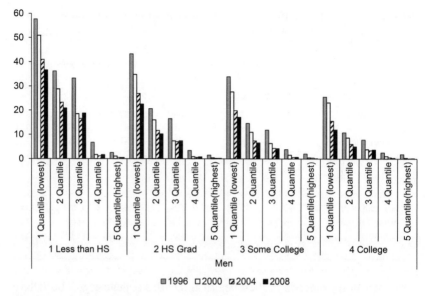

Fig. 8.5A   DI recipients by education and health quintile, age fifty-five to sixty-four (men)

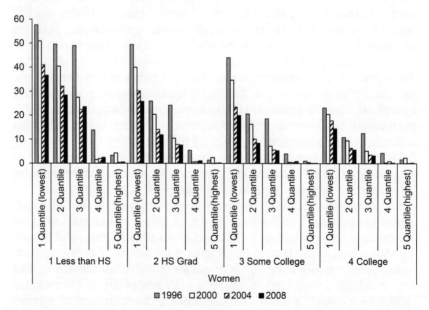

Fig. 8.5B   DI recipients by education and health quintile, age fifty-five to sixty-four (women)

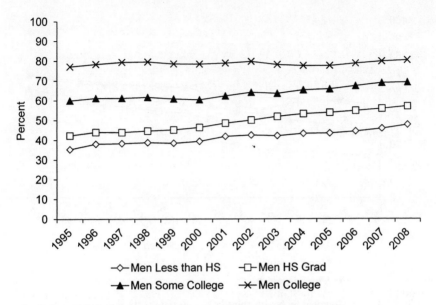

Fig. 8.6A   Employment by education, age sixty to sixty-four (men)

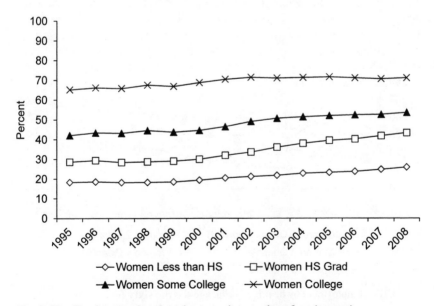

Fig. 8.6B   Employment by education, age sixty to sixty-four (women)

Figure 8.7A shows employment rates for age group sixty to sixty-four by health quintile over time for men, and women are shown in figure 8.7B. There is a clear health gradient in employment rates, with those in worst health having lowest employment rates, and those in the best two health quintiles having highest employment rates. Employment rates across all health quin-

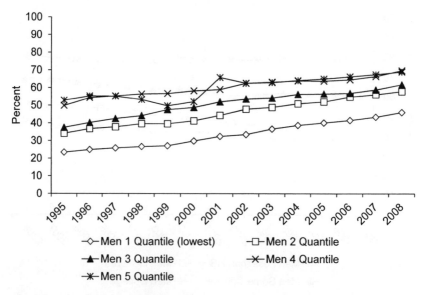

Fig. 8.7A   Employment by health quintile, age sixty to sixty-four (men)

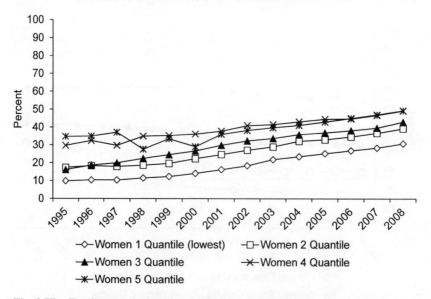

Fig. 8.7B   Employment by health quintile, age sixty to sixty-four (women)

tiles for men and women increase uniformly over the sample period. The increase in employment rates from 1995 to 2008 by about 20 percent points is similar to the difference in moving from the two worst health quintiles to the second best.

In summary, our years of observation (1995–2008) covers a period of falling DI participation, increasing labor force participation, and increasing employment for seniors, especially those age sixty to sixty-four. There are steep gradients in health, with those in worse health more likely to participate in DI and less likely to be in employment. There are similar and almost as steep gradients across the schooling distribution, with those without a high school diploma more likely to participate in DI and less likely to be in employment.

8.3   Empirical Approach

Our goal is to estimate the relationship between DI provisions and retirement age, given health status. In order to do this we need to consider all transfer programs relevant for the transition from work to retirement for seniors. These different pathways to retirement need to be combined in a weighted average measure that summarizes their relative potential importance. An inclusive option value framework will be introduced to characterize incentives implicit in the programs to retire at different ages. Finally, we need to condition on health in a way that is comparable across data sets and countries. The following four subsections present these elements of our empirical approach.

8.3.1   Pathways to Retirement

There are three main pension programs supporting income in retirement that are relevant for our analysis. First is a disability insurance program (*førtidspension*, hereafter DI) available for those age eighteen to sixty-six and later eighteen to sixty-four who have permanent social and/or health impairments that reduce work capacity. Second is a contribution-based but largely tax financed postemployment wage program (*efterløn*, hereafter SS), which is essentially unemployment insurance benefit without a job search requirement available for ages sixty to sixty-six and after 2006 from sixty to sixty-four. Third is old-age pension (*folkepension*, hereafter OAP), which is a demogrant available from age sixty-seven and after 2006 from age sixty-five, based on years of residence. Our period of analysis (1995–2008) is chosen to span reforms in DI stringency and SS/OAP incentives in order to provide variation by which to identify the effects of program provisions on the retirement age for older workers.

The SS program was introduced in 1979 for ages sixty to sixty-six and existed largely unchanged until reforms in 1992 and 1999. The 1992 rules are relevant for the first part of our sample period. Eligibility from 1992 to 1995 required membership of an unemployment insurance fund for at least twenty of the last twenty-five years. An individual was allowed to work for a maximum of 200 hours. If the 200 hours was exceeded, it resulted in a permanent disqualification from the program. The political motivation for the 200 hours restriction was the idea that youth unemployment would be reduced by cutting the labor supply. This, however, turned out not to be the case as shown in Bingley, Datta Gupta, and Pedersen (2010). For individuals claiming SS at ages sixty to sixty-two, the benefits for the first two years were at the level of unemployment insurance and reduced to 80 percent for the last four years. Delaying SS until age sixty-three or older gave benefits at 100 percent of the maximum unemployment insurance benefit level until age sixty-six. This policy obviously incentivized retiring at age sixty-three rather than at younger or older ages. In 1995 unemployment insurance fund membership history requirements were increased to twenty-five out of the previous thirty years. Until 1999, only payouts from life annuities in occupational pensions were means tested.

An SS reform was announced in March 1999 and enacted in July 1999. Means testing of payouts or returns from all contributory pensions—whether they were actually paid out or not—was introduced for those claiming SS at ages sixty and sixty-one. Those eligible for SS and not retiring now accumulate a quarterly USD 2,200 bonus beginning at age sixty-two. This reform shifted the retirement age incentive spike from age sixty-three down to age sixty-two. The previous limitation of working at most 200 hours per year was removed and replaced by a high effective marginal tax rate. The UI fund membership history requirements were further increased to thirty out of the last thirty-five years. Contributions were unbundled from UI and became separately elective.

An important element of the 1999 reform was the reduction in OAP age from sixty-seven to sixty-five. Those age sixty and older at enactment (born before July 1939) were unaffected and could first claim OAP at age sixty-seven, whereas those born later could claim OAP from age sixty-five. The change in OAP age was implemented from July 2004 through June 2006 and the maximum age for claiming SS benefits changed accordingly. This policy change was obviously running against the trend of pension reforms typically increasing the age of eligibility. The interpretation is fiscal considerations, in that the great majority of the sixty-five- and sixty-six-year-olds were in the DI or the SS program with benefits significantly higher than in OAP.

The DI program has existed in essentially the same institutional form in the period 1984–2002, but with some stringency tightening in the 1990s. It was available to those with permanent social or physical work impairments depending on three levels of severity/generosity. During this period, benefit levels were closely linked to the overall level of wages, but several stringency measures were introduced at different times. Three stringency reforms can be distinguished. First, during 1995–2002 a series of selective municipal award audits were undertaken, whereby each year two out of Denmark's fifteen counties were chosen and a random sample of new benefit awards was drawn for reassessment of eligibility. Second, in 1997 central government refunds to municipalities were reduced for expenditure on DI to individuals age sixty and older, bringing refunds into line with those for younger age groups. Third, in 1998 municipalities were required to first consider whether other locally administered programs, such as work rehabilitation or a program with disability wage subsidies, might be relevant before processing an application for DI.

In 2003, the government simplified DI for new awards by reducing the number of levels from three to one, but also introduced an array of condition- and needs-specific financial additions. These additions make net changes to incentives due to the reform difficult to characterize for systematic analysis.

Other relevant related programs for those in short-term poor health, with short-term or permanent work impairments but some remaining work capacity, are sickness benefits (*sygedagpenge*), rehabilitation benefits (*revalidering*), and disability wage subsidies (*fleksjobs*), respectively. We do not consider these programs as pensions financing retirement because they involve some degree of attachment to the labor market. Nevertheless, they are worth mentioning because of their relevance at the interface between health, work, and retirement. Work sickness absence benefits and rehabilitation are awarded temporarily. Disability wage subsidies are a payment at the level of the minimum wage for permanently reduced work capacity. Individuals in this program are classified as employed, or unemployed and seeking work, and therefore not retired for modeling purposes.

8.3.2   Calculating the Probabilities of Different Pathways

An option value incentive measure needs to combine provisions across different potential pathways to retirement. In order to integrate DI we need to impute to each person a probability that DI is a realistic option. These probabilities can then be used as weights to combine pathways into a single inclusive option value measure. We use a stock measure of calculating DI probabilities from the proportion participating in DI by different cells combining individual characteristics. Cells are calculated for those age fifty-five to sixty-four by level of schooling, gender, and year. Selected years of these DI weights are presented in figures 8.3A (men) and 8.3B (women).

8.3.3   Health Index and Health Quintiles

A continuous health index needs to be created and divided into quintiles so as to be comparable with other countries. Poterba, Venti, and Wise (2011) propose such an index be calculated from the first principal component of twenty-seven health indicators from the Health and Retirement Study (HRS). In the Danish administrative registers, we use the first principal component from hospital discharge records and prescription medicine purchases. The principal components analysis is conducted on the population age fifty to eighty during the years 1994–2007.

From hospital records we consider all encounters, for both day patients and overnight stays. Each encounter has a primary diagnosis code (ICD-10) and duration. We aggregate diagnoses to the three-digit level, giving 160 distinct diagnoses after twelve diagnoses with fewer than 100 cases are dropped. Durations of hospital stays are summed over a two-year period within each diagnosis for each person. In other words, hospitalization is characterized for each person as length of hospital stay over the previous two years with each of 160 primary diagnoses.

From prescription medicine records we consider all purchases from high street pharmacies. Each purchase has a drug code (ATC-5) and dosage. We aggregate drug codes to the three-digit level, giving 170 distinct drug types after eight drug types with fewer than 100 persons purchasing are dropped. Dosages are normalized according to World Health Organization (WHO)-defined daily dosages and summed over a two-year period within each drug type for each person. In other words, drug consumption is characterized for each person as number of standard daily doses over the previous two years for each of 170 drug types.

Principal components are calculated over hospitalizations and prescriptions together in two-year periods. For example, when modeling retirement behavior in 1996, principal components would be calculated for 1994–1995; for behavior in 1997, principal components would be based on 1995–1996, and so forth. The first principal component forms our health index. Figure 8.8A shows mean centile of the health index over age by gender, and schooling level is shown in figure 8.8B. By convention, a higher centile is taken to indicate better health. Men have a higher mean health centile than women. Note that it is conventional to observe that men have better self-reported health, less health care usage, but higher mortality than women of a similar age. Health declines with age and the gender health gap narrows from 5 centiles at age fifty to 1 centile at age seventy. The gender health gap at age sixty corresponds to the mean health decline over four to five years. According to our health index, based on health care usage, a woman age sixty is as healthy as a man age sixty-four. This is in spite of her having higher expected longevity. Figure 8.8B shows a health centile gradient in schooling with those with lowest schooling having worst health. The schooling health gradient narrows from 10 centiles at age fifty to 6 centiles by age seventy, however the 3 health centile difference of moving from high school graduation to some college persists.

8.3.4   Option Value Calculation

The goal of our analysis is to estimate the relationship between pension program provisions and age of retirement. Incentives implicit in pension program provisions can be characterized by the potential gain from postponing retirement until future ages. In order to do this we follow the option value approach of Stock and Wise (1990) and extend this to explicitly allow for different potential pathways to retirement in the form of an inclusive option value measure.

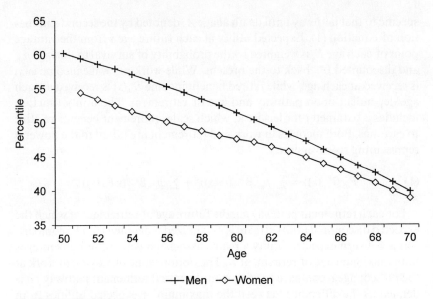

Fig. 8.8A   Health index mean by gender

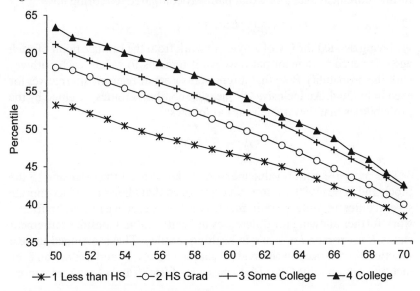

Fig. 8.8B   Health index mean by education

From the vantage point of each age *a* while in work, there are several possible pathways (*pa* = 1, . . ., *PA*) to retirement, each with an associated utility stream *V* dependent upon age of retirement time *r*. A pathway constitutes a number of years of continued work, denoted in the first summation of equation (1), followed by the number of years receiving pension benefits specific to that pathway until death at age A, denoted by the second summation of equation (1). Expected utility at each future age s from the vantage point of each age E_a is weighted by the probability of survival to that age $p_{s|a}$ and discounted β^{s-t} back to the present. While working, wage income $\omega(s)$ is received at each age, while retired benefit income $B_{rk}(s)$ is received at each age dependent upon pathway and age of retirement. The utility function includes a parameter for leisure κ, which scales retirement benefits relative to earnings. Both incomes in work and retirement are raised to the power γ representing risk aversion:

$$(1) \qquad E_a \{V_{ka}(r)\} = \sum_{s=a}^{r-1} p_{s|a}\beta^{s-a}(\omega(s))^{\gamma} + \sum_{s=r}^{A} p_{s|a}\beta^{s-a}(\kappa B_{rk}(s))^{\gamma}.$$

For each retirement pathway pa, the future age of retirement at which the expected discounted utility stream is maximized is denoted r^*. The comparison is between expected utility streams associated with all retirement ages until maximum age of retirement R. The option value of staying in work at the present age a compared to following eventual retirement pathway pa is defined as the difference between the maximum of expected utilities from future retirement ages along that pathway compared to retiring now:

$$(2) \qquad OV_{ka} \equiv \max_{a < r^* \leq R}[E_a\{V_{ka}(r^*)\}] - E_a\{V_{ka}(a)\}.$$

Having defined the OV of staying in work from the vantage point of each age a for each retirement pathway pa, it remains to weight each pathway with the probability P_k so that it represents a set of relevant alternatives for each individual. An inclusive OV measure combines routes weighted by the probabilities that they are relevant as follows:

$$(3) \qquad OV_a = \sum_{k=1}^{K} P_k OV_{ka}.$$

This inclusive option value measure makes explicit the extension to the Stock and Wise (1990) option value approach that allows us to incorporate several different routes to retirement. This can be cast in a regression framework further allowing for differences in health status. Consider retirement status R for person i of age a in health quantile j. This is assumed to be a function θ_j of exogenous individual characteristics X_{ia} and a function δ_j of inclusive option value OV_{ia}; H_j is a measure of health and ε_{iaj} is an error term:

$$(4) \qquad R_{iaj} = \sum_{j=1}^{J} [\theta_j X_{ia} + \delta_j OV_{ia} H_j] + \varepsilon_{iaj}.$$

Equation (4) is estimated as a probit model for year-to-year retirement. Retirement behavior is characterized as an optimal stopping problem in that an individual remains out of the labor force once retired. Benefit collection and retirement are assumed to be synonymous. Pathways from the labor force to OAP could be direct or via DI, SS, or a private pension drawdown.

Individuals are selected at ages fifty-seven to sixty-six and must be working in the first year of observation. We assume a maximum age of retirement R at sixty-seven and force those who are still working at age sixty-six to retire at sixty-seven on OAP. We use population life tables for survival probability s from age a published in 2009 by age and gender for ages fifty-eight to ninety-nine and impose zero survival probability at age 100. After retirement, an individual leaves the data set. Exits from the data set due to death, migration, or change of marital status are treated as missing at random. Observations for individuals who leave the data set are used in estimation until the year before the exit and the last observation is classified as working. Potential earnings profiles are assumed to be flat from age fifty-seven, with 1 percent real growth. Option value calculations assume knowledge of the pension and tax system as in place at the vantage point of observation. Individuals form expectations on the basis of that system and any future changes that had already been announced at that time. For the sake of comparison with other countries, preference parameters are fixed at the levels found in US data as discount rate $\beta = 0.97$, utility of leisure $\kappa = 1.5$, and risk aversion $\gamma = 0.95$.

It is informative to present examples of these option values in order to fix ideas. Figure 8.9A shows mean option value for the 1941 cohort by age for each retirement path as well as for inclusive option value combining all pathways for men, and women are shown in figure 8.9B. Option value falls with age. The fall is from a higher base for men compared to women, but the proportional fall over age is similar. The DI option value declines smoothly, whereas SS option value slows its decline just for age sixty-one and resumes a decline thereafter more slowly. This reflects an absence of age-related conditions for DI, but a postreform penalty for SS at age sixty-one due to means testing of private pension wealth, followed by bonus payments for delaying SS retirement for each quarter beyond age sixty-two. The ranking between OV profiles differs between women and men. For women the DI OV is lower than SS, while the opposite is found for men. The 1941 cohort of men typically have higher occupational pension wealth than women. As a consequence, benefits from SS are means tested to a higher degree for men than for women. Women, however, have a higher prospective rate of compensation from SS than men due to lower wages on average in a setting where benefits do not depend on preentry wages.

8.4   Results

In this section we present estimates of the models constructed in the previous section. Option value is the main explanatory variable of interest, and it is informative to first see how this evolves over age alongside retirement age to understand how it is driving the retirement decision modeling. Figure 8.10A shows the percent of men or women having reached maximum

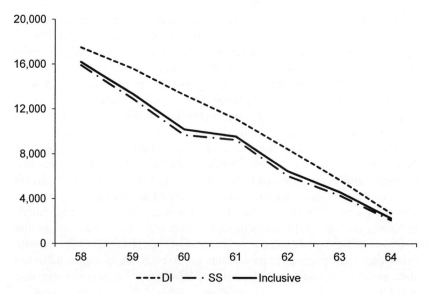

Fig. 8.9A   Mean OV by age for 1941 cohort (men)

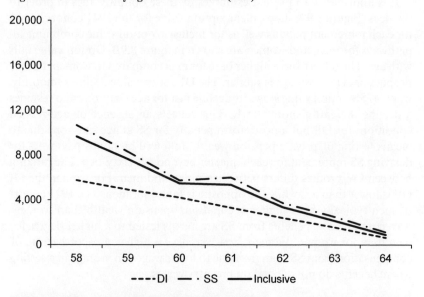

Fig. 8.9B   Mean OV by age for 1941 cohort (women)

utility, or minimum option value, by age for the prereform 1938 cohort, and the postreform 1941 cohort is shown in figure 8.10B. Also shown is the percent retired by age for men and women. The percent having reached minimum option value is higher for men than women and rises faster over age for women. The pattern is similar pre- and postreform, but with a bigger share reaching minimum option value by each age prereform.

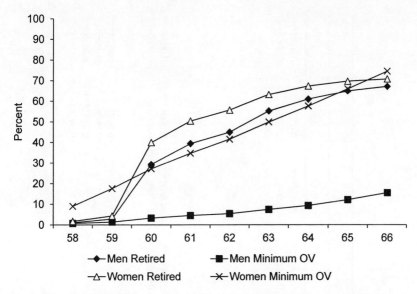

Fig. 8.10A   Percent having reached minimum OV and retired by age (1938 cohort)

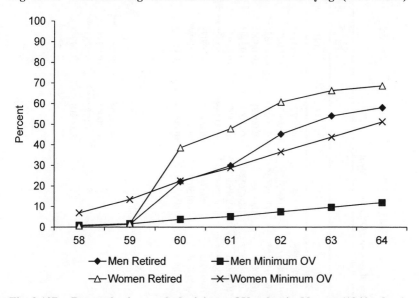

Fig. 8.10B   Percent having reached minimum OV and retired by age (1941 cohort)

The remainder of the section presents estimates of option value coefficients and controls for different specifications and samples. Table 8.2A shows estimates from retirement probit regressions with option value as the key explanatory variable and health measures as controls. Each column is for a separate regression to check sensitivity of results to the inclusion of linear age versus age dummies, inclusion of additional covariates, and to different

Table 8.2A **Effect of inclusive OV on retirement**

	Specification							
	(1)	(2)	(3)	(4)	(5)	(6)	(7)	(8)
OV_inclusive	-0.0907***	-0.0591***	-0.0775***	-0.0433***	-0.0903***	-0.0589***	-0.0773***	-0.0434***
	(0.0006)	(0.0005)	(0.0007)	(0.0005)	(0.0006)	(0.0005)	(0.0007)	(0.0005)
Health quint 2 (second lowest)	-0.0033***	-0.0190***	-0.0007	-0.0162***				
	(0.0008)	(0.0006)	(0.0007)	(0.0006)				
Health quint 3	-0.0101***	-0.0256***	-0.0089***	-0.0249***				
	(0.0008)	(0.0006)	(0.0008)	(0.0006)				
Health quint 4	-0.0098***	-0.0228***	-0.0116***	-0.0250***				
	(0.0008)	(0.0007)	(0.0008)	(0.0007)				
Health quint 5 (highest)	-0.0020*	-0.0150***	-0.0047***	-0.0180***				
	(0.0008)	(0.0007)	(0.0008)	(0.0007)				
Health index					-0.0060***	-0.0063***	-0.0061***	-0.0064***
					(0.0005)	(0.0005)	(0.0005)	(0.0005)
Age	X				X			
Age dummies		X	X	X		X	X	X
Female			0.0016*	0.0051***			-0.0001	0.024***
			(0.0006)	(0.0005)			(0.0006)	(0.0005)
Married			-0.0198***	-0.0184***			-0.0198***	-0.0188***
			(0.0010)	(0.0008)			(0.0010)	(0.0008)

	(1)	(2)	(3)	(4)	(5)	(6)	(7)	(8)
Spouse retired			0.0542***	0.0428***			0.0543***	0.0432***
			(0.0006)	(0.0005)			(0.0006)	(0.0005)
Total assets			−0.0000***	−0.0000***			−0.0000***	−0.0000***
			(0.0000)	(0.0000)			(0.0000)	(0.0000)
Occup. dummies			X	X			X	X
Educ: <High school			−0.0024***	−0.0045***			−0.0025***	−0.0046***
			(0.0006)	(0.0005)			(0.0006)	(0.0005)
Educ: High school			−0.0194***	−0.0154***			−0.0195***	−0.0156***
			(0.0008)	(0.0006)			(0.0008)	(0.0006)
Educ: Some college			−0.0509***	−0.0362***			−0.0510***	−0.0367***
			(0.0011)	(0.0008)			(0.0011)	(0.0008)
No. of observations	1,296,332	1,296,332	1,296,332	1,296,332	1,296,332	1,296,332	1,296,332	1,296,332
Pseudo R^2	0.081	0.207	0.103	0.229	0.081	0.205	0.103	0.228
Mean ret. rate	0.120	0.120	0.120	0.120	0.120	0.120	0.120	0.120
Mean of OV	9,898	9,898	9,898	9,898	9,898	9,898	9,898	9,898
Std. dev. of OV	10,110	10,110	10,110	10,110	10,110	10,110	10,110	10,110

Note: Coefficients are marginal effects of a 10,000-unit change in OV from probit models. Standard errors are shown in parentheses.

***Significant at the 1 percent level.

**Significant at the 5 percent level.

*Significant at the 10 percent level.

Table 8.2B   **Effect of percent gain in inclusive OV on retirement**

	Specification			
	(1)	(2)	(3)	(4)
Percent gain in OV	−0.2180***	−0.1236***	−0.1836***	−0.0806***
	(0.0018)	(0.0014)	(0.0020)	(0.0015)
Linear age	X		X	
Age dummies		X		X
Health quintiles	X	X	X	X
Other Xs			X	X
No. of observations	1,368,865	1,368,865	1,296,332	1,296,332
Pseudo R^2	0.071	0.194	0.099	0.223
Mean ret. rate	0.120	0.120	0.120	0.120
Mean of % gain in OV	0.356	0.356	0.356	0.356
Std. dev. of % gain in OV	0.365	0.365	0.365	0.365

Notes: Models are the same as models 1–4 in table 8.2A. Coefficients are marginal effects. Standard errors are shown in parentheses.
***Significant at the 1 percent level.
**Significant at the 5 percent level.
*Significant at the 10 percent level.

ways of controlling for health by quintiles in the health index. Option value has a negative and statistically significant effect on retirement. Estimates are similar regardless of how health is controlled for. The OV coefficients are somewhat smaller with inclusion of additional covariates and considerably smaller with age dummies rather than linear age controls. Other covariates are significant with expected signs. Compared to the reference group in worst health, the healthier are less likely to retire. However, among the four healthy quintiles there is no gradient in retirement. There is a clear gradient in schooling, whereby those with more schooling are less likely to retire early.

An alternative parameterization of option values is as percent gain in option value from delaying retirement. Table 8.2B shows estimates from retirement probit regressions with this as the key explanatory variable and health quintiles as controls. These show the effect of the utility gain from waiting to retire until the optimal age, scaled by the utility available by retiring immediately. Coefficients of interest are negative and statistically significant. Robustness across specifications is similar to that from table 8.2A, with somewhat smaller coefficients when including covariates and considerably smaller coefficients when controlling for age with dummies rather than a linear term.

The most flexible specifications run models separately by different cuts of the data. Table 8.3A shows estimates from retirement probit regressions with option value as the key explanatory variable, run separately by health quintile. Each cell of the table corresponds to a separate regression, with

Table 8.3A   **Effect of inclusive OV on retirement by health quintile**

	No. of obs.	Mean ret. rate (%)	Mean of OV	Std. dev. of OV	Specification (1)	(2)	(3)	(4)
OV: Lowest quintile (worst health)	273,552	14.363	8,862	9,392	−0.1055***	−0.0798***	−0.0966***	−0.0639***
					(0.0016)	(0.0014)	(0.0018)	(0.0015)
					[0.0566]	[0.0423]	[0.0499]	[0.065]
	R^2				0.045	0.142	0.064	0.161
OV: 2nd quintile	273,876	12.642	10,095	10,556	−0.0857***	−0.0665***	−0.0722***	−0.0490***
					(0.0015)	(0.0012)	(0.0017)	(0.0014)
					[0.053]	[0.0476]	[0.0405]	[0.0285]
	R^2				0.063	0.159	0.087	0.185
OV: 3rd quintile	273,816	10.524	10,738	11,049	−0.0772***	−0.0510***	−0.0594***	−0.0342***
					(0.0011)	(0.0009)	(0.0015)	(0.0011)
					[0.0673]	[0.0501]	[0.0436]	[0.0256]
	R^2				0.104	0.217	0.131	0.246
OV: 4th quintile	273,827	11.073	9,571	9,960	−0.0800***	−0.0428***	−0.0628***	−0.0282***
					(0.0012)	(0.0008)	(0.0015)	(0.0009)
					[0.0629]	[0.0387]	[0.0418]	[0.0186]
	R^2				0.120	0.269	0.144	0.293
OV: Highest quintile (best health)	273,794	11.249	10,217	9,381	−0.0897***	−0.0509***	−0.0765***	−0.0372***
					(0.0011)	(0.0009)	(0.0014)	(0.0010)
					[0.0835]	[0.0487]	[0.065]	[0.0283]
	R^2				0.127	0.266	0.147	0.286
Linear age					X		X	
Age dummies						X		X
Other Xs							X	X

Notes: Models are the same as models 1–4 in table 8.2A, but are estimated separately by health quintile; each coefficient on the table is from a different regression. Coefficients are marginal effects of a 10,000-unit change in OV from probit models. Standard errors are shown in parentheses. The effect of a one standard deviation change in OV is shown in brackets (this is estimated as the effect of increasing inclusive OV from the current value −0.5 std. dev. to the current value +0.5 std. dev.).

***Significant at the 1 percent level.

**Significant at the 5 percent level.

*Significant at the 10 percent level.

specifications differing by column and health quintile sample differing by row. Estimates differ across specifications according to a similar pattern seen in tables 8.2A and 8.2B. Those in worst health have the most negative option value coefficients, followed by those in the second worst health quintile, and the remainder in better health quintiles 3–5 have smaller-sized coefficients, but exhibit no obvious pattern between each other. So those in *worse health* are *more responsive* to pension incentives.

Using a more flexible specification than those presented in table 8.2B, table 8.3B shows estimates from retirement probit regressions with percent

Table 8.3B   **Effect of percent gain in inclusive OV on retirement by health quintile**

	No. of obs.	Mean ret. rate (%)	Mean of % OV	Std. dev. of % OV	Specification			
					(1)	(2)	(3)	(4)
OV: Lowest quintile (worst health)	273,552	14.363	0.34	0.36	−0.2128*** (0.0047)	−0.1310*** (0.0039)	−0.1897*** (0.0053)	−0.0924*** (0.0042)
R^2					0.032	0.127	0.056	0.153
OV: 2nd quintile	273,876	12.642	0.40	0.44	−0.1851*** (0.0038)	−0.1295*** (0.0031)	−0.1632*** (0.0042)	−0.0931*** (0.0032)
R^2					0.053	0.146	0.084	0.179
OV: 3rd quintile	273,816	10.524	0.39	0.36	−0.2043*** (0.0033)	−0.1235*** (0.0026)	−0.1538*** (0.0037)	−0.0744*** (0.0026)
R^2					0.094	0.204	0.128	0.240
OV: 4th quintile	273,827	11.073	0.30	0.29	−0.2352*** (0.0031)	−0.1155*** (0.0022)	−0.1839*** (0.0037)	−0.0678*** (0.0024)
R^2					0.117	0.261	0.145	0.290
OV: Highest quintile (best health)	273,794	11.249	0.31	0.27	−0.2321*** (0.0036)	−0.1145*** (0.0027)	−0.1930*** (0.0041)	−0.0739*** (0.0029)
R^2					0.118	0.253	0.144	0.280
Linear age					X		X	
Age dummies						X		X
Other Xs							X	X

Notes: Models are the same as models 1–4 in table 8.2A, but are estimated separately by health quintile; each coefficient on the table is from a different regression. Coefficients are marginal effects. Standard errors are shown in parentheses.
***Significant at the 1 percent level.
**Significant at the 5 percent level.
*Significant at the 10 percent level.

gain in option value from delaying retirement as the key explanatory variables, split by health quintiles. Each cell is the coefficient of interest from a separate regression. There is a familiar pattern of sensitivity across specifications, but no systematic differences in coefficients across health quintiles.

Table 8.3C shows estimates from retirement probit regressions with option value interacted with the health index as the key explanatory variables. This is the continuous health index version of table 8.3A, but further imposes that other covariates do not vary according to health, whereas they were allowed to vary in table 8.3A (not presented). Estimates of the interaction of option value with health index are negative, implying individuals in better health are more responsive to incentives. This is the opposite finding from table 8.3A and is likely due to the restriction that other controls are not allowed to also vary by health.

Analogously to splitting the sample by health quintile, the next two tables

Table 8.3C   **Effect of inclusive OV on retirement with health interaction**

	Specification			
	(1)	(2)	(3)	(4)
OV_inclusive	−0.0842***	−0.0492***	−0.0714***	−0.0348***
	(0.0012)	−0.0009	−0.0012	−0.0009
	[0.0643]	[0.0446]	[0.0502]	[0.0263]
Health index	−0.0003***	0.0002***	−0.0003***	−0.0002***
	(0.0000)	(0.0000)	(0.0000)	(0.0000)
OV_inclusive*health index	−0.0001***	−0.0001***	−0.0001***	−0.0001***
	(0.0000)	(0.0000)	(0.0000)	(0.0000)
Linear age	X		X	
Age dummies		X		X
Other Xs			X	X
No. of observations	1,296,332	1,296,332	1,296,332	1,296,332
Pseudo R^2	0.081	0.205	0.103	0.228
Mean ret. rate	0.119697	0.119697	0.119697	0.119697
Mean of OV	9,897.63	9,897.63	9,897.63	9,897.63
Std. dev. of OV	10,109.82	10,109.82	10,109.82	10,109.82

Notes: Models are the same as models 5–8 in table 8.2A, with the addition of an OV*health index interaction. Coefficients are marginal effects of a 10,000-unit change in OV from probit models. Standard errors are shown in parentheses. The effect of a one standard deviation change in OV is shown in brackets (this is estimated as the effect of increasing inclusive OV from the current value −0.5 std. dev. to the current value +0.5 std. dev.).

***Significant at the 1 percent level.
**Significant at the 5 percent level.
*Significant at the 10 percent level.

split the population by level of educational attainment. Table 8.4A shows estimates from retirement probit regressions with option value as the key explanatory variable, for samples split by schooling. Each cell of the table corresponds to a separate regression, with specifications differing by column and schooling-level sample differing by row. Once again, estimates differ across specifications according to a similar pattern seen in tables 8.2A and 8.2B. There is a clear gradient in coefficients across schooling samples, with those having the least schooling having the most negative option value coefficients, and gradually coefficients become less and less negative for samples with more and more schooling. The OV coefficients for those without a high school degree are about five times as large as OV coefficients for those with a college degree. The biggest difference in coefficients is at the high school graduation margin.

Finally, table 8.4B shows estimates from retirement probit regressions with percent gain in option value from delaying retirement as the key explanatory variables, for different samples split by level of schooling. This shows a similar gradient to that presented in table 8.4A.

Table 8.4A   Effect of inclusive OV on retirement by education group

	No. of obs.	Mean ret. rate (%)	Mean of OV	Std. dev. of OV	Specification (1)	(2)	(3)	(4)
OV: < High school	428,140	14.2	7,559	7,346	−0.1030*** (0.0016) [0.0605]	−0.0659*** (0.0013) [0.0375]	−0.1026*** (0.0021) [0.0596]	−0.0549*** (0.0016) [0.0266]
R^2					0.058	0.204	0.078	0.227
OV: High school	580,931	12.4	9,576	8,768	−0.0913*** (0.0010) [0.0683]	−0.0548*** (0.0008) [0.0417]	−0.0863*** (0.0012) [0.0608]	−0.0463*** (0.0009) [0.0304]
R^2					0.093	0.219	0.107	0.234
OV: Some college	268,381	8.9	11,798	11,554	−0.0614*** (0.0010) [0.0454]	−0.0374*** (0.0007) [0.0292]	−0.0595*** (0.0012) [0.0452]	−0.0328*** (0.0008) [0.024]
R^2					0.079	0.181	0.097	0.198
OV: College	86,920	4.1	17,979	17,053	−0.0218*** (0.0006) [0.023]	−0.0150*** (0.0005) [0.0186]	−0.0191*** (0.0007) [0.0186]	−0.0123*** (0.0005) [0.0137]
R^2					0.086	0.142	0.104	0.163
Linear age					X		X	
Age dummies						X		X
Health quintiles					X	X	X	X
Other Xs							X	X

Notes: Models are the same as models 1–4 in table 8.2A, but are estimated separately by education group; each coefficient on the table is from a different regression. Coefficients are marginal effects of a 10,000-unit change in OV from probit models. Standard errors are shown in parentheses. The effect of a one standard deviation change in OV is shown in brackets (this is estimated as the effect of increasing inclusive OV from the current value −0.5 std. dev. to the current value +0.5 std. dev.).
***Significant at the 1 percent level.
**Significant at the 5 percent level.
*Significant at the 10 percent level.

8.4.1   Model Fit

Estimates from table 8.2A, specification (4) are based on the full sample with option values, health quintiles, age dummies, and a full set of controls. Figures 8.11A and 8.11B show goodness-of-fit from this model in terms of observed and predicted hazard rates, separately for men and women. Hazard rate spikes at ages sixty and sixty-two are fitted well for both men and women. Estimates from table 8.3A, specification (4) are based on samples split by health quintile with option values, age dummies, and a full set of controls. Predictions by health quintile are presented in figures 8.11C and 8.11D and track the average hazard rate quite closely, with worst health always clearly more likely to retire at all ages and a more modest gradient in predicted retirement hazard across the better health quintiles. Estimates

Table 8.4B   **Effect of percent gain in inclusive OV on retirement by education group**

	No. of obs.	Mean ret. rate (%)	Mean of % OV	Std. dev. of % OV	Specification (1)	(2)	(3)	(4)
OV: < High school	428,140	14.21	0.31	0.31	−0.2269***	−0.1229***	−0.2241***	−0.0935***
					(0.0035)	(0.0027)	(0.0044)	(0.0031)
R^2					0.055	0.199	0.075	0.223
OV: High school	580,931	12.38	0.36	0.34	−0.2182***	−0.1113***	−0.2053***	−0.0861***
					(0.0026)	(0.0020)	(0.0030)	(0.0022)
R^2					0.088	0.209	0.103	0.228
OV: Some college	268,381	8.94	0.38	0.41	−0.1544***	−0.0844***	−0.1419***	−0.0679***
					(0.0032)	(0.0023)	(0.0036)	(0.0025)
R^2					0.074	0.173	0.091	0.192
OV: College	86,920	4.10	0.49	0.61	−0.0537***	−0.0322***	−0.0442***	−0.0246***
					(0.0044)	(0.0033)	(0.0045)	(0.0032)
R^2					0.067	0.121	0.091	0.149
Linear age					X		X	
Age dummies						X		X
Other Xs							X	X

Notes: Models are the same as models 1–4 in table 8.2A, but are estimated separately by education group; each coefficient on the table is from a different regression. Coefficients are marginal effects. Standard errors are shown in parentheses.

***Significant at the 1 percent level.
**Significant at the 5 percent level.
*Significant at the 10 percent level.

from table 8.4A, specification (4) are based on samples split by schooling level with option values, age dummies, and a full set of controls. Predictions by schooling are presented in figures 8.11E and 8.11F and track the average hazard rate closely for those with less than some college, but predicted hazards are more damped for those with some college and especially for college graduates.

8.4.2   Implications of the Results

Counterfactual simulations help us understand how the provisions of DI and SS programs differentially affect retirement ages. Figure 8.12A shows survival rates in work by age for simulating that only the DI retirement pathway is available or only the SS retirement pathway is available, and for those only ever receiving DI in figure 8.12B. Survival in work declines faster for simulations based on individuals who have ever received DI. For both the full population and those ever on DI, there is less survival in work simulating only the DI pathway.

A useful summary measure of the retirement consequences of our counterfactual simulations is the number of expected years of work after age fifty-seven. Figure 8.13 shows this together with two additional intermediate

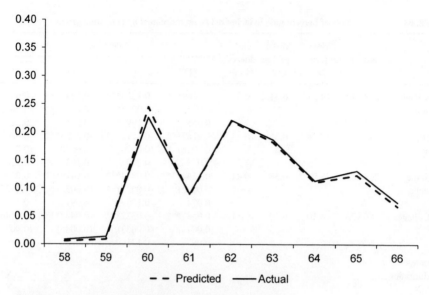

Fig. 8.11A   Actual versus predicted retirement age (men)

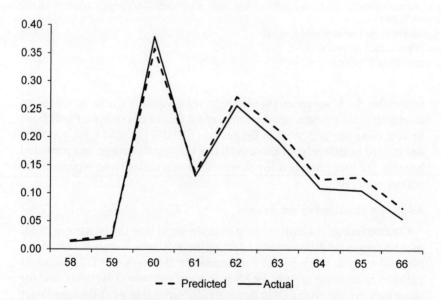

Fig. 8.11B   Actual versus predicted retirement age (women)

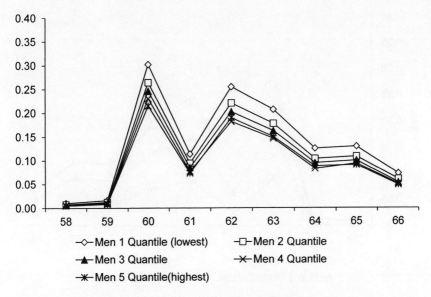

Fig. 8.11C   Predicted retirement age by health quintile (men)

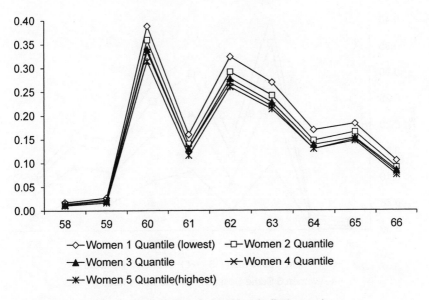

Fig. 8.11D   Predicted retirement age by health quintile (women)

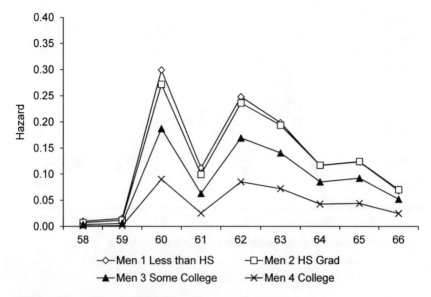

Fig. 8.11E   Predicted retirement age by education (men)

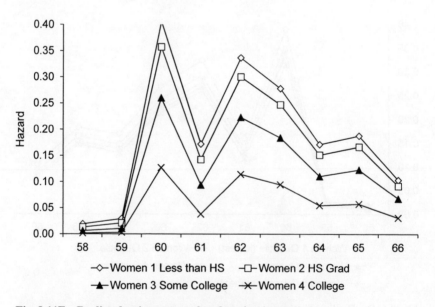

Fig. 8.11F   Predicted retirement age by education (women)

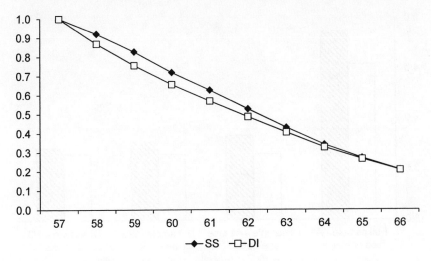

Fig. 8.12A   Simulated survival probabilities in work by pathway, for everyone

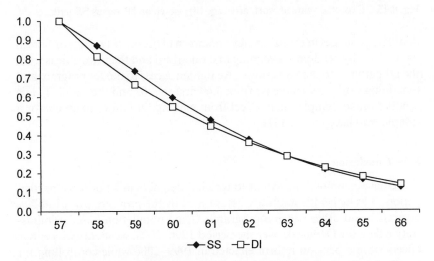

Fig. 8.12B   Simulated survival probabilities in work by pathway, for those having received DI

simulations, which are also conducted and presented for those ever receiving DI. The two new simulations involve first a random one-third assignment to the DI pathway and two-thirds assignment to the SS pathway, and second a two-thirds random assignment to the DI pathway and one-third to the SS pathway. For the full population, the SS pathway has 4.8 expected remaining years in work and the DI pathway has 4.5. For the sample of those who have ever received DI, the number of expected work years beyond fifty-seven for the SS pathway is 3.8 compared with 3.6 for the DI pathway.

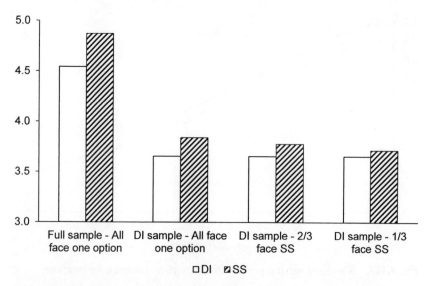

Fig. 8.13   **Expected years of work after age fifty-seven on DI versus SS path**

Simulated changes in DI stringency are shown in the other two sets of bars in figure 8.13. By randomly assigning first one-third and then two-thirds from the DI pathway to the SS pathway, we tighten access to the DI program and remaining work years increase from 3.60 first to 3.67 and then 3.73. This is a rather modest employment effect from making DI harder to access for a sample who have received DI.

8.5   Conclusion

We have examined the extent to which differences in labor force partici-pation rates by health status are determined by the provisions of disability insurance and other pension programs. Using population-based adminis-trative data for Denmark over the period 1996–2008, we identify incentive effects from a pension reform enacted in 1999–2006 while controlling for health care usage measured by hospitalization and prescription medicine purchase.

Descriptive analyses show that there is a gradient in DI participation rates by health status, with those in worse health being more likely to receive DI. A similar pattern is found for schooling, with those having less schooling being more likely to receive DI. The gradient of DI participation across health quintiles is almost twice as steep as across levels of schooling—when moving from having no high school diploma to graduating college. While the relationship between health status and DI participation is to be expected, the relationship with schooling is less well recognized, though it may largely be due to those who are in better health having more schooling.

In order to capture the incentives implicit in pension program provision, we characterize the potential gains from postponing retirement in an option value model that allows for different pension pathways to retirement. We find that pension program incentives in general are important determinants of retirement age. In order to understand how the provisions of DI and social security programs interact, we simulate increases in DI stringency by randomly allocating one-third, then two-thirds, of DI recipients to a social security pathway. These simulations show only rather modest changes in expected number of remaining work years, largely because of the availability of social security benefits for most people already at age sixty.

In our most flexible specifications, we estimate option value models of retirement age separately by health quintile and educational level in order to measure differential incentive effects. We find that individuals in poor health are significantly more responsive to economic incentives than those in better health. Similarly, those with less schooling are significantly more responsive to economic incentives than those with more schooling. The schooling effect partly reflects that the less educated have worse job prospects and therefore higher replacement rates from pension programs.

Our main finding is the existence of similar gradients in DI participation across health and education, and corresponding gradients in behavior in response to retirement incentives across health and education. Those in worse health and with less schooling participate more in DI and are more responsive to pension incentives. This suggests that reducing pension incentives to retire early will delay retirement most for those currently retiring earliest.

References

Bingley, Paul, Nabanita Datta Gupta, and Peder J. Pedersen. 2004. "The Impact of Incentives on Retirement in Denmark." In *Social Security Programs and Retirement around the World: Micro-Estimation*, edited by Jonathan Gruber and David Wise, 153–254. Chicago: University of Chicago Press.
———. 2010. "Social Security, Retirement and the Employment of the Young in Denmark." In *Social Security Programs and Retirement around the World: The Relationship to Youth Employment*, edited by J. Gruber and D. A. Wise, 99–117. Chicago: University of Chicago Press.
Høgelund, Jan, and Anders Holm. 2006. "Case Management Interviews and the Return to Work of Disabled Employees." *Journal of Health Economics* 25 (3): 500–19.
Jonassen, Anders Bruun, Brian Larsen, and Jan Høgelund. 2009. "Personer Med Handicap: Helbred, Beskæftigelse, og førtidspension 1995–2008." (Individuals with Disabilities: Health, Employment, and Disability Insurance), Report no. 09:21, SFI-The Danish National Centre for Social Research.
Milligan, Kevin S., and David A. Wise. 2012. "Health and Work at Older Ages:

Using Mortality to Assess Employment Capacity across Countries. NBER Working Paper no. 18229, Cambridge, MA.

Organisation for Economic Co-operation and Development (OECD). 2008. *Sickness, Disability and Work: Breaking the Barriers (Vol. 3): Denmark, Ireland, Finland and the Netherlands.* Paris: OECD.

———. 2009. *Employment Outlook.* Paris: OECD.

———. 2013. *Mental Health and Work: Denmark.* Paris: OECD.

Palme, Mårten, and Ingemar Svensson. 2004. "Income Security Programs and Retirement in Sweden." In *Social Security Programs and Retirement around the World: Micro-Estimation*, edited by Jonathan Gruber and David Wise, 579–642. Chicago: University of Chicago Press.

Poterba, James M., Steven F. Venti, and David A. Wise. 2011. "The Asset Cost of Poor Health." NBER Working Paper no. 16389, Cambridge, MA.

Stock, James H., and David A. Wise. 1990. "Pensions, the Option Value of Work, and Retirement." *Econometrica* 58 (5): 1151–80.

9

Pathways to Retirement and the Role of Financial Incentives in Sweden

Per Johansson, Lisa Laun, and Mårten Palme

9.1 Introduction

In the absence of a state early retirement scheme, the disability insurance (DI) program in Sweden is by far the most common pathway for labor market exit for those who exit before age sixty-five. In the early 1990s, the share of the age group sixty to sixty-four receiving DI was around 35 percent for both men and women. Although this share has decreased considerably following a series of reforms of eligibility rules, still about 17 percent of men and 25 percent of women in this age group receive DI. This is a larger share than in most other comparable countries (see, e.g., Wise 2012).

In Jönsson, Palme, and Svensson (2012), it was shown that historical changes in eligibility rules affected utilization of the DI program. However, an outstanding question is to what extent general changes in DI stringency will lead to increased labor force participation. This depends on the economic incentives induced by the old-age pension scheme and the DI program as well as on how people react to economic incentives in their retirement decisions. If the generosity in benefits is very similar in the old-age and DI programs or if people are not very sensitive to economic incentives in their

Per Johansson is a researcher at the Institute for Evaluation of Labour Market and Education Policy and professor of econometrics at Uppsala University. Lisa Laun is a researcher at the Institute for Evaluation of Labour Market and Education Policy. Mårten Palme is professor of economics at Stockholm University.

We are grateful for comments from Peter Skogman Thoursie and Olof Åslund and seminar participants at the ISS NBER meetings. Lisa Laun gratefully acknowledges financial support from the Swedish Research Council for Health, Working Life and Welfare, FORTE (dnr 2013-0209). Per Johansson gratefully acknowledges financial support from the Swedish Research Council for Health, Working Life and Welfare, FORTE (dnr 2013-2482). For acknowledgments, sources of research support, and disclosure of the authors' material financial relationships, if any, please see http://www.nber.org/chapters/c13333.ack.

retirement decisions, the effect of changes in the stringency of DI acceptance will lead to only very small changes in labor force participation rates. Conversely, if differences in economic incentives between the two schemes are very large and if people are very sensitive to these differences there will be comparatively large effects on labor force participation rates.

In this chapter we use an option value model (see Stock and Wise 1990) to estimate the effect of economic incentives on retirement behavior of older workers in Sweden. We consider two different pathways to retirement: the old-age pension path and the social insurance path. The latter includes unemployment insurance (UI), sickness insurance (SI), and DI, but we focus on the incentives provided by the DI program. We use data including the entire Swedish population between ages fifty and sixty-nine and estimate the model on the observed retirement behavior between 2001 and 2008. We use the estimated model to simulate the employment effect of different policy regimes for DI acceptance.

This chapter extends several aspects of the previous literature on how economic incentives affect retirement through the DI pathway using Swedish data (see, e.g., Palme and Svensson 2004; Skogman Thoursie 1999; Laun and Wallenius, forthcoming). The main contributions are that we use better data and model the Swedish income security programs relevant for the timing of labor market exit in a more detailed manner than previous studies. This allows us to make more precise inferences. The simulation exercises translate changes in DI screening stringency to economic incentives. This allows us to study how DI screening stringency affects retirement behavior, which has not been done in the previous literature.

We find that there is a significant effect of economic incentives on retirement. Our results also suggest that there is important between-group heterogeneity: the quintile group with the most inferior health status, as well as the low educated, respond more strongly on economic incentives. The simulation exercises, however, show that the effects of economic incentives, through changes in the stringency of DI admittance, overall are quite small.

The chapter is organized as follows. Section 9.2 gives a brief overview of Sweden's income security systems, describes recent developments in DI rates and employment among older workers and, finally, describes different pathways for exit from the Swedish labor market. Section 9.3 presents our data and the empirical approach. Section 9.4 presents the estimation results from the econometric models. Section 9.5 discusses the outcomes from the policy simulations. Section 9.6 concludes.

9.2   Background

9.2.1   Sweden's Social Security and Income Security Systems

In this section we describe the institutional details of Sweden's income security systems that we account for in this chapter. We consider both the public system as well as the centrally bargained plans. We also describe the simplifications we made in the calculations of the incentive measure. The empirical analysis includes individuals between ages fifty and sixty-nine during the period 2001 to 2008, that is, born between 1932 and 1958. We only describe the rules that applied to these cohorts.

The Old-Age Pension System

Sweden recently went through a major reform of its public old-age pension system. The old system was a pay-as-you-go defined benefit pension system, whereas the new system is a mixture of a notional defined contribution pay-as-you-go pension system and a fully funded pension scheme with individual accounts. The new pension system was implemented in 1999 and the first payments were made in 2001. The new system is phased in by cohort. Cohorts born before 1938 are completely in the old pension system. The 1938 cohort receives their pension to 4/20 from the new system and to 16/20 from the old system. Each successive cohort until the 1953 cohort receives an additional 1/20 from the new system and 1/20 less from the old system. The 1954 cohort receives their pension completely from the new pension system. Since we include individuals born between 1932 and 1958, we include those who are completely in the old system, different mixtures of the systems, as well as those who are completely in the new system.

The prereform old-age pension system consists of two main parts: a basic pension and an income-related supplementary pension. All Swedish citizens permanently living in Sweden are entitled to a basic pension, which is 96 percent of one basic amount (BA)[1] for singles and 78.5 percent for married. The BA is an indexation unit that price adjusts the Swedish income security system. It is politically determined, but has followed the Consumer Price Index (CPI) very closely. There is also a supplementary pension (ATP), which is determined by the average of the fifteen best years in the individual's income history up to 7.5 BA.[2] It is linearly reduced if the person contrib-

---

1. One BA was SEK 45,900/USD 6,600 in 2010.

2. From 1996 the ceiling was 7.5 increased price base amounts and from 2001 the ceiling is 7.5 income base amounts. The increased price base amount follows the prices in the economy, and the income base amount follows incomes. This means than the income price base amount is higher than the price base amount and, accordingly, the increased price base amount. The pensionable income is the annual income from labor earnings and public transfer systems below the social security ceiling of 7.5 price base amounts. To simplify calculations, we only account for the pensionable income that comes from labor earnings and the collection of disability benefits, but no other public transfer systems. The benefit level from the ATP is determined in several steps. First, the pension points for each year are calculated as the pensionable income above one price base amount divided by the current year price base amount. Since the social security ceiling is 7.5 price base amounts, the maximum number of pension points that can be collected each year is 6.5. Thereafter, the average pension points is calculated as the average of the individual's fifteen best years in terms of pension points collected. Finally, the individual's ATP pension income is calculated by applying the formula

$$Y_i = 0.6 \times AP_i \times \min\left(\frac{N_i}{30}, 1\right) \times BA,$$

where AP_i is the average pension points, BA is the price base amount, and N_i is the number of years with pension-rights income greater than zero.

uted less than thirty years to the scheme. The normal retirement age for both the basic and the supplementary pension is sixty-five, but both could be claimed in advance with a 0.5 percent actuarial reduction per month of early withdrawal from age sixty-one and delayed with an actuarial addition of 0.7 percent for each month of delay until age seventy. Individuals with no, or low, ATP are entitled to a special supplement of 56.9 percent of a BA, reduced on a one-to-one basis against the supplementary pension.

In the new public pension system contributions amount to 18.5 percent of pensionable income, of which 16 percent is credited to a notional defined contribution scheme and 2.5 percent is credited to a financial defined contribution scheme. In the calculations, we disregard the financial defined contribution scheme and attribute the full 18.5 percent to the notional defined contribution scheme. Therefore, we also do not describe the financial scheme but refer to Hagen (2013) for a detailed description.

In the notional defined contribution scheme, individuals collect notional pension rights based on their annual pensionable income and the annual contributions are used to finance current pension benefits in a pay-as-you-go system. The pensionable income is the total wage and public transfer income minus a 7 percent general pension contribution paid by all employees.[3] The maximum pensionable income is 7.5 income base amounts. Annual pensionable income must exceed a threshold of 42.3 percent of the price base amount to yield pension rights. The new pension system is based on the life-income principle and pension rights are accumulated from age sixteen or from year 1960. Accumulated pension rights are adjusted annually according to an income index reflecting the average wage growth. In this chapter, we assume an average wage growth of 1.6 percent throughout the period.

There is no normal pension age in the new public pension system, but the minimum age of withdrawal is sixty-one. Pension benefits at the age of retirement are calculated as the accumulated pension rights divided by an annuity divisor that is determined by average life expectancy for the given cohort at the given retirement age and an imputed real return of 1.6 percent. If the current year contributions are too small to cover the pension payments, an automatic balance mechanism is activated. In this chapter, we assume that funds are enough to finance the pension payments and disregard the automatic balance mechanism (for further details, see Hagen [2013]).

For individuals with no or low earnings, the new pension system also contains a means-tested pension supplement that replaced the universal basic pension and the special supplement in the old pension system from January 1, 2003. For cohorts born from 1938 onward, the so-called guaranteed pension amounts to 2.13 income base amounts minus public pension benefits if public pension benefits are smaller than 1.26 income base amounts. If public

---

3. The general pension contribution was introduced in 1999 and amounted to 6.95 percent in 1999 and 7 percent from 2000 onward.

pension benefits are larger than 1.26 income base amounts, the guaranteed pension is 0.87 income base amounts minus 48 percent of the public pension benefits that exceed 1.26 income base amounts. This implies that the guaranteed pension is phased out for individuals with public pension benefits above 3.07 income base amounts.

For those born before 1938, the rules for guaranteed pension are slightly different. For these cohorts, both public pension benefits and occupational pension benefits are taken into account. Given the sum of public and occupational pension (P), the formulas for the guaranteed pension benefits are:

$$P \times 1.5174 - 0.1193 - P, \qquad \text{if } 0.25 < P < 1.354 \text{ income BA}$$

$$P \times 1.343 + 0.1168 - P, \qquad \text{if } 1.354 \leq P < 1.529 \text{ income BA}$$

$$P \times 2.17 + (P - 1.51) \times 0.6 - P, \quad \text{if } 1.529 \leq P \leq 3.16 \text{ income BA.}$$

The Disability Insurance System

Before 2003, disability insurance was part of the old public pension system. Benefits were calculated in the same way as old-age pension, consisting of the basic pension and an income-related ATP supplement. As for old-age pension, the basic pension amounted to 96 percent of the basic amount for a single and 78.5 percent for a married disability pensioner. The special supplement for disability benefits was substantially larger than for old-age pension, however, at 112.9 percent of a basic amount, reduced on a one-to-one basis against the supplementary pension.

The supplementary pension in the old disability insurance system was based on an "assumed" income. The assumed income was calculated as the most favorable outcome from two different calculations. The first one was the average income of the two best out of the last four years before retirement. The second was the average income of half of the years during which the individual had positive pension points. The assumed income was used in the same formula as for old-age pension, but was not subject to the actuarial reduction for withdrawal in advance. The number of contribution years was calculated as the sum of the actual number of contribution years and the number of years between retirement and age sixty-four. If this sum was lower than thirty, benefits were reduced in the same way as for the old-age pension.

Since 2003, the disability insurance system is part of the social insurance system. Benefits are based on the assumed income, which is calculated as the average of the three highest annual earnings up to 7.5 income base amounts during the time frame immediately preceding labor force exit. The time frame is eight years for individuals below age forty-seven, seven years for individuals between ages forty-seven and fifty, six years for individuals between ages fifty and fifty-three, and five years for individuals above age fifty-three. Disability benefits amount to 64 percent of the assumed income. Individuals with low assumed income receive a guaranteed level of disability benefits (amounting to 2.4 income BAs). Individuals also collect pension points and pension rights during periods with disability benefits. The collection is based on the total assumed income, not only on the benefit payments, during the years until age sixty-five. At age sixty-five, individuals are transferred from the disability insurance system to the public pension system, with no reduction in public pension benefits due to early withdrawal.

The eligibility rules for the DI have been changed on several occasions since the early 1970s.[4] Since the early 1990s there have been a series of reforms leading to more stringent rules for DI admittance. In 1991 the right to receive DI for long-term unemployed workers older than age sixty was abolished, and in 1997 the right to DI for labor market reasons combined with health reasons was abolished. In 2003 the eligibility rules were further tightened. The rules changed so that the ability to work should be tested against the entire labor market, not just the job that the insured worker was on when applying for DI. Finally, in 2008 a number of changes affecting eligibility were implemented. Most importantly, eligibility now required permanent disability.

Occupational Pension Plans, Taxation, and Means-Tested Benefits

In addition to the public pension system, the most important pension schemes on the Swedish labor market are the occupational pension plans. Sweden has a highly unionized labor market. More than 90 percent of the labor market is covered by central agreements. These agreements contain, among other things, pension benefits and supplementary disability insurance. There are four main programs: one for white-collar workers in the private sector, one for blue-collar workers in the private sector, one for central government employees and, finally, one for local government employees. A main motivation for all these programs is to ensure earnings above the social security ceiling at 7.5 BA. Palme and Svensson (1999, 2004) give a detailed description of these programs. We also provide a detailed description of the rules that applied during our period of study in the appendix.

The option value of delaying retirement also depends on taxes. During the period under study there has been a tax bracket creep in the state income tax system, but also an introduction of an earned income tax credit in 2007. The details of the tax system during this period are described in the appendix. We further account for means-tested benefits, which are also described in the appendix.

9.2.2   The Development of Disability Rates and Employment

The DI program is one of the most important programs in Sweden's income security system. Figure 9.1 shows the participation in the DI program since the early 1960s by different age groups for males and females,

---

4. The institutional changes are described and their employment effects are analyzed in Karlström, Palme, and Svensson (2008) and Jönsson, Palme, and Svensson (2012).

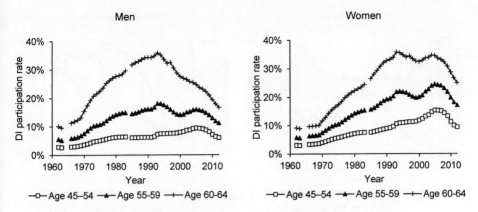

Fig. 9.1   DI participation rates by age and gender, 1962–2012

respectively. Figure 9.1 shows that there are huge variations in the participation rates, in particular for the age group sixty to sixty-four. This partially reflects the fact that, as described in section 9.2.1, the DI program has served somewhat different purposes over the period under study. In the 1970s and 1980s it was, for example, possible to get DI for labor market reasons. Older long-term unemployed workers were eligible for DI first for health reasons in combination with labor market reasons and then for labor market reasons alone. The decline in the DI participation rate reflects several changes in eligibility rules.

A key question in the study of how DI affects the labor market is, of course, to what extent the DI participation rate affects employment and labor supply. Figure 9.2 presents the development of employment along with the share receiving DI for each age and gender group. The development for females is affected by a strong trend toward higher female labor force participation in all age groups during the period under study. For males in all age groups, however, it is apparent that there is a relationship between employment and DI participation: when the DI participation rate increased from the early 1960s until the mid-1990s there was a trend toward a lower employment rate in this group. Likewise, when DI participation declined in the 1990s, there was an increase in the employment rate in this age group.

9.2.3   The Social Insurance Pathway to Retirement

Although the disability insurance program is by far the most common pathway for labor force exit for those who do not use old-age pensions, it is common that the insured worker starts his or her exit route in another program, such as unemployment insurance (UI) or sickness insurance (SI).[5] Although these are different programs with different requirements and

---

5. See Palme and Svensson (2004) for a detailed analysis of different exit routes from the Swedish labor market.

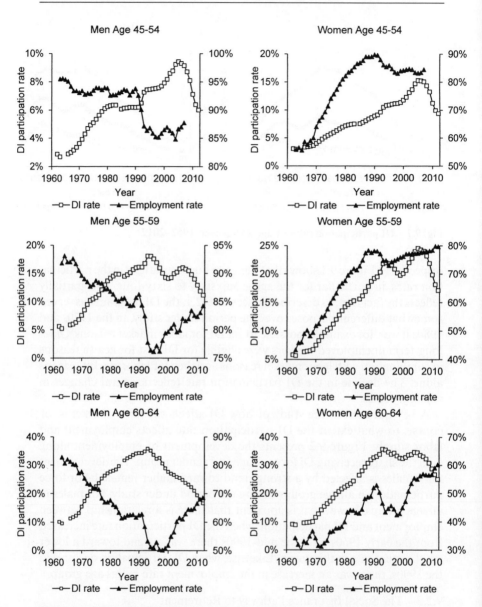

Fig. 9.2   DI participation rates and employment rates by age and gender, 1962–2012

regulations, the financial incentives in the programs are quite similar. In the option value calculations, we only model the incentives in the disability insurance program and let them represent the financial incentives in all of these programs as a simplification. In the definition of retirement we consider labor force exit through any of these insurance systems, or a combina-

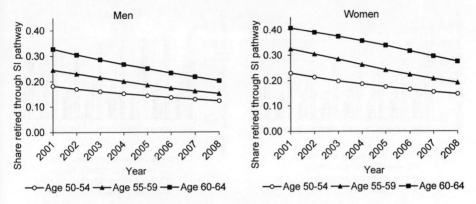

Fig. 9.3   Share retired through the social insurance pathway by age and gender, 2001–2008

tion of them, and label it the "social insurance pathway." In the empirical analysis we study retirement behavior between 2001 and 2008. Section 9.3 describes the data we use, the definition of retirement, and the pathways we consider in more detail. However, we will in this section give a brief overview of how the prevalence of the social insurance pathway has changed over time and how this prevalence differs within different population groups.

Figure 9.3 shows the share of individuals in the age groups fifty to fifty-four, fifty-five to fifty-nine, and sixty to sixty-four who have retired through the social insurance pathway between 2001 and 2008 among men and women, respectively. The social insurance pathway has been more commonly used among women than men in all age groups throughout the studied period. For both men and women, however, the share of the population who has retired through the social insurance pathway has decreased substantially over the studied period. The share has decreased from over 30 percent to about 20 percent among men in the age group sixty to sixty-four and from about 40 percent to less than 30 percent among women in the same age group between 2001 and 2008.

Figure 9.4 shows the share of individuals ages fifty to sixty-four in different education groups who have retired through the social insurance pathway between 2001 and 2008 among men and women, respectively. Retiring through the social insurance pathway is much more common in low-education groups among both men and women. The share of women retiring through the social insurance pathway is higher than for men in all education groups. The decrease in the use of the social insurance pathway over time is apparent for all education groups.

Figure 9.5 reveals that the higher disability rates among the low educated are also reflected in lower employment rates in the age group fifty to sixty-nine for males and females, respectively. The figure also shows that there is

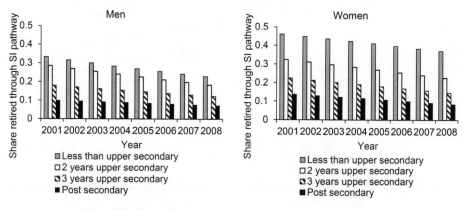

Fig. 9.4   Share retired through the social insurance pathway ages fifty to sixty-four by education and gender, 2001–2008

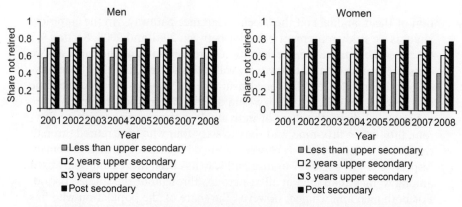

Fig. 9.5   Labor force participation ages fifty to sixty-nine by education and gender, 2001–2008

a much larger difference in employment by education group among women than men. Employment is almost twice as high—around 40 percent compared to almost 80 percent—for college-educated women compared to those with only compulsory schooling. The corresponding figures for men are 80 versus 60 percent, that is, the difference is that low-educated women work substantially less than the corresponding group among men.

Figure 9.6 shows the share of individuals ages fifty to sixty-four in different health quintiles who have retired through the social insurance pathway between 2001 and 2008 among men and women, respectively. The construction of the health measure is explained in section 9.3.3. The first quintile is the group with the most inferior health status. It is not surprising that the figure shows that the individuals in this group are most likely to retire through the social insurance pathway and that this likelihood decreases as

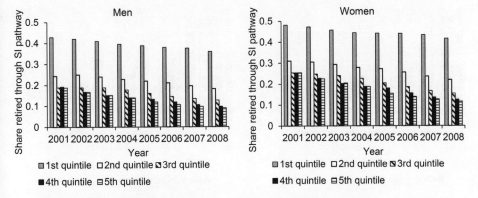

Fig. 9.6   Share retired through the social insurance pathway ages fifty to sixty-four by health and gender, 2001–2008

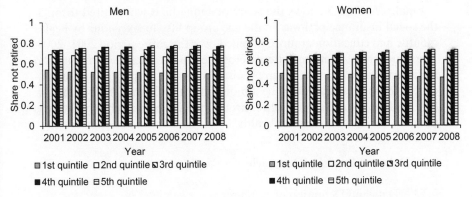

Fig. 9.7   Labor force participation ages fifty to sixty-nine by health and gender, 2001–2008

health improves across the quintiles.[6] It is interesting to note that the difference between the first quintile group and the other groups increases over time as the stringency in DI admittance increases. The likelihood to receive DI in the lowest health quintile is almost unchanged over time.

Figure 9.7 shows that the pattern from figure 9.6 on the probability of retiring through the social insurance pathway is repeated for labor force participation rates by health quintile in the age group fifty to sixty-nine for both men and women. The figure also shows that the increased labor force participation rate is primarily attributed to the groups with a good health status both among men and women.

6. As we explain in section 9.3.3, the health measure is improving over time due to more data. From 2005 we also have the drug prescription register, which improves the health index primarily for the highest quintiles.

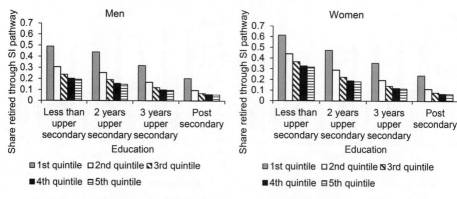

Fig. 9.8   Share retired through the social insurance pathway ages fifty to sixty-four by health and education, combined over the period 2001–2008

Finally, figure 9.8 shows the share of individuals who retired through the social insurance pathway in the age group fifty to sixty-four by health quintile and education group, combined over the entire period 2001–2008. The figure shows that the pattern across health quintiles seen in figure 9.6 is stable within education groups. It also shows that the pattern across education groups is stable within health quintiles, that is, the fact that the low educated are more likely to retire through the social insurance pathway is not only attributed to inferior health.

9.3   Data and Empirical Approach

9.3.1   Data and Definition of Retirement

We use data collected from different administrative registers including the entire Swedish population between ages fifty and sixty-nine. The registers were matched using the unique personal identification number (*personnummer*). Data on earnings by source of income along with different demographic characteristics are collected from the national tax register. We use the tax authority definition of spouse as either cohabiting or formally married (*samtaxerad*). This allows us to identify and match information on spousal income and demographic characteristics. Information on educational attainments is collected from the national education register. In section 9.3.3, we provide information about the registers used for obtaining individual measures of health status.

We use information on income from labor to define the year of labor force exit. In each year, a worker is defined as employed if labor earnings from employment or self-employment exceed one basic amount (BA), which corresponds to SEK 45,900 or USD 6,600 in 2010. A worker is defined as

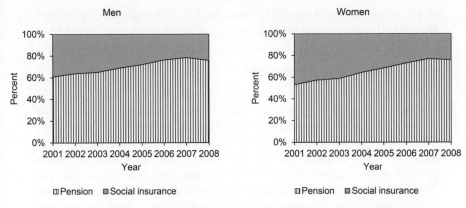

Figure 9.9   Pathways to retirement ages fifty to sixty-nine by gender, 2001–2008

retired in the year after the last observation of employment, if it is followed by at least two years of nonemployment. For a worker who is not observed in the data during the second year after the last year of employment, one year of nonemployment is sufficient to be defined as retired. The retirement age is the age in the last year of employment. An individual who is employed in the last year of observation has no retirement age. We have data of the Swedish population until 2010. Because of the way we define retirement, we are able to study retirement behavior until the year 2008. About 11.5 million person-year observations are included in the empirical analysis.

9.3.2   Pathways to Retirement

We consider two main pathways to retirement: the social insurance pathway and the old-age pension pathway. The pathway to retirement is defined on the basis of main income source during the years after the exit from the labor force and before age sixty-four. For each of these years we define the pathway from the largest income source. We then assign the pathway with most years to the individual. The social insurance pathway includes the total income from the sickness, disability, and unemployment insurances. The pension pathway includes the total income from occupational pension and public pension. A worker that retires at age sixty-five or later is assigned to the pension pathway, since eligibility for most social insurance benefits ceases at age sixty-five.

Figure 9.9 shows the pathways to retirement for men and women, respectively, during 2001–2008. The figure includes all individuals who retire between age fifty and sixty-nine during the period. The figure shows that the importance of the pension pathway has steadily increased for both men and women over the studied period. Although the pension pathway was less common among women than men in the beginning of the period, the importance of the pension pathway has increased more rapidly among women. By 2008, the pension pathway accounts for about 80 percent of all labor force exits in the age group fifty to sixty-nine among both men and women.

9.3.3   The Measurement of Health

We construct four different variables measuring health. The first one is the number of days the individual receives inpatient care during the year, that is, hospital care that requires the patient to stay overnight at the hospital. This information is available for the years 1986–2010 from the National Swedish Patient Register (see Socialstyrelsen 2009b). The second variable consists of the number of days receiving outpatient care during the year. This includes hospital care that does not require the patient to stay overnight at the hospital. The information for this variable comes from the National Swedish Patient Register and is available for the period 2001–2010.[7] The third variable consists of the total value of drug prescriptions to the individual during the year obtained from the National Prescription Register, available for the period 2005–2010. Finally, the fourth variable is subsequent mortality, which is available from the 1960s in the Cause of Death Register (see Socialstyrelsen 2009a).[8]

In a second step, we use these four variables to construct a health index for all individuals included in our sample. For each year, we create a health index based on the first principal component of the available health variables that year. We include the yearly values and two lags of inpatient care, outpatient care, and drug prescriptions, as well as two leads of mortality.

Figure 9.10 shows the average health percentile by age for men and women averaged for the years between 2001 and 2008. Men are on average in a higher health quintile than women, and health declines with age for both men and women. At older ages, however, the health of women is very similar to the health of men.

9.3.4   Option Value Calculations

We use the option value measure (see Stock and Wise 1990) for the economic incentive to remain in the labor force. The option value uses the value function measuring the utility for a particular individual at a particular age t for retiring at a particular age r as:

$$V(t,r) = \sum_{s=t}^{r-1} \beta^{s-t} [Y(s)^{\gamma}] \, probalive(s|t) + \sum_{s=r}^{\max age} \beta^{s-t} [kB(s,r)]^{\gamma} \, probalive(s|t),$$

---

7. The coverage of the outpatient care register is not complete during the first years of the period and increases for each year. However, since we construct a health index for each year separately, this is not a concern. The information contained in the register helps dividing individuals into health quintiles, and the increased coverage of the register over time may lead to better measures of health during the later years.

8. Johansson, Laun, and Laun (2014) uses ex post mortality to analyze changes in screening stringency in Sweden's DI program.

Fig. 9.10   Average health percentile by age for men and women

where $Y(s)$ is income from labor at age s, $B(s, r)$ is income from the income security system at age s if retiring at age r, β is the subjective discount rate $1/(1 + \delta)$, k reflects the marginal utility of leisure, and γ measures the marginal utility of consumption; *probalive*$(s|t)$ gives the probability of being alive at age s given survival until age t. The option value is then defined as the difference between the utility of retiring at age $t + 1$ compared to the utility of retiring at the optimal age r^*, the age yielding the highest utility value, that is,

$$\text{OVSS}(t) = V(t, r^*) - V(t, t + 1).$$

We do not estimate the parameters δ, k, and γ, but assign values similar to those that have been obtained in previous studies (see, primarily, Gruber and Wise 2004). We have chosen to set the subjective discount rate (δ) to 3 percent, k to 1.5, and γ to 0.75.

The income from the income security system depends, in addition to the retirement age, on how the individual leaves the labor force. As mentioned above, we consider two pathways to retirement: the social insurance pathway and the pension pathway. There is a possible endogeneity problem related to assigning a possible pathway to retirement for each individual in our sample. If we assign the more generous DI pathway to all, although we know that this is not an available option for a large share of the sample, it will appear as the individuals in the sample do not react on the more generous incentives to retire than they actually face and we will consequently underestimate the effect of economic incentives on retirement. If we instead assign the DI pathway when we observe that he or she has access to it, we will, of course, overestimate the effect of economic incentives.

To handle this endogeneity problem we use a probabilistic approach. This means that we calculate a weighted sum of the option value measure for the two pathways that we consider, that is,

$$\text{OVinclusive} = \text{DIweight} * \text{OVDI} + (1 - \text{DIweight})\text{OVSS},$$

where the OVDI is the option value measure for the DI pathway and OVSS is the option value for the old-age pension pathway; DIweight captures the likelihood that the DI path is available to the individual. These are determined based on the "stock estimator." The weight for the DI pathway is determined by the share of individuals between ages fifty and sixty-four who have exited through the social insurance pathway in each year, gender, and education group. The pathway probabilities were thus shown in figure 9.4.

In the data, the social insurance pathway includes income from the disability, sickness, and unemployment insurances. The major source, however, is disability insurance, with about 75 percent of the person*year observations including only disability benefits. Those who exit from the labor market through unemployment or sickness insurance switch, in most cases, to disability insurance after some time (see Palme and Svensson [2004] for a detailed analysis of different pathways). To simplify, we will only consider the economic incentives in disability insurance for the social insurance pathway.

The pension pathway consists of occupational pensions and the public old-age pension system. In the option value calculations, in addition to benefits from these two pension systems, we also take housing supplements as well as the special housing allowance for old-age pensioners, the so-called old-age support into account (see the appendix). For both pathways, we calculate the option value net of income taxes.

To make earnings backcasts and forecasts, we use earnings data for the entire population of Sweden during 1985–2010. Using an earnings equation as a function of age, age squared, and individual fixed effects, we backcast earnings to age twenty-three and forecast earnings until age seventy. That is, we assume that a worker starts working and collecting pension rights at age twenty-three. The option value is expressed in EUR 10,000 (2011).

We do not account for spouse or survivor benefits, but treat all individuals as if they were singles. Most of the financial incentives in the Swedish systems apply to the individual and not the household and the differences that do exist between married and singles are relatively minor.

Figure 9.11 shows the averages of the three different option value measures by age for men and women, respectively. The figure reveals some interesting features. First, it can be seen that the option value for the old-age pension pathway has a much steeper negative slope than the option value for the DI pathway and the weighted average reflected in the inclusive option value. This reflects the fact that the economic loss of retiring early is much larger for those who only have access to the old-age pathway. Second, it can be seen that the inclusive option value is as expected between the option value measures for the two main pathways, but much closer to the graph for the old-age pathway. This is because the weights, as reported in figure

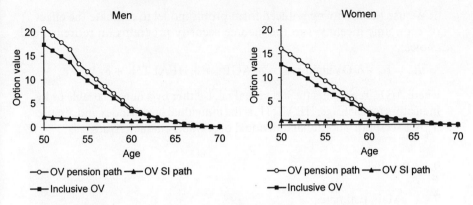

Fig. 9.11   Mean option value by age, gender, and pathway to retirement, 2001–2008

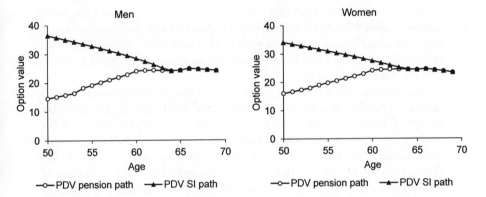

Fig. 9.12   Social security wealth (PDV) by age, gender, and pathway to retirement, 2001–2008

9.4, are larger for the old-age pension pathway. It should be noted, however, that these figures are based on a cross section and thus affected by sample attrition by age.

As a background to the option value figures, figure 9.12 shows the average social security wealth by age and pathway to retirement for men and women, respectively. It can be seen that the social security wealth for the DI pathway declines with retirement age, since the value of the DI payments that one gives up by delaying retirement exceeds the expected value of increases in the size of the benefits from longer work history. However, for the old-age pension pathway it increases up to age sixty, the minimum age for early withdrawal, and then reaches a horizontal phase. This suggests that, on average, the present value of the benefit payment one has to give up by remaining in the labor force is equal to the increase in the size of the future benefits from delaying retirement.

We use the following reduced form probit model to estimate the effect of economic incentives in the income security programs on retirement choice:

$$R_{it} = \delta_0 + \delta_1 \text{OVinclusive}_{it} + \delta_3 \text{AGE}_{it} + \delta_4 \text{HEALTH}_{it} + \delta_5 X_{it} + \varepsilon_{it},$$

where AGE_{it} represents the individual's age either by a linear variable or by indicators for each age, HEALTH_{it} is the individual health index and, finally, X_{it} is a vector of additional individual observable characteristics.

9.4   Results

9.4.1   Main Estimates

This section presents the results from the reduced-form retirement choice models. The estimates are obtained using probit models and are presented in three main sets. Tables 9.1A and 9.1B show the overall results for the entire sample. Tables 9.2A, 9.2B, 9.2C, and 9.2D describe sample heterogeneity in response to economic incentives with respect to health status and, finally, tables 9.3A and 9.3B show heterogeneity of the result with respect to differences in educational attainments.

The results for the coefficient of the option value variable should be interpreted as the effect of a 10,000-euro (measured in 2012 prices) change in the utility difference between retiring at a given age compared to retiring at the optimal age on the probability of retiring. The effect of a one standard deviation change in the option value measure is given in square brackets below the coefficients. In addition, all results are presented in a second version of the tables (9.1B, 9.2B, and 9.3B), where the coefficients are presented as the estimated response to a 1 percent change in the utility value of delaying retirement by one year.

Table 9.1A shows the results from eight different specifications. The first column shows the results when we, alongside the option value measure for retirement incentives and a linear age variable, have included dummy variables for each health quintile with the first quintile, and those with worse health status being the excluded category. As expected, there is a negative sign on the coefficient estimate for the option value measure. Thanks to an exceptionally large sample size, the precision of the estimate is impressively high and the estimate is highly significant. The magnitude of the estimate suggests that a 10,000-euro increase in the inclusive option value measure would lead to a 0.12 percentage point reduction in the retirement rate. The estimates also shows that those in the highest health quintile are on average about 1.6 percentage points less likely to exit the labor force compared to the quintile group with worse health status.

The second column in table 9.1A reports results from a specification where the linear age variable has been replaced by a more flexible specification with

Table 9.1A   **Effect of inclusive OV on retirement**

	Specification							
	(1)	(2)	(3)	(4)	(5)	(6)	(7)	(8)
OV inclusive	-0.0012***	-0.0020***	-0.0006***	-0.0015***	-0.0012***	-0.0020***	-0.0006***	-0.0015***
	(0.0000)	(0.0000)	(0.0000)	(0.0000)	(0.0000)	(0.0000)	(0.0000)	(0.0000)
	[-0.0118]	[-0.0176]	[-0.0057]	[-0.0133]	[-0.0118]	[-0.0177]	[-0.0059]	[-0.0134]
Health quint 2 (second lowest)	-0.0105***	-0.0109***	-0.0105***	-0.0109***				
	(0.0001)	(0.0001)	(0.0001)	(0.0001)				
Health quint 3	-0.0137***	-0.0142***	-0.0138***	-0.0142***				
	(0.0001)	(0.0001)	(0.0001)	(0.0001)				
Health quint 4	-0.0153***	-0.0158***	-0.0154***	-0.0159***				
	(0.0001)	(0.0001)	(0.0001)	(0.0001)				
Health quint 5 (highest)	-0.0159***	-0.0164***	-0.0161***	-0.0165***				
	(0.0001)	(0.0001)	(0.0001)	(0.0001)				
Health index					-0.0002***	-0.0002***	-0.0002***	-0.0002***
					(0.0000)	(0.0000)	(0.0000)	(0.0000)
Age	0.0070***		0.0071***		0.0070***		0.0071***	
	(0.0000)		(0.0000)		(0.0000)		(0.0000)	
Age dummies		Included		Included		Included		Included
Female	0.0048***		0.0048***	0.0040***			0.0046***	0.0038***
	(0.0001)		(0.0001)	(0.0001)			(0.0001)	(0.0001)
Married	0.0072***	0.0070***	0.0072***	0.0070***			0.0071***	0.0069***
	(0.0001)	(0.0001)	(0.0001)	(0.0001)			(0.0001)	(0.0001)

(continued)

Table 9.1A (continued)

	Specification							
	(1)	(2)	(3)	(4)	(5)	(6)	(7)	(8)
Spouse works			-0.0162***	-0.0149***			-0.0162***	-0.0149***
			(0.0001)	(0.0001)			(0.0001)	(0.0001)
Sector dummies			Included	Included			Included	Included
Two years upper secondary			-0.0016***	-0.0012***			-0.0016***	-0.0012***
			(0.0001)	(0.0001)			(0.0001)	(0.0001)
Three years upper secondary			-0.0052***	-0.0044***			-0.0052***	-0.0044***
			(0.0001)	(0.0001)			(0.0001)	(0.0001)
Postsecondary			-0.0109***	-0.0092***			-0.0109***	-0.0092***
			(0.0001)	(0.0001)			(0.0001)	(0.0001)
Observations	11,575,057	11,575,057	11,575,057	11,575,057	11,575,057	11,575,057	11,575,057	11,575,057
Mean ret. rate	0.0519	0.0519	0.0519	0.0519	0.0519	0.0519	0.0519	0.0519
Mean of OV	7.2557	7.2557	7.2557	7.2557	7.2557	7.2557	7.2557	7.2557
Std. dev. of OV	6.9829	6.9829	6.9829	6.9829	6.9829	6.9829	6.9829	6.9829

Note: Standard errors in parentheses, clustered by individual.

***Significant at the 1 percent level.

**Significant at the 5 percent level.

*Significant at the 10 percent level.

Table 9.1B **Effect of percent gain in inclusive OV on retirement**

	Specification			
	(1)	(2)	(3)	(4)
Percent gain in OV	–0.0104***	–0.0444***	0.0043***	–0.0315***
	(0.0003)	(0.0005)	(0.0003)	(0.0005)
Linear age	X		X	
Age dummies		X		X
Health quintiles	X	X	X	X
Other Xs			X	X
Observations	11,575,057	11,575,057	11,575,057	11,575,057
Mean ret. rate	0.0519	0.0519	0.0519	0.0519
Mean of % gain in OV	0.3145	0.3145	0.3145	0.3145
Std. dev. of % gain in OV	0.3311	0.3311	0.3311	0.3311

Note: Standard errors in parentheses, clustered by individual.
***Significant at the 1 percent level.
**Significant at the 5 percent level.
*Significant at the 10 percent level.

age dummies for each one-year age group. The results seem to be quite robust to this change. The coefficient estimate changes from –0.0012 to –0.0020, a change on the fourth decimal. The specification shown in columns (3) and (4) corresponds to those in the first and second columns, but we now also include controls for a number of observable demographic characteristics potentially correlated with the inclusive option value measure. The result for the inclusive option value measure in the specification in the fourth column does not change much compared to the one in column (2). However, the estimate in the third column is substantially smaller in absolute value compared to the corresponding one in column (1). The estimates for the demographic variables show, for example, that women on average retire earlier, since they have an about 0.5 percentage point higher retirement rate than men. The estimates of the dummy variables for the different education levels indicate large differences in the timing of the exit from the labor market between different educational groups: the group with college or university education has on average about a 1.1 percentage point lower retirement rate compared to those with compulsory education only.

The models shown in the fifth through the eighth columns of table 9.1A correspond to the ones shown in the first four columns with the difference that the dummy variables for the five health quintiles are replaced by a linear variable in the health index used for constructing the quintile groups. The estimates of the inclusive option value measure for these alternative specifications are very similar to the corresponding original ones.

To sum up, the results from the eight specifications shown in table 9.1A all give negative and significant estimates of the inclusive option value measure, that is, estimates show that economic incentives matter for the timing of the exit from the labor market. The preferred specification, which includes the most flexible specification in age and health differences together with controls for demographic variables shown in the fourth column, suggests that a 10,000-euro change in the inclusive option value would lead to a 0.15 percent change in the retirement rate. Since the average retirement rate is 5.19 percent in the age group under study, this implies that retirement would change by 2.9 percent. Table 9.1A also shows that a one standard deviation change in the option value would translate into a 1.34 percent lower retirement rate. The result in table 9.1B for this specification shows that a 1 percent increase in the option value would lead to a 3.15 percentage point reduction in the retirement rate.

Tables 9.2A and 9.2B show the same results as in tables 9.1A and 9.1B, but the sample is now divided by health quintile. For obvious reasons, we now only include the health index linearly as a control variable. The results reveal that the group with worse health status, the first quintile, reacts strongest on economic incentives. The coefficient estimates decrease monotonically across the five groups. However, if one relates the estimates to the average retirement rates in the groups, it can be seen that the percentage change is very similar in all groups. This is also true for the results of the response to the percentage change in the option value presented in table 9.2B.

Tables 9.2C and 9.2D present the results corresponding to results displayed in table 9.2A and 9.2B, but in which we instead have estimated a more restrictive model. Here the heterogeneous effects are estimated by adding an interaction between the option value and the linear health index to the regression model. In contrast to tables 9.2A and 9.2B, the marginal effects are decreasing with the level of health. Although statistically significant, the magnitude of the estimated heterogeneous effect is small.

Tables 9.3A and 9.3B show the results when the sample is divided into four groups by educational attainment. The first group includes individuals that have not obtained any education beyond the compulsory level, the second group consists of those with vocational education in addition to compulsory schooling, the third group consists of those who graduated from an academic track in their secondary education, and finally, the fourth group are those with college or university education. The specifications correspond to the first four specifications in table 9.1A, that is, all specifications include dummy variables for health quintiles; the specifications in the first and third columns includes linear controls for age, while those in the second and fourth columns use age dummies, and the specifications in the third and fourth columns include controls for the demographic characteristics shown in table 9.1B.

Although the estimates vary somewhat between the four different specifications, it seems that the low-education groups react more strongly on economic incentives in their retirement behavior. This result emerges more

Table 9.2A Effect of inclusive OV on retirement by health quintile

	Obs.	Mean ret. rate	Mean of OV	Std. dev. of OV	Specification			
					(1)	(2)	(3)	(4)
OV: Quintile 1 (worst health)	1,700,751	0.0814	5.7588	5.9693	-0.0022*** (0.0001) [-0.0144]	-0.0034*** (0.0001) [-0.0216]	-0.0010*** (0.0001) [-0.0068]	-0.0024*** (0.0001) [-0.0154]
OV: Quintile 2	2,254,529	0.0568	6.6553	6.4598	-0.0016*** (0.0000) [-0.0136]	-0.0025*** (0.0000) [-0.0201]	-0.0008*** (0.0000) [-0.0068]	-0.0019*** (0.0000) [-0.0150]
OV: Quintile 3	2,477,592	0.0476	7.3671	6.9350	-0.0011*** (0.0000) [-0.0112]	-0.0018*** (0.0000) [-0.0168]	-0.0005*** (0.0000) [-0.0052]	-0.0014*** (0.0000) [-0.0126]
OV: Quintile 4	2,560,048	0.0426	7.9134	7.3947	-0.0008*** (0.0000) [-0.0091]	-0.0014*** (0.0000) [-0.0140]	-0.0004*** (0.0000) [-0.0043]	-0.0011*** (0.0000) [-0.0110]
OV: Quintile 5 (best health)	2,582,137	0.0414	8.0067	7.4514	-0.0007*** (0.0000) [-0.0081]	-0.0012*** (0.0000) [-0.0128]	-0.0003*** (0.0000) [-0.0035]	-0.0009*** (0.0000) [-0.0098]
Linear age					X	X		
Age dummies							X	X
Other Xs					X	X	X	X

Note: ***Significant at the 1 percent level.

**Significant at the 5 percent level.

*Significant at the 10 percent level.

Table 9.2B   Effect of percent gain in inclusive OV on retirement by health quintile

	Obs.	Mean ret. rate	Mean % OV	Std. dev. % OV	Specification			
					(1)	(2)	(3)	(4)
OV: Quintile 1 (worst health)	1,700,751	0.0814	0.2474	0.2764	−0.0196***	−0.0700***	0.0070***	−0.0453***
					(0.0013)	(0.0017)	(0.0012)	(0.0017)
OV: Quintile 2	2,254,529	0.0568	0.2865	0.3026	−0.0162***	−0.0579***	0.0034***	−0.0404***
					(0.0009)	(0.0012)	(0.0008)	(0.0012)
OV: Quintile 3	2,477,592	0.0476	0.3189	0.3284	−0.0091***	−0.0420***	0.0049***	−0.0296***
					(0.0007)	(0.0010)	(0.0006)	(0.0009)
OV: Quintile 4	2,560,048	0.0426	0.3445	0.3541	−0.0047***	−0.0312***	0.0050***	−0.0230***
					(0.0006)	(0.0008)	(0.0005)	(0.0008)
OV: Quintile 5 (best health)	2,582,137	0.0414	0.3489	0.3574	−0.0031***	−0.0278***	0.0058***	−0.0200***
					(0.0006)	(0.0009)	(0.0005)	(0.0008)
Linear age					X		X	
Age dummies						X		X
Other Xs						X	X	X

Note: ***Significant at the 1 percent level.
**Significant at the 5 percent level.
*Significant at the 10 percent level.

Table 9.2C   **Effect of inclusive OV on retirement with health index interaction**

	Specification			
	(1)	(2)	(3)	(4)
OV	−0.0003***	−0.0012***	0.0003***	−0.0007***
	(2.44e−05)	(2.59e−05)	(2.30e−05)	(2.53e−05)
	[−0.0026]	[−0.0104]	[0.0029]	[−0.0063]
OV*health index	−1.86e−05***	−1.58e−05***	−1.76e−05***	−1.53e−05***
	(4.42e−07)	(4.33e−07)	(4.06e−07)	(4.05e−07)
Health index	−0.000149***	−0.000164***	−0.000156***	−0.000169***
	(2.28e−06)	(2.43e−06)	(2.20e−06)	(2.35e−06)
Linear age	X		X	
Age dummies		X		X
Other Xs			X	X
Observations	11,575,057	11,575,057	11,575,057	11,575,057
Mean ret. rate	0.0519	0.0519	0.0519	0.0519
Mean of OV	7.2557	7.2557	7.2557	7.2557
Std. dev. of OV	6.9829	6.9829	6.9829	6.9829

Note: ***Significant at the 1 percent level.
**Significant at the 5 percent level.
*Significant at the 10 percent level.

Table 9.2D   **Effect of percent gain in inclusive OV on retirement with health index interaction**

	Specification			
	(1)	(2)	(3)	(4)
OV	0.0131***	−0.0239***	0.0254***	−0.0121***
	(0.0005)	(0.0006)	(0.0005)	(0.0006)
OV*health index	−0.0005***	−0.0004***	−0.0004***	−0.0004***
	(9.75e−06)	(9.95e−06)	(8.66e−06)	(9.11e−06)
Health index	−0.0002***	−0.0002***	−0.0002***	−0.0002***
	(2.22e−06)	(2.39e−06)	(2.12e−06)	(2.29e−06)
Linear age	X		X	
Age dummies		X		X
Other Xs			X	X
Observations	11,575,057	11,575,057	11,575,057	11,575,057
Mean ret. rate	0.0519	0.0519	0.0519	0.0519
Mean of OV	0.3145	0.3145	0.3145	0.3145
Std. dev. of OV	0.3311	0.3311	0.3311	0.3311

Note: ***Significant at the 1 percent level.
**Significant at the 5 percent level.
*Significant at the 10 percent level.

Table 9.3A Effect of inclusive OV on retirement by education group

	Obs.	Mean ret. rate	Mean of OV	Std. dev. of OV	Specification			
					(1)	(2)	(3)	(4)
OV: < upper secondary	2,634,666	0.0709	4.4487	4.5582	-0.0019*** (0.0001) [-0.0109]	-0.0042*** (0.0001) [-0.0226]	-0.0011*** (0.0001) [-0.0062]	-0.0036*** (0.0001) [-0.0195]
OV: 2 years upper secondary	3,541,791	0.0519	5.9837	5.1799	-0.0015*** (0.0000) [-0.0104]	-0.0034*** (0.0000) [-0.0222]	-0.0015*** (0.0000) [-0.0105]	-0.0037*** (0.0000) [-0.0243]
OV: 3 years upper secondary	3,104,564	0.0455	8.4283	7.0607	-0.0003*** (0.0000) [-0.0029]	-0.0008*** (0.0000) [-0.0070]	-0.0002*** (0.0000) [-0.0023]	-0.0008*** (0.0000) [-0.0069]
OV: Post secondary	2,294,036	0.0385	10.8562	9.3225	-0.0003*** (0.0000) [-0.0035]	-0.0005*** (0.0000) [-0.0066]	-0.0002*** (0.0000) [-0.0032]	-0.0005*** (0.0000) [-0.0066]
Linear age					X		X	
Age dummies						X		X
Health quintiles						X	X	X
Other Xs					X	X	X	X

Note: ***Significant at the 1 percent level.
**Significant at the 5 percent level.
*Significant at the 10 percent level.

Table 9.3B   **Effect of percent gain in inclusive OV on retirement by education group**

	Obs.	Mean ret. rate	Mean of % OV	Std. dev. of % OV	Specification			
					(1)	(2)	(3)	(4)
OV: < Upper secondary	2,634,666	0.0709	0.1988	0.2176	−0.0173***	−0.1000***	0.0059***	−0.0828***
					(0.0013)	(0.0016)	(0.0013)	(0.0016)
OV: 2 years upper secondary	3,541,791	0.0519	0.2709	0.2552	−0.0086***	−0.0751***	−0.0063***	−0.0812***
					(0.0007)	(0.0010)	(0.0008)	(0.0010)
OV: 3 years upper secondary	3,104,564	0.0455	0.3693	0.3493	0.0065***	−0.0159***	0.0080***	−0.0153***
					(0.0005)	(0.0006)	(0.0005)	(0.0007)
OV: Post secondary	2,294,036	0.0385	0.4408	0.4414	0.0063***	−0.0062***	0.0060***	−0.0064***
					(0.0003)	(0.0006)	(0.0003)	(0.0005)
Linear age					X	X		
Age dummies						X	X	X
Health quintiles					X	X	X	X
Other Xs							X	X

Note: ***Significant at the 1 percent level.

**Significant at the 5 percent level.

*Significant at the 10 percent level.

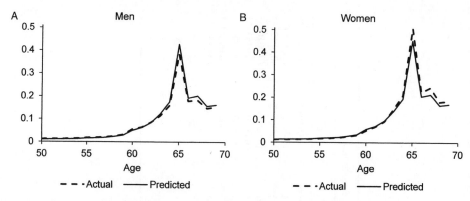

Fig. 9.13   Actual and predicted retirement hazard rates: *A*, men; *B*, women

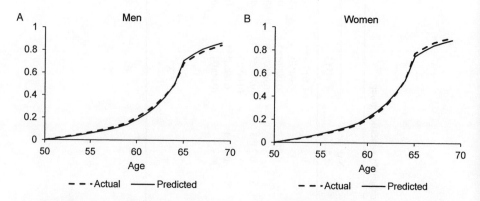

Fig. 9.14   Actual and predicted cumulative retirement hazard rates: *A*, men; *B*, women

clearly if one compares the lowest and the highest education groups. The coefficient estimates for the inclusive option value measure is significantly larger in all specifications for the low-education group.

9.4.2   The Model Fit

To evaluate the model we use the preferred specification, shown in the fourth column in tables 9.1A and B, 9.2A–D, and 9.3A and B. The evaluation of the model fit is of particular importance for the simulation analysis presented in section 9.5. Figure 9.13 shows the results when this model is used to predict the retirement rates by age and compare it with the actual retirement pattern. Panels A and B of figure 9.13 compare the hazard rates by age for males and females, respectively, and figure 9.14, panels A and B show the corresponding results for the cumulative distribution function.

From these figures it can be seen that the model underestimates retirement in relatively early ages and overestimates it in later ages for men. The

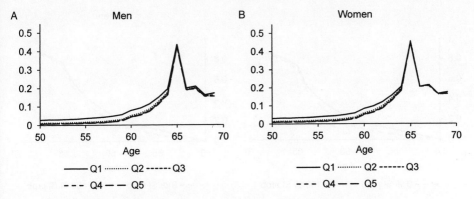

Fig. 9.15 Simulated retirement hazard by health quintile: *A*, men; *B*, women

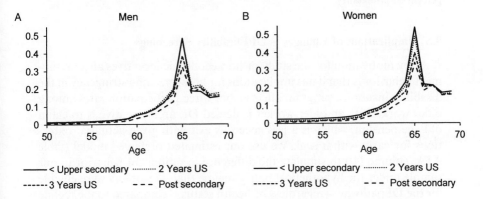

Fig. 9.16 Simulated retirement hazard by education group: *A*, men; *B*, women

opposite is true for women. Overall, however, it is apparent that the model gives a very good prediction of the actual outcome.

9.4.3   Descriptive Key Results in Graphical Form

Figures 9.15 and 9.16 show the results of tables 9.2A–D and 9.3A and B graphically. Panels A and B of figure 9.15 show the predicted retirement hazards by age for the five health quintiles, for males and females, respectively. It can be seen that the largest difference in retirement behavior is between the first quintile, those with worse health status, compared to the other four groups. This is true for both males and females.

Panels A and B of figure 9.16 show the differences in predicted retirement hazards between the four groups with different educational attainments. In general, it can be seen that the differences between groups with different educational attainments are somewhat larger compared to those between the quintile groups with different health status.

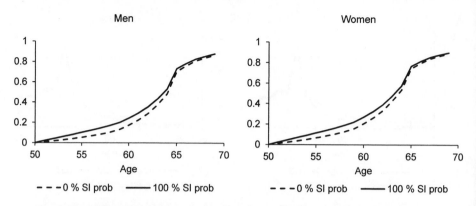

Fig. 9.17   Cumulative retirement hazard from simulations with 0 percent and 100 percent SI probability

9.5   Implications of Changes in DI Eligibility Screening

A key motivation for the study of how economic incentives affect retirement behavior is that it has implications for how screening stringency in the disability insurance program affects labor force participation rates among older workers. If an older worker is denied DI, an alternative is to claim old-age pension, which is a less generous exit path given actuarial reductions for early withdrawal. We use our estimated preferred model (table 9.1A, column [4]) to simulate the difference in retirement behavior in our sample under the hypothetical policy regime that *all* workers were eligible for the DI pathway—regardless of health status—compared to the regime where *no one* was eligible, that is, if only the old-age pension path is available. The driving force behind the observed differences is purely that the insured individuals are affected by economic incentives in their decision on when to leave the labor force.

Figure 9.17 shows the cumulative retirement hazards for these two policy simulations for males and females, respectively. As a summary of the effects of the policy simulations, figure 9.18 shows the expected remaining number years of work between ages fifty and sixty-nine of the two hypothetical policy regimes compared to the actual state. As expected, the cumulative hazard function for the policy regime where all workers are eligible for DI are everywhere above the corresponding regime with no DI. As can be seen in the summary measure in figure 9.18, the simulated difference between the expected lengths of the work life is 0.82 years, or a 5.9 percent prolonging of the work life after age fifty for men, and 0.75 years, or 5.6 percent, for women.

Disability insurance is not a relevant exit path from the labor force for quite a large share of the population. This implies that the simulations shown

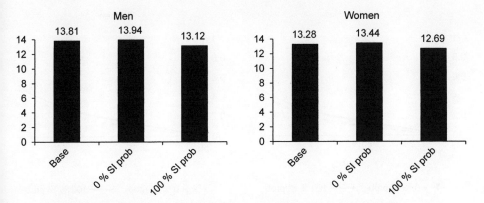

Fig. 9.18   Expected years of work between ages fifty and sixty-nine, base case and various simulations

above overestimate the effect though economic incentives of every relevant policy reform altering the DI screening stringency and should therefore be interpreted as an "upper bound" for possible effects of such reforms. However, the problem is that we do not know the size of the group for which DI is a relevant exit path depending on screening stringency. In addition, the group for whom it is a relevant exit path differs from those for which it is not on several observable as well as unobservable characteristics.

The most restrictive definition of the group for which disability insurance is a relevant exit path is to include only those who we observe use the DI pathway for exit from the labor force. As an alternative simulation strategy, we therefore repeat the simulations reported above on the subsample of individuals that we observe retiring through the disability insurance path separately. The economic incentives for retirement facing these individuals may differ from what we observe in the entire sample. These differences may generate differences in the result of the simulation. However, since we use the same estimated models as in the simulations reported above, possible heterogeneity parameters reflecting sensitivity to economic incentives in retirement behavior between the two samples are not taken into account.

Figure 9.19 shows the cumulative distribution functions for the subsample of DI recipients under different regimes of DI acceptance probabilities. The graphs stop at age sixty-three, that is, at the age when the individuals consider retiring at age sixty-four, which is the oldest age for DI eligibility. In addition to the simulation where we shut down the DI option—that is, zero probability of DI acceptance—and the simulation where everybody is eligible for DI, we also consider the cases where one-third and two-thirds of the group is eligible for DI. As expected, the differences between the simulations with 0 percent probability versus 100 percent probabilities, shown in

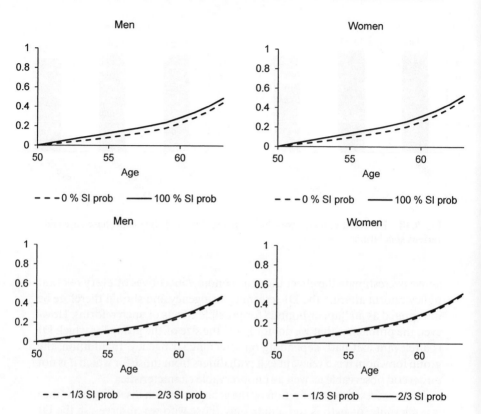

Fig. 9.19   Cumulative hazard functions for different DI probabilities: Males and females, respectively

the two upper panels of figure 9.19, are much larger than the simulation of two-thirds versus one-third DI probabilities, shown in the two lower panels of figure 9.19.

As a summary measure for the simulations, figure 9.20 shows the simulated expected remaining time in the labor force at age fifty under the different policy regimes described above. Comparing the results shown in figure 9.20 with the corresponding ones for the entire sample shown in figure 9.18, it can be seen that the simulated expected duration of the remaining work life is considerably shorter for those retiring through the DI program. This reflects the fact that these individuals on average have an inferior health status and lower educational attainments than the rest of the sample. However, comparing the simulated differences between the policy regimes in figure 9.20 with those in figure 9.18 suggest that the policy response is quite similar in the two samples. This suggests that differences in economic incentives in retiring through the DI path do not drive the observed differences in retirement ages.

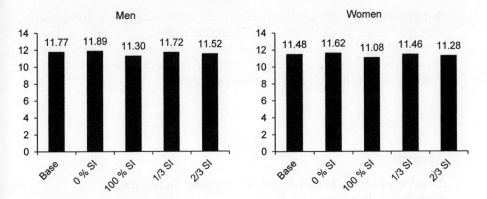

Fig. 9.20 Expected number of years of remaining work life at age fifty under different DI acceptance probabilities

9.6 Conclusions

In this chapter we first estimate an econometric model for the choice between staying in the labor market and leaving it for older workers in Sweden. We consider the economic incentives of two different exit paths from the labor force: the old-age pension path and a composite path consisting of other income security programs, where the DI program is the most important. We then simulate the effect if the probability of being admitted to DI is changed from 0 to 100 percent. The behavioral response to these changes comes through how the individuals in the sample respond to economic incentives in their retirement decision.

We find that the option value of retirement has a statistically significant impact on retirement behavior, that is, economic incentives generated by income taxes and the income security system significantly affects the timing of the exit from the labor market. We also find that there are statistically significant differences between different population groups. The quintile group with the most inferior health status reacts stronger on economic incentives and the strength of the reaction seems to decrease monotonically with health. The difference is even larger between groups with different educational attainments. People with lower education are more sensitive to economic incentives in their retirement behavior.

The simulation exercises, however, show that the effects of economic incentives, through changes in the stringency of DI admittance, overall are quite small. Going from 0 to 100 percent DI admittance probability in the male population would decrease the expected number of years in the labor force at age fifty from 13.93 to 13.17 years.

In Jönsson, Palme, and Svensson (2012), it was shown that changes in the rules for DI eligibility in the long run gave very sizable effects on labor force participation. Also, figure 9.2 in section 9.2.2 of this chapter shows that employment in the age group sixty to sixty-four increased from around 50 percent in the year 2000 to almost 70 percent in 2012. Our results suggest that such huge changes could not have been driven by economic incentives alone. Other factors such as social norms, credit constraints, and changes in population health may also have been important.

Appendix
Sweden's Occupational Pensions, Income Taxes, and Housing Allowances

Occupational Pensions

The Central Government Sector

The employees in the central government sector included in our sample are covered by two different pension agreements. Those born before 1943 are covered by the PA-91 Act, and the cohorts born from 1943 are covered by the PA-03 Act. The PA-03 replaced PA-91 in 2003. The pension age in both agreements is sixty-five, but pension can be claimed from age sixty under PA-91 and from age sixty-one under PA-03 with an actuarial reduction in benefits. Pension withdrawal can also be delayed with an actuarial increase in benefits.

The PA-91 Act includes a defined benefit pension and a supplementary defined contribution pension. The defined benefit pension in PA-91 is based on the average earnings up to 30 increased price base amounts during the five years preceding retirement. The pension from age sixty-five is 10 percent of the pensionable income below 7.5 increased price base amounts, 65 percent of the pensionable income between 7.5 and 20 increased price base amounts, and 32.5 percent of the pensionable income between 20 and 30 increased price base amounts. For each month of early withdrawal, benefits on the pensionable income below 7.5 increased price base amounts are reduced by 2.6 percent and benefits on the pensionable income between 7.5 and 30 price base amounts are reduced by 0.4 percent. For each month of delayed withdrawal benefits, all levels are increased by 0.4 percent. The pension below age sixty-five is 101 percent of the pensionable income below 1 increased price base amount, 65 percent of the pensionable income between 1 and 20 increased price base amounts, and 32.5 percent of the pensionable income between 20 and 30 increased price base amounts. In addition, benefits below age sixty-five are reduced by 0.4 percent for each month of early withdrawal. Benefits are also reduced proportionally if the number of contribution years from age twenty-eight is less than thirty.

The contributions for the supplementary defined contribution pension in PA-91 amounted to 1.5 percent of the pensionable income from January 1991 to March 1994 and to 1.7 percent from April 1995. Pension rights are collected between ages twenty-eight and sixty-five, and are also accounted for during years with disability benefits and early withdrawal of pension benefits. The defined contribution pension can be withdrawn lifelong or as a temporary pension. Pension rights collected under PA-91 are also accounted for the cohorts born after 1942.

The PA-03 consists of two defined contribution pensions and one defined benefits pension. The first defined contribution pension in PA-03 is the individual pension. The premium amounted to 2.3 percent of annual income during 2003–2007 and 2.5 percent from 2008 for income up to 30 income base amounts. Pension rights are collected between ages twenty-three and sixty-five and are also accounted for during years with disability benefits and early withdrawal of pension benefits. The individual pension can be collected from age sixty-one and is paid out lifelong.

The second defined contribution pension in PA-03 is the supplementary pension. The premium amounted to 1.9 percent of annual income during 2003 and 2.0 percent since 2004 for income up to 30 income base amounts. Pension rights were collected between ages twenty-eight and sixty-five until 2007 and between ages twenty-three and sixty-five since 2008. The supplementary pension is paid out lifelong or as a temporary pension.

The defined benefits pension in PA-03 is based on the pensionable income, calculated as the average income during the five years preceding retirement. In the long run, the defined benefits pension from age sixty-five will only be provided for individuals with income above 7.5 income base amounts and will amount to 60 percent of the pensionable income between 7.5 and 20 income base amounts and 30 percent of the pensionable income between 20 and 30 income base amounts. Cohorts born between 1943 and 1972 are covered by transitional rules, however. For the cohorts born between 1943 and 1958, included in this chapter, pension benefits amount to between 6.3 percent for the youngest cohort to 9.5 percent for the oldest cohort on the income below 7.5 income base amounts, between 62.60 percent for the youngest cohort, 64.85 percent for the oldest cohort on the pensionable income between 7.5 and 20 income base amounts, and between 30.9 percent for the youngest cohort and 32.4 percent for the oldest cohort on the pensionable income between 20 and 30 income base amounts. Benefits are reduced proportionally if the number of contribution years from age twenty-eight is less than thirty.

Individuals on disability benefits are also granted supplementary benefits from the state occupational pension plan from the retirement age up to age sixty-five. The supplementary disability benefits amounted to 21 percent on income up to 7.5 increased price base amounts, 81 percent on income between 7.5 and 20 increased price base amounts, and 40.5 percent on income between 20 and 30 increased price base amounts between 2001 and 2007. From 2008, the supplementary disability benefits amount to 15 percent on income up to 7.5 increased price base amounts, 75 percent on income between 7.5 and 20 increased price base amounts, and 37.5 percent on income between 20 and 30 increased price base amounts.

White-Collar Workers in the Private Sector

Private sector white-collar workers born before 1979 are covered by the ITP2 occupational pension plan. The scheme consists of a defined benefit pension and a defined contribution pension. The pension age is sixty-five, but pension can be withdrawn early from age fifty-five and delayed until age seventy. For each month of early or delayed withdrawal, benefits are adjusted according to the pension funds actuarially calculated guidelines.

The pensionable income under the defined benefit plan is the annual income up to 30 income base amounts in the year before retirement. The occupational pension is 10 percent of the pensionable income below 7.5 income base amounts, 65 percent of the pensionable income between 7.5 and 20 income base amounts, and 32.5 percent of the pensionable income between 20 and 30 income base amounts. Benefits are reduced proportionally if the number of contribution years from age twenty-eight is less than thirty.

The contributions for the supplementary defined contribution pension in ITP2 amounted to 2 percent of the pensionable income from 1977. Pension rights are collected between ages twenty-eight and sixty-five. If the individual retires before age sixty-five but after age sixty-two, pension rights are accounted for until age sixty-five based on the pensionable income at the time of retirement. The supplementary defined contribution pension is paid out lifelong or as a temporary pension.

Individuals on disability benefits are also granted supplementary benefits from the state occupational pension plan from the retirement age up to age sixty-five. The supplementary disability benefits amount to 15 percent on income up to 7.5 increased price base amounts, 65 percent on income between 7.5 and 20 increased price base amounts, and 32.5 percent on income between 20 and 30 increased price base amounts.

The Municipality Sector

Cohorts in the municipality sector born before 1938 are covered by the PA-KL agreement. The pension points (P) for the defined benefit pension in PA-KL are the average earnings during the best five years of the seven years preceding retirement up to 30 increased price base amounts divided by the increased price base amount. Gross pension points are calculated according to the following formula:

- $0.785*P + 0.1750$ if pension points are between 1 and 2.5 increased price base amounts,

- $0.6*P + 0.6375$ if pension points are between 2.5 and 3.5 increased price base amounts,
- $0.64*P + 0.4975$ if pension points are between 3.5 and 7.5 increased price base amounts,
- $0.65*P + 0.4225$ if pension points are between 7.5 and 20 increased price base amounts, and
- $0.325*P + 6.9225$ if pension points are between 20 and 30 increased price base amounts.

Gross pension points are reduced proportionally if the number of contribution years from age twenty-eight is less than thirty. The supplementary occupational pension from PA-KL is the difference between gross pension points and the pension payments from the public pension system. The pension age is sixty-five, but benefits can be claimed from age sixty with an actuarial reduction. The reduction is 0.3 percent per month if claimed at age sixty-four, 0.304 percent per month if claimed at age sixty-three, 0.339 percent per month if claimed at age sixty-two, 0.379 percent per month if claimed at age sixty-one, and 0.395 percent per month if claimed at age sixty. Benefits are increased by 0.1 percent for each month of delayed withdrawal up to age sixty-seven.

Cohorts in the municipality sector born from 1938 onward were covered by the PFA98 and PFA01 agreements until January 1, 2006. These agreements consist of a defined contribution pension scheme for all workers and a supplementary defined benefit scheme for workers with earnings above 7.5 income base amounts. Under the defined contribution pension scheme, the premium amounts to 4.5 percent of annual earnings up to 7.5 income base amounts and 2.1 percent of annual earnings between 7.5 and 30 income base amounts. Pension rights are collected between ages twenty-eight and sixty-five. Pension could be withdrawn early from age sixty-one and delayed to age sixty-seven.

The supplementary defined benefit scheme in PFA98 and PFA01 was based on the pensionable income, calculated as the average earnings during the best five years of the seven years preceding retirement up to 30 increased price base amounts. The supplementary pension amounts to 62.5 percent on pensionable income between 7.5 and 20 income base amounts and to 31.25 percent on pensionable income between 20 and 30 income base amounts. Benefits can be withdrawn early from age sixty-one and delayed until age sixty-seven, with a reduction in benefits of 0.4 percent per month of early withdrawal and an increase in benefits of 0.4 percent per month of delayed withdrawal. Benefits are reduced proportionally if the number of contribution years from age twenty-eight is less than thirty.

Since January 1, 2006, workers in the municipality sector are covered by the agreement KAP-KL, consisting of a defined contribution pension scheme and a supplementary defined benefits scheme. The premium for the defined contribution pension is 4 percent of annual earnings up to 30 income base amounts during 2006 and 2007, 4.25 percent during 2008 and 2009, and 4.5 percent from 2010 onward. For workers born between 1938 and 1943, however, the premium is the same as in the PFA agreements described above.

The pensionable income in the supplementary defined benefits scheme in KAP-KL is again calculated as the average earnings during the best five years of the seven years preceding retirement up to 30 increased price base amounts. For cohorts born before 1946, the supplementary pension is the same as under the PFA agreements, amounting to 62.5 percent on earnings between 7.5 and 20 income base amounts and to 31.25 percent on pensionable income between 20 and 30 income base amounts. For successive cohorts, benefits are gradually reduced to a level of 55 percent on earnings between 7.5 and 20 income base amounts and to 27.5 percent for earnings between 20 and 30 income base amounts, for cohorts born in 1967 or later. Benefits can be withdrawn early from age sixty-one and delayed until age sixty-seven, with a reduction in benefits of 0.4 percent per month of early withdrawal and an increase in benefits of 0.4 percent per month of delayed withdrawal. Benefits are reduced proportionally if the number of contribution years from age twenty-eight is less than thirty.

Blue-Collar Workers in the Private Sector

Since 1996, blue-collar workers in the private sector are covered by the SAF-LO agreement, which is a defined contribution scheme. Before then, workers were covered by the STP plan, which is a defined benefits scheme. Cohorts born after 1968 are fully covered by the SAF-LO agreement, whereas cohorts born between 1932 and 1968 are subject to special transitional rules between the two schemes. The premium under the SAF-LO agreement was 2 percent of annual earnings before the year 2000, and is 3.5 percent on annual earnings from 2000 onward. Pension rights are collected between ages twenty-one and sixty-five. Pension can be collected from age fifty-five.

The transitional rules for cohorts born between 1932 and 1968 are somewhat complicated and we have not been able to find any documents explaining these rules. We only had these rules explained to us by an employee at AMF Pension, administering the pension payments. For these cohorts, the pension wealth in 1996 was determined by the defined benefit pension under the STP plan based on the average income from all years from age twenty-eight until 1995. This pension wealth was brought along to the defined contribution STP plan. From 1996, individuals collected new pension points according to the STP rules. Since the transitional rules are rather unclear, we simplify our calculations by assuming that pension rights for the defined contribution plan SAF-LO was collected between ages twenty-one and sixty-five with a premium of 2 percent before the year 2000 and 3.5 percent from the year 2000 onward.

The Income Tax System

Individuals pay income taxes on earnings, public pension, sickness, unemployment, and disability benefits, and occupational pension. This is accounted for in the option value calculations. Individuals pay municipal income tax on the income, net of a basic deduction. If income exceeds a certain break point, individuals also pay a state income tax. In 2007, an earned income tax credit was introduced, which is also accounted for in the calculations.

The basic deduction is based on the total income (I) and is calculated according to the following formula, expressed in price base amounts:

- 0.423 if $I \leq 0.99$,
- $0.423 + (I - 0.99)*0.2$ if $0.99 < I \leq 2.72$,
- 0.77 if $2.72 < I \leq 3.11$,
- $0.77 - (I - 3.11)*0.1$ if $3.11 < I \leq 7.88$, and
- 0.293 if $7.88 < I$.

The municipality income tax varies across municipalities and may change over time. In this chapter, we do not take the municipality of residence into account but apply the average municipality income tax rate in each year for all individuals. The state income tax has two thresholds. Above the first threshold the state income tax is 20 percent, and above the second threshold the state income tax is 25 percent. These brackets have changed over time. Table 9A.1 presents the average municipality income tax and the two thresholds in the state income tax during the period 2001–2008, which is the period under study.

The earned income tax credit applied to earnings, but not to income from public pension or public transfers such as disability benefits. The tax credit was a function of earned income (E), the basic deduction (BD), and the municipality income tax rate (T). Furthermore, there was an age dis-

Table 9A.1   **Average municipality income tax rate and income thresholds for state income tax, 2001–2008**

	Average municipality income tax	Income threshold 20% state income tax	Income threshold 25% state income tax
2001	0.3053	271,500	411,100
2002	0.3052	290,100	430,900
2003	0.3117	301,000	447,200
2004	0.3151	308,800	458,900
2005	0.3160	313,000	465,200
2006	0.3160	317,700	472,300
2007	0.3155	328,600	488,600
2008	0.3144	340,900	507,100

continuity in the tax credit schedule. Individuals who had turned sixty-five at the beginning of the tax year received a substantially larger tax credit, roughly amounting to twice the size of the tax credit for individuals below age sixty-five. The formulas for the earned income tax credit in 2007 and 2008, accounted for in this chapter, are presented below.

For individuals below age sixty-five, the earned income tax credit in 2007, expressed in price base amounts, was:

- $(E - BD)*T$ if $E \le 0.79$,
- $(0.79 + (E - 0.79)*0.2 - BD)*T$ if $0.79 < E \le 2.72$, and
- $(1.176 - BD)*T$ if $2.72 < E$.

For individuals below age sixty-five, the earned income tax credit in 2008, expressed in price base amounts, was:

- $(E - BD)*T$ if $E \le 0.91$,
- $(0.91 + (E - 0.91)*0.2 - BD)*T$ if $0.91 < E \le 2.72$,
- $(1.272 + (E - 2.72)*0.033 - BD)*T$ if $2.72 < E \le 7$, and
- $(1.413 - BD)*T$ if $7 < E$.

For individuals above age sixty-five, the earned income tax credit in 2007, expressed in price base amounts, was:

- $(E - BD)*T$ if $E \le 1.59$,
- $(1.59 + (E - 1.59)*0.2 - BD)*T$ if $1.59 < E \le 2.72$, and
- $(1.816 - BD)*T$ if $2.72 < E$.

For individuals above age sixty-five, the earned income tax credit in 2008, expressed in price base amounts, was:

- $(E - BD)*T$ if $E \le 1.79$,
- $(1.79 + (E - 1.79)*0.2 - BD)*T$ if $1.79 < E \le 2.72$,
- $(1.976 + (E - 2.72)*0.033 - BD)*T$ if $2.72 < E \le 7$, and
- $(2.117 - BD)*T$ if $7 < E$.

Means-Tested Benefits

Housing Supplement

Individuals collecting public pension benefits or disability benefits can be granted a means-tested housing supplement if their income is low. The maximum housing supplement is 93 percent of the housing cost up to SEK 5,000 per month for singles, which is SEK 55,800 per year. For married individuals, the housing supplement is lower. The first step in the calculation of the housing supplement is to determine the individuals so-called "reduction income." It is the sum of public pension benefits, disability benefits and capital income, 80 percent of occupational income, 50 percent of earned income, and 15 percent of the wealth exceeding SEK 100,000, minus 2.17 price base amounts. The reduction income is based on gross income before tax. The housing supplement is then calculated as the maximum housing supplement minus 62 percent of the reduction income up to SEK 44,500 and 50 percent of the reduction income exceeding SEK 44,500.

Special Housing Supplement and Old-Age Support

Individuals with very low income can also be granted special housing supplement or old-age support. The rules are very similar. The calculation is based on the total net income, including housing supplement. The special housing supplement or old-age support equals 1.3546 price base amounts plus the housing cost of maximum 6,200 SEK per month minus net income.

References

Gruber, Jonathan, and David A. Wise, eds. 2004. *Social Security Programs and Retirement around the World: Micro-Estimation*. Chicago: University of Chicago Press.

Hagen, Johannes. 2013. "A History of the Swedish Pension System." Working Paper no. 2013:7, Uppsala Center for Fiscal Studies, Uppsala University.

Johansson, Per, Lisa Laun, and Tobias Laun. 2014. "Screening Stringency in the Disability Insurance Program." *B.E. Journal of Economic Analysis & Policy* 14 (3): 873–91.

Jönsson, Lisa, Mårten Palme, and Ingemar Svensson. 2012. "Disability Insurance, Population Health and Employment in Sweden." In *Social Security Programs and Retirement around the World: Historical Trends in Mortality and Health, Employment, and Disability Insurance Participation and Reforms*, edited by David A. Wise, 79–126. Chicago: University of Chicago Press.

Karlström, Anders, Mårten Palme, and Ingemar Svensson. 2008. "The Employment Effect of Stricter Rules for Eligibility for DI: Evidence from a Natural Experiment in Sweden." *Journal of Public Economics* 92 (10): 2071–82.

Laun, Tobias, and Johanna Wallenius. Forthcoming. "A Life Cycle Model of Health and Retirement: The Case of Swedish Pension Reform." *Journal of Public Economics*. doi: 10.1016/j.jpubeco.2013.11.002.

Palme, Mårten, and Ingemar Svensson. 1999. "Social Security, Occupational Pensions, and Retirement in Sweden." In *Social Security and Retirement around the World*, edited by Jonathan Gruber and David Wise, 355–402. Chicago: University of Chicago Press.

———. 2004. "Income Security Programs and Retirement in Sweden." In *Social Security Programs and Retirement around the World: Micro-Estimation*, edited by Jonathan Gruber and David Wise, 579–642. Chicago: University of Chicago Press.

Skogman Thoursie, Peter. 1999. "Disability and Work in Sweden." PhD diss., Swedish Institute for Social Research, Stockholm University.

Socialstyrelsen. 2009a. *The Swedish Cause of Death Registry*. Stockholm. http://www.socialstyrelsen.se/register/halsodataregister/cancerregistret/inenglish.

————. 2009b. *The Swedish National Patient Register. Inpatient Diseases in Sweden 1987–2007*. Stockholm. http://www.socialstyrelsen.se/register/halsodataregister /patientregistret/inenglish.

Stock, J. H., and David A. Wise. 1990. "Pensions, the Option Value of Work, and Retirement." *Econometrica* 58 (5): 1151–80.

Wise, David A., ed. 2012. *Social Security Programs and Retirement around the World: Historical Trends in Mortality and Health, Employment, and Disability Insurance Participation and Reforms*. Chicago: University of Chicago Press.

Health Status, Disability Insurance, and Incentives to Exit the Labor Force in Italy
Evidence from SHARE

Agar Brugiavini and Franco Peracchi

10.1 Introduction

Europe has witnessed a variety of policy interventions and reforms aimed at reducing the debt burden and public spending. Old-age spending is most prominent in such a landscape, and Italy has been at the center of the policy debate: on the one hand its debt over gross domestic product (GDP) ratio is one of the highest in Europe, and on the other hand, recent governments have legislated several social security reforms to guarantee sustainability. These reforms have tried to tackle the budgetary effects of the growth in longevity—which in Italy has been quite spectacular in the last decades (see Brugiavini and Peracchi 2012)—by increasing the old-age retirement age, by making early retirement less generous, in terms of both benefits and eligibility requirements, and by linking pension benefits to mortality in a more actuarially fair fashion.

It should be noted that Italy failed to reach the Lisbon target set by the

Agar Brugiavini is professor of economics at Ca' Foscari University of Venice and dean of Venice International University. Franco Peracchi is professor of econometrics at the University of Rome Tor Vergata and a research fellow of the Einaudi Institute for Economics and Finance.

This chapter uses data from SHARELIFE release 1, as of November 24, 2010, and SHARE release 2.5.0, as of May 24, 2011. The SHARE data collection has been primarily funded by the European Commission through the 5th framework programme (project QLK6-CT-2001-00360 in the thematic programme Quality of Life), through the 6th framework programme (projects SHARE-I3, RII-CT-2006-062193, COMPARE, CIT5-CT-2005-028857, and SHARELIFE, CIT4-CT-2006-028812) and through the 7th framework programme (SHARE-PREP, 211909 and SHARE-LEAP, 227822). Additional funding from the US National Institute on Aging (U01 AG09740-13S2, P01 AG005842, P01 AG08291, P30 AG12815, Y1-AG-4553-01 and OGHA 04-064, IAG BSR06-11, R21 AG025169) as well as from various national sources is gratefully acknowledged (see www.share-project.org for a full list of funding institutions). For acknowledgments, sources of research support, and disclosure of the authors' material financial relationships, if any, please see http://www.nber.org/chapters/c13329.

European Union, which required an employment rate for the age group fifty-five to sixty-four of 50 percent in the year 2010. Hence the challenge in Italy has been, for several years, to increase labor supply of workers in the age group fifty to sixty-five both by changing the incentives to retirement and by introducing stringent eligibility conditions. A "season" of pension reforms started in the year 1992 and the last—quite significant—reform took place in 2011.

However, the literature and the policymakers have paid little attention to the potential "substitutability" effects that could take place when the access to an exit route from the labor market, such as early retirement, becomes more limited. Indeed, for some workers in Italy a possible alternative to leave the labor force is to apply for disability benefits. Before 1984, disability benefits were awarded very generously on the basis of very loose health requirements. Eligibility conditions changed dramatically after 1984, in such a way that applicants had to undergo a very stringent medical test in order to qualify. The early retirement option has traditionally been extremely generous in Italy, and firms on the one hand and workers and unions on the other hand took advantage of such lenient rules to cushion negative shocks over the business cycle without having to fire employees or leave the labor force at young ages (Brugiavini and Peracchi 2004). The disability option was clearly less appealing at the time. It is therefore an open question whether a renewed interest by workers for disability pensions could stem from the recent pension reforms and the role played by health limitations in these choices. However, in order to capture the actual behavior of workers it is important, particularly in Italy, to take account of all possible options available in each year and to each individual.

In this chapter, we analyze the retirement behavior of Italian employees by considering distinct pathways to retirement such as old-age, early retirement, and disability insurance. In particular, we focus on the role played by health conditions and socioeconomic factors beyond and above the financial incentives associated to each pathway as measured by the "option value" of working an extra year vis-à-vis leaving the labor force through one of the alternative routes.

These financial incentives are used in a dynamic way, as in Gruber and Wise (2004): at a given age, a full benefit stream is computed for each future age, conditional upon survival and eligibility, and is then updated as extra years of work contributed to the pension calculation. Underlying long-term trends may partly confound the analysis, but we are able to control for cohort effects, which are particularly relevant in the Italian context, especially for women who increased their labor force participation only recently.

We contribute to the current debate on retirement behavior by referring especially to disability insurance (DI) benefits as a potentially utility-maximizing exit route and by analyzing the role played by health and other socioeconomic factors in the decision mechanism. To achieve this goal we combine Italian administrative data from the National Institute for Social Security (INPS) with the information on the subsample of Italian respondents in the Survey of Health, Ageing and Retirement in Europe (SHARE).

The administrative data—available in the form of a long panel—contain information on individuals' working careers and exits from the labor force at different years and ages, but lack information concerning health, education, and household characteristics, which is instead provided in SHARE.

This chapter is structured as follows. Section 10.2 outlines the institutional background of the Italian social security system and provides a first description of the data. Section 10.3 describes the available data in more depth, provides the methodology for constructing the incentive measure, and presents the empirical estimates. Section 10.4 discusses a series of policy reforms (simulations) and outlines their effect in terms of labor market behavior. Section 10.5 concludes.

10.1.1   Institutional Background

The Italian social security system is based on a variety of institutions administering public pension programs for different types of workers (private-sector employees, public-sector employees, self-employed, professional workers).[1] All programs are of the unfunded pay-as-you-go (PAYG) type. Despite a process toward convergence during the last two decades, the rules of the various programs remain somewhat different.

The main risks covered by the system are old age (through old age and early retirement pensions), disability, loss of the spouse or parent (through benefits to survivors), and unemployment. While all workers can access old-age and DI benefits subject to general eligibility conditions, unemployment insurance is not universal but is conditional to specific rules defining periods and types of firms undergoing financial distress.

Old-Age and Early Retirement Pensions

Public old-age and early retirement pensions are by far the largest public spending item of the Italian welfare budget.[2] In this section we briefly review the basic setup of the pension system and its recent reforms, and refer to Brugiavini, Peracchi, and Wise (2003) and to Brugiavini and Peracchi (2004) for further details.

The Italian pension system is characterized by a large first pillar and by almost negligible second and third pillars. Public pensions are organized by type of employment: private-sector employees pay contributions to the National Social Security Institute (INPS). The institute covers about nineteen million workers, twelve million of which are private-sector employees,

---

1. In this chapter we use the terms social security system and pension system synonymously. In fact, in Italy, social security is the main source of publicly provided income in old age.

2. In 2011, total expenditure on pensions reached 16 percent of GDP, with 11 percent of GDP spent on public old-age pension.

while the others are different types of self-employed workers. Another four million public-sector employees and civil servants pay contributions to a separate fund (INPDAP) now also managed by INPS. Only recently have some private retirement saving accounts been offered to workers, but the impact of the Great Recession has dwarfed the possibilities of growth for these forms of old-age insurance.

The system offers both an old-age pension, which depends on the years of age, and an early retirement (seniority) pension, which also depends on the years of contribution. Originally, seniority pensions were granted irrespective of age to retirees with at least thirty-five years of contribution, or even less for particular categories of workers (for example, female public-sector employees). The idea was to provide income to individuals who had started their working life early on, and also to women who had carried out both market and nonmarket activities during their lifetimes.

Until the 1980s, the statutory retirement age for old-age pensions was sixty for men and fifty-five for women, but a generous early retirement option was also available. The calculation of benefits changed over time, but was essentially of the "final salary" type, for both old-age and early retirement pensions, as averages of the earnings over the last years of work (pensionable earnings) formed the basis for the level of benefits. The initial pension was obtained multiplying pensionable earnings by a "rate of return" (accrual factor) approximately equal to 2 percent for each year of contribution (up to a maximum of 80 percent).

Starting in the early 1990s, the Italian pension system was modified through a long reform process. The most recent is the Fornero reform, legislated in 2011 and named after the labor minister in charge at the time. All these reforms aimed at increasing the retirement age and curtailing benefits, for example, by applying an actuarially fair basis for calculation. In this work, we focus on two major reforms, enacted in 1992 and 1995 and known, respectively, as Amato and Dini reforms from the names of the prime ministers of the time. The 1995 reform is particularly important because it completely redesigned the system by modifying the eligibility rules and by changing the calculation of old-age benefits from a defined-benefit (DB) basis to a notional defined-contribution (NDC) basis. However, because these changes were introduced gradually through a very long transitional period, the immediate effects of this reform were not as marked as those implied by the 1992 reform.

A common aspect of the reforms of the 1990s is the grandfathering approach, that is, the differential treatment of different cohorts of workers. For example, the 1992 reform explicitly distinguished between workers with at least fifteen years of contributions at the end of 1992 and workers with less than fifteen years of contributions; while the former group was kept under the status quo rules as far as benefits calculation and eligibility rules were concerned, for the latter group a new and much less favorable system was introduced. In particular, under the new system, the eligibility age for an old-age pension was increased gradually by one year of age every two years starting in 1994 until reaching age sixty-five for men and age sixty for women in the year 2000. The numbers of years of contribution required for an old-age pension was also increased gradually by one every two years starting in 1993 until reaching twenty years of contributions in 2001. One important change brought about by the 1992 reform, with relevant budgetary implications, was the indexation of pension benefits to price inflation only, rather than to nominal wage growth.

The grandfathering rule was maintained in the 1995 reform. In particular, the 1995 reform distinguished between three categories of workers depending on their number of years of contribution at the end of 1995: those with at least eighteen years of contribution, those with less than eighteen years, and new entrants into the labor force. Except for the changes to the eligibility rules introduced by the 1992 reform, very few changes applied to workers with at least eighteen years of contributions. On the other hand, for new entrants, the benefit computation method changed dramatically from DB to NDC.

Along the transitional phase, due to end in 2032 when all workers are expected to retire under the new (1995) regime, benefits are computed on a pro rata basis according to the number of years of contributions under the two regimes (contributions paid after 1993 count under the new regime). Furthermore, during the transitional phase, eligibility for a seniority pension depends on both years of age and years of contribution. For example, in 1996 a worker could take early retirement at age fifty-two if the worker had accumulated thirty-five years of contribution. These limits were gradually raised in such a way that, in 2002, eligibility required fifty-seven years of age and thirty-five years of contribution for both men and women. The minimum age for seniority pensions was legislated to increase until reaching age forty in 2008 (table 10.1).

The Fornero reform, introduced in 2011, touches three major points. First, concerning the calculation of the initial benefits, it stipulates the immediate transition (starting January 2012) to the contributive system pro rata. Second, the law still allows for two possible exit routes, the old-age pension and the early retirement pension, but the eligibility requirements become more stringent for both. On the one hand, for the old-age pension there will be a gradual increase in the legal age requirement in such a way that by 2018 there will be no difference between men and women, and by 2050 the age requirement will become sixty-nine years and nine months for all types of workers. On the other hand, for the early retirement option, the reform stipulates a gradual increase in the number of years of contributions needed to access this pathway (forty-six years for men and forty-five for women in 2050).

Table 10.1   **Rules for early retirement in the transitional phase for private sector employees**

Year	Age and years of contribution	Only years of contribution
1998	54 and 35	36
1999	55 and 35	37
2000	55 and 35	37
2001	56 and 35	37
2002	57 and 35	37
2003	57 and 35	37
2004	57 and 35	38
2005	57 and 35	38
2006	57 and 35	39
2007	57 and 35	39
2008	58 and 35	40
2009	58 and 35	40
2010	59 and 36 or 60 and 35 (quota 95)	40
2011	60 and 36 or 61 and 35 (quota 96)	40

Moreover, for those individuals whose retirement benefits are computed with the defined benefit method, the law sets a penalty if they retire before the age of sixty-two. Last but not least, the Fornero reform links the adjustment of the age requirement for an old-age pension to the increase in life expectancy. Starting in 2019, the adjustment will take place every two years.

Disability Insurance

A public invalidity pension was introduced in Italy in 1919 for individuals who, because of reductions in their working capacity, were unable to earn income below a given level. In particular, the cut-off point was established at one-third of the normal wage for a worker in the same activity in the same area of the country. Hence, DI benefits were granted on the basis of rather loose health eligibility requirements for those workers who qualified because of limited earnings capacity. In 1984, the public invalidity pension was changed through an important reform: workers would qualify only because of a certified mental or physical impairment. Also, a public "inability" pension was introduced for private-sector employees and self-employed workers with a physical or mental disease, certified by a medical test, which is permanent and makes it impossible to carry out any job. In addition, other forms of disability make individuals eligible for pensions on the basis of a medical test, even if the individual did not contribute to social security.

Currently, the Italian social security system currently provides two types of disability benefits:

1. Ordinary (civilian) disability benefits are granted to all citizens under certain health impairments (including deaf or dumb people older than eigh-

teen). In some cases, a monthly attendance benefit is also paid in order for the beneficiary to receive home care. For people older than sixty-five, a noncontributory pension (*pensione sociale*) is paid. Since 1971, an inability pension is also available to individuals age eighteen to sixty-five who cannot carry out any type of work. The handicap should be certified to be 100 percent of the working capacity of the individual.

2. Invalidity benefits are granted to workers registered with the Italian Social Security Institute (INPS) whose working capacity is permanently reduced by at least two-thirds because of physical or mental impairments. We will also include in this category of benefits "inability pensions" though these would—strictly speaking—follow different rules.

It is important to stress that, after the law passed in 1984, the eligibility rules for an invalidity pension became much more binding. First, benefits were subject to a medical test that certified that the claimed physical or mental disease caused at least a two-thirds reduction of the original working capacity. Second, at least five years of social security contributions were necessary, of which at least three in the five years were before applying for benefits. One of the important restrictions introduced by the reform was that the benefit would not be permanent: eligibility conditions had to be assessed every three years and only after three consecutive successful applications would the benefit become permanent. Furthermore, the law allowed to convert DI automatically into an old-age pension at the legal retirement age and could not be paid along with unemployment benefits.

10.1.2   Recent Trends in Program Participation and Benefit Take-Up

The Available Data

In this chapter we make use of two sources of data: a sample of administrative records from the INPS archives and survey data from the Survey of Health, Ageing and Retirement in Europe (SHARE).

The INPS sample is drawn from administrative records provided by the National Institute of Social Security.[3] The sample has four components: (a) information on the private-sector employees (a stock measure) paying social security contributions recorded at the end of each year; (b) information on beneficiaries (a stock measure) by type of benefit, regardless of the type of job previously held and labor market participation (hence including individuals with no labor market experience); (c) information on the flow of new pension and benefit awards at the end of each year; and (d) a panel of earnings histories, which can be linked to the stock information reported in (b). The years that are available to us are from 1985 to 2004. It should be stressed that the information on working histories described in (d) is

---

3. We are grateful to Fondazione Rodolfo Debenedetti for making available to us the INPS sample.

available only for a subsample of individuals: those who had any previous attachment to the labor force paying contributions to the social security administration and previously working as private-sector employees. Hence, for the stock and flow data we can observe dimensions such as participation to a program (benefit take-up), gender, age, and possibly previous occupation. When we link with earnings histories, we also obtain information on previous earnings and contribution histories, and detailed characteristics of the occupation held (only for private-sector employees).

In constructing our working sample, we selected only benefit recipients who could be linked with their earnings history (thus excluding, for example, widows who had no earnings ever in their lifetime but currently collect survivor benefits, or individuals who receive benefits that are not work related such as income maintenance for the elderly [*pensione sociale*]). Unfortunately, this choice also excludes public-sector employees because for these retirees no detail is available on the characteristics of their former job and their former contributions. There are two main reasons for our sample selection criteria: first, we are interested in the transition from work to other nonemployment states and want to focus on former (or current) workers only, and second, in Italy it is possible for people to work and collect benefits at the same time (for example, disability benefit), or to collect more than one benefit. In the latter cases we need to rely on a complete set of information regarding the worker/retiree in order to allocate individuals to the relevant category. In this sense, the information provided by the stock or even flow data is only partial. Finally, a further reduction of the sample was required as we had to select the population "at risk of retirement" (of age fifty and above) and focus on complete records in terms of relevant characteristics such as age and occupation. While the INPS data initially included 148,000 individuals, after our selection criteria we ended up with a sample of 81,246 individuals (631,844 records).

A large part of our empirical investigation, in particular the econometric study, is based on the Italian data from SHARE. The survey collects data on European citizens age fifty and over (and their spouses of any age). Questions posed to the respondents refer to different dimensions of their lives from economic conditions, labor supply, and retirement decisions to health status. Four waves of data are available at the moment: the baseline sample collected in 2004, the first panel wave of 2006, the SHARELIFE (retrospective, life histories) wave (that is, entirely panel, with no refresher component), and the second panel wave of 2011. The total number of countries involved in the first three waves is thirteen (Austria, Belgium, Czech Republic, Denmark, France, Germany, Greece, Italy, the Netherlands, Poland, Spain, Sweden, and Switzerland) and they provide a wide variety of institutional, cultural, and economic differences.

In this chapter we use both the panel component of SHARE for Italy (SHARE-IT sample) and the SHARELIFE component consisting of retrospective information. Through SHARELIFE, we can reconstruct sequences of events relevant to an individual, for example, employment spells or transitions into retirement. The initial SHARE-IT sample from the 2004, 2006, and 2011 waves contains 9,125 individuals. This is the sample used for the descriptive analysis of disability rates. However, as it will become clear in the following sections, some selection had to be made based on criteria related to the health information or to the occurrence of a transition, which required pooling all the data including the SHARELIFE component and further reducing the sample size.

Finally, we make use of mortality data for Italy from the Human Mortality Database (HMD). The database is the result of a joint project by the Department of Demography of the University of California at Berkeley and the Max Planck Institute for Demographic Research in Rostock, Germany, and provides data on mortality by gender, age, and birth cohort for a large number of countries.

Take-Up of DI Benefits

In this section we describe changes over time to DI participation in Italy. We do this by using both administrative and survey data. Administrative data help us characterize changes in DI participation by a set of characteristics such as age, gender, and type of occupation. On the other hand, survey data such as SHARE are much richer in terms of socioeconomic and demographic characteristics of the individuals and the households they belong to. This information can be exploited to analyze to what extent changes in DI reflect improvements in health conditions or in educational attainment for the population of interest. For the purpose of this study, the main advantage from using SHARE is the availability of a large set of variables on health conditions (physical and mental health) in connection with other socioeconomic characteristics, including educational attainment.

In order to get a first grasp of the relevance of DI benefits in Italy, we computed disability rates from the INPS sample, that is, the sample of administrative records provided by the National Institute of Social Security.

Figures 10.1A and 10.1B show the evolution of disability rates for men and women in Italy for three age groups, fifty to fifty-four, fifty-five to fifty-nine, and sixty to sixty-four. For each age group, the disability rates are computed by taking the ratio between the number of individuals collecting DI benefits and the number of individuals who are either working or collecting any type of benefits.[4]

Disability rates increase for men between 1993 and 1999 and then peter

---

4. Since in Italy retirees can receive more than one pension benefit and, under certain conditions, can also work and receive DI benefits at the same time, we had to use a general—though arbitrary—rule to decide if an individual is in disability, is a retiree, or is a worker. In all those cases where the DI benefit is not the only source of income, we regarded as a DI recipient an individual whose share of income from DI is prevalent (more than 65 percent).

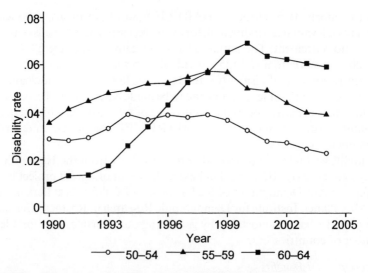

Fig. 10.1A   Disability rates by age group, men (INPS data)

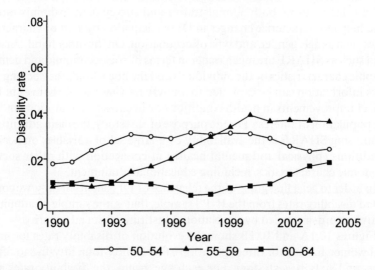

Fig. 10.1B   Disability rates by age group, women (INPS data)

out (figure 10.1A). This pattern may be related to the reforms of 1992 and 1995, which gradually increased both the legal retirement age and the contributive requirement. Individuals who qualified for disability benefits (plausibly those in poor health) may have opted for this less restrictive retirement route in order to maximize the probability of receiving the benefit and to minimize the waiting time. In fact, as it is clear from figure 10.1A, disability rates remained rather stable for the age group fifty to fifty-four, which

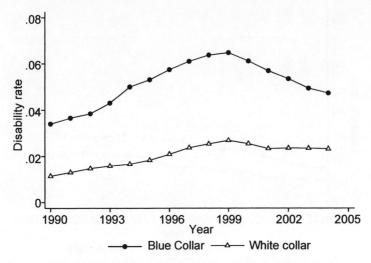

Fig. 10.1C   Disability rates by occupational status, men age fifty to sixty-four (INPS data)

was only mildly affected by the changes in eligibility rules for early retirement. Differently, for the age group fifty-five to fifty-nine, we observe a sharp increase in disability rates. An even sharper increase is observed for those in the age group sixty to sixty-four during the period 1993–2000, when the reform gradually changed the normal retirement age from sixty years (in 1993) to sixty-five years (in 2000).

Figure 10.1B shows disability rates for women in each age group. Again, no trend is observed for the age group fifty to fifty-four, which is unlikely to have been affected by the reform. However, we observe a sharp increase in DI take-up after 1993 for the age group fifty-five to fifty-nine, that is, for female workers who experienced the gradual increase in the eligibility age for an old-age pension from fifty-five years in 1993 to sixty years in 2000.

It would be interesting to explore the dynamics in DI participation by educational level. Unfortunately, the INPS data contain no information on education. To partially overcome this limitation, we use data on the type of occupation distinguishing between white-collar jobs and blue-collar jobs. Results are reported separately by gender.

Figure 10.1C shows disability rates for men age fifty to sixty-four, distinguishing by occupation. The DI participation increases over time for both blue-collar and white-collar workers during the observation period, reaching a maximum in 1999 (6 percent) and decreasing steadily afterward. It is interesting to note a significant difference in DI participation rates between the two occupational categories: the largest difference is observed in 1999 (around 3 percent). As already discussed, the change in the legal retirement age introduced by the 1992 and 1995 reforms is reflected in these trends.

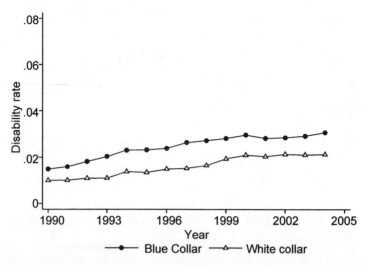

Fig. 10.1D   Disability rates by occupational status, women age fifty to sixty-four (INPS data)

Workers who qualified for disability benefits may have preferred to exit the labor force through the easiest route once early retirement became less favorable. The participation in DI for these years is always higher for blue collars (plausibly in worse health) than for white collars: a well-known result as also discussed in Case and Deaton (2005) who show a clear gradient in health status between individuals in low-skill occupations (blue collar) and high-skill occupations (white collar) for the United States.

Disability rates for women age fifty to sixty-four are reported in figure 10.1D, distinguishing by occupational status. Notice that female labor force participation is increasing in Italy for the youngest cohorts, and this trend may dominate the aggregate figures. Overall, a steady growth of the DI rate is observed over time, but the speed of growth is lower than for men. Further, the difference in disability rates between the two educational groups is not as significant as the one observed for men.

Several explanations can be put forward for the low disability rates observed for women. If DI rates reflect the health status of workers, then one possibility is self-selection of women into jobs with lower exposure to occupational risks or that are less physically demanding, leading to a lower demand for DI benefits. Another explanation could simply be that women find it harder to qualify for DI benefits. The fact that no significant difference emerges between white-collar and blue-collar women may again be due to sample composition: when aggregating over the age range from fifty to sixty-four, the trend in disability rates for women age fifty-five to fifty-nine (those mostly affected by the reforms and showing the highest DI take-up rates) may be partially compensated by the trends of the other two age

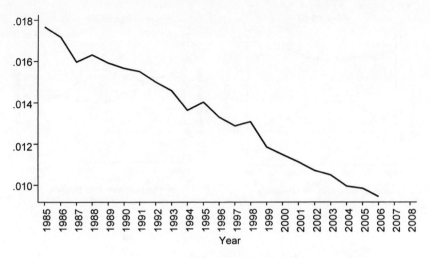

Fig. 10.2   Mortality rates at age sixty-five (Human Mortality Database)

groups. Finally, we cannot rule out that an increasing incidence of health conditions that are more common among women, such as depression, may have caused an increase in DI rates for the most recent years.

Some evidence for these competing explanations may be found in the next section where we look more closely at the relationship of benefits take-up and health conditions.

10.1.3   Disability Rates, Employment Status, and Health

Figure 10.2 shows the decline of mortality rates at age sixty-five between the mid-1980s and the early twenty-first century in Italy. The data are from the HMD. Mortality rates decline sharply over time. Yet, disability rates fluctuate widely over the same period (especially between 1992 and 1997), with a peak in 1999. What is relevant for this chapter is that there is little evidence that changes over time in disability rates could be directly attributed to a trend toward worse health, as crudely measured by mortality.

In order to better understand how reforms affected individuals' decisions, we explore the relationship between the time profile of employment rates and disability rates. As before, we show the two time series separately by gender and age group.

Figure 10.3A shows employment and disability rates for men by age group over the period 1990–2005. Disability rates are generally low (right scale) and show a hump-shaped profile over the period, which is particularly marked for the age group sixty to sixty-four. Employment rates (left scale) are fairly constant for both the age group fifty to fifty-four and the age group sixty to sixty-four. Hence, all the action is taking place in the age group fifty-five to fifty-nine: a negative correlation emerges between employment rates

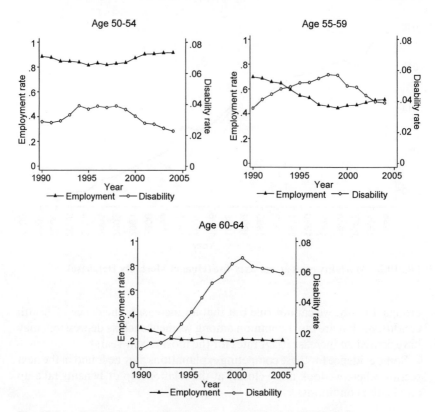

Fig. 10.3A   Employment and DI rates by age group, men (INPS data)

and disability rates for individuals that are mostly affected by the reforms of the 1990s.

When plotting the two time series for women (figure 10.3B) we notice a different pattern. Employment and disability rates seem to go in the same direction except for the age group fifty to fifty-five during the years 1990–1995 and 2000–2005. While disability rates seem to increase over time for the age groups fifty to fifty-four and fifty-five to fifty-nine, employment rates remain flat or increase at a low pace. Instead, for the age group sixty to sixty-four, both employment and disability rates tend to decrease.

So far we exploited patterns in DI participation based on the few sociodemographic characteristics that are available in administrative data, namely age, gender, and occupation. Using a richer survey such as SHARE allows us to extend our objectives by looking closely at the relationship between DI and health, as well as between DI and education.

Looking at the role of education, SHARE collects information on educational attainments that can be coded on the basis of standard educational

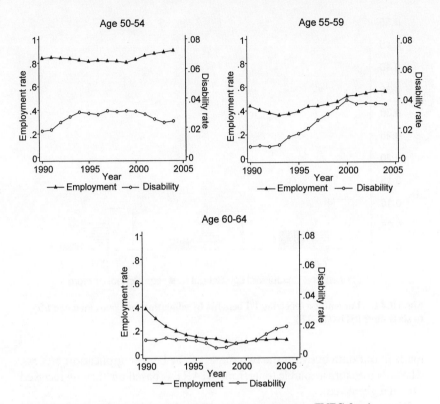

Fig. 10.3B   Employment and DI rates by age group, women (INPS data)

scales used in international surveys. In particular, we measure educational levels considering the highest degree obtained by each individual using the International Standard Classification of Education (ISCED) classification. Since the health status is a major focus of this research program, the measurement of health requires particular attention. As detailed in section 10.4 below, we construct an overall index of health via principal component analysis (a procedure first used in Poterba, Venti, and Wise [2011]) by exploiting the wide set of questions on health conditions that are recorded in wave 1, wave 2, and also in wave 4 of SHARE. Unfortunately, we cannot use for this purpose the data from SHARELIFE because it asks very little about current health status. A similar problem emerges for the information on DI participation in SHARELIFE, as the survey questions are not comparable with those in the other three waves of SHARE.

It should also be stressed that, unlike other surveys (e.g., the US Health and Retirement Study), SHARE does not distinguish between "having ever applied for DI" and "having ever received DI," hence no distinction can be

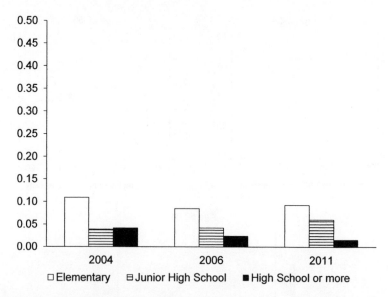

Fig. 10.4A   Percentage receiving DI benefits by education and year, men age fifty to sixty-four (SHARE-IT)

made in our data between the two stages of the benefit application process. The only measure available to us from SHARE is based on "having received DI" in a given year.

When analyzing the relation between DI, education, and health using the SHARE data, we condition on gender, age, education, and health quintiles, so we end up with a small sample size for each combination of characteristics. Hence, results should be interpreted with some caution.

Figures 10.4A and 10.4B show that the percentage of individuals receiving DI in Italy is very similar to that for the United States resulting from the HRS data. Across the three waves of SHARE (2004, 2006, 2011), the probability of receiving DI decreases with education (it is higher for those having completed, at most, elementary school and lower for those having a high school degree or more). This is what we expected, as more educated individuals tend to have better jobs on average or jobs in which the probability of suffering a physical limitation is lower.

The SHARE-IT sample allows us to study in more detail the relationship between DI receipt and health. Because many dimensions of health are recorded in SHARE, we would like to have a synthetic measure capturing the key aspects of the health status of an individual and pointing to the potential effects of health limitations. A single measure can be constructed in SHARE by making use of the principal component analysis (PCA): in particular, we focus on twenty-five indicators of health and extract the first component, which explains around 25 percent of the total variation in health. The PCA

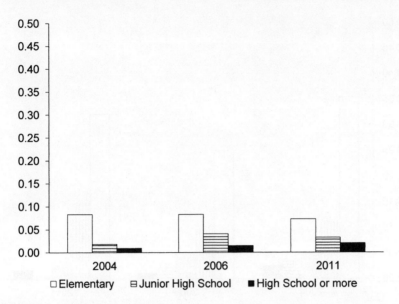

Fig. 10.4B   Percentage receiving DI benefits by education and year, women age fifty to sixty-four (SHARE-IT)

allows us to obtain a continuous health index that we use to classify people into health quintiles.

Figures 10.5A and 10.5B show that there is a negative relationship between health conditions and DI rates. The percentage of men age fifty to sixty-four who receive DI is more than 30 percent for those in the first health quintile (worst health) and less than 5 percent for those in the top health quintile (best health). This gradient tends to persist across waves. Women instead show low frequencies of DI for all health quintiles.

Since education and health tend to be positively correlated, it is interesting to look at DI participation conditioning both on health and education. Table 10.2 shows the percentage of respondents who receive DI benefits by health quintile and educational level. For education we consider three levels: elementary school or less (including those with no degree), junior high school, and high school or more. We used this classification since for the cohorts of interest (individuals age fifty and older) the percentage of Italian respondents having a college degree is very low.

We report DI participation separately by gender. The top panel shows the percentage of men receiving DI benefits. Looking at each row we see the percentage of men in DI by educational level over health quintiles. Vice versa, looking at the columns we see the percentage of men with DI for a given health quintile by education. The relationship between DI rates, education, and health is strong. However, we notice two things. First, the percentage of men with DI among the most educated and the healthiest

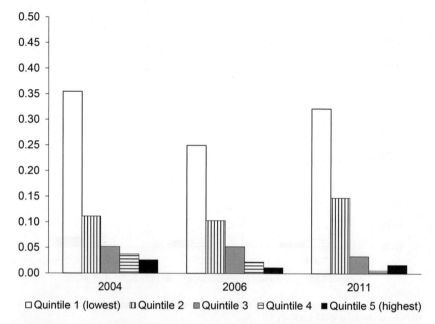

Fig. 10.5A   Percentage receiving DI benefits by health quintile and year, men age fifty to sixty-four (SHARE-IT)

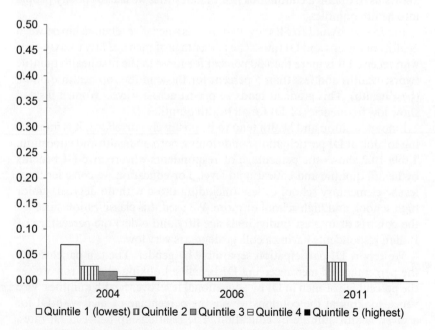

Fig. 10.5B   Percentage receiving DI benefits by health quintile and year, women age fifty to sixty-four (SHARE-IT)

Table 10.2   **Percentage of men and women age fifty to sixty-four receiving DI benefits by health quintile and education**

| | Percent approved Health quintile | | | | | |
Education	1	2	3	4	5	All
Men						
Elementary or lower	32.61	15.91	5.26	4.67	4.96	9.80
Junior HS	38.10	7.94	5.05	2.35	1.73	4.84
HS or more	18.75	10.34	3.85	0.85	0.37	2.54
All	31.33	11.90	4.61	2.14	1.76	10.35
Women						
Elementary or lower	23.86	8.70	3.30	1.98	1.78	8.02
Junior HS	11.43	7.09	1.44	0.00	0.00	3.16
HS or more	6.35	4.13	1.71	0.52	0.00	1.58
All	17.48	7.03	2.28	0.94	0.52	5.65

approaches 0. Second, the differences in DI rates by education seem not to be very sharp between those in elementary school and junior high school, even when looking over health quintiles. Thus, having at least a high school degree makes a difference.

A similar pattern is observed for women (bottom panel) in the same age group. In fact, the percentage of well-educated and healthy women receiving DI benefits is equal to 0.

To better highlight the information contained in table 10.2 we also report two figures (figures 10.6A, and 10.6B) showing the differences in DI by education over health quintiles (from the lowest to the top).

Employment Rates by Health and Education

Finally, to better understand the link between employment and DI, we explore the pattern of employment rates by health and education over time for the age group sixty to sixty-four. Because of the limitations of the INPS and SHARE data, we rely on the Italian data from the Labour Force Survey administered by Eurostat. These data allows us to study variation in employment rates by level of education by distinguishing between primary, upper secondary, and tertiary education (see figure 10.7). Unfortunately, the same analysis cannot be carried out for health conditions. We show the variation in the employment rate by educational level focusing on the age group sixty to sixty-four.

Figure 10.7 shows that employment rates are always higher for the more educated workers, but they seem to vary over the cycle in a similar fashion: a decline after the year 1992, a relatively stable pattern until the year 2008 and a slight reversal afterward, with an interesting rise for the highly educated workers after 2011. When more years of data become available we will be

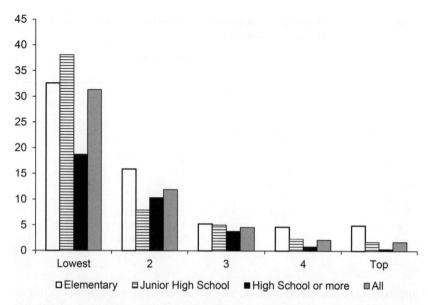

Fig. 10.6A Percentage receiving DI benefits by health quintile and education, men age fifty to sixty-four

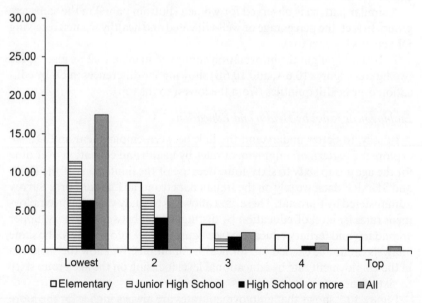

Fig. 10.6B Percentage receiving DI benefits by health quintile and education, women age fifty to sixty-four

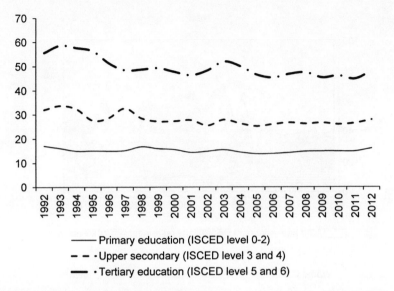

Fig. 10.7   Employment rate for the age group sixty to sixty-four by level of education (ISCED97 classification)

Source: Labour Force Survey (Eurostat).

able to see if the reform of 2011 (which also affected workers of the age group sixty to sixty-four) has had an effect in terms of employment rates.

10.2   Empirical Approach

The goal of this chapter is to investigate to what extent are the differences in employment determined by the provisions of the disability insurance program or other retirement program, for a given health status. Our empirical approach is based on the option value model described in detail in section 10.3: this empirical strategy requires information on the pathways to retirement from work that Italian workers have access to and a measure of health, along with other characteristics of the individual. We present in sequence a description of the relevant pathways to retirement, then the measure of the weights to be used in the option value calculation corresponding to the likelihood that a given pathway is chosen, and finally the measurement of the health of each individual through a specific index.

10.2.1   Pathways to Retirement

As it is clear from our previous descriptive analysis, three pathways to retirement are relevant for Italy: (a) old-age pension, (b) early retirement, and (c) disability pension. The number of exits observed for the first two routes is much higher than the number observed for disability. In order to

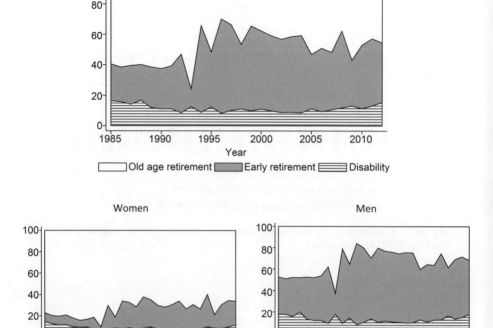

Fig. 10.8   Percentages of new entries in each pathway to retirement

show the relative importance of these three pathways, we consider a sample of individuals receiving a benefit (any of the three types of benefit, excluding other benefits) drawn from the INPS archive and look at the flows, that is, the "new entries" in each pathway.

Figure 10.8 describes a new entry into public pension and disability for individuals above age forty. We observe that there is an important announcement effect of the two main pension reforms of the 1990s. In 1993, the percentage of individuals that took the "old age" retirement route increased significantly for both men and women. Individuals who qualified for this type of pension preferred to immediately exit from the labor force, most likely in the expectation of tighter rules for both the "legal" retirement age and the number of contribution years after 1993. We also observe a slight increase in the number of individuals, especially men, who collect DI benefits. The peak in the old age and the disability exit routes seem to be correlated and appear every two years. This is interesting because, as shown in table 10.1, this is the time interval after which both the retirement age and the contribution years requirements increased by one additional year. In 1996 we observe a sharp increase of the share of the early retirement pathway, especially for men. This is the joint effect of the 1992 and 1995 reforms, as both introduced more stringent rules for the early retirement pathway, particularly in terms of eligibility age. In general, women cannot take advantage of such an exit route because they typically exhibit fewer years of contributions.

10.2.2   Weighting Pathways to Retirement

The trends observed in the pathways to retirement, based on aggregate flows (new entries) into retirement, offer an interesting description of the effects of the pension reforms in Italy. However, flow data provide only one type of representation and a choice has to be made as to how to assign robust weight to each possible pathway. There are three sets of weights which, in principle, could be considered: (a) weights based on "stock probabilities" (i.e., percentages) by year, gender, and age; (b) weights based on aggregate flow probabilities (percentages) by year, gender, and age; and (c) weights based on the estimates of a multinomial logit regression. To ensure comparability with the results for other countries, in this chapter we make use of the first type of estimates, that is, stock probabilities.[5]

Our calculations are based on the administrative data from INPS and our methodology consists in computing the percentage of individuals who enter into retirement separately for each age group and for each pathway. Instead of only considering the broad age range fifty-five to sixty-four, we distinguish between three age groups: fifty to fifty-four, fifty-five to fifty-nine, and sixty to sixty-four. This choice is motivated by the important changes in the Italian eligibility requirements induced by the pension reforms of the period 1992–2010. It is worth recalling that the "legal" retirement age for the old-age pension was revised by the 1992 reform and that the legal retirement age coincides with the time when a DI benefit is automatically converted into an old-age pension. In 1992, the retirement age was fifty-five years for women and sixty for men. Starting with 1994, this requirement increased gradually by one year every two calendar years up to 2000, when it was fixed to sixty years for women and sixty-five for men. Hence, the effect of the 1992 reform becomes clear when looking at the age group sixty to sixty-four for men and fifty-five to fifty-nine for women, as reported in figure 10.9. We observe a

5. We also made use of aggregate flow probabilities (percentages) and probabilities estimated through a multinomial logit, which are individual specific. The results of the econometric estimates are more precise in the latter case (multinomial logit), but are substantially coherent with the econometric results based on stock probabilities.

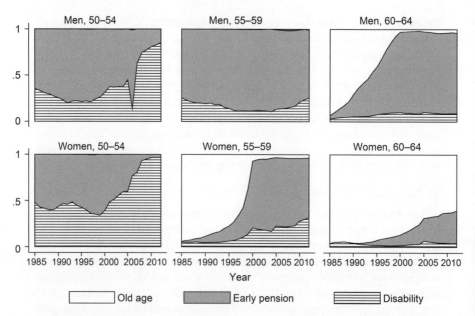

Fig. 10.9   Pathways to retirement using stock probabilities by gender and age group

dramatic decline in the percentage of fifty-five to fifty-nine-year-old females who use the old-age pathway as an exit route between 1993–2000, falling from approximately 90 percent in 1993 to around 0.03 percent after 2000.

A similar pattern, even if less sharp, is observed for men age sixty to sixty-four. The difference in the trend between men and women is probably due to the fact that women, characterized by more discontinuous careers, used to rely more on the old-age retirement route that had less stringent requirements from a contributive point of view. Differently, men relied more on the early retirement route.

10.2.3   Measurement of Health

We already motivated the use of an index aimed at capturing the overall health status of individuals starting from a large number of health dimensions. We construct our health index via PCA, following the paper by Poterba, Venti, and Wise (2011) and using data from wave 1 (2004), wave 2 (2006), and wave 4 (2011) of SHARE-IT. We employ twenty-four health indicators that provide a large amount of information on health conditions. These include six indicators for physical limitations (e.g., difficulties in walking for 100 meters, getting up from a chair, climbing, stooping, carrying, picking up a coin from a table, etc.), one for self-reported health (SRH) being fair or poor, one for having problems with activities of daily living (ADL), indicators for having experienced chronic diseases or conditions

Table 10.3   **Health index: Loadings of first component from PCA**

Question	Comp. 1
Difficulty lift/carry	0.2897
Difficulty push/pull	0.2864
Difficulty stoop/kneel	0.2838
Difficulty walking	0.2825
Difficulty climbing stairs	0.2799
Difficulty getting up from chair	0.2699
Difficulty with an ADL	0.2694
Self-reported health (fair or poor)	0.2566
Difficulty reach/extend arms	0.2406
Doctor visit (number)	0.2042
Difficulty sitting two hours	0.2012
Ever experience arthritis	0.1952
Difficulty picking up a dime	0.1871
Back problems	0.1836

(heart problems, high blood pressure, diabetes, stroke, cancer, arthritis, etc.), the body mass index (BMI), which is generated using self-reported data for height and weight, and indicators for having visited in the last twelve months a doctor, a nursing home, or a hospital. Most of these variables are discrete with value equal to 1 if the person is in poor health.

Differently from Poterba, Venti, and Wise (2011), we do not include an indicator for having received home care, as it is not available in the fourth wave of SHARE. Also, we do not pool the observations and compute the index separately by wave. The overall sample from the three waves contains 9,125 observations, whereas the balanced panel contains 3,852 observations. The health index is computed for only 8,859 observations due to the presence of missing values in some indicators. After extracting the first component index, we divide it in percentiles or quintiles according to the analysis at hand.

Table 10.3 shows the loadings for the first component extracted by PCA. We report the most important health conditions that explain most of the variation in the new measure.

Figure 10.10 shows the average health percentile by age and gender. Average health tends to decline with age for both men and women, although men seem to be better off than women at any age.

As an alternative to PCA, we also regressed self-reported health (1 = fair or poor, 0 = excellent, very good, or good) on the remaining twenty-three indicators using a logit specification and saved the fitted values. We then computed the correlation between the fitted values from this regression and the first component of the health. The two measures are highly positively correlated, with a correlation coefficient of 0.94.

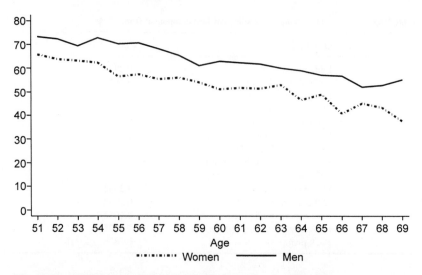

Fig. 10.10   Mean percentiles of the health index by age and gender

10.3   Data Construction and Estimation

The main objective of this chapter is to estimate the relationship between the provisions of retirement programs and retirement incentives. We pay particular attention to the provision of DI programs for which we perform some simulations later on.

We ask how changing the provisions of DI programs (and perhaps other programs) would change retirement decisions. More specifically, conditioning on health status, to what extent are the differences in labor force participation across countries determined by DI programs? The main idea is to analyze the incentives to delay retirement, measured by the potential gain from postponing retirement from today's age until some future age. To this purpose, we first introduce some key concepts from the classical retirement model of Stock and Wise (1990), assuming that there is only one pathway to retirement, and then extend the analysis considering multiple pathways to retirement.

Our analysis relies on SHARE data, and in particular on the SHARELIFE data discussed in the next paragraph. These data cover a wide range of variables useful for our study, such as information on employment pathways during lifetime (from the first job onward), health conditions, and other socioeconomic characteristics. The most important advantage from using SHARE is that it provides important details on individuals' earnings histories (see next section). However, compared with administrative data such as the INPS data, we end up with a smaller sample size, which may lead to loss of precision.

In particular, in our regression analysis, we consider year-to-year transitions into retirement using information from SHARELIFE. Our starting sample consists of about 2,700 observations (unbalanced panel), which falls to about 1,900 observations when we consider a broader set of covariates (e.g., education, health, etc.).

10.3.1   Retirement Incentives and the Option Value

First, we assume that there is a single retirement pathway into retirement. When our representative individual retires, he starts receiving a stream of benefits until death. If an individual retires at age t, the present discounted sum of his stream of benefits, or social security wealth, is denoted by SSW_t. If the person retires one year later, at age $t + 1$, the present discounted sum of his stream of benefits is denoted by SSW_{t+1}. The gain from postponing retirement from one year to the next then is given by $SSW_{t+1} - SSW_t$. Notice, however, that there could be larger gains from delaying retirement by two or more years.

Thus, to understand the incentives built into the design of the social security system we must consider all the possible future benefits associated to all possible retirement ages and then evaluate whether it is worth retiring today or continue working until a future date.

The benchmark model used for this evaluation is the option value (OV) model of Stock and Wise (1990). The model is based on a utility maximization approach, where a forward-looking agent decides at each time the retirement option. The expected utility for the worker from retiring at age r is assumed to be of the form

$$V_t(r) = \sum_{s=t}^{r-1} \pi_{s/t} \beta^{s-t} Y_s^\gamma + \sum_{s=r}^{S} \beta^{s-t}(kB^\gamma(r))^\gamma,$$

where t is the age (or time) when the worker decides, β is the intertemporal discount factor, and γ is a parameter of risk aversion. The parameter π captures the probability of survival and demographic projections till the time s conditional of being alive at time t. One may think of the parameter k as a leisure parameter because it captures the relative preference of benefits from retirement rather than income from work.

The option value of retiring at a specific age r is just the difference between the maximum utility for the worker from postponing retiring until some future time (r^*) and the utility gained from retiring at age r:

$$OV_t(r) = V_t(r^*) - V_t(r).$$

As already mentioned, the original model in Stock and Wise (1990) only considers one pathway into retirement. This is clearly not realistic for Italy, as we have three possible pathways: (a) old-age pension, (b) early retirement, and (c) disability insurance. In order to estimate the OV incentive on retirement when multiple programs are present, we use a weighted OV measure. For each pathway, we estimate the probability that a person considers that specific pathway along with the associated OV. Then we compute an "inclusive" OV by taking a weighted average of the OVs for each plan, as follows:

$$OV_{inc} = OV_{DI} * w_{DI} + OV_{Early} * w_{Early} + OV_{Old} * w_{Old}.$$

As for the parameters in the expected utility function, we set $\gamma = 0.75$, $k = 1.5$, and the discount rate to 0.03. The weighs for the inclusive OV are generally determined by the relationship between individual attributes and the possibility that a plan was already chosen in the past. In the next two paragraphs, we discuss the way we construct our data set and how we estimate the weights attached to each pathway into retirement.

10.3.2   Data Construction

Instead of pooling data across waves, we perform the analysis considering transitions into retirement from 2004 to 2011 with the help of SHARELIFE data.

The advantage of using year-to-year transitions is that, instead of seeing a worker just once between two waves with a unique OV, we follow him along all the years between two waves seeing him with his actual status in each year (some may work for some years and retire at some point between the two waves, for example, between waves 2 and 4). Since the time interval is long, one record would not be enough to describe the changes that happen along this period and with the OV corresponding to that particular year and status (work or retire). Another advantage is that we increase the number of available observations. Nevertheless, we must highlight the fact that the number of transitions is small due to the short panel length of SHARE.

To construct transitions into retirement we use SHARELIFE, since it allows reconstructing the working life of the respondents up to year 2011 (the year of the last available wave). Unfortunately, in wave 3 (2008) there is no question asking if the individual is retired or not, neither which is the retirement year. We only know if the respondent is still working (variable re_047), and hence we recover this information from wave 2 (variable ep329). In order to create year-to-year transitions into retirement, we make use of the following variables in SHARELIFE: re011_ (start of job spell), re026_ (end of job spell), re031_ (reasons left job), and the answer to the question re035_ (situation in after last job). These questions are asked for all job spells during life. The variable re035_ contains information on the situation after the last job with many alternatives (retired from work, out of the labor force, and so forth), so we are sure to pick up individuals retired after the last job. Considering only transitions means to drop out all records for the years that are subsequent to the transition year into retirement. Because the information on respondents from wave 3 stops in 2008–2009, for those individuals that declare in wave 3 (SHARELIFE) to be still at work we complete their

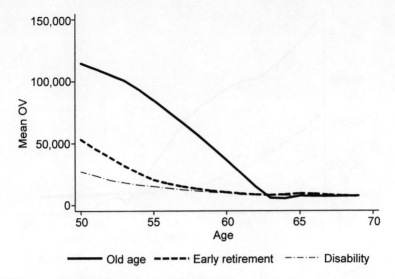

Fig. 10.11   Mean OV for men, cohort 1945–1949

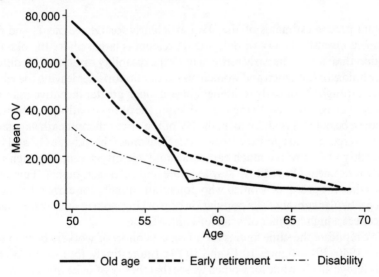

Fig. 10.12   Mean OV for women, cohort 1945–1949

working career with new information on possible retirement from wave 4 (2011) to extend our sample of transitions.

10.3.3   Descriptive Statistics for the Option Values

Figures 10.11 and 10.12 show the mean OVs for each of the pathways to retirement, separately for men and women, for the cohort born in 1945–1949. It is important to stress that the small sample size makes it hard to

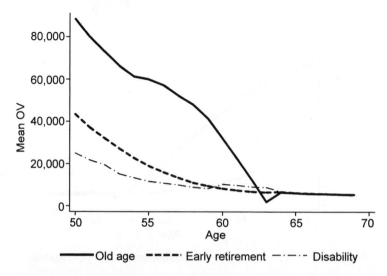

Fig. 10.13   Mean OV for men, cohort 1940–1944

obtain precise estimates of the OV, particularly for DI recipients and for women. Overall, the OV of delaying retirement is larger under the old-age option than under the early retirement or the disability options. This difference holds for both men and women: workers who consider leaving the labor force through DI or early retirement have a much greater incentive to retire at younger ages relative to those considering the old-age pathway. A further point to be noted is that, for men, the OV of the three different pathways tend to converge around age sixty-three, while for women the old-age OV and the disability OV converge much earlier, around age fifty-seven, although the early retirement OV tends to stay separate and is, in fact, higher. This suggests that the group of women who potentially qualify for early retirement is a particular subset of the population of working women as they managed to collect a high number of years of contribution.

We replicate the same figures for an earlier cohort of workers born in the years 1940–1944 (figures 10.13 and 10.14). Interestingly, for men things do not change much, while for women we see that the OV of delaying retirement is much higher under the early retirement pathway compared to the old-age pathway. Although the sample is too small to draw any inference, this result confirms that older women may find it particularly hard to collect an early retirement pension.

10.3.4   Empirical Specification and Results

We estimate a retirement model using probit regressions where the outcome variable is an indicator taking value 1 if the individual has a transition to retirement. Although the inclusive OV is the key predictor in the

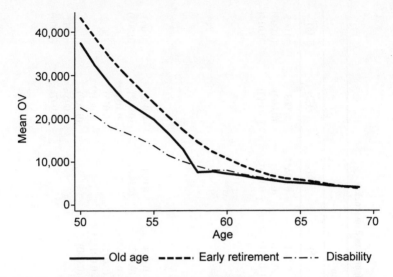

Fig. 10.14   Mean OV for women, cohort 1940–1944

model, we account for other individual characteristics such as educational level (using three categories: less than high school, high school, college or more), health status (using both a continuous index or indicators of health quintiles), gender, whether the person is married, and measures related to economic status such as total assets and occupation indicators (high-skill or low-skill job). We also account for age using two different specifications. The first includes a quadratic polynomial in age while the second includes a full set of age dummies. It is important to stress that the weights used to compute the inclusive OV measure are the weights based on the stock of individuals observed in each pathway for each year (by gender).[6]

In the tables with the estimation results we report marginal effects instead of simple coefficients. The OV coefficient is expressed in units of 10,000 euros. It is important to highlight that since the retirement decision is taken between year t and year $t + 1$, the health variable corresponds to health at time t. The main coefficient to look at is the estimated effect of the inclusive OV. The round brackets report the standard errors, while the square brackets report the effect of a one standard deviation change in OV. The latter are presented in order to cross-compare our results with those from other countries.

Table 10.4 shows the results for the different specifications. In columns (1) to (4) we use indicators for the health quintiles, while in columns (5) to (8) we use the health index as a continuous variable. Further, we control for age

6. We have also performed the same regression analysis by using the OV inclusive based on weights computed through a multinomial logit. The final results are similar and comparable, although the estimates based on the multinomial logit weighting procedure are more robust.

Table 10.4   Effect of inclusive OV on retirement (estimated probit retirement model—weights based on stocks)

	Specification							
	(1)	(2)	(3)	(4)	(5)	(6)	(7)	(8)
OV/10,000	-0.004*	-0.005*	-0.003	-0.004	-0.004*	-0.006**	-0.003	-0.005
	(0.002)	(0.003)	(0.002)	(0.003)	(0.002)	(0.003)	(0.002)	(0.003)
	[-0.015]	[-0.017]	[-0.012]	[-0.014]	[-0.016]	[-0.018]	[-0.013]	0.014
2nd Q	-0.010	-0.011	-0.007	-0.010				
	(0.008)	(0.010)	(0.008)	(0.011)				
3rd Q	-0.003	-0.002	-0.001	0.000				
	(0.008)	(0.010)	(0.009)	(0.013)				
4th Q	0.005	0.006	0.008	0.011				
	(0.009)	(0.012)	(0.010)	(0.014)				
5th Q (best health)	-0.017**	-0.021**	-0.016**	-0.023**				
	(0.007)	(0.009)	(0.007)	(0.010)				
Hindex					-0.003	-0.004	-0.002	-0.003
					(0.002)	(0.003)	(0.002)	(0.003)
Age	0.106***		0.099***		0.106***		0.100***	
	(0.015)		(0.014)		(0.015)		(0.015)	
Age2	-0.001***		-0.001***		-0.001***		-0.001***	
	(0.000)		(0.000)		(0.000)		(0.000)	
Female			0.007	0.013			0.005	0.011
			(0.006)	(0.009)			(0.007)	(0.009)

Married			0.010	0.014			0.010	0.014
			(0.007)	(0.010)			(0.007)	(0.010)
Educ.: <High school			-0.004	-0.002			-0.003	-0.003
			(0.009)	(0.011)			(0.010)	(0.011)
Educ.: High school			-0.003				-0.002	-0.002
			(0.008)				(0.009)	(0.009)
High skill			-0.001	-0.003			-0.001	-0.003
			(0.008)	(0.012)			(0.008)	(0.012)
Low skill			0.001	0.000			0.001	-0.001
			(0.007)	(0.010)			(0.007)	(0.010)
Assets			-0.000	-0.000			-0.000	-0.000
			(0.000)	(0.000)			(0.000)	(0.000)
Educ. >High school				0.004				0.002
				(0.013)				(0.013)
Observations	2,741	2,423	2,234	1,903	2,741	2,423	2,234	1,903
Pseudo R^2	0.115	0.119	0.122	0.121	0.111	0.116	0.115	0.114
Age dummies		X	X	X		X	X	X
Mean ret. rate	.0582	.0582	.0582	.0582	.0582	.0582	.0582	.0582
Mean of OV	2.357	2.357	2.357	2.357	2.357	2.357	2.357	2.357
Std. dev. of OV	2.821	2.821	2.821	2.821	2.821	2.821	2.821	2.821

***Significant at the 1 percent level.

**Significant at the 5 percent level.

*Significant at the 10 percent level.

through either a quadratic polynomial in age or a set of age dummies. For example, in column (1) we use a quadratic polynomial in age and in column (2) we use age dummies, whereas in columns (3) and (4) we add the other controls. The additional covariates are gradually included to check whether and how results are affected.

The sign and magnitude of the coefficients is in line with our expectations. The main OV coefficient is negative and almost always statistically significant, so that an increase of 10,000 euros in the OV at time t reduces the probability of retiring at time $t + 1$ by about 5 percentage points. Health conditions also appear to influence retirement, especially when we use indicators for health quintiles (excluded category is first quintile, i.e., being in worst health). From columns (1) and (3) we see that those in better health, especially those in the top fifth quintile, are less likely to retire. The sign is also maintained for the other indicators of health quintiles. We get similar results when including a continuous health index. An increase in the health index is associated with a decrease in the probability of retiring next period. The coefficient is not statistically significant, however, which may reflect lower variation in health when using transitions from year to year (we have to approximate health in year 2005 using health reported in year 2004). The other variables, such as education and type of occupation, have the right sign but are not statistically different from 0, while financial assets do not appear to matter for the retirement decision. Our results are robust to different specifications.

We also provide estimates of our retirement model separately for each health quintile (table 10.5). Estimates are presented in each of the five rows, with the columns corresponding to the different specifications. In column (1) we control for a quadratic polynomial in age, in column (2) we control for age dummies, and in columns (3) and (4) we add other covariates.

Similar to table 10.4 we get strongly significant results, especially for individuals in the fourth and fifth quintile. Being in very good health (either in the fourth or in the fifth quintile) lowers the probability of retirement by around 6percent. The estimates are always statistically significant at conventional levels, even when adding more covariates.

The same results hold when we interact the inclusive OV and the health (table 10.6) and when we estimate the effect of inclusive OV on retirement, distinguishing by the level of education (table 10.7). Again we notice a gradient, as individuals who completed a college degree are much less likely to retire compare to those with less than a high school degree.

10.4 Simulations

We perform different simulation exercises. In Gruber and Wise (2004) simulations were used to predict the impact on retirement of an increase in the eligibility age, finding large effects. Since this chapter focuses on DI

Table 10.5   **Effect of inclusive OV on retirement by health quintile (estimated probit retirement model—weights based on stocks)**

	No. of obs.	Mean ret. rate	Mean of OV	Std. dev. of OV	Specification			
					(1)	(2)	(3)	(4)
OV: Lowest quintile (worst health)	476	.076	1.921	3.09	0.0027	0.0072	0.0028	0.0020
					0.0032	0.0098	0.0030	0.0041
					[–0.003]	[–0.005]	[–0.001]	[–0.001]
OV: Second quintile	547	.049	2.380	2.580	–0.0187	–0.0541	–0.0095	–0.0422
					0.0046	0.0130	0.0057	0.0138
					[–0.023]	[–0.044]	[–0.024]	[–0.043]
OV: Third quintile	551	.063	2.688	3.048	–0.0066	–0.0207	–0.0050	–0.0185
					0.0029	0.0072	0.0034	0.0089
					[–0.024]	[–0.028]	[–0.036]	[–0.043]
OV: Fourth quintile	546	.062	2.384	2.663	–0.0079	–0.0123	–0.0073	–0.0121
					0.0031	0.0043	0.0030	0.0045
					[–0.028]	[–0.034]	[–0.032]	[–0.041]
OV: Fifth quintile	547	.032	2.351	2.569	–0.0061	–0.0097	–0.0050	–0.0082
					0.0021	0.0028	0.0022	0.0031
					[–0.018]	[–0.013]	[–0.037]	[–0.037]
Linear age					X		X	
Age dummies						X		X
Other Xs							X	X

Notes: Coefficients are marginal effects of a 10,000-unit change in OV from probit models. Standard errors are shown in parentheses. The effect of a one standard deviation change in OV is shown in brackets (this is estimated as the effect of increasing inclusive OV from the current value –0.5 std. dev. to the current value +0.5 std. dev.).

provisions, increasing the eligibility age would find obvious obstacles. Thus, here we ask how employment is affected when we change the eligibility stringencies in DI, and when we do it gradually.

This section is organized as follows. First we show the fit of our model, using specification (4) in table 10.4, by plotting actual and predicted retirement rates (hazard) by gender, health quintile, and educational level. Then we carry out some counterfactual analysis by changing the stringency of the criteria for admission into DI, separately for the overall population and the subpopulation of those who have received DI or early retirement benefits.

10.4.1   Model Fit

Our reference model is specification (4) in table 10.4, with the probability of retirement depending on the inclusive OV, dummies for age and controls for education, health quintiles, and so forth.

In figures 10.15 and 10.16 we show the actual and predicted retirement rates by gender. Because of the use of a full set of age dummies, our specification fits the data very well, especially in the case of men. The good fit of the model is also clear when we plot the actual and predicted probabilities

Table 10.6   **Effect of the inclusive OV, of the health index, and their interaction (estimated probit retirement model—weights based on stocks)**

	Specification			
	(1)	(2)	(3)	(4)
OV	−0.00535***	−0.00697***	−0.00477***	−0.00665***
	(0.00137)	(0.00158)	(0.00137)	(0.00174)
	[−0.019]	[−0.022]	[−0.018]	[−0.021]
OV*hindex	−0.00135***	−0.00175***	−0.00124***	−0.00174***
	(0.00039)	(0.00048)	(0.00038)	(0.00049)
Hindex	−0.00021	0.00005	0.00006	0.00039
	(0.00208)	(0.00261)	(0.00208)	(0.00287)
Observations	2.741	2.423	2.234	1.903
Pseudo R^2	0.122	0.128	0.128	0.128
Linear age	X		X	
Age dummies		X		X
Other Xs			X	X
Mean ret. rate	.0569	.0569	.0569	.0569
Mean of OV	2.345	2.345	2.345	2.345
Std. dev. of OV	2.810	2.810	2.810	2.810

Notes: Models are the same as models 5–8 in table 10.1, with the addition of OV*health. Coefficients are marginal effects of a 10,000-unit change in OV from probit models. Standard errors are shown in parentheses. The effect of a one standard deviation change in OV is shown in brackets (this is estimated as the effect of increasing inclusive OV from the current value −0.5 std. dev. to the current value +0.5 std. dev.). Robust standard errors in parentheses.

***Significant at the 1 percent level.

**Significant at the 5 percent level.

*Significant at the 10 percent level.

Table 10.7   **Effect of inclusive OV on retirement by education level (estimated probit retirement model—weights based on stocks)**

	No. of obs.	Mean ret. rate	Mean of OV	Std. dev. of OV	Specification			
					(1)	(2)	(3)	(4)
OV: < High school	1,232	.064	1.858	2.734	−0.0024	−0.0025	−0.0013	−0.0014
					0.0036	0.0038	0.0025	0.0028
					[0.000]	[0.000]	[0.000]	[0.000]
OV: High school	1,090	.051	2.543	2.614	−0.0050	−0.0126	−0.0020	−0.0101
					0.0018	0.0032	0.0013	0.0037
					[0.000]	[0.000]	[0.000]	[0.000]
OV: College or more	442	.056	3.289	3.237	−0.0025	−0.0054	−0.0009	−0.0011
					0.0016	0.0023	0.0009	0.0009
					[0.000]	[0.000]	[0.000]	[0.000]
Linear age					X		X	
Age dummies						X		X
Health quintiles					X	X	X	X
Other Xs							X	X

Notes: Coefficients are marginal effects of a 10,000-unit change in OV from probit models. Standard errors are shown in parentheses. The effect of a one standard deviation change in OV is shown in brackets (this is estimated as the effect of increasing inclusive OV from the current value −0.5 std. dev. to the current value +0.5 std. dev.).

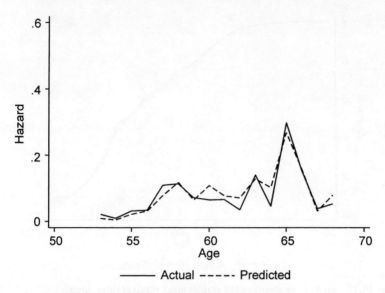

Fig. 10.15   Actual versus predicted retirement rates, men

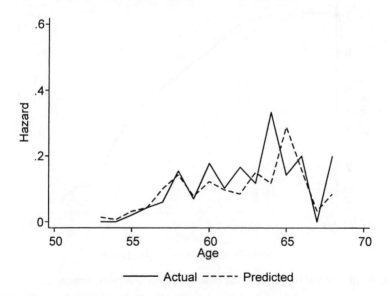

Fig. 10.16   Actual versus predicted retirement rates, women

of remaining employed, or "employment survival rates" (figures 10.17 and 10.18).

In figures 10.19–10.22, we also show the predicted retirement rates by education and health quintiles, separately by gender. It is clear from figures 10.19 and 10.20 that, for each age, the predicted retirement rate is higher for those in worse health (i.e., in the first and second health quintile) and

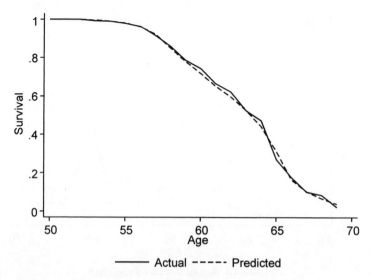

Fig. 10.17   Actual versus predicted employment survival rates, men

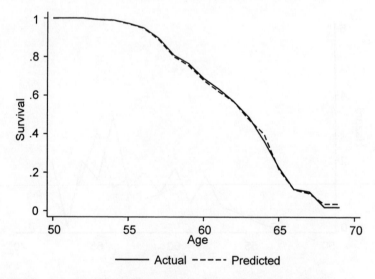

Fig. 10.18   Actual versus predicted employment survival rates, women

lower for those in better health (i.e., in the fourth and fifth quintile). This gradient is common to both men and women, although its age profile is somewhat different by gender.

Finally, figures 10.21 and 10.22 plot the retirement rates by educational level (less than high school, high school, college or more) separately for men and women. Similar to the previous figures, retirement rates tend to be

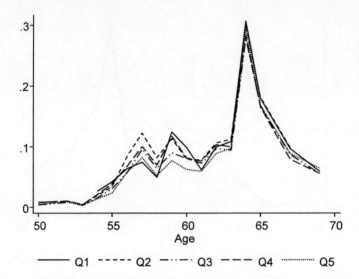

Fig. 10.19   Predicted retirement rates by health quintile, men

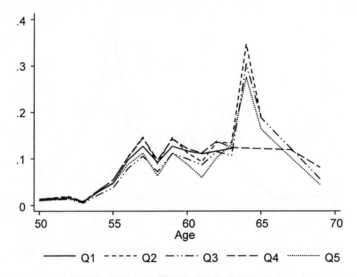

Fig. 10.20   Predicted retirement rates by health quintile, women

higher for those with less than high school and lower for those with college. Differences are more evident in the age range fifty-three to sixty-five, thus before both men and women reach the statutory retirement age. Generally, these figures show that specification (4) in table 10.4 allow the data to fit quite well when using the OV inclusive as the main variable (the weighted average of the OVs by pathway).

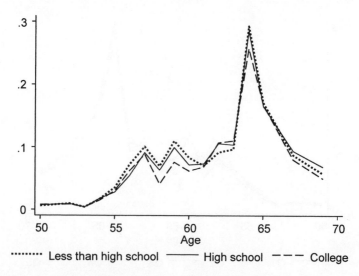

Fig. 10.21   Predicted retirement rates by education level, men

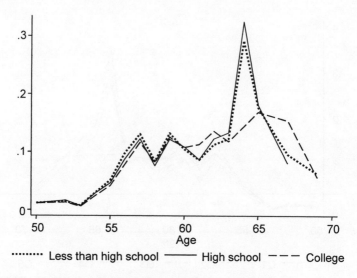

Fig. 10.22   Predicted retirement rates by education level, women

10.4.2   Counterfactual Simulations

We carry out some simulation analysis to evaluate the impact on employment participation of different incentives inherent in each retirement program. Since the focus is on disability, we ask whether employment is affected differentially by the provision of DI, compared to the provision of the old age or early retirement routes. Further, we want to see if this effect varies when we increase the eligibility stringency in DI.

Table 10.8   **Effect of incentive measures on years of work for the age group fifty to sixty-nine, results from three simulations**

Pathway	All face the same pathway	If all DI and early retirement recipients had faced each option	Two-thirds to DI and one-third to old age	One-third to DI and two-thirds to old age
	(1)	(2)	(3)	(4)
DI	12.97	9.33	—	—
Old age	13.38	9.74	9.49	9.56
Early retirement	13.14	9.25	—	—

Three types of simulations are used, depending on the stringency rules that we adopt. They are all based on the estimates obtained in table 10.4, specification (4), which represents our reference model and includes as regressors the inclusive OV and other control variables.

For each simulation, the first step is to calculate the OV separately for each retirement pathway: old age, early retirement, and DI. Then the estimated coefficients from specification (4) in table 10.4 are used to simulate retirement at each age under the different programs (with the inclusive OV associated to each program) for each person in the sample. We now discuss in detail the procedure and the final results.

The first simulation is intended to evaluate the differential effect of changing the stringency for each retirement route—as if all individuals were to face only one retirement pathway with probability 1. Then, for each program, we compute the mean predicted retirement rate by age, the employment survival rate, and calculate the expected years of work between fifty and sixty-nine years of age.

We find that the average expected number of years of work past age fifty is simulated to be 12.97 years if everyone faces the DI option, 13.4 if everyone faces the old-age option, and 13.13 if everyone faces the early retirement option (see table 10.8, column [1]). Thus, individuals need to work more if they all were to face the old-age option compared to the DI option. However, this result should be taken with care for two reasons. First, we have a small sample when using the year-to-year transitions into retirement. Second, we partial-out the age effects by using a set of the age dummies that capture most of the variation in retirement. If we drop age dummies, then we do observe higher differences in the incentives across pathways expressed by expected years of work for the age group fifty to sixty-nine.

Instead of making calculations for all persons in the sample, the second and third simulation would ideally consider only individuals who are DI recipients. Unfortunately, with the data at hand, one cannot perform this type of simulation as the subsample of DI recipients is very small and using the year-to-year transitions to retirement we get an even lower sample. We consider instead the subsample of individuals who are either DI recipients or early retirement recipients and force them to go in old age (we use the question ep071 in SHARE).

We ask how many extra years the individuals in this subgroup would work had they faced the OVs for the old-age pathway. The exercise is similar to that performed in the first simulation. We compute the mean retirement rate if they face the old-age program, the survival function, and calculate the expected years of work between age fifty and sixty-nine (results are shown in column [2]). We find that the expected years of work for this subgroup is 9.33 under the disability route, 9.74 under the old age, and 9.25 under the early retirement. The expected years of work for the disability route and early retirement do not differ much since the simulation is based on the subgroup of recipients of either disability or early retirement benefits.

The third simulation considers again the effect on retirement of greater stringency in DI rules. As in the second simulation, we consider the subgroup of individuals who receive either DI or early retirement benefits. We are aware that performing this simulation on the subgroup containing both DI and early retirement recipients does not allow us to separately identify the effect on labor force participation of a greater stringency in DI rules. However, in the Italian case, the DI and early retirement routes sometimes happen to be substitutes. Thus, we first randomly assign two-thirds of the group to the DI pathway and the other third to the old-age pathway. Then we calculate the mean retirement rate, the employment survival rate, and take the sum of the employment survival for the age interval fifty to sixty-nine. The same process is repeated by randomly assigning one-third of the respondents to the DI pathway and two-thirds to the old-age pathway. The idea of this simulation is to simulate the effect in terms of working years of making DI harder to access for a share of the population (see table 10.8, columns [3] and [4]). From the third and fourth columns we see, in fact, that by closing the DI pathway by one-third (hence by restricting two-thirds to go in DI and one-third in old age), the number of years of work under the old-age pathway reduces from 9.74 to 9.49, so there is an answer to the DI stringency, although we cannot identify the effect on the DI recipients only as explained above. The same occurs when we close the DI pathway by two-thirds; the number of years of work for the old-age pathway reduces from 9.74 to 9.56.

Thus, from these simulations we conclude that individuals respond to the incentives, although not very strongly. For future work, we need to consider a larger sample on which to perform the simulation analysis.

10.5   Conclusions

In this chapter we analyzed the retirement behavior of Italian employees considering distinct pathways to retirement such as old age, early retirement, and disability insurance.

We exploited the determinants of retirement behavior focusing on the role played by health conditions and socioeconomic factors beyond and above the financial incentives associated to each pathway. This was made possible thanks to the availability of SHARE data, which allowed considering a wide set of socioeconomic characteristics compared to administrative. However, we cannot neglect problems related to the small sample size when using SHARE at the level of a single country.

Although our estimated retirement model is standard in the literature, this chapter offers some new developments. First, we construct an overall or "inclusive" option value (OV) measure as the weighted average of the OVs associated to each of the three pathways into retirement using specific weights. Second, following Poterba, Venti, and Wise (2011), we construct an overall index of health via principal component analysis by exploiting the large amount of information on health conditions available in SHARE. Third, we again exploit the possibilities offered by the SHARE data and use year-to-year changes into retirement instead of considering a pooled panel.

Our results are in line with those found in the literature. An increase by 10,000 euros in the OV at time t reduces the probability of retiring at time $t + 1$ by about 5 percent, an effect that is statistically significant at the 5 percent level. Health conditions appear to influence retirement. In particular, being at the top quintile of the distribution of the health index reduces the probability of going into retirement by about 2 percent. Overall, the specification we use seems to fit the data quite well.

In the second part of the analysis, we devote particular attention to the provision of DI programs. In particular, we perform some counterfactual simulations and ask whether employment decisions are differentially affected by the availability of the DI pathway compared to the availability of the old-age or early retirement pathways. Further, we assess the effect of changing the stringency of DI rules.

References

Brugiavini, A., and F. Peracchi. 2004. "Micro-Modeling of Retirement Behavior in Italy." In *Social Security Programs and Retirement around the World: Micro-Estimation*, edited by J. Gruber and D. Wise, 345–99. Chicago: University of Chicago Press.

———. 2012. "Health Status, Welfare Programs Participation, and Labor Force Activity in Italy." In *Social Security Programs and Retirement around the World: Historical Trends in Mortality and Health, Employment, and Disability Insurance Participation*, edited by David Wise, 175–215. Chicago: University of Chicago Press.

Brugiavini, A., F. Peracchi, and D. Wise. 2003. "Pensions and Retirement Incentives. A Tale of Three Countries: Italy, Spain and USA." *Giornale degli Economisti e Annali di Economia* 61:131–70.

Case, A., and A. Deaton. 2005. "Broken Down by Work and Sex: How Our Health Declines." In *Analyses in the Economics of Aging*, edited by David A. Wise, 185–212. Chicago: University of Chicago Press.

Gruber, J., and D. A. Wise, eds. 2004. *Social Security Programs and Retirement around the World: Micro-Estimation.* Chicago: University of Chicago Press.

Poterba, J. M., S. F. Venti, and D. Wise. 2011. "Family Status Transitions, Latent Health, and the Post-Retirement Evolution of Assets." In *Explorations in the Economics of Aging*, edited by David A. Wise, 23–69. Chicago: University of Chicago Press.

Stock, J., and D. A. Wise. 1990. "Pensions, the Option Value of Work and Retirement." *Econometrica* 58:1151–80.

11

Financial Incentives, Health, and Retirement in Spain

Pilar García-Gómez, Sergi Jiménez-Martín, and Judit Vall Castelló

11.1 Introduction

Developed countries share a considerable concern about the financial sustainability of their social insurance systems. The origin of these worries can be found in two well-documented phenomena: an unfavorable demographic process (see Diamond 2007; Lutz, Sanderson, and Scherbov 2008) and a tendency toward reducing the age of retirement on those economies (see Gruber and Wise 1999, 2004; Fenge and Pestieau 2005). Changes in demographics are characterized by increases in life expectancy and decreases

Pilar García-Gómez is an assistant professor at the Erasmus School of Economics of Erasmus University Rotterdam. Sergi Jiménez-Martín is associate professor of economics at Universitat Pompeu Fabra, Barcelona GSE, and director of LaCaixa-FEDEA Chair on Health Economics at FEDEA. Judit Vall Castelló is a researcher at the Centre for Research in Health and Economics (CRES), Department of Economics, Universitat Pompeu Fabra.

We thank the Ministerio de Ciencia e Innovación for financial support (research projects #ECO2011-30323-C03-02 and ECO2014-52238-R). García-Gómez is a postdoctoral fellow of the Netherlands Organization for Scientific Research—Innovational Research Incentives Scheme-Veni. Vall Castelló thankfully acknowledges financial support from the Centre Cournot for Economic Research in Paris. This chapter uses data from SHARE wave 4, release 1.1.1, as of March 28, 2013, or SHARE waves 1 and 2, release 2.5.0, as of May 24, 2011, or SHARELIFE release 1, as of November 24, 2010. The SHARE data collection has been primarily funded by the European Commission through the 5th Framework Programme (project QLK6-CT-2001-00360 in the thematic programme Quality of Life), through the 6th Framework Programme (projects SHARE-I3, RII-CT-2006-062193, COMPARE, CIT5-CT-2005-028857, and SHARELIFE, CIT4-CT-2006-028812) and through the 7th Framework Programme (SHARE-PREP, N° 211909, SHARE-LEAP, N° 227822, and SHARE M4, N° 261982). Additional funding from the US National Institute on Aging (U01 AG09740-13S2, P01 AG005842, P01 AG08291, P30 AG12815, R21 AG025169, Y1-AG-4553-01, IAG BSR06-11, and OGHA 04-064) and the German Ministry of Education and Research as well as from various national sources is gratefully acknowledged (see www.share-project.org for a full list of funding institutions). For acknowledgments, sources of research support, and disclosure of the authors' material financial relationships, if any, please see http://www.nber.org/chapters/c13332.ack.

in fertility rates, which is the worst-case scenario for the sustainability of pay-as-you-go systems. Furthermore, despite growing immigration, the old-age dependency ratio has not improved in the last few years, particularly in European countries. On the other hand, labor force participation by older individuals has been recently increasing, induced in many cases by appropriate regulatory changes introduced in many countries.

The Spanish case is not an exception in this panorama. First, fertility rates are among the lowest in Europe with values below 1.4 in the last years (Eurostat 2013) while, at the same time, the country has experienced large gains in life expectancy. The increase in life expectancy at birth has also been translated in increases in life expectancy at age sixty-five. In 1960 women age sixty-five expected to live 15.3 more years, while the expectations were 21.9 in 2008. Similar improvements are also observed among men (from 13.1 in 1960 to 18.0 in 2008) (García-Gómez, Jiménez-Martín, and Vall Castelló 2012). In parallel, the behavior of the Spanish labor market is puzzling. After a period of strong growth in participation and employment rates (especially for females) between 1995 and 2008 at all ages, the recent economic crisis has dramatically increased unemployment rates, which are currently around 27 percent of the working force (in 2013).

In this work we provide further evidence on the role that financial incentives and health play in transitions out of employment among older workers. The literature on the effect of financial incentives on retirement is very large (see, for example, Samwick [1998]; Coile and Gruber [2007]; Börsch-Supan [2000], for the European case). Within this literature some studies try to identify the interaction between health and financial incentives. For example, Kerkhofs, Lindeboom, and Theeuwes (1999) study the interplay between financial incentives and health in a dynamic programming model. They find that incentive effects are relatively insensitive to alternative specifications for health. Hagan, Jones, and Rice (2009) analyze comparable European Union (EU) data and find a strong relationship between health and early retirement. In the Spanish case, García-Gómez, Jiménez-Martín, and Vall Castelló (2012) analyze the trends in labor force participation and transitions to benefit programs of older workers in relation to health trends as well as recent social security reforms. They find little evidence that health improvements at the population level increase the labor market participation rates of older workers.

In this work we take advantage of the detailed health information available in the Survey of Health and Retirement in Europe to explore the link between health, financial incentives, and retirement. With this purpose, we construct a health index and classify individuals into health quintiles and use this information to assess the extent to which differences in health are translated into differences in the responsiveness to changes in financial incentives. In addition, we construct a single-option value measure by compiling the information on financial incentives from the disability, old-age, and unemployment systems in order to consider the aggregate incentives from all the social security schemes used as pathways into retirement among individuals ages fifty to sixty-four in Spain.

Our results show that individuals in the worse health quintiles are, indeed, more responsive to financial incentives as they prove to be less likely to retire when incentives to continue working increase. We further perform a series of simulations to assess the expected changes in retirement choices of older individuals when some of the policy parameters are modified.

The rest of the chapter is organized as follows. In section 11.2 we discuss the recent trends observed in the Spanish labor market and regulation. In section 11.3 we present the key ingredients of our empirical approach. We discuss the main result obtained from the analysis in section 11.4. Last, section 11.5 concludes.

11.2 Background

In this section we first provide some graphical evidence about trends in employment and participation in different social security programs (disability insurance [DI], unemployment insurance [UI], and old-age pensions [OAP]). Next, we review the generosity and entitlement characteristics of these programs and explain the main recent reforms.

11.2.1 Trends in Employment and Participation in Different Social Security Programs

In this section we provide some graphical evidence on social security participation by age groups, gender, and educational attainment. Data on employment, unemployment, and disability come from the Spanish Labor Force Survey (*Encuesta de Población Activa* [EPA]). The EPA is a rotating quarterly survey carried out by the Spanish National Statistical Institute (*Instituto Nacional de Estadística* [INE]). The planned sample size consists of about 64,000 households with approximately 150,000 adult individuals. Although the survey has been conducted since 1964, publicly released cross-sectional files are available only from 1977. The 1977 questionnaire was modified in 1987 (when a set of retrospective questions were introduced), in the first quarter of 1992, in 1999, and 2004. The EPA provides fairly detailed information on labor force status, education, and family background variables but, like most of the other European-style labor force surveys, no information on health is provided. The reference period for most questions is the week before the interview.

Figure 11.1 shows the percentage of individuals in each social security program (unemployment, old-age benefits, and disability) for Spanish men in the age brackets fifty to fifty-four, fifty-five to fifty-nine, and sixty to sixty-four. The percentage of individuals who report receiving disability benefits has remained stable, as shown in previous research (Vall Castelló 2012;

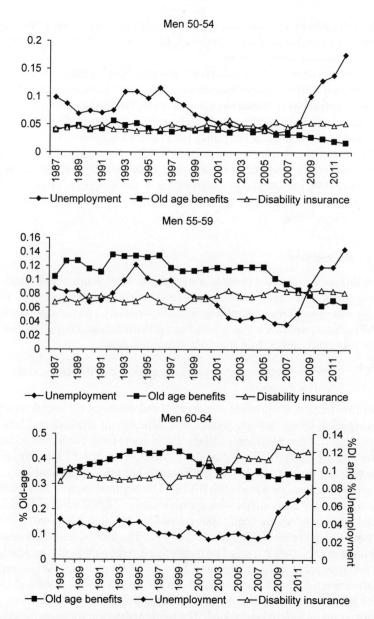

Fig. 11.1 Percentage of individuals in each social security program (self-reported). Men age fifty to sixty-four by age group

Source: Authors' own elaboration using data from the Spanish Labor Force Survey.

García-Gómez, Jiménez-Martín, and Vall Castelló 2012). While the inflow into DI has been growing steadily in a number of countries, this rate has remained quite stable in Spain (see Wise 2012). However, the percentage of individuals in disability has begun to increase at the end of the period for the elderly group of workers (as seen in figure 11.1). This could be the result of a worsening in labor market conditions as indicated by the increase in unemployment rates at the same time that early retirement becomes less attractive as the decreasing trends suggest.

The percentage of individuals in the old-age benefit system was increasing for both age groups until 1996, but since that date it has experienced a decreasing trend. Reforms introduced in 1997 and 2002 (especially the second one that delayed early retirement until age sixty-one) in the old-age benefit system (explained in detail in the next section) are partly responsible for this decreasing trend (see Jiménez-Martín 2006). The high fraction in old-age benefits in the fifty-five to fifty-nine age group showed by the Spanish Labor Force Survey is likely to be due to participation in preretirement schemes that do not involve automatic retirement (Dorn and Souza-Poza 2010; Boldrin, Jiménez-Martín, and Peracchi 1999). Alternatively, individuals may declare themselves as retired because they have exited permanently from the labor force even though they could be receiving benefits from another scheme. Therefore, in practice, individuals perceive this situation as a retirement path.

Last, we can see that the unemployment rates of the youngest group of workers are more sensitive to the business cycle compared to individuals entitled to early retirement benefits (see next section), although the severity of the current economic crisis in Spain has translated into increases in the unemployment rate for men in all age groups.

Figure 11.2 plots the share of men and women that report receiving DI benefits by age group (fifty to fifty-four, fifty-five to fifty-nine, and sixty to sixty-four). We can observe that contrary to the relatively stable trend observed for males (see figure 11.1), participation in the DI program has experienced a sizable increase among women in the three age groups. The increase in female DI participation rates in Spain begins in the mid-1990s and it slows down during the current period of economic crisis. This is an expected increase given the increase in female participation rates observed in the past that allow a larger share of women to be entitled to DI. In any case, for both men and women the strong economic crisis experienced by the Spanish economy does not seem to have increased or decreased the percentage of individuals in DI for any of the three age groups.

Figure 11.3 shows the evolution of the percentage of males and females in the labor force and receiving DI benefits. The increase in DI participation rates for both men and women in the age group sixty to sixty-four reported in figures 11.1 and 11.2 is linked to the increase in the labor force participation rates for both groups from the mid-1990s. For the case of men, however,

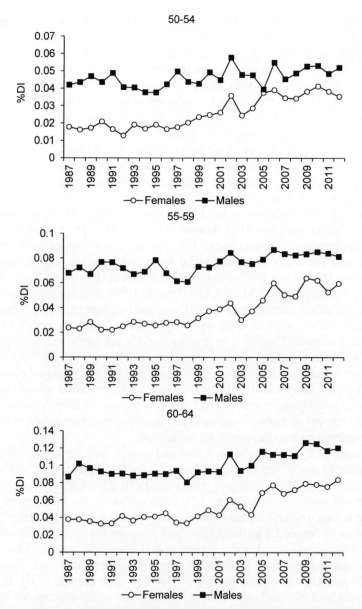

Fig. 11.2   The DI participation rates at ages fifty to fifty-four, fifty-five to fifty-nine, and sixty to sixty-four by gender

Source: Authors' own elaboration using data from the Spanish Labor Force Survey.

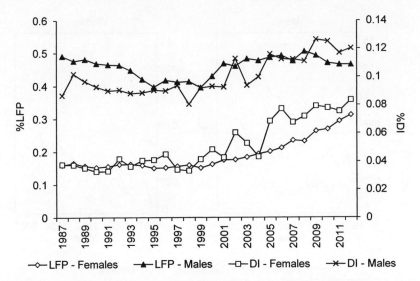

Fig. 11.3   Labor force and DI participation rates at ages sixty to sixty-four by gender
Source: Authors' own elaboration using data from the Spanish Labor Force Survey.

there is a change in this increasing trend from 2008 in which the participation in the labor force experienced a mild drop due to the economic crisis. This drop seems to have also been translated into a drop in DI participation rates for men, although with a two-year lag. Notice that labor force and DI participation rates are still increasing among women despite the economic crisis.

Figure 11.4 plots the evolution of DI participation rates by educational attainment. The figure shows the share of men and women age fifty-five to sixty-four who report being on disability insurance among those who have completed either primary education, secondary education, or hold a university degree. There is an educational gradient in these percentages for both males and females, but the differences are more striking among males. The percentage into DI is largest among individuals with primary education at most, and lowest among those with a university degree. Figure 11.4 also shows that the recent increase in the share of the population in DI among women age fifty-five to sixty-four is mainly driven by the increase in the percentage of low-educated women in the disability insurance system. It is difficult to disentangle whether this increase is due to business cycle conditions or to a number of reforms that were introduced in the retirement and DI system in 1997 (see next section).

Last, figure 11.5 shows the trends in employment for men and women age sixty to sixty-four in Spain by educational attainment. For both men and women we can see that the highest employment rates are for individuals

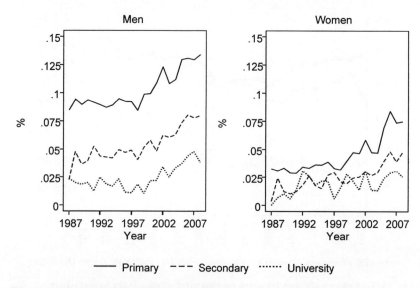

Fig. 11.4   Share of the population age fifty-five to sixty-four into disability insurance (self-reported) by educational attainment
Source: Authors' own elaboration using data from the Spanish Labor Force Survey.

with a university degree, which are also the ones with a lower percentage of individuals on the disability rolls. This difference in employment rates by education is more pronounced for the case of women. In general terms, we can see that employment has been decreasing from 1987 until 2008 for men with a university degree, while it has remained relatively stable for men with primary or secondary education (although both groups experience a drop in employment in times of economic slowdowns such as the first half of the 1990s, as well as in the recent economic crisis). On the contrary, female employment rates for the two lowest educational groups seem to be mildly increasing since the 1980s, and they seem to be less responsive to the business cycle conditions than the male employment rate.

11.2.2   Institutional Background

Disability Insurance

In Spain, there are two types of permanent disability benefits: (a) contributory, which are given to individuals who have generally contributed to the social security system before the onset of the disabling condition; and (b) noncontributory, which are given to individuals who are assessed to be disabled but have never contributed to the social security system (or do not reach the minimum contributory requirement to access the contributory

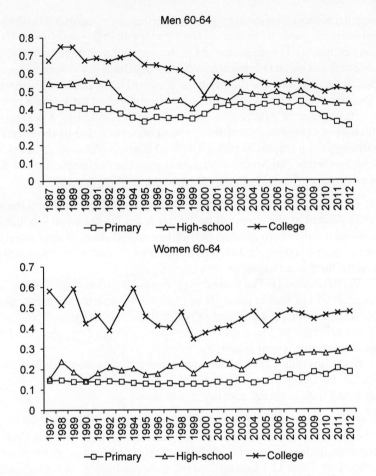

Fig. 11.5   **Employment rates for men and women at ages sixty to sixty-four by education**

Source: Authors' own elaboration using data from the Spanish Labor Force Survey.

system). Noncontributory disability benefits are means tested and managed at the regional level.[1]

The size of the noncontributory system is relatively small compared to the contributory system (195,986 individuals received noncontributory dis- ·ability benefits in October 2013, while 932,245 received contributory benefits during the same year). The amount of benefits received is also smaller in the

1. Income is evaluated yearly. The income threshold in 2010 was set at 4,755.80 euros per year for an individual living alone. This amount is adjusted if the individual lives with other members.

noncontributory case (the average noncontributory pension is 396.92 euros per month compared to an average contributory disability pension of 909.25 euros per month). For these reasons, in the remaining of this chapter we put more emphasis on the permanent contributory disability system in Spain.

Social security defines the permanent contributive disability insurance as the economic benefits to compensate the individual for losing a certain amount of wage or professional earnings when affected by a permanent reduction or complete loss of his/her working ability due to the effects of a pathologic or a traumatic process derived from an illness or an accident.

The Spanish Social Security Administration uses a classification of four main degrees of disability that depend on the working capacity lost:[2]

1. Permanent limited disability for the usual job. The individual loses at least 33 percent of the standard performance for his/her usual job, but the individual is still able to develop the fundamental tasks of his/her usual job or professional activity. Individuals in this level of disability only receive a one-time, lump-sum payment.

2. Partial disability. The individual is impaired to develop all or the fundamental tasks of his/her usual job or professional activity, but he/she is still capable of developing a different job or professional activity.

3. Total disability. The individual is impaired for the development of any kind of job or professional activity.

4. Severe disability. Individuals who, as a result of anatomic or functional loses, need the assistance of a third person to develop essential activities of daily living such as eating, moving, and so forth.

The eligibility requirements and the pension amount depend on the source of the disability (ordinary illness, work related, or unrelated accident or occupational illness), the level of the disability, and the age of the onset of the disability. Table 11.1 summarizes the main parameters of both the eligibility criteria and the pension formula. The two main features to highlight are that: (a) there are not contributory requirements if the health impairment is due to either an accident or an occupational illness, and (b) individuals older than fifty-five with a partial disability receive a higher replacement rate if it is considered difficult for them to find a job due to lack of education or the social and labor market conditions of the region where they live.

The total amount of the pension is obtained by multiplying a percentage, which varies depending on the type of pension and the degree of disability (as shown in the last rows of table 11.1) to the regulatory base, which depends on the source of the disability and on previous salaries.[3] The num-

2. Partial disability claimants represent 57 percent, total disability claimants represent 40 percent, and severe disability claimants represent 3 percent of all individuals in the DI system. The remaining 0.4 percent are individuals in the permanent limited disability system, which is being extinguished. These numbers are taken from the *Muestra Continua de Vidas Laborales*.
3. Benefit = Regulatory Base * Percentage.

Table 11.1   **Summary of the parameters to calculate permanent disability pensions**

	Ordinary illness	Work-unrelated accident	Work-related accident or professional illness
Eligibility	Age > = 31: Contributed 1/4 time between 20 years old and disabling condition. Minimum of 5 years Age < 30: Contributed 1/3 time between 16 years old and disabling condition. No minimum number of years required	No minimum contributory period required	No minimum contributory period required
Regulatory base	Average wage last 8 years of work*percentage[a]	Average annual wage of 24 months within the last 7 years of work	Average wage last year of work
Percentage applied to the regulatory base	Partial disability: 55% Individuals older than 55 with difficulties to find a job due to lack of education or characteristics of the social and labor market of the region where they live: 75% Total disability: 100% Severe disability: 100% + 50%		

[a] This percentage depends on the number of years contributed to the system at the age at which the individual enters the DI system. This percentage can range from 50 percent to 100 percent. This change was introduced in 2008 in order to make the formula to calculate the DI benefits closer to the formula used to calculate the old-age benefits.

ber of years included in the regulatory base depends on the source of the disability.

The income tax rules differ across disability types. Partial disability benefits are taxable under the general income tax rules, while total disability pensions are always exempted from income taxes. Furthermore, if the individual works while receiving the pension, there is a reduction in the earnings used to calculate the income tax of 2,800 euros per year if their degree of disability is low (between 33 percent and 65 percent) and of 6,200 euros per year if the disability level is higher (more than 65 percent) or if the disabled has reduced mobility. In addition, individuals receiving partial disability benefits can combine the benefits with earnings from work, as long as the type of job is compatible with his/her disability.

In general, to be granted a permanent disability benefit, the individual must come from a situation of sick leave (also called temporary disability/incapacity) and be observed as still presenting anatomic or functional reductions that decrease or cancel his/her capacity to work after following the prescribed medical treatment. The application can be started by the provincial office of the National Institute of Social Security (NISS), by the institutions that collaborate in the process (such as hospitals), or by the individual himself (in which case, more documentation is required). The Disabilities Evaluation Team evaluates the medical report and the professional background of the applicant and, on the basis of this analysis, the directors of the provincial office of the NISS decide on the type of disability pension granted (if any), the benefit level, and the date of the next medical check-up. All permanent disability pensions are automatically converted to old-age pensions once the individual turns sixty-five.[4]

Old-Age Pensions

Eligibility to the old-age pension benefits in Spain requires having contributed to the system for at least fifteen years and an individual can enter the system at the normal retirement age of sixty-five if the individual does not have any job that requires affiliation to the social security system.[5] The pension amount is calculated by multiplying a regulatory base[6] by a percentage that depends on the age of the individual and the number of years contributed to the system. If the individual enters the old-age system after the normal retirement age of sixty-five, there is an additional percentage that will also be multiplied to the regulatory base.

The regulatory base is obtained by dividing by 210 the wages of the last 180 months before retiring, and the percentage applied to this regulatory base is the following:[7]

$$\begin{cases} 0 & \text{if } n < 15 \\ 0.5 + 0.03(n - 15) & \text{if } 15 \leq n \leq 25 \\ 0.8 + 0.02(n - 25) & \text{if } 25 < n < 35 \\ 1 & \text{if } 35 \leq n \end{cases}$$

4. Most of the outflows from the permanent disability system are due to death or automatic transfer to old-age pensions. Around 4 percent of the outflows are due to improvement of the health condition and 2.7 percent to a judicial process. Monthly outflows in 2010 were around 2,500–3,000.

5. This condition was later relaxed in 2002 when partial retirement was introduced.

6. The benefit base is a weighted average of monthly earnings over the last eight years of work before retirement. This was changed to fifteen years of work before retirement from 1997. However, this change was introduced gradually from 1997 until 2002 and it affected all individuals in the same way. Therefore, we have reason to think that this change will not interfere in our results. See Boldrin and Jiménez-Martín (2007) for further details of the Spanish system and the reforms undertaken.

7. Both the calculation of the regulatory base and the percentage applied to this regulatory base was changed by a reform in 2011. However, we do not explain this reform in the current chapter as it is outside the years included in our sample period.

Unemployment Insurance

According to the current unemployment rules, there are two kinds of unemployment benefits. Unemployment insurance (UI) is available for eligible[8] workers that contributed while employed and have been fired from the previous job. After the exhaustion of UI benefits, unemployment assistance (UA) is available for individuals who have finished their UI contributory period. Individuals entering the UI scheme are entitled to receive 70 percent of the wages of the last 180 days of work during the first six months and 60 percent after that.[9] These quantities are subject to a minimum and a maximum amount. The minimum corresponds to 80 percent of the minimum wage and the maximum corresponds to 175 percent of the minimum wage. Both quantities are increased if the individual has, at least, one dependent child.[10] These benefits are paid for a period of one-third of the accumulated job tenure and are only paid for a maximum period of two years.

The UA benefits are only paid to individuals with an average family income below 75 percent of the minimum wage. There is a fixed amount paid that corresponds to 80 percent of the minimum wage. This benefit is only paid for a maximum period of twenty-one months if the individual has contributed for at least six months and if he/she has dependents.[11] There are, however, two special continuation programs for those who have exhausted their entitlement to contributory unemployment benefits: one for those age forty-five and older (UB45+ program), and the other for those age fifty-two and older (UB52+ program). The latter is a special subsidy for unemployed people that are older than fifty-two, have a family income lower than 75 percent of the minimum wage, have contributed to unemployment insurance for at least six years in their lifetimes and, except for age, satisfy all the requirements for an old-age pension.[12] Those in the UB52+ program keep contributing toward the pension, but at the minimum contributory base and they can receive 80 percent of the minimum wage until they reach the official retirement age. (García-Pérez, Jiménez-Martín, and Sánchez-Martín 2013; Jiménez-Martín and Vall Castelló 2013).

8. They must have accumulated 360 days of contributions to the Social Security Administration during the previous six years before becoming unemployed.

9. A reform introduced in 2012 decreased this amount to 50 percent (instead of 60 percent) of last earnings after the first six months receiving UI benefits.

10. For individuals with at least one dependent child, the minimum amount corresponds to 107 percent of the minimum wage and the maximum amount corresponds to 200 percent of the minimum wage.

11. If the person has contributed for at least six months but does not have dependents, the duration of the subsidy is six months. If the person does not have dependents and has not contributed for at least six months, he/she cannot receive the subsidy. There is also a special scheme in Andalucía and Extremadura for agricultural workers who have been employed for forty days during the year. They are entitled to receive 75 percent of the minimum wage for 90 to 300 days each year. The number of days depends on their age and number of dependents.

12. The age of fifty-two was changed to fifty-five in July 2012.

Main Reforms

Permanent disability benefits were used extensively as an early retirement mechanism for workers in restructuring industries (such as shipbuilding, steel, mining, etc.) or as a substitution for long-term unemployment subsidies in depressed regions during the late 1970s and 1980s (OECD 2001), which resulted in an increase in the inflows into the disability system and permanent disability benefits.

These events prompted a number of reforms introduced during the second half of the 1980s and beginning of the 1990s that aimed at reversing these trends (see table 11.2 for a summary). The main objective of these reforms was to abolish the incentive effects to permanently leave the labor market before reaching the legal retirement age through the disability system.

Here we focus on some distinctive features of the main reforms since the creation of the National Institute of Social Security in 1979, while we refer the reader to table 11.2 for a summary of all the reforms in the disability system in Spain during this period.

The first major reform of the disability system took place in 1997 and it included four main points:

1. Sickness benefits. Stricter control of the sickness status by doctors of the social security system, reduction of the level of long-term sickness benefits, and replacement of the old own-job assessment by a more objective definition of the usual occupation of the individual.

2. Permanent disability pensions of individuals at least sixty-five years of age are automatically transferred to the old-age pension system. This is just a change in the classification within the pensions system.

3. Organizational reform. All the permanent disability matters are transferred to the NISS. In the past, the permanent disability status was assessed and granted by local general practitioners and this reform created a group of experts (the disability assessment team inside the NISS) that would be in charge of assessing a person's ability to work on the basis of the available medical files and a special medical assessment done by one of the NISS doctors.

4. The individual does not lose entitlement to noncontributory disability benefits if he/she starts working. He/she will then still be entitled to receive noncontributory disability benefits if he/she loses his/her job.

Apart from this major reform in 1997, the 1998 budget law introduced the possibility for doctors from the NISS and mutual insurance companies to review the health situation and status of beneficiaries. However, in reality, very few individuals in the permanent disability system do effectively lose their benefits. In 2004 and 2005, monitoring of the use of sickness leave was tightened with the creation of a new subdepartment at the NISS and a new monitoring tool to reduce absence rates. In 2005, a general absence control

Table 11.2   **Main reforms since 1980 of the disability insurance, old-age, and unemployment systems in Spain**

1984	Introduction of temporary contracts. Introduction of unemployment assistance (UA) benefits (noncontributory). Special provision for workers age 55+; they can receive UA until retirement if comply with requirements to get old-age pension (except age requirement).
1985	The terms of eligibility for disability pensions are tightened. Increased the minimum mandatory annual contributions from 8 to 15. The number of contributive years used to compute the pension increases from 2 to 8. Several early retirement schemes are introduced; partial retirement and special retirement at age 64.
1989	Special scheme of UA (permanent until retirement) extended to workers 52+.
1990	Introduction of a means-tested noncontributory disability pensions for peopled age 65+ and for disabled people age 18+ who satisfy residency requirements.
1997	Stricter control of sickness status, reduction of long-term sickness benefit level, usual occupation replaces own job assessment. Permanent disability pensions to individuals 65+ are converted to old-age pensions. New INSS disability assessment team to assess permanent disability instead of the GP. Entitlement to noncontributory benefits is not lost if working, and can be collected if losing the job. The number of contributive years used to compute the pension increases from 8 to 15 (progressively by 2001). The formula for the replacement rate is made less generous. The 8% penalty applied to early retirees between the ages of 60 and 65 is reduced to 7% for individuals with 40 or more contributory years. Introduction of a new permanent contract with reduced severance payments targeted to certain population groups. Lower social security contributions for employers for the first two years if one of these new permanent contracts was signed.
1998	Possibility of doctors from INSS and mutual insurance companies to review the health situation of beneficiaries.
2001	Broaden the 1997 labor market reform. Extension of new permanent contract of 1997 to more population groups. Suppression or reduction of social security contributions to support permanent employment for certain groups of the population.
2002	Early retirement only from age 61. Impulse partial retirement; possible to combine it with work. Unemployed at age 61 can retire if contributed for 30 years and the previous 6 months registered in employment offices. Incentives to retire after age 65. Individuals age 52+ can combine unemployment benefits with a job. Extension of group of individuals that can benefit from the "integration contract" (program to help integrate the unemployed into the labor market).
2004–2005	Improve monitoring and control of sickness leave with new INSS tool. Possibility to combine noncontributory disability with some earnings.

(continued)

Table 11.2   (continued)

2007	Minimum contributory period to access permanent disability is reduced for young workers. The formula to calculate the regulatory base of the DI benefit gets closer to the formula for old-age pensions. Fifteen "effective" contributory years are used to calculate the old-age pension. Reduction from 8% to 7.5% of the per-year penalty applied to early retirees between 60 and 65 for individuals with 30 contributory years. Broaden incentives to stay employed after age 65. Increase contributions made by the Social Security Administration for individuals receiving the special scheme of UA for 52+ (they will receive a higher old-age pension when retiring).
2011	Gradual increase (from 2013 until 2027) of the normal retirement age from 65 to 67 depending on the age of the individual as well as on the number of years and months of contributions accumulated during his/her labor market career.
2012	The amount an individual receives from UI after the first six months is reduced from 60% to 50% of previous earnings.

was put in place for cases in which the absenteeism took longer than six months.

Finally, at the end of 2007, the minimum contributory period to access permanent disability pensions was reduced for young workers in order to adjust for the current later entrance into the job market of younger workers. At the same time, the formula to calculate the regulatory base of the benefit was slightly modified: the regulatory base of permanent disability due to a common illness is since then decreased by 50 percent if the individual had not contributed at least fifteen years, and it is lower the further the individual is from age sixty-five.

All these reforms have ensured the financial stability of the disability system in Spain as inflow rates have remained at stable levels and have not experienced any dramatic increases like in other countries.

The extent to which reforms in the disability system are able to decrease the outflows from employment at older ages will depend on the evolution of other programs that can be used as alternative early retirement routes. Therefore, in this section we summarize other important reforms that have taken place in other social security programs in Spain. In particular, we focus on reforms in the unemployment and old-age systems. Table 11.3 provides a chronological summary of these reforms.[13]

In 1984, both temporary contracts and noncontributory unemployment benefits (also called unemployment assistance benefits) were introduced.

---

13. A detailed exposition of the changes in the old-age pension system in Spain is provided in Boldrin, García-Gómez, and Jiménez-Martín (2010).

Table 11.3   The PVW first principal component index for Spain

Variable	Factor loading
Difficulty walking 100 meters	0.2737
Difficulties lifting or carrying weights over 100 pounds/5 kilos	0.3011
Difficulties pulling or pushing large objects	0.2938
Difficulty with an ADL (0 if no limitations; 1 if 1 or more limitations)	0.2826
Difficulty climbing stairs	0.3066
Difficulties stooping, kneeling, or crouching	0.3045
Difficulties getting up from a chair	0.2919
Self-reported health fair or poor	0.2594
Difficulties reaching or extending your arms above your shoulder	0.2514
Doctor has ever told you have arthritis, including osteoarthritis, or rheumatism	0.2007
Difficulties sitting two hours	0.2255
Difficulties picking up a small coin from a table	0.1828
Pain in back, knees, hips, or any other joint at least during the past six months	0.1952
Heart trouble or angina or chest pain during exercise at least for the past six months	0.1345
Hospital stay	0.1202
Home care	0.0884
Doctor visit	0.07
Ever experience psychological problems	0.0938
Doctor has ever told you have a stroke or cerebral vascular disease	0.0925
Doctor has ever told you have high blood pressure or hypertension	0.119
Doctor has ever told you have a chronic lung disease such as chronic bronchitis or emphysema	0.0899
Doctor has ever told you have diabetes or high blood pressure	0.0947
BMI	0.0844
Nursing home stay	0.0305
Doctor has ever told you have cancer or malignant tumor, including leukemia or lymphoma, but excluding minor skin cancers	0.036
Observations	7,480
Percent total variance explained	24.30

Note: Values based on SHARE data for 2004, 2006, and 2010.

In addition, a special provision was established for workers over fifty-five years of age who were allowed to receive unemployment assistance benefits until retirement age. To receive these benefits, individuals had to satisfy the entitlement requirements of the retirement pension, except for the age. The subsidy paid 75 percent of the minimum wage until reaching the age to be transferred to an old-age pension. Furthermore, the years spent unemployed under this special scheme were counted as contributive years toward an old-age pension.

In the following year, 1985, an old-age pension reform was passed that increased the minimum mandatory annual contribution to old-age pensions from eight to fifteen years, it also increased the number of years of contribution used to calculate the pension from two to eight years[14] and introduced several early retirement programs linked to hiring a new worker, such as the partial retirement program that allowed part-time retirement at sixty-three by combining part-time wages and old-age pension, and special retirement at sixty-four if the employer hired a registered unemployed.

In 1989 the special provision of unemployment assistance benefits until the retirement age of sixty-five for individuals at least fifty-five years of age was extended to individuals at age fifty-two, thus increasing the incentives of older workers to leave the labor market at younger ages. The expected decrease in the labor force participation rates of older individuals observed in Spain during the 1980s and the early 1990s prompted the government to adopt a change in the strategy, and to start a series of reforms to reverse these negative labor market trends. Therefore, the reforms introduced during the 1990s had the objective of keeping older workers active in the labor market for longer.

There have been two main reforms since the mid-1990s, one in 1997 and the other in 2002. In 1997 the number of contributory years used to compute the benefit base was progressively increased from eight to fifteen years and the formula to calculate the replacement rate was also made less generous.[15] On the other hand, the 8 percent penalty applied to early retirees between the ages of sixty and sixty-five was reduced to 7 percent for individuals with forty or more years of contributions at the time of early retirement. Some changes in the incentives on the demand side were also introduced in 1997 to reduce the unemployment rates and the share of temporary contracts among the disadvantaged groups, including individuals age forty-five or older who were either unemployed or had a temporary contract.

In 2002 changes in both the old-age and the unemployment systems were introduced. Before 2002, only individuals who had contributed to the system earlier than 1967 could benefit from early retirement at sixty, while the rest had to wait until the normal retirement age of sixty-five. In 2002, earlier retirement at age sixty-one was made available for the rest of the population. At the same time, there was an impulse to the partial and flexible retirement schemes with the possibility of combining income from work with old-age benefits and the introduction of incentives for individuals to retire after the legal retirement age of sixty-five (an additional 2 percent per additional year of contribution beyond the age of sixty-five for workers with at least thirty-

14. The change in the minimum mandatory annual contributions to have access to an old-age pension affected all individuals since 1985, but the number of years used to calculate the pension was progressively increased: during the first year, the last seventy months were used, seventy-two months in the second year, and eighty-four in the third year.

15. In 1997 the last 108 months are included, the last 120 months in 1998, the last 132 months in 1999, the last 144 months in 2000, the last 156 months in 2001, and the last 180 months from 2002 onward.

five years of contributions on top of the 100 percent applied to the regulatory base). At the same time, the possibility to access retirement was extended to individuals who are unemployed for reasons beyond their willingness at age sixty-one and who have contributed for at least thirty years and have been registered in the employment office for the previous six months.

On the other hand, the reform in 2002 opened up the possibility for individuals age fifty-two or older who are receiving unemployment benefits to combine the receipt of these benefits with earnings, as they could receive 50 percent of normal benefits and the employer would pay the remaining quantity in wages. In addition, it extended the program that helps to integrate unemployed persons in the labor market to all individuals at least forty-five years of age who have been unemployed for one month and to people with disabilities, among others.[16]

In 2007 the incentives to retire later than age sixty-five were further increased providing an additional 3 percent, instead of the 2 percent agreed on in 2002. Moreover, in order to have access to an old-age pension the individual must have contributed for at least two out of the last fifteen years and the proportional part related to the extra monthly salaries will not be taken into account when computing the number of contributed years. On the other hand, the 8 percent penalty applied to early retirees between the ages of sixty and sixty-five was reduced to 6–7.5 percent, depending on the number of years contributed, for those individuals with thirty years of contributions. In addition, the contributions for unemployed workers older than fifty-two were increased so that they would receive a higher old-age pension when retiring.

Last, in 2011 a new reform was introduced that gradually moved (from 2013 until 2027) the normal retirement age from sixty-five to sixty-seven, depending on the age of the individual as well as the number of years and months of contributions accumulated during his/her labor market career. However, as this last reform was introduced after the end of our sample period, we do not enter into the details of the policy change. Similarly, the amount an individual receives from UI after the first six months was reduced from 60 to 50 percent of previous earnings in 2012.

11.3 Empirical Approach

11.3.1 Pathways to Retirement

We use retrospective information available in the second quarter of the EPA regarding the labor status of individuals in the previous year to investigate which are the pathways used to leave the labor market in Spain. We calculate the percentage that transit from employment to each of the statuses

---

16. This program is called *Contrato de Integración* (Integration Contract).

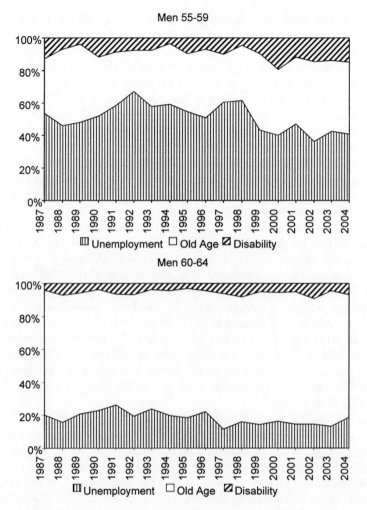

Fig. 11.6 Outflows from employment into unemployment, disability, and old age (men age fifty-five to sixty-four)
Source: Authors' own elaboration using data from the Spanish Labor Force Survey.

of interest. This is shown in figure 11.6. Unfortunately, the retrospective information does not distinguish between the different jobless statuses, which would have allowed us to identify the individuals that transit from unemployment or disability into retirement.

The share of individuals that leave employment and transit into unemployment is higher among the relatively younger individuals than among the older groups (50 percent of men age fifty-five to sixty that leave employment and transit to one of the statuses of interest go to unemployment compared to 20 percent among men age sixty to sixty-four). Disability insurance is the route less used to leave the labor market among older workers.

11.3.2   Option Value Calculations

In this section we describe the incentive measures used, as well as the necessary assumptions.

SS Incentives Measures

For a (representative) worker of age a, following Gruber and Wise (1999), we define social security wealth (SSW) in case of retirement at age $h \geq a$ as the expected present value of future pension benefits

$$\mathrm{SSW}_h = \sum_{s=h+1}^{S} \rho_s B_s(h).$$

Here S is the age of certain death, $\rho_s = \beta^{s-a}\pi_s$, with β denoting the pure time discount factor and π_s the conditional survival probability at age s for an individual alive at age a, and $B_s(h)$ the pension expected at age $s \geq h + 1$ in case of retirement at age s. Given SSW, we define the option value (OV) as follows:

$$\mathrm{OV}_a = \max_h\{V_h - V_a\}, \; h = a + 1, \ldots, R,$$

where

$$V_h = \sum_{s=a+1}^{h} \rho_s W_s^\gamma + \sum_{s=h+1}^{S} \rho_s [kB_s(h)]^\gamma$$

and ρ_s are the survival probabilities, S is age of (certain) death, and W stands for earnings. We have imposed that $\beta = .97$, $\gamma = 0.75$ and $k = 1.5$. The conditional survival probabilities are obtained from INE (2010). Note that future benefits include spouse and survival benefits.

Assumptions Made in Incentives Calculus

We have computed social security incentive measures (SSW and OV) for the sample of individuals in SHARE 2004–2011. In order to compute the above incentives, the basic ingredients are wages (contribution histories) and family characteristics. Since SHARE does not provide accurate wage histories, we match individuals in SHARE to average wage histories in the *Muestra Continua de Vidas Laborales* 2011.[17]

From every year-of-birth, education, and gender cohort in the ECVL 2011 sample we construct the median wage distribution in the period 1981–2011. For example, for the group of individuals born in 1940, we recover covered wages from age forty-one to seventy. In general, for individuals born in

---

17. See the appendix for a description of this administrative database.

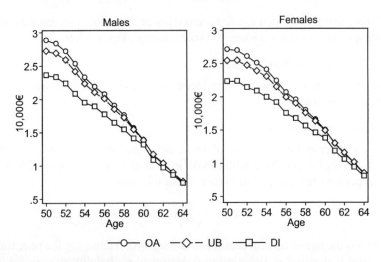

Fig. 11.7   **Average OV for different pathways by gender**

year j we recover wages from the years 1981 to 2011. Then we predict backward and forward in order to obtain a complete year of birth-gender-region wage profiles in the twenty to seventy age range. Wage profiles are projected assuming 1 percent real growth if there is no information (with 2 percent inflation after 2012). However, for ages fifty-nine and older we assume a 0 wage growth.

Regarding family characteristics, we use the information in SHARE for marital status. In addition, for both men and women, we assume that starting at age fifty-five and until a person reaches sixty-five, there are three pathways into retirement: unemployment benefits for individuals ages fifty-two and older (UB52+), disability insurance (DI), and early retirement (ER). At each particular age, the individual has an age-specific probability of going into retirement using any of these three programs. However, we have to take into account the following two restrictions: (a) a person has no access to the ER program before age sixty-one, and (b) after age sixty-one a person cannot claim UB52+ and can only claim ER or DI benefits.

Figure 11.7 plots the average OV for the three pathways considered (old age, unemployment, and disability) by gender. In all cases it is clear that the average OV is positive and decreasing with age, getting close to 0 as individuals approach sixty-five, as the incentives provided by the Spanish system to keep working beyond sixty-five are very low (see Jiménez-Martín and Sánchez-Martín 2007). We see that both for men and women the ranking in average OV among retirement pathways remains constant, that is, at any age the average OV for disability benefits is lower than the average OV for unemployment benefits, while the larger value is for the average OV for old-age retirement benefits.

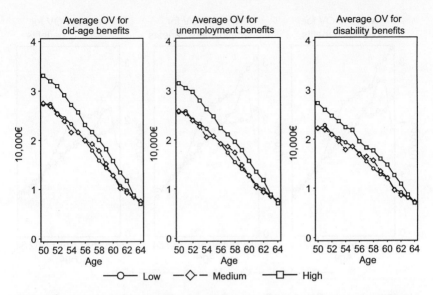

Fig. 11.8 **Average OVs for different pathways by educational attainment (males)**

We find that there is a clear gradient in the average OVs by educational attainment, as the OV for individuals with less than secondary education is lower than the OV for individuals with college for all the pathways into retirement (see figures 11.8 and 11.9). The difference disappears for individuals closer to the normal retirement age for males, and at ages sixty and older for females. In contrast, there are no differences in the average OV for individuals with low and medium educational attainment. In addition, the educational gradient is largest for unemployment benefits, implying that the gains from waiting are larger for educated individuals. This is not surprising since these individuals are less affected by incentives at the early retirement ages (for example, minimum pension incentives as pointed in Jiménez-Martín and Sánchez-Martín [2007]).

11.3.3   Weighting the Pathways

In the previous subsections we have seen that individuals in Spain use three different pathways to leave the labor market. Moreover, although the incentives to keep working in all cases decrease with age, the magnitude differs depending on the pathway used. Ideally, we would like to know how much weight an individual gives to each of the different possibilities, and use those to compute the financial incentives that he/she faces. However, the amount of information required for such a calculation may be very high and the assumptions needed very strong.

Instead, what we do is to impute to each observation the probability that each of the pathways (DI, unemployment, or old-age benefits) is a realistic

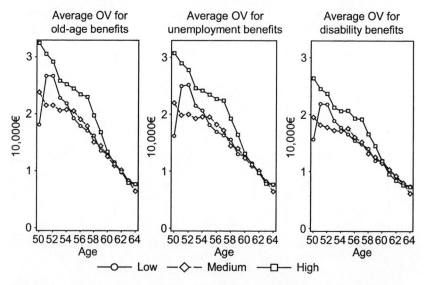

Fig. 11.9   Average OVs for different pathways by educational attainment (females)

option. These probabilities will then be used as weights in combining the paths into one option value number. We compute these probabilities using a set of exogenous characteristics of the individual. In particular, we use data from MCVL 2011 and compute for the population age fifty to sixty-four, the share that is receiving, in any given year, DI benefits, unemployment benefits, or old-age benefits. We calculate the probabilities separately by gender, year, and skill level.

These probabilities are reported in figure 11.10. We can see that the main difference between individuals with different educational attainment is related to the probability of being unemployed. Individuals with the lowest education (or skill level) are the ones with the highest probability of becoming unemployed in this age range. The administrative data also show that individuals in the highest skill level have the highest probability of being in the old-age benefits system, although the difference with respect to the other two groups is rather small. Last, the probability of being in DI is very similar for individuals in the medium- and low-skill level and slightly lower for the highest-skill group.

We then rescale these probabilities to one, and assign them to each of our individuals in our sample of analysis. We can think of this as an instrumental variable (IV) estimate of the probability, or the weight the person might assign to each of the possibilities.

The inclusive OV measure is therefore similar to the OV for unemployment benefits. This is due to two reasons. First, a large share of the population age fifty to sixty-four in Spain uses unemployment insurance as a

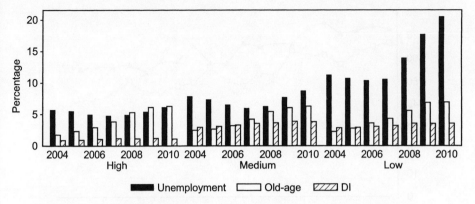

Fig. 11.10   Pathway probabilities by year and skill level for men ages fifty to sixty-four

Source: Authors' own elaboration using data from the *Muestra Continua de Vidas Laborales* (Spanish Social Security administrative data; see the appendix for details).

retirement scheme and, therefore, this is the scheme that may provide the largest incentives. Second, the OV for unemployment benefits lies in between old-age retirement benefits and disability benefits.

11.3.5   Health Index and Health Quintiles

We construct a single health index using a large set of variables available in the Survey of Health, Ageing and Retirement in Europe (SHARE) similar to Poterba, Venti, and Wise (2010). We use principal component analysis with all the observations and waves available. Notice that we exclude wave 3 as it does not contain health information.

Table 11.3 shows the factor loadings of the set of variables included in our synthetic health indicator. We see that the factor loading of all the variables have the correct sign. The variables with higher factors are those that capture whether the individual has difficulties with the (instrumental or basic) activities of daily living and self-assessed health. On the other hand, illnesses diagnosed by a doctor and health care use have a much lower factor loading.

We transform the health index so higher values are associated with better health. Then, we estimate for each individual in the SHARE sample his/her percentile in the health distribution. Figure 11.11 plots the mean percentile of the health index by age and gender. It shows that, as expected, there is a decreasing age trend in the average percentile of health index. In addition, at any age the average percentile among females is lower than the average percentile among males.

There are important differences in the characteristics of individuals in the different health quintiles. Table 11.4 shows descriptive statistics by health quintile for all individuals age fifty to sixty-four in our constructed database (see results section and appendix for data description). The group of indi-

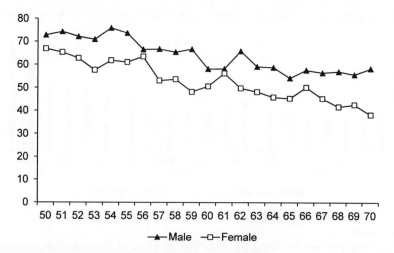

Fig. 11.11   Mean percentile of health index by age and gender

Source: We have used the entire Spanish SHARE sample from waves 1, 2, and 4 to calculate the health index and percentiles.

Table 11.4   Descriptives by health quintiles

	Health quintile				
	1st (worst health)	2nd	3rd	4th	5th (best health)
Male	0.281	0.369	0.425	0.512	0.570
Age	58.6	58.2	57.3	56.8	56.4
Less high school	0.666	0.557	0.427	0.372	0.361
High school	0.291	0.377	0.464	0.458	0.472
College	0.042	0.066	0.109	0.170	0.167
Employed	0.189	0.337	0.450	0.586	0.639
Unemployed	0.049	0.069	0.064	0.079	0.069
Retired	0.401	0.376	0.374	0.253	0.155
Disabled	0.187	0.059	0.046	0.011	0.012
OV inclusive	17,444	17,025	17,911	18,442	18,372

Note: The sample used to estimate shares of individuals in unemployment, retirement, or disability is smaller as it was not always possible to identify the exit route for those individuals who stopped working between SHARE waves.

viduals in worst health is characterized by having the largest share of older females with at most a primary education. In addition, the share of employed individuals is lower than in the other quintiles, while the share of disabled is much larger. It is worth noticing that while almost 20 percent of the individuals in the lowest health quintile claim to be receiving disability benefits, less than 6 percent of those in the second health quintile are on DI. There are not large differences in the average value of the inclusive OV, and they can be due to age differences.

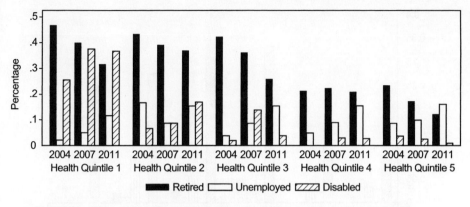

Fig. 11.12   Percentage of individuals in each social security program by health quintile (men age fifty-five to sixty-four)
Source: Authors' own elaboration using data from SHARE.

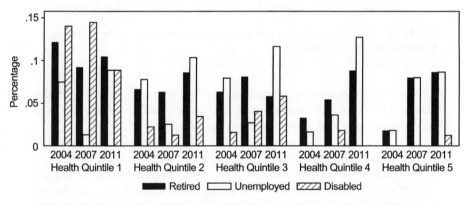

Fig. 11.13   Percentage of individuals in each social security program by health quintile (women age fifty-five to sixty-four)
Source: Authors' own elaboration using data from SHARE.

Figures 11.12 and 11.13 present the percentage of individuals in each social security program by health quintile for men and women ages fifty-five to sixty-four, respectively. As the results in table 11.4 showed, individuals in the worst health quintile are more likely to be disabled. However, figures 11.12 and 11.13 also show that the percentage of individuals in disability has increased for the other health quintiles in 2011, presumably as a result of the economics crisis. This is particularly important for women and for the second and third health quintiles.

Following with this evidence, figure 11.14 plots the percentage of individuals age fifty to sixty-four in DI for each health quintile and education level. Again, we observe that participation in DI is highly concentrated among

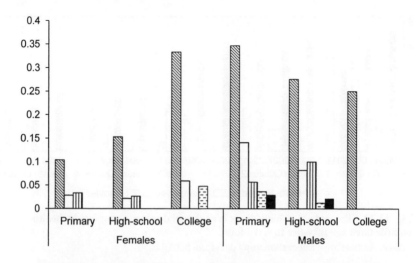

□Quintile 1 (worst)   □Quintile 2   □Quintile 3   □Quintile 4   ■Quintile 5 (best)

Fig. 11.14   The DI participation rate for men and women at ages fifty to sixty-four by health quintile and education
Source: Authors' own elaboration using data from SHARE.

those who report having very bad health. In fact, the percentage of individuals in DI for health quintiles other than the worst one is very low with the exception of men with a lower educational level.

Last, figure 11.15 shows that, although employment rates are generally higher for men than for women, both genders exhibit a similar pattern of employment by health quintile with those in the best health having the highest employment rates and those in the worst health having the lowest employment rates. The only exception to this pattern is for men age sixty to sixty-four, for which the highest employment rate is reported for those in the fourth health quintile.

Overall, we see that our health index measure captures reasonably well the well-known established facts with respect to the association of health and employment rates, DI participation, as well as education. In addition, it suggests that DI benefits in Spain are concentrated among those in the worst health, providing some evidence that the program is well targeted.

11.4   Results

We use the Spanish subsample from the Survey of Health, Ageing and Retirement in Europe (SHARE) to test the effect of financial incentives and health on transitions into retirement. We select the population age fifty to sixty-four (considering retirement at sixty-five) that respond to at least two waves and use an extensive definition of retirement that also includes

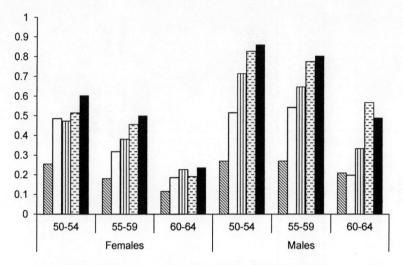

Fig. 11.15   Employment rates for men and women at ages fifty to sixty-four by health quintile

Source: Authors' own elaboration using data from SHARE.

unemployment and disability, as we have shown that these are also routes into retirement for the Spanish case. We combine retrospective employment information available in waves 2 and 4, with job episodes from SHARELIFE to construct a yearly panel from 2004 to 2010. We detail the procedure used in the appendix. We select individuals who are working at t and look at the probability that they are nonemployed in $t + 1$. Our final sample contains 1,682 observations for 451 individuals.

We use a series of probit models to estimate the probability of retirement as a function of the OV-inclusive measure, the health status measured in health quintiles, and a set of sociodemographic characteristics. Table 11.5 summarizes the results. The effect of the OV-inclusive measure always has the expected negative sign, that is, the larger the value of continuing working, the lower the probability of retirement, although it is not significant. The magnitude and significance of the effect are not affected by the specification of age (linear or age dummies), the health specification (health quintiles or continuous health index), or the inclusion of further covariates.

The sign of the effect of the rest of the variables is as expected. In particular, individuals in better health are less likely to stop working, although the difference is not statistically significant between individuals in the second lowest health quintile and individuals in the lowest quintile (omitted group). We see that individuals in all the other groups are at least 5.8 percentage points less likely to retire compared to individuals in poorest health.

As it has been found in many studies for the Spanish case (see, for ex-

Table 11.5 Effect of inclusive OV on retirement

	Specification							
	(1)	(2)	(3)	(4)	(5)	(6)	(7)	(8)
OV inclusive	−0.020	−0.008	−0.018	−0.005	−0.023	−0.011	−0.021	−0.009
	(0.017)	(0.015)	(0.020)	(0.017)	(0.017)	(0.016)	(0.020)	(0.018)
	[−0.014]	[−0.006]	[−0.012]	[−0.004]	[−0.016]	[−0.008]	[−0.015]	[−0.006]
Health 2 (second lowest)	−0.040	−0.040	−0.046*	−0.045*				
	(0.027)	(0.026)	(0.027)	(0.026)				
Health 3	−0.063**	−0.062*	−0.059**	−0.058**				
	(0.026)	(0.025)	(0.027)	(0.026)				
Health 4	−0.102***	−0.096***	−0.101***	−0.094***				
	(0.024)	(0.024)	(0.025)	(0.025)				
Health 5	−0.085***	−0.079***	−0.085***	−0.078***				
	(0.025)	(0.025)	(0.026)	(0.026)				
Health index					−0.001***	−0.001***	−0.001***	0.001***
					(<0.001)	(<0.001)	(<0.001)	(<0.001)
Age (linear)	0.010***		0.010***		0.010***		0.010***	
	(0.003)		(0.003)		(0.003)		(0.004)	

Age dummies	X	X	X	X
Male	0.008	0.008	0.009	0.009
	(0.017)	(0.016)	(0.017)	(0.017)
Married	0.018	0.019	0.018	0.019
	(0.017)	(0.021)	(0.021)	(0.021)
Educ.: High school	−0.011	−0.011	−0.010	−0.009
	(0.018)	(0.017)	(0.018)	(0.018)
Educ.: College	−0.041*	−0.045**	−0.039*	−0.043**
	(0.022)	(0.021)	(0.022)	(0.021)
No. Observations	1,682	1,633	1,682	1,633
Mean ret. rate	0.108	0.109	0.108	0.109
Mean of OV	18,309	18,256	18,309	18,256
Std. dev. OV	6,982	6,989	6,982	6,989

Note: Coefficients are average marginal effects of a 10,000-unit change in OV from probit models. Standard errors are shown in parentheses. The effect of one standard deviation change in OV is shown in brackets (this is estimated as the effect of increasing inclusive OV from the current value −0.5 std. dev. to the current value +0.5 std. dev.).

***Significant at the 1 percent level.

**Significant at the 5 percent level.

*Significant at the 10 percent level.

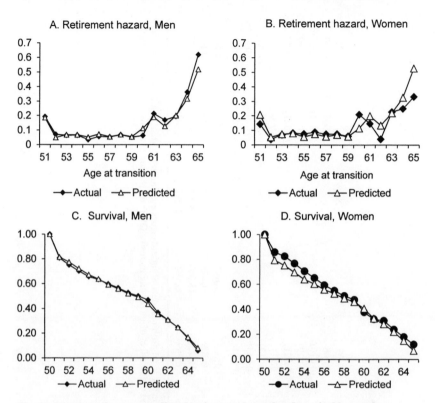

Fig. 11.16   **Actual versus predicted retirement hazard and survival by gender**

ample, Jiménez-Martín and Sánchez-Martín 2007), the hazard of retirement is lower for individuals with at least a high school education compared to individuals with lower educational attainment. Results show that individuals with a high school degree are around 1 percentage point less likely to retire compared to individuals with a primary education at most, although these differences are not statistically significant. Last, individuals with college are around 4 percentage points less likely to retire compared to individuals with less than high school education.

Figure 11.16 shows actual versus predicted retirement rates by age for both men (panel A) and women (panel B) and predicted survival rates for men (panel C) and women (panel D). The figures are based on estimates from specification (4) in table 11.5. The predicted hazard and survival curve rate are closer to the actual ones for males compared to females. This is not surprising because we have fewer observations for females, so the observed behavior is much more noisy. For example, only thirty-five women in our sample workers are at least sixty-three years of age.

Table 11.6 shows similar results where OV-inclusive has been substituted by the percent gain in utility units from delaying retirement, that is, the utility

Table 11.6   **Effect of percent gain in inclusive OV on retirement**

	Specification			
	(1)	(2)	(3)	(4)
Percent gain in OV	−0.044	−0.042	−0.033	−0.036
	(0.046)	(0.038)	(0.054)	(0.046)
Linear age	X		X	
Age dummies		X		X
Health quintiles	X	X	X	X
Other Xs			X	X
No. of observations	1,682	1,682	1,633	1,633
Mean ret. rate	0.108	0.108	0.109	0.109
Mean of % gain in OV	0.812	0.812	0.804	0.804
Std. dev. of % gain in OV	0.342	0.342	0.338	0.338

Notes: Models are the same as models 1–4 in table 11.5. Coefficients are average marginal effects. Standard errors are shown in parentheses.

gain from waiting to retire at the optimal date scaled by the utility available by retiring today. We have computed this measure as follows:

$$\%\text{Gain} = P_{\text{DI}} * \%\text{Gain}_{\text{DI}} + P_{\text{UI}} * \%\text{Gain}_{\text{UI}} + P_{\text{OA}} * \%\text{Gain}_{\text{OA}}.$$

The results are similar to those shown before. They are robust to the age specification and the inclusion of further controls.

As discussed above, there are large differences in the characteristics of individuals in the different health quintiles. In addition, we have seen that those in the best health are less likely to retire. Figure 11.17 shows the predicted hazard rate for each health quintile by gender. Hazard rates are constructed using estimates from specification (3) shown in table 11.5 that includes age linearly. The differences in predicted hazard rates between health quintiles are larger for males compared to females. Males in the two lowest health quintiles have a lower probability of retirement at any age compared to males in the highest two health quintiles. Males in the second-lowest quintile have the same hazard of retirement as those in worst health until age fifty-nine, but the hazard of retirement in the lowest quintile becomes higher compared to all the other health quintiles after age sixty.

Differences in health status may not only explain differences in the hazard of retirement but, in addition, individuals may react differently to changes in the financial incentives depending on their health status. It is not possible to get a priori any theoretical predictions as the health level may be an important determinant of several of the parameters that enter in the OV, as future string of income, the marginal disutility of labor, change in preferences, or the adjustment of the survival probabilities (Erdogan-Ciftci, Van Doorslaer, and Lopez Nicolas 2011).

In order to test this hypothesis, we further estimate the previous models

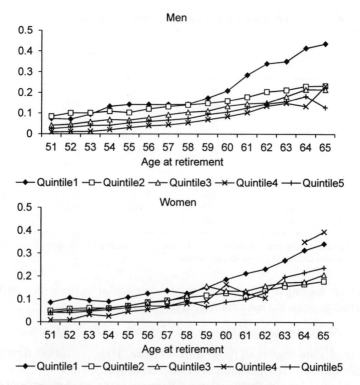

Fig. 11.17   Predicted hazard rate by health quintile and gender

separately for each of the five quintiles. We show only models that include a linear age specification, as the small number of observations in each of the subsamples prevents us from including age dummies. However, we would expect results not to be sensitive to this choice based on previous results (as shown in table 11.5). Table 11.7 shows results when the inclusive OV is included and table 11.8 when the percent gain is included.

In general, we see that the magnitude of the effect is robust to the inclusion of further controls. The differences by health quintile reveal an interesting pattern. We find that only individuals in the lowest health quintile respond to financial incentives. These results suggest that an increase of 10,000 units decreases the probability of retirement by 12 percentage points among individuals in the lowest health quintile, while an increase of one standard deviation increase in the OV-inclusive measure decreases the probability of retirement by about 8.5 percentage points.

We further explore the relationship between the inclusive OV and health, estimating the same model as the one shown in table 11.7 but including interactions between the inclusive OV and the health index. The marginal effects are shown in table 11.9. The conclusion one would draw from these

Table 11.7   **Effect of inclusive OV on retirement by health quintile**

	No. of obs.	Mean ret. rate	Mean of OV	Std. dev. of OV	Specification (1)	Specification (3)
OV: Lowest quintile (worst health)	337	0.184	16,604	6,878	−0.122*** (0.044) [−0.084]	−0.129*** (0.048) [−0.090]
OV: 2nd quintile	339	0.121	18,512	6,987	0.049 (0.036) [0.034]	0.039 (0.042) [0.028]
OV: 3rd quintile	334	0.102	18,358	6,749	−0.044 (0.044) [−0.030]	−0.024 (0.052) [−0.016]
OV: 4th quintile	342	0.056	19,916	7,126	0.002 (0.031) [0.002]	0.023 (0.033) [0.016]
OV: Highest quintile (best health)	330	0.076	18,128	6,794	0.005 (0.035) [0.003]	−0.002 (0.038) [−0.001]
Linear age					X	X
Other Xs						X

Notes: Models are the same as models 1 and 3 in table 11.5, but are estimated separately by health quintile; each coefficient in the table is from a different regression. Coefficients are average marginal effects of a 10,000-unit change in OV from probit models. Standard errors are shown in parentheses. The effect of one standard deviation change in OV is shown in brackets (this is estimated effect as the effect of increasing inclusive OV from the current value −0.5 std. dev. to the current value +0.5 std. dev.).

***Significant at the 1 percent level.
**Significant at the 5 percent level.
*Significant at the 10 percent level.

results is that there are no differences in the effects of the OV-inclusive for individuals with different values of the health index. However, the small magnitude and significance of the interaction shown in table 11.9 is due to the fact that only individuals in the lowest health quintile are affected by changes in the OV-inclusive, as shown in tables 11.7 and 11.8.

We have argued that there are some differences in the hazard rates by educational attainment. Figure 11.18 shows the predicted hazard rate for each of the educational groups by gender. Hazard rates are constructed using estimates from specification (3) shown in table 11.5 that includes age linearly. The results show that less-educated males are more likely to retire after the age of sixty (by the time the retirement program becomes available), while those with secondary education have the highest hazard rate at lower ages (by the time the disability program and the unemployment program are the only options). An educational gradient appears among females older than fifty-five and the differences in hazard rates widen with age.

Table 11.8 **Effect of percent gain on retirement by health quintile**

	No. of obs.	Mean ret. rate	Mean of % OV	Std. dev. of % OV	Specification (1)	Specification (3)
OV: Lowest quintile (worst health)	337	0.184	0.704	0.307	−0.334** (0.135)	−0.393*** (0.144)
OV: 2nd quintile	339	0.121	0.819	0.327	0.305 (0.513)	0.078 (0.115)
OV: 3rd quintile	334	0.102	0.813	0.366	0.033 (0.103)	0.059 (0.135)
OV: 4th quintile	342	0.056	0.894	0.351	−0.036 (0.086)	0.001 (0.106)
OV: Highest quintile (best health)	330	0.076	0.827	0.331	−0.007 (0.088)	0.036 (0.104)
Linear age					X	X
Other Xs						X

Notes: Models are the same as models 1 and 3 in table 11.6, but are estimated separately by health quintile; each coefficient in the table is from a different regression. Coefficients are marginal effects. Standard errors are shown in parentheses.

***Significant at the 1 percent level.
**Significant at the 5 percent level.
*Significant at the 10 percent level.

Table 11.9 **Effect of inclusive OV on retirement with health index interaction**

	Specification (1)	(2)	(3)	(4)
OV inclusive	−0.055 (0.035)	−0.024 (0.032)	−0.059 (0.036)	−0.026 (0.033)
Health index	−0.002*** (0.001)	−0.002** (0.001)	−0.002*** (0.001)	−0.002** (0.001)
OV*health index	<0.001 (<0.001)	<0.001 (<0.001)	<0.001 (<0.001)	<0.001 (<0.001)
Linear age	X		X	
Age dummies		X		X
Other Xs			X	X
Number of observations	1,682	1,682	1,633	1,633

Note: Coefficients are average marginal effects of a 10,000-unit change in OV from probit models. Standard errors are shown in parentheses. The effect of one standard deviation change in OV is shown in brackets (this is estimated as the effect of increasing inclusive OV from the current value −0.5 std. dev. to the current value +0.5 std. dev.).

***Significant at the 1 percent level.
**Significant at the 5 percent level.
*Significant at the 10 percent level.

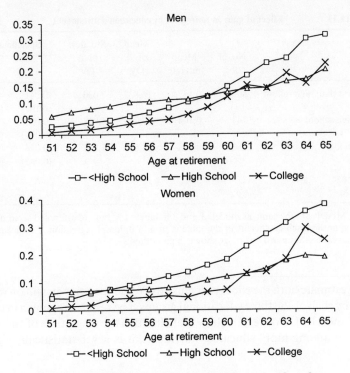

Fig. 11.18   Predicted hazard rate by educational attainment and gender

Table 11.10   Effect of inclusive OV on retirement by education group

	No. of obs.	Mean ret. rate	Mean of OV	Std. dev. of OV	Specification (1)	Specification (3)
OV: Less than high school	600	0.137	16,837	7,030	0.016 (0.035) [0.011]	0.008 (0.034) [0.066]
OV: High school	747	0.104	17,719	6,028	−0.017 (0.029) [−0.010]	−0.024 (0.030) [−0.014]
OV: College	286	0.063	22,639	7,511	−0.043 (0.033) [−0.033]	−0.050 (0.035) [−0.038]
Linear age					X	X
Other Xs						X

Note: Models are the same as models 1 and 3 in table 11.5, but are estimated separately by education group; each coefficient in the table is from different regression. Coefficients are average marginal effects of a 10,000-unit change in OV from probit models. Standard errors are shown in parentheses. The effect of one standard deviation change in OV is shown in brackets (this is estimated as the effect of increasing inclusive OV from the current value −0.5 std. dev. to the current value +0.5 std. dev.).

Table 11.11   **Effect of gain on retirement by educational attainment**

	No. of obs.	Mean ret. rate	Mean of % OV	Std. dev. of % OV	Specification (1)	Specification (3)
OV: Less than high school	600	0.137	16,837	7,030	−0.041	−0.016
					(0.101)	(0.096)
OV: High school	747	0.104	17,719	6,028	0.023	−0.019
					(0.079)	(0.087)
OV: College	286	0.063	22,639	7,511	−0.096	−0.090
					(0.082)	(0.095)
Linear age					X	X
Other Xs						X

Notes: Models are the same as models 1 and 3 in table 11.6, but are estimated separately by health quintile; each coefficient in the table is from a different regression. Coefficients are marginal effects. Standard errors are shown in parentheses.

We estimate both the effect of inclusive OV and the percent gain on retirement by each of the three educational groups. The results are shown in tables 11.10 and 11.11. The results show that although the magnitude of the effect is larger among more educated individuals, it is never statistically significant.

11.5   Conclusions

This chapter investigates the role of financial incentives and health in the retirement behavior of Spanish workers. We shed light on the different pathways that individuals choose to leave the labor market, and incorporate the incentives from the different systems (disability insurance, old-age retirement scheme, and unemployment insurance) in one single measure.

We use data from the Spanish sample of the Survey of Health and Retirement to model transitions out of employment. In general, although we find the expected sign in incentive variables, they are not significant. This is likely due to insufficient variability of simulated incentive indicators caused by the impossibility to construct individual wage profiles. Still, we are able to offer support for some interesting conclusions. For example, we show that the effects of the incentives from the different social security schemes on employment behavior seem to be concentrated among individuals in the worst health, while all the other groups seem not to be affected. In addition, health status plays an important role in explaining transitions out of employment as individuals in the worst health quintile are twice as likely to retire compared to individuals in the best health quintile.

In order to better understand the incentives provided by the different schemes, we provide a set of simulations in which we assume that individuals can only access one of the social security programs. The simulations show that there are small differences in the number of years a person would work if faced by different types of programs. This should not cause any surprise because there are small differences in the level of incentives provided by the various programs available to individuals in Spain.

Appendix

The Database *Muestra Continua de Vidas Laborales* (Continuous Sample of Working Lives)

The Continuous Sample of Working Lives (*Muestra Continua de Vidas Laborales* [MCVL]) is a microeconomic data set based on administrative records provided by the Spanish Social Security Administration. Each wave contains a random sample of 4 percent of all the individuals who had contributed to the social security system (either by working or being on an unemployment scheme) or had received a contributory pension during at least one day in the year the sample is selected. For these workers, the database contains the complete labor market and contributory benefits history since they entered the labor market for the first time.

There is information available on the entire employment, unemployment, and pension history of the workers, including the exact duration of employment, unemployment, and disability or retirement pension spells, and for each spell, several variables that describe the characteristics of the job or the unemployment/pension benefits. There is also some information on personal characteristics such as age, gender, nationality, and level of education.

Construction of Yearly Panel Using SHARE

We first use waves 1, 2, and 4 of SHARE. We identify all transitions between waves using retrospective information about all employment and unemployment spells, as well as transitions into retirement available in waves 2 and 4. We complement these transitions with information from SHARELIFE. In order to impute the date of interview (relevant for transitions and age at wave) we assume that the individual is interviewed in the same month as in the last wave in which he/she is observed.

We estimate health percentiles using information from waves 1, 2, and 4 and compute individual average annual growth rates to impute changes in health between waves. Education, date of birth, and gender do not vary over time and, therefore, information from existing waves can be used.

References

Boldrin, M., P. García- Gómez, and S. Jiménez- Martín. 2010. "Social Security Incentives, Exit from the Workforce and Entry of the Young." In *Social Security Programs and Retirement around the World: The Relationship to Youth Employment,* edited by Jonathan Gruber and David A Wise. Chicago: University of Chicago Press.

Boldrin, M., and S. Jiménez- Martín. 2007. "Evaluating Spanish Pension Expenditure under Alternative Reform Scenarios." In *Social Security Programs and Retirement around the World: Fiscal Implications for Reform,* edited by Jonathan Gruber and David A Wise. Chicago: University of Chicago Press.

Boldrin, M., S. Jiménez-Martín, and F. Peracchi. 1999. "Social Security and Retirement in Spain." In *Social Security and Retirement around the World,* edited by J. Gruber and D. Wise. Chicago: University of Chicago Press.

Börsch-Supan, A. 2000. "Incentive Effects of Social Security on Labor Force Participation: Evidence in Germany and across Europe." *Journal of Public Economics* 78 (1–2): 25–49.

Coile, C., and J. Gruber. 2007. "Future Social Security Entitlements and the Retirement Decision." *Review of Economics and Statistics* 89 (2): 234–46.

Diamond, P. A. 2007. "Top-Heavy Load: Trouble Ahead for Social Security Systems." *CESifo Forum* 8 (3): 28–36.

Dorn, D., and A. Souza-Poza. 2010. "'Voluntary' and 'Involuntary' Early Retirement: An International Analysis." *Applied Economics* 42 (4): 427–38.

Erdogan-Ciftci, E., E. Van Doorslaer, and A. Lopez Nicolas. 2011. "Does Declining Health Affect the Responsiveness of Retirement Decisions to Financial Incentives?" Netspar Discussion Paper no. 01/2011–005, Network for Studies on Pensions, Aging and Retirement.

Eurostat. 2013. "Towards a 'Baby Recession' in Europe?" *Statistics in Focus* 13. Brussels.

Fenge, R., and P. Pestieau. 2005. "Social Security and Early Retirement." Cambridge, MA: MIT Press.

García-Gómez, P., S. Jiménez-Martín, and J. Vall Castelló. 2012. "Health, Disability and Pathways into Retirement in Spain." In *Social Security and Retirement around the World: Historical Trends in Mortality and Health, Employment, Disability Insurance Participation and Reforms,* edited by D. Wise, 127–74. Chicago: University of Chicago Press.

García-Pérez, J. I., S. Jiménez-Martín, and A. Sánchez-Martín. 2013. "Retirement Incentives, Individual Heterogeneity and Labour Transitions of Employed and Unemployed Workers." *Labour Economics* 20:106–20.

Gruber, J., and D. A. Wise, eds. 1999. *Social Security and Retirement around the World.* Chicago: University of Chicago Press.

———. 2004. *Social Security Programs and Retirement around the World: Micro-Estimation.* Chicago: University of Chicago Press.

Hagan, R., A. M. Jones, and N. Rice. 2009. "Health and Retirement in Europe." *International Journal of Environmental Research and Public Health* 6:2676–95.

Instituto Nacional de Estadística (INE). 2010. *Tablas de Mortalidad de la Población Española.* Madrid.

Jiménez-Martín, S. 2006. "Evaluating the Labor Supply Effects of Alternative Reforms of the Spanish Pension System." *Moneda y Crédito* 222:271–312.

Jiménez-Martín, S., and A. R. Sánchez-Martín. 2007. "An Evaluation of the Life Cycle Effects of Minimum Pensions on Retirement Behavior." *Journal of Applied Econometrics* 22 (5): 923–50.

Jimenez-Martin, S., and J. Vall Castelló. 2013. "Business Cycle and Spillover Effects on Pre-Retirement Behavior in Spain." *Journal of European Labor Studies* 2:8.

Kerkhofs, M., M. Lindeboom, and J. Theeuwes. 1999. "Retirement, Financial Incentives and Health." *Labour Economics* 6 (2): 203–27.

Lutz, W., W. Sanderson, and S. Scherbov. 2008. "The Coming Acceleration of Global Population Ageing." *Nature* 451 (7179): 716–19.

Organisation for Economic Co-operation and Development (OECD). 2001. "Economic Survey-Spain." Paris, OECD.

Poterba, J. M., S. F. Venti, and D. A. Wise. 2010. "Family Status Transitions, Latent Health, and the Post-Retirement Evolution of Assets." NBER Working Paper no. 15789, Cambridge, MA.

Samwick, Andrew. 1998. "New Evidence on Pensions, Social Security, and the Timing of Retirement." *Journal of Public Economics* 70:207–36.

Vall Castelló, J. 2012. "Promoting Employment of Disabled Women in Spain: Evaluating a Policy." *Labour Economics* 19 (1): 82–91.

Wise, D., ed. 2012. *Social Security Programs and Retirement around the World: Historical Trends in Mortality and Health, Employment, and Disability Insurance Participation and Reforms.* Chicago: University of Chicago Press.

Option Value of Work, Health Status, and Retirement Decisions in Japan
Evidence from the Japanese Study on Aging and Retirement (JSTAR)

Satoshi Shimizutani, Takashi Oshio, and Mayu Fujii

12.1 Introduction

This study examines retirement decisions and their associations with health status in Japan, using the option value (OV) model proposed by Stock and Wise (1990a, 1990b). This model focuses on an individual's option value of continuing to work; that is, a utility gain achieved by keeping the option to retire in the future.

To our knowledge, only a few studies use the OV model to empirically examine retirement decisions in Japan. These studies include Oshio and Oishi (2004), which used cross-sectional data with limited information on an individual's background. Oshio, Shimizutani, and Oishi (2010) employed macrolevel data to explore the effect of OV on the labor force participation rate; they show that OV significantly correlates with labor force participation among the elderly.

More recently, Oshio, Oishi, and Shimizutani (2011)—whose study is closely related to that of Oshio, Shimizutani, and Oishi (2010)—used macrolevel data to construct several incentive measures vis-à-vis retirement, including OV. This study shows that since 1985, the labor force participa-

Satoshi Shimizutani is a visiting research fellow at the Institute for International Policy Studies. Takashi Oshio is a professor at the Institute of Economic Research, Hitotsubashi University. Mayu Fujii is an assistant professor at the Hokkaido University of Education.

This chapter was prepared for the Madrid meeting (September 2013) of the NBER International Social Security Project (ISS), Phase VII. The intermediate materials were presented at the Munich meeting (January 2012), Rome meeting (May 2012), and the Paris meeting (February 2013). Any remaining errors are our own. This study utilized microlevel data collected through the Japanese Study on Aging and Retirement (JSTAR), which was conducted by the Research Institute of Economy, Trade, and Industry (RIETI) and Hitotsubashi University in 2007 and 2009. For acknowledgments, sources of research support, and disclosure of the authors' material financial relationships, if any, please see http://www.nber.org/chapters/c13330.ack.

tion rate of the elderly in Japan has been significantly sensitive to both OV and social security reforms—the latter of which featured reduced benefits generosity and thus significantly encouraged the elderly to remain in the labor force longer.

The current study presents further evidence concerning retirement decisions in Japan within the framework of the OV model; it makes specific reference to Japan's disability pension program and individual health status.[1] It employs microlevel data collected through the Japanese Study on Aging and Retirement (JSTAR) (Ichimura, Hashimoto, and Shimizutani 2009), which is the Japanese version of the US Health and Retirement Study (HRS), the English Longitudinal Survey on Ageing (ELSA), and the Survey on Health, Ageing and Retirement in Europe (SHARE). The JSTAR study has a longitudinal design and features a rich variety of variables that touch on health status.

We calculate OV for each individual working in 2007, with the disability pension program considered a potential pathway from work to retirement; we also examine the effect of OV on retirement decisions in 2009, while controlling for individual health status. We find that OV negatively and significantly correlates with the probability of retirement, and that the individual's health does not confound the correlation.

The remainder of this chapter is organized as follows. Section 12.2 describes the institutional background. Section 12.3 explains, in detail, the study's empirical approach. Section 12.4 presents the empirical results, and section 12.5 assesses the fit of the model. Section 12.6 shows the results of the counterfactual simulation. Section 12.7 provides concluding remarks.

12.2   Background[2]

12.2.1   History of Japan's Social Security and Disability Program

This section provides an overview, from a historical perspective, of Japan's disability program and other related reforms to the social security program. We describe the "disability pension program" below, which is often referred to as a disability insurance (DI) program in other countries. The disability pension program is part of Japan's public pension program, and all revisions to the disability program have been linked to those made to core pension programs. Among several programs that assist the disabled, the disability pension program plays the most important role in terms of income compensation.

---

1. Ichimura and Shimizutani (2012) also employed similar JSTAR data (i.e., from the first and second waves) to explore retirement behavior in Japan. They grouped a variety of variables into health, family, and socioeconomic factors and explored the effect of each factor in the first wave (2007) on the probability of retirement and hours worked in the second wave (2009).
2. This section updates the discussion of Oshio and Shimizutani (2012).

Table 12.1   **Development of disability pension programs in Japan**

	National Pension Insurance (self-employed, agricultural, forestry and fishery sector)		Employee Pension Insurance (private firm employees)
	Disability Pension (with contribution)	Disability Welfare Pension (without contribution)	
1944			Grade 1 and Grade 2 (including mental diseases)
1954			Grade 3 was added
1959	Grade 1 and Grade 2	Grade 1	
1964–65	Covered mental diseases		
1974		Grade 2 was added	
1986–	Merged to Disability Basic Pension		Disability Basic Pension + Wage-proportional benefit

Source: Oshio and Shimizutani (2012).

The Japanese public pension program consists of three programs: Employees' Pension Insurance ([EPI]; *Kosei Nenkin*), whose pensioners are private employees; National Pension Insurance ([NPI]; *Kokumin Nenkin*), whose pensioners are self-employed or agriculture, forestry, or fishery cooperative employees; and Mutual Aid Insurance ([MAI]; *Kyosai Nenkin*), which covers employees in the public sector and in private schools. In terms of their numbers of pensioners, each of EPI and NPI contribute to the total by slightly less than half, and MAI occupies the remaining small portion. An overview of Japan's social security programs is provided in the appendix.

Below, we focus on the revisions made over time to Japan's disability pension program, while focusing on EPI and NPI (table 12.1). The disability pension program was included as part of the EPI program when it was launched in 1944.[3] Once disabled individuals were deemed to qualify for the program—based on functional ability to perform activities of daily living, rather than on loss of earning ability—they were rated through the use of two grades. Grade 1 refers to a condition that causes a person to be unable to perform activities of daily living (e.g., severe disability affecting both hands, or complete blindness). Grade 2 refers to a condition that causes a person to face very severe limitations in performing activities of daily living (any severe disability affecting either hand). The program at that time, from the very beginning, insured persons with mental disorders via EPI. The 1954 revision introduced Grade 3 to cover more disabled persons with conditions less severe than those in Grade 2.[4]

3. A brief review of development of the disability pension program is provided by the Ministry of Health, Labour, and Welfare (2009).
4. Before 1954, EPI had in the old-age pension program only a single layer of wage-proportional benefit. While EPI was reconstructed in 1954 so as to have a double-tier structure, the disability pension program had a single-tier structure until the 1985 revision.

Following the establishment of the EPI program the disability pension program was expanded, and there have been four major revisions during its development. The first revision was accompanied by the introduction of NPI in 1961. The NPI launched the universal pension system into the Japanese public pension program, substantially expanding the coverage of the disability pension program to more groups than just employees in the private sector. Unlike EPI, NPI did not cover mental disease at the time of its introduction. The NPI had two types of disability programs: one for recipients with premium contributions (Disability Pension Program [*Shogai Nenkin*]) and another for those without (Disability Welfare Pension Program [*Shogai Fukushi Nenkin*]). Eligibility to receive disability pension benefits is assessed at the time of the first doctor visit to survey the extent of the condition that rendered the person disabled; thus, those who had that first doctor visit before reaching the age of twenty or before 1961 were not insured by the Disability Pension Program under NPI. Instead, they were covered by the Disability Welfare Pension Program, which was financed by the government. Eligibility for this latter program was means tested, and its benefit amount was lower than that of the former program.

The second revision, in 1974, called for expanding coverage for mental disease. The NPI began to insure mental disorders in 1964 and mental deficiency in 1965, though coverage for mental disability was very limited. Whereas those who paid premiums were eligible to receive disability pension benefits once they satisfied Grade 1 or 2 criteria (NPI had no Grade 3), the disability welfare program insured the disabled only if they satisfied Grade 1 criteria. In 1974, the disability welfare program also began to cover those who satisfied Grade 2 criteria.

The third revision was implemented in 1985 (effective from 1986) as part of the major revision to core public pension programs, which harmonized all the public pension programs into an integrated form. For the first time, it reduced the benefit multiplier and flat-rate benefit in the old-age pension program, and sought to restrain increases in total pension benefits. Three revisions were implemented with respect to the disability pension programs.

First, a double-tier structure was introduced, wherein (a) the flat rate Disability Basic Pension" (*Shogai Kiso Nenkin*) benefit was in the first tier and replaced the Disability Welfare Pension funded by the government and by the premium contributions of NPI pensioners, and (b) the wage proportional Disability Employees' Pension (*Shogai Kosei Nenkin*) program was the second tier. The NPI pensioners, either with or without premium contributions, were entitled to receive (a). Second, both the disabled without premium contributions and those with premium contributions were entitled to receive the same Disability Basic Pension benefit, but the amount doubled for the former group. Third, the grading of disability conditions was harmonized across all programs. Nonetheless, the Disability Basic Pension covered only Grade 1 or 2 disabled individuals. The EPI additionally covered the disabled in Grade 3, and provided "disability compensation" for a disabled pensioner with a disability less severe than Grade 3, if that disability condition were fixed.[5]

Fourth, and finally, the government allowed Disability Basic Pension recipients age sixty-five years or older to additionally receive EPI benefits, if they had made any EPI contributions since 2006.

12.2.2   Current Scheme

Under the current scheme, a person who visited a doctor for the first time to consult about the cause of disability when he/she was under the age of twenty or when he/she was an NPI pensioner is entitled to receive the Disability Basic Pension benefit. There is no limitation in terms of age for receiving disability pension benefits. The formulas used to calculate the benefit are as follows:

Grade 1 = basic pension benefit × 1.25 + additional benefit for dependent children
Grade 2 = basic pension benefit + additional benefit for dependent children

The amount of the basic pension benefit is JPY 786,500 per year; that of the additional child benefit is JPY 226,300 for each of the first and second children, and JPY 75,400 for each for the third and subsequent children.

In addition to the Disability Basic Pension, any person who first consulted a doctor to identify the cause of disability when he/she was an EPI pensioner is entitled to receive a wage-proportional Disability Employees' Pension benefit or a Disability Mutual Aid Pension benefit (for the MAI recipients). The formulas used to calculate the second-tier benefit are as follows:

Grade 1 = wage-proportional benefit × 1.25 + additional benefit for a spouse
Grade 2 = wage-proportional benefit + additional benefit for a spouse
Grade 3 = max (wage-proportional benefit, JPY 589,900)

The amount of additional benefit for a spouse is JPY 226,300 per year.[6]

12.2.3   Change in the Disability Program Participation over Time

This subsection describes changes in disability program participation over time. The data source is the Annual Report of Social Security Administration (*Shakai Hoken Jigyo Nenpo*), which is published by Japan's Social

---

5. Since EPI pensioners were required to join the NPI as part of the 1985 reform, the entitlement to receive disability pension became contingent on NPI grading (Disability Basic Pension), even if the disabled person had been approved to receive disability pension benefits through the EPI or MAI programs. Additionally, the MAI program has a Grade 3.

6. Momose (2008) argues that the amount of benefits from Japan's disability employee pension (Grade 1 or 2) is larger than that of the United States or Sweden, while the amount from the disability basic pension (Grade 1) is much smaller in Japan, and that Grade 2 in Japan is one-half the standard benefit in the United States or Sweden.

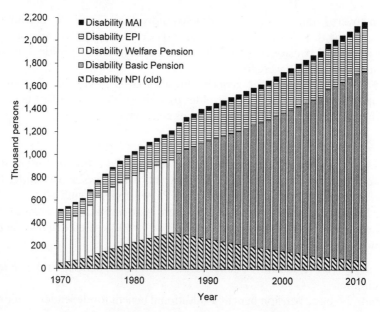

Fig. 12.1   The number of recipients of disability pension benefits

Security Agency. This report contains data on disability pension recipients, aggregated at the national level. However, it provides only the numbers of disability pension recipients by type of pension; no information on gender or age is available. Figure 12.1 reports the numbers of recipients who received disability pension benefits between 1970 and 2011.[7] The numbers of recipients have increased fourfold over these four decades, from 0.5 million in 1970 to 2.2 million in 2011. The proportions of NPI, EPI, and MAI pensioners have been about 80.0 percent, 17.6 percent, and 2.3 percent, respectively, in 2011.[8]

Figure 12.2 shows trends in the rate of disability pension receipt in comparison to those of the employment rate, during 1970 and 2011. Because of data unavailability, we make the strong assumption that the ratio of recipients age fifty to sixty-four to all total recipients in 2009—52.5 percent and 28.6 percent for disability EPI and NPI, respectively—has been the same over time; we also roughly estimate the total number of disability pension

7. In Japan, the fiscal year starts in April and ends in March. The figures are measured as of the end of the fiscal year.
8. The number of MAI pensioners receiving the disability pension is not available; the number of MAI pensioners eligible to receive benefits is available through the Annual Report on Social Security Statistics (*Shakai Hoken Tokei Nenpo*), compiled by the National Institute of Population and Social Security Research. We compute the number of MAI pensioners to receive the disability pension, assuming the proportion of those who receive out of those who are eligible—both of which are available in the Annual Report of Social Security Administration—to be the same for the EPI and MAI programs.

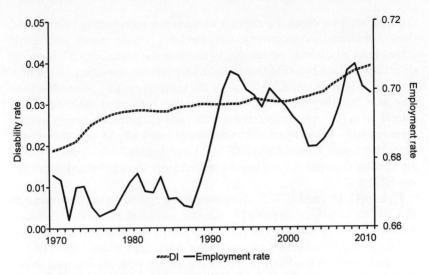

Fig. 12.2   DI and employment for those age fifty to sixty-four

recipients within this age group. As already suggested in figure 12.1, the disability pension receipt rate shows an upward trend, with some acceleration in the mid-1970s and early in the twenty-first century. More importantly, the movement of the disability pension recipient rate has been unrelated to that of the employment rate.

12.2.4   Disability Program Participation by Individual Characteristics: JSTAR

We use JSTAR data to explore the characteristics of individuals participating in the disability program. The JSTAR is a longitudinal survey that collects information on middle-aged and elderly individuals in Japan. The first wave of the survey was conducted in 2007, with a baseline sample of more than 4,200 individuals age fifty to seventy-five years who lived in five municipalities in eastern Japan. The respondents in the first wave were interviewed again in 2009; the response rate in the second wave among the respondents from the first wave was about 80 percent (i.e., an attrition rate of about 20 percent), with some variation across municipalities.

Although the JSTAR sample is not nationally representative and the sample size is not large enough to contain many disability pension recipients,[9]

9. The JSTAR project started in 2005. Its first wave was completed in five municipalities in 2007, and its second wave in seven municipalities (two new municipalities were added) in 2009. Ten municipalities (i.e., three new municipalities were added) were studied in 2011–2012. The baseline sample consists of individuals age fifty to seventy-five years. The JSTAR uses random sampling within a municipality rather than probabilistic national sampling; it places emphasis on securing a larger sample size within the same socioeconomic environment.

the data set does contain a rich set of variables representing individuals' demographic and socioeconomic characteristics, pension receipt, and health status, inter alia; hence, we are able to examine the probability of receiving disability pension by exploiting individual-level characteristics. In the first wave of JSTAR, about 1.3 percent of the sample (age fifty to seventy-five) answered that they were receiving a disability pension at the time of the interview; in the second wave that number was 1.2 percent (age fifty-two to seventy-eight). When restricted to the sample ages fifty to sixty-four, these percentages were 1.5 percent in 2007 and 1.6 percent in 2009—both of which are smaller than the percentages estimated from the aggregated data (figure 12.2).

Figures 12.3A and 12.3B illustrate the percentages of men and women age fifty-five to sixty-four, respectively, who are receiving a disability pension, by education level and year (i.e., 2007 and 2009). For both men and women and for both 2007 and 2009, we saw the general tendency that a more highly educated person is less likely to receive a disability pension. For men, however, the percentage receiving a disability pension in 2007 was much higher among those who had graduated from a two-year college/vocational school than that among high school graduates; this result may derive simply from the small sample size of men who had graduated from two-year college/vocational schools (60 of 864).

Figures 12.3C and 12.3D depict the percentages of men and women age fifty-five to sixty-four, respectively, who are receiving a disability pension, by health status and year (see subsection 12.3.3 on how the health index is computed). For both men and women, the probability of receiving DI benefits is highest among those in the lowest health quintile (those in the poorest health), while the probability is very small among the other health quintiles. This is not surprising, given that the eligibility requirement for a disability pension in Japan places emphasis on physical and mental conditions and functional limitations (Momose 2008).

In table 12.2, we present the percentage of disability pension receipt by education and health status to highlight those subpopulations in which disability pension receipt is particularly prevalent. As a general tendency, for both men and women, most recipients are concentrated within the lowest health quintile within each educational group. For example, among men the probability of disability pension receipt in 2007 of those who did not graduate from high school was 17 percent in the lowest health quintile, while it was 0–1.96 percent in the higher health quintiles. Within each health quintile, the percentage of disability pension receipt is lowest among those in the highest educational group. For instance, among men the probability of disability pension receipt in 2007 of those in the lowest health quintile was 17 percent in the lowest educational group, while it was 10 percent in the highest educational group.

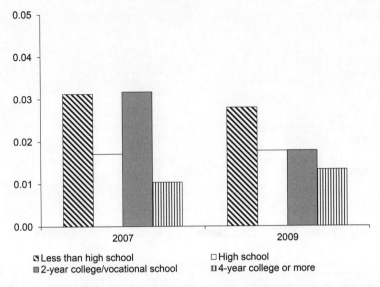

Fig. 12.3A   Probability of men age fifty-five to sixty-four in JSTAR receiving disability pension by education and year

Note: The total number of observations in 2007 and 2009 were 864 and 591, respectively. In 2007/2009, the sample sizes of those whose final educational attainment is less than high school were 218/137; high school, 399/263; two-year college/vocational school, 60/51; and four-year college, 187/140.

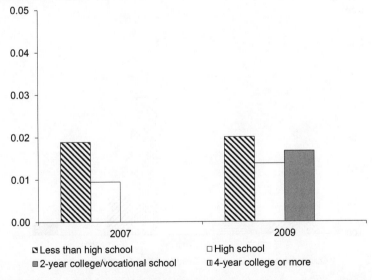

Fig. 12.3B   Probability of women age fifty-five to sixty-four in JSTAR receiving disability pension by education and year

Note: The total number of observations in 2007 and 2009 were 799 and 514, respectively. In 2007/2009, the sample sizes of those whose final educational attainment is less than high school were 202/96; high school, 409/274; two-year college/vocational school, 150/113; and four-year college, 38/31.

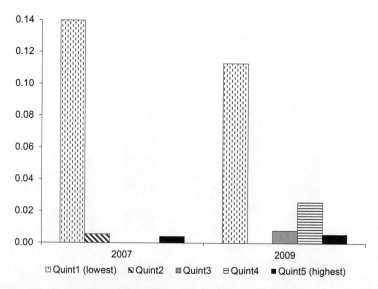

Fig. 12.3C Probability of men age fifty-five to sixty-four in JSTAR receiving disability pension by health quintile and year

Note: The total number of observations in 2007 and 2009 were 864 and 591, respectively. In 2007/2009, the sample sizes of those in the lowest health quintile were 93/62; the second health quintile, 181/117; the third health quintile, 206/125; the fourth health quintile, 154/116; and the fifth health quintile, 230/171.

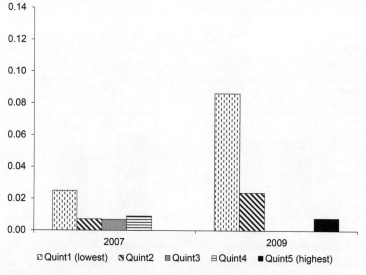

Fig. 12.3D Probability of women age fifty-five to sixty-four in JSTAR receiving disability pension by health quintile and year

Note: The total number of observations in 2007 and 2009 were 799 and 514, respectively. The sample sizes of those in the lowest health quintile were 119/58; the second health quintile, 142/84; the third health quintile, 146/91; the fourth health quintile, 223/155; and the fifth health quintile, 169/126.

Table 12.2   **Percentage of disability pension recipients: JSTAR men and women ages fifty-five to sixty-four by health quintile and education, 2007 and 2009**

	Percent receiving Health quintile				
Education	1	2	3	4	5
Year 2007					
Men					
Less than high school	17.24	0	0	0	1.96
High school	12.50	0	0	0	0
Two years college/vocational school	25.00	5.26	0	0	0
Four years college or more	10.00	0	0	0	0
Women					
Less than high school	9.09	2.04	0	0	0
High school	0	0	1.19	1.53	0
Two years college/vocational school	0	0	0	0	0
Four years college or more	0	0	0	0	0
Year 2009					
Men					
Less than high school	11.11	0	0	6.90	0
High school	14.81	0	0	2.08	0
Two years college/vocational school	0	0	6.67	0	0
Four years college or more	7.14	0	0	0	0
Women					
Less than high school	16.67	0	0	0	0
High school	2.94	4.26	0	0	1.59
Two years college/vocational school	25.00	0	0	0	0
Four years college or more	0	0	0	0	0

Note: For 2007, the total numbers of observations are 864 men and 799 women. For 2009, the total numbers of observations are 591 men and 514 women.

12.3   Empirical Approach

To examine the differences in elderly individuals' labor force participation across countries by the provisions of social security programs, we estimate an "inclusive" OV model, where it is assumed that an individual's retirement decision at age t depends on an incentive measure OV, his or her own health status, and other demographic and economic characteristics at age t. This section describes the data and sample used in the estimation, the empirical model used to estimate, and how we calculate individuals' OV figures and health status.

12.3.1   Data Source and Sample

The data we use to estimate the OV model come from the first and second waves of the JSTAR, conducted in 2007 and 2009, respectively. We restrict our sample to those who were interviewed in both waves, had answered in 2007 that they were working at all, and had provided information on their demographic, socioeconomic, and health-related characteristics in both waves. Individuals who answered in 2007 that they were working at all consisted of company executives, regular employees, part-time workers, casual or temporary workers, self-employed workers, employees on leave, and others. Our final sample consists of 1,575 individuals (996 men, 579 women) who were age fifty to seventy-five in 2007.

12.3.2   Empirical Model

We specify the empirical OV model as follows:

$$
(1)
\begin{aligned}
P(Y_{i,2009} &= 1 \mid OV_{i,2007}, Health_{i,2007}, X_{i,2007}) \\
&= \Phi(\varepsilon_i > -\beta_0 - \beta_1 OV_{i,2007} - \beta_2 Health_{i,2007} - \beta_3 X_{i,2007}),
\end{aligned}
$$

The dependent variable is an indicator that takes a value of 1 if individual i retired in 2009, and zero otherwise. We define an individual as "retired" if he/she answered that he/she was retired or doing housework. One of the main independent variables, $OV_{i,2007}$, is the OV of individual i in 2007; $Health_{i,2007}$ is another key independent variable because it represents the health status of individual i. Finally, $X_{i,2007}$ represents a vector of the remaining control variables, including age, gender, marital status (married), the existence of a working spouse, total assets, occupation, and educational attainment, all as measured in 2007.[10] In the following sections, we describe how the OV and health status are measured.

12.3.3   OV Calculations

The OV at age t is defined as:

$$
(2) \qquad OV_t = \sum_{k=1}^{K} P_k OV_{kt},
$$

where k refers to the kth pathway to retirement; P_k, the probability weight on the kth pathway, and OV_{kt}, the OV of the kth pathway at age t. Moreover, we define the OV corresponding to each pathway as:

$$
(3) \qquad OV_{kt} = E_t V_{kt}(r^*) - E_t V_{kt}(t),
$$

$$
(4) \qquad E_t V_{kt}(r) = \sum_{s=t}^{r-1} p_{s|t} \beta^{s-t} (y(s))^\gamma + \sum_{s=r}^{D} P_{s|t} \beta^{s-t} [\kappa B_{rk}(s)]^\gamma,
$$

where r^* represents the value of retirement age that maximizes $E_t V_{kt}(r)$; $p_{s|t}$ is the probability of survival at age s, given survival at age t; $y(s)$ refers to wage income at age s while working; $B_{rk}(s)$ refers to pension benefits at age

---

10. There are some missing data for each variable; this is especially true for the total assets. We impute the variable by allocating the average value of those who have attributes similar to those of the respondents.

s when retired at age *r* through the *k*th pathway; β is the discount rate; γ is the parameter of risk aversion; κ is the parameter of labor disutility; and *D* is the maximum age.

In the following sections, we consider in turn the essential components of the OV model: pathways to retirement; weights on the pathways to retirement; the measurement of health, profiles of wage, and pension income; and assumptions regarding model parameters.

Pathways to Retirement

Based on Japan's old-age pension system and its three related programs, we set up two pathways to retirement—namely, normal claiming and disability—for each of the EPI/MAI pensioners. More explicitly, for EPI/MAI pensioners, we assume:

A. Normal claiming: "Employed" to "normal claiming," which entails claiming at the normal retirement age. In this pathway, one claims wage-proportional benefits at ages sixty to sixty-five (depending on cohort) and a flat-rate benefit at age sixty-five. The benefits are reduced as per the results of the earnings test under the Zaishoku pension scheme, if one continues to work beyond the normal retirement age.[11]

B. Disability: "Employed" to "claiming disability pension benefit," which entails claiming EPI/MAI wage-proportional/flat-rate benefits at ages sixty to sixty-four.

For NPI pensioners, we assume:

A. Normal claiming: "Self-employed" to "normal claiming," which entails claiming NPI benefits at age sixty-five. Note that no earnings test is applied to NPI beneficiaries.

B. Disability: "Self-employed" to "claiming NPI disability pension benefit," which entails claiming disability benefits initially at ages sixty to sixty-four.

The Weight Given to Each Pathway

To compute the weight given to each retirement pathway in calculating OV, we employ a "stock estimator" that uses the share of the population taking each pathway in a combined age group at a given point in time.[12] In fact, since we assume there to be only two retirement pathways for each pension

---

11. In addition, there are "early claiming" (*Kuriage*) and "late claiming" (*Kurisage*) schemes, which actuarially adjust the benefit. Even when incorporating these claim schemes, we found the estimation results to remain virtually identical.

12. There are two alternatives to the stock estimator. One is the "age-specific flow" (i.e., the share of workers at each age who enter a pathway at that age),and the second is the "aggregated flow" (i.e., the share of workers starting at an initial age who eventually enter a pathway at any point). This latter approach reflects the actual ultimate experience of the cohort, but it does need to assume perfect foresight vis-à-vis future changes to stringency.

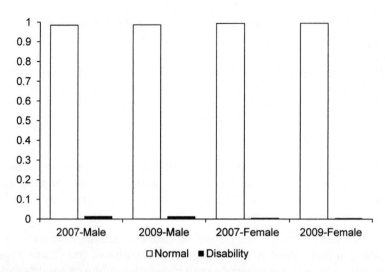

Fig. 12.4A   Weights on pathways to retirement, EPI

system (EPI/MAI or NPI), we estimate the weight of the disability pathway and assign 1—(the weight estimate on the disability pathway) to the normal claiming pathway. The stock estimator of the weight of the disability path is calculated by year, gender, and education. More specifically, we calculate the estimate of the weight of each pathway as follows:

A. EPI/MAI "Disability": Share of EPI/MAI disability pension enrollees ages sixty to sixty-four, among all EPI/MAI enrollees, by year, gender, and education.

B. EPI/MAI "Normal claiming": Others (1–[A]).

C. NPI "Disability": Share of NPI disability pension enrollees ages sixty to sixty-four, among all NPI enrollees, by year, gender, and education.

D. NPI "Normal claiming": Others (1–[C]).

Administrative data from the Annual Report on Social Security Administration are used to obtain information by gender; since administrative data lack information by education, data from the JSTAR are exploited to complement the information in terms of education.

Figures 12.4A and 12.4B illustrate the weight on each pathway for the EPI/MAI and NPI groups, respectively, by JSTAR wave year and gender. The proportion of disability is negligible for both the male and female EPI/MAI groups, while the amount is somewhat higher for the NPI group.

Earnings and Pension Benefits

The major components of the OV calculation are the labor income until retirement and the pension income between retirement and death. Labor income until retirement is calculated by taking the following steps. First,

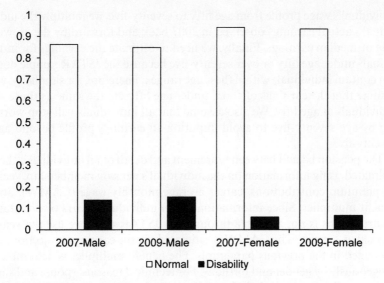

Fig. 12.4B   Weights on pathways to retirement, NPI

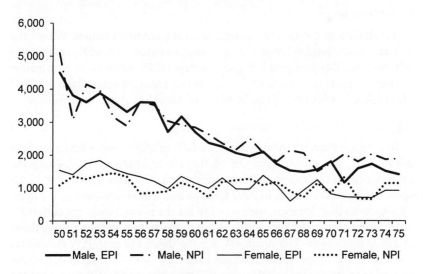

Fig. 12.5   Monthly wage projection (in 2011 euros), ages fifty to seventy-five

we obtain the median earnings by age, gender, and pension membership (NPI or EPI/MAI), using 2007 data (figure 12.5). Second, for each gender-by-pension-membership group, we calculate (median earnings among individuals age $A + 1$ – median earnings among individuals age A)/(median earnings among individuals age A) ($A = 50, \ldots, 74$) and assume that the rates represent how an individual's earnings grow as one ages. Then, to obtain an individual's wage profile from age fifty to seventy-five, we multiply the individual's actual earnings observed in 2007 back and forward by the growth rate of median earnings. Finally, we need to estimate the earnings for individuals under age fifty or over seventy-five because the JSTAR sample does not contain individuals within these age ranges. Therefore, for simplicity, we assume that the earnings of those under age fifty are the same as those of individuals at age fifty. We also assume that all individuals will stop working by age seventy-five to avoid imputing an earnings profile beyond age seventy-five.

The pension benefit between retirement and death of an individual is then estimated using information on the individual's pension membership, years of premium contributions, career average monthly wage (CAMW), and benefit multiplier. Since information on an individual's years of premium contributions is not available through the JSTAR data, we use the years worked as a proxy. The CAMW is estimated via the earnings projection, as explained in the previous paragraph. The benefit multiplier is determined exogenously by gender and birthday. For technical reasons, spouse and survivor benefits are not included.

Other Parameters

In calculating the OV, we assume several parameter values. We set the value of δ, the parameter of risk aversion, to equal 0.03; κ, the parameter of labor disutility, to equal 1.5; and γ to equal 0.75. All of these parameters are uniform across countries.[13] The mortality rates are taken from the 2007 "Life Table," published by the Ministry of Health, Labour, and Welfare.

OV Calculations and Descriptions

To examine the retirement behavior in 2009 of individuals who were working in 2007, we calculate the OV of these individuals in 2007, using the information described in previous subsections. Figures 12.6A and 12.6B show the mean OV by age in 2007 for men and women, respectively. Figure 12.6A shows that, for men, the mean OV for the normal claiming path (OV-normal) constantly declines with age, but remains positive even among those at age seventy-four. The mean OV for the disability path (OV-disability) levels off in the fifties and then begins to decline from the mid-sixties, where it overlaps with the mean OV-normal. The inclusive OV overlaps with the mean OV-normal because the weight of the disability path is very small. The result—that the inclusive OV decreases with age—indicates that the utility gained from working until the optimal retirement age, compared to that from retiring at the current age, tends to decline as people age. At the same time, however, the result that the inclusive OV remains positive until

13. The likelihood function is very flat, and the greater the assumed value for the risk aversion parameter γ, the lower the estimated OV coefficient will be. Given the flat likelihood function, we believe that little is to be gained from showing estimates based on other values.

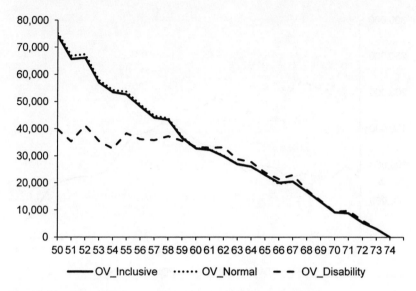

Fig. 12.6A   Mean OV by age for men (ages fifty to seventy-four)

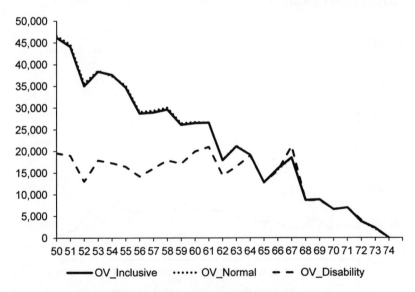

Fig. 12.6B   Mean OV by age for women (ages fifty to seventy-four)

age seventy-four implies that, in our OV model, it is optimal to delay retirement until age seventy-four. The relationship between the OV and age is similar for women, except that the OV level is much lower than that of men (figure 12.6B).

To further examine the relationship between OV and age, figures 12.6C and 12.6D illustrate—by age in 2007 and for men and women, respectively—

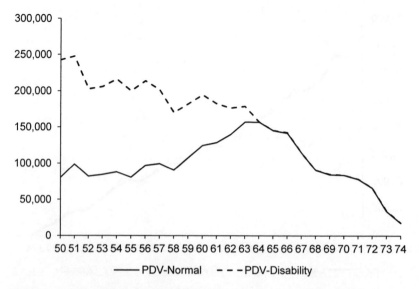

Fig. 12.6C   Mean PDV-normal and PDV-disability by age, men ages fifty to seventy-four (2011 euros)

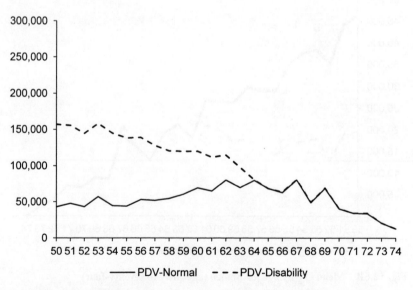

Fig. 12.6D   Mean PDV-normal and PDV-disability by age, women ages fifty to seventy-four (2011 euros)

the mean present discounted value (PDV) of pension benefits obtained, if retired. Figure 12.6C shows that, for men, the mean PDV of the normal claiming path (PDV-normal) rises until age sixty-five (i.e., the eligibility age for the basic public pension). Beyond age sixty-five the mean PDV-normal declines because by delaying retirement beyond age sixty-five, individuals must relinquish years of benefit receipt. In contrast, the mean PDV of the disability path (PDV-disability) declines continuously with age and beyond age sixty-five becomes the same as that of PDV-normal (i.e., the age at which the disability program is unified into the core public pension programs [EPI/ MAI or NPI]). Figure 12.6D shows that a similar pattern also holds for women. These results indicate that the mean OV remains positive until age seventy-four, not because the PDV increases with age, but because the additional earnings obtained through continued work more than compensate for the decline in the PDV.

12.3.4   Health Measurements

A measure of individual health status is calculated using the method of Poterba, Venti, and Wise (2010). The idea behind this approach is to construct a single index by using information from many health indicators. More specifically, using data pooled from the first and second JSTAR waves, we apply a principal component analysis to twenty-two health indicators and use the first principal component to construct a continuous health index.[14] The health index is then converted into percentile values, with 1 representing the worst health and 100 the best health. The appendix table 12A.1 reports the loadings on each health indicator.

Figure 12.7 shows the average percentile of the health index by age, for both men and women. We observe that (a) the mean percentile of the health index declines with age, (b) the speed of the decline is slightly higher in the sixties than in the fifties, and (c) men and women share almost the same pattern, although the mean is slightly higher for men in the late sixties.

12.4   Results

Table 12.3A reports the results of estimating the OV model in equation (1). Columns (1)–(8) relate to different model specifications, which vary by whether the effect of age is being controlled for linearly or with dummy

---

14. The twenty-two items are as follows: (1) difficulty in walking 100 m, (2) difficulty in lifting/carrying, (3) difficulty in pushing/pulling, (4) difficulty with an activity of daily living, (5) difficulty in climbing a few steps, (6) difficulty in stooping/kneeling/crouching, (7) difficulty in getting up from a chair, (8) self-reported health fair/poor, (9) difficulty in reaching/extending an arm up, (10) body mass index, (11) difficulty in sitting for two hours, (12) difficulty in picking up a dime, (13) ever experienced heart problems, (14) hospital stay, (15) doctor visit, (16) ever experienced psychological problems, (17) ever experienced a stroke, (18) ever experienced high blood pressure, (19) ever experienced lung disease, (20) ever experienced diabetes, (21) ever experienced arthritis, and (22) ever experienced cancer.

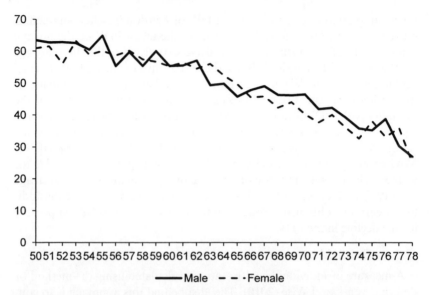

Fig. 12.7   Mean percentile of health index by age and gender (ages fifty to seventy-eight)

variables, whether the effect of health is being controlled for using quintile health dummies or a continuous health index, and whether covariates other than OV and health are included. Column (1), which controls only for a continuous age variable and health quintile dummies, shows that the coefficient on OV-inclusive is negative and statistically significant. The result indicates that OV-inclusive has a negative effect on retirement. More specifically, a 10,000-unit increase in OV decreases the probability of retirement by 2.1 percentage points; a standard deviation increase in the OV (shown in the brackets), meanwhile, decreases the probability of retirement by 4.8 percentage points. These results also hold for other specifications (columns [2]–[8]). The coefficients on the other variables generally have the expected signs. Columns (1)–(4) show that, compared to individuals in the lowest health quintile (i.e., those in the poorest health), those in the higher health quintiles are less likely to retire, although the health effects are neither monotonic nor statistically significant. Similarly, the results in columns (5)–(8) indicate that having a larger continuous health index value (i.e., being healthier) makes one less likely to retire, although again the coefficient is not significantly different from zero.

To confirm that the above results are robust to the scale of the OV measure, we also estimate the model using a percent gain in the inclusive OV as a key explanatory variable, instead of its level. Here, the measure of a percent gain in the inclusive OV is calculated by dividing the OV (i.e., the difference between the peak level and the current level of utility) by the current level of

Table 12.3A   **Effect of inclusive OV on retirement**

	Specification							
	(1)	(2)	(3)	(4)	(5)	(6)	(7)	(8)
OV_inclusive	-0.0213**	-0.0224**	-0.0204**	-0.0219**	-0.0216**	-0.0226**	-0.0207**	-0.0221**
	(0.0056)	(0.0056)	(0.0061)	(0.0061)	(0.0056)	(0.0056)	(0.0061)	(0.0061)
	[-0.048]	[-0.051]	[-0.047]	[-0.052]	[-0.049]	[-0.052]	[-0.047]	[-0.052]
Health quint 2 (second lowest)	-0.0159	-0.0154	-0.0179	-0.0166				
	(0.0184)	(0.0180)	(0.0173)	(0.0169)				
Health quint 3	0.0064	0.0068	-0.0004	0.0003				
	(0.0209)	(0.0205)	(0.0191)	(0.0187)				
Health quint 4	-0.0077	-0.0086	-0.012	-0.012				
	(0.0206)	(0.0200)	(0.0192)	(0.0186)				
Health quint 5 (highest)	-0.0047	-0.0054	-0.0069	-0.0073				
	(0.0205)	(0.0198)	(0.0193)	(0.0186)				
Health index					-0.000162	-0.00017	-0.000216	-0.00022
					(0.0003)	(0.0003)	(0.0003)	(0.0002)
Age	0.00355*		0.00321*		0.00335*		0.00300+	
	(0.0016)		(0.0016)		(0.0016)		(0.002)	
Age dummies		Included		Included		Included		Included
Female			0.0152	0.0128			0.0159	0.0136
			(0.0172)	(0.0167)			(0.0171)	(0.0166)
Married			0.0267+	0.0244			0.0271+	0.0247
			(0.0160)	(0.0159)			(0.0160)	(0.0159)

(continued)

Table 12.3A (continued)

	Specification							
	(1)	(2)	(3)	(4)	(5)	(6)	(7)	(8)
Spouse works			-0.0528**	-0.0512**			-0.0530**	-0.0513**
			(0.0161)	(0.0157)			(0.0162)	(0.0157)
Total assets			0.00003	0.00002			0.00002	0.00001
(in millions of euros)			(0.0001)	(0.0001)			(0.0001)	(0.0001)
Occup. dummies			Included	Included			Included	Included
Educ.: <High school			-0.0263	-0.0257			-0.0274	-0.027
			(0.0216)	(0.0210)			(0.0216)	(0.0209)
Educ.: High school			-0.0258	-0.0276			-0.0284	-0.0302
			(0.0217)	(0.0212)			(0.0216)	(0.0211)
Educ.: Two yrs. college/vocational school			-0.0036	-0.00286			-0.00537	-0.00451
			(0.0265)	(0.0262)			(0.0262)	(0.0259)
No. of observations	1,575	1,575	1,575	1,575	1,575	1,575	1,575	1,575
Mean ret. rate	0.096	0.096	0.096	0.096	0.096	0.096	0.096 ·	0.096
Mean of OV	32,185	32,185	32,185	32,185	32,185	32,185	32,185	32,185
Std. dev. of OV	20,581	20,581	20,581	20,581	20,581	20,581	20,581	20,581

Notes: Coefficients are marginal effects of a 10,000-unit change in OV from probit models. Standard errors are shown in parentheses. The effect of a one standard deviation change in OV is shown in brackets (this is estimated as the effect of increasing inclusive OV from the current value −0.5 std. dev to the current value +0.5 std. dev.).

***Significant at the 1 percent level.

**Significant at the 5 percent level.

*Significant at the 10 percent level.

Table 12.3B   **Effect of percent gain in inclusive OV on retirement**

	Specification			
	(1)	(2)	(3)	(4)
Percent gain in OV	–0.0416**	–0.0424**	–0.0416**	–0.0422**
	(0.0126)	(0.0131)	(0.0123)	(0.0126)
Linear age	X		X	
Age dummies		X		X
Health quintiles	X	X	X	X
Other Xs			X	X
No. of observations	1,575	1,575	1,575	1,575
Mean ret. rate	0.096	0.096	0.096	0.096
Mean of % gain in OV	1.380	1.380	1.380	1.380
Std. dev. of % gain in OV	1.011	1.011	1.011	1.011

Notes: Models are the same as models 1–4 in table 12.1. Coefficients are marginal effects.
Standard errors are shown in parentheses.
***Significant at the 1 percent level.
**Significant at the 5 percent level.
*Significant at the 10 percent level.

utility. Table 12.3B shows the results of the estimations. The estimated coefficients are again negative and significant, and robust to specification choice.

To investigate whether the effects of OV vary by individual health, we estimate the OV model separately for each health quintile; the estimations results are summarized in table 12.4A. Specifications (1)–(4) in columns (1)–(4) are the same as those in columns (1)–(4) of table 12.3A. The results show that the coefficient on the inclusive OV is negative for all the health quintile groups, but statistically significant only for the second, third, and fifth quintile groups. Similar results hold when we use a percent gain in the inclusive OV (table 12.4B). While insignificant coefficients on the OV among some of the health quintile groups may derive from the small sample size used in the estimations (indeed, the standard error of the coefficient on the OV is larger when the model is estimated separately for each health quintile), the results in table 12.4C also indicate that the effects of OV on the retirement decision do not vary monotonically with individual health. This table reports the results of estimating a model that includes an interaction between OV and the continuous health index, instead of estimating the model separately for each health quintile. While the estimated coefficient on the interaction term is negative—which may indicate that the financial incentives for retirement matter more for those in better health—it is not statistically significant.

In table 12.5A, we present the results of OV model estimation for each education group. The results show no consistent pattern of OV effects across the various education groups: the coefficient on the OV is negative and significant only for those who graduated from high school and those

Table 12.4A   Effect of inclusive OV on retirement by health quintile

	No. of obs.	Mean ret. rate	Mean of OV	Std. dev. of OV	Specification			
					(1)	(2)	(3)	(4)
OV: Lowest quintile (worst health)	311	0.1190	27,268.89	18,995.95	-0.0166 (0.0159) [-0.0322]	-0.0168 (0.0141) [-0.0329]	-0.00508 (0.0158) [-0.0104]	-0.00307 (0.0140) [-0.006]
OV: 2nd quintile	303	0.0957	30,907.59	21,073.72	-0.0270** (0.0103) [-0.08]	-0.0322** (0.0096) [-0.0969]	-0.0154+ (0.0088) [-0.0505]	-0.0212* (0.0085) [-0.0715]
OV: 3rd quintile	287	0.1185	31,893.59	20,732.61	-0.0394** (0.0134) [-0.0887]	-0.0393** (0.0139) [-0.0924]	-0.0488** (0.0159) [-0.135]	-0.0443** (0.0154) [-0.132]
OV: 4th quintile	306	0.0784	35,057.42	19,704.55	-0.00833 (0.0110) [-0.0172]	-0.00523 (0.0108) [-0.012]	-0.00883 (0.0100) [-0.02]	-0.00741 (0.0089) [-0.0188]
OV: Highest quintile (best health)	286	0.0944	34,728.72	21,178.41	-0.0168 (0.0108) [-0.04]	-0.0199+ (0.0107) [-0.0504]	-0.0171+ (0.0100) [-0.0455]	-0.0202* (0.0103) [-0.0531]
Linear age					X	X		
Age dummies							X	X
Other Xs					X	X	X	X

Notes: Models are the same as models 1–4 in table 12.1, but are estimated separately by health quintile; each coefficient on the table is from a different regression. Coefficients are marginal effects of a 10,000-unit change in OV from probit models. Standard errors are shown in parentheses. The effect of a one standard deviation change in OV is shown in brackets (this is estimated as the effect of increasing inclusive OV from the current value −0.5 std. dev. to the current value +0.5 std. dev.).

***Significant at the 1 percent level.

**Significant at the 5 percent level.

*Significant at the 10 percent level.

Table 12.4B Effect of percent gain in inclusive OV on retirement by health quintile

	No. of obs.	Mean ret. rate	Mean of % OV	Std. dev. of % OV	Specification			
					(1)	(2)	(3)	(4)
OV: Lowest quintile (worst health)	311	0.1190	1.217062	0.9589739	−0.035	−0.0452	−0.0331	−0.0395
					(0.0288)	(0.0277)	(0.0268)	(0.0250)
OV: 2nd quintile	303	0.0957	1.166729	0.8397144	−0.0602*	−0.0850**	−0.0403+	−0.0577**
					(0.0289)	(0.0256)	(0.0222)	(0.0217)
OV: 3rd quintile	287	0.1185	1.426323	1.122353	−0.0525	−0.0435	−0.0558+	−0.0464
					(0.0328)	(0.0342)	(0.0299)	(0.0302)
OV: 4th quintile	306	0.0784	1.572716	1.028707	−0.0362	−0.0236	−0.0319+	−0.0227
					(0.0242)	(0.0207)	(0.0193)	(0.0161)
OV: Highest quintile (best health)	286	0.0944	1.545694	1.059786	−0.0611**	−0.0676**	−0.0534**	−0.0604**
					(0.0190)	(0.0225)	(0.0169)	(0.0198)
Linear age					X		X	
Age dummies						X		X
Other Xs							X	X

Notes: Models are the same as models 1–4 in table 12.1, but are estimated separately by health quintile; each coefficient on the table is from a different regression. Coefficients are marginal effects. Standard errors are shown in parentheses.

***Significant at the 1 percent level.

**Significant at the 5 percent level.

*Significant at the 10 percent level.

Table 12.4C   **Effect of inclusive OV on retirement with health index interaction**

	Specification			
	(1)	(2)	(3)	(4)
OV	−0.0167	−0.019	−0.016	−0.0185
	(0.0116)	(0.0124)	(0.0113)	(0.0121)
OV*health index	−0.00005	−0.00003	−0.00004	−0.00002
	(0.0001)	(0.00005)	(0.0001)	(0.0000)
Health index	0.00004	−0.00002	−0.00002	−0.00007
	(0.00045)	(0.00046)	(0.00043)	(0.00044)
Linear age	X		X	
Age dummies		X		X
Other Xs			X	X
No of observations	1,575	1,575	1,575	1,575
Mean ret. rate	0.096	0.096	0.096	0.096
Mean of OV	32,185	32,185	32,185	32,185
Std. dev. of OV	20,581	20,581	20,581	20,581

Notes: Models are the same as models 5–8 in table 12.1, with the addition of an OV*health index interaction. Coefficients are marginal effects of a 10,000-unit change in OV from probit models. Standard errors are shown in parentheses. The effect of a one standard deviation change in OV is shown in brackets (this is estimated as the effect of increasing inclusive OV from the current value −0.5 std. dev. to the current value +0.5 std. dev.).

who graduated from a two-year college or vocational school. Using the measure of percent gain in OV-inclusive does not essentially change this result (table 12.5B).

12.5   Model Fit

To examine the fit of the OV model, we first compare the retirement hazard rate predicted by the OV model (specified in column [4] of table 12.3A) with the actual hazard rate. Two things should be noted, however, in conducting the examination. First, since our data set is a short panel, the hazard rate is obtained not by following the same individuals over time, but by assuming that the variation in hazard rates by cohort at a given point in time is the same as that by age of a single cohort. More specifically, we calculate the hazard rate by taking the average by age in 2007 of the probability of retirement within a year, given that the individual is working in 2007. Second, the retirement hazard rate averaged by age can be a noisy measure because the number of observations at each age is small. As an extreme example, in 2007, only three female individuals at age seventy-four were still working.

Figures 12.8A and 12.8B compare the predicted versus actual retirement hazard rates for men and women, respectively. Figure 12.8A shows that, for men, there are some gaps between the predicted and actual retirement

Table 12.5A Effect of inclusive OV on retirement by education group

	No. of obs.	Mean ret. rate	Mean of OV	Std. dev. of OV	Specification			
					(1)	(2)	(3)	(4)
OV: < High school	428	0.1332	22,958	17,059	0.00112	-0.0124	0.0122	-0.00545
					(0.0146)	(0.0125)	(0.0164)	(0.0144)
					[0.002]	[-0.022]	[0.022]	[-0.01]
OV: High school	690	0.0899	30,463	17,818	-0.0304**	-0.0305**	-0.0360**	-0.0347**
					(0.0081)	(0.0080)	(0.0085)	(0.0081)
					[-0.0613]	[-0.067]	[-0.0764]	[-0.0801]
OV: Two yrs. college /vocational school	177	0.0904	36,433	18,626	-0.0346*	-0.0339*	-0.0259*	-0.0217*
					(0.0138)	(0.0132)	(0.0116)	(0.0108)
					[-0.0708]	[-0.0704]	[-0.0653]	[-0.0585]
OV: Four yrs. college	195	0.0821	49,047	23,500	0.00135	0.00532	0.00814	0.0122
					(0.0093)	(0.0095)	(0.0105)	(0.0098)
					[0.00358]	[0.0158]	[0.02271]	[0.0423]
Linear age							X	X
Age dummies					X	X		X
Health quintiles						X	X	X
Other Xs								X

Notes: Models are the same as models 1–4 in table 12.1, but are estimated separately by education group; each coefficient in the table is from a different regression. Coefficients are marginal effects of a 10,000-unit change in OV from probit models. Standard errors are shown in parentheses. The effect of a one standard deviation change in OV is shown in brackets (this is estimated as the effect of increasing inclusive OV from the current value −0.5 std. dev. to the current value +0.5 std. dev.).

***Significant at the 1 percent level.

**Significant at the 5 percent level.

*Significant at the 10 percent level.

Table 12.5B   Effect of percent gain in inclusive OV on retirement by education group

	No. of obs.	Mean ret. rate	Mean of % OV	Std. dev. of % OV	Specification			
					(1)	(2)	(3)	(4)
OV: < High school	428	0.1332	1.007	0.762	-0.0477	-0.0598+	-0.0432	-0.0557+
					(0.0347)	(0.0326)	(0.0351)	(0.0320)
OV: High school	690	0.0899	1.372	0.954	-0.0745***	-0.0701**	-0.0753**	-0.0705**
					(0.0165)	(0.0170)	(0.0157)	(0.0157)
OV: Two yrs. college /vocational school	177	0.0904	1.692	0.815	-0.0118	-0.0185	-0.00832	-0.016
					(0.0337)	(0.0334)	(0.0256)	(0.0247)
OV: Four yrs. college	195	0.0821	1.819	1.306	-0.011	0.00103	-0.0118	-0.00073
					(0.0155)	(0.0147)	(0.0139)	(0.0116)
Linear age					X		X	
Age dummies						X		X
Other Xs						X	X	X

Notes: Models are the same as models 1–4 in table 12.1, but are estimated separately by education group; each coefficient on the table is from a different regression. Coefficients are marginal effects. Standard errors are shown in parentheses.

***Significant at the 1 percent level.

**Significant at the 5 percent level.

*Significant at the 10 percent level.

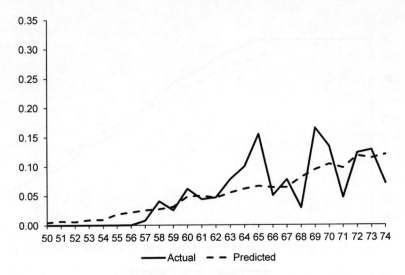

Fig. 12.8A   Actual versus predicted retirement rate (men ages fifty to seventy-four)

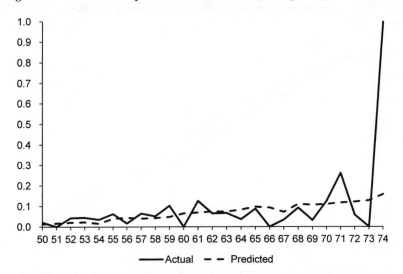

Fig. 12.8B   Actual versus predicted retirement rate (women ages fifty to seventy-four)

hazard rates; in particular, the actual retirement hazard rate is much higher at age sixty-five and ages sixty-nine to seventy. For women, the retirement hazard rate is underpredicted by the OV model at higher ages, particularly at ages seventy-one and seventy-four (figure 12.8B). These results indicate that the model does not seem to predict well the spike in the hazard rate at certain ages, as seen in the actual data.

Figures 12.8C and 12.8D illustrate the predicted versus actual survival

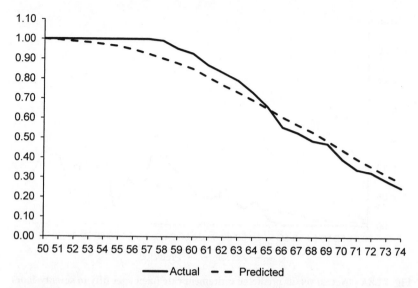

Fig. 12.8C   Actual versus predicted retirement survival (men ages fifty to seventy-four)

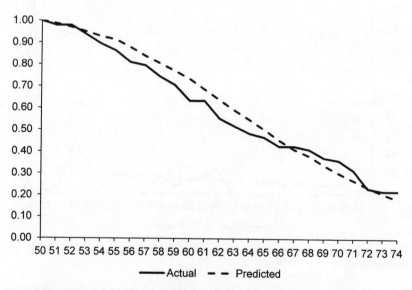

Fig. 12.8D   Actual versus predicted retirement survival (women)

rates of retirement for men and women, respectively. Figure 12.8C shows that, for men, the actual survival rate is close to 100 percent between ages fifty and fifty-six, declines quickly up to age sixty-six, and then decreases moderately up to age seventy-four. Meanwhile, the predicted survival rate declines steadily between ages fifty and seventy-four. The result that the predicted survival rate decreases monotonically with age is the same for women

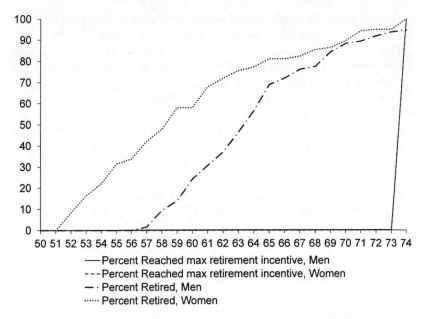

Fig. 12.9 Share having reached max OV-inclusive and retired (ages fifty to seventy-four)

(figure 12.8D): the difference in the rate of decline in the actual survival rate by age is not captured by the predicted survival rate.

Figure 12.9 shows the percentage of people for whom the maximum utility from retirement occurs (i.e., OV becomes zero) at a given age, according to the OV model. The figure also presents the actual proportion of individuals who have retired, at each age. We observe that, for most of the individuals in the sample, the maximum utility from retirement is not achieved until age seventy-four. In other words, the OV continues to be positive until the end point of our calculation. This is because, in our OV model, the additional earnings from continued work exceed the decline in the PDV of pension benefits (see figures 12.6C and 12.6D). In contrast, the actual proportion of individuals who have retired evolves more gradually with age. Hence, our model is not necessarily successful in predicting individuals' actual retirement behavior. The small sample size at each age may be one of the reasons for such results.

12.6 Counterfactual Simulation

As a counterfactual simulation analysis, we examine how individual retirement behavior would change if there existed only one retirement path—that is, either the normal retirement path or the disability path. More specifically, using the regression results in column (4) of table 12.3A, we calculate retirement probabilities and survival rates to retirement under the two counterfactual cases: when the weight placed on the normal retirement path in calculating OV is zero, and when the weight placed on the disability path is zero.

The results of the simulation are presented in figures 12.10A and 12.10B. If the probability of being part of the disability program is zero, then the probability of retirement would decrease over the age range of fifty to around sixty, compared to the case where individuals have no choice but to be on the disability program. Hence, if the possibility of being on the disability program were absent, the survival rate to retirement would be higher than the rate where the disability program were the only path to retirement: for example, at age sixty, the survival rate would be 80.8 percent in the former case, but 70.1 percent in the latter case. This leads to a difference in the simulated average number of work years over the ages of fifty to sixty-nine between the two counterfactual cases: 15.9 years in the case of there being no disability program, and 14.4 years in the case of there being no normal retirement. Thus, the average number of work years from age fifty to sixty-nine would be 9.5 percent higher if every individual were on the normal retirement path, rather than the disability path.

12.7   Conclusion

This study examined the factors that affect the retirement decisions of the middle-aged and elderly in Japan, focusing especially on their earnings, public pension benefits, and health status. Using two-year panel data from the JSTAR and applying the OV model proposed by Stock and Wise (1990a, 1990b), we found that the probability of retirement has a negative and significant correlation with the OV, and that the correlation does not depend on the health status. Our counterfactual simulation based on the OV model showed that, if the probability of being enrolled in the disability program were zero, the average years of work when individuals are in their fifties and sixties would increase. However, it should be emphasized that, in Japan—where being enrolled in the disability program is unlikely to make one a candidate for the retirement path—the result of this simulation does not indicate that the labor supplied by the middle-aged and elderly will increase by making the eligibility criteria for disability pension receipts more stringent.

We recognize that there remains much to be addressed in future research. First, we should further elaborate the specifications of the OV model. The value of an OV depends on the parameters of the utility function, such as parameters for converting income to utility and the discount rate; these parameters are tentatively assumed in the current study. Second, we should more precisely project wage profiles and capture different pathways to retirement on the basis of further information obtained from official statistical sources. Third, we should also model couples, rather than individuals, as retirement decisions are likely to be made jointly by elderly couples: we should therefore incorporate information about spouses' and survivors' pension benefits, which are ignored in this study.

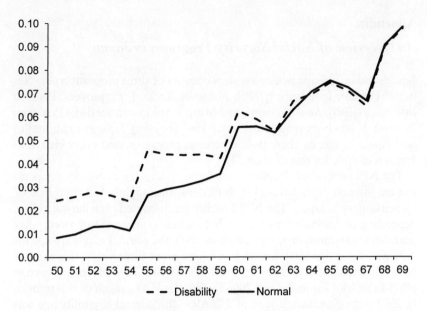

Fig. 12.10A   Retirement probabilities by pathway, disability, and normal retirement (ages fifty to sixty-nine)

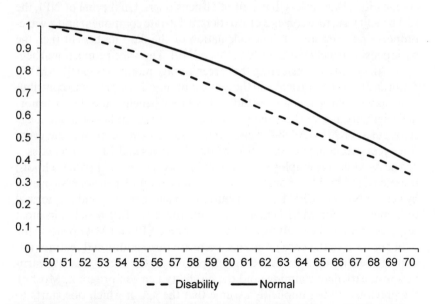

Fig. 12.10B   Survival probabilities by pathway, disability, and normal retirement (ages fifty to seventy)

Appendix
An Overview of Social Security Programs in Japan

Japan's public old-age pension system consists of three program types: National Pension Insurance ([NPI]; *Kokumin Nenkin*), Employees' Pension Insurance ([EPI]; *Kosei Nenkin*), and Mutual Aid Insurance ([MAI]; *Kyosai Nenkin*). It has been mandatory since 1961 for every Japanese national to participate in one of these public pension programs, and every citizen in Japan is eligible for one of them.[15]

The NPI covers self-employed workers, or forestry or fishery cooperative employees; those covered by NPI constitute slightly less than half of all pensioners in Japan. The NPI benefits are disbursed on a flat-rate basis, depending on the number of contribution years (minimum of twenty-five years and maximum of forty years). In 2000, the normal eligibility age for NPI was set at age sixty for both genders; every three years, this age has been scheduled to increase by one year to sixty-five. This reform has been in effect since 2001 for males and 2006 for females.[16] As a result of this reform, in 2007—the benchmark year of JSTAR—the normal eligibility age was sixty-three for males and sixty-one for females.

The EPI covers employees in the private sector, and the individuals it covers constitute slightly less than half of all pensioners. Unlike that of NPI, the EPI benefit structure consists of two tiers: a flat-rate component and a wage-proportional component. The calculation of the flat-rate benefit (i.e., the basic pension benefit) is identical to that of NPI. The wage-proportional benefit is calculated by considering the career average monthly wage ([CAMW]; *Hyojyun Hoshu Getsugaku*) and the number of months of premium contributions, as well as a gender and birthday-dependent benefit multiplier. The normal eligibility age for the wage-proportional component has been set at age sixty, but as of 2013 (2018) that age is scheduled to increase by one year every three years, reaching age sixty-five in 2025 for males and 2030 for females.

The MAI covers employees of the public sector and of private schools; those covered by MAI constitute the small portion of pensioners covered by neither NPI nor EPI. The contribution–benefit structure and the normal retirement age for MAI benefits resemble those for EPI benefits in most respects; thus, in the analysis below, we combine EPI and MAI pensioners.

In addition to the core programs, there are three additional features relevant to setting up Japan's retirement pathways: the social security earnings test, early/late claiming, and the disability pension program. Most of the previous studies implicitly assume that the age at which one starts to

---

15. The studies of Oshio, Shimizutani, and Oishi (2010) and Oshio, Oishi, and Shimizutani (2011) describe in detail Japan's old-age pension program.

16. Japan's social security program has undergone several large reforms over the last forty years. The studies of Oshio, Shimizutani, and Oishi (2010) and Oshio, Oishi, and Shimizutani (2011) provide detailed descriptions of past reforms.

claim pension benefits corresponds to the retirement age (i.e., marked by one's departure from the labor force). However, this is not the case in Japan, and such an assumption ignores some important aspects of the association between pension benefits and labor force participation among the elderly.

First, the social security earnings test (*Zaishoku Rorei Nenkin*) can result in a suspension of payment of part or all of one's pension benefits if one's labor income exceeds a certain threshold; the discouraging effect of this test on labor supply has been studied intensively in Japan and in other countries. Among recent studies in Japan, Shimizutani (2013) reveals the discouraging effect of the earnings test on the labor supply decisions of workers age sixty to sixty-four years. Shimizutani and Oshio (2013) show that the repeal in 1985 of the earnings test for workers age sixty-five to sixty-nine did not affect the earnings distribution of the elderly, but that its reinstatement in 2002 partially altered earnings distribution.

Under the current program, the earnings test focuses on the average monthly wage and bonus income.[17] For workers ages sixty to sixty-four, pension benefit payments are not suspended if the average wage and bonus income per month is less than JPY 280,000; however, benefits are suspended by JPY 0.5 per JPY 1 increase in labor income (i.e., a marginal tax rate of 50 percent) between JPY 280,000 and JPY 460,000, and suspended by JPY 1 per JPY 1 increase in labor income (i.e., a marginal tax rate of 100 percent) in excess of JPY 460,000. For workers age sixty-five and older, the pension benefit payment is not suspended if the average wage and bonus income per month is less than JPY 460,000, but it is suspended by JPY 0.5 per JPY 1 increase in labor income (i.e., a marginal tax rate of 50 percent) in excess of JPY 460,000. Note that the earnings test is applicable only to the second-tier (i.e., wage-proportional) benefit for EPI beneficiaries, and not at all to NPI or MAI beneficiaries.

Second, all three social security programs allow their beneficiaries to claim within a "window" period; indeed, a nontrivial proportion of those beneficiaries claim at ages other than the normal eligibility ages. First, NPI allows a ten-year window in claiming benefits, and an individual undergoes benefit reductions if he or she claims early, at ages sixty to sixty-four (*Kuriage Jyukyu*); alternatively, he or she receives a benefit reward if he or she claims late, at ages sixty-six to seventy (*Kurisage Jyukyu*). The actuarial adjustment rate differs across birth cohorts; for example, for those individuals born after April 2, 1941, the actuarial reduction rate before age sixty-five is 0.5 percent per month, and the actuarial credit rate after age sixty-five is 0.7 percent per month (Shimizutani and Oshio 2012). Second, EPI also allows some flexibility in terms of claim timing, and it differs between flat-rate and wage-proportional benefits. As of 2011, one cannot claim the special benefit (i.e., corresponding to the wage-proportional benefit prior to age sixty-five) earlier or later than the normal eligibility age of sixty years, regardless of gender;

---

17. The earnings test has been revised many times. Shimizutani (2013) and Shimizutani and Oshio (2013) review previous reforms vis-à-vis the earnings test, over long-term periods.

however, in 2007—when the normal eligibility ages for men and women were sixty-three and sixty-one, respectively—one could claim the flat-rate component earlier, at ages sixty to sixty-two for males and sixty for females.[18] Moreover, an EPI beneficiary can claim either the flat-rate or wage-proportional component later than age sixty-five, and thus enjoy an incremental benefit. Note that once one claims his or her benefits—either before or after the normal eligibility age—one cannot change his or her take-up decision.

Third, the disability pension program, which is not specific to the aforementioned old-age pension programs, covers some elderly individuals in Japan. While the participation rate in Japan with regard to the disability pension program remains low, many European countries have expanded their respective DI programs since the 1970s; in some countries, receiving DI benefits is a typical feature of early retirement (Wise 2012). Oshio and Shimizutani (2012) argue that this is not the case in Japan, and that the low participation in Japan's disability pension program can be attributed to the stringency of its eligibility criteria. Under the current program, if one consults with a doctor about the cause of disability for the first time before the age of twenty, or if one is an NPI pensioner, one is entitled to receive the Disability Basic Pension benefit, which is disbursed on the basis of disability severity (Grade 1 or 2) and the number of dependent children. In addition, if one consulted a doctor to identify the cause of the disability when one was an EPI (MAI) pensioner, one is entitled to receive a wage-proportional Disability Employees' Pension benefit or Disability Mutual Aid Pension benefit (for MAI recipients), the amount of which depends on the disability severity (Grades 1–3) and whether or not one has a spouse (Oshio and Shimizutani 2012).

Table 12A.1   Principal component analysis on health indicators (factor loadings of the first principal component health index)

1. Difficulty walking 100 m	0.311	12. Difficulty picking up a dime	0.248
2. Difficulty lifting/carrying	0.337	13. Ever experienced heart problems	0.094
3. Difficulty pushing/pulling	0.340	14. Hospital stay	0.109
4. Difficulty with an activity of daily living	0.242	15. Doctor visit	0.082
5. Difficulty climbing a few steps	0.315	16. Ever experienced psychological problems	0.017
6. Difficulty stooping/kneeling/crouching	0.309	17. Ever experienced a stroke	0.126
7. Difficulty getting up from a chair	0.304	18. Ever experienced high blood pressure	0.075
8. Self-reported health fair/poor	0.211	19. Ever experienced lung disease	0.040
9. Difficulty reaching/extending arm up	0.269	20. Ever experienced diabetes	0.071
10. Ever experienced arthritis	0.122	21. Body mass index	0.026
11. Difficulty sitting two hours	0.277	22. Ever experienced cancer	0.035

18. There are two types of early claiming in the EPI program: total early claiming (*Zenbu Kuriage*) and partial early claiming (*Ichibu Kuriage*). In the former, one can receive a flat-rate benefit at a reduced rate that is identical to that for an NPI beneficiary, but it is no longer eligible for the special benefit. In the latter, one can receive both part of the flat-rate component of the special benefit and part of the flat-rate component of the formal benefit (as well as the wage-proportional component). See Shimizutani and Oshio (2012) for the detailed formula. If the duration of EPI participation is lengthy, the flat-rate benefit of the special benefit and the formal component are almost identical, and partial early claiming is in general more advantageous than total early claiming. In the current study, we assume that an EPI beneficiary chooses partial early claiming if he or she claims benefits earlier than the normal eligibility age.

Table 12A.2   **Summary statistics of the variables**

		All	Male	Female
Continuous variable				
OV (in ten thousand euro)	M	3.22	3.59	2.58
	S.D.	2.06	2.16	1.70
Health index	M.	56.89	56.45	57.65
	D.S.	26.57	26.09	27.38
Monthly wage (in ten thousand yen)	M.	25.41	31.22	15.23
	S.D.	18.15	18.4	12.28
Enrolled years	M.	36.54	39.62	31.24
	S.D.	13.36	11.91	14.04
Assets (in million yen)	M.	11.37	13.44	7.99
	S.D.	68.07	85.48	15.45
Binary variables				
Age				
Less than 55		0.21	0.20	0.23
55–59		0.31	0.31	0.31
60–64		0.22	0.21	0.23
65–69		0.17	0.18	0.14
70–		0.10	0.11	0.08
Education				
Less than high school		0.29	0.31	0.25
High school		0.44	0.40	0.50
Two years college/vocational school		0.12	0.08	0.20
Four years college or more		0.15	0.21	0.06
Married		0.84	0.90	0.75
Spouse working		0.57	0.55	0.60
Occupation				
Specialist		0.10	0.10	0.09
Managers		0.08	0.11	0.02
Clerk		0.16	0.12	0.24
Salesperson		0.13	0.13	0.13
Service		0.14	0.07	0.26
Guards		0.01	0.02	0.00
Farmers		0.05	0.05	0.05
Trans and com.		0.05	0.08	0.01
Construction		0.25	0.29	0.17
Unknown		0.03	0.03	0.04
Retired in 2009		0.10	0.09	0.11
Public pension enrollee:				
EPI/MAI enrollee		0.60	0.67	0.50
NPI enrollee		0.40	0.33	0.50
		1,575	996	579

Note: M = mean; S.D. = standard deviation.

References

Ichimura, Hidehiko, Hideki Hashimoto, and Satoshi Shimizutani. 2009. JSTAR First Results: 2009 Report. RIETI Discussion Paper Series no. 09-E-047, Research Institute on Economy, Trade and Industry. http://www.rieti.go.jp/en/publications/summary/09090002.html.

Ichimura, Hidehiko, and Satoshi Shimizutani. 2012. "Retirement Process in Japan: New Evidence from the Japanese Study on Aging and Retirement (JSTAR)." In *Aging in Asia: Findings from New and Emerging Data Initiatives*, edited by James P. Smith and Malay Majmundar, 173–204. Panel on Policy Research and Data Needs to Meet the Challenge of Aging in Asia. Committee on Population, Division of Behavioral and Social Sciences and Education. Washington, DC: The National Academies Press.

Momose, Yu. 2008. "Income Security Systems for the Disabled with a Special Reference to the Disability Pension Programs (*Shougai Sha ni taisuru Shotoku Hosho Seido: Shougai Nenkin o Chushin ni*)." *Quarterly of Social Security Research* (Kikan Shakai Hosho Kenkyu) 44 (2): 171–85.

Ministry of Health, Labour, and Welfare. 2009. "Textbook for the Study Programme for the Senior Social Insurance Administrators (abstract)." http://www.mhlw.go.jp/english/org/policy/p36–37a.html.

Oshio, Takashi, and Akiko Oishi. 2004. "Social Security and Retirement in Japan: An Evaluation Using Micro-Data." In *Social Security and Retirement around the World: Micro-Estimation*, edited by Jonathan Gruber and David Wise. Chicago: University of Chicago Press.

Oshio, Takashi, Akiko Oishi, and Satoshi Shimizutani. 2011. "Social Security Reforms and Labor Force Participation of the Elderly in Japan." *Japanese Economic Review* 62 (2): 248–71.

Oshio, Takashi, and Satoshi Shimizutani. 2012. "Disability Pension Program and Labor Force Participation in Japan: A Historical Perspective." In *Social Security Programs and Retirement around the World: Historical Trends in Mortality and Health, Employment, and Disability Insurance Participation and Reforms*, edited by David Wise, 391–417. Chicago: University of Chicago Press.

Oshio, Takashi, Satoshi Shimizutani, and Akiko Sato Oishi. 2010. "Does Social Security Induce Withdrawal of the Old from the Labor Force and Create Jobs for the Young? The Case of Japan." In *Social Security Programs and Retirement around the World: The Relationship to Youth Employment*, edited by Jonathan Gruber and David Wise, 217–41. Chicago: University of Chicago Press.

Poterba, James, Steven Venti, and David Wise. 2010. "Family Status Transitions, Latent Health, and the Post-Retirement Evolution of Assets." NBER Working Paper no. 15789, Cambridge, MA.

Shimizutani, Satoshi. 2013. "Social Security Earnings Test and the Labor Supply of the Elderly: New Evidence from Unique Survey Responses in Japan." *Japanese Economic Review* 64 (3): 399–413.

Shimizutani, Satoshi, and Takashi Oshio. 2012. "Claiming Behavior of Public Pension Benefits: New Evidence from Japanese Study on Aging and Retirement (JSTAR)." RIETI Discussion Paper Series no. 12-E-068, Research Institute on Economy, Trade and Industry.

———. 2013. "Revisiting the Labor Supply Effect of Social Security Earnings Test: New Evidence from its Elimination and Reinstatement in Japan." *Japan and the World Economy* 28:99–111.

Stock, James, and David Wise. 1990a. "The Pension Inducement to Retire." In *Issues in the Economics of Aging*, edited by David Wise, 205–29. Chicago: University of Chicago Press.

———. 1990b. "Pensions, the Option Value of Work, and Retirement." *Econometrica* 58 (5): 1151–80.

Wise, David, ed. 2012. *Social Security Programs and Retirement around the World: Historical Trends in Mortality and Health, Employment, and Disability Insurance Participation and Reforms*. Chicago: University of Chicago Press.

Contributors

James Banks
Arthur Lewis Building-3.020
School of Social Sciences
The University of Manchester
Manchester M13 9PL
United Kingdom

Luc Behaghel
Paris School of Economics–INRA
48, boulevard Jourdan
75014 Paris
France

Paul Bingley
The Danish National Centre for Social
    Research
Herluf Trollesgade 11
1052 Copenhagen
Denmark

Didier Blanchet
INSEE–Timbre H230
18 Bd. Adolphe Pinard
75675 Paris Cedex 14
France

Axel Börsch-Supan
Munich Center for the Economics of
    Aging
Amalienstrasse 33
80799 Munich
Germany

Agar Brugiavini
Dipartimento di Scienze Economiche
Universita' "Ca' Foscari" Venezia
Sestiere Cannareggio, 873
30121 Venice
Italy

Tabea Bucher-Koenen
Munich Center for the Economics of
    Aging
Amalienstrasse 33
80799 Munich
Germany

Courtney Coile
Department of Economics
Wellesley College
106 Central Street
Wellesley, MA 02481

Klaas de Vos
CentERdata
Tilburg University
Warandelaan 2
5037 AB Tilburg
The Netherlands

Carl Emmerson
Institute for Fiscal Studies
7 Ridgmount Street
London WC1E 7AE
United Kingdom

Mayu Fujii
Hokkaido University of Education
2–1 Hachimancho
Hakodate 040–8567
Japan

Pilar García-Gómez
Erasmus School of Economics
Erasmus University Rotterdam
P.O. Box 1738
3000 DR Rotterdam
The Netherlands

Nabanita Datta Gupta
Department of Economics and
    Business
Aarhus University
Fuglesangs Allé 4, building 2621
8210 Aarhus V
Denmark

Sergi Jiménez-Martín
Department of Economics
Universitat Pompeu Fabra and
    Barcelona GSE
Ramon Trias 25
08005 Barcelona
Spain

Per Johansson
Institute for Evaluation of Labour
    Market and Education Policy
Box 513
SE-751 20 Uppsala
Sweden

Michael Jørgensen
ATP
Stradellasvej 24, 3
2450 København SV
Denmark

Alain Jousten
University of Liège
HEC Management School
Bât. B31, Boîte 41
Boulevard du Rectorat 7
4000 Liège
Belgium

Hendrik Jürges
Schumpeter School of Business and
    Economics
University of Wuppertal
Rainer-Gruenter-Str. 21 (FN.01)
42119 Wuppertal
Germany

Adriaan Kalwij
School of Economics
Utrecht University
Kriekenpitplein 21–22
3584 EC Utrecht
The Netherlands

Arie Kapteyn
University of Southern California
Center for Economic and Social
    Research
635 Downey Way, Suite 312
Los Angeles, CA 90089–3332

Lisa Laun
Institute for Evaluation of Labour
    Market and Education Policy
Box 513
SE-751 20 Uppsala
Sweden

Mathieu Lefebvre
University of Strasbourg, BETA
61, avenue de la Forêt Noire
67085 Strasbourg Cedex
France

Kevin Milligan
Vancouver School of Economics
University of British Columbia
997–1873 East Mall
Vancouver, BC V6T 1Z1
Canada

Takashi Oshio
Institute of Economic Research
Hitotsubashi University
2–1 Naka, Kunitachi
Tokyo 186–8603
Japan

Mårten Palme
Department of Economics
Stockholm University
SE-106 91 Stockholm
Sweden

Peder J. Pedersen
Department of Economics and
  Business
Fuglesangs Alle 4
Aarhus University
DK-8210 Aarhus V
Denmark

Franco Peracchi
Faculty of Economics
Tor Vergata University
via Columbia, 2
00133 Rome
Italy

Sergio Perelman
University of Liège
HEC Management School
Bât. B31, Boîte 39
Boulevard du Rectorat 7
4000 Liège
Belgium

Johannes Rausch
Munich Center for the Economics of
  Aging
Amalienstrasse 33
80799 Munich
Germany

Muriel Roger
Banque de France, Paris School of
  Economics–INRA
46–2401 DGEI-DEMS-SAMIC
Banque de France
31 rue Croix des Petits Champs
75001 Paris
France

Tammy Schirle
Department of Economics
Wilfrid Laurier University
75 University Avenue West
Waterloo, ON N2L 3C5
Canada

Morten Schuth
Munich Center for the Economics of
  Aging
Amalienstrasse 33
80799 Munich
Germany

Satoshi Shimizutani
Institute for International Policy
  Studies
Toranomon 30 Mori Bldg., 6F
3-2-2 Toranomon, Minato-ku
Tokyo 105-0001
Japan

Gemma Tetlow
Institute for Fiscal Studies
7 Ridgmount Street
London WC1E 7AE
United Kingdom

Lars Thiel
University of Wuppertal
Rainer-Gruenter-Str. 21 (FN.01)
42119 Wuppertal
Germany

Judit Vall Castelló
Pompeu Fabra University
Ramon Trias Fargas, 25–27
08005 Barcelona
Spain

David A. Wise
Kennedy School of Government
Harvard University
79 John F. Kennedy Street
Cambridge, MA 02138

Author Index

Subject Index